TEXAS
RANGER

ALSO BY JOHN BOESSENECKER

Badge and Buckshot: Lawlessness in Old California (1988)

The Grey Fox: The True Story of Bill Miner (with Mark Dugan, 1992)

Lawman: The Life and Times of Harry Morse (1998)

Gold Dust and Gunsmoke (1999)

Against the Vigilantes: The Recollections of
Dutch Charley Duane (1999)

Bandido: The Life and Times of Tiburcio Vasquez (2010)

When Law Was in the Holster: The Frontier Life of Bob Paul (2012)

TEXAS RANGER

The Epic Life of Frank Hamer, the Man

Who Killed Bonnie and Clyde

JOHN BOESSENECKER

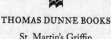

THOMAS DUNNE BOOKS

St. Martin's Griffin

New York

THOMAS DUNNE BOOKS.
An imprint of St. Martin's Press.

TEXAS RANGER. Copyright © 2016 by John Boessenecker. All rights reserved. Printed in the
United States of America. For information, address St. Martin's Press, 175 Fifth Avenue, New
York, N.Y. 10010.

www.thomasdunnebooks.com
www.stmartins.com

Frontispiece: Frank Hamer, about 1910. *Travis Hamer personal collection*

Designed by Michelle McMillian

The Library of Congress has cataloged the hardcover edition as follows:

Names: Boessenecker, John, 1953– author.
Title: Texas Ranger : the epic life of Frank Hamer, the man who killed
    Bonnie and Clyde / John Boessenecker.
Description: First Edition. | New York : Thomas Dunne Books, [2016] |
    Includes bibliographical references and index.
Identifiers: LCCN 2015048659 | ISBN 9781250069986 (hardcover) |
    ISBN 9781466879867 (ebook)
Subjects: LCSH: Hamer, Frank, 1884–1955. | Texas Rangers—Biography. |
    Barrow, Clyde, 1909–1934. | Parker, Bonnie, 1910–1934. | Police—
    Texas—Biography. | Law enforcement—Texas—History.
Classification: LCC HV7911.H35 B64 2016 | DDC 363.2092—dc23
LC record available at http://lccn.loc.gov/2015048659

ISBN 978-1-250-13159-1 (trade paperback)

Our books may be purchased in bulk for promotional, educational, or business use. Please contact
your local bookseller or the Macmillan Corporate and Premium Sales Department at 1-800-221-
7945, extension 5442, or by email at MacmillanSpecialMarkets@macmillan.com.

First St. Martin's Griffin Edition: July 2017

10 9 8

For Bobby and Randy

CONTENTS

TEXAS
RANGER

PROLOGUE

A late autumn breeze swept through the mesquite and the post oaks, rippling the surface of the stream. He leaned forward in the saddle as he spurred his horse up the riverbank. The musty scent of freshly harvested alfalfa hung in the air as the young cowboy cantered across the fields toward a cluster of small buildings along the rutted road.

He was a fine-looking youth, with sharp, angular features and a square jaw set off by piercing blue eyes and closely cropped light brown hair. He was big for a seventeen-year-old: six feet, two inches, tipping the scales at 190 pounds. Frank Hamer had not seen his family in a year, and he looked forward to returning home. For the occasion he wore his finest: a new Stetson hat, fancy neckerchief, high-heeled riding boots, and a hand-tooled belt. His parents' house was just twenty-five miles away, and his journey almost done.

The ride had been a long one, more than two hundred miles from the open ranges of the Pecos to the Texas Hill Country, and was hard on man and horse. The buckshot wounds in his back were almost fully healed, but days in the saddle had caused a constant ache up and down his spine. He was relieved to see, in the midst of the board-and-batten houses, a small country store. Its walls of limestone blocks promised a cool place to rest, its covered wood porch respite from the midday sun.

And he needed to rest. He needed food for himself and feed for his animal. What he did not need was the crowd of toughs loitering about the storefront, leaning on the hitching rail, drifting in and out through the double doors.

There wasn't much to do on a lazy afternoon in Winchell, Texas, in 1901. Farmers and field hands gathered to swap lies, drink forty-rod whiskey, arm wrestle, raise a little hell, and maybe hooraw any young stranger who happened by. Young Hamer tried to pay them little heed as he reined up in front of the store and swung slowly from the saddle. He tied his horse to the hitching post and stepped up on the porch and pushed through the doors.

One of the crowd called out, "Say, look there! That highpockets looks like he might give us a bit of fun!"

"My, my, ain't he pretty," drawled another.

Hamer ignored them. From the storekeeper he bought a can of sardines, a tin of crackers, and a small sack of grain. He stepped back outside, filled his nose bag with oats, and hung it on his horse's head. By now the crowd of roughs had surrounded him and his animal. One pointed at the youth and said, "Why, he ain't even wet behind the ears."

"Someone get the tar," yelled another, referring to the vigilante custom of tar and feathers. Others discussed the quality of his cowboy attire. One said he would take Hamer's spurs, another his belt, and another his hat. One rowdy threatened to yank off his boots and thrash him with them.

As his horse chewed, Hamer leaned calmly against the hitching rail. He drew his bowie knife and started to whittle a toothpick out of a match. The ringleader ignored the not-so-subtle warning and moved closer to him as one of the crowd hollered, "Don't tear his britches. They'll fit me just fine!"

Hamer knew he had to do something decisive and unexpected. As the antagonist stepped even closer, Hamer drew back and spat full in his face. That stunned the man, and for a moment he hesitated. Someone in the crowd yelled out, "Are you going to take it?"

The man took a long look at Hamer's unwavering gaze, his size, his steady hands, and the razor-sharp bowie in his fist. Then he wiped the spittle from his face and moved back. Calmly, slowly, Frank Hamer removed the nosebag, slipped on the bridle, and swung into the saddle. He turned his horse's head and rode slowly out of town.

He had recognized instinctively that any sign of weakness would have left him at the crowd's mercy. Of the ringleader, Frank recalled years later, "Had he reached for me I would have made two pieces out of him." For the rest of his life, Hamer would take great pride in the way he had stood off the crowd. It was one of the few stories his friends could coax out of him.

Extremely modest and humble, Hamer left behind but scant correspondence and no diaries or journals. Even to his closest friends he rarely spoke of the violent events of his long career. Yet his story is not lost. It lives on in moldering court records, yellowed newspapers, obscure archives, and the forgotten memoirs of his fellow lawmen. So now the full history of Frank Hamer's epic life appears in these pages for the first time.

I

A COWBOY OF
THE HILL COUNTRY

Texas bred tough men, and none came any tougher than Frank Hamer. He was to the Lone Star State what Wyatt Earp was to Arizona and what Wild Bill Hickok was to Kansas. His iron strength was hammered on the anvil of his father's blacksmith shop. His iron will was molded in forty tumultuous years as a peace officer. His iron character was honed by his struggles against horseback outlaws, Mexican smugglers, the Ku Klux Klan, corrupt politicians, the Texas Bankers Association, and Lyndon B. Johnson. His iron courage was forged in the flames of fifty-two gunfights with desperadoes. In an era when crooked police were a dime a dozen, he could not be bought at any price. Though a white supremacist of the Jim Crow era, he saved fifteen African Americans from lynch mobs. He was the greatest American lawman of the twentieth century.

Hamer was a son of the Hill Country, that undulating expanse of live oak, mesquite, and cedar brakes that stretches through central Texas from the Balcones Escarpment north and west to the Edwards Plateau. Rugged and isolated, its rivers and creeks rise from headwaters in the Edwards Plateau and slice through jagged limestone, flowing to the Gulf of Mexico. In the 1840s and 50s, settlers from the mountains of Missouri, Arkansas, and Tennessee poured into the Hill Country, long the domain of Apache and Comanche. Their battles against Indian raiders would, for generations to come, help define the character of Texans as fierce and unrelenting warriors. After the Civil War, the Hill Country was wracked by civil violence. With fewer Indians to fight, Texans turned on each other.

Beginning in the 1840s, feuds—between families, neighbors, and political rivals—became a tradition in Texas. Feuding, like vigilantism, was a notion of primitive law. After the Civil War, animosity between Northern and Southern sympathizers was the cause of feuds large and small. During the 1870s, Texas was wracked by infamous vendettas like the Horrell-Higgins feud in Lampasas County, the Mason County war, and, most notably, the Sutton-Taylor feud, the longest and bloodiest of them all. It lasted thirty years and left at least seventy-eight men dead. Notions of personal honor, coupled with an armed citizenry, excessive drink, lack of strong law enforcement, and a belief that social problems were best solved by individuals instead of government, all contributed to the plethora of feuds in frontier Texas. These concepts and conditions continued into the twentieth century. As late as 1912, when the leading partisan in the Boyce-Sneed feud was acquitted of cold-blooded murder, the jury's foreman explained the reasoning: "We in Texas believe a man has the right to safeguard the honor of his home even if he must kill the person responsible."[1]

The Hamer family—they pronounced their name "Haymer"—were relative newcomers to Texas. Frank's father, Franklin Augustus Hamer, was born in St. Louis, Missouri, in 1853, and grew up in Ohio and in Pennsboro, West Virginia. As a youth he worked as a railroad brakeman, but he wanted adventure in the West. In 1874 Franklin enlisted as a private in the U.S. Army in Pennsylvania and was assigned to the Fourth U.S. Cavalry, stationed in Fort Clark, Texas. The Fourth Cavalry was commanded by Colonel Ranald S. MacKenzie, a brilliant leader and famous Indian fighter. Its assignment was to stop raids by Comanche, Apache, and Kickapoo from their hideouts in northern Mexico.

The elder Hamer, a colorful, hard-drinking character with an offbeat sense of humor, displayed the same courage and quick-witted thinking that would be the hallmark of his son's career. One day, exhausted and separated from his cavalry unit, Hamer dismounted and lay down in the brush to nap. A nervous snort from his horse startled him awake in time to see that he had been surrounded by a Comanche war party. Hamer knew that his life depended on what he did next. Lurching to his feet, he staggered drunkenly through the brush, foaming at the mouth. Alternately singing in a loud voice and mumbling incoherently, he wobbled toward the astonished Indians. As he danced, whistled, and laughed, the warriors lowered their weapons. One of the Comanches exclaimed, "Muy loco!"

The Indians quickly retreated from the crazed soldier, fearful of the evil spirit that had possessed him. Swinging onto their horses, they galloped off. Hamer kept up his act until they disappeared, then caught his horse and raced hell-for-leather to Fort Clark.

Army life did not agree with Franklin Hamer. He received a medical discharge after just five months and settled in Fairview, a tiny Wilson County village of about a hundred, situated forty miles southeast of San Antonio. There, he worked as a farmer and blacksmith and wooed twenty-year-old Lou Emma Francis. The two were married by a justice of the peace in her parents' home in Fairview in 1881 and promptly set out to raise a large family. Their first child, Dennis Estill Hamer, arrived ten months later. The second eldest, Francis Augustus, destined for a legendary life, was born in Fairview on March 17, 1884. More children followed: Sanford Clinton, called Sant, in 1886; Harrison Lester in 1888; Mary Grace in 1891; Emma Patience, known as Pat, in 1894; Alma Dell in 1898; and the youngest, Flavious Letherage, in 1899. The Hamer family were a mixture of Scottish, Irish, English, and German blood. Frank, to distinguish him from his father, was often called Gus (for Augustus) in his youth.[2]

From his father Frank inherited a dry, sardonic wit and learned to speak in colorful and sometimes profane language. His father's heavy drinking was an attribute that the eldest son, Estill, inherited and that Frank was careful to avoid. As a young boy, Frank's most vivid memories were of his maternal grandfather, L. J. Francis. The old man, a jagged scar down the side of his face, regaled the youth with stories of his adventures on the frontier. In 1840, at age twenty-two, he accompanied an

Franklin Hamer, lower left, and three of his children, about 1915. Seated at right is son Harrison, and standing are son Flavious and daughter Pat. *Courtesy Harrison Hamer*

overland trade caravan from Texas to Chihuahua in northern Mexico. The traders were set upon by Indians, who killed seven of the party before Francis was shot in the head with an arrow. He was captured and almost killed but soon escaped. In later years he became a Presbyterian minister, and young Frank was inspired to follow his grandfather's religious life.[3]

Frank's father had a roving disposition. As Franklin's sister-in-law recalled, "Mr. Hamer was a great hand for moving from place to place."

In 1890, when Frank was six, his father brought his family to the Hill Country, settling at McAnelly's Bend (now called Bend), on the Colorado River, fourteen miles southeast of San Saba. There, he ran a blacksmith shop. In 1894 the elder Hamer moved his family south to Oxford, another small settlement, fifteen miles below Llano on the road to Fredericksburg. He opened another blacksmith shop in a two-story, barnlike building fronting the Llano-Fredericksburg road. Next to it was a simple, board-and-batten house, into which crammed the Hamers' growing brood. Estill and Frank helped their father, gathering firewood for the forge, pumping the bellows, and learning to hammer iron on his anvil. Years later, Frank and his good friend Bill Sterling, a Texas Ranger captain, happened to be traveling through Llano County. Recalled Sterling, "Hamer stopped our car in front of an old roadside blacksmith shop. He said that it had once belonged to his father. As a youth he had put in many hours of toil at the anvil, swinging a sledge hammer and working with other heavy tools. This was where Frank Hamer got his brawny arms."[4]

Like most youths in the Hill Country, the Hamer boys also learned riding, roping, branding, managing cattle, and basic farming. When not helping out with chores, the older Hamer children attended the public school in Oxford. Frank was extremely intelligent, with a near photographic memory. But he was no scholar. He did excel in mathematics, and the teacher would ask him to help instruct the class from time to time. Frequently, he would solve arithmetic problems in his head. His teacher would ask, "Frank, why didn't you work out the problem? Where is your paper?"

Hamer invariably answered, "I don't know how to work it out on paper, Ma'am, but I can give you the right answer to the problem." On one occasion, however, the teacher insisted that he stand before the class and explain how he arrived at the correct solutions. "I told the teacher I did not know how I reached the right answers and I refused to get up and talk to the class. She did not like this and I did not remain long in school." In later years he would jokingly boast that he was "the only Texas Ranger with an Oxford education." In truth, Frank had no formal schooling after the sixth grade. As Captain John H. Rogers of the

Texas Rangers later commented, "While he is not an educated man, he is bright and intelligent." Hamer himself freely admitted his paltry schooling, once saying, "The only education I got was on the hurricane end of a Mexican pony."[5]

Religion was one of the greatest influences on Frank's early life. His parents were devout Presbyterians. Camp revival meetings, coupled with the example set by his minister grandfather, reinforced Frank's desire to follow a career in the cloth. For most of his youth, from age six to sixteen, Frank believed he was destined to be a preacher. Most rural Texas families owned but one book, the Bible. Frank was then not much of a reader, but in addition to the Bible he devoured Josiah Wilbarger's *Indian Depredations in Texas,* published in 1889. The book was hugely popular among Texans, for it detailed how their ancestors had wrested the country from wild Indians. Hamer was fascinated by the tales of Comanche fights and Texas Rangers. But instead of being inspired to emulate the Rangers, the youth was most impressed by the underdogs—the Indians. "I made up my mind," he later recalled, "to be as much like an Indian as I could." His admiration for the underdog and his concern for those too weak or too outnumbered to protect themselves would become essential to understanding his character.[6]

Young Frank, when not working or attending school, and to escape the cramped confines of their tiny, crowded home, would often head alone into the hills. He took only his rifle, fishing gear, and bowie knife, exploring and living off the land. He recalled, "When a boy I liked to live in the woods . . . one to six weeks at a time. I got along fine for I fished, hunted, and slept upon the ground at nights. I was greatly fond of studying the habits of small animals and birds. I built an altar in the woods so I could talk to the Old Master."[7]

The Hill Country's heavily wooded slopes teemed with white-tailed deer, wild turkeys, and fowl of every type. There, Frank became intimately acquainted with nature, from insects to rodents, birds, and small and large game. As his friend and biographer Walter Prescott Webb once explained, "He studied bird calls and the animal cries and practiced imitating them until he could call them to him. Almost anyone can call crows, but Frank can call quail, deer, road runners, fox-squirrels, and hoot owls." He became an expert trailer, able—like an Indian in the old adage—to "track a fly across a looking glass." Hamer later said, with little exaggeration, that as a youth he slept outdoors for eight straight years. He took great pleasure in mastering woodmanship, Indian lore, and survival skills, not recognizing that he was simultaneously learning self-reliance, patience, endurance, and independence. To him, the dense, isolated timber of the Hill Country was not lonely and forbidding, it was home.[8]

Frank grew up around firearms. The Hamers, like all Texas families, kept a few rifles and shotguns in the house. All boys in rural Texas were expected to know how to load, shoot, and clean guns. Since the founding of the Republic of Texas, firearms had been a necessity to defend the frontier against raids by Comanche, Kiowa, and Kiowa Apache. Once the Indian danger was gone, Texans remained married to their guns. In the Hamer household, even the girls learned to use firearms. Frank's sister Pat carried a toy pistol as a child, wore a real one on her hip as a young woman, and in old age kept a handgun in her purse.[9]

It was on his boyhood journeys that Frank Hamer became a dead shot. Money was scarce and ammunition expensive, so he learned to hit what he shot at. Careful practice enabled him to kill a running deer or a bird in full flight. In a place and time when dead shots were a dime a dozen, Frank Hamer's marksmanship would become legendary. He also learned to use a knife, both as a tool and as a weapon. He hunted armadillos by throwing his bowie knife with such force he could pin the animal to the ground. Frank ate what he hunted and thought that armadillo meat tasted like fine-grained, high-quality pork.[10]

An extremely athletic youth, Frank excelled in both the high jump and the long jump. But organized sports did not interest him. The sports he liked most were horseback riding, hunting, fishing, and shooting. Other sports and leisure activities—football, bicycling, skating—became popular during the inaptly named Gay Nineties. Yet that 1890s America—of Frank Merriwell, of knickerbockers and celluloid collars, of baseball, pretzels, and beer, of tripping the light fantastic with Mamie O'Rourke—was utterly foreign to young Hamer. Instead, his boyhood in the Texas Hill Country was firmly grounded in the Old West, informed

The Hamer family home, left, and blacksmith shop, right, on the Llano-Fredericksburg road in Oxford, Texas. *Courtesy of the Texas Ranger Hall of Fame and Museum, Waco, Texas*

by the ethics and traditions of the Texas frontier. His heroes were not John L. Sullivan, "Gentleman Jim" Corbett, Cy Young, or Christy Mathewson—they were Captain Jack Hays, of the Texas Rangers, Colonel Ranald MacKenzie, of the Fourth Cavalry, and the Comanche war chiefs Buffalo Hump and Quanah Parker.

By his mid-teenage years Hamer was big for his age, tall and gangly, his sinewy limbs toned and hardened by long hours at his father's anvil. Quiet and modest, with a broad smile set off by large, even teeth, he possessed supreme self-confidence. With children and women he was gentle and caring; with strangers, awkward and bashful. At the same time, he was stubborn, hardheaded, and short-tempered, softened somewhat by a sardonic sense of humor. Early encounters with neighborhood tormentors made him despise bullies and ruffians, and his fighting blood was easily aroused. As an admirer once remarked, "At sixteen he was equipped with a personality forceful enough to impress a straw boss," adding, "He was the tall, silent youngster who invariably attracts the attention of schoolyard bullies." In those years both men and boys were expected to "kill their own snakes"—that is, to solve their own problems.

Boyhood disputes would often be resolved by angry wrestling matches, or by fisticuffs.[11]

Though Frank did not start fights, he became adept at ending them. Instead of punching his opponent, he would slap him with an open palm. He also learned to use his boots, said one observer: "He usually put a quick end to a scuffle with a mule kick to his opponent's groin." So adept was Hamer at fighting with his feet that his friend Bill Sterling thought Frank had been trained in savate, the French martial art. "From the way he performed," said Sterling, "I thought perhaps some adventure-seeking Frenchman had drifted into the Pecos country and shown him how it was done in France. His answer was that he had never taken any lessons other than those given by experience. In youthful fights, when older boys ganged up on him, he discovered that his feet could be turned into high powered weapons." Frank would later say, "My feet were always loaded."[12]

Early on, Hamer learned the concept of personal honor. As he once explained, "I was born and raised in Texas. I was born and raised not to take an insult. Any time a man insults me he has to back it up." This notion of honor was a vital component of masculine life in the American West of the nineteenth century. Honor was embraced by men of all classes in the West and the South. Honor meant courage, character, loyalty, respect for womanhood, and especially a firm resolve to never back down from an enemy. It was manifest in the code duello of the southern planter, the code of the West on the frontier, and the refusal to run from a fight so common to Texas feudists. It was codified in the Western legal doctrine of self-defense, known as "no duty to retreat" or "stand your ground," which authorized a man to resist attacks, even verbal ones, with deadly force. A man possessed honor only if his peers said he did. If his peers failed to accept him as an equal, his honor was gone, and only an act of violent retribution or heroic valor could retrieve it. This concept of personal honor is central to an understanding of the character of Frank Hamer and would explain many of the actions in his adult life.[13]

Personal honor was also an important component of Texas gun culture. The use of violence to resolve social problems was widely accepted on the frontier, especially in Texas. As a result, the Lone Star State became renowned for its plethora of gunfighters, feudists, and fast-shooting lawmen. A Texan who had "killed his man" proved that he could defend his honor and thus earned both respect and notoriety. From the anti-Hispanic racism of West Texas came the boast of gunfighters like John King Fisher, who bragged of killing twelve men, "not counting Mexicans." Texas gunfighter and killer-for-hire Jim Miller boasted, "I have killed eleven men that I know about. I have lost my notch stick on Mexicans I've killed out on the border." N. A. Jennings, who served with Captain Lee McNelly's Texas Ranger company in 1876, explained, "The taking of a Mexican's life by the white desperadoes was of so little importance in their eyes that they actually didn't count such an 'incident' in their list of 'killings,' as the murders were styled by them. Only white victims were reckoned by notches on their six-shooters."[14]

Frank Hamer deeply absorbed Texas gun culture, but he never considered himself a gunfighter. The term gunfighter first came into regular use in the late 1880s. The word "gunslinger" was unknown in the Old West; it was coined by fiction writers in the 1920s. During Hamer's youth, "gunfighter" held a negative connotation: a gunfighter was a man, often a hired killer, who sought trouble and who used firearms to settle personal quarrels. By the advent of motion pictures the term took on a more positive meaning, and by the television era of the 1950s the gunfighter had become a heroic figure, a quick-draw artist who wielded his guns for the common good. Of course, in the Old West, "fast draw" gunfights or "walk downs" on Main Street were all but unknown.[15]

By 1900, when Frank was sixteen, his father had moved the family again, this time to Regency, ten miles up the Colorado River in Mills County and about twelve miles northwest of San Saba. The town had just two hundred residents and a church, general store, and flour mill. That spring Frank went to work as a sharecropper for Dan McSween, a fifty-three-year-old widower and hardcase. He owned 340 acres on Spring Creek, which ran north from San Saba County and emptied into the Colorado River about four miles east of Regency. Hamer agreed to farm McSween's land in return for half the crop at harvest time. Frank was assisted by his twelve-year-old brother, Harrison.

When not planting McSween's fields, Frank practiced shooting.

McSween quickly recognized that the youth was a dead shot with six-gun, rifle, and shotgun. One June day he asked Frank if he would like to earn $150. Hamer's reply was typically sardonic: "Who do I have to kill?"

He was joking, but Dan McSween wasn't. McSween explained that he had been having trouble with a prominent local rancher and wanted to get rid of him. Hamer was shocked.

"Wait a minute, now, Mr. McSween, wait a minute," Frank exclaimed. "I was just kidding! I didn't mean that I was gonna kill anybody. That's the farthest thing from my mind. As a matter of fact, I want to be a preacher, and I just don't think that you can be a preacher and go about killing people."

To that, McSween retorted, "Well, if you're on that kind of bent, I'll up my offer to $200. I'll tell you what I want you to do. I'll hide you in a covered wagon and bring this man with me and we'll stand right in front of the wagon. While we're talking, take out your pistol and shoot him through a slit in the canvas. Nobody will ever find out what happened, and you'll be $200 richer."

"Hell no!" Frank exploded. "I'm not gonna kill that man for you! As a matter of fact, I'm gonna tell him what you've proposed."

As Hamer stormed off, McSween shouted, "If you let one word of this out, I'll kill you!"

A frightened Harrison, hiding behind a tree, heard the entire exchange. That night, the Hamer brothers mounted their horses, rode to the ranch of McSween's enemy, and told him about the plot. The grateful rancher thanked the youths and said he would be on the lookout for McSween. Two days later, on June 12, 1900, the Hamer boys were plowing in the field when McSween approached and ordered Harrison to bring some tools from the barn. Then he told Frank to go to his house and fetch some food. Frank left immediately, while Harrison, unseen by McSween, lingered behind to rest the plow next to a chinaberry tree. Suddenly, the boy heard a noise and turned to see that his brother had already returned. Frank had dropped several cans of food and was bending over to pick them up. Behind him crouched Dan McSween, squinting down the rib of a double-barreled shotgun.

"Look out!" Harrison screamed. Frank dove to one side as McSween's shotgun boomed. The heavy charge whined past harmlessly as the youth started to run. McSween fired the second barrel, and twenty buckshot slammed into Hamer's back and the left side of his head. The force knocked him to the ground, but he managed to pull a small revolver and open fire. One shot struck McSween, dropping him to the ground. Frank fired again at his assailant, narrowly missing Harrison and slicing a limb off the chinaberry tree.

Harrison rushed to help his brother while the wounded McSween staggered back to his house. Frank, though desperately wounded, was able to walk, and the two boys managed to cross a hill and hide in a ravine. Soon Dan McSween appeared on horseback, an old buffalo rifle in hand, hunting for the boys. As he rode close, Frank drew his revolver to fire, but Harrison urged him not to shoot. "He has that old rifle, and its bullet will reach a lot farther than your pistol, and carries a lot more weight."

As McSween rode off, the two boys made it back to their wagon. Bleeding heavily, Frank lay in the wagon bed in excruciating pain as Harrison took the reins. Frank later said that they were helped by an African American field hand who raced to bring a doctor to the Hamer home. The doctor was able to remove some, but not all, of the buckshot. Because Frank had lost so much blood, the doctor told his father, "I hate to say it, but the boy is not going to make it."

Hamer recalled, "I knew he was wrong. I knew I was going to make it, but I couldn't say it, because I was so far gone I couldn't talk. I could hear, but I couldn't speak. But, you see, I had talked to the Old Master about it, and I knew I was going to get well."

Frank had high praise for the black field hand. "A colored man was the best friend I ever had in my life," he recalled. "That colored man caused me to be living today." At home, his mother nursed him, and he slowly recovered. Years later, Frank explained, "Several of those bullets are in me yet. I'd rather have them in than go through the trouble of having them cut out."[16]

Hamer's close brush with death at the hands of Dan McSween was the most significant event of his youth and one that profoundly affected his nature. It showed him, at a very early age, that he could face gunfire without flinching and that he was tough enough to survive a shotgun blast that would have killed a lesser man. It taught him that he had the courage to defend himself from a deadly attack, as well as the ability and presence of mind to shoot an assailant despite being grievously wounded. It brought him an even deeper loathing of bullies and lawbreakers. And it instilled in him a lifelong affinity for African Americans. Because blacks and Hispanics were scarce in the Hill Country, he did not inherit the racial hatred so common to folk in East Texas, which had a large black populace, or to Anglos along the Rio Grande, where Spanish was more widely spoken than English. Though Hamer certainly harbored many of the racist notions of the era, such attitudes would not be expressed in his public career. And though he plainly did not possess modern-day notions of ethnic sensitivity, he never forgot the black man who helped save his life. To African Americans in Texas, it was a debt that Frank Hamer would pay back again and again.

Dan McSween was never charged in San Saba or Mills counties with attempting to kill Hamer. Harrison, in old age, claimed that when Frank recovered from his wounds, he returned to McSween's ranch and called him outside.

"I thought I'd finished you!" thundered the rancher.

"Not by a damned sight," declared Frank. "I've come to settle accounts."

As Harrison told the story, the two went for their guns, and McSween died instantly. That makes for a dramatic finale, but it never happened. Dan McSween sold his Spring Creek ranch in 1904 and moved to Kaufman, Texas, where he died of natural causes five years later.[17]

In fact, while Frank slowly recovered at the family home in Regency, his father had deep concerns about his safety. If McSween had tried to kill his son once, he certainly might try again. The elder Hamer had many friends in San Saba County, among them the Ketchum family. The Ketchums were San Saba pioneers. The eldest son, Green Berry Ketchum, had left the county in the 1880s to become a prosperous cowman in West Texas. Ketchum owned two ranches, one near Knickerbocker, south of San Angelo, and the other on Independence Creek, a tributary of the Pecos River, about nine miles southwest of Sheffield in Pecos County. He was best known as the older brother of Thomas "Black

Jack" Ketchum, one of the Old West's most infamous bandits. To all outward appearances, Berry Ketchum was an honest rancher. Although rumored to have benefited financially from the train robberies of the Ketchum gang, no proof ever surfaced.

Frank's parents sent him and Harrison to stay in safety with Berry Ketchum at his Pecos ranch. To pass the time while his wounds healed, Frank bought a fiddle in Sheffield. He practiced often, performing before an undiscerning herd of cattle. Recalled his son, Frank Jr., "He used to tell me he 'tortured the cowbrutes' playing that fiddle until he got good at it." When Frank was well enough, Ketchum put the Hamer boys to work, herding his horses and cattle on the Independence Creek ranges. The Ketchum ranch was a big one, encompassing 45,000 acres along the Pecos River. The Hamer brothers helped herd four hundred cattle and wrangle five hundred horses and mules. The Trans-Pecos desert was vastly different from the jagged Hill Country and the high savanna of the Edwards Plateau. The Pecos, flowing south from New Mexico to its confluence with the Rio Grande near Del Rio, was heavily alkaline and almost undrinkable for both man and beast. Above Sheffield the Pecos passes through a wide desert valley devoid of trees; below Sheffield it flows into a deep gorge to the Rio Grande. Frank's work as a cowhand and horse wrangler would take him throughout the Pecos country. Frank gained valuable experience working for Ketchum and became intimately acquainted with the vast expanse of Pecos County, the second largest in Texas, almost twice the size of the state of Delaware. His knowledge of its loamy deserts, limestone formations, and rugged mountains would prove of immense value in the years to come.[18]

By this time Berry's younger brother, gang member Sam Ketchum, had been killed by a posse, and Tom Ketchum was in prison in New Mexico under sentence of death. The Hamer boys were riding for Berry Ketchum when Black Jack was hanged in Clayton, New Mexico, on April 26, 1901. No doubt Frank read the newspaper accounts, for they were published extensively throughout the country. In one of the most notorious and horrific executions of that era, the hangman misjudged the drop, and Black Jack Ketchum was decapitated in the fall. From the ranch hands, and perhaps Berry Ketchum himself, Hamer heard many stories of the Ketchum gang, and he never forgot the bizarre hanging of Black Jack.[19]

Historically, West Texas had been open range, where cattle roamed freely. With the introduction of barbed wire in the 1880s, the free ranges were gradually fenced off. Nonetheless, much of the country west of the Pecos was isolated and unfenced, and it remained open range for many years. On the Pecos, Frank became a top hand and an expert horseman. He loved horses and felt that he could communicate with and understand them. Explained Walter Prescott Webb, "He believes that the endurance of a horse on long or hard journeys depends more on the rider's knowledge of how to ride than on his weight. Though Hamer weighed nearly two hundred pounds, he could help the horse. . . . One must sit deep in the saddle, bear a part of his weight on the stirrups, and catch the rhythm of the animal. If the ride is long, there must be no galloping, but only the trot and walk. The cinch must be neither too loose nor too tight. Long hills must be taken at a walk, and, if time permits, with loose cinch for easy breathing."[20]

Frank's study of animal life would make him an astute observer of humans. Said Webb, who knew Hamer as well as anyone, "Every type of human being reminds him of some animal, of something in nature. The criminal is a coyote, always taking a look over his shoulder; a cornered political schemer is a 'crawfish about three days from water.' . . . The merciless murderer is 'as cold-blooded as a rattlesnake with a chill.'" Frank considered himself most like an antelope, as he explained, "because antelopes are the most curious of all animals." On the Pecos ranges, the seventeen-year-old Hamer grew to a sturdy six foot two, soon adding another inch. He was strikingly handsome and spoke slowly in a deep, deliberate Texas drawl. Like many cowboys, he picked up the smoking habit, and for the rest of his life was rarely seen without a cigarette, a cigar, or a pipe.[21]

In 1903 Frank took part in an incident that he would deeply regret, telling Walter Prescott Webb, "Had I not gone with the law, I would have gone against it." As Frank candidly told the story to Webb, he was hired to help drive a remuda of horses to a buyer in San Angelo. Most of the wranglers were young, but one was an older man, an experienced

Frank Hamer, age twenty-two. *Author's collection*

criminal. As they herded the broncos outside San Angelo, the older hand filled the youths with tales of quick money. He explained how easy it would be for them to ride into town, hold up the bank, and escape into Mexico, where they could use the loot to start their own ranch. Hamer, like the other wranglers, was fascinated and agreed to take part. They hastily drew up plans and then took up positions on the street that led to the bank. They were about to make their play when the foreman rode up and ordered them to drive the horses to the corral. As Webb explained, "This interruption no doubt saved the man who has left his mark on the tradition of law enforcement in Texas." With time to reflect, Frank realized he had been a fool. He resolved that in the future he would think for himself. Said Hamer, "It was the adventure, and not the money, that appealed to me. Had I gone into it, things would have been different."[22]

In 1905 Frank was hired at the Carr ranch, located between Sheffield and Fort Stockton. For a time he was joined there by his nineteen-year-old brother Sant, who later drifted to Arizona to find work as a miner. One day two horses, with their bridles and saddles, were stolen. Frank took the trail alone, and for several days followed the meandering tracks eastward. Finally, he closed in on two riders. Dropping into a gully, Hamer circled around in front of them. As the horse thieves approached, Frank leveled his Winchester and took them by surprise. Hamer delivered his prisoners to the sheriff of Crockett County and returned the stolen mounts to his grateful boss at the Carr ranch.[23]

Frank had tasted his first manhunt, and it was exhilarating—just like hunting animals, but far more exciting and dangerous. The adventure, the adrenaline rush from taking his men alive, and the sense of pride and accomplishment in outwitting the horse thieves overwhelmed him. He wanted more of the same, and he would get it. Hamer was far too bright to be satisfied with the simple life of a drover. Growing bored with ranch life, he became heartily sick of driving, roping, and branding cattle. Two decades later, when invited to a rodeo, Frank declined, saying, "For many years I had a rodeo every morning by myself on the Pecos, and do not care to see another one."[24]

Hamer was fascinated by a newfangled contraption at the Carr ranch—a telephone. After 1900, telephone systems in Texas expanded rapidly as equipment improved and long-distance lines were extended. By 1906 there were more than one hundred thousand telephones in Texas. The telephone at the Carr ranch was on a party line, in which anyone could listen in on the neighbors' conversations. Hamer was often alone at ranch headquarters, and to relieve his boredom he spent much time on the phone, listening to neighboring ranchers' news, gossip, and complaints about the weather. One night in October 1905, he overheard a call from the Pecos County sheriff, Dudley S. Barker, in Fort Stockton.

Barker was asking his former deputy, Charlie Witcher, to intercept a horse thief who was headed Hamer's way on a stolen mount.

Witcher replied that he "was busy [and] did not want to get mixed up in the courts." Explained Witcher, "I'm sorry, Dud. I got my own things to take care of. Why don't you go after him yourself?"

"I can't," Sheriff Barker responded. "I'm so busy here at the jail in Fort Stockton that I hardly have time to leave and get my meals. Besides, that coyote has had such a jump, it would take me quite some time to catch up with him."

By this time Frank could not restrain himself. "I'll go get him, Sheriff!"

"Who the hell are you?" Barker demanded.

"I'm Frank Hamer, and I'm working on the Carr ranch."

"He's headed your way," said the sheriff, "and if you can catch him, I'll be mighty happy. I'll tell you what he looks like."

"No need to," Hamer replied. "I just heard you describe him to Charlie."

"I'd be much obliged if you do catch him. I'll ride out there tomorrow to give you a hand."

Frank knew that it would take the horse thief until daybreak to reach the Carr ranch. The only water on the route was at the Carr windmill, some distance from ranch headquarters. Hamer was sure the rider would have to stop there to water his horse. He awoke at 3:00 A.M., buckled on his gun belt and six-shooter, saddled his mount, and, with Winchester in hand, rode out to the windmill. At daylight, a rider appeared in the distance, headed straight for the windmill. As the stranger dismounted, Frank stepped out of the brush and covered him with his Winchester.

"You're under arrest," Hamer told him in an even tone. Within moments the horse thief was back in his saddle, headed toward Fort Stockton, with Hamer following twenty feet behind. Recalled Frank, "I sure felt good that morning going up and down the long slopes with that thief ahead of me. Finally, after riding sixteen miles, I saw Dud Barker top out on a hill two miles off. He was driving a couple of fast horses to a light buggy and they were sure stepping. I wouldn't have sold out very cheap that day."[25]

As Barker handcuffed the prisoner, he said to Hamer, "This is the second time you've done my work. You did a mighty fine job of catching this man, Frank. How'd you like to be a Texas Ranger?"

"I never gave it too much thought before," Frank answered. "It sounds pretty good, though. What do I have to do to get in?"

"You let me take care of that," replied the sheriff. Dud Barker, thirty-one, had served three years as a Texas Ranger and achieved repute for his role in breaking up the San Saba Mob in 1896. He recognized a good Ranger recruit when he saw one. On February 26, 1906, Sheriff Barker wrote to the Texas adjutant general, John A. Hulen, in Austin and recommended that Hamer be enlisted as a Ranger. Barker praised Hamer's capture of the horse thief and said he "has the ability to grasp the situation quickly." Soon after, John H. Rogers, captain of Company C, wrote to his sergeant, Jim Moore, and instructed him to have Hamer report for duty in Sheffield. At that time Company C was headquartered in Alpine, in the Big Bend country, seventy miles southwest of Fort Stockton. Sergeant Moore was in charge of a small detachment of the company that had a camp four miles outside Sheffield. In keeping with the state's failure to adequately fund the Rangers, they did not have housing. The lawmen slept outdoors in canvas army tents and cooked on open fires. If they were lucky, they might hire a local woman to do their cooking and washing.[26]

In mid-April Frank Hamer rode into the Ranger camp looking for Captain Rogers. But the captain was busy at his headquarters in Alpine, so Frank loitered about the camp, getting to know Sergeant Moore and Private E. S. McGee. Moore was an experienced Ranger, having served five years under Captain Rogers before being promoted to sergeant in 1905. But McGee had been a Ranger only seven months, and Captain Rogers had become dissatisfied with his performance. On April 15 the Rangers got a report that a Mexican had taken a horse "for the purpose of forcing the collection of a debt without any authority of law." McGee and Hamer (whom Captain Rogers referred to in his official report as "a citizen by the name of Haymer") started in pursuit and quickly caught their man. Wrote the captain, "They recovered the horse and delivered him to the rightful owner but not being able to make a case of theft . . .

against said Mexican they did not put him under arrest. The owner of the horse was entirely satisfied with the recovery of his horse."[27]

On April 21 Captain Rogers arrived in Sheffield to interview the gangly young recruit. At first he was disappointed, remarking, "Why, he's only a boy." But Rogers, impressed by Hamer's volunteering to help the Rangers, was soon satisfied with Dud Barker's recommendation. Calling the town's justice of the peace, he had Frank take the Ranger oath: "I do solemnly swear that I will faithfully and impartially discharge and perform all the duties incumbent on me as an officer of the Ranger Force according to the best of my skill and ability, agreeably to the Constitution and laws of the United States and of this State, and I do further solemnly swear that since the adoption of the Constitution of this State, I being a citizen of this State, have not fought a duel with deadly weapons; nor have I acted as second in carrying a challenge, or aided, advised, or assisted any person thus offending. And I furthermore swear that I have not, directly nor indirectly, paid, offered or promised to pay, contributed nor promised to contribute, any money or valuable thing, or promised any public office or employment to secure my appointment. So help me God."[28]

Every red-blooded Anglo boy in the Southwest dreamed of being a Texas Ranger. The new recruit, just twenty-two, was bursting with pride. Little did Captain Rogers realize how seriously Frank Hamer would take his Texas Ranger oath. Though his enlistment had been entirely coincidental, he was a Ranger born. His rugged life in the saddle had steeled him against hardship and privation. His massive size, physical power, superb marksmanship, and raw courage had melded him into a deadly adversary. A deep religious faith imbued in him strong notions of right and wrong. His lonely years in the wild country had made him so independent and self-reliant that he cared little for what others thought of him. His natural curiosity, his quick, analytic mind, and his near-photographic memory would mold him into a brilliant detective. Quiet and humble, rigid and unyielding, Frank Hamer now began his long ride into the halls of Texas legend and lore.

2

TEXAS RANGER

By the time of Frank Hamer's enlistment in 1906, the Texas Rangers had long since entered the pantheon of American myth. As famous as they were, there was no written history of the force for new recruits like Hamer to read. Instead, around a hundred campfires, Frank heard the stories, handed down by word of mouth, of the men who rode before him. The Rangers had been formed in 1835 as a small mounted paramilitary force. During the Texas Revolution the following year, they acted primarily as couriers and scouts. After the revolution they became a border-protection force and engaged in bloody war against the Indian tribes that opposed white settlement. In the Battle of Plum Creek in 1840, Rangers under Ben McCulloch helped defeat a huge Comanche war party led by Buffalo Hump. During the early 1840s, Captain John Coffee "Jack" Hays recruited tough frontiersmen, fought Indians, and established many of the Rangers' traditions. Under him rode such legendary leaders as McCulloch, Sam Walker, and "Big Foot" Wallace.

The Texas Rangers achieved worldwide recognition in the Mexican War. Mounted on the finest horses, clad in buckskin, and armed to the teeth with rifles, Colt revolving pistols, and bowie knives, they were perfectly adapted to desert warfare in northern Mexico. Their reckless courage helped the U.S. Army win victories in small skirmishes and major battles alike. At the same time, their ruthless tactics, including wanton killing of Mexicans, led the populace to dub them "Los Diablos Tejanos"—the Texas Devils. This was the beginning of the Rangers' long and troubled relationship with the Spanish-speaking people of Texas and Mexico. Nonetheless, Anglo Texans came to revere the Rangers second only to the martyrs of the Alamo.

During the 1850s Texas Rangers under John S. "Rip" Ford fought Indians and protected the Rio Grande from incursions by Mexican guerrillas. In the Reconstruction years after the Civil War, the Rangers were replaced by the Texas State Police. Because it was organized by Northern Republicans and its members included African Americans, the state police were despised by white Texans. In 1874 Democrats came back into power and reorganized the Texas Rangers. Captain Lee McNelly's Rangers broke up the infamous Sutton-Taylor feud and ruthlessly suppressed Mexican rebels, Anglo rustlers, and smugglers on the border. At the same time, Rangers under Major John B. Jones destroyed the raiding bands of Comanche and Kiowa and killed or captured countless outlaws, among them Sam Bass, the folk-hero bandit, and John Wesley Hardin, the king of gunfighters. With the Indian menace gone, the Rangers evolved from a quasi-military organization into a state police. Beginning in the 1890s, the force was led by the Four Great Captains: John A. Brooks, Bill McDonald, John R. Hughes, and John H. Rogers. Under their capable leadership, with exploits emblazoned in newspaper headlines, Rangers broke up feuds, battled lynch mobs, tracked down train and bank robbers, and fought smugglers on the Rio Grande.[1]

Unlike his fellow captains, Bill McDonald was a colorful self-promoter and responsible for the Rangers' best-known, but most apocryphal, story. One day a company of Rangers was called to stop a mob. When Captain Bill stepped off the train alone, the mayor and sheriff demanded, "Where's the rest of the outfit?" McDonald supposedly exclaimed, "Rest, hell! You ain't got but one riot, have you?" In truth, if only one Ranger responded to a call for help, it was because the parsimonious Texas legislature refused to hire enough of them. In further truth, a handful of Rangers could indeed face down a mob—so fearsome were their reputations as man killers.[2]

The lack of taxpayer funds was reflected in the Rangers' low pay: a paltry $40 a month, less than half the wage earned by the average city policeman. A new recruit like Hamer also had to supply his own horse, saddle, tack, and weapons. Frank spent his first few weeks with Captain Rogers at his headquarters in Alpine. The building was all that the state could afford to rent—a ramshackle wood house on the town's dusty main street, with a gaping hole in the rotting front porch. Alpine, the seat of Brewster County, was a cattle town of about twelve hundred people situated on the Galveston, Harrisburg, & San Antonio Railway. Laid out in a valley in the foothills of the Davis Mountains, it was surrounded by rolling grasslands. To the south lay the Big Bend country, its rugged peaks and deep chasms the center for many quicksilver mines. The Chisos Mountains, rising to more than seven thousand feet in elevation, and once the domain of Mescalero Apaches, stood among the highest in the state. Just south of the Chisos was the Big Bend of the Rio Grande, an area long dominated by American outlaws, Mexican bandidos, and smugglers of both nations.

The Texas Rangers, like most American police of that era, had no formal training; they learned on the job. Hamer could not have had a better teacher and mentor than John H. Rogers. One of the most famous lawmen in the Southwest, he did not look like a Ranger captain. At forty-two, he was modest, soft-spoken, and kind, as well as stocky, graying, and bespectacled. A teetotaler and deeply religious, Rogers carried a Bible in his saddlebags. He displayed an extraordinary combination of southern gentility and iron-fisted determination. He had been a Ranger since the age of eighteen and had killed several desperadoes in hairraising gun battles. Rogers had twice been wounded in shootouts, leaving one arm permanently injured. He carried a special rifle with a curved stock to compensate for his crippled limb. Hamer idolized his captain, and ever after sought to emulate him. Rogers became the most important influence in Hamer's professional life. As Frank's friend Bill Sterling once said, "Many Rangers who became noted in the service received their early training under Captain Rogers. . . . [Hamer] never missed an opportunity to express the highest regard for his first commander."[3]

Frank Hamer took to rangering like a duck to water. He was tough and resilient, used to making long rides, sleeping on the prairie, and eating wild game. He needed no training in tracking, riding, or gunfighting. Instead of hunting deer, he now hunted men. From Captain Rogers he would learn many other skills: to investigate crimes, to understand the statute books, to make arrests that would stick, to develop informants, to safely transport prisoners, and to give accurate and compelling testimony in court. Sheriff Dud Barker later said, "I never saw a better Ranger than Frank Hamer."[4]

Frank's first duties were routine. On May 9, 1906, Captain Rogers sent him to Terlingua, near the Rio Grande, with Robert M. "Duke" Hudson, who had a shock of red hair and, though short of stature, was a highly capable Ranger. Hamer and Hudson were ordered to relieve Private Marvin Bailey, whose horse had given out from extensive scouting along the border after fugitives and *tequileros*, or tequila smugglers. Liquor was then legal in many "wet" Texas towns, while illegal in "dry" communities. Smugglers brought it across the Rio Grande to avoid paying import duties. Hamer kept the peace in Terlingua, a rowdy quicksilver mining town of low adobe houses surrounded by craggy peaks. Its population of one thousand was mainly Mexican and Tejano miners and their families. When not policing the town and its mercury mines, he rode on scouts along the Rio Grande in search of horse thieves and tequileros. Terlingua was a dangerous place for lawmen: eight months earlier a Texas Ranger had been shot to death by a Mexican desperado.

On June 18, acting on complaints of the theft of quicksilver from the Terlingua mines, Hamer and a fellow Ranger, Wallace Howell, arrested three Hispanic suspects and recovered a flask of stolen mercury. Reported Captain Rogers, "The mine superintendent has been after my men for some time to break up the stealing of quicksilver ore but this is the first opportunity they have had to get cases against anyone. It is believed these parties have been stealing ore for some time and this will probably break it up as they not only have good cases against these men but they had others arrested in their investigation that no doubt got a good scare."[5]

A week later, on June 25, Captain Rogers dispatched Hamer and Howell after a band of cattle thieves. Lou Buttrill, who owned a ranch forty miles northeast of Terlingua, had complained to Rogers and provided him with the names of the men he suspected. Rogers advised Hamer and Howell how they should proceed. "I provided them with field glasses," the captain reported. He suggested that "by watching from a mountain top some miles away from the ranch of the suspects it is hoped they may be able to catch them in the act." Hamer and his partner dutifully spent the next thirteen days camped on the mountain top, carefully watching the suspects' ranch. But as Rogers reported on July 8, "They, however, failed to secure sufficient evidence to justify them in making any arrest." Frank Hamer was quickly learning that Ranger work was exactly that—a lot of hard work, often with nothing to show for it.[6]

A month later, Rogers sent him undercover to a ranch near Ysleta, thirteen miles southeast of El Paso, "as it is believed that certain parties are engaged in the stealing business." Hamer spent a month at the ranch, posing as a green cowboy. A few years later he told a friend, "That's the hardest job I ever had in my life." Frank appeared at the ranch in an ill-fitting wool suit, pretending to be an inexperienced hand. The range boss took one look at him and demanded, "What in the hell are you doin' out here?"

"Well," Frank replied, "I heard y'all was short of hands. I want a job."

As the group of cattle rustlers laughed at the gangly stranger, the ramrod barked, "What in the hell do you know 'bout workin' on a ranch? What can you do out here?"

"Oh. I don't know. 'Most any little thing. Dig postholes, stretch wire."

"We don't need none of that. What else can you do?"

"Oh, I can ride a little."

"Can you rope?"

"A little bit," Frank lied.

The ramrod was suspicious of Hamer but decided to give him a try.

He had the youth try his hand at roping and throwing cows. Frank did what he was asked, but made sure he didn't do the work very well. When the boss remarked that what he really needed was a good shot, Hamer saw his chance. The ramrod set up a target, but Frank deliberately missed his first shot.

"Gotta do better'n that," said the range boss.

"Well, gimme a chance," retorted Hamer. "I just missed one time."

Frank's next shots were dead on. The boss squealed with delight. "God damn! You're about as good as we got." Hamer got the job. He soon impressed the rustlers with two feats. They dared him to ride the wildest and biggest bronc on the ranch, Old Soandso, seventeen hands high. Hamer swung into the saddle. The animal started to buck, and Frank made sure he fell off. As the cowboys laughed uproariously, Hamer said, "I reckon he's a little shy. Ain't been rode in so long." The next day, Frank tried again. This time he stayed on, and no amount of bucking could throw him off.

Now, the rustlers tried another trick to embarrass the greenhorn. A neighborhood dance was coming up, and they asked if he could play any music. "Oh, I play a little fiddle," he said.

They got him a fiddle, expecting that he would make a spectacle of himself. At the dance, Frank struck up "Out on the Forty Thousand Acres" and played so well the revelers wouldn't let him stop. But despite all of Hamer's efforts to ingratiate himself with the cattle thieves, he was unable to develop enough evidence to make arrests. He finally returned to Rangers headquarters empty-handed.[7]

Frank was not discouraged, for he relished rangering. That fall he made several arrests, from minor ones like stealing railroad ties to the most serious of crimes. On September 23, 1906, a wealthy cattleman, Jim McCutcheon, was slain on his ranch fifty miles south of Pecos by a cowboy, Dick Riggs. The killer claimed self-defense and sent word to Captain Rogers in Alpine that he would surrender to the Rangers. Rogers promptly dispatched Sergeant John Dibrell and Frank Hamer to the Lackey ranch, where they quietly arrested their man. Riggs explained to the Rangers, "I was going to put some steers in a pasture, when Mr. McCutcheon rode up and asked me what I was going to do with those steers. I replied, 'To put them in the pasture.' McCutcheon then said I had no right to do so. I told him I had, and started to produce the papers, when he ran at me and commenced beating me over the head with his quirt. I tried to avoid the blows, but he pursued me, so I turned and fired." The fact that McCutcheon had been unarmed proved of little import to Texas jurors. A year later, when Riggs was brought to trial, the case ended in a hung jury. A change of venue was ordered to El Paso, and upon retrial in 1908 a jury agreed with Riggs and found him not guilty. Under modern law, Riggs was not entitled to use deadly force against such an attack and would at least be guilty of manslaughter. However, the rough frontier ethic of "stand your ground" was alive and well in Texas.[8]

Hamer would later recall that it was with Sergeant Dibrell that he made the longest horseback ride of his life. They first made a routine, weeklong scout on the Rio Grande, "riding around looking for border trouble," as Frank put it. The custom on such scouts was for the Rangers to ride parallel to the river, looking for the muddy tracks of cattle thieves and tequileros who had crossed the border. Once they "cut sign," they would follow the trail inland, hoping to catch up with the rustlers' herd or the smugglers' pack train. This was dangerous work, for Mexican tequileros rarely gave up without a fight. But on this scout, Hamer and Dibrell came up dry. Returning to camp near Sheffield, they were instructed to immediately report to headquarters in Alpine. The weary Rangers remounted and covered the 140 miles in two days.[9]

One of the toughest members of Company C, the one that impressed Hamer the most, was not a Ranger at all. Old Monk, a big pack mule, loyally served the Rangers for twenty years. The Rangers' mules were highly trained, and they carried food, cooking utensils, bedrolls, guns, and ammunition. Frank always insisted that Old Monk was the smartest of them all. "She knew more than any Ranger I ever knew," he asserted many years later. "Monk stood fifteen and one-half hands high and she always had her head up, watching, just like we did, for trouble. She was strong, too. I knew of three dead Rangers she packed out of the Big Bend country." Old Monk first saw service under Captain Rogers, and she was still on duty under Captain Will Wright on the Rio Grande in 1925.[10]

Frank Hamer, standing left, and other Rangers in Del Rio. At right is Duke Hudson. Captain John H. Rogers is seated, holding the German Luger pistol taken from Ed Putnam's body. *Author's collection*

During the fall of 1906, Hamer spent much of his time trying to capture Jesse Bass, a notorious horse and mule thief. In August Bass had stolen four animals in Irion County and brought them west into Brewster County. On September 17 Captain Rogers dispatched Sergeant Dibrell on a scout into Presidio County after Bass. "I sent Private Hamer to scout east of Alpine for the same purpose," wrote Rogers. Frank spent three days on the trail but found no trace of the slippery Bass. On October 1, however, Hamer and another Ranger, Oscar Rountree, spotted Bass in Alpine and arrested him without trouble. Frank then rode to Pecos County to round up witnesses and obtained a grand jury indictment against him.[11]

Two weeks later, Hamer and Howell left Alpine on a scout after a fugitive horse thief named Marse Contreras and in search of animals stolen by Jesse Bass. They managed to capture Contreras in Pecos County. Then, with Ken Oliver, a customs inspector, they made a weeklong scout along the Rio Grande after Bass's stolen horses. Captain Rogers believed that "Bass had turned them over to some Mexican comrade and that perhaps they had been carried by him into Mexico." Hamer left his companions on October 22 because he was under subpoena to appear as a witness in court in Fort Stockton. He only made it as far as Marathon. Despite superb skill with horses, Frank's ornery mount, according to Rogers, "severely kicked and disabled [him] in one limb." Hamer left his horse behind and came into Alpine by train. He recovered quickly, and a few days later was back on his cantankerous animal and headed for court in Fort Stockton.[12]

On November 3 Captain Rogers dispatched Hamer and Duke Hudson to Del Rio, "to aid me in preserving order and keeping peace during the election at the place." Del Rio was a dusty border town of two thousand, situated on the Rio Grande directly opposite its Mexican counterpart, Las Vacas (now Ciudad Acuña). Like all border communities, it had a large Spanish-speaking population; they resided in the neighborhood, or barrio, on the east side of town. Hamer's stay in Del Rio would prove anything but routine. In that era, many local Texas lawmen were inexperienced or incompetent. Those who were politically supported by the saloon and gambling element might be tough and capable, but they often avoided arresting their hardcase friends. As a consequence, Rangers were constantly called to all points in Texas to solve problems that should have been handled by local officers, if only they had had the experience, independence, and fortitude to do so. In Del Rio, Hamer and Hudson found that they were, to all practical effect, city police. They patrolled the town, kept peace at the polls, and arrested several townsfolk for public drunkenness, carrying weapons, and "using abusive language."[13]

In Del Rio, Hamer had his first of many experiences with Mexican revolutionists. For thirty years, Mexico's dictator, Porfirio Díaz, had ruled with an iron hand. Beloved by the ricos and hacendados, he was despised and feared by the common man. In 1906 followers of anarchist leader Ricardo Flores Magón presaged the Mexican Revolution by planning a rebellion in Del Rio. On September 25 eighty Magonistas attacked the Mexican village of Jiménez, on the Rio Grande, twenty miles south of Del Rio. They soon scattered, with Mexican forces in pursuit. Other raids quickly followed, but the rebels were ruthlessly suppressed by Díaz's army. A number of the ringleaders fled back to Del Rio, where they were arrested for violating U.S. neutrality laws, which prevented Americans from interfering in foreign affairs. President Díaz was outraged by editorials written by three prominent Del Rio newspapermen, Pedro N. Gonzales, R. V. Marquez, and Demetrio Castro, and accused them of inciting the Jiménez raid. His particular ire was directed at Marquez, a political cartoonist who had published caricatures of the dictator. Díaz demanded their arrest and extradition to Mexico. On November 21 a deputy U.S. marshal, Fred Lancaster, arrived in Del Rio with warrants for the three journalists. The next day, the marshal joined up with Captain Rogers, Frank Hamer, and Duke Hudson, and they arrested the newspapermen without trouble and jailed them in San Antonio. The three surely faced a firing squad if they were returned to Mexico, but two months later a sympathetic federal magistrate ordered their release.[14]

Frank Hamer would have many more encounters with Mexican rebels in the years to come. Meanwhile, he had his hands full with Anglo rowdies in Del Rio. Among them was a group of linemen working for the Western Union Telegraph Company. They lived in a pair of railroad cars parked on a spur track while they repaired the telegraph line between Del Rio and Comstock. On the night of November 28, five linemen—J. P. McKinney, C. J. Neckerson, E. L. Smith, L. B. Mitchell, and W. Offer—finished their supper, got fighting drunk, and headed for a cantina in the Mexican barrio of East Del Rio. After several rounds of drinks and billiards, they pulled revolvers and shot up the saloon, then called for a hack to take them back to their railcars. Deputy Sheriff Serapio Andrade responded to the sound of gunfire and, with the aid of his brother, arrested all five of them as they tried to leave in the hack. With Deputy Andrade inside the hack and his brother on the back, they started for the jail. But Andrade had failed to properly search his prisoners. One of them jumped out and drew a pistol on the deputy's brother. When Andrade seized the gunman, his companions drew pistols and opened fire, hitting the deputy with two bullets in the head and another in the back. Serapio Andrade died instantly, the first Del Rio lawman slain in the line of duty.

The five murderers scattered and ran, but Offer was immediately caught by a Hispanic citizen. Captain Rogers, asleep in his hotel room, got a telephone call and raced to the scene. "I found the deputy sheriff prostrate in the middle of the street having been killed instantly," he later reported. Rogers was quickly joined by Frank Hamer and Duke Hudson. The three Rangers, accompanied by a deputy sheriff, staked out the railcars and waited for the linemen to return. Two hours later, McKinney, Neckerson, Smith, and Mitchell showed up, and the Rangers clapped them in irons, then hauled the killers to the Val Verde County jail.[15]

At daybreak, Captain Rogers and his men began gathering evidence against the five murderers, but their work was soon cut short by a jarring sequence of bloody events. Eleven days earlier, on November 18, a stranger had appeared in town, calling himself A. R. Sibley and claiming to be a livestock dealer. His real name was Ed Putnam, a thirty-year-old ex-convict from Edwards County, north of Del Rio. For the previous seven years, he had drifted back and forth between West Texas and New Mexico, where he was suspected of smuggling. He had last been in Kerrville, Texas, where he always seemed to have plenty of money and paid a deposit for the purchase of a $20,000 ranch. Putnam intended to raise the rest of the money quickly, without working for it. On November 23 he visited the sheep ranch of John W. Ralston in Rocksprings, seventy-five miles northeast of Del Rio. The sheepman agreed to sell his herd to Putnam for $6,000. Putnam handed over a check for $1,000, and the two climbed into Putnam's buggy so they could complete the deal at the First National Bank in Del Rio. As they reached a spot nine miles north of town, Putnam shot Ralston in the head. To avoid leaving a blood trail, he draped an oat sack around the sheepman's head and dragged his body into a roadside gully. Then Putnam continued on alone into Del Rio.

Meanwhile, Ralston's sons drove the flock of sheep to a pasture seven miles outside Del Rio, known as the Four Mile Tank, to await their father's return with the rest of the purchase money. A few days later, Putnam met a wealthy stockman, Blake M. Cauthorn, who owned a sheep ranch near Del Rio. Putnam told the sheepman that he had a large flock for sale outside town. Cauthorn was interested, so he and Putnam rode out to the Ralston boys' camp to look over the flock. There, Putnam told the boys that he had paid their father in full and that the elder Ralston had gone to Kerrville to buy horses. Putnam announced that Ralston wanted his boys to turn over the sheep and meet him at the family ranch in Rocksprings. Cauthorn was satisfied with the sheep, and he and Putnam returned to the bank in Del Rio, where Cauthorn handed the killer a certified check for $4,500.

By this time the Ralston boys had become suspicious. While one stayed with their flock, the other rode to Rocksprings, where he sent a telegram to Kerrville and learned that their father was not there. He raced back to the sheep camp. The next morning, November 30, Blake Cauthorn rode out to the Four Mile Tank to pick up the flock, telling his wife he would return by noon. There, he met Ralston's sons, who were now extremely alarmed by their father's disappearance. They refused to turn over the sheep. Cauthorn was very surprised and immediately started back to Del Rio to find Ed Putnam and stop payment on the check. He never got there. About four miles from town, he encountered Putnam, who had been waiting for him in a livery rig. Putnam apparently tried to convince Cauthorn that Ralston's sons were mistaken and got him to turn his buggy around so they could go back to the sheep pasture at Four Mile Tank. As Cauthorn turned his buggy, Putnam fired once. The bullet passed through the rear of the buggy seat and struck Cauthorn in the lower back, a fatal wound. The sheepman's team spooked at the gunfire and raced a half mile off the road, finally breaking loose from the buggy. Now, Putnam whipped up his team and headed north on the road toward Sonora, Texas.[16]

By early afternoon, Cauthorn's wife became worried by her husband's failure to return home. She telephoned her brothers, who in turn notified the Rangers. Captain Rogers investigated and quickly learned of the mysterious disappearance of John Ralston after his business dealings with the stranger known as Sibley. Several citizens had seen the stranger late that morning in a livery rig, headed north out of town at a rapid gait. It didn't take the experienced captain long to connect the dots, and he promptly called in the Val Verde County sheriff, John Robinson. Sheriff Robinson and Duke Hudson started in pursuit of Ed Putnam. They hadn't gone far when they met a rider on the way into town, who had seen Putnam's livery rig abandoned twelve miles north of Del Rio. Robinson rushed to a nearby ranch house that had a telephone and notified Rogers to bring the sheriff's bloodhounds and a small posse to the scene of the abandoned buggy. Recounted the captain, "I took Private Hamer and a citizen and proceeded to the designated point of meeting, met Sheriff Robinson and Hudson there and we spent the night circling and trying to find a trail that the dogs could take up and follow but failed."[17]

In the meantime, Ralston's sons started for Del Rio in search of their father. On their way into town that evening, they spotted Cauthorn's buggy and found his corpse slumped in the seat. They raced into Del Rio and reported their discovery. At daybreak, December 1, 1906, a messenger from Del Rio brought word of the murder to Captain Rogers and Sheriff Robinson. The townsfolk were whipped up to a frenzy of excitement and believed that Ralston and Cauthorn had been robbed and murdered by Mexican bandits or revolutionaries. Rogers and the sheriff immediately started for Del Rio, leaving Hamer and Hudson with the bloodhounds and a small posse to continue the hunt for Putnam. The fugitive was on foot, and Hamer knew it would be no easy task to find him. As Rogers explained, the terrain was "very rough and jagged and containing many caves that would furnish convenient hiding places for a criminal."[18]

While Hamer and Hudson kept up the manhunt, Captain Rogers and Sheriff Robinson proceeded to the scene of Cauthorn's murder. They found his body in the buggy's seat, examined the wounds and the buggy tracks, and then returned to Del Rio. They suspected that the killer might have circled back to Del Rio to board a railroad train. While Rogers watched all westbound trains, Sheriff Robinson assigned several men to keep an eye on the eastbound coaches. Said Rogers, "I advised Sheriff Robinson to remain in Del Rio, attend to all telegraphing, receive all information and, in short, to command the situation, as [a] system is always necessary in handling any situation, especially where such excitement exists among the citizens."[19]

When a westbound freight train started to pull out, Captain Rogers swung aboard with three volunteers. They stayed on for thirty miles, but no one tried to board, and at Comstock they got off and returned to Del Rio on a passenger train. Rogers found Sheriff Robinson waiting for him at the depot. The sheriff said that he had learned that Sibley's true name was Ed Putnam and that he believed he was holed up in a brothel owned by Glass Sharp, situated just north of the railroad tracks on the outskirts of town. The two quickly raised a posse and were joined by Frank Hamer and Duke Hudson, who had just returned to Del Rio. The lawmen crowded into two hacks and quickly drove to the Sharp house, arriving at six in the evening.

Sheriff Robinson stationed seven men in front of the Sharp brothel, while Captain Rogers, Hamer, Hudson, and another man covered the rear. Robinson ordered all the women in the house to come out, telling them that he knew Ed Putnam was inside. Explained Rogers, "At first one of the women denied that he was there, afterwards they admitted that he was inside and they carried him word from Sheriff Robinson to come out and surrender." Sharp's daughter, Georgia, was allowed to re-enter the house and talk with Putnam. "He won't come out," the girl told the officers. "He's got a funny look in his eyes and says he won't give up."

Thirty minutes passed and Sheriff Robinson lost patience. By this

The murderer Ed Putnam, shot to death by Frank Hamer
in Del Rio, Texas, on December 1, 1906. *Author's collection*

time a crowd of more than a hundred townsfolk had gathered, some of
them carrying firearms. Robinson then ordered the possemen to fire
on the house. Hamer, armed with a Winchester Model 1894 saddle-ring
carbine, had taken up a position behind a hackberry tree, which gave
him a good view of the back windows. The possemen opened up,
pumping thirty or forty rounds through the wood walls. Frank held his
fire and patiently watched the rear windows. Several times, he saw a
curtain move, then spotted the barrel of a revolver protruding from
behind the curtain. Hamer quickly drew a bead on the six-gun barrel
and squeezed his trigger. The heavy Winchester slug slammed into the
crouching Ed Putnam just under the left eye, ripped downward, and
shattered his jaw, then entered the neck, severing the jugular vein, passed
out of the neck, tore into the left shoulder, and exited through his left
arm. Ed Putnam dropped to the floor, and in seconds was dead.

The lawmen heard a thud, as if Putnam had fallen. Said Rogers,

"However, not knowing whether he was dead, wounded or feigning to be dead, the house was not entered for a time and our party reloaded and fired many times after this until, perhaps, something like two hundred rounds had been fired, when the house was entered and Putnam found to be dead having received one fatal shot." A loaded six-shooter was still in his hand. Captain Rogers took three guns from Putnam: a .32 caliber Colt Single-Action Army revolver, a .32 caliber Winchester rifle, and a newfangled German Luger automatic pistol. In Putnam's pockets the lawmen found three hundred cartridges and $3,500 in cash. The house was completely riddled; one newspaper reported that five hundred shots had entered it. According to an eyewitness, "The furniture in the Sharp home was completely wrecked, even the stove legs being shot off."[20]

John Ralston's sons viewed Putnam's corpse and identified him as the man who had "bought" their father's sheep. The next day Ralston's body, mutilated by scavenging animals, was found where Putnam had dumped it. A Del Rio photographer, Noah H. Rose, had watched the fatal gunfight. He took a postmortem image of Ed Putnam and invited Captain Rogers and his men to sit in his studio for commemorative portraits. Rose took four images of the Rangers. Two were group shots, with Captain Rogers seated, holding Ed Putnam's Luger pistol. Next to him were Frank Hamer, Duke Hudson, and an unidentified friend, with their rifles in prominent display. Then Rose had Hamer and Hudson take off their coats, so their gun belts and six-guns were exposed, and photographed them kneeling and standing, rifles in hand. The images Noah Rose took that day have become iconic in Texas Ranger lore.[21]

Captain Rogers gave Ed Putnam's Colt .32 revolver to Frank Hamer, saying that since this was his "first gunfight as a Ranger he thought he should have a memento of the occasion." Then Rogers left for Alpine, leaving Hamer in Del Rio. The captain had been hugely impressed with Frank's coolness and deadly marksmanship. He began to view the young recruit as one of his most trusted and reliable men.[22]

Hamer stayed in Del Rio long enough to testify against the killers of Deputy Andrade, and before Christmas he was back at company headquarters in Alpine. Rural Texas towns got rowdy during the Christmas season. Cowboys and roustabouts had time off work to attend country dances and blow off steam by drinking and fighting. In mid-December the sixty-nine-year-old sheriff of Brewster County, D. A. T. Walton, wrote to Captain Rogers, asking him to send Rangers to Marathon, a one-horse town thirty miles east of Alpine. Its population of five hundred was too small to have a jail. Sheriff Walton told Rogers that "some complaint had been made of rowdyism during the approaching Holidays." On December 22 Captain Rogers dispatched Frank Hamer and Wallace Howell, ordering them "to keep the peace during the Holidays."

On Christmas night Hamer learned that a "bad hombre," Ed Harris, had been "whipping anybody who would fight at the ranch dances." Alone, Hamer found Harris at a dance in Marathon and told him he was under arrest "for being drunk, disorderly, and disturbing the peace." The tough replied contemptuously, "Arrest, hell. Where's your jail?"

Harris tried to resist, but he didn't have a chance. The brawny young Ranger dragged his struggling prisoner down the street to a windmill. "There's the jail," Frank said, and handcuffed his man to one corner. There, Harris stayed all night until Frank could deliver him to a justice of the peace in the morning. After the justice ordered Harris fined, Hamer mounted his horse and rode back to Alpine. The Marathon townsfolk, both surprised and pleased, watched him go, and the story of Frank Hamer, "the man who made a jail out of a windmill," was repeated in West Texas for two generations.[23]

During the new year, Hamer continued to rapidly gain experience. In mid-January 1907, Captain Rogers dispatched him to Sierra Blanca, halfway between Alpine and El Paso, on another undercover assignment. A local rancher, Tom Love, had suggested this plan as the only way to get evidence against a gang that was stealing cattle and running stolen horses. Frank went to Sierra Blanca, posing as a cowboy, which wasn't hard because that is what he was. On his first day there, however, acquaintances immediately recognized him as a newly minted Texas Ranger. His cover blown, a disappointed Hamer rode back to Alpine. A few days later, Rogers sent him with Duke Hudson back to Terlingua, instructing them to ride on scouts with the U.S. customs inspectors

Frank Hamer, left, and Duke Hudson, right, the day after the gunfight with Ed Putnam in Del Rio. *Author's collection*

stationed in Lajitas. The pair wasted little time in tracking down an accused murderer, Luis Sosa, and delivering him to Brewster County authorities.[24]

Neither of Hamer's mentors, Sheriff Barker and Captain Rogers, were drinking men. Consequently, Hamer sought to follow their example. His fellow Ranger Wallace Howell, however, was a heavy drinker. On February 1, 1907, Captain Rogers got a complaint that, the day before, Howell had been drunk on duty in Marfa. Rogers, a stickler for sobriety, immediately journeyed to Marfa to investigate. The captain reported that he "satisfied myself of the truthfulness of the report, and promptly discharged him the same day." This lesson was something Frank Hamer never forgot, for he never drank on duty and, for that matter, rarely imbibed socially. Years later, when handed a celebratory glass of champagne in front of the adjutant general of Texas, he politely declined and poured it down a sink.[25]

From their headquarters in Terlingua, Hamer and Duke Hudson made numerous scouts along the Rio Grande, looking out for Mexican outlaws. The two Rangers, reported the Alpine newspaper, "have been 'keeping tab' on their movements on this side of the river." Early in February, they crossed the river at Lajitas to confer with Mexican officers about a fugitive they were hunting. On the ride back, while they were still in Mexico, gunfire exploded from the rocks above them. One bullet whined past Hudson's head and splattered into a rock wall behind him. He and Hamer leaped from their horses, rifles ready, but they could not spot their assailant. Fearing an ambush, they remounted and galloped back to Lajitas without further trouble.[26]

In March Duke Hudson was replaced in Terlingua by Oscar J. Rountree. An experienced twenty-nine-year-old officer, he had served three years as an Arizona Ranger before enlisting in Captain Rogers's company. Rountree bore the distinction of being one of the few men to serve in both the Arizona Rangers and the Texas Rangers. Hamer and Rountree kept Terlingua's rough element under control, arresting several desperadoes as well as an accused murderer, Patricio Pena. In April Hamer got violently ill and was laid up in his hotel room in Terlingua for a week. A doctor looked him over and said he could not ride on horseback. Private Rountree loaded Frank into a wagon and brought him back to Alpine. The rough, eighty-five-mile trip must have been agony, but once back at headquarters Hamer quickly recovered. Within a few days, he was again in the saddle, stationed with Sergeant Dibrell in Comstock, thirty miles northwest of Del Rio.[27]

The boy Ranger was quickly learning investigative skills that would prove invaluable in his later career. Hamer's natural curiosity and uncanny powers of observation contributed greatly to his development as a detective. On May 3 he rode to the Gerlach ranch, thirty miles from Comstock, to investigate the mysterious poisoning of Gerlach's cattle, sheep, and goats. A five-day investigation led him to arrest Peyton Boyd, who, upon close questioning, made a full confession. He led Hamer to places on the range where he had set out poison. The next day, May 9, Frank brought his prisoner into Comstock and turned him over to Sheriff Robinson. Boyd was convicted and sentenced to jail.[28]

A week later Hamer and Sergeant Dibrell received word that "a very suspicious character" was in Juno, an isolated ranch town forty miles north. The stranger, who called himself Jones, matched the description of David Barker, a Wells Fargo cashier who had vanished from Hot Springs, Arkansas, two months earlier with $14,000 in company funds. On May 16 the two Rangers boarded a mail hack for Juno. Once there, they looked over the suspect, finding scars and other marks that did not match Barker's description. The stranger was well dressed, educated, and almost effeminate in appearance. But Hamer noticed "the way his eyes slid from one object to another, alertly and fearfully." He had what Frank called "the hunted look."

The young Ranger told Dibrell, "Let me arrest that man and search his luggage. He's wrong. He's done something criminal."

Dibrell rejected that idea outright. "You're too curious," he snapped, and ordered Jones released. As it turned out, Frank's instincts were right on the money. Jones was indeed David Barker, who, after fleeing Arkansas, had bought an interest in a ranch near Juno. Later, he slipped away to San Angelo, where he consorted with prostitutes, spent money freely, and lived the high life. In June 1909, when his cash finally ran out, he killed himself with poison in a San Angelo bordello. Wells Fargo detectives soon identified the dead libertine as the much-wanted David Barker. The case made newspaper headlines, and Hamer felt fully vindicated. He told Dibrell, "You see, I could have arrested him and saved his life. And we'd have gotten ten per cent of that money for returning it!"[29]

Frank Hamer's first year as a Texas Ranger had been an eventful one. He acquired more experience in twelve months than many modern law officers get in a decade. He rode several thousand miles throughout the border region and the Big Bend, obtaining intimate knowledge of the country and its people. He learned to conduct surveillance, work undercover, and investigate a myriad of crimes. He arrested seven men for murder. In the Del Rio gunfight, he proved his coolness and deadly marksmanship by killing Ed Putnam. Captain Rogers was more than pleased with his new recruit. One day, the captain ran into Sheriff Barker and told him, "If you have any more kids like Hamer out there, send 'em in. I can use 'em."[30]

3

ONE RIOT, ONE RANGER

In May 1907 Adjutant General J. O. Newton directed Captain Rogers to move the headquarters of Company C from Alpine to the state capitol building in Austin, more than four hundred miles east. They replaced Captain John R. Hughes and his Company D, who were ordered from Austin to Marfa. Newton instructed Rogers "to dismount his company." Each Ranger had to sell or let out his beloved horse, for once in Austin they would travel primarily by train. Most of Rogers's men were cowboys, used to life in the saddle on the open ranges of West Texas, and they were not happy with their new assignment. On May 22 Sergeant Dibrell, Hamer, and five other privates boarded an eastbound train for Austin. They arrived the following day and moved into a rooming house at 1314 San Bernard Street, a mile east of the state capitol building. The state paid their lodging, for no Ranger could afford rent on his forty-dollar-a-month wage. A day later, Captain Rogers arrived with his wife and children. He leased a house and moved into an office in the adjutant general's headquarters in the capitol building. Rogers's company was now charged with maintaining order in a wide swath of the eastern part of the state.[1]

In his entire life, Frank Hamer had never set foot in East Texas. It was a world away—geographically, culturally, and racially—from the

Hill Country, the Pecos, and the Big Bend. East Texas is green and lush, with a humid subtropical climate. Many of the Rangers, accustomed to the dry heat of West Texas, did not like the humidity and claimed it was bad for their health. In the north, the Piney Woods extended into Louisiana, Arkansas, and Oklahoma. East Texas's grassy, rolling hills faded into flat coastal plains north of the Gulf of Mexico. Countless rivers and creeks crisscrossed the grasslands and pineries. Here the settlements were among the oldest in Texas. Nacogdoches had its beginnings when the Spanish built a mission in 1716; Americans began settling there in 1820. The oldest Anglo settlement was San Augustine, near the Louisiana border, thirty-five miles east of Nacogdoches, founded in the 1820s.

While West Texas and South Texas had large Hispanic populations, East Texas was home to most of the state's blacks. By 1910 there were 690,000 African Americans in the Lone Star State, representing 18 percent of the state's population. Because East Texas was where most

Ranger Company C in Alpine, Texas, in 1907. Back row, left, is Frank Hamer; third from left, Marvin Bailey; and at far right, Duke Hudson. Seated, third from left, is Captain Rogers, and at far right is Sergeant John Dibrell. *Author's collection*

slave owners had lived, much of the black population was still centered there. And although after Reconstruction African Americans retained the right to vote, they were often intimidated at the polls or otherwise disenfranchised. Jim Crow laws kept blacks segregated from whites; Jim Crow customs made blacks inferior to whites in every way. Blacks could never argue with whites, they had to step aside for whites on public sidewalks, and they had to refer to whites as "Mr." or "Mrs.," while, in turn, they were always called by their first names. And, especially, no black man could ever touch or even appear familiar with a white woman.

Even worse for blacks was the state's long history of summary justice, or "Judge Lynch." During the 1890s, 95 percent of those lynched in Texas were African American, and most hangings of blacks took place in East Texas. Between 1900 and 1910 more than one hundred African Americans were lynched in the state, mostly in East Texas, making the Lone Star State the third worst in the nation. The worst year was 1908, with twenty-four blacks lynched in Texas. In addition to being hanged for rape and murder, blacks were strung up by mobs for property crimes and also for acts that were entirely legal, such as "testifying against whites" and "suing whites."[2]

The tradition of lynching in Texas and the South was grounded in notions of personal honor and nostalgia for the lost cause of the Confederacy. The "Lost Cause" was an intellectual and literary movement in the South that sought to portray the region's defeat as noble and its antebellum way of life as chivalrous while denying responsibility for the horrors of slavery and civil war. During Reconstruction, lynching helped reinstate white dominance. It also became a purification ritual in which the honor of family, white womanhood, and community were sustained; "evil" blacks were exterminated; and racial reforms that had been forced on the South were resisted. Judge Lynch helped restore Southern self-esteem, which had been lost in the war. And just as dueling in the antebellum period washed away the stain of a personal insult, so lynching in the postwar era removed the "stain" of any African American who dared oppose the established racial order.[3]

Yet not all Texas blacks kowtowed to whites; some refused to accept Jim Crow customs. To whites and blacks alike they were known as "bad niggers." Some were gamblers, some career criminals, and many others simply tough men who refused to cower. Best known today is Jack Johnson (1878–1946), the champion boxer and native Texan who flouted conventions by marrying three times, all to white women. Far more representative of the refusal to accept Jim Crow was the now obscure Lewis Kimball of Dallas, slayer of Texas lawman Tom C. Smith. The latter was a dangerous character who figured prominently in the Jaybird-Woodpecker feud of the 1880s and who was a leader of the "Invaders" in Wyoming's Johnson County War of 1892. When Tom Smith and two other deputy U.S. marshals, riding on a train from Texas to Oklahoma, walked through a segregated smoking car, Lewis Kimball ordered them out, declaring, "If negroes could not ride with white folks, the whites should not ride with negroes." Hot words followed, and Kimball jerked his pistol and shot the white lawman dead. One of the deputy marshals fired back, killing Kimball instantly. During the Jim Crow era, many other white Texas lawmen were shot by black desperadoes.[4]

For several decades the Rangers had little contact with East Texas. Then, beginning in the 1880s and 90s, Rangers were increasingly called there to put down mob violence. They were not popular, for East Texans had their own way of life and didn't like state Rangers telling them what to do. In East Texas towns, the Rangers, with their wide-brimmed Stetsons, riding boots, Winchesters, and heavy cartridge belts, stood out like sore thumbs. Many lawmen there saw the Rangers as interlopers, though some local police and sheriffs welcomed the Rangers' help and worked closely with them in opposing lynch mobs. While modern riot control tactics involve the deployment of large numbers of police, organized into military-style platoons, to prod and push mobs at the weakest points, the Rangers had no such luxury. Budget and manpower restrictions guaranteed that rarely more than a handful were available to fight mobs. Instead, Rangers depended on long tradition and fearsome reputations. Even the most racist, murderous lyncher would think twice when faced with a group of lean, sunburned, heavily armed border men.

Hamer's first assignment was to maintain order in Groveton, seat of Trinity County, one of the rowdiest and most lawless towns in East

Texas. A logging community, its principal business was the Trinity Lumber Company, which ran one of the largest sawmills in the United States. The county was embroiled in conflict over the banning of saloons. Prohibition of liquor had long been an issue in Texas, pitting "wets" against "drys." In 1903 bootleggers had attacked the antiliquor county attorney, H. L. Robb, who in turn shot one of his assailants in self-defense. In 1906, two bootleggers, one of them a notorious desperado named H. O. Park, assassinated a private detective in Groveton who had been investigating them. Hamer hunted Park in Trinity County but was unable to capture him.[5]

One of the main reasons for Hamer's presence in Groveton was the attempted assassination of a Texas Ranger, Sergeant James D. Dunaway, five weeks earlier. Dunaway, who would later become a close friend of Hamer, had been stationed in Groveton following the murder of the private detective. Dunaway was short, stocky, and clean-shaven and had red hair topping an oval face. A veteran lawman, the former city marshal of Llano, and a member of Captain Bill McDonald's Company B for three years, he was also quarrelsome in the extreme. On April 26 Sergeant Dunaway and the county attorney, H. L. Robb, were walking down the main street to the courthouse when R. O. Kenley, a young attorney who represented the saloon element, fired on them from a second-story window of his law office. Dunaway was hit six times; Robb was wounded in the head and leg. Jim Dunaway was as cool as he was tough. He dictated a succinct telegram to the adjutant general: "Send Rangers at once. Waylaid and shot all to pieces; not serious." Said Bill Sterling later, "Jim's classic message, with variations usually occurring at each retelling, has become famous in Ranger annals. It has been widely quoted in camps from the Red River to the Rio Grande."[6]

Kenley promptly surrendered, claiming that he had acted in self-defense. He said that Dunaway had assaulted him a few days before and that he had complained to the governor and asked for the sergeant's removal. He claimed that Jim Dunaway then threatened to kill him in retaliation, which, given the Ranger sergeant's quarrelsome nature, was probably true. According to Kenley, when he saw Dunaway approaching, he thought the Ranger was coming to his law office to kill him, and so he opened fire in self-defense. Jim Dunaway quickly recovered from his wounds, but H. L. Robb died on May 2. Kenley and his two accomplices were charged with murder.[7]

On August 1 Frank Hamer, with Captain Rogers and two other Rangers, acted as bodyguards for Dunaway when he returned to Groveton to testify before the grand jury about the attack. This was the beginning of a long friendship between Hamer and Dunaway. Afterward, Hamer helped guard Dunaway on the train out of town, because, as Rogers said, "it was believed by some that he would scarcely get out of Trinity County alive." A year later Kenley stood trial on charges of attempting to kill Dunaway. In a flagrant miscarriage of justice, a Houston jury acquitted him. Nonetheless, charges against Kenley for killing Robb would hang over his head for many years. To his credit, Kenley went on to a distinguished career as a lawyer and judge, but he was destined to have more trouble with Jim Dunaway, which in turn would tarnish Hamer's reputation.[8]

A few weeks later, Hamer was sent back to Groveton. The Trinity Lumber Company was building a logging railroad twelve miles from town. They had hired black laborers, but white workers had objected. Some whites threatened the blacks and ordered them to leave. The African Americans refused, and a race riot was feared. All work stopped on the logging road as the company appealed for Texas Rangers. On September 14 Hamer and Sergeant Dibrell were hurriedly dispatched. They spent a week investigating the case and obtained a warrant for a white ruffian, Charles Mossenton, charging him with "intimidation of the railroad construction hands." Then Hamer and Dibrell rode out to the railroad camp and arrested Mossenton, putting an end to the labor troubles. Frank Hamer would soon find that handling such racial conflicts would be a major part of his job in East Texas.[9]

On October 1 Captain Rogers was ordered to take his company to protect a black prisoner, Dock Bailey, who had been charged with murder in Nacogdoches County. Three weeks earlier, Bailey had killed a young white farmer, D. G. Owens, the day before his wedding. When Owens failed to show up for the ceremony, a search was begun and his beaten and bullet-riddled body was found in the woods. Bailey was arrested soon afterward, and he confessed to shooting Owens in a gambling quarrel. He had dragged the body by horseback into the pinewoods, then fled to Rusk, where he was captured and placed in the state penitentiary to keep him safe from lynch mobs. Captain Rogers took four privates, among them Frank Hamer, to the prison at Rusk. Their assignment was to transport Bailey by rail to Nacogdoches and protect him during his murder trial. On arrival, Rogers, Hamer, and the other Rangers found that Adjutant General J. O. Newton and his assistant, Colonel L. T. Rogers, were already there. The white population of Nacogdoches was whipped into a frenzy of racial hatred, and Newton had been warned that they intended to seize and hang Bailey as soon as the train arrived with him on board.[10]

General Newton sent for two more Rangers, Sergeant Dibrell and Private J. C. White, and then, on October 3, accompanied by the sheriffs of Rusk and Nacogdoches, the eleven-man posse boarded the train for Nacogdoches. The cowed mob gave the Rangers no trouble. The lawmen safely lodged Bailey in the Nacogdoches jail, which they guarded all night. However, as one newspaper reported, "Considerable indignation is expressed by citizens because of the rangers being brought here, it being the prevalent opinion that this precaution was not needed." That was hardly true, for Nacogdoches had a bloody history of mob violence. In 1897 a black man accused of the attempted rape of a white girl was publicly lynched in the town square. In 1900 a mob tried to hang a white man who had killed a woman but the lynchers were outwitted by the county sheriff. In 1902 Nacogdoches saw the legal hanging of Jim Buchanan that—for all practical effect—was a lynching. Buchanan, an African American desperado, had murdered a white family. He was promptly captured, confessed to the triple murder, and was brought to trial in less than a week. While a huge mob screamed for his neck outside the courthouse, Buchanan was tried, convicted, and summarily executed in three hours, making a mockery of due process. The following year a mob in the eastern part of the county flogged eight black men and forced them from their homes; a ninth was hanged.[11]

Frank Hamer and the other Rangers knew that they had a dangerous assignment. Dock Bailey's trial began the following day, October 4, as large, angry crowds filled the streets and surrounded the courthouse. The town's population was about two thousand, but twenty-five thousand people lived in the county, and many had flooded in from the country-side, hoping to see a hanging. Captain Rogers assigned Hamer and the rest of his men to guard all the entrances to the courthouse, and he ordered them not to allow anyone to enter unless they had a written permit from him or Adjutant General Newton. Reported the captain, "There was intense interest in the trial and there seemed to be a nervous restless feeling among the citizens. In the afternoon, ex-sheriff A. J. Spradley was making improper and imprudent talks on the street, which was calculated to incite citizens already nervous and with the mob spirit uppermost in their minds, to violence." Spradley, fifty-four, was the best-known sheriff in East Texas. An expert detective, he had solved many famous cases during the previous two decades and was known for his populist bent and his fair treatment of African Americans. But by 1907 Spradley's liberalism had cost him the sheriff's office, and he abandoned his populist, egalitarian beliefs. As a result, he had gone from opposing lynch law to leading a mob.[12]

Captain Rogers asked the county sheriff, George Blackburn, to get a witness to Spradley's inflammatory language so that he could be charged with inciting a riot. Rogers then approached the district judge, James Perkins, and told him of Spradley's conduct. The judge replied that he "was friendly with Spradley and could approach him easily . . . and influence him to do right." As a result, recounted Rogers, "No arrests were made at this time. The situation in the afternoon appeared very critical from our standpoint, as we stood in the upper story of the court house and watched the excited mob below. They had even brought lumber into the open square with which to erect a gallows, and news reached us that two wagon loads of guns had been brought in from the country for the use of the mob."[13]

That afternoon, the jury announced that it had reached a verdict. It was a disgraceful example of Texas justice for African Americans: Bailey had been brought to trial less than a month after the crime, giving his counsel little time to prepare, and his trial had lasted less than a day. But those were not the Rangers' concerns. Their job was to protect Dock

Bailey from the mob. Captain Rogers ordered his men to clear the upper floor of the courthouse. Hamer and the rest herded the spectators downstairs, then took up positions to prevent anyone else from entering. When the jury filed out to give the verdict, it was a foregone conclusion: guilty of first-degree murder, with a sentence of death.

Instead of placating the mob, this result inflamed them further. Many of the townsfolk believed that Dock Bailey, like Jim Buchanan five years earlier, would be hanged immediately after the trial. When Judge Perkins warned that this was not true, they became even more determined to lynch him. Loud shouts rang out as vigilantes threatened to storm the courthouse and hang the prisoner. Reported Captain Rogers, "For a time it looked as if the surging mob would attack us in spite of everything that could be done; but we kept our positions of advantage firmly allowing no one to even start up the stairs from the bottom." A number of responsible citizens attempted to placate the mob, many of whom were friends of the murder victim. Finally, a heavy rain began to fall, and the mob sought refuge under nearby awnings. But Hamer and the others could see them "in large numbers on the streets talking in groups on the sidewalks under shelter."[14]

Captain Rogers decided it was too risky to return Bailey to the county jail, so he ordered his men to settle in for the night. As Rogers explained, "the upper story of the court house afforded us much better advantage for his protection." It was a long, nerve-wracking night, but daybreak finally arrived without any attack by the mob. At 9:30 Spradley, the ex-sheriff, emerged from the crowd and strode brazenly up the courthouse stairs. Dibrell, Hamer, and the other Rangers called for him to halt, but he refused. Sergeant Dibrell stopped him on the stairs, and Spradley announced that he was "on his way to deliver an important message to the judge and demanded that he be allowed to pass." However, as Rogers later pointed out, it was a Saturday, court was not in session, and Spradley had no legitimate reason to enter the courthouse. Dibrell nonetheless relayed the message to Judge Perkins, who refused Spradley's admittance. Dibrell then pulled his six-shooter and forced the ex-sheriff downstairs.

By now Spradley was yelling and cursing loudly, and Captain Rogers came downstairs and placed him under arrest. Said Rogers, "He struggled and resisted all in his power and was very unruly and hard to handle." The captain had had enough. Jerking his Colt revolver, Rogers "bent the barrel" on the ex-sheriff's head, inflicting a deep gash from which blood flowed freely. Still struggling, Spradley was dragged off to jail by the Rangers. Later Rogers stopped by the cell to check on the bloodied sheriff, remarking to his men, "I only meant to tap him." To that, one of the Rangers exclaimed, "Cap, if that's what you call tappin' a man I would hate to see one who was really hit!"

Judge Perkins, upon getting Spradley's promise of good behavior, ordered him freed. But as Rogers said, "Immediately upon being released he disregarded his promise to Judge Perkins and proceeded to act very ugly and created much excitement in town. His friends, however, got him away from the Court House and he remained away, over in town until we left and could be seen talking in an excited manner." Then Rogers and his men, brandishing rifles and shotguns, marched Dock Bailey past the mob to the railroad depot. They boarded the 12:40 train and safely returned Dock Bailey to the state penitentiary in Rusk. On November 7 Sheriff Blackburn returned Bailey to Nacogdoches for execution of his sentence. More than five thousand people gathered to see the public hanging. On the scaffold, before Sheriff Blackburn dropped the trap, Bailey again admitted killing Owens.[15]

The arrest and pistol-whipping of Spradley caused a sensation in Nacogdoches, and locals criticized the Rangers for brutality. Judge Perkins directed the grand jury to investigate, and it issued a lengthy report, exonerating Rogers of any wrongdoing but concluding that "the Rangers and Mr. Spradley acted indiscreetly." Frank Hamer, by observing Captain Rogers, learned several valuable lessons in Nacogdoches. First, Rogers showed that he did not subscribe to the "One Riot, One Ranger" ethos. Instead, to protect the prisoner, he rounded up every Ranger he could find, including one from Captain Hughes's company, as well as two local sheriffs. Second, Rogers carefully organized the men to work together as a team. Third, Rogers firmly opposed racist violence and impressed this ethic on his men. In his official reports, he railed against "outrageous lynchings" and "outrageous violence against inoffensive negroes and Mexican laborers." Fourth, Rogers demonstrated an iron-fisted determination to enforce the law against overwhelming opposition. Despite the fact that the Rangers were completely outnumbered by a mob that was thousands strong, he never flinched. And lastly, the captain singled out the leader of the mob, despite the fact that he was one of the most powerful politicians in the county, and did not hesitate to forcefully subdue him. Though Frank Hamer lacked much formal education, he quickly absorbed these practical and moral lessons. Dock Bailey was but the first of numerous African Americans whom Frank Hamer helped protect from lynch mobs.[16]

Within a few weeks, the young Ranger saw more racial violence. On October 25, 1907, Captain Rogers left Austin with Hamer and J. T. Laughlin for the isolated town of San Augustine, near the Louisiana line. Rogers had received a report that "three men had been killed within the last few days, and that the situation was beyond the control of the local authorities." Train service was so slow that it took the Rangers two days to travel the 280 miles. San Augustine County, situated in the Piney Woods, had changed little since the antebellum period. The county's ten thousand people subsisted on lumbering and growing cotton and corn. Clannish, stubborn, and independent, they frequently turned to violence to solve personal problems. From 1900 to 1904, San Augustine County saw the Border-Broocks-Wall feud, in which six men were killed, including the county sheriff. The latest trouble had been caused by a notorious twenty-five-year-old bootlegger, Henry A. "Harry" Head. In 1906 he had killed a black man with a shotgun and escaped punishment. Four months before the Rangers' arrival, one of Head's brothers had been killed by an African American, and several blacks had been slain in revenge.[17]

Then, on the night of October 19, 1907, there was more bloodshed. Harry Head, his brother Lewis, Charlie Alvis, and Jack Davis, a young man, were gambling with six black railroad section hands in a house on the outskirts of San Augustine. Davis started a quarrel and pulled a pistol on the railroad men. A black section hand, Monroe King, disarmed Davis and was thrashing him soundly with the revolver when Harry Head came to the youth's aid. At that, King opened fire, mortally wounding Davis, killing Lewis Head, and slightly injuring Harry Head. Not wishing to experience East Texas justice, the six African Americans then fled into the woods. Harry Head, after getting his wounds treated, gathered together a band of five friends and relatives, Lucius Jenkins, Charlie Alvis, Robert Kennedy, Steve Fussell, and Steve's son, Dan. Arming themselves with shotguns, they mounted horses and began hunting King and the other section hands. They learned that King had been seeing the sister-in-law of a black woodcutter, Oscar Garrett. Two days later, they found Garrett and Abe Greer cutting wood in a bayou bottom two miles south of town. The two had nothing to do with the shooting and had good reputations among the whites. Harry Head questioned them about Monroe King's whereabouts, but they insisted they had not seen him. Harry decided to kill them both, but several of his comrades objected. Finally, Harry Head, Jenkins, and Alvis shot them to death. Then Harry led the band on a rampage, ordering blacks to leave the county, shooting into at least one house, and setting another on fire. Reported Captain Rogers, "They continued to parade the county with their guns intimidating negroes and causing them to leave, regardless of whether they were innocent or had any connection with the former killing."[18]

Captain Rogers and his Rangers investigated and learned that Harry Head, Jenkins, and Alvis were the probable killers of the two woodcutters. On October 30, Rogers took Frank Hamer and J. T. Laughlin to the bayou where the woodcutters had been murdered. Hamer's extraordinary tracking skills became immediately evident. As the captain reported, they "succeeded in following the tracks of the murderers, notwithstanding they were a week old and a few rains had fallen upon them, we connected sufficient tracks of these men, both horseback and on foot, to complete a case against these parties." They managed to identify Kennedy and the Fussells from their tracks and from witnesses who had seen them hunting the blacks. Rogers interrogated Kennedy and the Fussells and got two of them to admit that the killers were Harry Head, Jenkins, and Alvis, who had disappeared. Captain Rogers then swore out warrants for their arrest and sent Hamer and Laughlin in search of the murderers.[19]

Meanwhile, forty blacks had fled San Augustine, and Rogers feared a full-scale race war. He sent for the balance of his company, three more Rangers, but no further trouble arose. Rogers swore out warrants for the six black section hands, but they had fled the county, and the Rangers could not find them. The lawmen had better luck with the white killers. On November 5 Duke Hudson and J. C. White captured Charlie Alvis in San Augustine, and the next day they picked up Harry Head. Lucius Jenkins was arrested by a local deputy sheriff, and all three were brought into court. Kennedy and the Fussells turned state's evidence, and all three of the killers were held to answer on charges of murder. Because the jail in Beaumont was more secure, they were taken there for safekeeping. That was not the last Frank Hamer would see of Harry Head.[20]

Captain Rogers left several Rangers in San Augustine and sent Hamer and Laughlin to Hempstead, a busy railroad town and cotton-shipping center located fifty miles northwest of Houston. In 1905 it got its nickname, "Six-Shooter Junction," following a bloody gun battle that left a U.S. congressman and three other men dead. For six weeks Hamer went back and forth on the railroad between Hempstead and Navasota, twenty miles north, helping local officers control the criminal element. He made numerous arrests for petty offenses and became well known to the townsfolk in both communities.[21]

Some years later, Hamer's Ranger friends would repeat a story about one of his first encounters with Navasota's toughs, who had been bullying a local constable. Frank arrived on the morning train, looked the town over, then took a seat in a barbershop, where he quietly whittled pecan shells with his pocket knife. Soon one of the leading hardcases swaggered into the shop.

"Where's this damned Ranger they sent over here to clean up the town?" he demanded. "I can whip him just as easy as I can handle that constable."

"Well, you might be talking about me," Frank replied in his easy drawl. "I'm a Texas Ranger."

He slowly folded his knife blade and slipped it into a pocket. In an instant the hardcase got the fight he asked for, but it didn't last long.

According to an early account, "In ten minutes he was in a doctor's office getting a badly cut head sewed up. Hamer had taken him there after subduing him with a pistol butt."[22]

Such pistol whippings—known as buffaloing—were not always condoned, even in Texas. On November 30 Hamer and Laughlin arrested a black man, Sam Cain, for drunk and disorderly conduct in Hempstead. Cain was obstreperous, and Frank struck him several times over the head with his six-gun. Some townsfolk thought he had used excessive force, and a few weeks later Hamer was charged in court with aggravated assault. Either the charges were dropped or Hamer paid a fine, but he was never suspended from duty.[23]

In the new year, 1908, Captain Rogers called Hamer back to headquarters in Austin. On January 12 Hamer, with Rogers, Hudson, and White, picked up Harry Head, Lucius Jenkins, and Charlie Alvis at the jail in Beaumont and brought them to San Augustine to face murder charges. The Rangers, concerned that Harry Head's friends would try to break them out of jail, guarded them day and night. Defense attorneys obtained a change of venue to Beaumont, and the Rangers returned them to jail there. For the next two months, Hamer was stationed in Navasota, until Rogers sent him back to San Augustine to prevent more violence. Harry Head's trial was scheduled in Beaumont, and on April 16 Rogers dispatched Hamer to Fort Worth to bring two of the witnesses, Steve and Dan Fussell, to court. The Fussells feared for their lives; Frank guarded them in court until the judge continued the case to June.[24]

Hamer had thoroughly cowed the desperadoes of San Augustine, but as soon as he was gone, they began to terrorize the black residents. As Captain Rogers reported, the local hardcases "cause much trouble when the Rangers are not present." On May 25 he sent Frank back to San Augustine, accompanied by a veteran Ranger, Oscar Latta. Hamer and Latta became close friends. Latta was a capable lawman and a dangerous man in a gunfight. In 1897, while a deputy sheriff in Kimble County, he and other officers engaged in a pitched gun battle with bank robbers, killing two of them. The next year he enlisted in the Rangers. Both Hamer and Captain Rogers thought very highly of him.[25]

Meanwhile, the killers Harry Head, Lucius Jenkins, and Charlie Alvis were released on bond and returned to their homes in San Augustine. Hamer kept an eye on them, and on June 4, 1908, he and Oscar Latta arrested Harry and a companion, W. C. Scott, for "whitecapping"—that is, threatening someone while masked. The ineffectual courts promptly released them, so, two days later, Hamer and Latta arrested Harry Head and Lucius Jenkins for gambling, taking a pistol away from Head.[26]

Early in the morning of June 21, Hamer and Latta were awakened by Sheriff W. S. Noble with a startling report. At 8:30 the previous evening, a young white stockman, Aaron Johnson, had been murdered on his ranch near Geneva, about midway between Hemphill and San Augustine. Johnson had just finished his supper and was sitting with his wife and infant baby when someone fired a shotgun through the window, striking him in the head and splattering blood and brains all over his wife and child. Johnson's nearest neighbor, who lived a half mile away, clearly heard the wife's bloodcurdling screams. The news spread like wildfire, creating a public uproar. Because there was no nighttime telephone service to Hemphill, the county seat, an emergency call was made to the nearest lawman, Sheriff Noble, in San Augustine.[27]

At 3:00 A.M. Hamer and Latta piled into a buggy and raced the twenty miles to Johnson's ranch. A quick investigation led them to arrest Johnson's hired hand, Perry Price, a nineteen-year-old black youth. Price promptly confessed to the murder, saying that Johnson's brother-in-law, Robert Wright, had paid him five dollars to do it. By this time an angry crowd of 150 gathered at the scene and threatened to lynch Price. By then the local sheriff arrived and asked Hamer and Latta to bring Price to the Sabine County jail in Hemphill, but the Rangers were concerned about its security. Instead, Hamer and Latta spread the word that they had to take Price "to point out other offenders" and would soon return. They bundled him into their buggy and started off. By the time the enraged mob found out they had been duped, the Rangers were halfway to San Augustine. Once there, Oscar Latta called out the local militia company to help guard the jail. Still not trusting the security of the local lockups, and eager to get Price farther away from Sabine

Frank Hamer, left, and Oscar Latta in 1908. *Author's collection*

County, they took him by rail to Center, eighteen miles north, where they lodged him in jail overnight.

In the morning, Hamer and Latta found that they had exercised good judgment in avoiding the jail in Hemphill. At one in the morning, a mob had broken into the county jail and taken out six black prisoners charged with murdering a white man. They shot and killed one who tried to escape and hanged the rest from the same tree. Three other accused blacks were killed by Sabine County vigilantes the same night. Nine African Americans had died in one of the biggest lynchings in Texas history. But, once again, the Rangers avoided losing a man to a mob.[28]

While at the jail in Center, Hamer and Latta heard that Robert Wright, who had incited the murder, had appeared in Center and then left for his home near the Johnson ranch. To townsfolk, Wright had feigned surprise, as Captain Rogers said, "pretending at Center that he had just heard of the crime and . . . to be very much grieved." Hamer and Latta telephoned Sheriff Noble in San Augustine, who sent a deputy to arrest Wright at his home. The next morning, Hamer and Latta boarded a southbound train with their prisoner, Perry Price, and then picked up Wright and Sheriff Noble when the train stopped in San Augustine. Due to widespread rumors that a mob would try to stop the train in Sabine County, forty-two militiamen accompanied them part of the way. The Rangers then continued on to Beaumont, where they lodged both prisoners in jail. The newspapers praised Hamer and Latta, one saying, "A lynching was only averted . . . from the fact that . . . the rangers from San Augustine County outwitted the mob." Perry Price's confession was discredited when an investigation showed that Wright had acted alone. Before the murder, he had publicly threatened to kill his brother-in-law. Price was released, while Robert Wright was convicted of murder and legally hanged in Hemphill on December 17, 1909.[29]

Meanwhile, Hamer and Latta, on their arrival in Beaumont, found Captain Rogers waiting for them. The Rangers were all under subpoena to testify in Harry Head's murder trial, which began on June 23. Three passenger coaches filled with witnesses arrived in town before the trial. The defense claimed that Harry Head, Jenkins, and Alvis were innocent and that the two woodcutters had been slain by Kennedy and the Fussells. Captain Rogers was incensed when three of Harry Head's cronies took the stand and testified to a fabricated alibi. One of them, H. J.

"Judge" Wilkinson, claimed to have been with the band in the bayou, stating that he, Harry Head, Jenkins, and Alvis had separated from the rest. He swore that they heard the fatal shots from a half mile away, implying that the killing had been done by Kennedy and the Fussells. Harry Head took the stand and spun a similar yarn. The prosecution, however, used the testimony of several witnesses to prove clearly that Wilkinson had been in Louisiana, fifty miles away, at the time of the murders.

Captain Rogers arrested Wilkinson and the two other witnesses and charged them with perjury. But the damage had been done; most of the jurors believed that Harry Head had not killed the two black woodcutters. On July 4 the jury announced that it was deadlocked, eight for acquittal and four for conviction. Captain Rogers was not ready to throw in the towel, and he sent Hamer to Louisiana to gather further evidence against Wilkinson. According to Rogers, Hamer "secured very material evidence against said Wilkerson [sic]." But it was almost impossible to convict white men of involvement in murders of blacks. Wilkinson was brought to trial in November 1908, and the result was the same: a hung jury. In the end, Harry Head and his fellow thugs were never punished for killing the two woodcutters near San Augustine. And for African Americans, the ultimate insult was when Wilkinson was later elected sheriff of San Augustine County, a post he held throughout the 1920s.[30]

Captain Rogers sent Hamer and Latta back to San Augustine. On July 9 they received a report of a murder at the house of Charley Teal, a black man who lived twelve miles west of town. With Sheriff Noble, the two Rangers rode out and found the dead body of an African American, Elijah Richardson, in the house. He had been shot to death. There were several young black men at the home who claimed to be Richardson's friends, but all denied any knowledge of the murder. Finally, Hamer and the other officers arrested one of them as a material witness and took him to jail in San Augustine for questioning. The next day, he broke down and admitted that Teal's son, Charles Jr., had killed Richardson. Hamer and White returned to the scene, arrested young Teal, and locked him in jail.[31]

Five days later, on July 15, Frank boarded a train bound for Beaumont to testify before the grand jury in the Wilkinson perjury case. Beaumont was a bustling, modern city of twenty thousand, but its citizens' attitudes toward race relations were as primitive as those in rural areas. Situated just twenty miles from Louisiana, it was a southern community, not a western one. When Hamer arrived, he found the place in an uproar. The day before, in the northern outskirts of the city, a thirteen-year-old white girl, Ada Bell Hopkins, left home to look for her horse and was brutally raped and beaten unconscious. When an African American youth stumbled onto the crime after hearing the girl's cries, he saw a black man fleeing the scene. Two other African Americans spotted and pursued the culprit as he raced on foot into the nearby timber. Beaumont police immediately began a proper investigation. While officers cordoned off the crime scene, mounted policemen scoured the woods for clues. At the same time, other lawmen unsuccessfully tried to track the killer with bloodhounds and a huge armed mob fanned out through Beaumont. One of the mob shot and killed a shotgun-carrying black man, who turned out to be an innocent squirrel hunter. Despite the fact that African Americans had reported the crime, provided descriptions of the suspect, and voluntarily joined the manhunt, that night a mob of three hundred whites burned two black-owned saloons and several black-owned houses in the neighborhood where the rape had taken place. African Americans stayed in their homes and workplaces to avoid getting beaten or lynched. Beaumont police were forced to curtail their investigation to respond to senseless mob violence.[32]

In such high-profile cases of murder, rape, and black-on-white assault, police came under tremendous public pressure to arrest culprits. A common law-enforcement practice of the nineteenth century was the police dragnet, in which officers would literally "round up the usual suspects" and submit them to third-degree interrogations. This technique had its origins in urban centers, where criminals operated in anonymity and were usually identified by appearance, suspicious behavior, or associates. The police dragnet was rarely used in rural areas, where everyone knew one another. Rural police and sheriffs, who likewise knew their communities, had no need to make such wide sweeps in order to identify suspects. After 1900, because the police dragnet mollified the public—and occasionally succeeded—its use increasingly spread to smaller towns and rural communities. It continued to be a popular law-enforcement tool until banned by the U.S. Supreme Court in 1969. Yet the dragnet was rarely, if ever, used by astute police detectives, who saw it as a lazy, incompetent investigative technique. For the most part it did not work, distracted attention from the real suspects, and resulted in the arrest of the wrong persons. And nothing was as embarrassing, or politically risky, for law officers as obtaining a conviction in a high-profile crime only to have the true culprit surface later.[33]

When the initial Beaumont investigation and manhunt turned up empty, city police resorted to the dragnet. Officers rounded up and jailed ten blacks whom they deemed suspicious. But they were scapegoats, not suspects. One, an African American who had chased the rapist from the crime scene, was jailed as a material witness. Of another arrestee, a newspaperman frankly reported, "It is not contended or even suspected that this negro had anything to do with the crime, and the arrest was probably made to appease public sentiment, which is inclined to criticize the officers for not apprehending the fugitive."[34]

Jefferson County's sheriff, Ras Landry, on the other hand, conducted an astute investigation. He and his deputies found African American witnesses who had seen thirty-year-old Claude Golden talking with Ada Bell Hopkins just before the assault. Golden had been arrested twice before for sex offenses. When located by Beaumont's city marshal the next day, July 15, Golden had burned his shirt, but lawmen found a bloodstained cuff left behind in the ashes. Sheriff Landry also picked up a teenager, Matthew Fennell, and lodged both black suspects in the county jail. Word of the arrests spread like wildfire. Before a huge mob could descend on the jail, the sheriff sent a deputy out in a buggy with the two prisoners handcuffed together, concealed on the floorboards. For several hours they were surreptitiously driven about town, then hidden, first in a Catholic church, next in a schoolhouse, and finally in the sheriff's barn. Rumors spread that lawmen were attempting to spirit the prisoners out of Beaumont on the evening train, and a seething mob of two thousand descended on the Southern Pacific railroad depot. Vigilantes armed with shotguns searched the train but found no officers or prisoners aboard.[35]

It was evening when Frank Hamer stepped off an inbound train. His tanned, rawboned features, set off by a large Stetson hat, high-heeled boots, and heavy cartridge belt, marked him plainly as a Texas Ranger. But the frenzied horde paid him no heed. The vigilantes, brandishing Winchesters, shotguns, and revolvers, surged excitedly between the city's two railroad depots and the jail, searching in vain for the suspects. Hamer immediately hunted up Sheriff Landry and offered his assistance, which the lawman eagerly accepted. The sheriff told Hamer that he had secreted Golden and Fennell in his barn. By now it was dark, and Frank slipped into the barn, where he, alone, guarded Golden and Fennell for several hours while a deputy sheriff tried secretly to bring a buggy to the barn. But bands of enraged vigilantes were hunting everywhere for the two suspects, yelling and firing their guns in the air. One of the mob searched the barn and passed within a few feet of Hamer and his terrified prisoners. They kept deathly quiet, and the vigilante passed on.

Unable to secure a buggy without alerting the mob, Hamer, with Sheriff Landry and Beaumont police detective E. E. Cowart, took their prisoners on foot into the swamps four miles west of the city. The mob got wind of this, and hundreds of armed men headed into the swamp, carrying lanterns and torches. Hamer and the rest lay facedown in the mud. The prisoners were beyond terrified as vigilantes came within ten paces of their hiding place. Miraculously, they stopped and came no farther. The mob gradually melted into the dark, but then shots rang out, and the acrid smell of gunpowder drifted through the warm night air. Distant shouts from the vigilantes became louder. The lawmen and prisoners crawled on their bellies deeper into the swamp, its black waters infested with copperhead snakes and alligators. Soon, they could see lanterns and torches approaching, and again members of the mob came within thirty feet of them. Hamer and the others hugged the boggy ground and held their breaths, and yet again the lynchers passed by. This scene was repeated again and again. Frank and the rest spent the entire night crawling with their manacled prisoners through the swampy underbrush, barely avoiding the lynchers.

Finally, at daybreak, the posse managed to crawl to a church near Hamilton, four miles west of Beaumont. Hamer and Cowart hid with the terrified prisoners underneath the church while Sheriff Landry slipped back into Beaumont on foot. He boarded a Galveston-bound train and ordered the engineer to stop at Hamilton. Hamer, Cowart, Golden, and Fennell rushed from the church to the railroad tracks and swung aboard. Before long, the suspects were safely locked in the Galveston jail. Frank immediately received newspaper praise for this exploit. He never sought publicity and must have been amused that he was variously identified as "F. A. Homer," "F. A. Hammer," and even "Oscar Hammer." He recognized that newspapers could, and often did, make egregious errors in their reporting, a fact that would profoundly affect his relationship with the press in the coming years.[36]

Hamer had acted entirely on his own sense of duty by offering to protect the two black prisoners; he had received no orders to do so. His initiative in making that quick decision, coupled with his stubborn refusal to give in to the mob, would prove a hallmark of his later career. Captain Rogers was ecstatic with his performance. Frank may have looked a boy, but his acts were those of a veteran lawman. Though Rogers rarely singled out individual Rangers for praise in his official reports, this time he made an exception: "Ranger Hamer's presence of mind, coolness and courage on this occasion, as on all other like occasions, is indeed very commendable."[37]

And what of the two prisoners he had saved from the mob? Young Matthew Fennell confessed to the assault soon after he was arrested. Sheriff Landry did not believe him and asserted that, while in jail, Claude Golden had convinced Fennell to take the rap. It is also possible that officers used third-degree methods to coerce a confession from the youth. When the victim, Ada Bell Hopkins, came out of her coma days later, she picked Golden out of a photographic lineup. Ada did not know his name, but she had seen him from time to time in the neighborhood. The girl said that he had offered to help find her horse, then lured her into the woods. Matthew Fennell was released a month later when the grand jury found that there was no evidence against him. With Claude Golden it was a different story: he was convicted of rape—a capital crime in Texas—and executed by hanging on February 12, 1909.[38]

From Beaumont Frank was sent back to Hempstead. On the night of September 23, Hamer, with Rangers Bailey and White, got a tip that an escaped convict, Ernest Mullins, had been spotted stealing a ride on an incoming freight train. Mullins, an African American, had burglarized a railroad boxcar and a house in Fort Worth and had been sentenced to eight years in the Allen prison farm near Navasota. He had served less than six months of his sentence when he escaped. Hamer and the other two Rangers rushed to the railroad yards. As the freight train pulled in, Hamer took one side while Bailey and White took the other. It was very dark, but Frank's keen eyes caught the sight of Mullins jumping down from a boxcar. Hamer pulled his six-shooter and raced after the fleeing escapee, jumping fences and crossing an open field, all the while repeatedly calling for Mullins to halt. Suddenly, the young Ranger lost his footing and fell into a ditch. Springing to his feet, Frank recognized that he could not catch Mullins. He took dead aim and squeezed the trigger of his .45. The heavy slug tore into Mullins's upper thigh, and he crumpled to the ground. Hamer brought him to a doctor and then to jail. Commented Captain Rogers in his report, "The negro is believed to be not badly hurt. This is considered to be an important catch as he was an eight year man." The next day, Frank delivered the wounded Mullins to a prison officer in Navasota.[39]

In later years, Frank prided himself on never shooting an unarmed suspect. As one of his admirers wrote in 1929, "It is Hamer's record that he never shot a man who had not first shot at him." However, as the Ernest Mullins shooting demonstrates, this was not true. Modern police officers are not allowed to shoot fleeing felons unless they are armed or pose an immediate threat to the public safety. But in Hamer's day American lawmen were legally authorized to use deadly force to shoot unarmed, fleeing felons, such as burglars and thieves. The reason was that under English common law, dating to the Middle Ages, all felonies were punishable by death. As a consequence it was lawful to kill fleeing felons. This tradition was continued in the United States, where for more than a century American police followed the so-called "fleeing felon" rule. It became controversial, both because of the frequency of such shootings and the fact that many unarmed suspects were shot in the back. Beginning with the increasing professionalism of U.S. police in the 1960s, many states abandoned the rule in favor of the "defense of life" policy. Nevertheless, it was not until 1985 that the fleeing-felon rule was declared unconstitutional by the U.S. Supreme Court.[40]

Hamer reported in person to Rangers headquarters in Austin, where he received hearty congratulations from Captain Rogers for his crack shooting. Rogers immediately sent him back to Hempstead, because, as he explained, "Reports have reached my detachment at Hempstead from several sources that the lawless element at that place was contemplating and planning to assassinate the rangers stationed there." One of the officials who called for the Rangers was the county sheriff, J. J. Perry. Said Rogers, "Sheriff Perry has heartily cooperated with my men in their efforts to break up this hot bed of lawlessness, and has proven himself to be a good man who would like to perform his duty, but who was entirely unable to cope with the situation, and his life was believed at the time the rangers went there to be daily in danger. This lawless element even talked of waylaying and assassinating the rangers as the only means of getting rid of them, and for a time the rangers had to be very cautious and watchful." But the ruffians of Six-Shooter Junction had enough sense not to tangle with Hamer or the other Rangers. With J. T. Laughlin and Marvin Bailey, Frank helped keep order during a session of the district court and prevented jury tampering and intimidation of witnesses.[41]

But Hamer's most important work continued to be protection of African Americans from white mobs. On September 12, 1908, John Buchtein, owner of a large cotton plantation on Brazos River south of Hempstead, quarreled with one of his tenant farmers, a black youth named Raymond Newton, over $1.50 in past-due rent. Newton promised to pay, but Buchtein fired at him with a pistol. Newton in turn gave the planter a fatal shot in the back with a Winchester rifle. Then Newton, with his father, David, and his brother Daniel, fled the scene. Daniel

Newton was quickly captured and placed in the Brookshire jail. Despite the fact that he had not been involved in the killing, a mob took him out and hanged him to a telegraph pole. To save their necks, David and Raymond Newton rushed to Hempstead and surrendered to Sheriff Perry. The sheriff kept their whereabouts secret for a month while he moved them from one county jail to another, one step ahead of a determined lynch mob. Finally, Sheriff Perry had no choice but to bring the Newtons back to Hempstead for a court hearing. On October 15 he recruited Frank Hamer and Marvin Bailey, and the three lawmen left for Brenham on the noon train. They picked up the Newtons, loaded them on the return train, and brought the prisoners into Hempstead the same day. The presence of the Rangers was enough to dissuade any further lynching attempts. David Newton was eventually released, but Raymond was convicted of second-degree murder and sentenced to ninety-nine years in prison. In 1910 his sentence was reversed by the Texas Supreme Court because of grossly prejudicial errors by the trial judge.[42]

Hamer and his fellow Rangers had brought peace to Waller County. On October 28 they were ordered to pack up and return to Austin. A local newspaperman reported, "This move was unexpected. . . . They made good, quiet citizens while here, and will be missed by all the people who know them." Several of Frank's friends in Company C, including John Dibrell, J. T. Laughlin, Oscar Latta, and Duke Hudson, left the Rangers in search of higher-paying jobs. The $40 monthly pay was so low that it was customary for Rangers to seek more lucrative work as deputy sheriffs, city police, or federal officers. At that time an Austin policeman made $70 a month; sergeants and detectives got ninety-five. The federal service paid even more: a U.S. mounted customs inspector earned $100 monthly.[43]

On November 18, 1908, Captain Rogers granted Frank a leave of absence so he could visit his family. His parents and younger siblings Pat, Alma, and Flavious were then living in the tiny village of Streeter in Mason County, about seventy-five miles southwest of San Saba. It had been an unhappy year for the Hamer family: Frank's younger brother Sant had been working as a miner in Arizona, where he died from mercury poisoning. He was impoverished, and Frank's older brother, Estill, himself a miner in Mexico, paid for the funeral. The death of Sant, a carefree sort, deeply affected the entire family.[44]

Upon Frank's return to Austin, he learned that officials in Navasota were looking for a new city marshal. The pay was more than twice what he earned as a Ranger, and he decided to apply for the position. After receiving verbal assurances from Navasota officials that he would get the job, Hamer resigned from the Rangers on November 30, 1908. But it was far from the end of his career with the Rangers.[45]

In the previous two and a half years, he had developed into a seasoned lawman. From the mountains and canyons of the Big Bend to the pineries and plantations of East Texas, he honed his skills as a tracker and manhunter. He learned the fine points of criminal investigation and testified in court many times. He shot two men in the line of duty, killing Ed Putnam and wounding Ernest Mullins. Most significantly, from Captain Rogers he learned never to bend in front of a lynch mob. In East Texas he repeatedly arrested whites for violence against blacks and helped save six African Americans from vigilantes. His protection of Claude Golden and Matthew Fennell was one of the greatest exploits of his career and laid bare his two most significant attributes: moral and physical courage. In the years to come, he would need them both.

4

MARSHAL OF NAVASOTA

Navasota was a tough town. Situated in Grimes County near the confluence of the Brazos and Navasota Rivers, it had long been the home of King Cotton. Navasota was the county's center for growing, shipping, and commerce, reflected by three different railroads that had depots along Railroad Street. Like most other communities in East Texas, it was more of a southern village than a western one. Although Navasota was the county's largest town, with a population of 3,200, the county seat was in Anderson, sixteen miles northeast, with only about six hundred residents. Grimes County was as well known for its violence as for its cotton.

For three decades, much of the county's political history had been written by its controversial sheriff, Garrett L. Scott, who served several terms in the 1880s and 1890s. According to one early account, he won the elections because "the influence of himself and his relatives was strong with the negroes, their former slaves, who held the balance of political power in the county." At that time African Americans made up a little more than half of the county's population and had exercised the right to vote since Reconstruction. Sheriff Scott was supported by the People's Party, an agrarian reform movement of the 1890s that found its support among small farmers, sheep ranchers, laborers, and blacks.

Local Democrats strongly opposed Scott and considered his Populist system "negro rule." Yet Scott, like most Populists, enjoyed significant support from poor whites.

In 1899 prominent Democrats secretly organized the White Man's Union. Its members assassinated two African American Populist leaders, then voted out Sheriff Scott in 1900. The day after the election, a wild gun battle broke out between the two groups. Scott was badly wounded, and his brother was slain. Protected by National Guard troops, he left Grimes County and never returned. The White Man's Union had achieved complete victory. Between 1900 and 1910, more than 30 percent of the African American population deserted Grimes County. For the next half century, blacks were excluded from Grimes County politics. The White Man's Union remained the county's dominant political institution until the 1950s.[1]

This was the racially charged atmosphere that prevailed when Frank Hamer sought appointment as city marshal of Navasota. For the previous five years, the marshal had been W. B. Loftin, who had his hands full trying to police the town. In 1907 he was shot in the hand—losing one finger—while trying to stop a gunfight. During the next year, Texas Rangers, among them Frank Hamer and John Dibrell, were repeatedly sent to Navasota to help Loftin suppress lawlessness. On March 8, 1908, a black man, John Campbell, stabbed, but did not kill, a prominent white politician. Marshal Loftin locked Campbell in the Navasota city jail, but that same day a mob broke in and seized him. They hanged Campbell to a telephone pole, then fired shots into his dangling body. According to one account, a white woman who stumbled across the hanging corpse wrote to the governor, demanding that he take action to clean up the town.[2]

Marshal Loftin had been unable to protect his prisoner, and he struggled to keep the tough element in check. Finally, on November 4, 1908, Loftin tendered his resignation. The city council first offered the position to the former Ranger sergeant John Dibrell, who declined but recommended Frank Hamer. On December 2 Hamer came into town by rail, and the next day the *Navasota Examiner-Review* reported that he "at once qualified as police officer of the city." But civic leaders objected that, at age twenty-four, he was too young for the job. Apparently the city council reconsidered, and after looking into Hamer's record as a Ranger, reaffirmed their decision. On December 17 the council held a special meeting and reported that Frank "was ready to accept an offer of $85.00 per month. . . . After a short discussion, the committee was given further consent to close contract with Mr. Hamer."[3]

The office of city marshal—tantamount to a chief of police—should not be confused with the U.S. marshal, a federal lawman appointed by the president. The city marshal's jurisdiction was within city or town limits. As a general rule, smaller towns with a few officers had city marshals; larger communities had a chief of police. By the late nineteenth century, police in Texas cities were uniformed, but small-town marshals like Frank Hamer wore civilian dress. The city marshal's duties were set both by custom and by law. By custom, marshals would patrol the streets on foot and horseback and respond to calls for assistance. At night they walked back alleys, shook doorknobs, and looked out for prowlers, burglars, and rowdy drunks. Under Texas law, marshals were specifically required to identify and arrest all vagrants in their jurisdiction; to suppress gambling and confiscate gaming tables and gambling paraphernalia; to enforce public health, sanitary, and quarantine statutes; to enforce antiprostitution laws; and to maintain a fee book of all court costs in civil and criminal cases. In many communities they were also charged with such mundane tasks as keeping roads and bridges in good repair, maintaining public windmills, and picking up stray dogs.[4]

The White Man's Union, with many members from prominent planter families, firmly controlled Navasota. They were still in conflict with their old opponents, blacks and landless white laborers. Some members of the White Man's Union enjoyed visiting town, raising hell, and bullying both African Americans and white sharecroppers. Frank Hamer encountered this problem on his very first day on the job. Will H. Brown, who had been the first graduate of Texas A&M College in 1880, was a colorful and notorious Navasota character. He decided to teach the new marshal a lesson. Followed by a crowd of cronies and onlookers, Brown walked along the board sidewalk next to the muddy street until he stood opposite the city marshal's office. Then, throwing back his head, he let loose with an ear-splitting rebel yell. When Hamer poked his head out the office door to see what the commotion was, Brown continued to bellow at the top of his lungs.

The young lawman took slow but deliberate steps across the street. "I'm Frank Hamer, the new city marshal," he announced in a quiet voice. "You know there's an ordinance against disturbing the peace. If you yell again, I'm going to put you in jail."

Will Brown eyed Hamer carefully, then let loose another rebel yell. Frank understood the situation perfectly. "I knew that it was going to be decided right then and there whether or not I would continue as marshal of Navasota," he later recalled. "I just reached up with my left hand and grabbed a handful of white beard, put one foot up on the sidewalk, stepped back, and threw him like you would throw a cow. I put him right out in the middle of that mud. Then I turned to the crowd and said, 'Now, I told him what was going to happen. He's going to jail.'"[5]

Word got around fast about the youthful upstart marshal. A week later, a prominent citizen dropped by Frank's office to have a helpful talk with him. He explained that he and other community leaders—who presumably were members of the White Man's Union—enforced certain laws themselves. "We don't allow our kind to be arrested," he told Hamer, even if they got drunk and disorderly in town. He suggested that the marshal "confine his duties to the negroes and outsiders" and provided the names of men who were not subject to arrest. The taciturn Hamer did not argue with him. That night, one of these "influential citizens" loaded up on whiskey and shot up a saloon. Hamer was quickly on the scene and elbowed his way through the patrons. Staring down the hostile crowd, he said calmly, "I understand you don't allow 'your kind' to be arrested."

For several moments he watched them with his hands on his hips. No one challenged him. Then, with a toothy grin, he hauled the drunk off to jail.[6]

To make a further impression on Navasota's roughs, Hamer at first carried an extra revolver in his gun belt. One of the "self appointed town protectors" made a sneering comment that "the new marshal was a coward because he carried two pistols." Frank heard about this remark and soon encountered the man on the street. The young marshal stepped forward, unbuckled his gun belt, and dropped it on the sidewalk. Then, using his massive arms, Hamer "cuffed the man all over the place." Today it would be called police brutality. Then it was simply rough justice.[7]

There was a reason for his displays of brute force. For every thousand people in small towns today, there is an average of two full-time police officers. Under that formula, a town like Navasota, which then had 3,200 people, would have six officers. But in 1908, no community that small had a tax base large enough to pay for six police. As a result, western and rural villages often hired the toughest marshal they could find, knowing that for the most part he would have to handle criminals and rowdies alone. Only in cases of emergency would the county sheriff or his deputies be able to help. The typical town marshal was a muscular

Frank Hamer on horseback, far left, leading a parade in Navasota in 1909. *Travis Hamer personal collection*

bruiser, but when it came to investigating crime or shooting it out with real desperadoes, he was often found wanting. Frank Hamer, on the other hand, embodied all the characteristics required of a small-town marshal: he was big and tough; extremely intelligent; a crack, intuitive investigator; and a deadly shot who did not flinch from gunfire.

Hamer was well aware of Navasota's long history of violence and racial unrest. He fully recognized that it was up to him alone to maintain order by intimidating the hardcases. Modern police are trained to never make an arrest alone and always to have a backup officer in case a suspect resists. But Frank had no help; his backup was his hands and feet. Hamer's tactics were described by his Ranger friend Bill Sterling: "His usual method of subduing a tough . . . was to slap him on the ear with his open hand. [His] forearms were extremely well developed. When he boxed a man alongside the head, it reminded me of a grizzly bear cuffing a steer. If he ever used his pistol as a club, I never heard of it. . . . Hamer's open palm always took the fight out of the hardiest ruffian."[8]

Yet Hamer was a mass of contradictions. On the one hand, he was modest, unassuming, and humble. He shied away from attention and sought assiduously to avoid newspaper publicity. On the other hand, he was supremely self-confident and aggressive, willing and able to handle any task, no matter how difficult or dangerous. He did not bluster or threaten; he spoke quietly, said little, and meant exactly what he said. He possessed—in spades—what modern police officers call command presence: the ability to exert his authority simply by his stature and physical demeanor. But his body language was the opposite of erect military bearing. He did not swagger but walked with a lazy, rolling gait. He did not stand erect; he slouched, often leaning against walls or doorways, a cigarette dangling from his lips. Even on horseback, he slouched in the saddle, swaying left and right in rhythm with the animal. Despite his barrel chest, massive shoulders, and oaklike legs, he carried himself with graceful ease. At the same time, he had a temper that was easily aroused. In the presence of women and children, he was the paragon of Texas gentility, but when his blood was up, he swore like a longshoreman.

Frank soon befriended a fourteen-year-old African American boy, Mance Lipscomb, the son of an ex-slave and sharecropper. Young

Lipscomb had first seen Hamer a year earlier, when the big Ranger had been stationed in town. Lipscomb was so impressed with Frank's size and presence that he believed fellow Ranger Marvin Bailey—five years the elder—was Hamer's deputy. Mance idolized Hamer and always considered him a Ranger rather than a city marshal. "He was a bad man," Lipscomb recalled years later, in his East Texas drawl, using "bad" as a synonym for "tough." "Talkin' 'bout *bad* man. He was a Ranger! You know what they is? Texas Ranger. . . . No purdy bad in 'im. He's as bad as they git." He vividly recalled the marshal's fighting abilities, saying that those who resisted arrest often met his boot heels. Hamer would kick a hardcase all the way to the city jail. "But if he hit ya, he knock you down. He did'n have no branch or nothin, jest fistiz. One lick, you goin' down. An' when he did'n wanta hit you wit' his fist, he'd kick you." Mance recalled that Hamer would walk the streets, whistling softly and keeping an eye out for trouble.[9]

Young Mance followed Hamer everywhere, often driving the marshal's buggy and showing him around town. The teenager was highly musical and loved to sing and play guitar. From an early age, he performed with his musician father at local dances. Mance Lipscomb later became one of America's legendary blues musicians, and by the 1960s he influenced an entire generation of artists, including Bob Dylan and Janis Joplin. A mutual love of music seems to have cemented the bond between the unlikely pair. For two years, Mance drove with Hamer in the buggy. "And he carry me all through the fields. . . . An' I'd stick up targets, bones and bottles, so he could shoot at 'em, see could he hit 'em."[10]

Though he admitted being afraid of Hamer at first, Lipscomb was both touched by the marshal's kindness and sense of justice and awed by his toughness and skill with firearms. Lipscomb said, "Now he wad'n 'fraid a black or white. He wad'n no *piece* a man, he was a *whole* man." Lipscomb, who always called the marshal "Mista Hayman," recalled: "See, the people runnin' this place—the white folks—had said, 'Well, I'm gonna run this place.' Mista Hayman say, 'I think you got that pitched over some ways. I'm running this place. When you do wrong, you got to go to jail. And lay there, until the term's come. Don't care how much money you got.'" Hamer explained to Mance that he had told local whites, "Now, I'm strictly for right. And if y'all handle me that way, we can get along. But when I tell you something, I mean that. And if you don't do what I say, I'm gonna put you in jail, white or black."[11]

Some of Navasota's merchants were not happy to have quiet streets. After all, if the town was wide open, and the vice laws not enforced, people came in from the farms and plantations to have a good time, and saloons, liquor dealers, gamblers, and hotel keepers prospered. When Hamer had a run-in with the owner of the town's leading hotel, he further antagonized the influential citizens. The hotelkeeper owned a powerful bulldog that had killed several dogs and bit a number of passersby. Finally, the city council ordered Frank to watch for the cur and have the owner keep it off the street. Soon after, the young marshal came across the bulldog attacking a bird dog that was leashed to a wagon. The bulldog's powerful jaws had a death hold on the other animal's throat when Hamer drew his gun. With a single blow of the barrel, he knocked the bulldog unconscious.

The hotelkeeper rushed outside and tore into Hamer for mistreating his pet. The young officer replied, "Now, if you want a watchdog, that's fine, but keep him on your premises or put a muzzle on him."

"What'll you do if I don't?" the hotel man asked scornfully.

"If he ever attacks another animal or person without cause, I'll have to shoot him."

The hotelkeeper let out a contemptuous laugh and went back inside with his dog. A few days later, the bulldog again ran loose and killed a bird dog. Diplomacy was never Frank Hamer's strong suit, and perhaps his temper got the better of him. He promptly strode into the hotel lobby, pulled his six-shooter, and shot the bulldog dead. Holstering his weapon, Hamer turned to the stunned spectators and said, "Maybe now you'll believe me that when I say I'm going to uphold the law, I mean what I say."[12]

At that time Texas courts had ruled that local ordinances that authorized police to shoot loose, unmuzzled dogs were unconstitutional. The reason was that dogs were considered property, which could not be

taken or destroyed by the government without due process of law. Frank
Hamer's action in killing the bulldog, while understandable, was nonetheless unlawful. An officer could impound a dog, but he could not ar-
bitrarily shoot it. That distinction was of little moment to the young
marshal: he intended to use overwhelming force to intimidate Navasota's hardcases and lawbreakers.[13]

After this incident, as Walter Prescott Webb later wrote, "The town
split into Hamer and anti-Hamer factions with the hotel man leading
the anti-Hamer group which was recruited from saloon toughs, some of
whom had felt the heel of the Hamer boots—and some the toe. The
young marshal's struggle for supremacy was desperate, and in the course
of time more of the toughs made contact with his boots. The situation was
one that would permit no compromise, one in which the officer could
show no weakness without complete loss of prestige. . . . This does not
mean that anyone was killed, but some were pretty well marked for
future identification."[14]

Hamer also employed a far more sophisticated approach to policing
Navasota.

Soon after he became marshal, the Throop Saloon was burglarized.
Frank spent the entire night investigating the case, questioning employees and patrons of the saloon. He quickly recovered the stolen
money, then arrested a black suspect who was indicted by the grand
jury. A few months later, Long's grocery store was victim of a mysterious
burglary. Because there were no signs of forced entry, Frank concluded
that the burglar had concealed himself inside during store hours. Hamer
interrogated all the patrons who had visited the store that day. Finally,
he brought in a black youth who confessed to the theft. Commented the
editor of the *Navasota Examiner-Review,* "Officer Hamer deserves special mention for the quick work he did on a case which is remarkable
on account of the flimsy clue he had to work on." On another occasion
that fall, a thief burglarized a home and two shops in one night. Hamer
worked nonstop until he arrested the culprit. The experience he gained
investigating such minor thefts would lead to expertise in important
murder and corruption cases in the years to come.[15]

One of Frank's primary duties was to enforce laws against the carrying of concealed weapons. Mance Lipscomb recalled such an arrest one night. Hamer told a white gun toter, "I thought I told you to put that pistol up, next time you come around here."

When the man denied having a gun, Hamer unleashed a kick and demanded, "I want that pistol."

"Yassuh!" the man replied.

"Well give it here! I mean hand it to me careful. Don't make no funny moves. If you do, I'll blow your brains out."

Hamer took hold of the weapon and said, "Now get in front of me," and marched him to the jail. There, they were met by the prisoner's wife, who begged Hamer to release him. "How much money would you take to let my husband out so he can go home?"

Hamer ignored the proffered bribe and quietly explained that she could post his bail in court in the morning: "Well, Miss, he's my prisoner tonight. That money don't talk til tomorrow. He's got to stay all night with me tonight."

The woman began to cry, saying, "Oh, Mr. Hamer. I can tell you are mean. That's a white man."

Hamer's blunt and angry retort revealed volumes about his character: "Yeah, that's what's the matter with this town: white. I'm a white man, but I'm doing my job. He can come out in the morning. But he can't get out with no amount of money that you offer me. 'Cause money don't buy me."[16]

For African Americans in Texas, Juneteenth was one of their most popular celebrations. It marked the anniversary of June 19, 1865, when Union troops landed in Galveston and announced that all slaves in Texas were free. On May 20, 1909, black leaders met in the Navasota firehouse to plan the Juneteenth celebration that year. Frank Hamer consulted with one of them, Sam, as he later recalled: "When I was marshal . . . the Brazos bottom had a lot of plantations with many field hands, who picked cotton and raised other field crops. I found that this fellow was the unofficial boss of all the rest down there, and anytime they had a parade or anything, such as a Juneteenth celebration, I'd go over to this man, and say, 'Now, Sam, I'm gonna make you the parade marshal. I want you to keep all the rest of the boys in line, so pick out three or four helpers and make sure everyone behaves.' I'd given Sam a great big, wide red sash and he'd put this around his shoulders and wear a tall black silk top hat. All of the time I was there, we never had any trouble at a negro celebration, thanks to Sam."[17]

Navasota's Juneteenth celebration that year was a huge one. It was widely advertised and the railroads provided cheap fares into town. Crowds of blacks and whites viewed an elaborate parade, followed by speeches at the local picnic ground. A barbecue dinner, paid for by Navasota's whites, was capped off with a grand ball that night. Frank Hamer's judgment was affirmed by the editor of the *Examiner-Review*, who reported, "The Juneteenth celebration was the most orderly conducted affair ever witnessed at Navasota. Although some 2–3 thousand negroes were about the streets and grounds all day, not a single arrest was made nor was there occasion for arrest. The negroes in charge of the celebration deserve great praise for the successful event."[18]

While Hamer maintained good relations with the African American community, he continued to collar numerous blacks for stealing. In August he captured a black youth who had tapped the till of Fischer's bakery; he also recovered the stolen money. When he picked up a clothes thief in September, the *Examiner-Review* remarked, "It would seem that the negroes about town would learn after awhile that it is a mere waste of energy to steal. There is absolutely no way to get off with the goods for keeps, consequently the only thing they can figure on as a cinch is that Hamer will not only arrest them but in nine cases out of ten find the goods." Frank's success lay in his ability to cultivate informants. In the coming years, he would often make deals with the criminal element to solve crimes. His word was his bond, and never once would he renege on an agreement with a snitch—black, white, or Hispanic.[19]

In Navasota, racial tension was always just under the surface. On Saturday night, September 25, 1909, a ten-year-old white boy, Michie Coe, quarreled with a black youth and hit him over the head with a rock. The injured boy's father, Minor Baker, rushed to the scene and took his son to a drugstore to treat the wound. They were intercepted by Michie's father, Oscar Coe, a hardcase butcher and former constable, who began to beat the elder Baker with a club. Minor Baker pulled a pocketknife and stabbed Coe three times in self-defense. Bystanders were unable to separate them for fear of getting cut. But Hamer rushed up and stopped the fight, arresting Minor Baker. He lodged him in the town lockup, and soon after took him to the county jail in Anderson. Although Coe quickly recovered from his wounds, it is noteworthy that no attempt was made to lynch Minor Baker. After all, many blacks had been hanged by mobs in East Texas for far less. It is to Frank Hamer's great credit that while he was marshal of Navasota, no mob violence ever took place.[20]

Mance Lipscomb recalled that Hamer was all business when on duty. "He didn' laugh and carry up wit' nobody." He was also protective of the boy. Once, when a white man kicked Mance, Hamer arrested him by ordering, "You be at that jail when I get there." On another occasion, Frank was sitting under a shade tree with young Lipscomb when a white man approached and said, "Mr. Hamer, what are you doing letting Mance ride here with ya? He oughta be in the field."

Hamer turned around and growled, "What did you say?"

"That boy there's big enough to plow."

"His damn hands don't fit no plow as long as I'm with him," snapped Hamer. "Who told you his hands fit the plow?"

"Well, I didn't mean no harm," the interloper answered.

"Well, I don't mean no harm telling you," said Hamer. "He's doin' what I want him to do, and he ain't gonna plow til he quits drivin' 'round and opening gates for me."[21]

Not all African Americans in Navasota shared Mance Lipscomb's warm feelings toward Hamer. Years later, one of them was working as a porter in an Austin barbershop. When a customer brought in several photos of Texas Rangers, one of the barbers pointed out Hamer and asked the porter, "Do you know that man?"

"Yes, suh," he replied with a huge grin. "An' when I sees him comin' I jes' steps aside."[22]

Frank Hamer surely was, like many white Americans of the time, especially those living in Texas, a white supremacist. This commonly held idea maintained that blacks were biologically and intellectually inferior to whites. Though Hamer did not hold modern views of racial sensibility, he treated the African American community with fairness and dignity. He never exhibited the cancerous and intransigent racial hatred then so common to white East Texans and southerners. And Captain Rogers had instilled in him a deep conviction for justice and a strong notion that his duty as an officer was to protect the weak from the strong. At the same time, Hamer was extremely strong-willed, stubborn, and pugnacious. As would become increasingly evident in the coming years, he did not hesitate to take unpopular positions, defend unpopular causes, and antagonize powerful businessmen and politicians. It is possible that some of his acts in protecting African Americans were motivated as much by a sense of contrariness as by a belief in racial justice. But he seems to have been primarily influenced by the debt he felt he owed to the black man who saved his life after he had been shot down by Dan McSween. Either way, if any of the Navasota townsfolk considered calling their hard-nosed young marshal a "nigger lover," they had enough sense to keep their thoughts to themselves.

As city marshal, Hamer put on many impromptu exhibitions of his shooting prowess. Mance Lipscomb was astounded by Hamer's ability with his .45 Colt and helped him with pistol practice: "I set up somp'n right here, an' git back, an' let him shoot that off. Stick or bottle. . . . An' sometime he git a crowd of white folk. I'd git them tawgits set up and every time his gun popped, one of 'em bust open. One of 'em say, 'Well, I ain't seed nobody take a dead aim like this man done.' 'Cause he could shoot a gun better'n inybody ever been in this county. An' they figgered that he's the best mawksman they ever saw in their life. When he shot at you . . . he hit you. . . . Where he shot at, he knowed its going where it hit you at." The reserved Hamer was no show-off. His public shooting exhibitions were simply a none-too-subtle warning to Navasota's rough element.[23]

Traveling circuses and carnivals were—and still are—the bane of any lawman's existence. They drew large, often unruly crowds, and at night were frequently the scene of drunken brawls and cutting scrapes. On the night of October 6, 1909, Navasotans flocked to a "tent show." The *Examiner-Review* reported that one of the carnival workers, "a wild and wooly negro . . . got on the warpath and cut a negro woman in the hand." Word was sent to Marshal Hamer, but when he tried to arrest the culprit, the latter fled through the crowd and raced down the railroad tracks. Frank, afraid to shoot because so many people were milling about, kept his six-shooter holstered and sprinted after the man. According to the newspaper, Hamer succeeded in "finally outrunning the negro in a fair and square race, a feat not often accomplished by a white sprinter." The marshal overpowered the suspect, relieved him of a pistol and a pair of brass knuckles, and hauled him to the calaboose.[24]

Although he antagonized many in Navasota, Hamer also made many friends. He joined the town's Masonic lodge and the Navasota Hunting and Fishing Club. Frank's favorite duck-hunting spot was Yarboro Lake, nine miles east of Navasota. Although Frank enjoyed hunting wild fowl, he also loved pet birds. He often stopped by Jimmy Lee's saloon—not to drink, but to view the owls and parrots on display in a large cage. Navasotans must have been perplexed by the paradoxical sight of the nails-tough young lawman petting the birds and treating them with peanuts. On one occasion, Hamer and a friend shot two mammoth pelicans at Yarboro Lake and caught a third that had a broken wing. Frank brought the injured bird, which had a nine-foot wingspan, to Jimmy Lee so he could treat the wound and add it to his menagerie. Hamer also enjoyed visiting the Candy Kitchen, an ice cream parlor downtown. Ice cream was a rarity in West Texas, and in Navasota Frank acquired a lifelong addiction to it. One day, he was seated at the Candy Kitchen counter, enjoying a sundae, when a friend crept up behind him and slapped his back. Hamer reached for his six-shooter but stopped when he recognized his comrade's image in the mirror behind the counter. The marshal warned his chagrined friend never to do that again.[25]

Among Hamer's new friends was the Cameron family in Hempstead. William and Cassie Cameron had two sons and three attractive daughters. Frank was especially interested in the middle daughter, Mollie. She was twenty-two, with a round, cherubic face, long brown tresses, and an hourglass figure. Mollie, educated and cultured, was a schoolteacher and skilled bookkeeper. But Frank was intrigued by her tomboy personality. She loved to ride horseback, wearing a broad-brimmed Stetson

Frank Hamer's first wife, Mollie Cameron. She sent him this photo when they began courting in 1908. *Courtesy Kathy Hatchett*

and split skirt, considered scandalous in an era when women were expected to ride sidesaddle. She was also a crack shot. A few months before they met, Mollie had been practicing with a rifle in the Brazos River bottoms west of Hempstead. When she spotted a six-foot-long alligator sunning itself on a log, she took aim and killed it with a single shot. Frank, when he heard the story, must have been more than impressed. Not surprisingly, Mollie was attracted to Frank, for, as Mance Lipscomb once said, "He was purdiest white man I ever laid eyes on." Recognizing his athleticism, Mollie nicknamed him "Tige." At first the young marshal, too humble and too oblivious to understand that she had a romantic interest in him, called her "little sis." He took the train from Navasota to visit her family on occasional Sundays, and for months she sent him postcards and photos of herself. Finally, almost in despair, she wrote him, "Think of me sometimes. . . . Hope I'll see you again some day." Frank got the message, and a long but cautious courtship began. Mollie taught school in Waller, thirty miles south of Navasota, and Frank's duties as marshal kept him from seeing her regularly.[26]

On one occasion, in 1910, Frank and a friend borrowed a motorcar to chase down and kill a rabid dog. This was the first known use of an automobile by Frank Hamer in law enforcement. Previously, he had always traveled by horseback and train, and in Navasota by buggy, with Mance Lipscomb often driving. Horseless carriages had been manufactured commercially in the United States since the late 1890s. At first they were a fad, then a craze, and finally a necessity. By 1905 dealers in Texas were offering "machines" at high prices, ranging upward to a whopping $5,500. Most automobiles were beyond the means of the average American. Then, in 1909, Henry Ford released his Model T at a cost of $850; due to mass production, the price dropped to $550 in 1913. By 1911 there were thirty thousand automobiles in Texas, and another five thousand the following year. Two-seat autos were known as roadsters; four seaters or larger were touring cars. At that time all highways in Texas were dirt, which was perfectly adequate for travel by horse and buggy. But motorcars bogged down on muddy roads, and, as early as 1903, citizens formed "good roads" associations in Texas in order to promote better highways. Even then, it would not be until the 1920s that the Lone Star State's major connecting highways were paved. Frank did not earn enough money to own an automobile, so, like most Texans, he continued to rely primarily on the horse or the railroad.[27]

On the night of May 25, 1910, Hamer was aboard a northbound train from Hempstead when the engineer spotted an obstruction on the tracks ahead. Setting his sand brakes, he managed to reverse his engine enough so that the locomotive slowed before it harmlessly struck two heavy railroad ties that had been jammed between the rails and held in place by piles of rock. It was a very close call. The engineer and fireman told Hamer that they had seen two black men walking along the track, not far from the obstruction. While the train continued on, Hamer jumped down from the cars and raced off after the suspects on foot. In short order, he tracked the pair to a house near the tracks. They said they were farmhands and gave their names as Henry Clay and Levi Ellis. Hamer tricked them by asking if they had caused a disturbance on the northbound passenger train out of Hempstead. As Frank hoped, they denied it but admitted that they had walked down the tracks from Navasota. The marshal arrested them both and started north with the pair on foot, headed for Navasota. Soon a southbound train approached, so Hamer flagged it down and brought his prisoners to jail in Hempstead.

Train wrecking was common at the time. It was also an extremely serious offense. Beginning with the Jesse James gang's wrecking of a train at Adair, Iowa, in 1873, there had been scores—even hundreds— of them in the United States. Many were for the purpose of robbery, others out of sheer malice, and numerous trainmen and passengers had been killed. Several states, Arizona, California, and Wyoming among them, made train wrecking a capital offense. Frank Hamer's investigation was an important one, and the *Examiner-Review* was effusive in its praise: "This is one of the prettiest pieces of detective work pulled off in this part of the country for months and adds another feather to Mr. Hamer's cap. He certainly does deserve unstinted credit for the smooth manner in which he trailed the negroes and caught them and while he is too modest, perhaps, to say anything about it, the railroad company is certainly under obligations, for there is no question but what the attempt would have been repeated at the earliest possible moment and maybe with disastrous results to both passengers and the railroad."[28]

Navasota's city council was pleased with Hamer's performance, and that spring they increased his salary to $100 a month. Equally impressed was C. M. Spann, the county attorney. In June 1910 he presented Frank with a fancy, engraved single-action Colt .45 revolver, F. A. HAMER inscribed on the back strap. This was the first time Hamer had ever received such a magnificent gift, and he was deeply touched by the gesture. He would carry this Colt—his favorite—through many trying years in the Texas Rangers and nicknamed it Old Lucky. Resting today in a private collection, it is one of the most famous and valuable of all Colt firearms.[29]

By the summer of 1910, Hamer was eager to visit his family, whom he had not seen since coming to Navasota. Frank secured permission to visit them in Mason County on a two-week vacation. As was the custom, Hamer asked Captain Rogers to assign a Texas Ranger as a temporary substitute. On July 9 Frank left town, and he was replaced by Ranger Private Ed Avriett from Austin. At nine o'clock on the night of July 17, Avriett was making his rounds in an alley behind the Navasota bank and post office when he was shot at by a would-be assassin. Drawing his pistol, Avriett fired twice at shadows of two fleeing men. A crowd quickly gathered, and their lanterns showed a trail of blood leading out of the alley, but no trace of the gunman could be found. Captain Rogers investigated and concluded that Avriett had stumbled upon a pair of yeggmen—itinerant burglars—preparing to break into the bank or the post office. The people of Navasota thought differently, reported the *Examiner-Review*: "Certainly it was not the work of anyone lurking about the post office, with a view to robbery, because the hour was entirely too early, and the moon shone [sic] as bright as day. Mr. Averetts [sic] has no enemies in Navasota because he has only been here about

Frank Hamer's Colt revolver, "Old Lucky," presented to him in 1910. *Photo © Paul Goodwin from Little John's Auction Service*

ten days, taking Officer Hamer's place who is off on a vacation. The only theory which would seem to hold water is that someone who had it in for Hamer must have figured that the assassination of Mr. Averetts might have a depressing effect upon Hamer, probably causing his resignation to be handed in. This idea seems to prevail and has been advanced several times since the shooting by a number of citizens."[30]

On Frank's return to Navasota, he ignored the danger and returned to his duties. While serving as city marshal, he shot two men in the line of duty. The first incident was related by Mance Lipscomb. Hamer was notified of a burglary at the telephone office. As he was searching the ground floor, the culprit fled down the stairs. According to Lipscomb, Hamer could hear him "hittin them gravels . . . goin' nawth . . . right through town. Down where the bank used to be, and the Smith Hotel." Frank ordered the burglar to stop, but he kept running, and the marshal shot him in the leg. Hamer ran up and immediately recognized the suspect, whom Mance said was "a half-crazy boy named Doach. . . . They'd git him ta dancin' fur a nickel, and they'd give him a dime to stop." Doach thought he was killed and kept yelling, "Oh Lawdy! Oh Lawdy!"

Chuckling, Frank said, "If I'd a knowed that was you, I wouldn't have hurt you. But I had to give an account of who you were. I had to shoot you because you would outrun me. I didn't mean to kill you. You ain't dead." Hamer got a doctor for the wounded burglar and did not arrest him. The next morning, Doach hopped up to the marshal's office on a crutch with his leg in bandages. Frank told him, "Now you go home. Stay off these streets, and stealing and trying to break in. Because you're liable to get hurt sure enough next time."[31]

The marshal's second shooting had no comical overtones. At ten o'clock on the night of February 28, 1911, E. N. Simmons, an International & Great Northern Railroad foreman, reported to Hamer that his home had been burglarized. With little to go on, Hamer decided to take Simmons with him and watch the I&GN depot for any burglars or other suspicious characters. At midnight, just before the arrival of the northbound train, Frank spotted a black man emerge from the dark and slip into the depot waiting room. The marshal followed him inside and asked him where he came from.

"Hempstead, about ten minutes ago," the stranger replied.

Hamer knew that no northbound train had arrived in the past ten minutes, and said, "Hempstead, eh?"

"No, I means Waller," was the quick response.

Frank ordered the suspect outside, had him raise his hands, and searched his pockets. The first thing he found was a watch. Marshal Hamer called Simmons over, who immediately identified it as his. At that, the man whirled around and bolted from the station. Hamer jerked his pistol and yelled, "Halt!"

The burglar kept running, so Frank sent two pistol shots very close to his head. That only made him run faster, so Hamer shouted, "I'll kill you if you don't stop!"

This command also had no effect. The marshal took dead aim and sent two shots to kill. One passed through his right arm; the other struck dead center in the back, tearing out through the abdomen. The suspect staggered forward a few steps and then collapsed. Hamer brought him to jail and summoned a doctor. The badly wounded man turned out to be a notorious burglar, Manny "Kid" Jackson, alias Granville Johnson. In his pockets Frank found other items stolen from the Simmons house. Jackson confessed to the Simmons burglary as well as numerous others in Hempstead and Brenham a few nights before. The next day, Kid Jackson died. Hamer's enemies took advantage of the incident to spread a rumor "that the negro was shot while handcuffed." The *Examiner-Review* immediately pronounced the story "absolutely untrue."[32]

As was customary in an era when police internal affairs investigations were unheard of, the young marshal immediately surrendered and asked for a hearing so that he could be exonerated. The next morning, he appeared in court and was released on $200 bond. In a subsequent court examination, Hamer was found to have acted in the lawful discharge of his duty.[33]

A week later, on March 19, 1911, Frank married Mollie Cameron in Hempstead, after almost two years of courtship. The Camerons were present, but not the Hamers, because they could not make the long journey by horse and buggy. While on a short honeymoon to Dallas, Mollie wrote to Frank's mother, telling her they had wed. The union was a happy one. Mollie was a good cook, and Frank's weight went from a lean 190 pounds to a sturdy 240. His angular, strikingly handsome features started to become rounded until, finally, he was moon-faced. Hamer loved the Camerons and spent much of his free time with them in Hempstead.[34]

But Frank was growing bored in Navasota. He told Mance Lipscomb, "I'm just foolin' 'round here. Ain't nothin' in Navasota to fit me. I want to go to a bigger town."

Hamer's reputation as a town tamer had spread beyond the city limits of Navasota. For several months, Horace Baldwin Rice, the wealthy, progressive mayor of Houston, had been trying to recruit him to come to the crime-ridden Gulf city. But neither Hamer nor the Navasota city council had been able to find a substitute marshal until Frank talked his old friend, Ranger Sergeant Marvin Bailey, into taking the position. Bailey had been promoted to captain of Company B in 1910, but in February 1911, in a political shakeup, he was demoted to sergeant. Bailey needed little urging from Hamer to take the Navasota job. He would serve for years in various law-enforcement positions in Grimes County.[35]

Marshal Hamer tendered his resignation on April 20, 1911. Commented the *Examiner-Review*, "Mr. Hamer has made a most efficient officer since coming to Navasota and is universally liked. He plays no favorites in the discharge of his duty—everybody looks alike to him and if an offender of the law labors under the impression that he can raise a disturbance and get off with it all he has to do is to try him on. Of course such a man has his enemies; it is natural to suppose that he would have, but as an impartial peace officer he holds the championship so far as we are informed. He leaves Navasota with the best wishes of the city council, with whom he has always been in harmony and the further knowledge of having made many warm personal friends."[36]

To that, A. P. Terrell, a prominent Navasota merchant, added, "He is the best officer we have ever had. Mr. Hamer is not only a good officer but is a perfect gentlemen in every respect, sober, honest, reliable and fearless. . . . [H]e has no pets and treats every one kindly, but when one disobeys the law he lays friendship aside and does his duty." And Mance Lipscomb had nothing but praise for Frank's performance in

Navasota: "Boy, he cooled that town down. Po' colored folks was scared ta meet white folks on the street. . . .'cause they was white and they was niggas, they don't wanta touch up against no white folks. But them white folks commenced ta lettin' the colored folks git by. Give some room fur them. But wad'n no room fur nobody but whites until *he* come there."[37]

5

FROM HOUSTON TO THE
OPEN RANGE

Frank Hamer found Houston a booming city of eighty thousand people, 30 percent of them African American. In 1901 oil had famously been discovered at Spindletop, near Beaumont, ushering in the modern petroleum industry. The Gulf Coast became the hub for oil exploration, with Houston and Beaumont the principal centers for refineries and shipping. Between 1900 and 1910, Houston's population almost doubled. Tall buildings sprouted everywhere. A thousand automobiles and countless horse-drawn vehicles clattered along a hundred miles of paved streets. The city was served by several railroads, while electric streetcar service encouraged residential development in outlying areas that were once but bayous and marshland. By 1913, Houston was home to twelve petroleum companies, most significantly Humble Oil Company (now ExxonMobil). The city boasted six department stores, nine hotels, eight large office buildings, nine banks, six schools, and four motion picture theaters. Houston was divided into six wards; the "Bloody Fifth," situated northeast of downtown and largely black, was known for its violence.[1]

With the booming economy came trouble. The city's beleaguered police could not control an explosion of crime. During the first four months of 1910, Houston saw thirteen murders, including the butchery of a family of five and the killing of the city's assistant police chief. In addition, "pistol toters" engaged in numerous shooting affrays. Houston's wealthy mayor, Horace Baldwin Rice, a progressive reformer, publicly expressed his lack of faith in the city police. In April 1910 he hired two tough former Texas Rangers, Henry L. Ransom and Jules J. Baker, to work directly for him as special officers in an effort to stop the violence. Rice hoped that their reputations would intimidate the city's lawless element.[2]

Henry Ransom would prove by far the most controversial Texas Ranger of the twentieth century, later achieving infamy in the Bandit War of 1915. Thirty-nine years old, standing five foot eight and weighing only 140 pounds, he was hard as nails. In 1892 he quarreled with two African American brothers, then shot them both dead. He was indicted for murder, but because the victims were black he escaped punishment. From 1899 to 1901 Ransom saw bloody service in the Philippine insurrection, when U.S. troops destroyed villages and murdered both military prisoners and civilians. On his return to Texas, he drifted from one law-enforcement job to another: deputy sheriff, Texas Ranger, city marshal, and deputy sheriff again. "He was represented to me to be a brave and fearless man," explained Mayor Rice. "I brought him here to help run this shooter brigade out of Houston."[3]

Trouble followed Henry Ransom like horseflies on a cow pony. In October 1910, while on duty as a special officer, he shot and killed a lawyer who had insulted him in court. He was tried for murder but testified that the attorney had reached for a pistol. The jurors reached a verdict that was then customary in Texas. Despite the fact that the lawyer died with two bullets in his back, they found that Ransom had killed him in self-defense.[4]

On April 21, 1911, during Henry Ransom's trial and the day after Frank and Mollie left Navasota, Hamer was sworn in as special officer for Mayor Rice. The mayor came from a prominent family; his uncle founded Rice University. Nine days earlier, Rice had conducted the biggest shakeup in the history of the Houston police, firing the chief and thirteen officers. Hamer was one of the replacements, and, like the other special officers, he reported directly to the mayor. Rice had already hired several other special detectives, including Joseph Lee Anders, a former Ranger sergeant. Ransom, Baker, Anders, and another special officer lived together in a house in the Bloody Fifth ward. Frank and Mollie rented their own place at 810 Walker Avenue, near the downtown. The mayor's special officers earned $100 a month, which provided a comfortable living for Frank and his bride.[5]

According to Houston newspaperman H. C. Waters, Mayor Rice brought in Hamer as a restraining influence on Henry Ransom and the other special officers. Waters was highly critical of the specials and called them "the wild bunch." The journalist explained that Hamer disapproved of Ransom: "In fact, he and Henry Ransom had been at sword points, and it was generally believed he was brought here by the mayor to sort of hold the wild bunch, which the mayor had got entangled with, in restraint." Frank, in fact, strongly disliked Ransom, calling him "cold-blooded as a rattlesnake. One of the most dangerous men I ever knew."[6]

Hamer's other principal duties were to arrest pistol toters and gamblers. He wore plain clothes, with a six-gun in his waistband and a special officer's badge pinned inside his coat. He later told Mance Lipscomb that he was ordered to focus on black gamblers and to ignore whites who wagered at the Rice Hotel and other swank resorts. Hamer refused, saying, "Now the coloreds and whites are all gonna get arrested, if I catch 'em gambling down there." According to Mance, the white cardsharps tried to bribe him, to no avail. Hamer then staked out one of the principal illegal gambling halls. On several nights, he tried to gain entry but was turned away by the door guard. Then, disguised in an old pair of overalls and a floppy hat, he climbed in through the fire escape, raided the game, and marched thirty-eight white gamblers downstairs to waiting police wagons.[7]

During the fall of 1911, a railroad strike resulted in a violent confrontation in which a Southern Pacific guard was shot dead. The Southern Pacific swore in thirty-five special officers to protect strikebreakers and railroad property in Houston. One of them was Hamer's pal Jim Dunaway, who as a Ranger sergeant had been badly wounded by R. O. Kenley in Groveton. Burly and round-faced, Dunaway was a pugnacious sort. In 1906, while stationed as a Ranger in Odessa, he quarreled with Ector County's sheriff, George "Gee" McMeans. Dunaway pistol-whipped McMeans, who was himself destined to have a deadly encounter with Frank Hamer. In 1909 Dunaway even threatened the venerable Captain John R. Hughes, resulting in his discharge from the Rangers. In Houston, Dunaway and Hamer became boon companions.[8]

Frank also worked closely with Houston's police detectives. When they got a tip that an African American jailbreaker, Owen Matthews, was believed to be hiding out in the Fourth Ward, Hamer and Detective George Peyton were assigned the case. After learning that the fugitive had been staying in his father's house at 406 Robin Street, the officers hired a black informant to keep an eye on the place. Early in the morning of February 3, 1912, their stool pigeon told them that Matthews was at home. At 1:30 A.M., carrying a police "dark lantern," they slipped inside the house and found a black man asleep in a front room. He was not Matthews, so Hamer told Detective Peyton to take the lantern and search the back bedrooms while he guarded the first man. As Peyton entered one room, Matthews leaped from the bed, snatching an automatic pistol from under his pillow. He fired twice at close range. One shot struck the lamp, knocking it down and powder-burning Peyton's hand. A second bullet missed as the detective backtracked into the hallway. When Matthews charged him in the flickering light from the fallen lantern, Detective Peyton shot twice, killing the fugitive instantly. Frank Hamer had not fired a shot.[9]

To the general public, Hamer and his fellow special officers were all plainclothes policemen; few recognized that four worked for Mayor Rice, and Dunaway for the railroad. They carried fearsome reputations as ex-Rangers, and common rumor claimed that all of them were gunfighters. On February 28, 1912, Mayor Rice appointed Henry Ransom chief of police of Houston. Rice believed that Ransom had been justified in killing the lawyer, and he wanted a tough man in charge of the force. It would prove a serious error in judgment.[10]

Houston then had three principal daily newspapers: the *Post*, the *Chronicle*, and the *Press*. The *Chronicle* was a strong supporter of Mayor Rice. The upstart *Press*, established in 1911 by the Scripps-Howard newspaper chain, emphasized local politics and muckraking journalism.

Paul C. Edwards, its first editor, was no fan of Mayor Rice or his special officers. As Edwards recalled years later, "For a number of years the mayor had maintained a sort of private police force under his personal command composed of a group of former Texas Rangers, most of them men with notches on their gun stocks. They wore big Stetson hats, rode cow ponies, were equipped with lariats and big six-shooters, and were genuinely terrifying to most of the populace." Soon after the appointment of Henry Ransom, editor Edwards sent reporter H. C. Waters to meet the new chief in his office. When Waters tried to introduce himself, Ransom barked, "Well, I don't want to know you, but get out of this room or I'll beat your brains out." When Ransom reached for a billy club, Waters scampered away.[11]

Detractors of the *Press*, most notably the *Post*, accused it of manufacturing sensational "news" to increase its budding circulation. Undeterred, the *Press* directed its barbs at the city police. It published stories and issued wire reports claiming that Ransom had hired as police officers "numerous Texas border 'gun men,' the present day representatives of the so-called desperado spirit of the old west." Given that Ransom had brought only a few former Rangers to his ninety-man force, the *Press*'s claim referred mainly to Hamer, Dunaway, and the other special officers, none of whom were city police. "The charges," said the *Press*, "include unwarranted and brutal attacks upon citizens; third degree methods that have resulted in lasting injury to persons and in some cases even death, and reckless use of guns, clubs and other weapons." What the *Press* failed to mention was that between 1910 and 1912, three Houston policemen, one constable, and one railroad special officer had been murdered. In June 1912, Mayor Rice announced that a full investigation of the police by city commissioners would begin immediately. During a weeklong public hearing, more praise than complaints was heard. The most serious charges came from several black men who reported that they had been beaten by uniformed officers on the street and in the police station. No complaints were made against Hamer or any of the special officers. Henry Ransom had been vindicated, but he could not leave well enough alone. A week after the hearings ended, he savagely beat a witness in the police station. Though he quickly resigned as chief of police, Mayor Rice gave him his old job back as a special officer.[12]

On the afternoon of November 18, 1912, Hamer and Lee Anders ran into Jim Dunaway on Main Street. Dunaway invited them to join him for a soft drink and a cigar in Rouse's drugstore at 319 Main, near the corner of Preston Avenue. The three stepped inside Rouse's, which had a long, narrow interior. On one side was an ornate soda fountain, with a white marble countertop that extended along the entire side of the store. Cushioned stools lined the counter, and behind were large mirrors framed with marble columns along the wall. Across the store's single aisle was a long row of glass display cases. Dangling from the high copper ceiling were numerous large fans, a self-evident necessity in Texas.

As Hamer took a seat at the soda fountain near the front door, Dunaway was shocked to see his deadly enemy R. O. Kenley, the lawyer who had shot him up so badly—and killed county attorney H. L. Robb—in Groveton five years before. Although Kenley had been acquitted of shooting Dunaway, the case against him for killing Robb had never come to trial. Kenley, with his wife and young children, was seated at the opposite end of the long counter, eating ice cream. The drugstore and the sidewalk in front were crowded with shoppers. When Kenley spotted Dunaway, he asked for the receipt from the soda clerk, hurriedly gathered up several packages, and started with his wife and children toward the cash register. By this time Hamer also recognized Kenley and stepped quickly toward Dunaway. As the lawyer approached the cash register, he and Dunaway suddenly clashed. Dunaway yanked his Colt .45 and struck the barrel several times over Kenley's head. Hamer grabbed the gun from Dunaway's hand, and then he and Anders escorted the former Ranger sergeant to the police station. Kenley's wounds were dressed at a nearby doctor's office.[13]

The crusading *Houston Press* had a field day with this story, headlining its account, MAN BRUTALLY BEATEN WHILE COPS LOOK ON. Its reporter began by saying, "The assault . . . was similar to some which occurred while Henry L. Ransom was chief. This time not only the victim was outraged, but it was in the presence of many women and children." According to the *Press*, "One of the soda fountain boys says two of Mayor Rice's plain clothes men stood by and watched the assault. It is alleged Dunaway is a friend of these two officers, who were themselves state rangers until Mayor Rice brought them to Houston."

The *Press* gave full coverage to Kenley's version, saying that he "had his pocket book in one hand and the pay check in the other and had some bundles under his arm. To save trouble, he let his wife and children walk on the side next to Dunaway. But Dunaway walked around his wife." Declared Kenley to the *Press*, "He pointed the gun at me and I dropped my head. When I ducked, he beat me over the head with the weapon." The *Press* identified Hamer and Anders as the special officers and reported, "Judge W. H. Gill was standing in the store and grabbed Dunaway's gun. He says a plain clothes man walked up to him and said, 'Don't you dare take that gun from him.' As he said this he pulled his coat back, showing he was an officer." Judge Gill told the *Press*, "I would like to know who that officer was. I would make it hot for him. It is a case where the officers, paid by the people, turn against their paymasters, and protect the assaulters and disturbers." The *Press* concluded its account: "After the assault, Officer Frank Hamer arrested Dunaway. He was taken to the station, but immediately given his liberty."[14]

The *Press* had not interviewed the special officers or tried to get Jim Dunaway's side of the story. The *Chronicle*, on the other hand, did so, and provided Dunaway's version: "When he put his hand in his pocket, coming toward me all of the time, I naturally thought he was after a pistol. I struck him several times and that ended it. I said nothing to him prior to that." Hamer supported Dunaway's account, saying, "I was calling for something to drink. I think Anders called for a cigar and Dunaway probably the same. We were standing near the cashier's desk and cigar case. I saw Kenley at the counter, but paid little attention to him. He walked rapidly toward Dunaway then, at the same time running his hand into his pocket. In an instant the two were together and Dunaway drew his pistol and rapped him over the head several times. The two were finally separated and Anders and I accompanied Dunaway to the police station. We had him in custody, and after the matter was explained he was released on his own recognizance."[15]

The next day, Hamer was irate when he read the account of the affair in the *Press*. He described his subsequent meeting with the *Press* reporter: "I went to the office in the presence of a witness and asked them to desist, saying at the time that I had no objection as an officer of the law in appearing in the paper; but making a specific request that when I was quoted as saying anything in print that they use my direct words." Hamer then gave a detailed statement, which the *Press*, to its credit, printed in full: "Such a report as you had in your paper yesterday does me a great injustice and my friends all over the state will tell you so. To say that I stood by and watched a man brutally beat up another man without interfering is to state something that was not true. If Judge W. H. Gill said what he is quoted as saying he is either badly mistaken or intentionally stating something that is not true. He is quoted as saying that a plain clothes man walked up to him and said, 'Don't you dare take that gun from him.' The inference is that I was protecting Dunaway. That is not the case. I grabbed Dunaway's gun and was holding it pointed toward the floor to keep him from shooting when a man I did not know came up and tried to seize the gun. I told him not to interfere, meaning of course that I had Dunaway in custody. I do not see how it is possible to put any other interpretation upon my actions. I do my duty as an officer and my record is absolutely clean. To try to give the impression that I was a party to the assault in the drug store is a gross misrepresentation that I resent."[16]

Edwards, the editor of the *Press*, was dissatisfied with Hamer's explanation. In a long editorial headlined, LIFT THE VEIL JUST ONCE, he wrote, "The fact that two of Mayor Rice's 'special officers' were in company with a six-shooter deputy who created a scene in Rouse's drug store . . . brings up the question: Who are these officers? Why are they maintained? What salaries do they draw? What duties do they perform for the protection of the people of Houston?" Terming them a "squad of secret police" and "special six-shooter men," he demanded, "Why, then, does the mayor need to keep about him a bunch of gun men in plain clothes? Is not the police department sufficient and efficient enough to keep down crime in Houston?" Edwards, who had first moved to Houston in 1911 to establish the *Press*, was either unaware of, or indifferent to, the crime wave of 1910 that had prompted Mayor Rice to hire the specials in the first place. His opinions, however, were shared by many Houstonians.[17]

Jim Dunaway, after being released from the police station, left town that night on railroad business. A warrant was issued for his arrest charging him with aggravated assault and battery and carrying a pistol. Hamer promised Sheriff Frank Hammond that Dunaway would return the next day, but Hammond was not happy. "I have told Hamer I will arrest Dunaway on the street when he returns if he doesn't beat me to the office," the sheriff declared. "I am going to see that all law violators are arrested, whether they be officers, friends of officers, or private citizens." Reported the *Press*, "Sheriff Frank Hammond doesn't like the idea of the mayor having special officers. But he says if the mayor appoints them, he has no right to disarm them." When a *Press* reporter asked Police Chief Edward C. Noble about the specials, he equivocated, saying, "I have nothing to do with the special officers. The city charter gives the mayor the right to appoint them; he has had that right a long time. It is not up to me to criticize that power." Jim Dunaway stayed in Houston and kept his job as a railroad officer. Ten months later, he was brought to trial on the assault charges. He claimed self-defense, and the jury, in true Texas style, acquitted him.[18]

By this time Hamer had begun work on one of his most serious cases as special officer. More than a year earlier, on June 14, 1911, Constable Edgard E. Isgitt had been shot to death while attempting to arrest Matt Young, a black man accused of whipping his wife. The killing took place at a craps game near Harrisburg, now part of Houston. Young, known as Mississippi Red, fled the scene. Although he was a gambler and hardcase, the African American community believed that he killed Isgitt in self-defense. A black clergyman, Elijah C. Branch, charged, "All the Harrisburg officers are quick to kill a Negro, with a little exception. . . . [The] officers made three shots at Red when Red was about to run, so Red pulled his gun and made one shot." Constable Isgitt, mortally wounded, died the next day. Despite a determined manhunt and a $250 state reward, Mississippi Red eluded capture.[19]

In November 1912 Frank Hammond, the newly elected sheriff of Harris County, made it a priority to find the fugitive. Despite his opposition to the special officers, he fully recognized Hamer's abilities as a detective and manhunter. The sheriff enlisted Frank's aid, and for the next few weeks Hamer ran down leads, finally learning from a tipster that Mississippi Red had been seen gambling in Opelousas, Louisiana. Hamer discovered that he was using the alias Poorboy Taylor and frequently slipped into Opelousas to play craps. On Christmas Eve Hamer and Sheriff Hammond quietly boarded a train for the 240-mile trip to Opelousas. There, Frank learned that the fugitive had been seen near Baton Rouge, sixty miles east, so they boarded another train for the capital city, where they discovered that Mississippi Red was working on a levee near Melville, fifty miles away.

Hamer and Hammond arrived in Melville on January 3, 1913, having spent eleven days on the trail of Mississippi Red. According to Sheriff Hammond, "Hamer disguised himself as a Baptist preacher, black frock coat, bible and all. . . . Hamer found the boarding house where Red lived. As a man of the cloth he learned from the boarding house keeper where Mississippi Red worked." Their quarry was at the nearby settlement of Redcross. Explained Hammond, "Young was practically buried from the rest of the world in the bottoms of the Mississippi delta near Redcross, on the Atchafalaya River, among the gangs engaged in repairing the Melville levee. There are no less than 5,000 negroes in the bottoms engaged in that work, many of whom are evidently outlaws. . . . It is so easy to evade capture in the woods and brakes throughout that region that we succeeded in our efforts only through strategy and utmost care and precaution. On arriving at Redcross we were joined by a constable of that place and engaged a negro guide. After arriving at the camp where Young worked, we had to crawl along on our hands and knees through the brakes and marsh to a place where we could cover him as he passed. The men were barrowing dirt from a pit 200 yards from the place where it was dumped. We hid close to the place where he must pass and the guide stood, hat in hand, on the dump and watched. When Young passed, the guide replaced his hat, the prearranged signal. We then sprang forward and covered the prisoner with Winchesters."[20]

Hamer and Hammond returned to Houston the following afternoon with Mississippi Red. The two officers split the $250 bounty, but Sheriff

Hammond told newspapermen that their expenses—travel, lodging, and paying informants—exceeded the amount of the reward. On April 22 Matt Young pled guilty to second-degree murder and was sentenced to twenty years in prison. The public accolades and positive press notices that Hamer received for his manhunting skill should have helped dispel the criticisms of the *Houston Press*. Instead, they would soon be eclipsed by a violent quarrel with its editor and reporters.[21]

Less than three weeks later, Mayor Rice announced that he would not run for reelection. Hamer decided to stay on until April 21, the day Rice was to leave office. For months, Frank had been seething over his dispute with the *Press*. On April 14, 1913, the *Press* ran a purported interview with Police Chief Noble in which he was quoted as saying that "the special officers on Mayor Rice's staff interfered with his officers" and that "when his men found a vice resort or gambling joint and encountered some of the special officers there, the latter would warn them to get out and they would handle the situation." Although the story did not mention any special officer by name, Hamer was infuriated by the implication that the specials were protecting vice. The next morning, he confronted Chief Noble, who later explained, "I did not make the statement, and the views expressed in the paper are not my own. In fact, I wasn't even in Houston in time for that interview to have been given the paper."

Hamer, with Chief Noble and Lee Anders, immediately went to the *Press* office, where they encountered Edwards, its editor, and H. C. Waters, the reporter. Chief Noble produced a copy of the article and demanded to know why it had been published. Waters insisted that Noble had authorized the story. Edwards wrote in the *Press*, "Chief Noble said he would never have authorized the publication of such a story because he considered it ill-advised." Edwards said that Hamer then declared, "I notified this paper some time ago that if it ever wrote anything against me I would fix somebody. The next one of you fellows I see on the street, I am going to smoke him off the earth." Continued Edwards, "He slapped at the reporter and then placed his hand on his hip as though to pull a gun, but he did not do so. He repeated the threat that he would shoot persons connected with the *Houston Press* if he saw them on the street. Chief Noble stood by in colloquy and then he and the two special officers left."[22]

Hamer wasted little time in carrying out his threat. Late the following night, Waters, with his brother George and Ed Fox, fellow reporters for the *Press,* stepped out of the Houston Press Club, then located in the Prince Theater building across from the courthouse on Fannin Street. The trio walked south on Fannin and stumbled upon Frank Hamer, Lee Anders, and a couple of other men who were coming out of the Stratford Hotel. H. C. Waters described what happened: "We were coming along Fannin Street when Mr. Hamer saw my brother and knocked him to the pavement. I ran to the Field bar and there telephoned to the police station. . . . In the meantime my brother and Fox had run to the corner." H. C. Waters struggled with Hamer on the sidewalk, shouting, "Let me go, I only want to take my brother to the hospital, he's hurt. I want to take him to the police station." As Waters later recalled, "George was bleeding profusely and we jumped into an automobile which was standing in front of the saloon and went to the police station. When we arrived Hamer was in the officers' rest room washing his hands. I entered the door and started to say, 'What is the mat—.' No sooner had I said that than Hamer came to the door, and after a very few words struck me with his fist. He then kicked me out of the station into the street."

Several witnesses said that Hamer then clouted H. C. Waters over the head with his six-gun, knocking him unconscious. His brother George, seeing this, fled down Caroline Street and turned onto Preston Avenue. Hamer followed, and when he reached the corner, he pulled his revolver and fired two shots. George Waters claimed that one of the bullets grazed his finger, which seems improbable given that several witnesses, as well as Hamer himself, reported that he had fired into the air. Then Frank returned to the police station, where the night chief placed him under arrest. Hamer posted a twenty-five-dollar bond and was immediately released.

Frank's temper had got the better of him, and he knew it. Early the next morning, April 17, he went to city hall, looking for Mayor Rice. The mayor was not there, so Hamer told the city controller that he was

Frank Hamer with Mollie's niece, Marie Mills. This photo was taken
when he was a special officer in Houston. *Courtesy Kathy Hatchett*

resigning and picked up his last paycheck. That afternoon, Mayor Rice
telephoned Frank and asked him to come to his office. After a long meeting, Hamer emerged and made a lengthy statement to a journalist: "The
fight between myself and Waters is the result of a disagreement of over
five months standing. . . . At the time of this interview I told a reporter
that if he wanted trouble all he would have to do was to 'write me up,' as
he had been doing, and that I would 'smoke him up.' I've kept my word.
When a certain article appeared in a newspaper yesterday afternoon I
knew a certain man was hunting trouble, for I had repeatedly asked him
to give me a fair deal and not to misquote me. I did hit George Waters
with my six-shooter, though I never turned the butt end of the revolver

against him. I used the barrel. When I shot at Mr. Waters as he was running down Preston Avenue last night I did not shoot to hit him. I am a good shot with a revolver, but I am not a gun fighter. I wanted to scare him."[23]

Edwards later recalled that he devoted the front page of the *Press* to the story of the assault and an editorial condemning the special officers. "They created a sensation. That day marked the beginning of the end of the cowboy police force. One by one they left Houston. . . . Public wrath had effectually vanquished them." That was hardly true. The Houston *Chronicle* and *Post* promptly published statements of support for Hamer, one saying, "He has the reputation of being quiet, steady, and a gentleman . . . and no complaints against any of his actions as an officer or a citizen have ever been made." The other declared that he "bears the reputation of being clean, clear-cut and fearless." Still, when the new mayor was sworn in the following week, he fired the rest of the special officers.[24]

Despite the fact that the Waters brothers had been pistol-whipped by Frank Hamer, H. C. Waters later wrote that he did not consider him a bad officer. "Hamer was not exactly in the class referred to by [Chief] Noble and had probably caused the regular force no embarrassment in law enforcement, as his record seems generally to have been on the side of the law." When Frank had told the newspapers that his record was "clean," he meant that he did not accept bribes. At a time when petty graft was commonplace among American police, Hamer prided himself on the fact that he was scrupulously honest. When he said he was not a "gun fighter," he meant that he did not fit the image as it was then commonly understood—a disreputable hardcase who used his guns without just cause. In fact, he had certainly used his pistol unlawfully against the Waters brothers. And, in retrospect, his claim was extraordinarily ironic, for Frank Hamer would prove to be one of the greatest gunfighters of the American West. Despite his protestations, Hamer's ignominious conclusion to his career as a Houston lawman was one of the lowest points of his official life.[25]

Frank told newspapermen that he had no fixed plans and intended to take a sixty-day vacation and go hunting. He and Mollie stayed in

Houston until June 10, when he appeared in court and pled guilty to charges of assaulting the Waters brothers. He paid a fine of $88.70 and was released. Frank and Mollie then moved back to Navasota. There, unable to find work, Hamer was faced with months of idleness. Cracks in his marriage began to develop. Unfortunately, no details are known, but several possibilities exist. Frank's long period of unemployment and his frustration with inactivity may have led to friction between the couple. Mollie was educated, independent, and highly employable as both a schoolteacher and a bookkeeper. Perhaps she wanted, or needed, to return to work, a result that would have amplified Frank's sense of helplessness and restlessness. Mollie liked Houston and may not have wished to leave; she also may have feared that she would face a nomadic life as the spouse of an itinerant Texas lawman. Lastly, Frank's love of children would have made him anxious to begin a family, but Mollie was either unable or—perhaps because of their precarious finances— unwilling to conceive a child. Some or all of these factors must have contributed to serious marital discord.[26]

Hamer's seven idle months were suddenly interrupted in late November when Texas was hit by one of its worst floods. He was immediately hired as a temporary Navasota police officer and assigned to work with City Marshal Marvin Bailey. They had their hands full evacuating people from the Brazos River bottoms. When the floodwaters finally receded, hundreds were found dead along the river. The 1913 flood was a major impetus for construction of flood control dams on the Brazos in the 1930s and 1950s.[27]

Mance Lipscomb was delighted with Frank's return to Navasota. Mance, then eighteen, attended a party one night at the house of his cousin, Gainesville Lipscomb, twenty-nine. Such "Satiddy Night Suppas" were the scene of drinking, dancing, gambling, and, sometimes, fighting. When one of Gainesville's enemies slashed his head with a knife, Gainesville responded by stabbing his assailant in the leg. A general brawl broke out, and the assailant's brother-in-law, Robert Howard, rushed forward to join the attack on Gainesville. Mance snatched up a Winchester and threw it to his cousin, who was bleeding heavily from his head wound. Gainesville opened fire, hitting Howard in the hip. A second shot struck Cercy Walker, deflected off a small tobacco can in his pocket, and passed through Walker's side. As the bloodied Gainesville dropped to the floor, Mance seized the rifle and fired several shots into the air to scatter the crowd.

Frank Hamer and Marvin Bailey, alerted by the gunfire, rushed to the house and arrested Gainesville. Hamer was sympathetic, as he understood Mance's cousin may have acted in self-defense, and told him, "Now, Gainesville, we got to arrest you 'cause you shot a couple of people."

Gainesville responded, "I ain't gonna lie. I did some shootin'."

"Well," said Hamer, "I want you to tell me the truth. But you got to pay for it, one way or the other."

As Frank was speaking, Bailey struck Gainesville in the head, saying to Hamer, "Don't let him talk to you!"

"Don't you touch that man," Hamer retorted. "Let him talk. We got him arrested. We need ten more Gainesvilles like him. That's what's the matter with this damn Navasota. Ain't nobody here nervy as Gainesville."

Bailey paid no heed, and when he drew back to unleash a kick, Gainesville prepared to defend himself, warning Bailey, "I'll make you kill me."

At that, Hamer, flush with anger, barked, "Bailey, you better not touch that nigga! Let him talk 'til he gives out. He ain't hurting nobody."

Mance recalled that Bailey "didn' like that, but Mista Hayman was the boss." When Gainesville showed them his wound and explained that he had shot in self-defense, Frank replied, "You ain't done nothing bad. You're gonna get out easier than you think. But I just want the truth about it."

Hamer was true to his word, said Mance: "An sho' 'nuff, he let him out that next day."[28]

In the new year of 1914, Hamer kept up his aggressive police work. He and Bailey captured numerous commercial burglars in Navasota and neighboring towns. But that summer, the Hamers' marriage continued to deteriorate. By August, he and Mollie were on the verge of separating. When Frank was offered a job as a livestock detective in Kimble County, he quickly accepted. Hamer was probably recommended by his old Ranger comrade Oscar Latta, a longtime resident of Kimble County who later served as sheriff. In late August, Jim Dunaway, no longer a railroad officer, visited the Hamers in Navasota. The cultured Mollie could not have been pleased by Frank's friendship with the rough, hard-drinking Dunaway. Mollie's younger sister Adice came to Navasota to stay with her and to offer emotional support. On August 29 Hamer and Dunaway entrained for the latter's hometown of Llano, two hundred miles distant, leaving Mollie behind.[29]

Kimble County, situated at the western edge of the Hill Country, had long suffered from the depredations of goat thieves and fence cutters. That spring, the Kimble County Angora Goat Raisers and Breeders Association met in Junction and offered a $500 standing reward for goat and sheep thieves. The reward did not stop the stealing, so the association elected to hire Hamer. Somewhere, Frank had acquired his favorite saddle horse, a powerful bay named Bugler. Much too poor to own an automobile, Hamer would ride Bugler throughout the Hill Country for the next year. Junction, the Kimble County seat, was isolated, with no railroad connections and accessible only by rough dirt roads. From Llano, Hamer and Dunaway rode eighty miles southwest to Junction, situated in a pretty valley surrounded by high hills and bluffs at the junction of the North and South Llano Rivers. They found a bustling rural town of one thousand people, with two hundred houses, fifteen shops, a bank, four churches, and even a couple of drugstores. It was the center of a vast sheep- and goat-raising district. The county was extremely remote, with the nearest railroad more than fifty miles away on dusty roads that turned into quagmires when it rained. Its sheep and goat raisers eked out a precarious living, always on the edge of financial disaster from drought, poor soil, and primitive transportation.[30]

Jim Dunaway did not stay long in Junction, instead continuing on to Rocksprings, in Edwards County, where he hired on as a deputy sheriff. Not surprisingly, he soon stirred up trouble and lost his badge. Hamer, for his part, was commissioned a Kimble County deputy sheriff and paid a salary by the goat raisers' association. Frank learned from the stockmen that Fletcher Gardner, son of a prominent family, was the suspected ringleader in the thievery. The ranchers thought that Hamer could break up the gang in a month, but the job proved far more difficult. He would spend almost a year in Kimble County. Just as he had done in Navasota, Frank, acting alone, used overwhelming displays of force to intimidate the county's numerous thieves and hardcases. Dayton Moses, a stockmen's lawyer, recalled that "there were a great many undesirable citizens in that county at that time." He said that many residents thought that Hamer was "a first class man and a first class officer," but "there were a great many good citizens of the county who believed that some of the methods that [Hamer] used towards suspects were too harsh." On one occasion, in October 1914, Frank was charged with assault and paid a ten-dollar fine in the Junction courthouse. Although the case files from that period have long since disappeared, there can be little doubt that the charges grew out of his campaign to eliminate the livestock thieves.[31]

There was also a lighter side to his work, as Hamer later recalled. One day a horse was stolen in Junction, and Frank learned that the thief was headed west toward the town of Sonora, in Sutton County, sixty miles away. He telephoned Sheriff Robert H. Martin in Sonora and warned him to be on the lookout. Then Frank started in the saddle after the horse thief. When he reached the Allison ranch, thirteen miles from Sonora, he found a telephone message asking him to call Sheriff Martin, a prominent rancher and civic leader. Martin was well known for his sense of humor but handicapped by a serious speech impediment. Hamer called Martin on the ranch telephone, saying, "Hello, Sheriff. What is it?"

"Hello, F-Frank," Martin stuttered. "F-F-Frank, I got him."

"Y'did?" exclaimed Hamer. "Well, that's fine. Tell me about it."

"C-C-C-Come on in, Frank. You c-c-can r-r-r-ride it b-b-b-before I c-c-can tell you."[32]

On December 2, 1914, the Kimble County commissioners appointed Coke R. Stevenson as county attorney, giving him one instruction: "Get the thieves." He promptly teamed up with Frank Hamer. Stevenson was four years younger than Frank, but the two had much in common. Born into poverty, Stevenson was a self-educated, self-made man. As a youth, he worked as a laborer, freighter, and cowhand. At twenty, he managed to land a job in the Junction bank, and "read law" on his own at night and in his spare time. After five years of diligent study, and one year before Hamer's arrival in Junction, he passed the state bar. Stevenson was tall, quiet, earnest, and scrupulously honest. A strong bond developed between the pair, the advent of a close friendship that would last decades, through Stevenson's terms as one of the Lone Star State's most popular governors, and, finally, in 1948, through one of the most important cases of Frank Hamer's life.[33]

On the morning of January 13, 1915, Hamer and Stevenson piled into the latter's touring car and made the 125-mile drive southwest on the rough, winding road to Del Rio. There, they attended the first annual meeting of the Texas Angora Breeders Association. Stevenson later recalled that the main purpose of the conference "was an effort to stop the large-scale stealing of sheep and goats." The conclave lasted two days, giving Frank time to hobnob with powerful ranchers. He longed to return to his beloved Texas Rangers, and no doubt lobbied for support in his quest for an appointment. But there were no openings in the Rangers.[34]

The Mexican Revolution was then raging, and its unrest had spread across the border into Texas. Criminals, both Anglo and Hispanic, took advantage of the turmoil to raid and pillage along the Texas-Mexico border and to smuggle arms, liquor, and stolen livestock. These violent events later inspired numerous Hollywood films, most notably Sam Peckinpah's *The Wild Bunch* (1969). Though most of the cross-border raids were by Mexican bandits, in March Captain J. Monroe Fox, of the Texas Rangers, blamed Americans as much as Mexicans for cattle stealing in the Big Bend region. The entire 1,254-mile border was guarded only by a handful of mounted U.S. customs inspectors, known as "river guards," local sheriffs and their deputies, fewer than thirty Rangers, and scattered army posts.[35]

On February 24, 1915, the powerful state senator Claude B. Hudspeth introduced a bill to appropriate $10,000 for ten additional Rangers, "to protect the border from Mexican depredations." Since Hudspeth owned cattle ranches in the Big Bend region, he had a personal interest in its passage. Newspaper reports resulted in a flood of Ranger applications to the adjutant general. A few weeks later, the bill was approved by the governor. Captains John J. Sanders, of Company A, and Monroe Fox, of Company B, were allocated five privates each. Senator Hudspeth knew of Frank Hamer's quest for appointment and recommended that he and Jim Dunaway receive two of the commissions. However, Captain Sanders and L. A. Clark, the Edwards County sheriff, strongly objected to Dunaway. Sanders and Dunaway despised each other, and Sheriff Clark complained—correctly—that Dunaway was a troublemaker, pointing out that he had recently fired him as a deputy. At the same time, Captain Fox was not interested in either Dunaway or Hamer and asked that two other recruits be sent to his company. In a letter to Adjutant General Henry Hutchings, Fox explained that Hamer "does not speak" to Sheriff Milt Chastain, of Presidio County, or to Sheriff Allen Walton, of Brewster County. They were the two principal lawmen of the Big Bend region—Captain Fox's district. Since Hamer had not worked in the Big Bend since 1907, his dislike of Chastain and Walton must have been of long standing. Despite the animosity, Senator Hudspeth insisted that Hamer and Jim Dunaway "be enlisted and detailed for this service." As a result, the newly elected governor, James E. Ferguson, personally ordered General Hutchings to hire them both.[36]

Hutchings, not wanting to alienate Captains Sanders and Fox, devised a compromise. He ordered that Hamer and Dunaway be sworn in and assigned to Captain Edward H. Smith, a new appointee to the Rangers, "in order that these men might not be forced on a Company Commander." Smith was in charge of Company C, which at that time had only one man—Captain Smith—who handled administrative duties at Ranger headquarters in Austin. Frank must have thought over his reenlistment long and hard. Ranger pay was still a dismal $40 a month, but it was a chance to stay in West Texas, where he had always been happy in the saddle on the open range. In addition, service on the simmering border offered excitement and adventure. It was exactly what he needed to get Mollie off his mind.[37]

Although the two captains wanted neither Hamer nor Dunaway, Sheriff John W. Almond in Del Rio was eager to have both assigned to

Val Verde County. Almond, a political ally of Senator Hudspeth, favorably recalled Hamer from his daring service as a young Ranger in Del Rio in 1906. So Frank rode from Junction to Del Rio, where he and Dunaway met Captain Smith and Sheriff Almond and then signed enlistment papers on March 29, 1915. Their assignment was to stop widespread goat stealing in Val Verde and the adjacent counties of Edwards and Kinney. Frank, however, was first ordered to return to Junction and carry on with his work in running down livestock thieves in Kimble County.[38]

Hamer knew that Fletcher Gardner, the suspected ringleader, was the son of John F. Gardner, one of Kimble County's biggest and most popular pioneer ranchers. The elder Gardner had two daughters and five sons. Two of them, Fletcher and Buck, were hardcases. Buck was especially notorious, and Frank heard rumors that he had been mixed up in the 1911 murder of a Mexican goatherd. Hamer was determined to get the goods on the Gardner brothers.[39]

As Coke Stevenson later recalled, "The talk in Kimble County was that someone was doing a lot of stealing, but nobody was able to catch them." But he had utmost faith in the abilities of his new friend, declaring, "Frank Hamer was a natural born detective." Hamer was unable to track the thief, said Stevenson. "We found out he would go out into a pasture, stretch a wagon sheet in the gate and drive the sheep across. The wagon sheet kept them from leaving tracks." Stevenson recalled that he and Frank "lay out" in the hills for many nights, staking out various sheep and goat pastures. Finally, on April 22, 1915, they captured Fletcher Gardner and his partner in crime, Willis Cross, a part-time court bailiff.[40]

The arrest and prosecution of Fletcher Gardner displeased many in Kimble County. The Gardner family announced that he was innocent and claimed that Stevenson was prosecuting him merely to make a name for himself as the new county attorney. Others believed that Gardner was guilty but that he should have been released because of his family's high standing in the community. Stevenson refused to respond to any of the criticism. In the end, Gardner was convicted of theft.[41]

Now, Hamer turned his attention to Buck Gardner. Little or no effort had been made to investigate his murder of the sheepherder four
years earlier. After all, who cared about a dead Mexican, especially
when the suspect was the scion of a prominent family? But Hamer ignored the ethnicity of the victim and the status of the suspect. Following up on rumors, he managed to locate the victim's skeletal remains in
a remote canyon. He learned that Gardner had shot and killed the
sheepherder so he wouldn't have to pay him several months of back
wages. Gardner then dismembered the body and used it to bait his wolf
traps. Frank reported that he "actually fastened the traps to the legs,
arms, and head of the dead Mexican." He arrested Buck Gardner for
murder, but when the case went to trial in the fall, a jury acquitted him.
The desperado didn't live long. He took part in a number of shooting
scrapes and finally met his match in 1922, when a Junction storekeeper
ended his career with a fatal load of buckshot.[42]

During the spring of 1915, Frank continued his antirustling campaign, and in May he picked up a pair of horse thieves in Kimble
County. But he wanted horseback service on the Rio Grande. He must
have complained to Senator Hudspeth, because on July 6 Governor Ferguson ordered that Hamer report for duty to Captain Fox in Marfa. He
spent a week wrapping up his affairs in Junction, then mounted Bugler
and made the three-hundred-mile ride west, across the open ranges. A
week later, Frank was in camp with Fox's company in the rugged mountains of the Big Bend.[43]

In 1913 and 1914, Hamer's career and his personal life had both
reached a nadir. His fine work as a special officer for Mayor Rice had
been overshadowed by his unseemly public feud with the Houston *Post*.
His pistol-whipping of the Waters brothers—to say nothing of his
shooting at George Waters—was flagrantly unlawful and exposed his
raw temper. And this would not be the last time he would be accused of
police brutality.

The failure of his marriage to Mollie was one of the greatest disap-
pointments of his life. At some point in late 1914 or early 1915, they
divorced, for in March 1915 Hamer listed himself as single in his

Ranger application. Frank and Mollie had loved each other deeply, and their breakup seems to have been a relatively amicable one. In later years, both spoke fondly of the other. Mollie's family in particular thought highly of Frank, and, ever after, the Camerons remembered him in very positive terms.[44]

Nonetheless, Hamer must have been desperately lonely and discouraged. He was thirty-one and impoverished. He had no money, no home, no land. His only possessions were the clothes on his back, his rifle, six-gun, saddle, and horse. But he loved the Ranger service and looked forward to the camaraderie it offered. He was more than happy to be back on the border. From the lowest point in his life, he had nowhere to go but up.

6

THE BANDIT WAR

In the blackness, he sensed death. Frank Hamer stepped cautiously along the railroad tracks, his high-heeled boots skittering on the ties and the gravel. With Captain Fox at his side, he approached the bullet-riddled linemen's shack. Hamer swung up the barrel of his Winchester and shoved open the door. Bursting inside, he was stopped cold by a horrendous sight. The insurgents had done their deadly work. Before him lay the body of an aged Mexican woman, weltering in her own gore. The back of her head had been blown entirely off. Beside her, clustered on the blood-drenched floor, cowered several terrified railroad hands and their wives. Never was a group of Mexicans so happy to see a Texas Ranger.

Frank had joined Company B at just the right time. Its captain, forty-eight-year-old James Monroe Fox, was a stocky, oval-faced professional lawman. He had long served as a deputy sheriff and constable in Austin, where in 1902 he shot and killed a black prisoner attempting to escape. Political connections got him appointment as a Ranger captain in 1911. He was active and energetic but seriously deficient in leadership. Captain Fox's biggest problem came in the form of a notorious revolutionary leader, robber, and smuggler named Francisco "Chico" Cano. Chico Cano's gang numbered about one hundred, formerly followers of Mexican revolutionary leader Pascual Orozco. Cano and his bandidos rustled cattle on the Mexican side and smuggled them into Texas, then stole horses in Texas and sold them in Mexico.

Just before Frank joined Fox's outfit, two of its Rangers had been slain and the company badly demoralized. In May 1915 a posse led by veteran lawman and river guard Joe Sitter, which included three men from Company B, was ambushed by Chico Cano and his band near Pilares on the Rio Grande. Joe Sitter and Ranger Eugene Hulen, a rookie recruit and brother of the former adjutant general, died in a hail of gunfire. Cano and his riders escaped. Two weeks later, on June 7, Ranger Lee Burdett was killed in a gunfight with Mexican desperadoes in Fabens, southeast of El Paso. The Rangers hunted in vain for Chico Cano; he was never captured and died in Mexico of natural causes in 1943.[1]

Six weeks after the Burdett killing, Hamer, mounted on Bugler, rode slouch-saddled into Ranger camp in the mountains of the Big Bend. He brought experience, judgment, marksmanship, and morale to the company, all of which were sorely lacking. Frank's natural leadership qualities, combined with utter fearlessness, never failed to inspire fellow Rangers. In his scabbard he carried a lever-action Winchester Model 1895 rifle. This was by far the most popular weapon among river guards and Rangers during the Mexican Revolution. It was a huge improvement over the old Winchester Model 1873 and fired the powerful, smokeless .30-06 cartridge that was accurate at ranges up to a thousand yards. The rifle's box magazine held five rounds. Frank carried extra ammunition in a U.S. Army–issue canvas bandoleer. Most important to Hamer and his ill-paid comrades, its ammunition was the same as that fired by the army's standard-issue Model 1903 Springfield rifle. When low on bullets, Rangers could get them for free from the soldiers. One Company B Ranger, Ivey Finley, a former El Paso policeman, recalled how impressed he was with Hamer: "The man wasn't afraid of the devil himself." Of Frank's skill with a Winchester, Finley said, "A rifle was his favorite weapon. I never saw him fire a pistol. We used to throw coins and small pebbles into the air, and he would break them almost every time with bullets from a high-powered rifle. He practiced constantly."[2]

The Mexican Revolution had sparked unrest along the entire Rio Grande, from El Paso to the Gulf of Mexico. Its most populated region

Frank Hamer mounted on his favorite horse, Bugler, during the Bandit War of 1915. *Courtesy of the Texas Ranger Hall of Fame and Museum, Waco, Texas*

was the river's lower reach, the Rio Grande Valley, extending inland one hundred miles from its mouth near Brownsville. The Rio Grande Valley includes Starr, Cameron, Hidalgo, and Willacy Counties. Historically the region had been an arid, chaparral-covered desert, but the introduction of large-scale irrigation in 1898, coupled with the arrival of the railroad six years later, transformed the valley into an important agricultural center. Farmers and laborers from both sides of the border flocked to the Rio Grande Valley. For several generations past, Tejanos (Mexican Americans born in Texas), who were in the majority, had lived in relative harmony with Anglos. White political bosses had the electoral support of the Spanish-speaking population. Political power was concentrated in the hands of big landowners, lawyers, and merchants.

South Texas had long been dominated by political bossism, and James B. Wells was *the* boss. A Brownsville attorney, he exercised control from the mid-1880s until 1920. Jim Wells County was named in his honor in 1912. Though corrupt, Wells was hugely popular with both Anglos and Hispanics. Like a *patron* in old Mexico, he provided jobs, protection, and support for the Hispanic poor in exchange for bloc voting. Mexican American rancheros and ricos freely participated in his machine. And by attracting railroads and agribusiness, he secured the support of Anglos. But after 1900 the infusion of American farmers from the Midwest brought change, and the political balance began to shift in their favor, eventually spelling doom for Wells's machine. The new Anglo farmers also brought racial trouble. Not knowing Tejanos or Mexicans personally, they relied on stereotypes: Hispanics were ignorant and lazy, a people to be treated with contempt. The result was bitter and justifiable resentment of Anglos by Hispanics.[3]

At the same time, revolution was brewing in Mexico. Its dictatorial president, Porfirio Díaz, had been in power since 1876. Widespread corruption and mistreatment of citizens had made Díaz extremely unpopular among the masses. Especially brutal were the rural police, known as *rurales,* who institutionalized the practice of *ley de fuga*—law of flight—which used alleged escape as a pretext for the killing of prisoners. In the election of 1910, Díaz was challenged by Francisco I. Madero, an aristocratic reformer. President Díaz had Madero jailed and then defeated him through massive ballot fraud. Madero obtained his release and fled to Texas, where he called for a popular uprising against Díaz, thus igniting the Mexican Revolution. The Battle of Juárez, watched by many in its American sister city of El Paso, took place on May 8, 1911. Rebels supporting Madero, and led by Pancho Villa and Pascual Orozco, defeated Díaz's forces and captured the city. Porfirio Díaz was forced to sign the Treaty of Ciudad Juárez, after which he resigned the presidency and fled to Spain.

Thus began an extraordinarily confused and anarchic period of Mexican history. During the next ten years, the country would see no less than ten presidents. Francisco Madero proved a weak leader and incurred the wrath of both Pancho Villa and Pascual Orozco by failing to offer them political appointments. In a bloody coup led by General Victoriano Huerta, Madero was assassinated. General Huerta served as president for one year, during which time he was violently opposed by Venustiano Carranza, a politician and rancher. In 1914 U.S. forces seized the port city of Vera Cruz, cutting off arms shipments to Huerta from Germany. After a crucial defeat by Pancho Villa two months later,

Huerta resigned the presidency and went into exile. A civil war broke out as Venustiano Carranza, Pancho Villa, and Alvaro Obregón battled one another for control. Though Pancho Villa had been a lifelong criminal and robber, he enjoyed the most American support until he made the foolish decision to raid Columbus, New Mexico, in 1916. President Woodrow Wilson refused to extend official recognition to any of them. Venustiano Carranza later obtained the presidency until he was finally assassinated in 1920.

The Mexican Revolution had a momentous effect on Texas, and particularly on the border region. As the Revolution disintegrated into an armed struggle between rival chieftains, a flood of Mexican refugees poured across the border. These newcomers supported the various factions—those of Huerta, Villa, Obregón, Carranza, and others. The result was that both Mexicans and Tejanos, many of the latter with close family ties to Mexico, favored different sides. The revolution would also profoundly affect the Texas Rangers.

Frank Hamer's reenlistment was immediately preceded by two more events that were pivotal in the history of the Ranger force. In January of 1915 a new governor took office—James Ferguson, known as "Farmer Jim" or "Pa" Ferguson. The most corrupt Texas governor of the twentieth century, Ferguson had opposed urban Democrats and was supported by rural tenant farmers, working men, and pro-liquor forces. One of Ferguson's first acts was his refusal to reappoint Ranger Captain John R. Hughes, the legendary "Border Boss," and the last of the "Four Great Captains." Although Ferguson's stated reason was Hughes's age—sixty—in fact he intended to pack the Rangers with political supporters. Captain Hughes's forced retirement ended the institutional professionalism imposed by the four great captains and marked the beginning of the blackest chapter in the annals of the Texas Rangers.[4]

The second pivotal event was one of the most infamous in Texas history—the Plan of San Diego. A radical manifesto supposedly drawn up in San Diego, seat of Duval County, it called for a full-scale race war in the Southwest. According to the plan's exhortations, on February 20, 1915, all Mexicans were to rise up in arms against U.S. tyranny. Territory lost in the Mexican War—Texas, New Mexico, Arizona, Colorado, and

California—would be "freed" and annexed to Mexico. Every North American male over sixteen would be put to death. Six other states were to be given to blacks as an independent nation, a buffer region between Mexico and the United States. All plan members must be Hispanic, black, or Japanese, and they would carry a white battle flag with red fringe.

This harebrained scheme had absolutely no chance of success. It became public when one of its adherents was arrested with a copy in his possession. The judge who heard the case thought he was a crackpot. But Texas lawmen took the Plan of San Diego very seriously, as did many impoverished, disaffected Hispanics in the Rio Grande Valley. They suffered from ethnic, political, and economic discrimination and were willing to join any movement that gave them hope for a better future. To disenfranchised Tejanos and Mexicans, the Plan of San Diego seemed to provide just that. Newspapers reported the details of the plot, which created panic among Anglos on the border. But February 20 came and went without any uprising, and for the next several months Anglos in the Rio Grande Valley breathed easy.[5]

Just after Hamer rejoined the Rangers, the Plan of San Diego suddenly took on new life. It came to be known as the Bandit War. In early July a band of rebels, or *sediciosos* (seditionists), led by Luis de la Rosa, appeared wraithlike from the rugged brush country north of Brownsville. De la Rosa was a former shopkeeper, ex–deputy sheriff, and suspected cattle thief. On July 4, 1915, his riders attacked a ranch near Raymondville, fifty miles north of Brownsville, then reportedly killed two Anglos near Lyford. They fled into the dense chaparral with posses and U.S. troops in pursuit. Three days later, the foreman of the vast King Ranch caught five members of the band with stolen cattle. They opened fire, and he shot back, killing one raider and wounding another. On July 12 the marauders robbed a store near Lyford, and five days afterward one raider killed an Anglo youth in a pasture eighteen miles east of Raymondville. On July 25 the band torched and destroyed a railroad bridge near Sebastian. Six days later, they raided Los Indios ranch and killed a Mexican. These brazen attacks terrorized the Anglos, who demanded protection from U.S. troops and Texas Rangers.[6]

In response, Governor Ferguson appointed Henry Ransom a captain of the Texas Rangers. Ransom had remained in Houston after he and the rest of the special officers had been fired. Never one to stay out of trouble, he was arrested in October 1913 for beating a Houston *Post* reporter and shooting a jailer in the neck. Henry Ransom had been hardened by his shooting scrapes in Texas and his service in the Philippine insurrection. As a corporal in the company of Captain John A. Hulen, he had saved Hulen's life by killing a Filipino who attacked him with a bolo knife. Hulen, later adjutant general, was eternally grateful. Ransom's friendship with Hulen and former mayor Horace Baldwin Rice was crucial to his appointment as Ranger captain. Governor Ferguson ordered Ransom to form a new outfit, Ranger Company D. As Hamer's friend Bill Sterling observed, "Ransom's . . . service in the Philippines had caused him to place small value on the life of a lawbreaker." Sterling recalled a conversation in a Mexican border camp between Ransom and an army captain who had served in the Philippines: "The tales they told about executing Filipinos made the Bandit War look like a minor purge."[7]

Governor Ferguson was later quoted as ordering Ransom to use drastic measures against the Plan of San Diego rebels. The governor instructed Ransom "to go down there and clean it up if he had to kill every damn man connected with it. . . . I firmly told Ransom that if he didn't do it—if he didn't clean that nest up down there that I would put a man down there that would." Ferguson offered Ransom and his Rangers official protection from prosecution for murder: "I have the pardoning power and we will stand by those men." Ransom was eager to follow Ferguson's orders, telling Bill Sterling, "The Governor sent me down here to stop this trouble, and I am going to carry out his orders." Referring to Porfirio Díaz's use of ley de fuga, Ransom said, "There is only one way to do it. President Diaz proved that in Mexico." His ideas of justice also applied to those who assisted the raiders: "Anyone who has guilty knowledge of crimes committed, or anyone who harbors bandits should be killed." William T. Vann, sheriff of Cameron County, was very unhappy with Ransom's appointment, telling Governor Ferguson, "I don't like his style. I have heard a good deal about Captain Ransom, and I don't want him down there." This was the beginning of a long conflict between Sheriff Vann and the Rangers, one that would later involve Frank Hamer. Henry Ransom would prove one of the most disreputable captains in the history of the Texas Rangers. He recruited former prison guards and tough characters from South Texas. It is noteworthy that Ransom, who insisted on handpicking his own men, did not have Frank assigned to his company. Mayor Rice had hired Hamer to keep a lid on Ransom, who knew that Frank would not stand for cold-blooded murder. Captain Ransom's company, stationed in Harlingen, would soon be called into gory action.[8]

On August 2, 1915, a band of fifty Mexican riders was spotted crossing the Rio Grande near Brownsville. Caesar Kleberg, manager of the huge King ranch, and political boss Jim Wells wired Adjutant General Henry Hutchings in Austin, urging him to come personally. Hutchings sent a telegram to Captain Fox in Marfa and ordered him to bring his entire company to Brownsville. Then Hutchings boarded a train for Brownsville, arriving on August 6. He discovered that on that very morning fifteen *sediciosos*, led by Luis de la Rosa, had attacked the little settlement of Sebastian, forty miles north of Brownsville. They looted the two general stores, then captured an Anglo farmer and his son and shot them to death. Before escaping, the raiders threatened to kill other prominent citizens. Reported *The Dallas Morning News,* "Today's encounter dissipated the idea that the bandits were from across the Rio Grande. Reliable Mexicans and Americans who saw them recognized several members of the band as having lived in the northern part of this county for years."[9]

That night, August 6, a posse led by General Hutchings and Captain Ransom shot and killed three suspected raiders on the McAllen ranch near Paso Real. Sheriff Vann, who was present, later insisted that the suspects were unarmed. The following noon, Captain Fox and seven of his Rangers, including Frank Hamer and Jim Dunaway, arrived in Brownsville by train. On the morning of August 8 they received a telephone message from Caesar Kleberg, manager of the King ranch, advising that Mexican raiders had been spotted on his range south of Kingsville. Adjutant General Hutchings quickly organized a strong posse:

Captains Fox and Ransom with Frank Hamer and thirteen more Rangers, plus Corporal Allen Mercer and seven privates from Troop C, Twelfth Cavalry. They boarded a special train and headed for Norias, headquarters of the Norias division of the sprawling King ranch, the largest in Texas. A U.S. mounted immigration inspector, D. Portus Gay, lounging on the front porch of the Immigration Service office near the depot, was surprised to see the special train with a large posse aboard. Seeking excitement, he decided to head for Norias himself, and at 3:30 boarded the northbound passenger train. On the way, he picked up Deputy Sheriff Gordon Hill and two customs inspectors who were former Rangers, Pinkie Taylor and Marcus "Tiny" Hines, plus two civilian volunteers, Sam Robertson and a youth named Vinson.[10]

Meanwhile, Frank Hamer and the rest had arrived in Norias. Situated on a flat plain seventy-five miles north of Brownsville, Norias was an isolated cattle-shipping point for the King ranch. The headquarters, a two-story wood frame house, was fifty feet west of the railroad tracks. A hundred yards south stood a railroad section house, and just across the tracks was a toolshed and a pile of cross ties. A hundred feet north of the ranch headquarters were two bunkhouses. The Rangers found Norias occupied by only a handful of people: foreman and Special Ranger Tom Tate; cowboys Frank Martin, Luke Snow, and Lauro Cavazos; the carpenter, George Forbes, and his wife; and the black cook, Albert Edmunds, and his wife. Several Mexican railroad hands and their wives, including an elderly woman, Manuela Flores, lived in quarters connected to the section house.

Tom Tate supplied the Rangers with King ranch horses. Then General Hutchings, the two captains, Frank Hamer, and the rest of the Rangers mounted up, and Tate led them toward a water hole twelve miles southwest, hoping to strike the trail of the raiders. The eight cavalrymen were left behind to guard the ranch house. At 5:30 the northbound train stopped in Norias, dropping off Portus Gay and his posse. They were invited into the ranch house to eat supper. After the meal, they stepped onto the front porch and spotted riders approaching from the east. Tiny Hines remarked, "There come the Rangers back."

But Portus Gay, squinting into the bright evening light, saw Mexican sombreros and exclaimed, "Look at those big hats and that white flag. They are damned bandits!"[11]

Sixty bandoleer-draped riders, armed with Mauser rifles, were closing fast. Some were Carranza's soldiers; others, Tejano adherents to the Plan of San Diego. Carrying a battle flag and commanded by Luis de la Rosa and at least one Carranza officer, they planned to wreck and rob a train at Norias. Quickly, the U.S. cavalrymen took up prone positions behind the low railroad bed, between the tracks and the house. Corporal Mercer was big and burly, but his soldiers were mere boys, most only eighteen or nineteen years old. As the raiders closed to 250 yards, the soldiers opened up with a barrage from their Springfield rifles. The guerrillas dismounted and returned the fire. Frank Martin and two of the soldiers were wounded almost immediately. The rebels charged forward as one band circled to the south to try to flank the defenders. Lawmen and cowboys took up positions along the tracks, while the six-foot-four, three-hundred-pound Tiny Hines, armed with a ten-gauge Winchester Model 1887 lever-action shotgun, squeezed behind a large water barrel.

The biggest battle of the Bandit War was under way. Deadly fire from the defenders forced the sediciosos to take up positions behind the railroad toolshed, the section house, and the pile of cross ties. Then they broke into the section house, where one of their leaders, Antonio Rocha, demanded that Manuela Flores tell them how many defenders were at the ranch headquarters. She answered defiantly in Spanish: "Why don't you go over there and see, you cowardly bastard of a white burra." Rocha jammed the muzzle of his revolver into her mouth and blew out the back of her head.[12]

As rebels on foot and horseback fired on the defenders from two sides, the raiders in the section house rained bullets on the soldiers. The defenders, afraid of hitting railroad hands in the section house, did not fire at it. Lauro Cavazos managed to shoot the horse out from underneath one of the rebel leaders. Meanwhile, the three wounded defenders were carried into the ranch house. Several attackers got caught behind a barbed wire cattle fence east of the tracks and were shot down by the defenders. Seeing that the raiders could not get past the fence, the rest of the defenders rushed inside the ranch house and returned the fire from doors and windows. The young troopers, with only ninety rounds per man, carefully chose their targets. The black cook, Albert Edmunds, crawled out the door to a telephone hanging on an outside wall. Amidst the shattering roar of gunfire, he managed to reach Caesar Kleberg in Kingsville, told him of the raid, and begged for help. Then, braving the fire, Edmunds crawled from one defender to another, bringing each of them water. While the man was drinking, Edmunds took over his rifle and fired at the marauders.[13]

The battle raged for more than two hours. The defenders were almost out of ammunition, and it appeared that they would be overwhelmed. Just at dark, about 8:30, the raiders mounted a final charge, "shooting and yelling like Indians," as Portus Gay recalled. At a range of forty yards, Pinkie Taylor shot and killed the leader, and the attack faltered. The raiders, who had only expected to encounter a few cowboys, lost heart in the gathering darkness. The rebels loaded their wounded onto horses and rode off in the blackness, shouting, *"Gringos cabrones!"* Portus Gay later said that they had wounded half the raiders, some of whom had to be tied to their saddles. The defenders, believing that the fighters in the toolshed and section house had stayed behind, held their positions.

An hour later, Frank Hamer and the rest of the Rangers, oblivious to the battle, returned to Norias. The defenders first thought the approaching horsemen were raiders, until Lauro Cavazos recognized Tom Tate's voice. They yelled at the Rangers to "fall off" their horses "as Mexicans had the house surrounded." Hamer and Captain Fox quickly ran up the tracks and approached the two outbuildings. Fox later recalled, "In a dark room of one shack we stumbled over the body of a dead Mexican woman, and in the road outside we found a horribly wounded Mexican man." Next to the corpse of Manuela Flores they found several terrified section hands and their wives huddled together. The Rangers returned to the ranch house, where they were both embarrassed and chagrined to learn how narrowly they had missed the marauders. The loudmouthed Captain Ransom began to lecture the defenders on how they should have conducted the battle. At that, Pinkie Taylor exploded: "Listen—*we* were here—we did not get a man killed—we were here when they came, we were here when they left, and we are still here, and I don't know what you all would have done if you had been here, but I do know there was not a goddamn son of a bitch of you here!"[14]

Deputy Sheriff Gordon Hill was just as angry. He barked at the Rangers, "If you all are such hell-roaring fighters, why don't you go after them? They can't be so very far away, as they have not been gone very long." But General Hutchings and Captains Fox and Ransom, concerned about an ambush in the dark, prudently elected to delay pursuit until morning.[15]

The Rangers found four bodies on the plains east of the ranch house. Nearby, they discovered a white battle flag emblazoned with a large letter *E*. The badly wounded raider gave his name as Jose Garcia and said he was from San Benito, Texas. He claimed, improbably, that he had been forced to join the attackers and admitted that their goal was to reclaim the Rio Grande Valley for Mexico. Recalled Portus Gay, "Just after making this statement, he died. I will not state just how or why he died." The obvious inference was that one of the posse murdered him. Gordon Hill's father, Lon, who arrived on a special train with Sheriff Vann soon after the battle ended, also talked with Garcia, who told him, "Now, you all will kill me, and I want you to tell my folks that I am killed." Based on these accounts, Jose Garcia is often considered to have been murdered by Texas Rangers. However, contemporary wire service reports differ. They identified the captured man as Jesus Garcia of Brownsville and said he died the following day from his battle wounds.[16]

In the morning, a northbound train rolled in. On board was Robert Runyon, an energetic and enterprising photographer from Brownsville who had created a cottage industry photographing scenes from the Mexican Revolution—many of them morbid images of dead bodies—and selling them as real-photo postcards, which were distributed widely in the United States and Mexico. Now, Runyon unlimbered his heavy camera and took numerous photos, including the Norias ranch headquarters and the six uninjured troopers standing on the front porch. He then carried his camera to the spot where the dead bodies lay in preparation

Frank Hamer, right, posing with dead raiders at Norias, August 9, 1915. The Ranger on the left appears to be Jim Dunaway. They are holding the captured battle flag between them. *Author's collection*

for burial and made several exposures of the corpses. He took two images of Frank Hamer and another posseman, who appears to be Jim Dunaway, posing on horseback behind the dead bodies and holding the captured battle flag between them. In the photos, Hamer is slouched easily on his horse, wearing a baggy canvas brush jacket with a U.S. Army–issue canvas cartridge belt slung across his chest. Runyon also took several photographs of Captain Fox, Tom Tate, and other lawmen with their lariats tied around three dead bodies as they prepared to drag them across the prairie.[17]

In accordance with the jingoistic ethos of that era, the Rangers posed proudly. The dead Mexicans were blood relics, trophies of war, representing triumph in battle. Ironically, the Rangers had nothing to do with killing the raiders. According to Lauro Cavazos, he and another King Ranch cowboy came up with the idea of dragging the bodies to a nearby sandbank, where they could easily be interred in a mass grave. After posing for the images, the Rangers prepared to bury the bodies. One of them intoned over the grave, "Dust to dust, if the *cabrones* don't kill you, the Rangers must."[18]

These images, especially the "dragging" photographs, became the most infamous in the Texas Rangers' history. They circulated widely as picture postcards in the United States and Mexico, and some were even published in newspapers. Many Americans considered the photos callous and disrespectful. Mexicans were outraged, since the images confirmed every negative stereotype of Rangers brutalizing Hispanics. Hamer's judgment in posing with the dead bodies was extremely poor, because the photographs inflamed further violence by Tejanos and Mexicans. As one federal immigration officer pointed out, the photos "did more perhaps than anything else to incite the Mexicans against the Americans."[19]

The Norias raid created a sensation and was reported on the front pages of newspapers throughout the United States. The foray, taking place so far north of the Rio Grande, illustrated the depth and danger of the insurrection. Now began a massive manhunt for the Norias raiders, which quickly turned into a pogrom. The U.S. Army commander, General Frederick Funston, ordered additional troops, heavy guns, and an airplane to the border. On August 11 San Antonio's *La Prensa,* the leading Spanish-language newspaper in Texas, reported that, in the previous forty-eight hours, ten Mexicans and Tejanos had been shot dead or hanged in the Rio Grande Valley. Governor Ferguson's ley de fuga order was apparently not much of a secret. Reported the *Brownsville Herald,* "Rangers now working under special orders from General Hutchings have 'certain instructions' that may help to clear the air of lawlessness in short order. It is not unlikely that the 'certain instructions' order them to shoot to disable suspicious characters on sight."[20]

Three days later, a journalist from *The Dallas Morning News* visited the valley and reported, "To all practical intents and purposes a condition of guerilla warfare exists along the border. Nobody knows how many Mexicans have been killed out in the brush the last few days—and nobody will ever know. . . . From the Nueces to the Rio Grande most of the men, and a good many boys, have buckled on their artillery. Texas Rangers, regular soldiers, sheriff's posses, and individual groups of citizens are scouring the country. . . . Whenever armed Mexicans are encountered it is understood the situation is not open to debate." The *News* reporter, with other journalists, questioned a "lean, sunburned Texas Ranger" about the deaths of three Mexicans found in the brush near Santa Maria, not far from the Rio Grande. "Well, boys," the Ranger remarked, "it's been pretty hot today—maybe they died of sunstroke. I ain't so sure of that though." Grinning sarcastically and hefting a 30-30 rifle, he continued, "You see, it could have been spinal meningitis, and then again, for all I know, they might have had leprosy—you never can tell."[21]

Meanwhile, Frank Hamer, Captain Fox, and the rest of Company B, after posing for the controversial photographs, started in pursuit of the Norias attackers. A few miles south of the ranch house they found a dead Mexican on the trail. He had a rifle bullet in his body, his face was powder-burned, and the top of his head had been blown off. Captain Fox believed that the man's compadres had killed him when he could ride no farther. Fox later claimed that he and his company pursued the band for thirty miles, exchanging rifle fire at long distance, and killed many of the marauders. No documentation has been found to support his claim. If true, it would account for one or more of Hamer's numerous gunfights along the Rio Grande.[22]

While scouting for raiders in the Rio Grande Valley, Hamer first met twenty-four-year-old Bill Sterling, who would become one of his closest friends and, years later, a Ranger captain and adjutant general of Texas. Though tall and powerful like Hamer, Sterling was very different. He came from a successful ranching family and had attended Texas A&M College for two years. He loved attention, wore gaudy boots and fancy pistol belts, and reveled in the image of a border roughrider. During the Bandit War, Bill Sterling was a deputy sheriff and a civilian scout for the Third U.S. Cavalry. Bill Sterling was hugely impressed with Frank Hamer and considered him the finest Ranger he ever knew.[23]

On the morning of August 10, Captain Fox got a tip that a band of marauders was holed up at El Merino ranch, two miles west of Sebastian. As Fox and members of his company rode toward the ranch house, a group of Mexican raiders leaped onto their horses. The Rangers opened fire, killing two, but the rest escaped. Four days later, Captain Fox and some of his men were told by local Mexicans that one of the Norias raiders was at a ranch near Raymondville. They tracked him down and killed him. That night, in a telephone report to Brownsville, Fox announced cryptically, "We got another Mexican—but he's dead." His blunt boast hit the wire services and was published in newspapers nationwide. The next day, Fox returned to Brownsville and reported that "virtually all of the Mexican bandits . . . have either been killed or driven back into Mexico."[24]

By now, Captain Fox, who had taken Mexican bandits alive in the Big Bend country, had changed his tactics. Evidently, Captain Ransom had told him of the ley de fuga order from Governor Ferguson. On August 20, Fox led a group of his Rangers to the house of Tomas Aguilar, a suspected insurgent, located near Raymondville. According to reports in Spanish-language newspapers, which presumably originated with Captain Fox, Aguilar first tried to hide, then grabbed a Winchester rifle and ran for his horse, firing at the Rangers. Fox and his men shot back and killed him. However, the next day Captain Fox, from his hotel in Raymondville, wrote a chilling report to Adjutant General Hutchings: "Yesterday we caught a Mexican by name of Tomas Aguilar, one of the 3 that robed [sic] the depot at Combs and set the R. R. bridge on fire to which he admitted and was also in the killing of Mr. Austin & son. Of course he tried to make his escape but we killed him. Everything very quite [sic] here now & don't know whether Captain Ransom boys caught the other two last night or not. They had them located near Harlingen." By Fox's own admission, Aguilar had first been caught, made a confession, and then was murdered.[25]

A week later, Captain Fox and Company B were ordered back to the Big Bend country. Senator Hudspeth, whose ranches were being raided by stock thieves, had demanded their return. Fox, Hamer, and the rest left the Rio Grande Valley on August 28. Meanwhile, the Bandit War continued unabated, and Captain Ransom carried out his command to eliminate Mexican raiders. Though he failed to mention such "evaporations" in his official reports, on September 25, Ransom and two of his Rangers were at the Young ranch in Hidalgo County when a pair of Hispanic farmers rode up and reported they had been forced to give food and bandages to a party of raiders. After they rode off, Ransom and his men jumped into an automobile, raced after the pair, and shot them to death. The next day, Ransom and his Rangers made a scout on the road near Ebenezer, in Hidalgo County. Two days later, the dead bodies of ten or eleven Mexicans were found near the road. On October 18, marauders wrecked and robbed a train north of Brownsville, killing three and wounding four. Captain Ransom and seven Rangers responded, along with Sheriff Vann. Ransom captured four suspects and, despite Vann's protestations, took them into the brush and executed them. Ransom would have murdered a fifth Mexican had he not been rescued by Sheriff Vann and Inspector Portus Gay, who subsequently proved that the man was innocent. In the next few days, the bodies of seventeen more Mexicans were found in the nearby brush, presumably killed by Rangers or vigilantes.[26]

On November 19, 1915, Governor Ferguson finally ordered a stop to "summary executions of Mexicans" after receiving complaints from General Funston. Nonetheless, in Texas the terms "Rangered," "evaporated," and "Ransomized" would become synonymous with the unlawful execution of Hispanic suspects. And in the end, it was not evaporations by Rangers, local lawmen, and vigilantes that brought a finish to the Bandit War. Although many of the Carranza forces supported the Plan of San Diego, Carranza himself was desperate to gain official recognition from the United States, which he finally achieved in October. He quickly took action against the bases of the sediciosos, and the raids sharply declined. Soon U.S. troops began to pursue raiders back into Mexico. Then, following the March 1916 raid on Columbus, New Mexico, by Pancho Villa's band, General John J. Pershing led his expedition deep into Mexico in a fruitless hunt for Villa. Finally, in response to the international crisis caused by the Pershing expedition, President Woodrow Wilson mobilized the National Guard and sent a hundred thousand troops to the border. That combination of political and military pressure put an end to the Bandit War.[27]

The suppression of the Plan of San Diego had been critical to the economic development of South Texas. The bloody raids and counter-raids damaged business, depressed property values, and dissuaded Anglo settlement. Jim Wells, for example, was forced to sell ninety thousand acres of land at a steep loss. After the Bandit War, business boomed again, and immigration soared. New arrivals cleared thousands of acres of brush and planted enormous orchards and vast croplands and cotton fields. By 1920, the value of farmland in Cameron County increased almost threefold, and in Hidalgo County more than fourfold. Four years later, Hidalgo County was America's highest-producing agricultural county. Yet the influx of newcomers spelled doom for the Jim Wells political machine, which collapsed in 1920. However, as we shall see, bossism in South Texas would be a significant problem for Frank Hamer in the years to come.[28]

In 1920 the U.S. Senate conducted hearings into violence on the border. Evidence was submitted that, between 1910 and 1919, 365 American civilians and 59 U.S. troops had been slain in Mexico, while along the border on the American side the toll was 62 American civilians and 64 U.S. soldiers. The Senate committee found that "[d]uring the bandit troubles between August 4, 1915, and June 17, 1916, 100 Mexicans have been executed by the Texas Rangers and deputy sheriffs without process of law. Some place the figures at 300. Most of these executions, it has been asserted, were by reason of data furnished the Rangers, implicating the particular Mexicans in the raids." Other Texas Ranger critics claimed that the number of evaporations was as high as 5,000, a wildly improbable figure. Jim Wells, who opposed the use of Rangers in the Bandit War, estimated that 250–300 Hispanic men had been summarily executed in Cameron and Hidalgo Counties. Wells tellingly pointed out that in Starr County, where no Rangers were sent, no such executions took place.[29]

The "One Riot, One Ranger" ethic, coupled with the Rangers' fearsome reputation as border warriors, had now proved to be the Rangers' greatest weakness. In any law-enforcement agency, then or now, it is the supervisors' role to keep the young fire-eaters in line and to direct their aggressive energies into lawful and productive police work. During the Bandit War, Captain Ransom, and to a much lesser extent Captain Fox, utterly failed to do that. Instead, Ransom in particular led his men in flagrant violations of civil rights, including cold-blooded murder. The captains' failures in leadership and willingness to obey unlawful orders from Governor Ferguson caused the darkest epoch in Texas Ranger history.

And what of Frank Hamer? Did he evaporate Mexican raiders? Was he involved in the supposed murder of Jose Garcia at Norias? Was he present when Captain Fox and his men murdered Tomas Aguilar? Because Fox's scout reports are so spotty and vague, it is impossible to tell. If Hamer participated, it would have been the blackest episode in his career and a damning indictment of his character. What we do know is this: as a young Ranger, Captain Rogers had drummed into him strong notions of justice, fairness, and, especially, an unwavering duty to protect the weak from the strong. Hamer demonstrated that he had absorbed those lessons by repeatedly risking his life to protect African Americans in East Texas. That he would suddenly abandon these ideals and follow Captain Fox, whom he had only known for a month, into cold-blooded murder—even during what was in effect a guerrilla war— is most improbable. And later events would show that Hamer had a very poor opinion of Fox as a lawman. The subsequent state and federal investigations of the Bandit War revealed many instances of Ranger brutality, but no evidence of any unlawful force or illegal shooting by Frank Hamer was ever produced.

Perhaps the closest answer comes from Judge W. H. Mead, a pioneer of the Rio Grande Valley, who, in recalling Frank Hamer and the Bandit War twenty years later, explained, "Hamer was no ordinary old type ranger. He had a heart. He was not the killer type with an itching trigger finger but any bad man whom he knew had it coming to him surely got it sometime somewhere." To his son, Frank Jr., Hamer insisted that he had a clear conscience: "I've always been able to sleep a good night's sleep every night." Though in later years Hamer would rarely discuss any of his fifty-two gunfights, he insisted that all of his shootings were proper: "The men I have shot down have all been criminals in the act of committing a crime or resisting arrest. I'm hired to do that work. It's my job. I do it because I have to. I don't like to talk about it or think about it. It's something to be forgotten."[30]

7

THE JOHNSON-SIMS FEUD

The lone rider emerged wraithlike from a billow of alkali dust, spurring his horse gently as he crested the Caprock and descended into the Llano Estacado. His leather gear creaked as he slouched easily in the saddle, his body swaying with the rhythm of the horse. Reaching toward the butt plate of the Winchester in its scabbard, he struck a match and lit the cigarette dangling from his lips. Before him, looking west as far as the eye could see, was endless prairie, blanketed with wild grasses. It was there on the Staked Plains that Frank Hamer first rode the ranges of Scurry and Garza Counties as a mounted cattle inspector. Little did he know that his lonely horseback scouts on the plains would bring him a new bride and plunge him headlong into the last blood feud in Texas.

After the Bandit War, Frank had applied for a higher-paying position as inspector for the Cattle Raisers Association of Texas. Hamer was disillusioned with the leadership of Captain Fox and had no desire to serve under him any longer. And the wages of a Texas Ranger were still so low that many men continued to leave the service in search of better opportunities. His old captain, John Rogers, then U.S. marshal of the Western District of Texas, recommended him for the new job. Rogers wrote the association an effusive letter: "Mr. Hamer is one of the most active officers I have ever known. He is absolutely void of fear, and while he is not an educated man, he is bright and intelligent, very industrious, and a splendid detective. He was raised and grew up in the West, and when I first enlisted him he was a typical cowboy. . . . The harder the criminal and more dangerous and hazardous the work, the better he likes it. . . . I have never recommended a man for this position that I recommend so heartily and unqualifiedly as I do Mr. Hamer. . . . He is a live wire beyond a doubt, and the lawless element stand in awe of him wherever he has worked."[1]

Hamer quickly got the job. On November 1, 1915, the association's secretary, E. B. Spiller, wrote to Adjutant General Hutchings, "We have employed as one of our field Inspectors Mr. F.A. Hamer. . . . In view of the character of service that Mr. Hamer renders it will be very valuable to us if he could receive a commission as a Texas Ranger. We, of course, would not ask the state to pay any expense or any salary, but simply desire that he be clothed with the authority which this commission will give him."[2]

The Cattle Raisers Association of Texas had been organized in 1877 to combat stock theft. It attracted large and small ranchers, who were assessed a membership fee per head of cattle. The association lobbied for cheap railroad shipping rates, kept track of cattle brands, offered rewards for thieves, hired brand inspectors, and even provided a lawyer to help local prosecutors bring charges against rustlers. By 1916 the association employed fifty-two inspectors, who were stationed throughout central and West Texas and even at the principal stockyards in Chicago and Kansas City. The association wielded great economic and political power, and its request that Hamer be commissioned a special Ranger was promptly granted. Frank was happy, for the Cattle Raisers Association paid its men from $75 to $250 a month, far more than a Ranger's meager forty-dollar paycheck.[3]

General Hutchings was very friendly with Frank and offered the Cattle Raisers Association his own recommendation: "Personally and officially I think very highly of Mr. Hamer, and feel sure he will prove a valuable man to you." Special Rangers had existed as early as the 1880s. They had the same authority as regular Rangers, including the right to carry firearms. Because they were unpaid, the state got free law

enforcement. Railroad conductors, brakemen, private detectives, cattlemen, and livestock inspectors all had legitimate reasons to be special
Rangers. But anyone with enough political pull who wanted to carry
the storied title of Texas Ranger was given a commission. They were allowed to call themselves Texas Rangers, and the public generally did
not know the difference between a special and a regular Ranger. Over
time, hundreds of special Ranger appointments were made. With no
training and no supervision, the bad ones brought discredit to the force.[4]

Most of the association's inspectors were based at railroad shipping
points. Hamer, on the other hand, was one of five field inspectors who
rode the ranges hunting stolen cattle, investigating thefts, and tracking
down rustlers. Frank's base was San Angelo, an important cattle-shipping
center served by two railroads. His headquarters were lodgings in the
Landon Hotel, an impressive, three-story brick building with one hundred rooms. He began work with his customary energy and aggressive-
ness, and on November 16 wrote to Adjutant General Hutchings, "We
are dealing the cow thieves misery here."[5]

In 1916 Hamer was working a case near Snyder in Scurry County,
situated a hundred miles due north of San Angelo. His brother Harrison
was employed at the ranch of William A. "Billy" Johnson, a prominent,
wealthy rancher and banker in Snyder. Frank visited Harrison at the
Johnson ranch, twelve miles northeast of Snyder. Hamer must have been
impressed by the ranch house, which was well suited for a cattle baron
of Billy Johnson's stature. It had two stories and sixteen rooms, with ga-
bled roofs and a sun deck that circled the top story and a columned porch
surrounding the ground floor. Frank and Harrison were as close as ever,
and Harrison introduced him to the Johnson family: Billy, the patriarch,
then fifty-four; his wife, Nannie; daughter, Gladys; and sons Sid and
Emmett. Hamer was welcomed warmly by the Johnson family, especially
Gladys. Twenty-five, petite, dark-haired, with full, pouty lips, and very
pretty and sensuous, Gladys was immediately attracted to Frank. He towered quietly above her, but she found him easygoing, with blue eyes that
sparkled whenever he smiled, which, when he looked at her, was often.

At that time Frank Hamer was well known only in Navasota, Houston, and parts of the Hill Country. Although popular in the far-flung

community of current and former Rangers, he was years away from gaining a statewide reputation. But the gregarious Harrison had entertained the Johnsons with stories of his brother's exploits as a Texas lawman, so Gladys already knew much about him. She recalled her first impression: "He was daring and handsome." Referring to his ability to solve dangerous problems, she said, "The Lord seemed always to be tapping him on his shoulder." Gladys was going through a vicious divorce, and she and her two little girls, Trix, nine, and Beverly, seven, lived with Gladys's parents. Frank Hamer was likewise attracted to Gladys, and he quickly grew fond of her girls. Beverly in particular delighted in his attentions. Just as he was in his friendship with young Mance Lipscomb, Frank was patient and kind with Gladys's children. He had no way of knowing it, but his meeting with the Johnson family would change his life forever.[6]

At first Frank and Gladys were merely friends. His cattle-detective work took him all over that section of Texas, and he had little time for romance. In addition, his divorce from Mollie had made him gun-shy. But he was intrigued by Gladys, for he had never known a woman like her. She was extremely strong-willed, hot-headed, and thoroughly spoiled by her wealthy father. But Billy Johnson had not always been rich. In 1878, as a dirt poor, sixteen-year-old cowhand, he had settled in a dugout on Ennis Creek in Scurry County on the Texas frontier. There, he claimed cheap government grazing land. He raised cattle, worked hard, and continually bought adjacent parcels of grassland until he owned more than thirty thousand acres plus a controlling interest in the First National Bank in Snyder, the county seat. While Billy Johnson was affable and easygoing, his wife, Nannie, was mean-spirited and ill-tempered; her daughter-in-law later remarked that "ugly blood" flowed in her veins.[7]

Billy taught his sons, and also Gladys, to ride and shoot. He allowed no sidesaddle for Gladys. Although it was considered unladylike, he had her wear split skirts and ride like a man. Billy Johnson spoiled his only daughter terribly and always let her have her way. Nannie disapproved and often fought with both Billy and Gladys about his indulgent parenting. Gladys and her brother Sid grew up very close. Both were strong-willed, and as Sid got older, he became a heavy drinker. As a teenager, Gladys often carried a pistol, for Billy ingrained into her psyche both Texas gun culture and notions of personal honor. One day she was out riding the family range alone when two strangers accosted her. Enraged by their attentions, Gladys pulled a pistol and shot them both. Her wealthy father managed to cover up the incident, probably by paying money to the wounded men.[8]

In 1905, when Gladys was but fourteen, Billy, over Nannie's objections, allowed Gladys to marry twenty-one-year-old Ed Sims, who was from a prominent ranching family in neighboring Garza County. Ed's father, Dave Sims, raised ten children and large herds of cattle on more than twenty-five thousand acres of ranch land. In 1907 Gladys and Ed Sims welcomed their first daughter, Trix, and two years later their second, Beverly. But Gladys's marriage was an extremely unhappy one. A child bride, a mother at sixteen, she was too spoiled, too temperamental, and far too young to shoulder the responsibilities of a wife and mother. Nothing Ed Sims did could make her happy. The two fought incessantly, and several times Gladys moved out and took the girls to her parents' home. Gladys's mother, Nannie, instead of acting as peacemaker, stoked the fires and encouraged the estrangement. But, each time, Gladys would go back to Ed.

While Ed found solace in the bottle, Gladys began to seek joy in the company of other men. In 1913 she had a clandestine affair with a young man named Garland Mellard. But few things were secret in rural Texas, and Ed Sims heard rumors of the dalliance. Ed intercepted her mail and found salacious letters from Mellard. He and Billy Johnson angrily confronted her, and she tearfully admitted that she and Mellard had sexual relations on three separate occasions. Billy could not believe what he was hearing. He had spoiled and indulged his only daughter, and now, overcome with rage, he threatened to kill her. Billy eventually calmed down, and Gladys begged Ed for forgiveness, promising that she would behave if he took her back.[9]

Ed Sims finally agreed to reconcile. He had no such feelings about Garland Mellard. He sent a warning to Gladys's lover to stay out of Scurry County and threatened to shoot him on sight. Mellard prudently obeyed. But the marriage of Gladys and Ed continued its downward

Gladys Johnson, age fourteen, and Ed Sims on their wedding day in 1905. Their disastrous marriage ignited the Johnson-Sims feud. Gladys married Frank Hamer in 1917. *Courtesy Scurry County Museum, Snyder, Texas*

spiral. Later that year, Ed suspected her of having an affair with a local man; the following year, he accused Gladys of illicit relationships with two other young mashers. For her part, Gladys accused Ed of having an affair with one of her girlfriends and of buying the woman a $900 diamond ring. Finally, in November 1914, Gladys and the girls moved into her parents' home again. Gladys and her mother managed to convince Billy Johnson that the problems had all been caused by Ed's drinking and cheating. Billy eventually forgave his daughter and warned Ed Sims "at his own peril" never to set foot on the Johnson ranch.[10]

During 1915 Gladys and Ed made a few half-hearted attempts to reconcile. Early in 1916, she learned that Ed was still seeing her former girlfriend. Enraged, she moved back to the Johnson ranch and instructed her attorney, Cullen Higgins, to file for divorce in Scurry County. Ed's lawyers managed to get the case continued, and then filed Ed's own divorce action in Garza County. Ed had good reason to believe that the courts in Scurry County would favor Gladys, while the courts in his home county would favor him. In May Ed had his attorneys prepare a will that disinherited his daughters. He was worried that if anything happened to him, his estate would pass to the girls, and thereby into Gladys's hands. Gladys immediately retaliated by obtaining an injunction from a friendly judge that prohibited Ed from taking custody of Trix and Beverly. Ed's lawyers sought to modify the injunction, and the judge relented, giving Ed custody for alternate ten-day periods until school reopened in September. The judge ordered that custody be exchanged at the Manhattan Hotel on Snyder's town square.[11]

The divorce created a public sensation and triggered a bitter feud between the Johnson and Sims families. Most people in Scurry County supported the Johnsons, while those in Garza County sided with the Sims family. More than fifty witnesses were subpoenaed to appear in Post City, the Garza County seat, for the first court hearing in Ed's divorce case. On July 24, 1916, witnesses and partisans showed up armed with six-shooters, Winchesters, and shotguns. Many in the opposing factions took rooms in the Algerita Hotel. One of them was Ed's forty-year-old brother-in-law, Gee McMeans, the former Texas Ranger and enemy of Jim Dunaway. McMeans was a tough character. In 1901 he was sent to prison for assault with intent to commit murder but was pardoned after serving only five months. The pardon cleared the way for McMeans to join the Rangers in 1903. He served two years under Captain Rogers, and in 1905 married Ed Sims's older sister, Ada. McMeans then became sheriff of Ector County. Ranger Captain John A. Brooks once called him "the only man I ever dreaded." McMeans nonetheless earned a good reputation as sheriff, but he did have a hot temper. In 1906 the ever-quarrelsome Ranger Sergeant Jim Dunaway pistol-whipped him following an altercation in Odessa. McMeans later moved to Ysleta, near El Paso, where he farmed and served as deputy sheriff. During an election in El Paso in 1910, he was charged with assaulting a precinct judge. A year later, McMeans was arrested again, this time for misappropriating $400 from a cattle dealer.[12]

Though Gee McMeans was Gladys's brother-in-law, she hated him. Upon leaving her upstairs room in the Algerita Hotel, she ran into the former lawman in the hallway. The two immediately began arguing and shouting. Gladys later claimed that McMeans kicked her in the stomach. She pulled an automatic pistol, while McMeans yanked his six-shooter. Hotel guests poured out of their rooms as the two squared off, guns in hand. Sheriff E. J. Robinson and police officer J. E. Cash rushed upstairs. Cash pleaded with the raging Gladys to hand over her pistol, but she refused. Cash reached for the gun, and as the two scuffled, the weapon discharged with a deafening bang. The slug narrowly missed Cash. As the pair struggled, Gladys's pistol dropped to the floor, and Sheriff Robinson grabbed it. By now the hallway was jammed with armed Johnson and Sims partisans. Sheriff Robinson managed to calm them down, then confiscated a small arsenal of firearms.[13]

At the courthouse the next morning, Sheriff Robinson searched all the men for weapons. The hearing itself was anticlimactic. Gladys's attorney, Higgins, argued that the proper venue for the case was back in Snyder, where she had first filed for divorce. The judge continued the hearing until the Scurry County court could rule on the correct venue. Then Gladys and the rest of the Johnsons and their friends piled into automobiles and drove back to Scurry County. In September the lawyers appeared in court in Snyder, where the judge ruled that he had jurisdiction and that grounds for divorce existed. He granted dissolution of their marriage.[14]

Billy Johnson was alarmed by his daughter's violent clash with Gee McMeans. He wanted a bodyguard for his family and turned to Harrison Hamer. Frank's younger brother was tall, handsome, and capable. He and his wife lived with their children in a small house in Snyder. He worked part-time as a deputy game warden and may have carried a commission as a special Ranger. Like his brother Frank, Harrison was an expert cowboy, a superb horseman, and a dead shot with rifle and revolver. Harrison became a fixture at the Johnson ranch and, always heavily armed, accompanied Billy Johnson and Gladys whenever they made automobile trips into Snyder or nearby communities.[15]

Meanwhile, Ed Sims married his paramour and continued to fight with Gladys over visitation with the girls. Nine-year-old Trix acted coldly, and Ed charged in court papers that the Johnsons were "prejudicing his children against him." Beverly, age seven, was too young to be manipulated and remained affectionate with her father. On the evening of December 15, 1916, Ed drove into Snyder to make arrangements to pick up the girls for the regular change of custody the next day. He was prepared for trouble and brought along a rifle and two pistols.

Billy Johnson was working late at his bank, and at 9:30 he ran into Ed in a drugstore on the town square. Ed, on seeing his former father-in-law, exploded in rage. He accused Johnson of trying to turn the girls against him, then drew down on him with a pistol. A deputy sheriff quickly appeared and seized Ed's two handguns. Billy Johnson returned to his ranch, angry and humiliated. His household went into in an uproar. Gladys and her brother Sid were furious that their prominent father had been publicly cowed. Ed's actions were a public affront, an unforgivable attack on the Johnson family honor.

The next morning, Sid accompanied his father to the bank in Snyder, carrying a pump shotgun for protection. Sid took the weapon inside the bank. Meanwhile, Gladys reluctantly packed the girls' suitcases and drove them into Snyder. Billy Johnson, concerned about more trouble, asked Sheriff W. A. Merrill to supervise the custody exchange. Sheriff Merrill disliked Harrison Hamer, which may explain why Harrison did not accompany Gladys. At noon, Sheriff Merrill and Snyder's city marshal, O. P. Wolf, stood with Ed Sims next to his parked automobile in front of the First National Bank on the north side of the square. It was Saturday, and the square was filled with the buggies, wagons, and motorcars of holiday shoppers. Sheriff Merrill spotted Sid Johnson walking from the bank to his parked auto. The sheriff asked him to go back into the bank. Sid complied and stood watching from a window, his shotgun within reach.

Thirty minutes later, Gladys drove up to the bank, with Trix and

Bev in the backseat. Ed and Sheriff Merrill got into Sims's car, which Ed drove out from in front of the bank and then pulled up behind Gladys's machine. As Wolf watched from the sidewalk, Ed and the sheriff got out and stepped up to Gladys's car. Ed leaned inside the driver's-side window to kiss Trix and Beverly. At that, Gladys loudly complained about being made to bring the girls, saying she could not force them to accompany Ed. She had obviously prepared and prejudiced her daughters, for they began crying and telling their father that they would not leave with him. Ed immediately responded, "Oh, yes. You must go with me."

He reached into the backseat, pulled out a suitcase, and placed it on the running board. The girls kept crying and insisting they would not go with him. When Ed reached for Beverly and tried to pull her from the car, Gladys snapped. Jerking out her automatic pistol, she fired three times at point-blank range. The first bullet tore through the brim of Ed's hat. The next two hit him in the chest and the left leg.

"God damn you!" Ed barked, and grabbed for the pistol. At the same time, Sheriff Merrill lunged forward, trying to grasp the gun. Gladys fired another shot before dropping the weapon behind the seat. As the sheriff pulled Ed aside, the wounded man yelled at Gladys, "You see what you have done! I am unarmed!"

His wounds were not serious, and he managed to stay on his feet as he staggered away from the motorcar. Suddenly, Sid Johnson burst out of the bank, pump shotgun in hand. He fired a blast of buckshot into Ed's right side, slamming him to the ground. As Sid cracked a second shell into the chamber, Sheriff Merrill wrestled the weapon from his grasp.

"No man can curse my sister and her children!" Sid yelled at his prostrate victim. "You cannot shoot and do around here like you can at Post City."

Billy Johnson darted outside, scooped up his granddaughters, and rushed them into the bank. Bystanders carried Ed into the drugstore, where he died a few minutes later.

The killing, involving two of the most prominent families in West Texas, created a sensation, and the story—featuring a quick-shooting Texas female—hit the wire services and was published in newspapers throughout the United States. Gladys and Sid were charged with murder and released on bail to await trial.[16]

Billy Johnson understood that Ed Sims's family would seek retribution. Friends and relatives of Ed Sims made open threats to kill the Johnsons. Soon Gee McMeans encountered Harrison Hamer in the lobby of the Algerita Hotel in Post City, where McMeans and Gladys had drawn guns five months earlier. Harrison was with a friend, H. L. "Hod" Roberson, an inspector for the Cattle Raisers Association. Roberson was a hard-bitten border lawman and former Ranger who had taken part in a number of fatal shooting scrapes, some justifiable, others not. McMeans, wearing two pistols, walked up to Harrison and kicked him in the feet, trying to provoke a fight. Harrison's guns were upstairs in his room. He wisely kept cool, and McMeans swaggered off, snickering loudly. Harrison, perhaps concerned about the reaction by his hot-tempered brother, said nothing to Frank. However, Hod Roberson went to see Frank, who later recalled, "I was stationed in Big Spring, Texas, working after cattle thieves when one of the field men for the Texas Cattle Raisers Association came to see me and informed me that my brother was liable to be killed."[17]

Within a few days, Frank Hamer arrived at the Johnson ranch, accompanied by a fellow cattle inspector from Amarillo, Eben M. Holman. Frank Hamer's protective instincts came to the forefront, and he was determined that no harm would come to his brother or the Johnsons. Hamer knew McMeans's reputation, but he boldly confronted the Sims's partisans at McMeans's ranch. "I informed the bunch," Frank later said, "that if anyone murdered my brother that they would pay dearly for it and immediately thereafter the hatred of the entire bunch was directed toward me. McMeans openly boasted the fact that he would kill me on sight." Now, Frank, Harrison, and Holman, all heavily armed, accompanied the Johnsons everywhere and made sure everyone knew it, telling residents they were Texas Rangers. As was his custom, Hamer created a show of overwhelming force to scare off the Sims partisans.

But Sheriff Merrill did not like Hamer's tactics a bit. On December 20 he and Wolf, the city marshal, fired off a telegram to Governor Ferguson: "From all appearances we are likely to have more [trouble] in next few days. We want you to send two good experienced Rangers to Snyder to remain after the holidays. There is two men here that claim to be Rangers but they are acting as body guards for one side. That is the trouble and are only agitating the trouble more." The next day, Sheriff Merrill and local officials sent a detailed letter to the governor, complaining that the "Johnsons have three men acting as private body guards, carrying six shooters but claiming to be State rangers, these men stay with Johnsons, ride around with Johnsons in their automobiles with big cartridge belts and guns, making rather a display of their arms. One of these men, whose name is Harrison Hamer, I have found upon investigation is a deputy game warden, and that W. A. Johnson, father of Sidney Johnson made Hamer's official bond as deputy game warden. . . . These extra guards and gun displays are only agitating trouble, rather than keeping it down. These men, the Hamers, are antagonistic to the local officers of this County. Harrison Hamer has paid two fines in this County, recently for drunkenness and disturbing the peace, on which occasion he unnecessarily displayed his pistol, and made threats against the local officials [and] stated that the sheriff, nor no other man could arrest him."[18]

The officers did not know Harrison's brother, who was a stranger in Snyder, but they quickly identified him. The county attorney insisted that "Harrison Hamer's commission be canceled as deputy game warden or that he be removed from this county." Of Frank Hamer, he demanded "to know by what authority he is going armed, if he is a State Ranger I ask that he be removed from this county." Governor Ferguson promptly ordered Adjutant General Hutchings to contact Sheriff Merrill "and find out just what ought to be done." The result was that Hutchings dispatched two of Captain Fox's men to Snyder. The presence of the Rangers had a calming effect on the Johnson and Sims partisans, for they reported to Hutchings after Christmas: "Every thing is very quiet here just now but the Sheriff & City Marshal have ask us to stay here until after their round up ball that is to be given next Monday night as there would be lots of people here from both sides of this faction that we were called up here on."[19]

With the two Rangers present, the Roundup Ball on New Year's night passed without incident. Meanwhile, Hutchings wrote Governor Ferguson and asked whether he wanted "the Game and Fish Commissioner to revoke the commission of Harrison Hamer and for me to have Frank Hamer withdrawn from Scurry County." Ferguson instructed him to "confer with the county attorney and sheriff and be guided largely by their recommendations." Hutchings did so and canceled Frank Hamer's warrant of authority as a special Ranger. And in response to a further request from Sheriff Merrill, he ordered that the Rangers stay in Snyder until after the March term of the district court.[20]

Frank was deeply stung by the revocation of his Ranger commission. He decided to take a leave of absence from the Cattle Raisers Association to act as full-time bodyguard for the Johnsons. He was strongly attracted to Gladys, and she saw him as her family's savior. Frank plainly considered his role in protecting Gladys and her family as one of legitimate law enforcement. But the fact was that Gladys and Sid had precipitated the feud by shooting down an unarmed man. Hamer, instead of maintaining the requisite impartiality of a professional lawman, had taken sides in a vicious and unlawful dispute between two wealthy families. On January 10, 1917, he sat down in an office in Billy Johnson's First National Bank and penned a letter to General Hutchings asking him to reconsider: "As I have resigned my position as inspector for the Texas Cattle Raisers I feel it my duty to inform you of same. However my resignation is only temporarily with them. I am still engaged in the same line of work. Before very long I expect to take up my work with the association again. My special Ranger commission is very valuable to me and I would like very much to keep it in this work. However, I felt it my duty to inform you of the change and I will appreciate it very much if you will allow me to keep it."[21]

Hamer also asked his friend Sam H. Hill, a prominent San Angelo cattle rancher, to intercede on his behalf. Hill telephoned Hutchings in Austin, but the adjutant general would not be swayed. As much as he liked Frank Hamer, he could not have a special Ranger mixed up in a brewing feud. Hutchings wrote to Hill, "Personally I am very favorably disposed toward Mr. Hamer, but conditions in Scurry and Garza Counties are such that it is desirable the warrant should be revoked, unless he should again be in the employ of the Cattle Men's Association, and stationed in some other section of the State." Hutchings followed up with a letter to Hamer: "Conditions are such that this department cannot reconsider its action in revoking your warrant of authority as a Special Ranger." To assuage Hamer's feelings, he added, "This is in no sense a personal reflection on you, but is purely a matter of policy which may be modified at a later date when conditions have changed." Hamer's note in response was characteristically obedient: "Have just received your letter in regard to my commission as Special Ranger. I am very sorry that I will be unable to keep it and am enclosing same to you. Any time I can be of service to you let me know."[22]

Special Ranger commission or no, events would soon show that Frank Hamer's judgment was sound. His "gun displays," though they might have exacerbated the tensions, would prove to be fully warranted, for Billy Johnson and his family were in deadly peril. Dave Sims was seeing to that. The Sims patriarch fully understood that it would be almost impossible to obtain justice for his dead son in Texas courts. Texas juries were extremely lenient with women who shot men in domestic disputes. No jury would ever convict Gladys for trying to "protect" her children from their father, despite the fact that the girls had not been in danger and Gladys had no reason, other than spite and anger, to shoot Ed. Convicting Sid in court would be almost as difficult. For in 1917, personal honor remained an important component of Texas life.

Under English common law, a man had a duty to retreat from an attacker—to literally "retreat to the wall" before he could legitimately kill in self-defense. But in the American South and West of the nineteenth century, the value of honor over cowardice took precedence over the value of human life. Government was minimal, and especially on the frontier, police protection often nonexistent. Men—and women—were expected to defend themselves and their property. Texas culture, a violent mix of the deep South and the frontier West, helped give rise to the no-duty-to-retreat doctrine: a man could stand his ground and kill in self-defense. It became so deeply embedded into Texas lore and law that it was referred to by lawyers and legal scholars as the "Texas rule." By 1900 the doctrine had been widely adopted by state courts throughout the U.S. But in Texas, the "stand your ground" defense was expanded and corrupted by juries that refused to convict those who killed in any altercation even remotely resembling mutual combat. Attacks with non-lethal weapons, fists, or even verbal threats could be resisted with deadly force, and such killings were often condoned by Texas juries.[23]

If Dave Sims could not get justice in the courts, there were plenty of hard men in West Texas who could get it for him. He asked his son-in-law, Gee McMeans, and an old friend, Thomas A. "Uncle Tom" Morrison, to "bump off" Billy Johnson and Frank Hamer. Morrison, sixty-five, was a prominent ranchman and, as a young man, had served as a Texas Ranger. One day in the spring of 1917, McMeans and Morrison set up an ambush along a route they expected Johnson and Hamer to take. Their plan was to open fire from the roadside; McMeans would shoot Johnson, and Morrison would kill Hamer. However, when John-son's auto approached, with Frank at the wheel, Gee McMeans got cold feet. Morrison insisted, "This is our chance. Let's do the work." But Mc-Means would not go through with it, so the unsuspecting targets passed safely by.

A dissatisfied Dave Sims now quietly offered a $4,000 bounty to anyone who would kill Billy Johnson. McMeans and Morrison were happy to spread word of the blood money. Morrison recruited Felix R. Jones, who had once been tax assessor of Coryell County and later a horse trader in Abilene. But Jones's real profession was killer for hire. He had been charged with at least three murders, but each time man-aged to wriggle out of trouble. Felix Jones's principal henchman was W. G. Clark, a notorious forty-year-old hardcase. In the spring of 1917, Morrison offered Felix Jones the $4,000 to kill Billy Johnson and pre-vent him from testifying as an eyewitness for Gladys and Sid. But Felix Jones had his hands full. He had already been hired to kill Thomas Lyons, the principal cattle baron of southwestern New Mexico. Jones agreed to find another assassin for the Johnson job. On May 1 Jones met his henchman, Clark, in Abilene and suggested that he handle the job. Clark decided to think it over.[24]

Frank was not yet aware of the details of the murder plot, but he knew instinctively that Billy Johnson was in grave danger. Meanwhile, he and Gladys, thrown together during a time of peril and turmoil, had grown close and passionate. They were polar opposites: he was poor; she was rich. He was reserved; she was outspoken. He was modest; she was extravagant. His huge size dwarfed her tiny frame. Matching hot tempers were one of the few things they had in common. While Billy Johnson admired and respected Hamer, his wife Nannie did not share his opinion. She believed that a minimally educated ex-cowboy and itinerant lawman was hardly good enough for her precious, high-toned daughter. But Gladys considered Frank strong, silent, and steady, and she desperately needed a stabilizing influence in her tumultuous young life. When he proposed, she was ecstatic. Years later, Gladys freely admitted that "her ready acceptance when he asked her to marry him was all but immodest." The couple wasted little time. Leaving Trix and Beverly with the elder Johnsons, Frank and Gladys boarded a train for New Orleans, where they were married on May 12, 1917. Frank was thirty-three; Gladys, twenty-six. After a short honeymoon in the Crescent City, they were back at the Johnson ranch near Snyder.[25]

News of their marriage spread like wildfire among the Sims partisans. They realized that Frank Hamer was there to stay, and if they were going to get Billy Johnson, they would have to kill Hamer, too. On May 21, nine days after the wedding, Uncle Tom Morrison called W. G. Clark in Abilene by telephone and asked him to come to Colorado City that day. Clark entrained for Colorado City, and Morrison met him at the depot that night and took him to see Felix Jones at his rooming house. "We sat up and talked about killing Bill Johnson, of Snyder," explained Clark later. "Jones told me there was $4,000 for anyone who would bump Johnson off. . . . It was all talked over and said if I killed Johnson, I'd have to kill F. A. Hamer too. . . . I agreed to kill him for this $4,000." Tom Morrison insisted that "whoever would kill Johnson would have to kill Hamer, his son-in-law, as the two were always together."[26]

Several days later, Gee McMeans showed up at Felix Jones's boarding house in Colorado City. He had come there to deliver the blood money from Dave Sims. McMeans was extremely nervous and asked for a room in the back, telling the landlady that a price had been put on his head. Rightly or not, McMeans was convinced that Billy Johnson wanted him dead. The former Ranger met with both Jones and Morrison, who had taken a room in the lodging house, and turned over the cash. W. G. Clark later said that Morrison then telephoned him from the boarding house: "He told me to come up there, and I went to see that money to be given for killing Bill Johnson." Clark went to Morrison's room, and the old rancher produced a gripsack and pulled out $4,000 in $50 bills. "He didn't count it, but said there was $4,000," Clark related. "He then told me how to go about killing Johnson."[27]

Clark later claimed—improbably—that he had no intention of killing Billy Johnson and that he had only played along with the scheme. True or not, before he and Jones could go to Snyder, the plot was derailed by events that had taken place a few days before. In El Paso on May 17, while Frank and his bride were in New Orleans, Felix Jones assassinated the cattle baron Thomas Lyons. Four days later, Jones met W. G. Clark at his Colorado City lodging house to plan the murder of Billy Johnson. But Clark soon learned that Lyons's widow had offered $10,000 for the arrest and conviction of her husband's assassin. This was a much better offer than $4,000 to bump off Billy Johnson and risk death at the hands of Frank Hamer. Clark elected to turn in his partner, Felix Jones, for the reward. He turned state's evidence, and Jones was promptly arrested and jailed in El Paso.[28]

The preliminary examination of Felix Jones and two accomplices began in El Paso on June 13. W. G. Clark was the star prosecution witness. He not only testified about the plan to murder Thomas Lyons but also described in detail the plot with Gee McMeans to bump off Billy Johnson and Frank Hamer. The next day, Hamer himself was on hand to listen to the testimony. When Felix Jones spotted the big lawman entering the courtroom, he asked a bailiff if he could speak to him. Frank approached the hired killer to see what he wanted, and Jones smiled broadly, held out his hand, and exclaimed, "Hello, Hamer."

Frank, who towered over Jones, glared down at him, his anger and hatred unconcealed. As spectators and an *El Paso Times* reporter looked on, Jones visibly cowered and grabbed the back of a chair for support. Wrote the newspaperman, "Jones appeared to wilt under the piercing look Mr. Hamer gave him as he [Hamer] turned on his heel and walked away. Jones attempted to carry off the incident by smiling, but it was rather a chagrined and sickly smile which parted the corners of his mouth." At the end of the hearing, the judge held Jones and his accomplices to answer for the murder of Lyons. Jones's arrest and prosecution put an abrupt end to his part in the plot to kill Billy Johnson and Frank Hamer. Felix Jones was convicted of first-degree murder and sentenced to twenty-five years in prison. Thus ended one of El Paso's most sensational murder cases.[29]

With Felix Jones in jail and W. G. Clark locked up as a material witness, Dave Sims turned again to Gee McMeans. The former sheriff was no fool and would not risk tangling with Frank Hamer alone. So he sought the help of Robert N. Higdon, a notorious sixty-two-year-old gunman from Lampasas. A showdown between Frank Hamer and the Sims gunfighters was becoming inevitable. At the same time, Frank's gun-toting bride was still facing murder charges. Because of Billy Johnson's influence, Scurry County prosecutors believed that they could not get a fair trial in Snyder. They obtained a change of venue: Sid was to be tried in Baird, west of Abilene, and Gladys was to stand trial in Lamesa, sixty miles west of Snyder. Brother and sister remained free on bail. Gladys's trial occurred first, on September 17. She appeared in court with her lawyer, Cullen Higgins, Frank Hamer, and her parents, family, and supporters. Dave Sims and his family, friends, and witnesses were also present. Higgins moved for a dismissal of the charges, presumably on the legal grounds that Gladys had not fired the fatal shots and on the emotional grounds that she was a wife and a mother. The judge refused to empanel a jury and instead dismissed the case, despite the fact that the evidence was uncontroverted that she had shot an unarmed man. This result was exactly what Dave Sims feared, and he and his supporters left the courthouse in a rage.[30]

Soon afterward, Gee McMeans and three armed hardcases concealed themselves in the brush near the road between the Johnson ranch and Snyder. Frank and Harrison, as was their custom, accompanied Billy Johnson on all his trips into Snyder. As Billy's touring car approached the ambush site, Frank fortuitously glimpsed a large gray wolf, the bane of every cattleman. The auto jerked to a halt, and Hamer leaped out, firing his rifle at the wolf. He was shocked to see McMeans and his three accomplices burst out of the brush. The desperadoes thought they were under fire. They ran to a nearby car and fled toward Snyder. For Frank Hamer, this was the last straw.

He and Harrison raced into Snyder, hoping to find the would-be assassins. The sharp-eyed Frank saw them first. "Look over yonder next to that cafe," he exclaimed.

Two of McMeans' companions could be seen inside a storefront. The Hamer brothers waited, and soon the two came outside and walked across the square toward Billy Johnson's First National Bank.

As they approached the men on the sidewalk in front of the bank, Frank asked his brother, "Which one do you want?"

"It don't make a damn to me," replied Harrison. "Take your pick."

The brothers stepped close, and one of the toughs blurted out repeatedly, "Hello, hello there."

Frank Hamer didn't say a word. With his open palm he slapped the man off his feet. At the same time, his partner threw up his hands and pleaded with Harrison, "Don't hit me, don't hit me!"

Said Harrison later, "I grabbed him by the collar and shoved him up against the abutment of that First National Bank building and smashed his nose and lips and all. Frank was jest stompin' the hell out of his man."

Frank yanked the gunman to his feet and barked, "Pull out that pistol you've got in your pocket and use it!"

"But the man wouldn't use it," said Harrison, "and Frank then kicked him plumb out in the street. Hell, he wouldn't do nothin' so Frank turned him loose, and I let mine go too."[31]

The trial of Sid Johnson was fast approaching. On the morning of October 1, Sid appeared in court in Baird with his wife, Ruth, and his attorney, Cullen Higgins. Dozens of witnesses were there under subpoena, among them Billy Johnson; Gladys and her daughters, Trix and Beverly; and her brother, Emmett, and his wife, Rocky. Frank and Harrison Hamer came along as bodyguards. The Sims faction was also present, including Gee McMeans, Bob Higdon, and two other desperadoes, Si Bostick and H. E. "Red" Phillips. The latter was a redheaded youth who worked as a hired hand for Gee McMeans. Local lawmen and a Texas Ranger were on hand to maintain order. The legal proceedings proved anticlimactic. Either the lawyers or the judge were not ready for trial, for the parties agreed to continue the case until the spring term of court. Disappointed witnesses and spectators poured out of the courthouse.

Gee McMeans and Red Phillips left town first, headed for Sweetwater. The Hamers and Gladys apparently took Billy, Sid, Ruth, and the girls to the railroad station to see them off. Then Frank, Gladys, Harrison, Emmett, and Rocky all piled into a Cadillac touring car for the hundred-mile drive back to Snyder. The trip would take them west to Abilene, then through Sweetwater, and finally north to Snyder. Before they could gas up and leave town, Frank got a warning. He recalled, "While making preparations to return to Snyder, Texas, a bunch of men came to me and advised me not to go through Sweetwater (which was on the road to Snyder), as McMeans and others were in Sweetwater for the purpose of murdering me."[32]

Frank, characteristically but foolishly, ignored the warning. He later said, "I quietly informed them that I had always gone where I pleased and that I was going through Sweetwater, as it was on my way home." With Frank at the wheel, his party left town and drove the twenty miles west to Abilene. The highways in West Texas were still dirt, and many would not be paved for another ten years or more. As they passed through Abilene, Frank spotted a lawyer he knew looking down on them from his second-story office window. The attorney was a friend of Gee McMeans, and had a broad grin on his face. Hamer took it as a warning, as his son Frank Jr., later explained: "Dad seldom carried two guns. But he had one of those hunches of his he always trusted." He was wearing a .44 Smith & Wesson Triple-Lock revolver in a shoulder holster on his left side. He picked up his favorite weapon, Old Lucky, and shoved it into his waistband on the right side. Then they proceeded another forty miles to Sweetwater, arriving at one thirty in the afternoon.[33]

"Immediately after entering the city limits of Sweetwater," Frank recalled, "I had a puncture and drove to a garage which was located on the southeast corner of the square. . . . I walked from my car to the office of the garage to get someone to fix my tire." The City Garage was situated at the corner of Locust and Broadway, directly across from the courthouse. A large brick building, it was seventy-five feet long with two wide entrances. Harrison and Emmett walked outside and across an adjacent alley to find a men's room. Just then, a motorcar veered into the south doorway, driven by young Phillips, with Gee McMeans in the passenger seat. They parked in the entrance to the garage. Phillips would later contend that he and McMeans stopped there for gasoline and encountered the Hamer party by accident. That is not how Frank Hamer saw it. He stepped out of the office and ran straight into Gee McMeans. Hamer said that McMeans instantly drew his Colt .45 automatic pistol and raised it to fire. "I jumped at him and slapped the gun down, receiving a forty-five bullet through my right leg above the knee."

McMeans exclaimed, "I've got you now, God damn you!"

At that, explained Hamer, "I clinched him and received another bullet through my left shoulder, which badly shattered the bone." Frank was wearing a coat, and by habit he always carried his pocket watch in the outside left pocket, with the chain looped through the buttonhole of his lapel. That may have saved his life. The heavy slug struck his breast, deflected on the watch chain, then flattened and exploded, driving shards of metal deep into his left shoulder and lung. Stunned and in excruciating pain, his left arm dangling useless at his side, Hamer grabbed for McMeans's pistol with his right hand, seizing the barrel and knocking it downward.

Gee McMeans's powerful Model 1911 Colt .45 was the standard sidearm of the U.S. Army. It had been adopted because of its stopping power—its ability to knock down an opponent. Despite being hit twice at point-blank range, Frank stayed on his feet and grappled with his attacker. McMeans tried to fire again, but his Colt was jammed. When Hamer grabbed the barrel, he stopped the slide from ejecting the last round, jamming the cartridge in the chamber. The .45 automatic was now useless. Hamer, bleeding heavily, tore the pistol from McMeans's hand, then cuffed him in the face with his open palm. Remarkably, Frank made no effort to draw either one of his six-guns to kill Gee Mc-Means.

Gee McMeans, shot dead by Frank Hamer in Sweetwater, Texas, October 1, 1917, in the climactic gunfight of the Johnson-Sims feud. *Author's collection*

Meanwhile, Gladys, inside the car, saw Red Phillips jump out of his auto, carrying a semiautomatic shotgun. Gladys later said that as Phillips approached her husband from behind, she shrieked a warning, then pulled a small automatic pistol and opened fire. Phillips jumped for cover behind his motorcar. Every time he showed his head, Gladys fired, keeping him pinned down. Finally, her pistol was empty, and Phillips swung his shotgun toward the Hamers' car. Phillips fired at least one blast at the Cadillac, putting three holes in the fender and radiator. He then started after Frank Hamer, who was still struggling with McMeans.

Explained Hamer, "While we were clinched, this man [McMeans] called to another man [Phillips] who came running toward me with an automatic shotgun. The man I was clinched with jerked loose from me and the other man fired at my head with the shotgun, the muzzle of the gun being about three feet from my head, cutting my hat brim off." Hamer dropped to his knees, stunned by the concussion and shaking his head to clear his vision.

"I got him! I got him!" cried Phillips jubilantly. McMeans, seeing that Hamer was still alive, ran back to his car and grabbed a pump shotgun from the seat. It was the worst mistake of his life. As McMeans turned to face Frank Hamer, the desperately wounded lawman struggled to his feet, reached across his body with his right hand, and seized the grip of his Smith and Wesson. "I then pulled my pistol and shot him through the heart, killing him instantly," said Hamer later. "He fell on the sidewalk out of sight from where I was standing. I staggered to the front door, and the stranger who had shot my hat brim off with his shotgun was hunkered down by the side of the dead man with his shotgun across his lap. I invited him to get up and fight me face-to-face, but he immediately broke and ran down the sidewalk with his shotgun in his hand. I called for him to turn around, not caring to shoot him in the back, regardless of the fact that they had tried to murder me."

By now, Harrison and Emmett had heard the gunfire and raced back to the garage. Harrison seized a Winchester rifle from their motorcar and took dead aim at Phillips as he fled down the sidewalk.

"Don't!" Frank called to his brother. "Not in the back."

Phillips, still carrying his shotgun, ducked into the side door of a restaurant. Recalled Harrison, "I was going to kill that son of a bitch, but then he ran into that side door. I quit Frank and went after him, and Phillips just flattened himself up against the door, which was a big old swinging door. I couldn't see anything. I just stood there ready for him, and he never did show up."[34]

Walter Prescott Webb later asked Frank why he had not shot Phillips. Hamer's reply was as blunt as it was profane: "I couldn't shoot the damned coward in the back."[35]

A deputy sheriff rushed to the scene, disarming and arresting Red Phillips. Sweetwater's chief of police, W. R. "Buck" Johnson, placed Frank, Harrison, Gladys, Emmett, and Rocky under arrest. Chief Johnson confiscated every firearm at the scene: seven revolvers, three rifles and shotguns, and two automatic pistols. He lodged everyone in jail except Frank, who was carried into the courthouse. After his wounds were treated by a physician, who was unable to remove all the metal fragments, Hamer joined the rest in jail. Soon after, the Sims's gunman Bob Higdon arrived in Sweetwater by train. According to the Hamers, he had come to Sweetwater to help McMeans ambush them. Higdon, seeing a shrouded figure being brought into a funeral parlor, assumed it was Frank. He loudly complained "that he'd planned to kill Frank Hamer and that McMeans hadn't the decency to wait for him."

At that, a bystander told him that "the job was still open. Frank Hamer was still in town. Gee McMeans hadn't hogged all the glory after all." Higdon blanched and finally grumbled that "it wouldn't do to take on a wounded man, not a decent thing at all." When the next train pulled in, Higdon got aboard and quietly slipped out of town. The body of Gee McMeans was shipped to his widow and eleven-year-old son in Aspermont, where he was buried the next afternoon. Meanwhile, word of the shootout spread quickly by telephone. Two Rangers rushed to Sweetwater to help protect the Johnsons and the Hamers.[36]

Frank needed protection, for McMeans had friends in Sweetwater. But then so did Hamer. One of them was S. D. Myres, the leading saddle maker in West Texas. Myres later recalled that a group of townsfolk were determined to lynch Hamer. He and Chief Johnson stopped the mob, and Myres warned them, "If you want him, go get him. He's down to the jail and the door's not locked. But I ought to warn you fellows he has a 30-30 and a sawed-off shotgun and a case of ammunition for each of 'em. Buck and me are going home to bed." The mob decided to go home as well. Myres always enjoyed telling this story, and would invariably add, "I told them folks a lie. Frank didn't have but one box of shells for that shotgun!"[37]

Gladys later claimed that the grand jury immediately convened after the gunfight and "absolved Hamer on the spot." That was hardly true. Frank, Gladys, Harrison, Emmett, and Ruth, as well as Red Phillips, remained in the Sweetwater jail for five days while the grand jurors took evidence. The grand jury records are lost, but apparently numerous witnesses testified about the bad blood between the two factions. The two

Rangers and local officers were on hand to prevent trouble. Finally, on October 6, the grand jury adjourned without bringing charges against any of the participants. All were released from jail that afternoon. Hamer later said, "The most of this fight was viewed by the grand jury which had convened that morning and was in plain view of the jury room in the court house. The grand jury not only refused to indict me, but complimented me very highly for not shooting the man in the back as he ran away."[38]

Frank was brought home to the Snyder ranch to recover from his wounds. Within two weeks, his strength and toughness enabled him to get about on crutches. He spent the Christmas holidays with Gladys's family and recovered quickly. Billy Johnson owned a summer home in Altadena, California, just north of Los Angeles. Touring by motorcar was all the rage, and early in 1918 Frank and Gladys decided to make a long drive to California. Gladys was pregnant, and they both sorely needed to escape the danger, stress, and recrimination in Scurry County. Frank may have also seen an opportunity to get Gladys away from her dysfunctional family. With Trix and Beverly, they headed west in a brand-new touring car. It was likely a wedding gift from Billy Johnson, since Hamer could never have afforded such a luxury on his meager pay. The journey was a long one on rutted dirt highways through New Mexico and Arizona, but they arrived in Southern California without incident. The Hamers spent more than six months in California, where Frank rapidly recovered his strength. On April 11, 1918, Gladys gave birth to their first son, Frank A. Hamer Jr., in Pasadena Hospital. He would always maintain that he was the only Hamer not born in Texas.[39]

During the Hamers' vacation on the West Coast, the Johnson-Sims feud continued unabated. Dave Sims was beside himself with grief and rage. His son was dead and his daughter a widow. He loathed Cullen Higgins, who not only had represented Gladys in the divorce but also had gotten the attempted murder charges against her dismissed. Sims had to do something about the attorney, whom he now feared would also get Sid Johnson acquitted. On the night of March 17, 1918, Bob Higdon and two other hired killers assassinated Higgins in a hotel in Clairemont, north of Snyder. All three were quickly arrested. Two Texas

Rangers from Captain Henry Ransom's company took one of the murderers, Si Bostick, to jail in Sweetwater. He confessed and revealed where the murder weapon was hidden. The next morning, Bostick was found strangled in his cell. It was first ruled a suicide, but the Rangers were later suspected of killing him during a harsh interrogation.[40]

While Captain Ransom supervised the investigation into Cullen Higgins's death, he made his headquarters in Sweetwater's Wright Hotel. On the night of April 1, just eleven days after the death of Bostick, he was shot dead outside his hotel room. Officially, the death was ruled an accident. However, the fatal bullet had passed through his left shoulder, slashing up through his left jaw into his head. This showed that he must have been on the floor when he was shot. As the most disreputable captain in the history of the Texas Rangers, Ransom had made many enemies. He had taken part in numerous cold-blooded murders, and no doubt many men had the motive to kill him. One of them was Dave Sims, who may have wanted to stop the investigation into Cullen Higgins's assassination by having Bostick and Ransom killed. Perhaps Captain Ransom's death was in fact an accident, or perhaps he was the last man slain in the Johnson-Sims feud. Either way, it was the editor of the *Houston Chronicle*, recalling Ransom's bloody reign in that city, who provided his most fitting epitaph: "The gun fighters all go the same route, sooner or later."[41]

The conclusion of the Johnson-Sims feud was anticlimactic. Sid Johnson got a new lawyer, and, after a short trial in September 1918, he was found not guilty of the murder of Ed Sims. Even though he had shot an unarmed man, the jury believed he was justified in "protecting" his sister. Bob Higdon and his accomplice were indicted for the murder of Cullen Higgins, with Dave Sims posting bond for Higdon, his hired gunman. Because the principal witness against them—Si Bostick—was dead, it was no surprise that the prosecution was eventually dropped for lack of evidence.[42]

Frank Hamer's role in the Johnson-Sims feud remains a controversial one. On the one hand, it was wholly inappropriate for a professional peace officer to get mixed up in a blood vendetta. Hamer was well aware of that, for in his only surviving detailed account of the Sweetwater gunfight—a 1932 letter to his friend Sam Hill—he claimed it was a deliberate ambush and assiduously avoided making any mention of the feud, the Johnson and Sims families, or Gladys's role in the shootout. Frank's first involvement had arguably been proper: he meant simply to protect his brother Harrison. Then his passion for Gladys, coupled with his sense of personal honor, blinded his judgment. By falling in love with her, he found himself connected to the Johnson family and responsible for their safety, which in turn made him a partisan. He was more than just a paid warrior for Billy Johnson, he was his son-in-law. But the same was true of Gee McMeans. In later years Frank, Gladys, and Harrison consistently asserted that McMeans was a gunman for hire and failed to acknowledge that he was Dave Sims's son-in-law. By the Hamers' own standard, both Gee McMeans and Frank Hamer were hired gunfighters.

Hamer did nothing unlawful during the Johnson-Sims feud, but his killing of Gee McMeans may well have been mutual combat rather than self-defense. Frank, Harrison, and Gladys Hamer would forever claim that the Sweetwater gunfight was an ambush by McMeans and Phillips. Their story is the one that has survived, and it has been repeated over the years in numerous books, magazines, and newspapers. McMeans's descendants, on the other hand, assert that it was Hamer who ambushed Gee McMeans. Both accounts may be wrong, for contemporary wire service reports all stated plainly that the two parties encountered each other by accident in the City Garage.[43]

An alternative—albeit conjectural—reason for the gun battle is suggested by Gladys's history of violent and unprovoked use of firearms. Upon seeing the hated Gee McMeans approaching her husband, she may well have grabbed her pistol and shot first, provoking the gunfight. The ultimate truth may never be known, for Gee McMeans was dead, and the Hamers were alive, and history is written by the victors.

8

GUNSMOKE ON THE
RIO GRANDE

The Johnson-Sims feud was a mere Texas footnote in 1917. When the nation plunged into World War I that year, the Lone Star State was at the forefront of enlistment into the armed services. After all, Texans loved a good fight, and here was a chance to do it legally and with the most modern weaponry. At the same time, many Tejanos, long subject to ethnic discrimination, were loath to fight for a nation which treated them like second-class citizens. Hispanic draft dodgers, or "slackers," repeatedly slipped across the Rio Grande to avoid conscription. As the war raged in Europe, Governor Ferguson was fighting his own desperate battle at home. In September 1917 the state legislature impeached him on charges of embezzlement and misappropriation of public funds. Though disgraced and removed from office, Jim Ferguson would remain a powerful force in Texas politics for another twenty years.

While the Johnson-Sims feud gradually subsided, Frank and Gladys were enjoying their extended vacation in Southern California. Billy Johnson's summer home in Altadena was just north of Pasadena and fourteen miles from downtown Los Angeles. A comfortable, modern, two-level cottage, it boasted an expansive lawn in front. The Hamers enjoyed the many activities so popular in Southern California: motorcar tours of the endless orange groves, trips to the ocean beaches, and visits to the new motion picture studios in Hollywood. Because their stay was a prolonged one, they enrolled the girls for the spring session in a local elementary school.[1]

Los Angeles was home to many silent film stars, and few were bigger than Tom Mix. Although a genuine cowboy and superb horseman, studio publicity hacks created a phony history for their star: they claimed that he hailed from El Paso, rode with the Rough Riders in Cuba, acted as chief of scouts in the Philippines, served in the Boxer rebellion in China, and was a deputy U.S. marshal in Oklahoma and a Texas Ranger. In fact, Mix had been born into a poor lumbering family in Pennsylvania. After deserting from the army, he moved to Oklahoma with the first of his five wives. Mix became a rodeo performer, and his trick riding and roping, coupled with rugged good looks, soon brought him to the attention of the burgeoning motion picture industry. He moved to Southern California and made his first western film in 1909. Handsome features, natural horsemanship, and his ability to perform his own dangerous stunts led to enormous popularity. By 1918 Tom Mix was one of the highest-paid stars in Hollywood.[2]

It was probably Trix and Beverly who wanted to meet the king of the cowboys. Certainly the reserved, rodeo-hating Frank Hamer could have cared less about seeing another cowhand, film star or not. Yet he took the girls and Gladys to one of Mix's film sets. In those years many movie locations were open to the public, and there Frank was introduced to Tom Mix. Hamer was still an obscure figure—highly regarded in Texas law-enforcement circles but totally unknown outside the state. Someone—either Gladys or the girls—boasted that Frank was a Texas Ranger, recovering from gunshot wounds suffered in a shootout with desperadoes. Mix, who sometimes believed his own publicity and often falsely claimed to have been a Texas Ranger, was hugely impressed.

The two men were polar opposites. Mix was talkative, loud, and flamboyant; Hamer, quiet, modest, aloof. The actor wore fancy cowboy boots, huge batwing chaps, flashy embroidered shirts, and ten-gallon hats. Frank, on the other hand, favored simple boots, dress slacks, and a collarless striped cotton shirt, topped off by a narrow-brimmed Stetson hat. But Tom Mix had lived in the West long enough to spot a real westerner. And Hamer was the very embodiment of the heroic lawmen whom Mix portrayed on the silver screen. As a general rule, Frank despised what he called "drugstore cowboys"—phony westerners. However, probably influenced by the gushing of Gladys, Trix, and Beverly, he was flattered by attention from one of film's biggest stars. Tom Mix spent the next few days showing the Hamers around the movie studios. On one set, he commented to Frank, "Watch that so-called cowboy yonder try to get on that horse. He don't even know how to mount. He'd just as soon mount on the right side as the left. That's what we've gotta put up with around here."[3]

Mix remarked to Gladys that he "liked to watch the way Hamer walked and talked." At that, Frank just laughed and told the actor "he had seen too many of his own movies." But Mix was serious, and he tried to convince Frank to stay in California and pursue a career acting in western films. He said that Hamer "had the looks, the bearing, and the athletic ability to be a great cowboy star." Frank shrugged off the suggestion, but this was the beginning of a close friendship that would last until Tom Mix's death.[4]

The vacation in Los Angeles did much to solidify the Hamers' marriage. Frank affectionately called his bride "Bunch"—short for "Honey Bunch." Gladys had time to ruminate on her past behavior and seems to have finally recognized that her selfish and spiteful actions had helped spark a deadly feud that left as many as five men dead. Frank, for his part, was no fool and certainly had heard the stories of Gladys's past extramarital exploits. They had been detailed in her divorce and were a matter of public record. He had also seen firsthand her poisonous relationship with her mother, her explosive temper, and her self-indulgent nature. Either as a result of Frank's forceful personality or, perhaps, through heartfelt discussions about her failings as a daughter, mother, and spouse, Gladys began to change and to mature. She worshiped Frank and was desperate to make their relationship a success. The foundation for a long and happy marriage was first set during those pleasant months in Southern California.

Frank Hamer, right, and Tom Mix, in front of the capitol building in Austin, 1927. *Taronda Schulz collection*

That summer, when Frank Jr. was a few months old, the Hamers started on the return trip to Texas. Instead of the direct route due east, they took a long, sightseeing drive to visit Yellowstone National Park, then becoming a popular destination for auto tourists. The Hamers drove north, and while passing through Reno, Nevada, Frank was flabbergasted when an African American jumped off the sidewalk and yelled, "Hello, Cap!" (To Texas blacks, every white man who carried a pistol was "Cap" or "Cap'n.") The man was Sam, whom he had made the unofficial parade marshal in Navasota ten years before. Hamer, astonished to see Sam so far from home, greeted him warmly before heading across the Nevada desert. On the long tour, they first visited Yellowstone and then meandered south through Utah, Colorado, and New Mexico before returning to West Texas. For all of them, the trip had been an adventure, and it was the farthest Hamer had ever strayed from his home state. He had slowly recovered his strength, and he was as vigorous as ever by their return in late August.[5]

Frank and Gladys moved back into the big ranch house and got Trix and Beverly started in the fall school session in Snyder. Earlier that same year, 1917, Frank's parents had moved to Snyder, where his father opened a blacksmith shop, and later a secondhand-goods store. Hamer found that the violence of the Johnson-Sims feud was over. Dave Sims was now suffering from cancer and beyond seeking further vengeance. Bedridden in his home, he died the following year. Yet the bad blood stirred up by the feud would take several generations to dissipate.[6]

Frank, not used to idleness, was eager to rejoin the Rangers. Cashing in on his father-in-law's connections, he was soon commissioned a Ranger. Gunsmoke in the Rio Grande Valley had created an opening for him in the Texas Ranger force. On the night of August 21, Privates Joe Shaw and S. T. Chavez, of the Rangers, were scouting the river on horseback at Los Tomates, a bend in the Rio Grande notorious as a crossing for smugglers (today it is the site of the Veterans Memorial International Bridge in Brownsville). Shaw, a rookie with just two months on the force, carried a shotgun loaded only with bird shot. The Rangers spotted seven Tejanos approaching the river, preparing to cross into Mexico. They turned out to be Teofilo Solis, accompanying his four sons to Mexico to evade the draft. They were led by two professional smugglers; one of them was later identified by Rangers as a notorious desperado, Encarnacion Delgado. As Chavez headed through the brush to cut them off, Shaw approached the group. A gun battle broke out, leaving Joe Shaw dead from two rifle bullets—supposedly fired by Delgado— and Francisco Solis wounded with bird shot from the Ranger's shotgun.

Jim Wells, the political boss who opposed the Rangers, later claimed that the shooting was the result of mistaken identity. He said that Francisco Solis thought Shaw was a thief who had entered the family farm to steal corn and melons and that the two had opened fire simultaneously.[7]

A month later, Frank Hamer was directed to report for duty on the border, as the replacement for Shaw. From Snyder he drove six hundred miles on dirt roads in his touring car. On October 1 he met with a new captain, William W. Taylor, in Brownsville, where he was sworn in as a private in Company F. Brownsville, situated about twenty miles from the mouth of the Rio Grande, was a modern, booming border town of about eleven thousand people, two-thirds Spanish-speaking. As usual, the cash-strapped state government provided no lodging for the Rangers; their headquarters was a tent encampment in an empty city lot. Although the Bandit War had ended in 1916, the Mexican Revolution was still under way, and unsettled conditions made the border extremely unsafe. Revolutionists, arms smugglers, and draft dodgers crossed the Rio Grande almost at will. In 1918 alone, four Rangers were killed in the line of duty between El Paso and Brownsville; two others, including Captain Ransom, were slain in other parts of the state.[8]

Captain Monroe Fox continued Ransom's murderous exploits on the Rio Grande. Earlier in 1917, his company took part in one of the blackest incidents in the history of the Texas Rangers. On Christmas Day a band of Mexican raiders, believed to be followers of Pancho Villa, attacked the Brite ranch in the Big Bend, murdering two Hispanics and one Anglo. Local ranchers concluded that the Mexican residents of Porvenir, a tiny adobe settlement on the Rio Grande, were guides for and harborers of the bandidos. The ranchers complained to Captain Fox, and on the night of January 28, 1918, a group of Fox's Rangers "rounded up" Porvenir. Instead of leading such an important raid himself, Fox put a private in charge of seven Rangers. They were accompanied by four ranchers and a detachment of U.S. cavalry. While the troopers surrounded the village, the Rangers and ranchers, wearing bandanna masks, searched the adobe huts, finding some of the loot stolen in the raid of the Brite ranch. They arrested every able-bodied man in Porvenir—

fifteen of them—and herded the group a quarter mile out of town. After telling the cavalrymen to ride off, the Rangers and ranchers lined up the fifteen Mexicans in front of a rock wall and shot them to death.

Word of the Porvenir massacre did not leak out for more than a week, finally hitting the wire services on February 8, 1918. Captain Fox claimed self-defense, but numerous witnesses proved beyond any doubt that the Texas Rangers had committed a massacre. The Rangers involved were fired and Fox's company was disbanded; Fox resigned in protest. None of the posse was ever charged with a crime, and in Ranger lore Porvenir was considered a victorious battle with bandidos. Later writers—most notably the bestselling author Stuart N. Lake—claimed that Frank Hamer had been with the Rangers at Porvenir. If true, it would have been the most despicable act of his life. Yet his participation was impossible, for he was then an ex-Ranger, recovering from his wounds in Southern California with Gladys and the children.[9]

The dangerous border conditions were complicated by bitter political divisions in the Rio Grande Valley. In Brownsville, the sheriff of Cameron County, William T. Vann, who had opposed Captain Henry Ransom during the Bandit War, was in open conflict with a number of the Rangers, soon to include Frank Hamer. Vann was a highly capable and principled sheriff. Unlike many Texas lawmen, he had never been a Ranger and owed them no institutional loyalty. Following Jim Wells's lead, Vann was sympathetic to and protective of Mexican Americans, while his enemies accused him of being a machine politician. During the Bandit War, Vann had vigorously opposed the appointment of Captain Ransom and was the most prominent lawman to accuse him of murdering Mexican suspects.[10]

In 1918 Sheriff Vann and Jim Wells engaged in a bitter feud with Ranger Captain Charles F. Stevens. The bespectacled fifty-year-old Stevens, who soon became one of Hamer's closest friends, had served for twenty years as a lawman before being appointed a Ranger captain in 1917. Like Sheriff Vann, "Cap'n Cholly," as his Rangers called him, was aggressive, capable, and principled. He trained his men to protect prisoners and never mistreat them. But although Stevens spoke Spanish fluently, he had difficulty understanding the border culture. He assumed that Tejanos were German sympathizers, failing to recognize that it was Anglo racism, not anti-Americanism, that compelled many Hispanic males to dodge the draft. In South Texas his vigorous enforcement of the law brought him into conflict with the Wells machine. When Stevens and his men jailed Mexicans in Brownsville, the suspects were released on worthless "straw bonds" and often fled to Mexico. Stevens blamed Sheriff Vann, whom he considered a toady of Jim Wells and indebted to the Hispanic vote. He began sending arrestees to Sheriff A. Y. Baker, a former Ranger and the political boss of Hidalgo County. Things got so heated that Captain Stevens and Sheriff Vann refused to speak to each other. Stevens clashed with Jim Wells himself over the captain's practice of entering Hispanic homes on the river and confiscating firearms. Wells rightly considered the practice unlawful, but Stevens responded that the country was at war, requiring extraordinary measures. On one occasion, Wells threatened to shoot Stevens. Adjutant General James Harley was flooded with complaints about Stevens, and in August he transferred the captain and his men to the Big Bend country and replaced them with Captain Taylor and his company.[11]

Hamer soon discovered that the violence on the Rio Grande was exacerbated by the efforts of American interventionists who sought to influence the Mexican Revolution. Chief among them were the corrupt oil tycoon Edward L. Doheny and his political strongman, Senator Albert Bacon Fall, both of whom would achieve infamy in the Teapot Dome scandal. Doheny had invested in Mexican oil, and he stood to lose heavily when President Carranza threatened to seize Doheny's oil wells in 1917. Fall's mining interests in Mexico were likewise devastated by the revolution. In Texas, Carranza was strongly opposed by Francisco A. Chapa, a wealthy and influential Tejano merchant and newspaper publisher. Chapa, a confidant of several governors, held a colonelcy in the Texas National Guard and had fervently supported Porfirio Díaz. In January 1918 Chapa arranged with Governor William Hobby to have William M. Hanson, a close friend of Senator Fall, appointed senior captain of the Rangers and special investigator for the adjutant

Frank Hamer with his stepdaughter, Beverly, and his first automobile, about 1918. *Travis Hamer personal collection*

general. Hanson immediately became the most powerful man in the Rangers, and he would soon become a bitter enemy of Frank Hamer.[12]

The close relationship between American oil and mining companies and Governor Hobby, Chapa, and Hanson was made clear in 1918 when Captain Stevens was called to the governor's office in Austin for a conference with Chapa and Hanson. During the meeting, Hobby asked Chapa, "When are you and Hanson going to get me those mining concessions in Mexico?" Chapa answered, "Well, Governor, you will have to wait until our faction is successful." A stunned Stevens left the meeting with a firm belief that Hobby, Chapa, and Hanson were violating U.S. neutrality laws—which prevented American involvement in Mexican affairs—and intended to use the Rangers for their own financial interests. Hamer would soon come to the same conclusion.[13]

Meanwhile, Hamer settled into his new duties with Company F. His closest comrade in the outfit was its sergeant, Delbert "Tim" Timberlake, whom Frank had known for years. Timberlake, two years older than Hamer, had been a cowboy before commencing a two-year hitch with the Rangers in 1905. He was then a deputy sheriff in Galveston, a special Ranger (in 1916), and city marshal of Del Rio before rejoining the Rangers in June 1918. Hamer, Timberlake, and the rest of Captain Taylor's men were desperate to capture Encarnacion Delgado, the suspected killer of Ranger Joe Shaw. Delgado, age twenty-seven, led a double life. He made his home in Matamoros and was popular in Brownsville, where he was a member of the local lodge of the Woodmen of the World fraternal organization. He worked as a "cart man," legally hauling goods across the border. Captain Hanson later reported that "for the last five years he has been a murderer, opium and mescal smuggler, thief, and a very bad and dangerous character. He had a passport that allowed him free access from this country six days in each week, and very few had any idea that the seemingly innocent cart-man that plied his vocation between Matamoros and Brownsville was as dangerous a character that he later proved to be." Delgado smuggled deserters into Mexico at five to ten dollars a head. Sheriff Vann also recalled that Delgado was a dangerous man who "said he was going to kill anyone that said a word to him, told us that every time we talked to him." Vann later said that he and the Rangers got a tip that Delgado's gang of smugglers would be bringing in a load of mescal at Los Tomates bend: "Somebody had given us some dope that they were coming across the river." On the evening of October 10, 1918, just nine days after Hamer rejoined the Rangers, Sheriff Vann and Captain Taylor gathered their men in a plan to capture or kill Delgado.[14]

During the preceding seven weeks, two lawmen had been murdered outside Brownsville. This made Sergeant Timberlake extremely apprehensive. When Hamer came into the Ranger camp, he found that his friend had packed his bags and was burning a bundle of personal letters.

"What in the hell are you doing, Tim?" asked Hamer.

"Frank, I've got the feeling I won't be needing this stuff anymore after tonight."

"Aw, stop that nonsense," Hamer replied. "Nothing's going to happen to you tonight that hasn't happened in the past. That Delgado is the one who's going to get it."

"I just can't help it, Pancho," he said, calling Frank by his nickname. "I've got a funny notion that things are going to end for me down at Tomates."

It was dark when the posse left Brownsville. With Hamer and Timberlake were Sheriff Vann, Captain Taylor, Deputy Sheriff Fred Winn, Ranger Thomas M. Dunagan, and two U.S. customs inspectors, Ben Tumlinson and Clint Atkins. Sheriff Vann, who had scouted the spot near Los Tomates the night before, led the way. Vann insisted that they try to take the smugglers alive. Hamer recalled his just-healed gunshot wounds and, though only a private, objected vehemently.

"Sheriff, you know that sidewinder Delgado isn't going to surrender as long as he has a chance to shoot his way out of the trap," Hamer exclaimed. "If you try to arrest him, you'll get yourself shot for sure."

"I'm sorry, Frank," responded Vann. "But I'm not going to take any chance of shooting an innocent person."

"Now, what in hell is an innocent person going to be doing down at Tomates at this time of night?" demanded Hamer. "I am in favor of giving him the works first and the orders afterwards."

"We might kill an innocent man," interjected another of the posse.

"No, we won't kill an innocent man," Hamer insisted, "because no innocent man is going to be on this trail at this time of night."

Vann overruled Hamer, and the posse continued on toward the river. Hamer was carrying his favorite rifle, a .25 caliber Remington Model 8 semiautomatic. In the darkness, he was surprised to see what looked like a shotgun in Timberlake's hands. Sheriff Vann also carried a double-barreled shotgun. Hamer knew that Ranger Joe Shaw had been criticized for carrying a shotgun loaded with bird shot in his fatal gunfight. Shotguns also did not have the necessary range for border duty. A typical load of 00 buckshot consisted of nine .32 caliber pellets, deadly at close range but ineffective at distances of more than forty or fifty yards.

"Tim, what kind of gun is that?" Hamer asked.

"A shotgun," Timberlake replied.

"What do you mean coming out on a deal like this with a shotgun?"

"Well, Pancho, the way I feel tonight, one gun will do me about as much good as another. I have a feeling that I'll get mine any way you take it."

The posse arrived at the ambush site at dusk. It was the intersection of two trails that led through heavy brush to Los Tomates. The informant said that Delgado would come across alone to the American side and would give a signal, the bleat of a goat, for his confederates to follow across the river. Sheriff Vann and Timberlake took positions close together, while Hamer and the rest were strung out in a rough line along the trail. Two tense hours passed, and a half-moon rose on the horizon. Suddenly, they heard the snapping of twigs and the bleat of a goat. Encarnacion Delgado, acting as guide, was about twenty yards ahead of the rest of the gang. Delgado appeared first, as Vann recalled: "He did come along, and I expect passed within six or eight feet of me and Timberlake. I let him go thirty or forty steps before I said anything. . . . [H]e was going into the light and not into the brush."

Frank Hamer and Sheriff Vann jumped to their feet. Vann yelled, "Alto!" ("Halt!")

Delgado, clutching a .45 revolver in his right fist, fired a single shot at the sheriff's voice. The bullet struck the ground about eighteen feet in front of Timberlake, who was in a prone position. It skipped across the ground, pancaked, and tore into his left side. The sergeant rolled over and gasped to Taylor, "Cap, he got me through the guts."

Sheriff Vann fired two loads of buckshot and missed. Not Frank Hamer. Swinging up his Remington, he aimed at Delgado's pistol flash and opened up. Hamer squeezed the trigger so quickly the blazing muzzle looked like the flame of a "pear burner" torch, which was used to singe the thorns off a cactus so it could be eaten by cattle.

"Good God!" exclaimed one of the posse. "Watch Frank use the pear burner on him!"

Frank Hamer in action. His rifle is a Savage Model 1899. *Taronda Schulz collection*

One of Hamer's bullets hit Delgado in the hand, another in his right side, a third in the leg, and two more ripped into his chest near the heart. The outlaw ran forward a few feet, then crumpled dead, sprawled on top of a cactus. Hamer and the others cautiously approached. They found Delgado's .45 in his right hand, a fistful of cartridges in the other. Then they turned their attentions to Timberlake, who was bleeding heavily. The bullet had torn through his side above the left hip, crossed through his stomach, and then slammed into his pocket watch on his right side. The watch had stopped at 9:27 P.M., fixing the exact time of the gunfight. Several of the posse rushed Timberlake to the hospital in Brownsville while the rest pursued Delgado's fleeing compadres. After hunting through the brush, they found nothing but ten gallons of abandoned mescal.[15]

Three of the best surgeons in Brownsville worked on Timberlake, but there was nothing they could do. His intestines had been shredded by the exploding lead slug. Reported Captain Hanson, "The surgeons then called in Capt. Taylor and Hamer and informed them that it would be impossible to save Timberlake's life, therefore, they closed him up and eased his pain as much as possible with opiates." A distraught Frank Hamer stayed at Timberlake's bedside all night as he suffered. Timberlake was still conscious at 7:00 A.M.

"Pancho, there's no chance for me, is there?" he gasped.

"No, Tim," answered Hamer dejectedly. "There's not a chance for you."

"Did he get away?" Timberlake asked.

"No."

"That helps a whole lot," said the Ranger. A tremor passed over his body, and then he died. Hamer slowly pulled the white bedsheet over his face. Then he stepped outside, where the rest of the posse waited by the hospital-room window.

"Well, he's cashed in," said Frank quietly.

At that, one of the officers—probably Sheriff Vann—remarked, "Hamer, if we had followed your advice, things would have been different. We made a mistake."

Hamer's eyes flashed with anger. Then he nodded toward the white sheet through the hospital-room window and snapped, "Yes, and there is your mistake."[16]

Bill Sterling later provided another detail that may have contributed to Timberlake's death: "Like all Southwest Texas ranchmen and horseback Rangers, he used a short brush jacket made out of heavy duck. This was for protection against thorns. It had been laundered many times by native washerwomen, and the homemade lye soap they used had bleached it out. In contrast to the darkness of the river bank, this white garment made a plain target for the cat-eyed *guia* [guide]."

Captain Taylor and other Rangers took Timberlake's body by train to his father's home in Uvalde, where the popular sergeant was buried. U.S. Army aviators flew over the funeral procession and dropped flowers on the grave. Encarnacion Delgado's obsequies were not so grand. His friends and family laid him to rest in Brownsville's Old City Cemetery, where his engraved headstone can still be viewed today.[17]

Hamer was immediately promoted to sergeant to succeed Timberlake and placed in charge of the company during Taylor's absence. The financial benefit was significant: he now earned $100 a month. Captain Hanson went to Brownsville to investigate the shooting. In Hanson's report, he stated that Sheriff Vann had fired all the shots into Delgado. However, Walter Prescott Webb later interviewed both Hamer and Captain Taylor, who confirmed that Vann had been armed with a shotgun and could not have fired the fatal rounds. Bill Sterling also talked with members of the posse. He wrote, "Ben Tumlinson . . . frankly told me that the action was so sudden and the night so dark that he did not get off a shot. All the survivors agreed that if it had not been for the coolness and marksmanship of Frank Hamer, the slayer of Sergeant Timberlake would have made good his escape." Captain Taylor even repeated the comment made during the fight, telling Sterling, "Bill, it looked like Frank was burning him up with a pear burner." Ever after, Rangers would say, "Hamer used Old Lucky during the day, but always took his pear burner with him at night."[18]

Hamer's deadly marksmanship and coolness under fire were made abundantly clear in the Los Tomates gunfight. At the same time, his "shoot first and ask questions later" ethic was entirely contrary to the law. Police, then and now, are constrained to use deadly force only when lives are endangered. Yet, instead of following his instincts, Hamer obeyed the dictates of Sheriff Vann by holding his fire until Delgado shot first. A year to the month earlier, he had almost lost his life in a deadly close-quarters gun battle, so his desire to take no chances was entirely understandable given the circumstances. Timberlake's murder had a profound effect on Hamer and would influence his actions in future gunfights. Illegal as it would have been, his proposal to shoot first certainly did not rise to the level of the cold-blooded murders of captured Mexican suspects by Rangers commanded by Captains Ransom and Fox. But it would not be the last time this issue would arise in Hamer's career.

9

"THIS RUFFIAN HAYMER"

Frank's first assignment as the new sergeant of Company F was to assist Captain Hanson in investigating complaints from the Mexican government about violence against Mexicans in the Rio Grande Valley. H. N. Gray, who was an intelligence agent employed by the Mexican consul in Brownsville, conducted his own investigation. Jose T. Canales, a Brownsville lawyer, state legislator, and Tejano, had also received many complaints from Hispanics. Shortly after the killing of Sergeant Timberlake, Canales and Gray met with Hamer to discuss the Los Tomates fight. Canales had never met Hamer; he later said, "He impressed me as a good man." After Hamer explained how the ricocheted bullet hit Timberlake, Gray tried to defend Delgado, saying that "he didn't try to kill him [Timberlake]." A surprised Canales remarked, "Well, he intended to kill somebody, and if the bullet glanced and hit somebody, he has committed murder in my judgment."[1]

A few days later, about the fifteenth of October, Hamer got a tip that smugglers were bringing mescal to U.S. soldiers stationed in San Pedro, nine miles northwest of Brownsville. As Agent E. H. Parker of the Bureau of Investigation (now the FBI) later explained, the troopers "had been in the habit of . . . coming over there [Mexico] for quite a while, and it has been our business there to catch these people, mescal sellers, who have been peddling mescal into Texas from the Mexican side, and they have been in the habit of trading with the soldiers." Parker pointed out that the smugglers "could sell it to soldiers when they could not sell it to anyone else, as the soldiers would not report it, as they knew they themselves would be put in the guardhouse." Parker said that, as a consequence, the Mexican smugglers "were almost safe in selling it to a soldier."

Hamer, Agent Parker, Ranger Lee Rosser, Deputy Sheriff Fred Winn, two customs inspectors, and two soldiers piled into a pair of motorcars and drove to the farm of Santiago Tijerina at San Pedro, half a mile from the Rio Grande. Parker later described Tijerina as a supporter of Venustiano Carranza and charged that he had violated the federal neutrality laws. The lawmen passed Tijerina, who was supervising fifteen or twenty Mexican hands as they harvested corn in the field. Two hundred yards down the road, the officers parked next to some brush so their vehicles would not be visible from the river and then hid in the tall grass while the two soldiers walked down to the Rio Grande to buy liquor. From their place of concealment, Hamer and the others watched the soldiers speak with several Mexicans across the river, who then got into a buggy and disappeared, apparently to obtain mescal. Hamer and the rest left their position to move closer to the river, crouching low among the cornstalks. As they did so, they spotted Santiago Tijerina, hunching over as he made his way through the corn toward the Rio Grande. The posse took up a new position at a bend in the river, waiting for the Mexican smugglers to return with the mescal. After a long wait and no smugglers, Hamer exclaimed, "Someone has given it away."

Soon the troopers returned and announced, "Someone had tipped it off, and this was the man," meaning Tijerina. The posse stopped Tijerina on his return from the river, but he did not speak English. As Agent Parker later explained, "Mr. Hamer I don't think speaks Spanish very well, in fact I don't think he speaks it at all." Hamer told Lee Rosser, who did speak the language, "I want you to tell this man that he went down there and tipped this play off, that we are officers and came here to catch these smugglers that came to smuggle mescal over here, and I want you to tell him if we come here again, not to interfere with officers."

Tijerina later claimed that the lawmen threatened to kill him. Perhaps the hot-tempered Hamer did, but Parker denied it, saying, "they might have used a few curse words or something like that, but he was not abused or anything, and they told him not to tell anyone about this, that is to notify the smugglers that they intended to come again and catch them." To that, Tijerina promised, "I will not notify them. I will say nothing to them."[2]

Santiago Tijerina was related to a prominent Tejano family. His first cousin was Jose Canales, the lawyer and state legislator. Tijerina complained to Canales, saying that he had gone to the river not to warn the smugglers but to trail some stolen cattle. This story was obviously contrived, for he certainly had not told the posse that. Had he informed the officers that his cattle had been stolen, they surely would have acted. Any border lawman would have been far more interested in capturing cattle thieves than petty mescal smugglers. Tijerina said to Canales, "I believe those men meant to kill me. I believe they insulted me for the purpose of me making some demonstration and to be killed by them on the spot, and then say I was resisting arrest." Canales accepted his cousin's story, apparently unaware that there were numerous field hands present who would have been witnesses to any violence. Said Canales, "He . . . wanted me to get him a passport for him and his family to go into Mexico for fear of his life. I dissuaded him from doing so and promised to report the incident." Shortly after, Canales met Captain Hanson on a train from Brownsville to Austin and related the Tijerina affair. "I know all about it," Hanson replied. "They went to catch some fellows who were bringing in mescal or whiskey from the other side, and they saw him going over there and making signals to men on the other side . . . and for that reason those fellows were angry and they abused him, and I don't blame them."[3]

Although Canales believed that Hanson would take no action after that response, the captain did reprimand Hamer and the other Rangers present. Hanson nonetheless was hugely impressed with Hamer, both for his role in the Tomates Bend gunfight and for his detective abilities. He later wrote to the Ranger quartermaster in Austin, "He is a good man and his expenses are more than he gets out of the service. Help him all you can as he is the best Ranger in Texas." Frank later recalled that "Hanson was a likable fellow" and said that they became very good friends. Hamer's warm feelings toward Hanson would not last.[4]

One of Frank's most important assignments was to help Captain Hanson investigate election frauds in the Rio Grande Valley. While Jim Wells was political boss of Cameron County, for forty years Archie Parr ruled Duval County as the "Duke of Duval." In the Democratic primary of July 1918, Parr ran for reelection as state senator. He met strong opposition from a lawyer, D. W. Glasscock. Despite the Rangers' poll monitoring and investigation, Parr and Wells used massive election fraud and bloc voting by Hispanics to defeat Glasscock in one of the most crooked elections in Texas history. Glasscock, undaunted, launched a write-in campaign for the general election in November. In October Governor William P. Hobby, who supported Glasscock, ordered the Rangers to again investigate fraud by Parr, Wells, and their supporters. The state, just as it required Rangers to supply their own horse, saddle, and weapons, provided no automobiles for official use. Since Hamer was one of the few Rangers who owned a motorcar, he was dispatched to Duval County to assist Captain Hanson. Their efforts proved fruitless, for once again Parr controlled the balloting, allowing unregistered Hispanics to vote and invalidating hundreds of Glasscock ballots. He won reelection and kept his state senate seat until 1934. This was not the last time Frank Hamer confronted the Parr machine; thirty years later, he would return to South Texas to investigate one of America's most important cases of election fraud.[5]

Meanwhile, Frank missed his wife and family terribly. The girls attended school in Snyder, and Gladys and baby Frank were at the Johnson ranch, almost six hundred miles away. Hamer's promotion to sergeant created a vacancy in the company, and he was hopeful that his brother Harrison could fill it. Frank's marriage into the Johnson family, coupled with his reappointment to the Rangers, seems to have mollified Sheriff W. A. Merrill, of Scurry County. The previous year, Merrill had strongly opposed the Hamer brothers because of their involvement in the Johnson-Sims feud. Now, Sheriff Merrill, along with the Scurry County judge and the local state senator, wrote to General Harley, asking that Harrison Hamer be appointed a special Ranger. Harley did one better and ordered Harrison to Brownsville, where on October 23 he was mustered into Company F by Captain Taylor as a regular Ranger. Frank was delighted to have his brother working with him.[6]

At that time the influenza epidemic of 1918 was sweeping the globe, and it eventually killed more people than World War I. The virus affected about 28 percent of all Americans, killing 675,000. A week after Harrison arrived, Frank came down with the flu and became deathly ill. His brother and fellow Rangers could not care for him in camp,

Gladys Hamer and the children in 1919. Baby Frank is on her lap and Beverly is at left. Trix is standing. *Photo © Paul Goodwin from Little John's Auction Service*

and Frank was too poor to afford a stay in a hospital and too proud to accept money from his in-laws. He took a room in the Miller Hotel on the corner of Thirteenth and Elizabeth Streets and sent for Gladys. She rushed to Brownsville by train, bringing the seven-month-old baby, Frank. It was a risky proposition, but she was still nursing the infant and had no choice. Gladys cared for her husband for fifteen days until he could finally get back on his feet. Frank was one of the lucky ones, and Gladys stayed with him for much of November. When Captain Hanson arrived in town, Hamer appealed for financial help. He owed the hotelkeeper $1.50 a day plus a five-dollar doctor's bill, almost a third of his monthly pay. Hanson urged the quartermaster to pay the bill and allow Hamer to keep his room in the Miller Hotel. The quartermaster grudgingly did so, but allocated only fifteen dollars a month for rent, writing Hamer, "This is out of the ordinary, but is being done because urged by Captain Hanson."[7]

Soon after recovering, on December 11, 1918, Hamer was walking toward the Miller Hotel when he spotted Jose Canales approaching him. The attorney was on his way to his office in the Merchants' National Bank building. Hamer, still seething over the Tijerina incident and smarting from Hanson's reprimand, had evidently learned that Tijerina was Canales's cousin. He hailed the legislator, saying, "Here, I want to see you."

Canales stopped, and the big Ranger ordered, "Come here."

As Canales approached, Hamer demanded, "What is the name of that son of a bitch that complained to you about the Rangers cursing him and abusing him over at Rio Grande City?"

"I don't know that anyone from Rio Grande City complained about the Rangers cursing and abusing him."

"Yes, you have," insisted Hamer. "You have said that to Captain Hanson—the man you told, Captain Hanson."

"Now let me tell you," Canales answered. "The man that I spoke to Captain Hanson of is Santiago Tijerina."

When Canales tried to explain that Tijerina lived nine miles from Brownsville, and not in Rio Grande City, Hamer interrupted. "Now what did that son of a bitch tell you?"

Canales was shocked by Hamer's belligerent tone, and replied, "I don't believe such testimony is for you to know, that is my own business about it."

Canales later recalled, "He looked at me in a very angry way, his eyes glistened and . . . I have been practicing law for twenty years and I know when men mean business."

By now Hamer's temper got the better of him. He seems to have thought that Canales was a corrupt politician trying to cover up his cousin's crimes. The hulking lawman barked, "You are hot-footing it here, between here and Austin complaining to the Governor and the Adjutant General about the Rangers, and I am going to tell you if you don't stop that you are going to get hurt."

"What?" asked the stunned Canales. He could not believe what he was hearing.

"If you are not going to quit it, you are going to get hurt."

"Mr. Hamer, will you repeat that to somebody?" the incredulous Canales requested. "I would like to have a witness to that."

The two were standing in front of a garage owned by Jesse Dennett, an auto dealer and Brownsville city commissioner who was friendly with both men. Canales led Hamer to Dennett's office in his garage, calling him outside.

"Mr. Jesse Dennett, come here. I call you to listen to what this man has to say."

At that, Hamer started to explain himself, when Canales interrupted. "Don't explain matters. I want you to repeat what you told me. Didn't you just tell me that if I didn't quit making complaints against the Rangers to the Governor and the Adjutant General, that I was going to get hurt?"

Dennett interjected, "Did you say that to Mr. Canales?"

"Yes, sir," replied Hamer, and again started to explain himself.

"I don't want to hear any more," snapped Dennett, who walked back into his office.

As Hamer stalked off, Canales returned to his law office. He later said, "I didn't know who Mr. Hamer was or his reputation." However, he did know that a few weeks earlier the big Ranger had shot and killed a Mexican desperado. Canales was shaken and frightened and went to see Sheriff Vann. The sheriff, still rankled by Hamer's harsh criticism over the death of Sergeant Timberlake, exploded. "My advice to you is, take a double-barreled shotgun and I will give you a man and you go over there and kill that man. No jury would ever convict you for that." Canales ignored Vann's ill-considered advice.[8]

Frank Hamer's hot temper had led him into the most serious blunder of his professional life. Jose Canales was no crooked politician. Nor was he a rowdy from the streets of Navasota or Houston who could be intimidated with threats, rough language, and an imposing physique. By any measure, the slender, forty-one-year-old legislator was a remarkable man. Born into a wealthy ranchero family in Nueces County, he was raised on both sides of the border, speaking Spanish and English fluently. After graduating from the prestigious University of Michigan law school in 1899, he moved to Brownsville and opened a law practice, then served in various official positions before being reelected to the legislature in 1917. In an era of deep racial prejudice, Canales was extremely proud of his ethnic heritage. As a lawyer, he defended impoverished Mexicans and Tejanos. An intense American patriot, he had been a lifelong supporter of the Texas Rangers. As a boy, the Rangers had often camped on his family's ranch, and he was a friend and admirer of Captains Rogers and Hughes. At the height of the Bandit War, Canales recruited a company of Mexican American scouts to gather intelligence for the U.S. Army. But the excesses and evaporations by Rangers, local lawmen, and vigilantes troubled him deeply.[9]

Though shaken by his encounter, Canales was determined to do something about the Rangers in general and Hamer in particular. The next day he dictated a long letter to Governor Hobby: "I write you this to inform you that one Frank Haymer who is Sergeant of Rangers in Captain Taylor's Co., stationed in Brownsville has threaten[ed] to do me bodily injury if I would continue to complain to the Adjutant General's Department or to you, for the abuses and outrages committed by Rangers in this part of the State. He met me on the street yesterday and in the presence of a respectable citizen, to wit, Jesse Dennett, repeated this threat." Canales then described the Tijerina incident and lambasted Captain Hanson for doing nothing about it. He charged that Hanson had instead ordered Hamer to threaten him. "The trouble with this ruffian Haymer is nothing personally but [he] is acting under instructions, I am sure, of Hanson, who is using this method to gag me." Canales complained that Hanson had told Hamer and the other Rangers about his complaint, then leveled a blast at the captain. "This man Hanson is a corrupt Republican intriguer. . . . He served as secret service man for General Diaz, President of Mexico; was a co-conspirator of General Huerta; was expelled from Mexico for intriguing . . . and ever since has been plotting against that Government and working to force intervention in Mexico by the United States." Canales concluded with an appeal "to protect me from this corrupt Republican intriguer and his gang of ruffians, who are called state rangers."[10]

Canales's complaint that Hanson should not have discussed the Tijerina incident with Hamer and the other Rangers was nonsensical.

Hanson could not investigate it without questioning the people who were there. However, his other charges against the captain were entirely true. The handsome, mustachioed Hanson, fifty-two, had been appointed U.S. marshal for the southern district of Texas in 1902. He later resigned and went to Mexico, where he prospered by investing in oil and cropland. More politician than lawman, he took sides in the Mexican Revolution in an effort to protect his holdings. In 1911, as a private detective for the Porfirio Díaz government, he spied on Mexican revolutionists in Texas. The revolution devastated his investments in Mexico, and in 1914 Carranza forces seized his huge El Conejo ranch and accused him of being a spy for Victoriano Huerta. Hanson was jailed, then expelled from Mexico. A year later, he plotted to sell five million rounds of Mauser rifle ammunition to Mexican revolutionists. Working on behalf of Senator Fall, he promoted U.S. intervention and labored consistently for and against Mexico's various revolutionary governments in a decade-long effort to regain his lost fortune.[11]

Governor Hobby had Adjutant General Harley respond to Canales and advise him that Captain Hanson had reprimanded Hamer and the other Rangers for their conduct toward Tijerina. Of Hanson, he said, "I do not believe he instructed them to make any threats against you. He has assured me he gave no such orders . . . to any of the men, but on the contrary had instructed them to treat all people with respect and fairness." Regarding Hanson's unsavory involvement in the Mexican Revolution, Harley declared, "that matter has been thoroughly investigated and was found to be a thing of the past." One comment in Harley's letter especially irked Canales: "You understand, of course, that the Rangers like everyone else, make mistakes sometimes, but I do not believe they would do any intentional wrong." Harley closed by inviting Canales to visit him in Austin "and see if we cannot straighten out the whole situation."[12]

Harley's response was wholly unsatisfactory to Canales. Earlier that year he had complained to General Harley and Captain Hanson about Ranger brutality, and they had done nothing to correct it. Now, he believed that he was being stonewalled. He fired off a reply, insisting that "the action of Sergeant Frank Haymer in threatening me is no mistake, my dear General. . . . If this threat on my life by a State Ranger is a mistake it is better to correct it by putting him out where he can do no harm." He then brought up Hanson's investigation of two controversial shootings of Mexicans by Sergeant John Edds, a Mexican American Ranger. "When he investigated Ranger John Edds . . . for the murder of a poor man near Hebbronville, in Jim Hogg County, he reprimanded him so well that he, John Edds, within a short time murdered another man named Munoz near Rio Grande City. . . . Judging from that I am sure Hanson will reprimand this fellow Haymer by making him Captain of the Rangers."[13]

On December 23, immediately upon receipt of Canales's letter, General Harley sent a stern telegram to Hamer: "Under Governor's orders you are instructed not to make any threats against the lives of any citizens especially J. T. Canales and that he is to be given proper protection as a citizen. Complaint has been filed that you have made some threats. Without going into the truth of the matter you are instructed to be careful and courteous at all times and not to make a personal matter of your official duties. Undertake to adjust differences as best you can without causing any trouble."[14]

By this time Hamer, oblivious to the trouble he had stirred up, was spending the Christmas holidays with his brother Harrison at Bill Sterling's family ranch in western Hidalgo County. As much as the Hamers would have wanted to celebrate the season with their wives and children in Snyder, they were not authorized to leave the Rio Grande Valley. Bill Sterling never forgot Frank Hamer's displays of marksmanship during the weeklong visit. On a deer hunt, Hamer spotted a buck leap over a clump of cactus more than a hundred yards distant. Shouldering his .25 Remington, he squeezed off a single round that hit the animal square in the head. After examining the buck, Frank joked that he "was going to give the gun away on account of defective sights, for he had missed the deer's eye by almost half an inch." The ranch foreman, Edgar McGee, had been an Arizona Ranger and a Texas Ranger and was not easily impressed. With McGee, the Sterling family, their guests, and vaqueros looking on, Hamer was asked to demonstrate his ability with a handgun. He borrowed from Bill Sterling a .45 Colt single-action with a five-and-a-half-inch barrel. Although Hamer had never fired Sterling's revolver before, he took aim at a blackbird perched atop a tall willow tree. Despite a strong wind that swayed the tree, Hamer hit the bird with one shot. Edgar McGee announced that "never again would he doubt any story told about the marksmanship of Frank Hamer."[15]

After Christmas, Frank finally got permission to visit his family in Snyder for a few days, then left for Austin on Ranger business. Meanwhile, Representative Canales had been mulling over a plan to reform the Texas Rangers. On January 13, 1919, he was in Austin for the new session of the state legislature, making the rounds of the hotels to meet with lawmakers before the caucuses the next day. While talking with a fellow representative in the Driskill Hotel, Canales later said, "I saw Mr. Frank Hamer, and his presence was made known to me very marked by passing in front of me, as though he simply wanted me to know that he was here and on the force. From there I went to the Avenue Hotel and I find him there. He came after I left the other hotel, and showed

Frank Hamer as a Texas Ranger sergeant in 1919. *Photo © Paul Goodwin from Little John's Auction Service*

himself that he was here. He wanted me to know it and I know it, of course."[16]

Canales claimed that Hamer "had been transferred from Brownsville and placed on the force here [in Austin]." That was incorrect; Hamer was stationed in Brownsville and had come to Austin on state business, not to menace Canales. But that is not how the legislator saw it: "He has not done anything that I know of to carry out his threat on me, but has just made it known that he is here and is still on the ranger force. I took his action as a challenge that I would be intimidated if I would make any charges against these rangers or introduce any law attempting to regulate them." That Frank intended to intimidate Canales is unlikely. He had received a direct order not to do that, and he never disobeyed lawful orders. However, Canales was undoubtedly correct in concluding that Hamer was trying to make a point—that he was still on the Texas Ranger force. Hamer's poor judgment would prove a gross miscalculation.[17]

That night, Canales met with General Harley in the Driskill Hotel and attempted to persuade him that Captain Hanson, instead of exposing the wrongdoing of Rangers, was trying to cover it up. Harley was unconvinced. The next morning, a frustrated Canales drew up legislation that would prove momentous in the history of the Texas Rangers. His bill was a modest one, calling for a reduction of the force to twenty-four men, for a pay increase, and for a requirement that each man be bonded, be at least twenty-five years old, have two years of law-enforcement experience, and possess good moral character. It prohibited the use of excessive force and required Rangers to allow bail and to promptly bring prisoners to the nearest jail. When Canales brought these common-sense proposals before the House of Representatives, they were met with outrage by reactionary legislators, who saw them as a frontal attack on a beloved institution. For the Texas Rangers were far more than a state police force. They were the heart and soul of the Lone Star State, a breathing manifestation of its frontier birth, of its very existence.

In heated debate, one representative after another defended the Rangers as Canales made public his charges, ones that were familiar to every Spanish-speaking person on the border: Rangers had murdered innocent Mexicans, made unlawful searches, beaten prisoners, and verbally and physically abused citizens. He charged that Captain Hanson's investigations into Ranger wrongdoing were instead designed to bury it. In reply, Canales's opponents gave fiery speeches, summoning up the Alamo and the Battle of San Jacinto to burnish the glorious image of the Texas Rangers. General Harley had a much more pragmatic—and cynical—response. He called for a joint legislative investigation to look into allegations of Ranger misconduct and to determine whether the force should be abolished. It was a masterful tactical move, for Harley knew that no Texas politician would ever vote to disband the Rangers. Now Canales was on the defensive. He needed to prove his charges of abuse, but he was primed for the fight.

The hearings began in the capitol building on January 30. Canales filed a total of nineteen specific charges against the Rangers. These ranged from the threats made against him by Frank Hamer and the killings by Ranger John Edds to such atrocities as evaporations during the Bandit War and the Porvenir massacre. General Harley was so confidant—or arrogant—that he assigned Hamer as one of three Rangers to serve witness subpoenas in the Rio Grande Valley, a gross conflict of interest, given that Hamer was a subject of the investigation. Eighty witnesses testified over two weeks. Several legislators supported Canales, but the majority ridiculed him repeatedly. Many witnesses were shills brought in by Harley to muster praise for the Rangers. But slowly, witness by witness, the truth came out. Numerous Rangers hired by Governor Ferguson's administration were shown to be embarrassments to the force. In many cases, the principal requirement for a new Ranger seemed to be skill with a six-gun and willingness to use it. For the first time, Ferguson's ley de fuga orders to Captain Ransom were publicly confirmed. Sheriff Vann and Jim Wells testified in detail about the evaporations by Ransom and his men. Others told of men abused by Rangers and of Mexicans arrested by Rangers who were never seen again. Pathetic affidavits from grieving widows of the men murdered at Porvenir spoke volumes of the need for reform.[18]

Among the many pro-Ranger witnesses was Dayton Moses, attorney for the Cattle Raisers Association. Moses had been district attorney of Burnet County during Hamer's stint breaking up the Kimble County goat thieves in 1914. He testified in detail about the need for both regular and special Rangers and declared that the livestock industry would be decimated by rustlers if the force was disbanded. But his testimony backfired when he was asked about Frank Hamer. At first Moses hemmed and hawed, finally saying, "I do not want to shirk answering any question that ought to be answered. . . . I knew Mr. Hamer in Kimble County first. It was a county that was overrun by goat thieves . . . and the danger was so great and they were losing so much stock that Mr. Hamer was employed by the local citizens there and paid a salary." He explained, "There was one element in that country that believed that Mr. Hamer was a first class man and a first class officer and there was another element, and they were not all bad men, there were a great many good men who believed that he was entirely too harsh and too harsh as an officer in the discharge of his duties."[19]

Hamer's friend Bill Sterling, on the other hand, stoutly defended him. "I think his reputation is one of the best in the whole force," he testified. "I don't think any man who is not a criminal has anything in the world to fear from him. I don't think he would touch one of them. He is an awful good officer and absolutely not a bully." Sterling also pointed out—correctly—that during the Bandit War, Rangers were often blamed for things done by local lawmen, federal officers, and vigilantes. "[To] the common Mexican class, everybody that wears a six-shooter is a Ranger, it may be an immigration officer, Customs, or a deputy sheriff or a cowman with a six-shooter—Rangers." His father, Edward A. Sterling, testified that he had known Frank Hamer for ten or twelve years and confirmed that he was a "conscientious, fearless officer." When asked if it was true that Hamer carried twenty-six bullets in his body "that were placed there by the bandits and thieves and desperadoes," Sterling answered, "Well, I couldn't tell you exactly. I know that he has been pretty badly shot up."[20]

Jose Canales provided his own testimony, explaining his lifelong support and admiration of the Rangers and the deterioration of the force during the Ferguson administration. Most of his testimony concerned the atrocities committed by Rangers and other lawmen during the Bandit War. But he also described in detail his menacing encounter with Hamer in Brownsville and introduced into the record the letters he wrote in protest. Jesse Dennett fully confirmed Canales's account. News reporters ate it up, and the story was widely published in Texas newspapers. It was the first time Hamer's name had appeared prominently in the statewide press, an inauspicious beginning. Frank, on duty in Brownsville, was never called as a witness to defend himself. For the proud and confident Frank Hamer, the newspaper reports of his encounter with Canales were especially embarrassing and humiliating, and he must have deeply regretted his rash actions. It was a valuable lesson, for never again would he make a public spectacle of himself.[21]

When Canales's opponents accused him of wanting the force abolished, the Tejano legislator made his position clear: "I know that we need Rangers, but we don't need the kind of Rangers we have had and the class of Rangers we mostly are getting now; we want simply to purge the Ranger force of its bad element so as to preserve its vitality and go back to the old days of Captain Rogers and Captain Hughes and Captain Brooks." Captain Rogers himself was one of the most important witnesses. Now U.S. marshal for the Western District of Texas, he sat through some of the testimony and was apoplectic, wondering what had become of the beloved force he had worked so hard to professionalize. Rogers testified that although his deputy marshals were bonded, an unpropertied, poorly paid Ranger could never qualify for and obtain a bond. While emphasizing the need for reorganizing the force, he was most concerned about Ranger brutality. "I have heard a good deal of complaint about . . . illegal killings," he declared. "Such conduct is a blot on the history of this state."[22]

During the hearings, Canales overplayed his hand. Instead of focusing on the most egregious offenses, he used a shotgun approach, bringing too many charges that he could not clearly prove. The result was a mass of meandering testimony that filled a fifteen-hundred-page transcript. A number of the Ranger shootings that Canales complained of were shown to be lawful. His attacks on the popular, politically connected General Harley and Captain Hanson were doomed to failure from the start. On occasion, he was guilty of exaggeration and dramatization, once claiming, "If you kill this bill, you had just as well sign an order to send my body home feet first." Nonetheless, Canales had presented clear evidence of Ranger incompetence and brutality. Still, most legislators were unmoved. By convincing themselves that murdered Mexican suspects simply got what they deserved, they ignored the obvious: that the rule of law is paramount, that constitutional liberties are sacred, and that a well-regulated police force is essential to a free society.[23]

The result of the Canales hearings was a watered-down bill that passed both houses overwhelmingly. The force was reduced to four companies, each consisting of a captain, a sergeant, and fifteen privates. There would also be a headquarters company of six men, led by a senior captain in Austin and charged with responding to trouble spots all over Texas. The governor retained the authority to increase the force as needed. All recruits had to submit evidence of good character, and all special Ranger commissions were temporarily suspended. Although Rangers still had to supply their own weapons, horses, and automobiles, wages were substantially increased in an effort to attract higher-quality men. Privates now earned ninety dollars a month and were given a monthly allowance of thirty dollars for food and fifty dollars for automobile upkeep. Captains would receive $150 a month; sergeants, $100. To allow captains to monitor their activities, each Ranger was required to file a weekly report. The act also created, for the first time, a formal system for investigating misconduct.

In addition to these reforms, the committee criticized the Rangers for "gross violation of both civil and criminal laws" and charged that unnamed captains had been "arbitrary and overbearing in the discharge of their duties." However, the legislators fully exonerated General Harley and Captain Hanson of any wrongdoing. They commended Harley for "the able, efficient, impartial, and fearless manner in which he has discharged the duties placed upon him as the head of the Ranger Force," ignoring the fact that the Porvenir massacre had occurred on his watch. On February 19 a jubilant Captain Hanson sent telegrams to several Rangers, including Hamer in Brownsville, exulting, "Committee report all we could ask for. Vindication complete."[24]

The committee also found, dismissively, "Hon. J. T. Canales has been prompted by no improper motives." To that, the editor of *The Dallas Morning News* angrily responded, "It seems to that the service which Mr. Canales has rendered in this matter merited a more generous recognition than it received from the committee. Merely to admit that Mr. Canales was 'prompted by no improper motives' is to ignore that he rendered a large public service in disclosing a state of affairs which neither the people nor the Legislature knew anything about and which would probably . . . continue indefinitely if he had not had the courage and sense of responsibility necessary to force a consideration of it. . . . The salient fact is that he proved the existence of a shocking and intolerable condition that demands correction." Such praise was little solace to Canales. "I do not recognize my child," he said plaintively of his bill. Disillusioned and faced with hostility from many legislators, he declined to seek reelection in 1920. As a result of his courageous and principled stand, Jose T. Canales sacrificed his political career on the altar of justice.[25]

No such nobility can be assigned to Frank Hamer. His encounter with Canales was one of the most ironic in Ranger annals. By threatening the legislator, he both abused his authority and unwittingly triggered a series of events that laid bare Ranger wrongdoing and resulted in significant reforms of the force. The testimony in the hearings largely supported the need for a law-enforcement body like the Rangers. After all, the force was not all bad, it just had a lot of bad eggs. And truth be told, Frank Hamer—at least on that December day in Brownsville—was one of them. The extraordinary coolness, skill, and courage he demonstrated in the Los Tomates shootout—which barely made a ripple in the Texas press—had been totally eclipsed by his angry threats against Jose Canales.

In fairness to Hamer, it must be emphasized that he had long worked in a place and time that was extremely dangerous for lawmen. Texas then and now leads the nation in peace-officer fatalities. As a young Ranger, because of budget restraints and manpower shortages, he had been sent repeatedly into trouble spots with only a handful of other Rangers when it would have been prudent to assign an entire company. And because local lawmen in those communities were often incapable or incompetent, Frank learned to rely primarily on himself or his fellow

Rangers. Over and over again, he had faced lawbreakers and lynchers who greatly outnumbered him. On the streets of Navasota and the ranges of Kimble County, Hamer had been forced to act alone against the hardcases and thieves. Because he had no backup other than his open palm and his boots, he had routinely used harsh language and overwhelming force—unlawful force by modern standards—to maintain his authority. As a result, Hamer and other Rangers relied on their fearsome reputations—amplified to mythic proportions during a century of fighting Mexicans, Indians, and bandits—to enforce the law. In the ensuing years, Hamer would continue to use the forceful methods of the frontier Rangers, though now combined with a more measured, increasingly sophisticated approach to law enforcement.[26]

As would become clear in the decade to come, the modest reforms of the Canales hearings were a turning point for the Texas Rangers, just as they were a turning point for Frank Hamer. The hearings, coupled with the end of the Mexican Revolution in 1920, made possible a new era for the Rangers. No longer would they be primarily a border-protection force. As troubles on the Rio Grande gradually subsided, Rangers would increasingly be used to assist local officers in keeping the peace and investigating serious crimes throughout the state. They would still serve on the border, but their duties would become much broader and more complex than scouting the Rio Grande and fighting Mexican bandidos. The Canales hearings began the long process that would eventually turn the Texas Rangers into a modern, professional law-enforcement body, one of the most capable—and by far the most fabled—in American history.

THE LONE RANGER

Under a merciless sun, the horsemen rode single file along the north bank of the Rio Grande, their morning solitude interrupted only by the steady clip-clop of ponies' hooves and the riders' low murmurs. Then the dull thud of distant gunfire rolled across the river. Frank Hamer and his fellow lawmen quickly dismounted and tethered their animals in a cluster of brush. They crawled along the embankment on hands and knees to a pile of boulders overlooking the river. Training field glasses across the Rio Grande, they watched a battle unfold. Hamer, as he squinted through the dust and smoke, thought that the fight pitted President Carranza's troops against forces led by General José Gonzalo Escobar. Much of the combat in the Mexican Revolution was bloody and no quarters, but this fight seemed to be more comic opera than anything else. The Carrancistas, blowing bugles, charged from behind a hill, yelling like demons. Then the Escobar force counter-attacked, shouting, cursing, and firing as the Carrancistas retreated behind the hill. Hamer and the other lawmen looked on as the skirmishing lasted most of the day, with each side alternately taking long rests and then attacking. Finally, the Carrancista commander charged his horse through the enemy lines, splashing into the Rio Grande. Shouting curses and waving his sword, he tried in vain to rally his men, when suddenly his horse balked and pitched him headfirst into the river. The soggy commander climbed into the saddle and raced back to his men. As the back-and-forth skirmishing went on, Frank and his comrades counted more than two thousand shots fired. Then, as evening approached, the exhausted fighters abandoned the battlefield. The lone casualty of the entire fight was the Carrancista commander's horse, which he finally shot out of anger and frustration.[1]

The Mexican Revolution continued to be Hamer's greatest challenge. In December 1918 he had received a tip that a large shipment of arms and ammunition was to be sent from the Bering-Cortes Hardware Company in Houston and smuggled to Pancho Villa's forces across the border near Brownsville. By this time Senator Albert B. Fall, at the behest of Edward Doheny, later of Teapot Dome infamy, was secretly supporting Villa because he was the strongest opponent of Carranza. Indeed, Hamer later charged that Villa bribed Fall in exchange for the senator's support. Although the United States had recognized the Carranza government since late 1915, there was an embargo on all private arms shipments to Mexico. Frank reported the smuggling plot to Adjutant General Harley in Austin and advised that he would try to intercept the shipment. Several days later, Captain Hanson showed up in Brownsville and invited him to dinner. There he ordered Hamer "to let this shipment reach Villa." A shocked Hamer adamantly refused, whereupon Hanson told him "that these were the orders of Adjutant General J. A. Harley." Frank replied that he "didn't care if they were orders of the President of the United States—that it was a violation of the neutrality laws and he didn't propose to have anything to do with it." Hamer told Hanson that he "was crooked or he would not have come . . . with such a proposition." Frank later said that Hanson left the restaurant "in considerable anger."[2]

Soon after, on the last day of 1918, Captain Taylor and several members of his company, ostensibly in a cost-cutting measure, were discharged, and Company F was disbanded. Hamer retained his job but was kept on detached service in Brownsville, assigned to no company captain. Frank later insisted that Hanson and Harley did this so that he would be "left alone on ninety miles of border . . . for the purpose of getting [me] killed off."[3]

Hamer had never failed to follow a direct order, but he had no obligation to obey an illegal one, even from a captain who had been one of his admirers. Explained his friend Walter Prescott Webb, "Frank Hamer . . . knew that when the Rangers were withdrawn, the bandits would come from the other side and clean up the Texas ranches. . . . If his body should be found in the brush or floating down the Rio Grande, the assumption would be that the smugglers and thieves had killed him for meddling with their affairs." As Hamer later said, "I was positive that gun smuggling was wrong. So I gave the smugglers of guns and ammunition hell."[4]

Harley and Hanson elected to leave Hamer alone, apparently fearing that the maverick Ranger might cause trouble. As Walter Prescott Webb later pointed out, Hamer's "superiors knew he would talk, and it is barely possible that they feared he might make the issue personal." Frank now worked independently, but he knew he needed help. In mid-February 1919 he crossed the international bridge between Brownsville and Matamoros and met with Lieutenant Colonel Manuel Bernea, the Carrancista commander of the Tamaulipas state police. This force, similar to the old rurales under Porfirio Díaz, had recently been organized by Tamaulipas's governor, Andrés Osuna. Its recruits, from the Mexican interior, had no family loyalties along the border. Explained Webb, "As a result of this conference, Hamer . . . became the virtual head of a large squad of Mexican soldiers who combed ninety miles of border. When stolen property or stock was located and identified, the possessors were invited to back up against an adobe wall about thirty feet from a military firing squad, and the stolen goods were assembled and returned to their owners in Texas." For example, on February 19, twenty miles upriver from Brownsville, rurales captured a Mexican riding a horse stolen in Texas. They promptly strung him up a tree.[5]

One day, Hamer got a tip that a gang of horse thieves was going to cross the border into Mexico. He notified Colonel Bernea, who dispatched his men in pursuit. Frank rode to the river crossing, hid his horse, and crawled to a vantage point atop a hill. Soon, a band of riders came into view, leading a remuda of stolen horses across the Rio Grande. They disappeared into a side canyon, and fifteen minutes later Hamer heard a distant volley of gunfire. Finally, a commander of the rurales appeared, spurred his horse into the river, and yelled for Hamer, who mounted and rode to meet him. The officer said, "I appreciate your information, *amigo*. All of the *cabrones* are dead, and here are your horses." Frank accepted the stolen herd and returned the animals to their owners in Texas.[6]

By February 23, 1919, little more than a week after Hamer's meeting with Bernea, Mexican mounted police had summarily shot or hanged nineteen outlaws along a twenty-mile stretch of the border above Matamoros. Wire service reports did not name Hamer, but they described the process: "The police have been supplied with the names of 'bad men,' and their method, it is said, is to enter the home of the man wanted, identify him, and if he is unable to give a plausible explanation of his means of livelihood, to execute him, either by shooting or hanging." Eight of the ill-fated outlaws had been found in a single village. Soon after, eight more desperadoes were rounded up and sentenced to be hanged. Colonel Bernea sent official invitations to American and Mexican dignitaries to witness the execution. The chosen spot was on the bank of the Rio Grande, opposite San Benito, Texas. On March 10, scores of spectators gathered on the American side to watch the mass hanging across the river, carried out by Bernea and his rurales. In all, at least twenty-eight outlaws had been slain by the Mexican mounted police in the previous month. This was clearly a message to the American government that President Carranza was cracking down on the border raiders.[7]

By this time Frank had been joined by his brother Harrison, who was now a member of Captain Will Wright's Company K. Colonel Bernea's purge caused many Mexican desperadoes to flee across the river into Texas. On a single day in early March, the Hamer brothers and other officers captured nine fugitives, including several draft dodgers, one army deserter, and a Mexican raider who had taken part in a 1915 attack on the Galveston ranch, which had left two U.S. soldiers dead. When Harrison got a letter from Captain Wright advising that he would be discharged on April 1, Frank became alarmed and suspected machinations by Captain Hanson. On March 23 he wrote to General Harley, "I am very sorry of this as well as [are] our friends who stayed with us through the [Canales] investigation, as we have been here just long enough to get this work lined up and get acquainted with the people. And I think the work we are doing in the way of cooperating with the officials on the other side we can put an end to the thieves for a long time to come and maybe for good. And in this work I kneed [sic] my brother very much and I would be very glad if you would let him stay here with me at least two months longer. . . . I feel that Cap Hanson has suggested that [Harrison] be discharged in order to bring about other results but I don't think Cap Hanson is as well acquainted with present conditions as we are, especially here on the river."[8]

Hamer's complaint was fairly direct: that Captain Hanson wanted Harrison discharged to hamper Frank's efforts to protect the border. Instead of responding to this inflammatory charge, Harley ignored it. Harley replied in defense of the captain, telling Hamer that "you are taking the wrong view of the situation in believing that anyone suggested [Harrison's] discharge. Captain Wright was merely notified by me that he was to discharge a certain number of men until he carried only fifteen men on his company and he naturally suggested the men who did not belong to his company throughout the year and your brother was one of these." On receiving this response, Hamer promptly sought help from his friend Caesar Kleberg, the influential manager of the King ranch. A single telegram from Kleberg was enough to change General Harley's mind. He reversed himself and saw to it that Harrison remained in Wright's company, albeit not with Frank on the border.[9]

International relations were gradually warming along the Rio Grande, due largely to the Allied victory in World War I and the end of German meddling in Mexican affairs. On April 7, Governor Hobby and his staff met in Nuevo Laredo with Governor Osuna, along with the governor of Nuevo León, representatives for the governor of Coahuila, and their military advisors. Enthusiastic Mexican crowds greeted Hobby for what *The Dallas Morning News* called "the largest border conference ever held." Free commerce, removal of restrictions on travel, and cooperative extradition of criminals were all discussed. For the first time in five years, U.S. soldiers were allowed to freely visit the border cities. It was a new era of cooperation with Mexican authorities, one that would eventually reduce the constant need for Rangers on the border.[10]

On March 26 Hamer was reassigned to Captain Charles Stevens's company, then stationed in Sanderson in the Big Bend. However, he remained on detached duty, alone in Brownsville. In April Frank was delighted when Gladys brought the girls and baby Frank to Brownsville. They took rooms in the San Carlos Apartments near the train depot and did some sightseeing. Frank had passport photos taken and obtained a visa that allowed them to visit Matamoros. Four years earlier, at the height of the Bandit War, such a family visit to Mexico would have been unthinkable. The fact that they could cross the border as tourists spoke volumes of how safe the Rio Grande Valley had become. Hamer had plainly missed his family. The fact was that he had not been particularly welcome at the Johnson ranch since his marriage. Billy liked Frank tremendously, but Nannie had never warmed up to him. Hamer was grateful for the time with Gladys and the children, free from his meddling mother-in-law. Yet even that was short-lived, for at the end of May the ill-tempered Nannie came for a visit, staying with them in their apartment.[11]

The new Ranger law, which resulted from the Canales hearings, took effect on June 20, 1919. It provided that all Ranger commissions were automatically canceled on June 19. Those desiring to remain in the service were required to reapply through their respective captains. In keeping with Captain Hanson's desire to isolate and nullify Hamer, he was never informed of this requirement. It was the responsibility of the new quartermaster, Captain Roy Aldrich, to notify Hamer, but he never did so. Aldrich—whom Frank would come to deeply despise—may have acted on his own, but more likely at the behest of Hanson. Unlike Hamer, Aldrich was politically astute, manipulative, and eager to permanently secure a position of power in the Ranger organization. Instead of notifying Hamer, he made the following notation on his service record: "resigned June 19, 1919." It was a flagrant lie.[12]

That very day, preoccupied with his work and unaware that he had "resigned," Hamer sent a detailed report directly to General Harley. After complaining that the penurious state government still had not paid the undertaker who had handled Sergeant Timberlake's funeral, Frank explained, "We had a little killing up the river a few days ago and I have run it down and have fastened the crime on a bunch of Mexicans on the other side but haven't been able to get much assistance over there yet owing to the unsettled conditions existing here." The state's failure to reimburse vehicle expenses rankled him. "General, I feel that I should have some allowance for the use of my car as I use it in my work and haven't been allowed a cent for it for several months and I have run it many hundreds of miles." Though he signed the letter, "I remain as ever your friend," it soon became evident that Harley did not reciprocate those feelings.[13]

Five days later, on June 24, Roy Aldrich wrote to Hamer, advising him for the first time of the new Ranger law and saying that he had been "automatically discharged" on June 19. Hamer was stunned to learn he was no longer a Texas Ranger. He promptly sought assistance from influential friends in the Rio Grande Valley. On June 26, Frank Rabb, a prominent landowner and customs collector in Brownsville, wired Harley, "Sergeant Hamer has made good in this section and would regard it as a personal favor if he was retained in office here." The next day, Caesar Kleberg sent his own telegram: "Understand Frank Hamer has made application reenlistment Ranger service. I feel he should be reappointed. He is making good." Most telling was a detailed letter from Oscar C. Dancy, the prosecuting attorney for Cameron County. Unlike Sheriff Vann, he had a very high opinion of the big Ranger. "I hear with regret that you are contemplating having Mr. Frank Hamer removed from this place," he wrote, unaware that Hamer was no longer a Ranger. "I trust you can reconsider and have him remain. He and I are working together on certain matters of importance. . . . Mr. Hamer is a very efficient officer and he and I work in complete harmony. He has always been more than willing to work with me in the enforcement of the law. . . . [H]e and I understand each other and have the fullest confidence in each other."[14]

General Harley and Captain Hanson were determined to get Hamer out of the service and away from the border. By telegram, Harley advised Rabb that all Ranger commissions had been terminated on June 19, that captains had the right to select their own men, and that no reenlistment application had been received from Hamer. To Dancy, he sent a letter saying the same thing. However, in his response to Kleberg, he asserted that "as you know there is a great deal of opposition in the Legislature to Hamer on account of his conduct up in the Burnet County district. . . . [A]nd under the new law, the Captains have the right to select their own men and submit them for appointment to this office. Up to the present time no Captain has selected Hamer, and we have no authority to make the appointment unless it is requested through some Captain and then we have the right to either accept or reject the selection." Harley's statements were, if not an outright fabrication, at least highly misleading. There was no opposition to Hamer "on account of his conduct up in the Burnet County district." Harley was referring to the testimony in the Canales hearings by Dayton Moses, former district attorney of Burnet County, in which he said that some people in Kimble County had thought Hamer's methods there were "entirely too harsh," while others considered him "a first class officer." Moses had expressed no personal opposition to Hamer. Harley simply used Moses's testimony as an excuse for not reenlisting Hamer.[15]

Frank stayed on with his family in Brownsville, hoping to gain reinstatement. When Kleberg sent him Harley's letter alleging that there was opposition to him in the legislature, Hamer was both perplexed and angry. On July 8, writing from the Miller Hotel, he fired off a long letter of complaint to General Harley. He blasted Captain Hanson, saying "all the Rangers they know what he is. I also feel that I haven't been treated fair by any means. I was not notified as to the reorganization of the ranger service as were the others. My friends here in the Valley were solid for me and were going to send in a petition, the same men who fought far up in the [Canales] investigation, but I told them no. These men are my friends and they know what I have done to stop stealing. They know that through my influence on the other side I have had about eighteen men hung who were thieves and operated on this side.

Mr. Caesar Kleberg sent me the letter you wrote him in which you informed him that my conduct in Burnet Co. had caused some comment in the Legislature. I don't know who made this report as I haven't been in Burnet Co. since I was a small lad. All of these reports should be investigated and I should have a chance to defend myself and that I am going to have and soon. You know General that I turned down several positions on promises that were made to me and I don't think that I am getting a square deal, something I always contend for."[16]

When the Canales hearings started, Frank had been in Brownsville, and he was helping the rurales hunt down bandits in Mexico when they concluded. He was obviously unaware of Moses's testimony, or he would have understood that the complaints had come from Kimble, not Burnet, County. General Harley was then in Chicago, and he answered Hamer a month later. Of Roy Aldrich's role, Harley asserted, "It seems there is some mistake with reference to you not being notified as to the reorganization as Cap. Aldrich informs me that he has written to you two or three times in which he stated that it would be necessary for all applicants to apply through some Captains." Of course, Aldrich had done no such thing. He had indeed written to Hamer on June 6, forwarding his paycheck, but said nothing about his Ranger commission expiring in thirteen days and the need to reapply. Then Aldrich waited until five days after the deadline to finally notify Hamer. As it was, Frank desperately needed his sergeant's pay and would never have ignored timely reenlistment instructions.

In his letter, General Harley defended Hanson and tried to mollify Hamer: "I also wish to disabuse your mind with reference to Capt. Hanson's attitude toward you. He has always been a warm supporter of yours and he and Capt. Caesar Kleberg went to the Governor and made a special plea for your appointment and also made the same to me. Personally I think you are a splendid officer and my friend but sometime we cannot do all we would like to and in this case the reason given in my letter to Kleberg was the only thing that was against you." Harley's statements were plainly untrue, for Hanson was furious with Hamer for disobeying his smuggling order. Governor Hobby himself was unwilling to authorize Frank's reappointment. Hamer heard the death knell for his Ranger career. Like Jose Canales, he had made his own principled stand, bucking powerful forces in Austin, and lost.[17]

Meanwhile, he waited in Brownsville for his final paycheck. His subsistence was hand-to-mouth, and he could not afford the trip back to Snyder until he was paid. He sent several telegrams to Aldrich, pleading with him for his wages, which finally arrived in mid-July. Frank piled Gladys, the children, and their belongings into the touring car and made the long drive back to Snyder. To avoid conflict with his mother-in-law, he took a room at the Manhattan Hotel on the town square instead of staying at the Johnson ranch. Now, Nannie Johnson, just as she had done in Gladys's first marriage, attempted to cause trouble between Frank and Gladys. Nannie also tried to turn Beverly and Trix against him, but little Bev adored Frank and called him "Daddy." In old age, she fondly declared, "Frank Hamer was the best man I ever knew." Trix, on the other hand, was influenced by her grandmother, and just as she had acted coldly toward her own father, now acted the same way toward Frank. When Hamer visited the big ranch house, Nannie was openly hostile to him. Frank did not kowtow to her, and, after one argument, Nannie exclaimed in frustration, "Oh, I wish I were a man for one minute!"

To that, the terse Hamer growled meaningfully, "Believe me, madam, so do I."[18]

Hamer's domestic life had him trapped, something no desperado had ever been able to do. He could not afford to support his family or to buy his own home. He was humiliated that his wife and children were financially dependent on Billy and Nannie Johnson. His hundred-dollar-a-month salary as a Ranger sergeant had been ample, but now he was unemployed, with barely a cent to his name. He was so broke that he was unable to pay a bill from a clothing store in Brownsville; the storekeeper later appealed to the adjutant general for collection. Hamer wrote to his friend Captain Stevens, then stationed in Ysleta, begging for a commission. "Cap'n Cholly" was eager to enlist him, and on August 16 Hamer penned a note to General Harley, saying that Stevens "would like very much to have me enlist in his Co. which I would be very glad to do if it is agreeable to you." Harley, instead of handling the matter himself, turned it over to Captain Hanson. On August 26, Hanson sent Hamer an application form, saying, "Please fill it out carefully and return to me, and I feel sure it will go through O.K."[19]

It was an empty promise. Both Harley and Hanson were determined to keep Hamer out of the service. While Frank languished in Snyder, his application languished in Austin. That summer the state had failed to allocate enough funds for the Rangers' budget, resulting in the men going without paychecks for almost three months. Then, on September 3, Captain Hanson left for Washington, D.C., to act as special investigator for Senator Fall, whose committee was examining the years of violence on the Mexican border in an effort to force U.S. intervention in Mexico. A month later, Harley resigned as adjutant general to take a higher-paying job with an oil company. With Harley and Hanson gone, opposition to Hamer vanished. In November the capable new adjutant general, William D. Cope, approved his application. An ecstatic Hamer was instructed to report to Austin, where, on November 25, Cope enlisted

Frank Hamer, far right, with Texas Rangers and Mexican rurales on the border near El Paso, 1919. Captain Charlie Stevens is center, holding field glasses. *Courtesy of the Texas Ranger Hall of Fame and Museum, Waco, Texas*

him as a private in Company B under Captain Stevens. When Hanson learned of this, he fired off several letters protesting Hamer's appointment, to no avail.[20]

Frank could not have been pleased with his first assignment, a mundane one: to proceed by train to Fort Worth, where an oil boom was underway, and to guard some newly constructed state buildings. A few days later, however, he reported to Ysleta, where Captain Stevens promptly promoted him to sergeant. Hamer was happy to be back on the border, and Stevens was happy to have his help. Stevens reported to General Cope that "smuggling and illicit traffic of liquor is being carried on in a wholesale manner between El Paso, Texas, and the Texas oil fields, namely Ranger, Eastland, and Desdemona and between El Paso and Wichita Falls, Dallas, and Fort Worth." Stevens first ordered Hamer to raid the Franklin Tavern, seven miles east of El Paso. It was a notorious dive and the scene of at least one murder. At two in the morning on December 9, Frank, with Privates Stafford E. Beckett and Arch Miller, barged into the Franklin Tavern, seizing four cases of smuggled Canadian Club whiskey worth $500. They also arrested the tavern keepers and hauled them into federal court, where each was forced to post a $1,000 bond. At three o'clock the next morning, Hamer, again with Beckett and Miller, stopped two Buicks five miles east of El Paso. They arrested one Anglo and two Hispanics and hauled in eighteen five-gallon jugs of Mexican whiskey. Reported Captain Stevens, "During the investigation that followed the arrest of these men they all admitted that they were going to Ranger, Texas, to dispose of the liquor. . . . [I]t is my idea that such immense profits are great inducements to criminals, such as safe blowers, train hold ups, and bank robbers who will flock here to engage in this business."[21]

Captain Stevens had been roundly disliked in the Spanish-speaking community of the Rio Grande Valley for entering homes without warrants and disarming Hispanics. However, in El Paso he enjoyed good relations with the Mexican government. Stevens, who spoke Spanish, crossed the border several times to confer with Mexican officials about the smuggling problem. On December 31, 1919, Stevens and Hamer visited Ciudad Juárez for one such meeting. On another visit, a cameraman came along and took snapshots of Stevens, Hamer, and the rest of the company riding their horses across the Rio Grande and holding a parley with Mexican rurales. One of the images showed Captain Stevens shaking hands on horseback with his Mexican counterpart while Hamer and the other Rangers look on. It was certainly a huge change from the days of the Bandit War.[22]

Just as Stevens had been aggressive in making warrantless searches in the Rio Grande Valley, so too he now had his men aggressively stop and search motorcars for contraband. Unlike his previous searches of homes near the border, the captain was now on solid legal ground. Although the Fourth Amendment prohibits unlawful search and seizure, American law had long recognized the so-called "border search exception," which provides that officers do not need warrants or probable cause to make routine stops and searches along the country's borders. In the early morning hours of December 10, Stevens, with Hamer, Beckett, and Miller, stopped and searched two new Buicks on Val Verde Street near the river. They seized a hundred gallons of Mexican whiskey and arrested three suspects.[23]

On Christmas Eve Sergeant Hamer was in charge of a squad of five Rangers at a roadblock on a bridge five miles east of town. One of them was Antonio "Tony" Apodaca, a twenty-seven-year-old former El Paso deputy sheriff, whose presence illustrated a fact often forgotten today: numerous Hispanics served in the Texas Rangers. Hamer's squad halted a number of automobiles, one of which was driven by a reporter for the *El Paso Herald*. According to that newspaper, the Rangers were courteous: "They explained as soon as the car was stopped that they were officers and wished to see if there was any liquor in the car. On finding none, they said, 'Drive on.'"[24]

That same night another group of motorists claimed a different experience with Hamer's men. Louis Lay, an insurance agent, was driving a touring car, accompanied by his brother Horace; a friend, Paul Atkinson; and two of their wives. Louis Lay gave his version of what happened: "As we approached the five mile bridge, we saw a flash light thrown across the road. I slowed down, threw the car into second, and stopped as soon as I saw three armed men. I saw a revolver stuck in my face and felt a hand at the back of my neck. . . . The man tried to pull me out of my seat over the door. I asked him to hold on and asked him what he wanted. He said he wanted to search the car and kept pulling at me. I asked him to release me and asked him for his authority for searching the car, and if he had a warrant. He said he didn't need a warrant and struck at me with his gun." Lay said that his hand was bruised when he warded off the blow.[25]

Paul Atkinson later said that he leaped out of the backseat "and asked one of the men what he meant by such violence. The only answer I got was a cursing. I asked him who he was and he . . . responded by saying it was none of my damn business. I thought we were held up. I told him we had nothing in the car and I offered him my watch and chain. He . . . struck me over the head with a pistol. Blood gushed from my head and the women began to scream. The blow made an awful sound and my wife thought I was shot and began to scream, 'He's shot, he's shot.'" At that, Horace Lay stepped forward, but one of the Rangers struck him in the face and kicked him five or six times. When the motorists threatened to report the incident to El Paso's mayor, one Ranger retorted, "To hell with the mayor," adding that they "didn't have anything to do with them. We are Rangers." The motorists were allowed to leave. After taking Atkinson to a hospital, they complained to the district attorney, to a state senator, and to the newspapers.[26]

When Captain Stevens investigated the incident, his men claimed that the driver had fallen against his car, cutting his head. Years later, Hamer gave Walter Prescott Webb his version of the affair, which seems to have been more truthful than the motorists' account. Hamer said that the group had approached in a high-powered touring car. When it failed to stop, the Rangers shot out its tires. One of the occupants—Atkinson—wanted to fight, and Hamer slapped him to the ground with his open palm. As a stunned Atkinson struggled to his feet, he reached into his pocket for a handkerchief. Tony Apodaca thought he was going for a gun and struck him over the head with his revolver. Wrote Webb, "Tony made a mistake, but in a good cause. Hamer reported that when he slapped the man down, he struck his head on the running-board of the car." The fact that the *El Paso Herald* reporter found the Rangers to be courteous is a strong indication that the motorists precipitated the incident. Similarly, Hamer's frank admission that he had lied to protect one of his men tends to confirm his version of the affair. And Horace Lay's account that he was struck in the face and repeatedly kicked sounds very much like something Hamer would do to a troublemaker.[27]

The incident created an uproar in El Paso, where misunderstanding of the border-search law was widespread. Even R. B. Rawlins, an El Paso justice of the peace, demonstrated his ignorance of the law when he lambasted the Rangers in the columns of the *El Paso Herald*: "The recent action of the rangers on the lower valley road is an outrage. The law does not give any authority to peace officers to search a car without a warrant." He demanded that the Rangers involved "be removed from office."[28]

Captain Stevens begged for cooperation from the public: "My men are trying to cope with a very trying situation here and we need the help of the people if the law is to be enforced, not their antagonism." He explained that his Rangers "stop many dozens of cars every night in our search for contraband liquor. There is much smuggling of liquor along the border and a lack of cooperation with the officers on the part of many leading people." He also defended his Rangers: "My men are not thugs and brutes. I know them and I am in close touch with them all the time." In response to charges that his men drove their autos too fast, Stevens said that they "have to drive fast to overtake bootleggers. . . . Cars full of liquor often escape us by outrunning us. The occupants of the car often throw bottles of liquor out onto the pavement when we start after them, in the hope that the glass will cut our tires."[29]

Complaints about Stevens's company flooded into the governor's office. On December 30, General Cope wired Stevens, "You are directed to immediately suspend from the force all rangers implicated in the detention and search of the Lay party Christmas night pending investigation. You will suspend all operation in the vicinity of El Paso until further directed."

Assistant Adjutant General H. C. Smith promptly entrained for El Paso to investigate. On January 2, 1920, he conducted an informal hearing in the office of the district attorney, assisted by the district judge and three El Paso legislators. Several witnesses accused the Rangers of "overstepping their authority and conducting themselves in a manner unbecoming state officers." Captain Stevens insisted that his men had the right to stop and search vehicles that they suspected were used in smuggling. As a result of the hearing, Governor Hobby telegrammed Sheriff Seth Orndorff, saying that he had received many complaints of illegal liquor being brought through El Paso to the Texas oil fields but that he would withdraw the Rangers if the sheriff could control smuggling. Orndorff responded that it was "best that the Rangers be removed from the county at present." Hobby then ordered Captain Stevens and his company out of El Paso. As General Cope explained, "If the people of El Paso County do not want the Rangers, we will not force the Rangers upon them. We are short of men and can readily use the company . . . in other sections of the state." It was the second time Stevens and his company had been removed from the border. The captain was bitter and disappointed.[30]

Frank Hamer's sojourn in El Paso had lasted but three weeks. Now Stevens's company was ordered to the oil fields near Burkburnett, on the Red River, nine miles north of Wichita Falls. Black gold had been discovered there in 1912, and by 1918 twenty thousand people had flocked to the oil fields, events later dramatized in the popular 1940 film *Boom Town,* starring Spencer Tracy and Clark Gable. Texas and Oklahoma had long disputed their true boundary along the Red River. Oklahoma officials argued that the Louisiana Purchase and later treaties provided that its territory extended to the south bank, or Texas side, of the river, while Texans contended that the border was in midstream. The dispute became critical when the oil fields expanded north from Burkburnett to the Red River. Wells were drilled along the Texas bank, and even in the river itself. By January 1920 the tract along the river, known as the Burk Divide, was valued at $100 million. Not only did a great deal of private litigation take place, but the state of Oklahoma filed suit against the state of Texas in the U.S. Supreme Court. An Oklahoma court placed the wells of the Burk Divide in the hands of a receiver, thus depriving the Texas oil companies of their revenue.

Oklahoma deputy sheriffs, reinforced by armed guards, crossed the river and took possession of the oil wells.

Governor Hobby, heavily influenced by oil interests, ordered the Rangers in. Ostensibly, their job was to prevent violence between the two sides. On January 20, 1920, Hobby sent fifteen Rangers under Captains Joe Brooks and William M. Ryan to Wichita Falls. They were soon joined by Adjutant General Cope, along with Captain Stevens, Frank Hamer, and the rest of Company B. On January 24, after representatives from Texas and Oklahoma were unable to settle the dispute, the entire force of twenty-eight well-armed Rangers left Wichita Falls in an automobile convoy. They pitched tents and set up their camp on a bluff overlooking the Red River. The Rangers' encampment was squarely on land claimed by both states. Armed Oklahomans were still in possession of the Burk Divide wells. Texas officials claimed that the Rangers were present only for "suppressing gambling, bootlegging, and other vice." However, on January 26, Cope and a party of Rangers, including Hamer and Private Tom Hickman, armed with an injunction from a Texas judge, seized the Burk Divide wells. Explained John Hornsby, who had been appointed receiver by the Texas court, "Waiting a favorable time, when some of the Oklahoma guard was relieved, Hamer and Hickman slipped in, seized it, and refused to be dislodged." According to Hornsby, "They found twenty Oklahoma guardsmen, armed to the teeth, holding it. Hamer decided on strategy. He slipped in while the guardsmen were away, seized the land and defied the guards to oust him. The guards retreated." As a result of the Rangers' actions, the disputed oil was promptly marketed in Texas, which received a one-eighth share royalty.[31]

Two days later, in response to a telegram from Sheriff Ed Clarkson, Hamer and Arch Miller were dispatched to Paris, Texas, 180 miles to the east. "Whitecappers," probably members of the Ku Klux Klan, had been threatening local blacks and ordering them to move out of Lamar County. By the time Hamer arrived in Paris, he was extremely ill, probably a relapse of the Spanish flu. When notified of Hamer's condition by Sheriff Clarkson, the adjutant general wired him to "see that Mr. Hamer receives the best of attention." The big Ranger was brought to St. Joseph's

Infirmary, where he stayed for a week. Sergeant Charlie Blackwell of Headquarters Company came from Austin to take charge of the investigation. From his hospital bed, Frank told Blackwell that Sheriff Clarkson was "playing politics" by sending the Rangers after the suspects, whose identities were known to the sheriff. Hamer believed that Clarkson lacked the political will to tackle the whitecappers himself. Blackwell reported to General Cope that he would not have any difficulty bringing in the suspects.[32]

Frank recovered quickly and returned to the Burk Divide. By this time an attorney for the Oklahoma claimants had criticized Hamer's actions there, charging that "the Texas Rangers successfully carried out a coup d'etat . . . by suddenly rushing into the bed of Red River armed with rifles and revolvers and overpowering the Burk Divide guards, seized the property. The Rangers were in boots and big hats. There were twenty Rangers; five went to each well." According to Captain Stevens, General Cope now ordered him to take over from the other captains and "repel, by force and arms, any attempt of the Oklahoma claimants to regain possession." Stevens was convinced that the Rangers were being used not as lawmen but as partisans in the dispute. Already smarting from his removal from El Paso, and long believing that Governor Hobby was in the pocket of oil interests, Stevens concluded that the orders were unlawful. He abruptly resigned on February 3, writing to Hobby, "I would not take command of an armed band of men, having no authority from any Court or otherwise practically engaged in a Civil War with another State, ignoring its laws and courts." He declared that he could not "reconcile my duty as an officer with the Adjutant General's conception of his authority over me" and insisted, "I would not be a lawbreaker simply to protect private claimants of valuable oil holdings." Three of his men also resigned, and a furious Hobby disbanded his entire company. Stevens quickly landed on his feet; the following month, he took a higher-paying job as San Antonio agent with the newly created U.S. Prohibition Unit. Sergeant Hamer was placed in temporary command of a new Company B.[33]

Captain Stevens was correct. His orders to hold the oil field—Texas court injunction or no—were entirely unlawful. It did not require a

Frank Hamer, second from left, and other Rangers on the Red River bridge near Burkburnett, Texas, during the boundary dispute with Oklahoma in 1920. *Courtesy of the Texas Ranger Hall of Fame and Museum, Waco, Texas*

Harvard law degree to understand that a state judge had no jurisdiction to determine a boundary dispute between two states. Only the U.S. Supreme Court could do that. Texas officials acted both out of a desire for the oil profits and in blind adherence to the doctrine of state's rights. Oklahoma's governor, on the other hand, acted with prudence, refusing demands that he send in National Guard troops and putting his faith in the U.S. Supreme Court. General Cope soon withdrew most of the Rangers, including Hamer, leaving six men to guard the disputed wells under Private—and later Captain—Tom Hickman. Then, on March 11, a federal judge in Oklahoma ruled that the state boundary was on the south bank of the Red River. Newspapers reported that deputy U.S. marshals would enforce the order and predicted "a serious clash between the Texas and Oklahoma authorities."[34]

The next day a deputy U.S. marshal served the court order on the Rangers. Governor Hobby foolishly elected to defy the federal judge. On March 16 General Cope, after consulting with Hobby, ordered that Captain Joe Brooks, Sergeant Hamer, and a third Ranger proceed to the Burk Divide to reinforce the Ranger detachment there. Cope ordered them to "prevent the dispossession of any receiver appointed by [the Texas] court and otherwise maintain the sovereignty of the State.... Captain Brooks will properly preserve peace and order, enforce the laws of Texas, protect the lives and property of citizens from unlawful depredations by outside armed bands, and will disarm every individual found armed who is not a duly qualified or acting Peace Officer under the laws of Texas." Cope's meaning was clear: he was ordering the Rangers to arrest Oklahoma deputy sheriffs, who were the only armed Oklahomans in the Burk Divide.[35]

Just as the Texas Rangers had no authority to arrest Oklahoma deputy sheriffs, they could not legally oppose a deputy U.S. marshal who was enforcing a federal order. That legal doctrine had long been established. In 1889, Dave Neagle, a noted gunfighter and former chief of police of Tombstone, Arizona, while acting as bodyguard for U.S. Supreme Court Justice Stephen J. Field, shot and killed Judge David S. Terry after Terry assaulted Justice Field. Neagle was charged in a California state court with murder, but in a famous constitutional decision that greatly expanded the scope of federal authority, the U.S. Supreme Court ruled that the state of California could not prosecute a federal officer for an act performed in the line of duty. Under this precedent, the Texas Rangers could not interfere with a deputy U.S. marshal.[36]

Hamer's thoughts on receiving Cope's order are not recorded, but he could not have been happy. Foremost in his mind was the resignation of his friend, Captain Stevens, after refusing to follow an identical command. On the other hand, another friend, Walter Prescott Webb, later noted approvingly that Hamer "assisted in defending the rights of Texas in the contest with Oklahoma over the Red River boundary." Hamer obeyed General Cope, while Captain Brooks blustered to journalists, "We are seeking no trouble, but we will execute our orders to the limit." Frank and the other Rangers made camp in tents next to the Burk Divide's number one well, which was pumping five hundred barrels of oil a day. Nearby, armed guards employed by the Texas oil companies erected barbed wire fences and prepared to defend the wells from a supposed invasion by Oklahoma forces—which never materialized. Had Captain Brooks followed the governor's order "to the limit," he would have arrested the armed Texas guards. While a federal judge in Oklahoma held hearings to determine whether to hold the Rangers in contempt of court, Governor Hobby had Cope send even more Rangers back to the Burk Divide. Then, on April 1, the U.S. Supreme Court abruptly put a stop to the Texans' saber rattling by issuing an injunction that stopped Texas from exerting control over the disputed wells. In the end, the Supreme Court came down firmly on the side of Oklahoma, ruling in 1921 that the correct boundary was the south bank of the Red River.[37]

Hamer and the other Rangers left the Burk Divide oil fields in mid-April 1920. The Rangers' involvement in the border dispute was yet another illustration of Governor Hobby's use of the force as a political tool. Frank began to recognize that true professionalism could not be achieved until the Rangers were immunized from politics. Hamer, probably influenced by Captain Stevens, was now considering leaving the Rangers and following his old commander into the U.S. Prohibition Unit. This move would result in one of the most violent chapters of Frank Hamer's life.

II

HELL PASO

On January 16, 1920, the Volstead Act took effect. It made the manufacture or sale of alcoholic beverages a federal crime. Even before that, in 1918, Texans had voted to outlaw liquor statewide, but the statute was set aside by a state appellate court, which ruled that it conflicted with the local-option law. The Volstead Act provided stiff sentences for violators: for selling liquor, a thousand-dollar fine and up to a year in prison; for possessing liquor, the same fine and six months' imprisonment. A second offense could result in a $2,000 fine and five years in prison. Texas passed its own prohibition law, the Dean Act, which provided even tougher penalties. But as the public would quickly find out, Prohibition didn't work. It made liquor more appealing and helped increase its social acceptance among both men and women. People clustered in speakeasies to imbibe illegal drinks, leading to disrespect for the law and the growth of organized crime. Before Prohibition, respectable women did not drink, smoke, or wear provocative clothing. After Prohibition, however, these customs became socially acceptable, as young, cigarette-puffing, short-skirted "flappers" and "jazz babies" ushered in the Roaring Twenties.

Congress created the Prohibition Unit to enforce the new law. In Texas, the director was Clifford G. Beckham, a Fort Worth lawyer whom Hamer respected immensely. The Texas unit had four districts, with headquarters in Fort Worth, San Antonio, Houston, and El Paso. Each district was commanded by a chief agent, under whom were ten federal Prohibition agents. Legislators were under no illusion that such a small force could ban booze in Texas. Instead, agents were expected to encourage and assist local lawmen in enforcing Prohibition. Frank Hamer was not a drinking man, and when he was offered a position as a federal Prohibition agent, he had little compunction about accepting it. The salary was as much as $2,000 a year, well above his sergeant's pay. On May 11, 1920, Hamer resigned from the Rangers and began work in San Antonio as a Prohibition officer, popularly known as a "prohi" or "dry agent."[1]

Just three days later, in Austin, Frank Hamer announced his presence with a bang. During the war, a popular confectionary and soft drink parlor, the Liberty Corner, had opened on the corner of Thirty-fourth and Guadalupe Streets. The owner, Sidney Warren, was known for dispensing lubricants considerably stronger than Coca-Cola, and his patrons included soldiers from Camp Mabry and students from the University of Texas. A warrant was issued, and Hamer teamed up with his old captain, the U.S. marshal John H. Rogers, to serve it. On the afternoon of May 14, Hamer, Rogers, and several deputy U.S. marshals stepped inside the Liberty Corner. According to the *Austin American*, "the government officers were not satisfied with a little 'snort,' but called for 'everything on the bar.'" Warren, unaware they were lawmen, poured bottles of "whiskey, Jamaica ginger, forty rod, chain lightning, and other popular brands of bravo." When the officers placed Warren and his wife under arrest, patrons quickly slunk out of the bar. At that point, an automobile pulled up to the curb, and a prominent Austinite alighted and called out, "Give me two bottles." Then, seeing Warren in handcuffs, he gulped, "Of, oh, soda water." Sid Warren was fined $250 and sentenced to three months in jail.[2]

Hamer's supervisor in San Antonio was chief Prohibition agent Thomas R. Stevic. He was a thirty-three-year-old former army captain who had seen service in France during the war. Strong political connections got him the job: his uncle was Dr. Charles E. Sawyer, President

Warren G. Harding's close friend and personal physician. Stevic was no lawman, and Frank had little respect for him. Unknown to Hamer was the fact that Stevic was on the payroll of the Black Hand in Chicago. A precursor of the Mafia, the Black Hand was a criminal syndicate in New York, Chicago, and other cities with large Italian populations. Since the 1880s it had specialized in extortion and kidnapping. With the advent of Prohibition, the Black Hand increasingly turned to bootlegging. Stevic's position allowed him to ignore moonshining and smuggling and to thus protect the activities of organized crime. In July 1920 Stevic—a newcomer to Texas—foolishly approached Hamer and offered to let him in on the action. Frank promptly notified the Department of Justice—presumably Captain Rogers—of Stevic's overtures. Hamer was authorized to play along and collect evidence against Stevic.

Before long, Stevic and his associates became suspicious of Hamer. On August 9, 1920, on a pretext, Stevic instructed Frank to drive him out in the country. As they bumped along an isolated dusty road, Hamer became convinced that Stevic "was trying to muster the courage to kill." Frank stared coldly into Stevic's eyes, as if daring him to try. Nervous and sweating profusely, Stevic finally whispered hoarsely, "Let's go on back to town."

Arriving back at headquarters, Hamer told him, "Well, it's all up now. I've got enough evidence to put you away, and I guess I'd better do it before you get any other foolish notions."

Stevic was jailed and charged with "conspiring to import, transport, and sell liquor." Three local members of the gang, J. O. Merchant, V. S. Caldwell, and Polk C. Neal, were also picked up and charged with violating the Volstead Act. The four were accused of traveling to Laredo a month earlier to buy smuggled liquor on the border. In December, based in part on Hamer's evidence, all four of them were indicted by a U.S. grand jury. Stevic claimed that he was the victim of a frame-up and that two Prohibition agents had planted liquor in his car. But in January 1921 he pled guilty and was sentenced to a fifty-dollar fine and one year and a day in federal prison in Leavenworth, Kansas. Stevic's replacement was Hamer's friend Charlie Stevens.[3]

Thomas R. Stevic, the chief prohibition agent in San Antonio, as he looked upon entering Leavenworth prison in 1921. *Author's collection*

Much to Hamer's disgust, Stevic served only two months before a federal judge freed him on grounds that his grand jury indictments were defective: he had been charged with a misdemeanor but convicted of a felony. San Antonio authorities were ignorant of this development until they read a Kansas newspaper story two weeks after Stevic was released from Leavenworth. Federal prosecutors insisted that there were no errors in the indictments and pointed the finger of suspicion at Stevic's uncle, Dr. Charles Sawyer. Interviewed by reporters, Sawyer vehemently denied using his influence with President Harding to get Stevic released. He admitted that Stevic was his wife's nephew, saying rather unconvincingly, "I hardly know the boy, but I understand that he had a good army record and his mother insists that his conviction was on circumstantial evidence. I don't know anything much about the case." Dr. Sawyer himself received national notoriety two years later, when he was accused of providing negligent medical care resulting in the death of President Harding. Thomas Stevic was never brought back to San Antonio for retrial, but that was not the last heard of him. In 1923 officers in Chicago arrested him for taking a cabin cruiser out of state and failing to pay for it. Stevic admitted to police that he used the boat to smuggle liquor from Canada.[4]

The arrest of Thomas Stevic, and rumors of widespread bribery in the Prohibition Unit, resulted in a shakeup. James Shevlin, the respected chief Prohibition agent for the state of New York, was appointed to take charge of the newly organized Border Department, consisting of Texas, Oklahoma, New Mexico, and Arizona. His headquarters were moved to El Paso, the hot spot of smuggling operations. Shevlin brought in agents from the East and Midwest who were honest but inexperienced. Smuggling whiskey and tequila had long been a problem on the border, but now that alcohol was banned in the United States, much bigger profits could be made in Mexican liquor. Tequila and whiskey could be bought for two to three dollars a gallon in Mexico and sold in Texas for as much as ten dollars a quart. The result was a huge increase in smuggling, while the mounted tequileros—whom the Rangers called "horsebackers" to distinguish them from motorized smugglers—became ever more violent in efforts to protect their contraband.[5]

During the latter part of 1919, in anticipation of the Prohibition Act, Mexican smugglers in Juárez and El Paso grew aggressive. Some—perhaps most—were former members of Villa's army, rendered jobless after his final defeat in the Third Battle of Juárez in June 1919. In August, two smugglers were shot dead in a fight with American troops; their bodies were left where they fell across the border. In November, two El Paso deputy sheriffs exchanged fifty shots with a band of whiskey runners in East El Paso. A month later, one smuggler and a U. S. Army provost guard were slain in an hour-long gun battle on the international line. In 1920 the violence continued, with numerous shootouts on the border between Mexican smugglers and U.S. soldiers and lawmen.[6]

The Prohibition Unit sorely needed a man of Hamer's abilities in El Paso, and by January 1921 he was in the border city with fifteen other Prohibition agents, who were responsible for patrolling fifty miles of the Rio Grande. El Paso, the gateway from Mexico to the American Southwest, was a prosperous, important center for commerce that was served by multiple railroads. In 1920 it was home to 77,000 people, a majority Spanish-speaking, with a modern downtown of multistory buildings surrounded by sprawling barrios of cheap wood frame and adobe homes. El Paso was the biggest city in all of West Texas, New Mexico, and Arizona. It also had, next to San Antonio, the largest Mexican population of any city in the United States. Across the Rio Grande was its sister city, Ciudad Juárez, an impoverished, war-ravaged community of about twenty thousand. Prohibition was especially un-popular in El Paso, as one newspaperman pointed out: "At nearly all taxicab stands or second rate hotels liquor of a fair grade is sold, and also is for sale at hundreds of small residences to individuals who can give references." El Paso held a reputation as one of the wildest towns on the border. Hamer later recalled, "El Paso was one of the toughest towns I'd ever been in. There was a gunfight for 236 straight nights."[7]

El Paso had long been home to legions of western gunfighters, out-laws, and lawmen, whose exploits gave the town its well-deserved nick-name, Hell Paso. The El Paso Salt War of 1877 pitted local Mexicans against Texas Rangers and a band of American gunfighters from New Mexico. After the arrival of the railroad in 1881, Dallas Stoudenmire was hired as city marshal to ride herd on rowdy patrons of the dance halls, gambling parlors, saloons, and bordellos. Stoudenmire was victor of the 1881 "Four Dead in Five Seconds" gunfight, in which he shot to death three men, one an innocent bystander. The resulting feud led to Stoudenmire's bloody demise in a shootout the following year. He was succeeded as city marshal by the noted Texas Ranger James B. Gillett, who avoided Stoudenmire's propensity for killing. During the 1890s, El Paso hosted such noted shootists as John Wesley Hardin, John Selman, George Scarborough, Jeff Milton, Pat Garrett, George Herold, and Manning Clements. Only two of them—Milton and Herold—died of natural causes. In 1895 John Selman gunned down Wes Hardin; Sel-man, in turn, was killed by George Scarborough a year later. Manning Clements and Pat Garrett, the slayer of Billy the Kid, were assassinated in separate shootings in 1908.

A decade later, El Paso remained a perilous place for lawmen. The most dangerous spot was Cordova Island, a chamisal-choked, 385-acre tract situated on a large horseshoe bend of the Rio Grande, a mile south of downtown. In 1899, to control flooding, the U.S. and Mexican governments had jointly cut a channel across the south end of the horseshoe, diverting the river through it. The result was a cut-off section of land, which was surrounded by dry riverbed on the north and located entirely in Mexico. Smugglers made their headquarters in adobe houses on Cordova Island and dug trenches along the north end of the island for protection. They used the adobes to store liquor and the trenches to bring it close to the boundary. Nearby was a dirt county road, and the contraband would be carried across the riverbed and loaded onto automobiles for transport into El Paso.

Soon after Hamer arrived in El Paso, during the early morning hours of January 9, 1921, he and several fellow dry agents were in a motorcar, guarding the border at Cordova Island. They spotted two shadowy figures cross over and ordered them to halt. The pair jumped into a waiting automobile, then opened fire on the lawmen. The smugglers' high-powered vehicle roared off at great speed, with Hamer and the rest in pursuit. A looping, twisting chase led north into the center of the city. As one newspaper reported, "Toward El Paso at a 60-mile rate the cars raced. They sped around corners on two wheels." When the smugglers' auto approached the intersection of Copia Street and Alameda Avenue, Hamer and the other agents opened fire. Four shots pierced its gas tank, and one hit the left front wheel, shattering the spokes. The wheel exploded in shards of wood and rubber, and the motorcar crashed into the curbstone sidewalk. As the occupants fled, agents recognized one of them as Manuel Osollo, a taxi driver and suspected smuggler. The lawmen recovered ninety quarts of tequila from the vehicle. They picked up Osollo a few hours later and jailed him on federal smuggling charges.[8]

Six weeks later, on February 25, 1921, Hamer was in the U.S. Customs House when he received news of a desperate battle with horsebackers. Three customs inspectors led by Joe Davenport, a former Ranger, were hiding in the brush and watching the border in Anapra, New Mexico, seven miles west of El Paso. They spotted a caravan of six mounted men, followed by a train of packhorses, approaching their position. Two hundred yards behind the riders was another pack train loaded with contraband liquor and led by a single horseman. Davenport waited for them to close within twenty feet. "I called to them to halt," he later said, "and had no sooner done so than there was a volley from the smugglers."

One of the first bullets struck Davenport, who crumpled to the ground. He still managed to get his rifle into action and, with his companions, sent a withering fire at the gang. The tequileros tried to stampede the burro train back into Mexico but were forced to flee for their lives, abandoning animals and cargo. News of the gunfight was telephoned to the Customs House in El Paso, and soon Hamer, Inspector J. D. Reeder, and several other officers raced to the scene. The smugglers were long gone, but Hamer and the rest confiscated 407 quarts of tequila, twenty-two pints of whiskey, and all the pack animals. They brought Joe Davenport into El Paso, where he recovered from his wound.[9]

A week later, on the morning of March 2, a farmer and an El Paso policeman were fired on at a range of two hundred yards by a pair of Mexicans on Cordova Island. The desperadoes had hidden liquor in the brush and were trying to protect it. While the police officer returned fire, the farmer raced for help. Hamer and fellow Prohibition agent Ernest W. Walker jumped into an automobile and rushed to the scene. They were joined by fellow agents Stafford E. Beckett and Charles A. "Arch" Wood. The lawmen began searching the brush when they suddenly encountered an armed band of twenty-five tequileros, who were headed toward the booze cache. As the Mexicans opened up with rifles, Hamer and Walker darted for cover, shooting as they ran. A steel-jacketed round slammed into Walker's abdomen, and he fell, desperately wounded. Hamer kept up a hot fire with his rifle, driving the smugglers back onto Cordova Island, where they took cover in the trenches and adobe houses. Soon a dozen reinforcements arrived from El Paso—soldiers, policemen, and Prohibition agents—and engaged in a raging two-hour gun battle with the fortified gang in which more than a thousand rounds were fired. Unknown to the Americans, the desperadoes managed to slip away, and the officers' constant firing finally prompted a Mexican official to cross the border and demand that they stop shooting.

Walker, in critical condition, was brought to a hospital. The next day, Hamer and other officers returned to the scene to search for a pistol that the wounded officer had dropped in the fight. As they rummaged through the brush, smugglers on the island again opened fire, and another pitched battle raged until the Mexicans disappeared into the trenches and the chamisal. Two days later, Ernest Walker died of his wounds. It was the second time in Frank's career that a fellow lawman had been mortally wounded just a few feet from him. Hamer's boss, James Shevlin, then crossed into Ciudad Juárez to meet with Rafael Davila, chief of the Mexican border guards. Davila agreed to work more closely with the American forces and promised to tear down the adobe houses and fill in the trenches on Cordova Island. To reporters, Shevlin said that "the smugglers are more desperate now than they have been. . . . [T]hey go in bands of fifteen to twenty-five instead of two and three as formerly . . . and are heavily armed and ready to fight any time rather than sacrifice their contraband."[10]

Less than three weeks later, on March 22, Prohibition Agents Arch Wood and Stafford Beckett, Frank's friend and former Ranger, were slain in a violent gun battle with bootleggers at a ranch five miles east of El Paso. A. L. Raithel, a lanky, six-foot-four federal narcotics agent who had been recently assigned to El Paso, recalled that Hamer was flabbergasted that so many officers had been shot in and near El Paso. "Most of the agents were from the East and the Midwest," Raithel said. "They were green to the border. This was like sending banty roosters after hen-killing coyotes." He recalled that Hamer met with the federal officers and demanded, "What are you people doing to lose so many men?"

"Well, Frank," answered Raithel, "We go to the river when we hear that smugglers are coming over. We stake out in the brush. When they come across, we stand up and holler, 'Manos arriba!' ['Hands up!'] But they always start shooting. And then we start shooting. And it seems one or two of our boys always end up dead."

Hamer shook his head. "All wrong. I'll show you how it's done."

One night, Frank led a posse to the river. Its members were Raithel and two other Prohibition agents, one of whom was Elmer B. McClure, a former Ranger and brother-in-law of the murdered Ernest Walker. They took up a position on a sand dune overlooking the dry streambed.

By the light of a yellow moon, they spotted six smugglers, guns in hand and liquor cases on their shoulders as they crossed over.

According to Raithel, Hamer whispered, "Don't do anything until I give the word. When I give the word, do exactly as I do."

The moment the smugglers reached the U.S. side, Hamer cried out, "OK!"

At the same time, he opened up a barrage with his Remington .25 and was promptly joined by McClure. "I got in just one shot," recalled Raithel, who said that another of the possemen "didn't get a shot at all. It was Hamer and McClure's party. All six of the smugglers were dead."

As the posse stepped forward, Hamer toed the smugglers' bodies with his boot. Then, looking squarely at the young agents, he said, "Now holler 'Manos arriba' at these sons of bitches and see how many of them shoot you."[11]

Texas newspapers did not report a gunfight such as the one Raithel described. However, as one El Paso newspaperman wrote that spring, "A score of minor engagements have been fought here recently between officers and smugglers, but they are not always reported, especially if nobody is hurt or no liquor is captured." Years later, Texas Ranger "Lone Wolf" Gonzaullas told his biographer about this gunfight and said that Hamer and McClure had killed six or seven Mexican desperadoes. If the shooting took place on Cordova Island, that was Mexican territory, and the lawmen may have been loath to report it. Raithel's claim that Frank ordered the posse to shoot first rings true. That is exactly what he had proposed to Sheriff Vann before the Los Tomates shootout, when his recommendation went unheeded and his friend, Sergeant Timberlake, had been slain. However unlawful by modern standards, Frank was taking no more chances with desperadoes. And this gunfight was the beginning of a strong friendship between Hamer and McClure.[12]

Years later, Frank recalled yet another shooting scrape in El Paso. He was on foot and attempted to stop an auto driven by Clarence and Walter Willmering, two notorious bootleggers from Amarillo. When they tried to run him down, Frank shot through their windshield, wounding one of the brothers. When Hamer told the story to his friend,

Elmer B. McClure in 1922. He took part in Hamer's deadly ambush of Mexican smugglers near El Paso in 1921. Fourteen years later, their friendship would profoundly affect Hamer's career. *Travis Hamer personal collection*

historian J. Evetts Haley, he could not recall which brother he had shot.[13]

Hamer's instincts of self-preservation, though sometimes cold-blooded and of questionable legality, were nonetheless sorely needed in El Paso. On the night of April 30, 1921, Prohibition agents John Watson and W. B. Holzman were approaching the New Mexico–Texas line on their way to El Paso when they stopped to help people in a stalled motorcar. It was filled with Mexican smugglers and a load of liquor. A gun battle broke out, leaving Watson mortally wounded and Holzman with a bullet in the arm. Then, on June 13, Captain Harry Phoenix and another officer, both of the El Paso police force, stopped to question two suspicious Mexicans, who drew pistols and opened fire. Phoenix died with a bullet in the head while his fellow policeman was badly wounded. Captain Phoenix was the fifth lawman slain in the El Paso area in less than four months. Every one of these killings was a direct result of Prohibition, showing plainly the disrespect for law that the act had generated as well as the utter futility of the ban on liquor.[14]

Hamer, in his spare time, quietly investigated the schemes of Senator Fall and Captain Hanson. The senator's attempts to use Pancho Villa had been widely reported in the press. Frank's murdered friend Stafford Beckett had obtained a copy of a check from Pancho Villa to Fall. Hamer believed that it was a payment for Fall's help in assisting Villa, one part of Fall's efforts to compel U.S. intervention in Mexico. Hamer followed up on widespread rumors in El Paso that Villa's agent, J. Todd McClammy, a notorious gun runner and associate of Fall, had helped organize bloody raids on Glenn Springs and Boquillas, Texas, in May 1916. There, Villa forces had reprised their assault on Columbus, New Mexico, by attacking the two settlements and killing four Americans. Hamer was not shy about making public his charges against Fall. His claims were investigated by FBI agents during the height of the Teapot Dome scandal in 1925. Although the case was not pursued, Fall was famously convicted of taking a $100,000 bribe when he was secretary of the interior, and he was sent to prison in 1929.[15]

In May 1921 Hamer was reassigned to Austin and promoted as chief Prohibition agent for the district surrounding the state capitol. This was to be a permanent assignment with a higher salary, and for the first time in his life Frank could afford to purchase his own home. In June he moved Gladys and the children from Snyder to Austin. For three months, they lived in a hotel while searching for a house to buy or rent. Finally, the Hamers bought a new home at 1007 Riverside Drive, located in Travis Heights, south of downtown and across the Colorado River. In keeping with Frank's character, it was a modest, single-story, sixteen-hundred-square-foot bungalow on a bluff overlooking the river. Years later, an interviewer of Gladys observed that, "At that time, Travis Heights consisted of a few scattered houses, and the Hamers thought they were living practically in the country." The house was shaded by huge trees. Fifteen steps up a stairway from the street led to a front veranda. Behind the house was a small garden, a dog run, and two board-and-batten garages. For the first time, Frank had a domestic life, far from the gunsmoke on the border. He could come home after work and spend time with Gladys and the children without Nannie's meddling influence. Hamer was immensely proud of his new home and would live there until his death.[16]

On May 28, 1921, Hamer led the biggest liquor raid in central Texas since the start of Prohibition. Frank's posse, consisting of a fellow agent and four Texas Rangers, went to Thorndale, fifty miles northeast of Austin. On two farms outside town, they seized eight whiskey stills, several hundred gallons of corn mash, and large amounts of sugar and cornmeal. Mash was corn that had fermented enough to be distilled into liquor. Corn liquor was a favorite of bootleggers because it was so easy to brew. All they needed was a large supply of corn, a boiler, a gas stove, and a coil of tubing. Hamer and his men jailed the culprits, a group of moonshining farmers. On July 20, Hamer and a local sheriff made a number of raids near Taylor, just west of Thorndale. On one farm, they seized a still and 125 gallons of mash and arrested its operator; nearby, they caught two more moonshiners and confiscated a supply of wine and corn whiskey.[17]

One night in July, Hamer raided a booze party in the brush hosted by a politically connected Austinite, George Nunelee. As an Austin newspaper reported, "George didn't know Frank very well and he threatened to use his influence on the job that Frank was holding. Somehow the threats didn't scare the intruder. . . . He offered to pass the man named Frank Hamer a few plunks and let it go at that, but a few plunks didn't seem to interest the officer; he then raised his ante to one thousand plunks, and then the officer made him shut up, they say he does that way sometimes. George shut up, they say he snapped his mouth together so hard he loosened three molars and one bicuspid." Hamer brought Nunelee in, but the bootlegger's connections resulted in his case never coming to trial.[18]

Frank never shied from arresting those with political pull. A month later, on August 25, 1921, an Austin motorcycle officer pursued and stopped a vehicle driven by two state legislators, Thomas Brinkley and Homer Hendricks, and found a jug of liquor inside. The pair were turned over to Hamer, who charged them both with transporting and possessing illegal alcohol. Frank also confiscated their auto. The same week, in a series of raids around New Braunfels, Hamer and his men seized 362 gallons of wine and other liquors, making six arrests. Frank personally collared Ed Moeller, city marshal of New Braunfels, for bootlegging. Commented the Austin *American,* "Since Mr. Hamer's appointment as chief prohibition officer with headquarters in Austin, he has become well known for the large number of raids and arrests which he has made in the enforcement of the Federal prohibition laws."[19]

In January of that year a new governor, Pat Neff, had taken office. Unlike most Texans, he did not hunt, fish, play cards, smoke, or drink. A Waco lawyer and the son of a Texas Ranger, he had been active in fraternal and religious groups. He was a progressive Democrat and a strong supporter of Prohibition. Many saw him as a crusading moralist, but most of his progressive reforms were successfully resisted by the legislature. Neff believed in strong law enforcement and a professional Ranger force; he demanded the resignation of any Ranger who drank or gambled. Hamer's friends immediately began lobbying the governor for his appointment as a captain. Most prominent among them was John H. Rogers. Frank's old commander wrote to Neff, "I feel that I am able to give you first-hand information about Mr. Hamer, having enlisted him myself in the Ranger service about fifteen years ago when he was a mere lad. It was interesting to note with what rapidity he developed in the work, soon coming to the front as a shrewd, courageous officer, and for a number of years now he has been recognized as one of the most courageous and energetic officers in Texas. . . . He is sober and dependable and I consider him trustworthy in every way. Should you appoint him I can assure you that the law violators in the territory assigned him would either have to amend their way, leave the country, or go to the penitentiary, as a criminal cannot ply his vocation in the same section where Hamer resides."[20]

But Frank had little political pull. He could rely only on his record, and his application gathered dust. In February Governor Neff reorganized the Rangers into one headquarters company and four line companies, with a total of seventy-five men. In August, however, Neff's opponents in the legislature cut funding for the Rangers by $50,000 and reduced the force to fifty. Captain Aaron W. Cunningham, a former sheriff who had been appointed only six months earlier and placed in charge of Company C in Del Rio, soon came under fire. A local legislator complained that Cunningham's men "were 'jelly beans' and not real law enforcing officers." In the slang of that era, a "jelly bean" was a dandy or a fop. When Cunningham made it known that he would resign at the end of August, Governor Neff approached Hamer and offered him a captaincy in the Rangers. This was a chance to rejoin his old company and to follow in the footsteps of Captain Rogers, and he jumped at the offer.[21]

At the end of August 1921, he tendered his resignation as chief Prohibition officer. His decision to rejoin the Rangers received much favorable comment in the newspapers. "Ranger Captain Hamer is perhaps one of the best known officers in Texas," commented the *Austin American*. "Mr. Hamer is now 37 years old and has been in continuous service as an officer of the law for the last sixteen years." When asked by a reporter, the taciturn Hamer said that he was happy to take command of "my old bunch." He added, "Of course, in a way, I hate to leave Austin, but I will sure be glad to throw my leg over a horse again and to see some real canyons."[22]

Frank's life had made a complete turnaround. Exactly two years earlier he had begged to be commissioned a private. Now, a new governor appointed him a captain. By this time Hamer's career had seen many ups and downs. Before the Canales hearings, his record was a mixed one. As a young Ranger under the supervision of Captain Rogers, his performance had been outstanding. As marshal of Navasota, his tactics had been heavy-handed, but he had shown great moral courage in protecting the African American community from racial violence. Hamer's successful two-year stint as a special officer in Houston had been tainted by his violent assault on the reporters of the *Houston Press*. His aggressive actions in cleaning up the stock thieves of Kimble County in 1914–15 had also proved controversial; at one point he was charged with assault. His close friendship with the hard-nosed, hard-drinking Jim Dunaway was troubling, his posing for photographs with the dead Mexican raiders at Norias a serious error in judgment. Hamer's participation in the Johnson-Sims feud, while not unlawful, again brought his judgment into question. His angry confrontation with Jose Canales in Brownsville—and Canales's public branding of him as a ruffian—blackened his reputation. His killing without warning of the six armed smugglers at the end of the Mexican Revolution, while understandable due to the numerous murders of El Paso lawmen, was of dubious legality. If viewed as a preemptive military strike against former Villistas, it was justifiable. But if viewed as a local police action, it was murder.

Yet Hamer learned from his mistakes. He became acutely aware of his responsibility as a new Ranger captain, and he strove to avoid anything that would bring his beloved Ranger service into disrepute. He quickly began to demonstrate increasing maturity as a leader and sophistication as a peace officer and detective. His leadership would be a significant factor in bringing the Rangers out of the Old West and into the modern era.

12

GUNFIGHTER

On September 1, 1921, Adjutant General Thomas D. Barton, in his office in the state capitol building, swore in Frank Hamer as a captain of Texas Rangers. It was surely one of the proudest moments in Hamer's life. After completing his federal reports and other unfinished Prohibition business, he took a short vacation to visit his parents and go fishing. A week later, he was in Del Rio, commanding Company C. Speaking of the complaints about the company, Captain Roy Aldrich commented, "The Del Rio territory is where we had most of the 'kick' from, and Frank will have plenty to do to get things straightened out." Hamer was likewise unimpressed with the way the company had been run, wiring headquarters, "Things have been running mighty loose around here." He fired several men and established a policy of cooperation with Mexican police. Among his privates were two who would become lifelong friends. One was Charlie Miller, twenty-six, a former deputy sheriff who had been a Ranger the previous two years. Miller was the opposite of Hamer. Boisterous and full of fun, he habitually wore his Colt .45 auto "cocked and locked" in his holster. Once, late in his long career, a young range master asked him whether he realized that was a dangerous way to carry an automatic pistol. Miller retorted, "Son, if the damned thing wasn't dangerous, I wouldn't be carrying it!" On another occasion, Miller and a fellow Ranger tried to order coffee from an inhospitable café owner. After a long wait while they were ignored, Miller finally drew his pistol and shot two holes in the coffee urn. While patrons ducked for cover, Miller calmly filled two cups with java spurting from the bullet holes.[1]

Frank's other friend was Manuel T. "Lone Wolf" Gonzaullas, one of the best known, most interesting—and peculiar—Texas Rangers of the twentieth century. Gonzaullas, who would rise to the rank of captain and achieve Ranger fame second only to Hamer, claimed to have been born in Spain in 1891 to a Spanish father and Canadian mother who were naturalized U.S. citizens. He said his full name was Manuel Trazazas Gonzaullas, that his family had been killed in the great Galveston flood of 1900, and that he spent the rest of his boyhood in El Paso. When Gonzaullas first joined the Rangers, he gave his birthplace as Spain; in another enlistment, he claimed Port of Spain, Trinidad. Sometimes he claimed to be Portuguese or said that his father was half Spanish and half Portuguese. As one of his Rangers recalled many years later, "No one ever got really close to 'Lone Wolf' unless it was his wife Laura. No one knew exactly where he was born or anything much about his life before he enlisted in the Ranger service about 1921."[2]

Gonzaullas's claims about his background were almost certainly false. Census records show that his true name was Manuel T. Gonzales and that both he and his father were born in Texas. He seems to have attempted to de-Hispanicize his last name by changing it to Gonzaullas—a spelling that is unknown in the Spanish language. In that era, it was common, both in Latin America and the United States, for *hueros*—light-complected Hispanics—to claim they were Spanish. It was a class-conscious effort to deny their mestizo heritage, despite the fact that almost everyone in Latin America was mestizo—a mixture of Spanish and Indian blood. Light-complected African Americans did it, too; it was called "passing." Lone Wolf Gonzaullas's denial of his Tejano heritage was only eclipsed by the abject racism of that era, which compelled him to do it.[3]

Once, when asked about his ethnicity, Gonzaullas exclaimed, "I ain't no damn Mexican." As if to draw attention away from the issue, he wore fancy two-gun rigs, with engraved matching pistols, their grips embedded with semiprecious stones. He adorned himself with diamond jewelry and loved to ride horseback on an elaborate hand-tooled saddle. In 1932 he even mounted a Thompson submachine gun in the passenger seat of his Chrysler scout car, a flashy but, since it could only be fired in one direction, largely useless appendage. Of average height, he wore high-heeled boots and large Stetson hats to make himself appear taller. He reveled in his nickname, Lone Wolf, a moniker given him early in his career by newspapermen, and amassed a collection of more than five hundred firearms. Despite his flamboyant and self-aggrandizing nature, he was a highly capable lawman, an astute detective, and a dangerous man in a personal encounter. In thirty-one years as a Ranger and Prohibition agent, he killed at least three armed lawbreakers and wounded several others in the line of duty. He was one of the best Rangers on the force.[4]

Lone Wolf Gonzaullas was first assigned to the company of Captain Tom Hickman, stationed in Wichita Falls and sent out to the North Texas oil fields. Hickman, colorful, publicity-loving, and bipolar, took an immediate dislike to Gonzaullas. Captain Aldrich wrote that, as a result, Adjutant General Barton "ordered his transfer to Captain Hamer's company at Del Rio," adding, "I am sure that it will be much more pleasant for Gonsaullas [sic], and I want to do all I can for him." Hamer and Gonzaullas hit it off immediately. Frank affectionately dubbed him "Gon," a nickname that Gonzaullas disliked but accepted with good humor. Lone Wolf considered Hamer one of the toughest men he had ever known. He reciprocated Hamer's warm feelings, once saying, "Frank Hamer was a great captain. I loved him and he taught me many things."[5]

Gonzaullas, more than any other Ranger of that era, thoroughly adapted to modern technology. He would become an expert in forensic science, fingerprints, and ballistics. Although Hamer would also come to embrace technology, he kept one foot firmly planted in the nineteenth century. Perhaps because he had a near-photographic memory for names and faces, he placed little value in reports or paperwork. Much to Frank's annoyance, Captain Aldrich, the quartermaster, frequently pestered him to correctly fill out reports and requisition forms. Gonzaullas recalled that one day in 1921 he came in from a long scout and, finding that Hamer was not in camp, sat down and wrote out a detailed report. It was so thorough, he thought, "I ought to get a medal for it." When Hamer returned, he perused the report, then tore it to shreds and tossed it into the campfire.[6]

Although Gonzaullas spent but two months with Hamer in Del Rio, he later recalled that the company had "numerous gunfights with Mexican smugglers" and that, as a result, local Hispanics dubbed them "Hamer's murderers." Only one of these shootouts is recorded, but it was one of the greatest exploits of Hamer's long career. Ironically, it did not involve Texas lawbreakers, and, for that matter, it did not even take place on Texas soil.

The bizarre and bloody series of events that led to one of Hamer's most important gun battles began nine years earlier in distant Bingham, Utah. Situated in the Oquirrh Mountains twenty-five miles southwest of Salt Lake City, Bingham was an important center for silver and lead mining. It attracted cheap immigrant labor—Serbs, Greeks, Scandinavians, Italians, Japanese, and Mexicans. In the big strike by the Western Federation of Miners in 1912, nonunion men had been brought to the mills and drift tunnels. One of them was Rafael "Ralph" Lopez, who was reportedly born in Coahuila, Mexico. He was twenty-six, handsome, light-complected, and spoke fluent English. Numerous stories later circulated about Lopez: he had been a horse thief in Wyoming's Powder River country, a rebel marksman during Francisco Madero's revolution in Mexico in 1911, and even a sharpshooter with Buffalo Bill's Wild West Show.[7]

When the labor strike was over, Lopez stayed on in Bingham. He and a partner leased a section of the Apex Mine in Carr Fork in Bingham Canyon, fruitfully working the tailings and tunnels. They made up to forty dollars a day, far beyond what a union laborer could earn. Lopez came to know the tunnels and shafts of the Apex Mine like the back of his hand. He lived in a boardinghouse in Bingham and was well liked by Anglos. In his spare time he would practice shooting with his pistol and could hit silver dollars thrown into the air. Lopez got into minor trouble in Bingham. On one occasion, he was brought before a justice of the peace and fined for taking part in a cutting scrape. In July 1913 Salt Lake County Deputy Sheriff Julius Sorensen arrested Lopez for assault and battery at the Highland Boy Mine. Lopez spent twelve days in jail in Salt Lake City, and thereafter nursed a bitter grudge against the officer. One day, he threatened to "get all the deputies in Bingham Canyon." Later that same night in a saloon, Lopez boasted that he would "kill some of the deputy sheriffs for what they have done to me and Sorensen will be among the first."[8]

Rafael Lopez and another young miner, Juan Valdez, were both courting the same girl, Ynez Ocariz, known as the "belle of the Mexican quarter of upper Bingham." On the evening of November 20, 1913, Lopez walked to the Ocariz cabin, located near the Highland Boy

Captain Frank Hamer on the border, about 1921. *Travis Hamer personal collection*

Mine, with a box of candy for Ynez. When he got there, he found that she was visiting with his rival and refused to see him. An enraged Lopez went to his boardinghouse, changed into rough clothes and boots, then armed himself with a Winchester Model 1895 rifle and two automatic pistols. Returning to the Ocariz place, he waited in ambush. At 1:00 A.M. Juan Valdez stepped out into the darkness. He had gone only a few steps when Lopez fired once; Valdez collapsed, screaming in agony. Word was sent to Deputy Sorensen at the Highland Boy Mine, who rushed to the scene and found Valdez dead.[9]

Rafael Lopez scrambled up the mountain behind the Highland Boy Mine, then fled south on foot. Meanwhile, Deputy Sorensen raised a small posse: Bingham's chief of police, J. W. Grant, and deputy sheriffs Otto Witbeck and Nephi Jensen. They caught up with him the next evening at a ranch near Saratoga Springs on the west shore of Utah Lake. Lopez took cover in a drainage ditch and opened fire, killing Chief Grant and Deputy Jensen. As Deputies Sorensen and Witbeck galloped forward, Lopez fired again, killing Witbeck. He then escaped in the darkness.[10]

By daybreak a massive manhunt was underway amidst intense public excitement. As news of the quadruple murders filled headlines nationwide, deputy sheriffs, policemen, and volunteers guarded roads, trails, and bridges throughout central Utah. Late the next afternoon, November 22, a posse encountered Lopez eighteen miles south of Saratoga Springs. He opened fire with his pistols, the possemen fired three hundred shots in return, and again Lopez vanished.[11]

In an act of extreme endurance and audacity, Lopez walked and then limped sixty-five miles through sleet and snow back to Bingham, eluding posses all the way. On the night of November 26, he quietly knocked on the door of a cabin owned by a friend, Mike Stefano, an Italian miner who lived near the Highland Boy Mine. Stefano gave him dry socks, a pair of overshoes, blankets, and food. Lopez exchanged his empty rifle for Stefano's Winchester 30-30 and fresh ammunition. The fugitive hobbled off and disappeared into a nearby mine tunnel.[12]

The terrified Stefano kept quiet about the encounter until the next day, when he reported it to the mine foreman. Soon more than one hundred men were on the scene, guarding the mine's seventeen tunnel entrances at different elevations. The mine levels were connected by twenty-five miles of tunnels and shafts, which honeycombed the mountain. During the next two days, several miners, who were still working in the shafts, reported seeing and talking with Lopez. Salt Lake County's sheriff, Andrew Smith, decided to try smoking the fugitive out. On the afternoon of November 29, a six-man posse led by Deputy Sheriff J. Douglas Hulsey entered a tunnel carrying a kerosene-soaked bale of hay. They took a lift to the three-hundred-foot level and then made their way nine hundred feet in a tunnel. When they reached the mouth of a shaft known as the "Larson stope," the deafening roar of gunfire shattered their ears. Flames from Lopez's rifle spurted from the blackness as one bullet tore into Deputy Hulsey, passing through both lungs, killing him. Another slug slammed into posseman Thomas Manderich, splitting his heart. Lopez had fired on them from the top of the stope, only twenty feet distant.[13]

The mine was cordoned off, and lawmen lit dozens of fires in the tunnels and shafts in a fruitless effort to smoke him out. Sheriff Smith, hugely embarrassed that he and his men were unable to locate Lopez, officially declared that the fugitive had died somewhere in the labyrinth. But because his body was not recovered, the public remained skeptical. Soon, the fact that Lopez managed to escape the mine was proved beyond question. The Winchester rifle he had taken from Mike Stefano was found under a railroad trestle in Carr Fork. Next to it was a full cartridge belt and an empty holster. The rifle was shown to Stefano, who identified it by a mark he had filed into the stock. Lawmen surmised that Lopez escaped the mine soon after shooting Hulsey and Manderich; fled along the railroad tracks, abandoning the rifle and gun belt but keeping his pistol; and then swung aboard an outbound ore train.[14]

Rafael Lopez's killing of five lawmen remains the worst law-enforcement tragedy, and the greatest manhunt, in Utah's history. In the ensuing years, there were numerous reported sightings of Lopez. Suspects were picked up in Utah, Colorado, Arizona, Wyoming, Wisconsin, and even British Columbia, but none proved to be the right man. Frank Hamer, like most experienced peace officers, believed that Lopez had returned to his native state of Coahuila, Mexico. In October 1921, just weeks after taking over as captain of Company C in Del Rio, Hamer got a tip that the long-missing Lopez was riding with a band of smugglers that operated on both sides of the border, between Coahuila and Del Rio. Frank investigated and learned that his informant, a guide for the band, was reliable. Hamer's source told him that Lopez and his gang would soon be crossing the Rio Grande in the dark.

On the designated night, Hamer, accompanied by Ranger Private Charlie Miller, several other men from his company, and the Mexican informant, proceeded to the river at a spot west of Quemado and thirty-five miles south of Del Rio. Frank knew all about Lopez's deadly accuracy with a rifle and later said that he was certain that Lopez, if found, would be armed with a rifle and not a handgun. The *confidente* led Hamer and his men to an irrigation ditch, which, as later events would show, was actually on the Mexican side of the Rio Grande. As we have seen, over the years Hamer had made frequent trips across the border, both official and unofficial. Given how elusive and dangerous Rafael Lopez was, Frank Hamer had no scruples about slipping into Mexico to get his man.

The informant told Hamer, "Now get in this ditch right here, and when you come out you can raise up and get them."

The notorious Rafael Lopez, who murdered five Utah lawmen in 1913. He was slain by Frank Hamer while resisting arrest on the Rio Grande in 1921. *Randy Lish collection*

He then left to join Lopez, explaining that he was to guide the outlaws across the river. After a short wait, Frank grew suspicious. It was another of those hunches that he always trusted. To Miller, he confided, "Charlie, I think we're being put on the spot."

Hamer mulled over his next move, then announced to his men, "I've got a feeling we've been led into a trap." The captain decided, as he said later, "to move over about two ditches." The irrigation ditches ran parallel to one another from the Rio Grande. Frank and his men crawled to the new location, where the Rangers lay prone in the ditch. Hamer himself took up a position behind the wooden irrigation gate. His left shoulder wound from the Sweetwater gunfight was bothering him, and he eased the pain by leaning his shoulder into the cedar gatepost.

Hamer's suspicions were well founded. After a short wait, the Rangers spotted a score of shadowy figures approach the ditch where they had been hiding. As the smugglers peered into it, Frank shouted in Spanish, "Halt! We're officers of the law!"

The desperadoes instantly opened up with a fusillade of rifle fire. Rafael Lopez, in the lead, sent a rifle shot at Hamer, grazing the captain's cheek and drawing blood. The bullet thudded into the cedar post Frank had been leaning on. Unfazed, Hamer fired back, his .25 Remington rifle barking as fast as he could squeeze the trigger. One of his bullets slammed into Rafael Lopez's chest, shattering his heart and killing him instantly. The other Rangers aimed at the smugglers' muzzle flashes, unleashing a barrage. After a short exchange of fire, they could hear the outlaws running away in the dark. Frank and his men waited thirty minutes, then cautiously approached the ditch. Inside were eleven dead smugglers, among them Rafael Lopez. He was wearing a pair of blue bib overalls, and one of Hamer's shots had struck a gold watch in his top pocket. Frank took the watch as a memento of his encounter with one of the most desperate outlaws of the Southwest. His brother Harrison admired the timepiece, and Frank gave it to him. When Harrison Hamer joined the U.S. customs service in 1923, he hung the pocket watch in the Del Rio customs house, where it remained for ten years as a grisly warning to smugglers.[15]

Hamer made no official report of the Lopez shootout, probably

Gold pocket watch taken from the body of Rafael Lopez. It
has been pierced by a bullet from Frank Hamer's rifle. *Photo
© Paul Goodwin from John Robinson Collection*

because it took place in Mexico. Nor was the gunfight reported in newspapers, although Ranger Charlie Miller was not shy about telling the
story in later years. As a journalist wrote in 1934, "Much of Hamer's
early activities were along the Texas-Mexico border, and the facts on
these episodes of his life have never been preserved." Frank knew there
was a $1,000 reward offered for Lopez in Utah, but he never claimed it.
Reticent in the extreme, he had no use for publicity and never sought
any recognition for killing Rafael Lopez. To him it was just another of
his fifty-two gunfights.[16]

Nonetheless, in 1945, Ed Kilman, a noted reporter for the *Houston
Post,* managed to coax the story out of him while they shared a cup of
coffee with a mutual friend, Carl Jarrell. When Hamer finished his account, Jarrell asked, "Well, what became of the Mexican informer who
tried to put you on the spot for Lopez?"

"Oh, him?" Hamer replied. "Well, he had an accident the next day. Fell off his horse, I believe, not far from there."

"Broke his neck, I presume?" Jarrell asked, suggesting that the Rangers had a hand in his death. Hamer did not take the bait and merely grunted, "Yeah—it killed him."[17]

At the height of the Utah manhunt in 1913, a Salt Lake City policeman who knew Rafael Lopez was asked by a reporter to describe the fugitive's character. The officer responded, "He is a desperate man and will die with his boots on." Though his words were prophetic, in the end Lopez proved no match in a stand-up gunfight against Frank Hamer. And perhaps it was no surprise that vengeance for the five dead Utah officers was carried out by the deadliest manhunter in the Southwest. Frank Hamer was indeed a living manifestation of the mythic western gunfighter.[18]

Eight years before, he had declared plaintively to a Houston journalist, "I am not a gun fighter." In fact, he was one of the greatest gunfighters of the American West. By the early 1920s, it was widely believed in Texas that he had killed between twenty-three and twenty-seven men. The lower number may not have been too far off the mark. Hamer had personally slain Ed Putnam, Kid Jackson, Gee McMeans, Encarnacion Delgado, and Rafael Lopez. If one can credit the body count of his fatal El Paso gunfight, he and Elmer McClure killed six smugglers. In the fight with Rafael Lopez's band, Hamer and his Rangers shot to death eleven outlaws. By 1921 he had probably killed, or participated in killing, at least twenty-one desperadoes.

Years later, in a rare interview, Pulitzer Prize–winning journalist A. B. MacDonald asked Hamer, "How many men have you killed?"

"I won't talk about that," he replied.

"They say you have killed twenty-three men, not counting Mexicans," MacDonald pressed.

"I won't discuss it. All my killings were in line of duty. It was an unpleasant duty."

"Does your conscience bother you?"

"Not a bit."

"How many gunfights with criminals have you been in?"

"I don't mind telling you that. I have been in fifty-two of them, counting the scrimmages we had with Mexicans and smugglers along the Rio Grande."

Frank explained why he had been victorious in so many shootings. After pointing out that his preferred weapon was a rifle, he explained how he used a revolver. "The great thing about shooting with a six-gun is to hold it steady and not to shoot too quick. What I mean is this: a man who is afraid, who is nervous, cannot shoot straight with a six-shooter grasped in his hand. The muzzle of the gun will wobble with every nervous pulse beat in his hand. . . . When you've got to fight it out with a six-shooter the only sure way is to make the first shot count. . . . Take it slow and cool. Don't get excited."

Hamer insisted to MacDonald that "the chances are always with the man who has the law on his side. The criminal knows at heart that he is in the wrong. He is a coward at heart, generally. He will be nervous. You can always count that, ninety times in a hundred, he will be so nervous that his first shot will be wild. That's where your coolness and deliberation count and decide the issue between his life and yours. What is the use of you getting the first shot if you fail to hit the mark?

"The one superlative thing you want to achieve is to hit your mark. That mark should be the broadest part of his body. Draw quickly and aim, not at his head or legs, but at his stomach, for that is the widest part. Be deliberate, pause, and aim with the utmost deliberation, and when you are sure your muzzle will land the bullet squarely in the middle of his stomach, pull the trigger and it's all over. Really it is very simple. Just keep cool and take time to aim straight, and that's all there is to it."[19]

However, those were mere techniques. To his friend J. Evetts Haley, Hamer credited God for his gunfighting prowess. "They say I am a good shot. I know I am. But as long as I'm doing what is right—and I'm always trying to cut it square—there's something of higher help that's looked down the gun barrel with me and told me when to pull the trigger."[20]

13

BOOMTOWN

The Roaring Twenties were a time of unprecedented prosperity, accompanied by rapid urbanization and wrenching social change. Politically and economically, the decade was dominated by three successive Republican presidents who espoused unlimited and uncontrolled economic expansion. Culturally, the 1920s were dominated by the newfound popularity of automobiles, motion pictures, radio, and jazz. As the population of Texas rose by more than a million, the state became increasingly urban. At first these changes were barely perceptible to Frank Hamer, for his traditional horseback duties as a border Ranger were little different from those of the captains who rode before him: John S. "Rip" Ford, Lee McNelly, and John Hughes. All that would quickly change.

Governor Neff and his adjutant general, Thomas D. Barton, became convinced that Frank Hamer was indeed, as Captain Hanson had pointed out three years earlier, the best Ranger in Texas. On January 1, 1922, Neff had Hamer transferred to Austin, placed him in charge of Headquarters Company, and made him senior captain of the Rangers. Although the pious Neff planned to use Hamer as his point man in a wide-scale attack on lawlessness, there was more to Frank's life than crime busting. A few weeks before, on December 3, 1921, he and Gladys welcomed a second son, Billy Beckham Hamer, named after his father-in-law,

Billy Johnson, and his Prohibition boss, Clifford Beckham. Beverly, now twelve, attended a local grammar school, and fourteen-year-old Trix was a freshman at Austin High School. Hamer's house on Riverside Drive was but a two-mile drive from his office in the state capitol building, allowing him to spend time at home with his family. The Hamers added a second story to accommodate their growing brood.[1]

Frank's friend Walter Prescott Webb later described his new role as captain of Headquarters Company: "The duties of this company differ somewhat from those of the other companies, either border or interior. Whereas the other companies operate in a particular section, the head-quarters men operate all over the state. One week they make a raid in the Panhandle of north Texas; the next week we may hear of them investigating a murder case in the Rio Grande Valley of the Mexican border. All the members of this company are stalwart men, physically strong and of proved courage."[2]

The new senior captain, fully aware of his visible role, was determined to instill professionalism in the force. This extended to the Rangers' dress. In the state's rapidly growing urban areas, tall boots, ten-gallon hats, loud neckerchiefs, and heavy cartridge belts looked increasingly out of place. During the Canales hearings, there were many complaints about Rangers dressing and acting inappropriately—parading in border towns in cowboy gear with six-shooters prominently worn. Four years earlier, the sheriff of Scurry, W. A. Merrill, had criticized Hamer himself for such displays. The Rangers' 1919 rules and regulations, enacted after the Canales hearings, expressly prohibited "the wearing of boots, spurs, wide belts, etc., or having a pistol exposed while visiting cities or towns." In the parlance of the day, phony westerners were known as "jelly beans" and "drugstore cowboys." As Hamer once remarked, "Boots were made for riding, and I've got no desire to look like a 'pharmaceutical Ranger.'" He put away his cowboy boots, wide-brimmed hat, and western gear and rarely wore them, except on hunting trips. Instead, he donned business suits and narrow-brimmed Stetsons, tucking Old Lucky into his waistband and out of sight.[3]

As Frank belatedly joined the twentieth century, Texas oil presented him with a new set of challenges. Governor Neff decided to crack down

on the rowdy oil boomtowns of North Texas. After 1910, as automobiles had become increasingly popular—and then indispensable—the
nation's thirst for oil grew unquenchable. Major discoveries of black
gold in Oklahoma in 1912 and 1913 led to exploration in North Texas.
When a gusher erupted at Ranger in 1917, it set off a mammoth oil
boom. The unprecedented finds made Texas the nation's leading oil pro-
ducer and ushered in an era of extraordinary development and industri-
alization. In the next few years, oil boomtowns exploded throughout
North Texas. Burkburnett, Ranger, Desdemona, Cisco, Breckenridge,
Mexia, and, later, Borger, Wink, and Kilgore became household names
in the Roaring Twenties.

Gambling, bootlegging, prostitution, and drug peddling flourished
in all the boomtowns. Local lawmen were often too few, too underpaid,
and too powerless, and some took bribes to look the other way. In 1920
Rangers were called in to suppress lawlessness in Desdemona, west of
Fort Worth, and then into nearby Ranger. They were led by Captain
Roy Aldrich, who, with Lone Wolf Gonzaullas and others of the force,
were stationed in Fort Worth for a year while they repeatedly raided
nearby oil towns, arresting numerous bootleggers and gamblers. But
when brought to trial, the culprits were generally acquitted by all-male
juries, for women were not allowed to serve as jurors in Texas until 1954.
Sympathetic juries reflected the fact that most of the residents of the
boomtowns were men, few of whom objected to the popular pastimes of
whoring, gambling, and drinking. In April 1921, following complaints
about heavy-handed tactics, Governor Neff finally ordered the Rangers
out of all the North Texas boomtowns, leaving one detachment in Fort
Worth.[4]

With the Rangers gone, and local lawmen either overwhelmed, incompetent, or on the take, the oil towns went from bad to worse. In
August 1921 a sensational strike was made near Mexia (pronounced
"Ma-hay-ya"), a cotton-growing town of 2,500 situated ninety miles
south of Dallas. It was the biggest oil discovery in Texas since Spindletop. Mexia had been a sleepy Old West town, where horses were tied to
hitching posts and where the bell in the city hall tower, clogged with
cobwebs and bird nests, had not been tolled for years. Almost overnight,

the population exploded, reaching 55,000 by year's end. Amidst a forest of derricks, shacks, and tents, crisscrossed with muddy streets, oil rough-necks mingled with bootleggers, gamblers, hijackers, drug peddlers, and prostitutes. No small rural community could afford to police so many people, and vice ran rampant. Bordellos operated openly, and stills in the outlying woods operated night and day to supply the thirsty popu-lace. A local deputy sheriff sold gamblers four acres of land four miles north of town, near the Mexia-Wortham highway, where they built a gambling house facetiously named the Chicken Farm. It had trap-doors to allow patrons to flee and was surrounded by high watchtow-ers manned by armed guards. It operated in full view of the deputy, who, though he lived only two hundred and fifty yards away, later claimed, "I do not know what was going on in this building after it was opened. They told me that they were going to build a dance hall and restaurant."[5]

Just as elaborate was the Winter Garden, four miles east of town on the Mexia-Teague highway. A large, whitewashed, wood-frame build-ing with a huge sign on the front, it was owned by four Oklahoma gamblers. Inside were two roulette wheels; a chuck-a-luck game; black-jack, crap, and poker tables; as well as a full bar and restaurant. It even boasted a dance floor complete with jazz orchestra. Armed guards were posted on the driveway between the Winter Garden and the highway, and bouncers searched everyone who entered. More guards, with rifles and shotguns, were perched on platforms overlooking the main gam-bling hall. Its patrons included deputy sheriffs from nearby counties, with four to five hundred people spending thousands of dollars daily. On one occasion, a crowd of Chicago gamblers visited the Winter Garden and lost more than $30,000 in a single night. The wide open gambling and drinking encouraged contempt for the law. In November 1921 three Fort Worth police detectives went to Mexia to recover stolen motorcars but were run out of town by an armed mob. A month later, a town mer-chant was slain in a gunfight with robbers. Complaints flooded into the governor's office.[6]

Neff took decisive action. After meeting with General Barton and federal officials, he sent detectives into Mexia to gather information.

Undercover Prohibition agents visited the Chicken Farm and the Winter Garden and made detailed diagrams of each.

Governor Neff, General Barton, and David H. Morris, chief Prohibition agent in Texas, drew up plans for a major raid. Barton intended to lead it. A former drugstore owner and army veteran, he was politically ambitious but had no law-enforcement experience. Morris insisted that Hamer be placed in charge, because, as the Prohibition agent later explained, "In my judgment he is the most efficient officer in the service." Hamer handpicked fourteen men from Company C in Del Rio and Tom Hickman's Company B in Fort Worth, including Sergeants John Gillon and James McCormick, and Privates Charlie Miller, J. B. Wheatley, Charley Carta, and William M. Molesworth. With them was a force of Prohibition agents, among them Lone Wolf Gonzaullas, who had recently joined the feds, and Elmer B. McClure, who drove in from Del Rio.[7]

Before dawn on January 7, 1922, Hamer quietly led a convoy of automobiles out of Austin. In addition to Frank's posse, the group included General Barton, Assistant Attorney General Clifford Stone, Captain Roy Aldrich and eight other Rangers, plus six Prohibition agents. Tom Hickman and half a dozen of his men drove south from Fort Worth. They met in Groesbeck, twelve miles south of Mexia, where they firmed up their plans and waited for dark. Late that night, the lawmen simultaneously converged on Mexia. At 11:00 P.M. Hamer and his Rangers, armed with shotguns, rifles, and a Thompson submachine gun, raided the Winter Garden. Frank was taking no chances with armed guards. As he burst in the main door, he spotted a closed door with a peephole at the end of a hallway. Hamer fired a single shot through the door, but the guard, fortunately for him, was not at his post. As *The Mexia News* reported, "This represented the only gun shot fired in the entire proceedings." The Rangers met no resistance and arrested and disarmed everyone in sight. When a carload of surprised customers pulled up, the Rangers ordered them away. At the same time, Hickman led an assault on the Chicken Farm, kicking open the front door and capturing the occupants. In all, twenty men and five women were seized, along with the gambling equipment, two automobiles, and ten thousand dollars' worth of corn liquor.[8]

Hamer and his men carried all the gaming tables outside the Winter Garden and set up headquarters inside. In the morning, Assistant Attorney General Stone sent word for the county officials, judges, and sheriffs of both Limestone and Freestone Counties to meet the state officers at the Winter Garden. According to a disgusted General Barton, "All of these officials claimed ignorance of any such resorts and seemed amazed that such could have been running." Sheriff Horace Mayo, of Freestone County, professed to be surprised by the raids, saying that he had been "sick for the past four weeks" and "had never found any gambling devices or lawlessness." The same day, Hamer and his men destroyed the captured liquor. "We burned 165 gallons of whiskey," said Barton, "while the spectators shed tears." From Austin, the state attorney general issued a warning: "This is . . . but the beginning of a systematic campaign to drive out the hijackers, gamblers and

Texas Rangers with confiscated liquor and gambling paraphernalia behind the Winter Garden in Mexia, 1922. Hamer is in dark coat at left side of roulette table, and Governor Pat Neff is standing behind the roulette wheel. General Jacob F. Wolters is second from right. *Author's collection*

lawbreakers. While it may take some time we intend to accomplish our purpose."[9]

He was deadly serious. While Lone Wolf Gonzaullas left for Waco to file charges in federal court, Rangers and Prohibition agents fanned out through Mexia and the adjacent oil fields, arresting more bootleggers and gamblers. They even raided a Mexia drugstore, seizing a supply of illegal narcotics. But the officers soon encountered resistance: judges, local lawmen, and prosecutors would not cooperate, witnesses were afraid to testify, and the jails could not hold so many prisoners. Governor Neff had had enough, and on January 11 he declared martial law in the Mexia oil fields. "We intend to give Texas at least one clean oil town," proclaimed Adjutant General Barton. General Jacob F. Wolters, a prominent Houston lawyer, politician, and militia leader, arrived with forty soldiers of the Texas National Guard. He set up headquarters in city hall and announced that local officials had suddenly become cooperative. Wolters remembered Hamer well from his service as a special officer in Houston, and in Mexia the pair became friends.[10]

The declaration of martial law obviated the need for search warrants and cleared the way for wholesale arrests. The following night, Hamer and his men continued their raids. When an African American bootlegger shot twice at the Rangers, one of them fired back, wounding him in the leg. They arrested two deputy sheriffs for possessing liquor, but the officers claimed that they had taken it as evidence. Orders were issued prohibiting loitering and loafing, the carrying of firearms, and the assembly of crowds in the streets. The tiny two-cell jail in Mexia quickly filled, and overflow was sent to Groesbeck; soon arrestees were being released for lack of space. The Rangers then began locking prisoners in the back gambling room of the Winter Garden, while they and the soldiers set up barracks in the main hall. The soldiers were ordered to shoot any of the twenty-eight prisoners who attempted to escape. The crackdown began a massive exodus, as hundreds of "undesirables" filled departing passenger trains and freight boxcars.[11]

The next morning, January 13, Hamer led a raid on two stills operating in a creek bottom not far from the Winter Garden, capturing four

African American moonshiners. Assistant Attorney General Stone and a civilian volunteer marched them across the prairie to the barracks. To add to the tumult, the following day a massive fire, caused by a gasoline accident, raged through Mexia, destroying a large section of the business district. Fifteen thousand spectators gathered while General Wolters detailed twenty-five of his men to help fight the flames, leaving the rest on guard duty at the Winter Garden. The Rangers patrolled the streets and alleys to prevent looting. In the week following the first raids, Rangers, Prohibition officers, and soldiers made 158 arrests, while an estimated three thousand people—many of them gamblers, bootleggers, drug addicts, and prostitutes—fled Mexia. The Rangers even arrested the prosecuting attorney of Limestone County, Lon Eubanks, for violating the liquor laws. Fifteen stolen autos were recovered, and six more illicit stills seized.[12]

During the next week, Hamer and the other lawmen made more than one hundred additional felony arrests. Fourteen prisoners, most charged with armed robbery, were held in the tiny city jail. On January 15, Frank and his men captured a fifty-gallon still on Plummer Creek, south of Mexia. That afternoon, they arrested a man running a tobacco shop in a roadside tent; he had been selling something stronger than cigars. In a dugout behind the tent they found the contraband. As a reporter explained: "A spade in the hands of a husky Ranger soon unearthed the wet goods." The newspaperman described the Ranger chief for his readers: "Captain Hamer is a typical Texas Ranger, over six feet in height and a most pleasing man to meet, that is if you are not a violator of the law." Frank told the journalist that "it would be only a short time before Mexia would be free of all law violators."[13]

A military court was set up in Mexia, and the Rangers dragged both arrestees and witnesses before it. More than 1,000 people were interviewed, and their testimony laid bare rampant corruption. Among the revelations was that gamblers, moonshiners, and prostitutes paid bribes in the form of "fines" to local police and deputy sheriffs. It was reported that Sheriff Mayo enjoyed playing roulette in the Winter Garden, while Limestone County's sheriff, W. A. Loper, and three of his deputies, as well as the county attorney, Lon Eubanks, frequented the place. Eubanks had also been seen visiting brothels. On one occasion, Sheriff Mayo led a purported raid on the Winter Garden, but the owners had been tipped off in advance, and the raid was a sham.[14]

According to a story that became popular some years later, one night Hamer staked out a still in a cabin near Mexia. At 4:00 A.M. the moonshiner lit a kerosene lamp, then kindled a fire under the boiler. Frank, his six-gun holstered, stepped to the door, swung it open, and strode inside. The moonshiner snatched up his shotgun, then whirled around to face the Ranger captain. Hamer, without reaching for his revolver, said calmly, "Well, what are you going to do with that thing? Are you coming up or going down with it?"

"I think I'll go down," the moonshiner wisely answered.[15]

On the night of January 25, Hamer, Lone Wolf Gonzaullas, and other officers raided a vacant building in Mexia, where they found a false wall and a sliding panel that led to a hiding place under the floor. They discovered 827 bottles of corn liquor valued at $1,650 and carted them off to the Winter Garden. The next day, soldiers dumped out 425 gallons of liquor, which flowed out into the road. "The smell of liquor wafted up from the muddy street," wrote a reporter, and "lingered long after the bottles had been broken and the spirits of the 'corn' mixed with the mud in the gutter."[16]

Three days later, Frank left Mexia to meet with Governor Neff in Austin. Based on his discussions with Hamer, Neff declared that "considerable clean-up work was yet to be done" and that martial law would remain in place. General Wolters explained that they had broken up two large gangs of professional gamblers, adding, "I would like to point out that of all the arrests since martial law went into effect, only three have been residents of Mexia who were here prior to the oil boom." Up to that point, the Rangers had been well behind the times by failing to photograph and fingerprint prisoners; the state legislature had refused to pay for it. Now, the Rangers brought in a fingerprint expert from the Houston police. Said Wolters, "All professional crooks have 'mugged' and their fingerprints registered."[17]

By this time, as things began to quiet down in Mexia, the Rangers received reports of large-scale liquor operations in eastern Freestone County. A private airplane was engaged to make a surveillance of the Trinity River bottoms east of Mexia. Its pilot found and photographed numerous illegal stills. Rangers went in undercover and found that the stills were operated by a ring led by a notorious bootlegger with the help of local lawmen. Manufacture of liquor was being done on a gigantic scale, with carloads of corn shipped in from Kansas. On February 2 Governor Neff expanded martial law across all of Freestone County. At the same time, Captain Hickman and General Barton led Rangers, Prohibition officers, and troops on a raid into the eastern part of the county. First cutting the telephone lines to prevent news of the raid, they entered a rough country, heavily wooded and crisscrossed with ravines. As the airplane circled overhead to spot the targets, moonshiners opened fire, hitting the wings but missing its pilot. The Rangers fired into the brush with a Thompson submachine gun, and the moonshiners' shooting quickly stopped. The officers rounded up eleven stills and fifty-seven prisoners, who were loaded into military trucks and brought to the Winter Garden.[18]

The National Guard troops, some of them expert marksman, were eager to see a shooting exhibition by Frank Hamer. Word got out, and a salesman for the Remington Arms Company drove down from Dallas to watch. Targets were set up behind the Winter Garden. Hamer disliked fully automatic weapons, for they represented the opposite of his careful, accurate shooting style. Nonetheless, he tried a Thompson submachine gun with a fifty-round drum. A photographer took a still shot of him preparing to fire at a gambling table that was leaned on its side. According to Ranger Bill Molesworth, Hamer fired fifty rounds at a range of twenty-five yards. Shooting from the hip, he put forty-eight slugs into the three-foot-square table. With a crowd looking on, the big Ranger also demonstrated his skill with a Colt single-action army revolver. Several of the soldiers began throwing confiscated three-inch butter dishes into the air so Frank could shoot them with his .25 Remington rifle. The Remington man took motion pictures of Hamer as he shattered more than a hundred dishes in the air, without a single miss. The salesman sent the film to company headquarters with an account of

Frank Hamer, left, and Ranger Captain Tom Hickman with a captured still in Mexia, 1922. *Author's collection*

Hamer's exploits with that very weapon. Remington officials were so impressed they prepared a beautifully scroll-engraved .30 caliber Model-8 semiautomatic rifle, inscribed CAPT. FRANK HAMER OF THE TEXAS RANGERS on the left side of the frame. They shipped the rifle to Petmecky's sporting goods store in Austin, where it was later presented to the unsuspecting lawman. He was surprised and greatly pleased, and it became his favorite deer-hunting rifle.[19]

Hamer was not as pleased with the Rangers' three new Thompson submachine guns. Roy Aldrich, as quartermaster, had recently purchased two from Petmecky's for $185 each. The adjutant general bought a third directly from the manufacturer, Auto-Ordnance Company of New York City. The Thompson had been introduced in 1919 and was heavily marketed to law-enforcement agencies. Soon dubbed the "tommy gun," it would become the favorite weapon of gangsters of the 20s and 30s. Many of the Rangers were enthusiastic about the new weapon, which was extremely well made and also extremely expensive. That summer, Aldrich bought two more from Petmecky's at the reduced price of $342 for the pair. Yet the Thompson was the antithesis of Hamer's style of combat shooting. He believed in calm, deliberate marksmanship, firing as few shots as possible, thus reducing the danger to innocent civilians. The Thompson, on the other hand, had a rate of fire of more than six hundred rounds per minute. A fifty- or hundred-round drum magazine could be emptied in a few seconds. It fired the .45 automatic pistol cartridge and was accurate only up to fifty yards. For those who carried a Thompson, calmness, deliberation, and deadly marksmanship were not part of the equation. Hamer recognized that its threatening appearance would be useful in cowing mobs, but he never once used a fully automatic weapon in a gunfight.[20]

On February 18, Governor Neff attended a large public meeting in Mexia, accompanied by Hamer, Wolters, and other state officials. Neff railed against the lawlessness and threatened to remove from office Sheriff Loper and the county attorney, Eubanks, of Limestone County, whom he believed were in cahoots with the criminal element. After obtaining assurances from local citizens that they would cooperate in suppressing crime, he ended martial law on March 1. The raids on Mexia had been a resounding success. The Rangers and other lawmen had made 602 arrests, seized 27 stills and 2,270 gallons of liquor, recovered 53 stolen automobiles, and confiscated thirteen rumrunners' cars as well as four thousand dollars' worth of cocaine and other narcotics. Hamer's friend Albert Mace, an ex-Ranger and former sheriff, took over as Mexia's police chief and put together a new force of officers, who kept the town clean.[21]

The Mexia cleanup took forty-seven days and was one of the biggest of that era. It was trumpeted in newspaper headlines nationwide. Mexia was also important for other reasons. It demonstrated Governor Neff's willingness to send in Rangers despite opposition from local officials. As he declared at the height of the raids, "While I am Governor, no band of criminals will ever take charge of a community as long as a Texas Ranger can pull a trigger." It featured the first known use of an airplane in Texas law enforcement and introduced the Rangers to modern police photography and fingerprinting. Governor Neff and the Rangers received wide praise in the Texas press for their stubborn stand against lawlessness. Frank Hamer's leadership had been essential in the professional and relatively violence-free way the campaign was carried out. The governor was grateful, and he wrote to Hamer: "I desire to express to you my appreciation for the effective service which you rendered. . . . The bearing and conduct of the individual members of the entire organization was in every way consistent with the ideals of our Ranger service, and I have heard from the citizens of Mexia and the surrounding community many words of commendation for the accomplishments and demeanor of the Texas Rangers."[22]

The Rangers had come a long way since the disgraceful days of Captain Ransom and the Bandit War six years earlier. They had joined the twentieth century.

14

THE KU KLUX KLAN

Screams shattered the night air.

"Lynch him! Lynch him!"

An enormous mob, shouting and cursing, surrounded the county jail, jamming the sidewalks and overflowing into the street.

"Let's get the nigger!"

The throng grew larger by the minute. Dozens carried ropes as the shouts got louder.

"Send the black rat out here or we'll tear down the jail and get him!"

The sheriff and the county judge appeared on the front steps.

"Let the law take its course," cried the judge. "If this man is guilty he will be punished by the law. Look at yourselves. Have you gone mad?"

"Don't try to stop us!" yelled one of the mob. "We're coming in!"

As they began to surge forward, a touring car pulled to a stop at the edge of the infuriated throng. Inside were five grim-faced men. One of them climbed out, then stepped forward in a slow, slouching gait. Elbowing his way through the mob, he climbed the courthouse steps. He wore a conservative business suit, silk tie, and a white felt hat, but clutched in one massive fist was a Thompson submachine gun. Shaking hands with the sheriff, he sat down on the top step, casually resting the

Thompson gun on his knees, the blue steel barrel aimed directly at the center of the mob. Immediately, a buzzing swept through the horde.

"That's Frank Hamer. . . . Captain Hamer . . . Ranger Captain of headquarters company . . . came from Austin . . . Yeah, that's him. . . . Frank Hamer . . . a killer . . . He's shot down twenty-seven men. . . . That's him."

Hamer did not say a word. He simply sat and stared the mob down. None dared climb the steps. His Rangers then poured out of the motorcar, taking up positions around the jail. Within fifteen minutes, the deflated mob had drifted away, leaving behind only a handful of gawkers.[1]

Of the many who fought long and hard to end lynching in Texas, none was as dogged—or as effective—as Frank Hamer. The Ku Klux Klan saw a resurgence in Texas during the early 1920s. On February 28, 1922, the day before martial law in Mexia was lifted, members of the local Klan, Klavern number 47, held a secret meeting, then publicly announced full support for Governor Neff's cleanup. The Klansmen also issued a warning: "We hereby serve notice on the lawless element of our population that because of the withdrawal of the State Constabulary forces, we will not countenance any of the acts of lawlessness and violence that was so prevalent in our midst sixty days ago." Continued the pronouncement, "If the courts cannot . . . we will handle it ourselves in our own way." One can only wonder where those hooded cowards were before the Rangers came to Mexia.[2]

The Klan had first appeared in Texas during Reconstruction in 1868, targeting African Americans and white Republicans. Within a few years, it was suppressed by Reconstruction officials and the short-lived Texas State Police. In 1915 a new Ku Klux Klan was organized in Georgia, and after World War I, feeding on nationalist fervor, its membership quickly spread through the South, the Midwest, and East Texas. The new Klan tapped into an emerging nativist movement that sowed distrust of blacks, Catholics, Jews, and "foreigners." The First Red Scare of 1919–20, which featured widespread fear of anarchism, bolshevism, and labor unions, attracted many to the Klan. After 1920 the Klan drew prohibitionists and white supremacists and grew rapidly, boasting two million members nationwide, as many as 150,000 in Texas. Because of its anti-Catholicism, it was embraced by many Protestant clergymen. The Klan became especially strong in Dallas and Fort Worth, even influencing the two cities' governments.

The Roaring Twenties was a decade of extraordinary social and economic upheaval, especially in the South and in Texas, where the oil boom fueled unprecedented prosperity. The increasing availability of automobiles, coupled with paved highways, quickened the pace of life, made the population highly mobile, and helped trigger the migration of rural workers and families into the cities. Women became more independent as they increasingly entered the work force and exercised their newly won right to vote. Society changed rapidly as motion pictures and newly invented broadcast radio quickly disseminated the latest news, music, dance, and fashions. The first commercial radio stations appeared in Texas in 1922; within six years, the state had thirty-two broadcasters, and a radio set was in most households. Jazz music and dances like the Charleston were viewed by traditionalists as provocative and decadent. It didn't help, especially in Texas and the South, that jazz and modern dance had a strong African American influence. In response, Protestant fundamentalist preachers railed against the seemingly immoral new social order. For many Texans, caught in the rapid urbanization of the decade, the Ku Klux Klan represented a return to their traditional rural and southern values.

The Klan focused not only on blacks accused of crime but also on white bootleggers, moonshiners, adulterers, and others considered immoral. In addition to lynchings of blacks, some eighty floggings—primarily of whites—took place in Texas during 1921 for such offenses as gambling, wife beating, fraternizing with blacks, performing abortions, marital infidelity, and even speaking German in public. Tarring and feathering was another Klan punishment. The victim was stripped naked, covered with hot tar, and dusted with feathers. If warm pine tar was used, the victim was generally not injured. However, boiling hot pitch would often cause severe burns and excruciating pain. The tarred and feathered victim would often be loaded into a cart or placed on a fence rail and paraded around town in a ritual of shame and humiliation. Vigilantes came to use it to punish offenses for which flogging or hanging were judged too harsh.[3]

No doubt many Texas lawmen were either members of the Klan or quietly supported its anticrime agenda. According to one account, Frank Hamer himself briefly joined the Austin chapter of the Ku Klux Klan when it was first organized in 1921. Wrote a Texas journalist in 1962, "Somehow he was hoodwinked into joining the Klan by friends who said its most important mission was to aid in law enforcement." Hamer reportedly joined up because he believed that "Texas law enforcement could use all of the aid it could get." He attended a Klan meeting one night when its leader proposed that they tar and feather a well-known Austin prostitute. Frank listened as the plan was met with enthusiastic approval. Then he stood up, walked to the center of the hall, and announced in a loud voice, "You tar and feather that woman and I'll throw every man in this room in jail." Then he stormed out in disgust, and ever after was a staunch opponent of the Ku Klux Klan. He was not alone, for a strong anti-Klan movement would soon emerge in Texas.[4]

On March 22, 1922, three weeks after leaving Mexia, Hamer was ordered to lead a detail of Rangers to Waco and guard two African Americans accused of murdering a married couple, W. H. and Loula Barker, and a thirteen-year-old boy, Homer Turk. On February 11 the three victims had been shot and hacked to death on a farm seven miles northeast of Waco. As was customary in that era, local lawmen promptly instituted a police dragnet and rounded up numerous suspects: two whites, nine blacks, and eight Mexicans. One was Roy Mitchell, the African American chauffeur of a white businessman in Waco. Mitchell was able to prove an alibi through his employer. Two other black suspects, Cooper Johnson and Bennie Young, were wearing bloody clothes that they explained was from butchering hogs. After third-degree questioning, both allegedly confessed and were held for trial. Lynching sentiment was strong in Waco; six years earlier, an accused murderer, Jesse Washington, a seventeen-year-old black youth, had been roasted alive in a bonfire in the city plaza. The incident became known as the Waco Horror and blackened the city's reputation.

Frank Hamer now found himself in Captain Rogers's shoes, and memories of his dangerous experiences with lynch mobs as a young Ranger must have flooded back. The McLennan County sheriff, Bob Buchanan, a staunch opponent of the Klan, was determined to avoid a lynching. The previous year Buchanan had been shot and seriously wounded while courageously stopping a Klan parade. Incredibly, the county's grand jury lambasted the sheriff and his deputy, Marvin "Red" Burton—later a noted Ranger—for their efforts against the Klan, which were in fact heroic, and refused to indict the Klansmen who shot Buchanan. Captain Hamer was determined to cow the Waco Klan. He first sent Rangers J. B. Wheatley, Bill Molesworth, Claude Darlington, and Joe Orberg directly to Waco. Then he and Private Edgar McMordie picked up the two prisoners, Johnson and Young, at the jail in Waxahachie, where they were being held for safekeeping, and drove them into Waco. The next day, Hamer had his men search all spectators before bringing the prisoners into the courtroom. The two trials lasted a week, with Johnson sentenced to hang and Young given ninety-nine years. As we will see, both were entirely innocent. Because of the presence of the Rangers, no attempt was made to lynch the pair. Hamer employed his old tactic—a demonstration of overwhelming force—and armed one of his men with a Thompson submachine gun. That prompted a reporter to note, "Recalling the old days when a six-shooter and a Winchester was considered full armament for a Ranger to face an army, we are driven to the conclusion that either Rangers or mobs have changed."[5]

That spring saw an outbreak of whippings by the Klan, particularly in Dallas and Fort Worth. In March several white men were kidnapped, driven to the Trinity River bottoms, and savagely flogged. When one victim demanded to know whether his tormentors were Klansmen, they did not deny it, but declared, "That is none of your damned business and it doesn't matter what we belong to." One of the masked lynchers boasted that they had flogged sixty-three other men in the previous few months, but the actual number was a fraction of that. Governor Neff had been vocal in his opposition to vigilantism. Two months earlier, he had declared, "Lynching is one of the worst forms of lawlessness known today. During 1920 there were more lynchings in Texas than any other state. This means that Texas led the civilized world in this species of uncivilized lawlessness." Now, he ordered Frank Hamer to Dallas and threatened to send in the National Guard. "Mob rule must stop," Neff proclaimed. "Whippings like those that have occurred in Dallas will be stopped, even if Rangers and militiamen have to patrol the streets of Texas' chief city."[6]

Hamer and several of his men arrived in Dallas on April 1 and met with city police detectives. To inquisitive journalists, Frank claimed the Rangers were after auto thieves. "Captain Hamer denied he was in Dallas to investigate the whipping cases," reported one. In fact, the close-mouthed lawman was there to assist Dallas police in the investigation of the floggings and to make a point of enforcing the Prohibition laws. Much to the anger of Dallas civic leaders, Governor Neff had publicly charged them with ignoring the floggings and being soft on crime. This was unfair to Mayor Sawnie Aldredge, who opposed the Klan, and to the Dallas police, who had already arrested one of their own officers and suspended two more for involvement in the whippings. Yet the policemen were quickly exonerated and reinstated. At the same time, Dallas officials pressured Neff to withdraw the Rangers. The governor responded by telling them that "the combined official forces of your city and county have not been able to bring to the bar of justice even one" of the floggers. He complained about open bootlegging in Dallas and refused to remove the Rangers, insisting instead that local officers cooperate in a joint investigation of the whippings. Hamer was unable to identify any of the vigilantes, but, to emphasize the governor's statements, he arrested five bootleggers in Dallas.[7]

Governor Neff's pressure worked. On April 4, a crowd of five thousand, led by former Governor Oscar Colquitt, met at the Dallas city hall to protest the Ku Klux Klan. They formed an anti-Klan group, the Dallas County Citizens' League. In response, five thousand Klansmen held a mass rally a few days later and refused to disband. Klan leaders, shaken by the outpouring of opposition, sent a letter to *The Dallas Morning News* denying responsibility for "the recent illegal and outrageous whippings of Dallas people at the hands of law-breakers" and promising to forego any further parades of masked Klansmen. The whippings in

A Ku Klux Klan parade in Beaumont, Texas, 1922. *Author's collection*

Dallas suddenly stopped, but the Klan did not go away. In elections the following year, the anti-Klan mayor, Sawnie Aldredge, and the rest of his ticket were overwhelmingly defeated. The Ku Klux Klan, for the present, remained a powerful force in Texas.[8]

Governor Neff's next Klan assignment proved even less successful for Frank Hamer. On May 4, a seventeen-year-old white schoolgirl was found murdered near Kirvin, in Freestone County, seventeen miles northwest of Mexia. She had been dragged from her horse, carried into the woods, then raped and stabbed to death. A huge manhunt resulted in the arrests of three black suspects: McKinley "Snap" Curry, John Cornish, and Mose Jones. All of them worked for the dead girl's family. Two days later, despite the efforts of Sheriff Horace Mayo, a mob of five hundred broke into the county jail. The three prisoners were taken to Kirvin, where a pyre was built in an empty lot. The mob castrated at least one of them, then tied Curry to a stake and burned him alive. Despite savage beatings, Cornish and Jones maintained their innocence until they too met the same fate—roasted alive on the roaring flames. It was one of the most brutal lynchings in Texas's bloody history.[9]

Sheriff Mayo, who had claimed ignorance of corruption and lawlessness in Mexia, had failed to call on the Rangers to help guard his prisoners. On May 8, Sim Cornish, brother of John Cornish, was reportedly found lynched to a tree near Kirvin, and another black man, Shadrick Green, accused of participating in the girl's murder, was shot and hanged. The same day, after sensational news accounts of the lynchings appeared, Sheriff Mayo finally called Governor Neff and asked for ten Rangers. His reason was not to prevent further killings of African Americans but to guard against a feared uprising of vengeful blacks against the white populace. Hamer and his Headquarters Company rushed from Austin, while Tom Hickman and his men responded from Wichita Falls. Whether the Rangers actually reached Freestone County is unclear, for the following day Sheriff Mayo realized the rumors of black mobs were false and withdrew his request. Hamer, Hickman, and their men were ordered to return to their posts. Meanwhile, white vigilantes—presumably the Klan—continued to menace African Americans in Kirvin, yet Neff did not send the Rangers back. In the end, it developed that John Cornish and Mose Jones were likely innocent and that two white suspects held by Sheriff Mayo were probably the killers, assisted by Snap Curry. In a damning indictment of Texas racism and injustice, the white suspects went free.[10]

By this time leaders of the Dallas County Citizens' League, in public letters to the governor, demanded that he respond to rumors that "almost every officer and private of the Ranger forces is a member of the Ku Klux Klan" and that "a number of officers of the National Guard hold office under the imperial wizard of Atlanta and his invisible empire." The Citizens' League demanded the names of all Rangers and Guard officers who were Klansmen. On May 11 Governor Neff ordered an investigation, and a month later Adjutant General Barton reported that he had interviewed "the Captains of the companies, all Rangers and members of the Adjutant General's department, and have failed to find any who were members of the Ku Klux Klan." Yet Barton himself was reputed to be a "big shot" in the Klan. The governor pointed out that most of the Rangers—with the exception of Hamer's and Hickman's companies—were stationed in West Texas and along the border, where Klan influence was minimal.

Soon after, Harry Warner, a rival candidate for governor, alleged in speeches that Neff turned a blind eye to the Klan. *The Dallas Morning News* lambasted Neff for his reticence, and the governor was forced to state that he had never been a member of the Ku Klux Klan. Although Neff repeatedly spoke out against vigilantism and sent in the Rangers to stop lynchings, he notably failed to criticize the Klan or to mention it by name. The reason was that his strongest political support came from the law-and-order faction, many of whom either belonged to the Klan or sympathized with it. Neff's lieutenant governor, T. W. Davidson, explained the administration's paternalistic, Jim Crow attitude toward lynch law: "In this land of white supremacy we make the negro our ward. It is our duty to give our ward legal protection." This was an ethic that Frank Hamer adhered to.[11]

A few weeks later, Hamer once again confronted mob violence in Waco. Following the Barker killings, several more mysterious murders and sexual assaults had taken place in McLennan County. On May 9, 1922, William P. Driskell was found in his Waco home, his head splintered by an ax. Among the suspects questioned was Roy Mitchell, the same black chauffeur who had been picked up in the Barker case. Mitchell, light-skinned with a gold front tooth, was well known in Waco. Once again, his white boss gave him an alibi. Even though Mitchell had been questioned three months earlier, Waco lawmen failed to investigate him any further. Ten days later, a young couple, William Cottrell and Marjorie Sheffield, were parked in an auto in Waco's Cameron Park, a popular trysting place. A black man approached with a drawn pistol and ordered them out. When they refused, he shot them both in the face and fled. Neither was killed.[12]

By the 1920s, automobiles had become a staple for courtship. They allowed young couples to escape front porch swings, living room sofas, and the prying eyes of parents and siblings. Almost all earlier motorcars were convertibles, which offered little or no privacy. But hardtops of the twenties were ideal for sex. Because autos were viewed mainly as tools for transportation, it became increasingly acceptable for courting couples to go for long drives, ostensibly for sightseeing, but just as often for "heavy petting" in a lover's lane. And just as Texas introduced the first drive-in restaurant in 1921, it had now produced one of the first lover's-lane killers.[13]

On the night of May 25, a week after the Cameron Park attack, another young couple, Harrell Bolton and Margaret Hays, were driving on the Corsicana road, four miles north of Waco, when they were stopped by a light-complected black man with a gold tooth. He shot and killed Bolton, then dragged the young woman into the woods and raped her. The next day, a citizen picked up a taxi driver, Jesse Thomas, who fit the killer's description. Instead of turning him over to the police for a proper lineup, he and several other citizens brought Thomas to Margaret Hays's home. The hysterical young woman took one look at Thomas and exclaimed, "That's the man, papa!"

Her father, Sam Harris, immediately jerked out an automatic pistol and pumped seven bullets into the hapless taxi driver, killing him. As the body was taken to an African American undertaker, Waco residents flocked to Harris's house to congratulate him. "You've done a good day's work," exclaimed one. "It was a fine job," declared another. Then a mob forced their way into the funeral home and hauled the body outside. Tying it to a truck, they dragged it down Franklin Avenue to the plaza behind city hall. While a crowd of five thousand gathered, the body was stripped and tossed into a huge bonfire. Then what remained of the blackened corpse was pulled from the ashes, tied to the rear of a motorcar, and dragged to the Harris home. Finally, the triumphant mob dragged it back through downtown Waco for all to see. Men vied with one another to pry off body parts as souvenirs—blood relics. It was a savage replay of the Waco Horror of 1916. The victim in that case had been burned alive in the same plaza. His corpse had also been dragged by an automobile in an equally barbaric display. The 1916 lynching—and graphic photographs of the charred corpse—brought Waco international notoriety and condemnation, but in the ensuing six years its citizens had learned nothing.[14]

Earlier that day, May 26, Waco officers had locked five other black suspects in jail. One of them, Sank Johnson, also had a prominent gold tooth. When a huge lynch mob surrounded the jail, the prosecuting attorney telephoned Adjutant General Barton for the Rangers. Frank

Hamer and his men rushed one hundred miles to Waco by auto, arriving that evening—just an hour after Jesse Thomas had been incinerated in the plaza. Hamer, with Sergeant McMordie and Privates Charlie Miller, J. B. Wheatley, and William M. Molesworth, drove up to the jail. The lockup was a large four-story building directly behind the courthouse. Hamer found county officials, including Sheriff Buchanan and Judge Irvin Clark, on the front steps, pleading with the mob to disperse.

As the enraged crowd surged forward, Frank Hamer left his men in the motorcar, climbed the steps with a Thompson submachine gun in hand, and faced the lynchers alone. Many of the hardcases recognized the Ranger captain from his sojourn in Waco two months earlier. His personal reputation, coupled with his brazen fearlessness and the yawning barrel of the Thompson gun, were enough to intimidate the mob. The huge throng quickly dispersed as his Rangers set up a guard around the jail. According to a breathless reporter, "They are armed with machine guns, high-powered rifles, and automatic pistols." It wasn't "One Riot, One Ranger," but it came close.[15]

Sank Johnson and the other four black suspects were soon released from jail. Sam Harris, who had slain the hapless Jesse Thomas in cold blood, was never charged with a crime. Hamer stayed in Waco until May 29, then returned to Austin, leaving two men behind to keep an eye out for trouble. But the mob's bloodlust was satiated, and Waco remained quiet for six months. Then, on the night of November 21, nineteen-year-old Grady Skipworth and his girlfriend, Naomi Boucher, were parked in an automobile at Lover's Leap in Cameron Park, overlooking the Bosque River. Suddenly, a black assailant appeared from the dark, pulling young Skipworth from the car and shooting him to death. He dragged the body to the edge of the cliff and threw it over. After raping Naomi Boucher, the killer vanished. The attack created an uproar in Waco, and more racial violence was feared. Hamer arrived the next day and stayed until the city settled down. When he left, Ranger Rudolph D. Shumate was assigned to assist in the investigation.

The similarity of this attack to the ones on William Cottrell and Marjorie Sheffield and on Harrell Bolton and Margaret Hays, and the occurrence of two of the attacks in the same park, should have been enough to convince even the most simple-minded harness bull that a serial killer and rapist was on the loose. Instead, Ranger Shumate conducted one of the most bungled investigations in Ranger history. On January 12, 1923, in a priceless moment of buffoonery, he arrested the rape victim, Naomi Boucher, and two of her brothers for conspiring to kill young Skipworth. Their innocence would soon be proved in the bloodiest way possible.[16]

A week later, on the night of January 19, W. E. Holt and a young woman, Ethel Denecamp, were shot to death while parked in their car on the Mexia road, five miles east of town. Their bodies were discovered two days later. Several weeks later, Roy Mitchell was picked up for gambling. He was the same gold-toothed, light-complected African American chauffeur who had been twice questioned in the prior killings but released after establishing alibis. In Mitchell's house, officers found items that had belonged to some of the murder victims: Grady Skipworth's watch fob; W. E. Holt's pistol, pocketbook, and fountain pen; and William Driskell's razor and shaving mug. Roy Mitchell then made a full confession, admitting to all seven Waco murders: Driskell, the Barkers and young Homer Turk, Harrell Bolton, W. E. Holt, and Ethel Denecamp. He acknowledged several rapes and the shooting of William Cottrell and Marjorie Sheffield in Cameron Park. Mitchell also revealed the location of other property stolen from the victims, which was subsequently recovered.[17]

Roy Mitchell affirmed that the imprisoned Cooper Johnson and Bennie Young, as well as the incinerated Jesse Thomas, were entirely innocent. Naomi Boucher and her brothers were promptly released. Cooper Johnson soon died of illness while awaiting execution, and in a gross miscarriage of justice, Bennie Young remained in prison until he was finally pardoned in 1934. Roy Mitchell, with Hamer again providing protection, was tried and convicted on six charges of murder and sentenced to hang. On July 30, 1923, a crowd of eight thousand jammed into the Waco plaza to get a glimpse of the condemned man as he climbed the gallows stairs in the jail yard. Mitchell's death on the scaffold was the second-to-last legal hanging in Texas, which subsequently adopted the electric chair. Waco had long been known as the "Athens of Texas" because of its fine schools and colleges, yet the lynchings of 1916 and 1922 revealed a disturbing undercurrent to the city's veneer of respectability and left a dark stain. In Waco, Frank Hamer twice demonstrated how his hard-nosed, intransigent tactics prevented mob violence in a time and place when profound racism and the Ku Klux Klan ruled supreme.[18]

The Ranger captain was soon called on to handle more trouble with the Ku Klux Klan. This time, however, Klansmen were the victims. Although the Klan was not strong in either West or South Texas, it did have a presence in Corpus Christi, a picturesque port city of ten thousand on the Gulf Coast. During the Democratic primary election on July 22, Hamer and Captain Will Wright were sent to maintain order at the polls. Because Texas was overwhelmingly Democratic, the only real election battles were between Democrats themselves in the primaries. The election pitted the machine of Judge Walter Timon, Nueces County political boss, who was supported by blacks, Hispanics, and Catholics, against Prohibitionists and a Klan-backed slate of candidates. Fred Roberts, a prominent cotton raiser, political leader, Klansman, and close friend of Governor Neff, supported the Klan slate. He had quarreled with Nueces County's sheriff, Frank Robinson, and its constable, Lee Petzel, incumbents who ran for nomination on the anti-Klan platform of Judge Timon's machine. Just before the primary, Hamer, with two Rangers, and Wright, with five, arrived in Corpus Christi. A Klan supporter was delighted at the arrival of the Rangers, writing, "Hamer is the man they all dreaded, and when he got here they all got good and remained so. . . . This is all that saved the day for us and prevented the election being grabbed for Timon." But in the next breath he complained, "they permitted niggers, Mexicans, priests and nuns at the polls." Under Hamer and Wright the balloting passed off peacefully, with Robinson and Petzel winning the nomination. Fred Roberts was so impressed with Hamer and Wright, and so grateful for their protection, that he collected funds to purchase a Colt presentation revolver for each of the captains.[19]

Roberts never lived to make the gifts. He and other members of the Klan contested Sheriff Robinson's nomination, but their complaints of ballot-box stuffing were overruled by the Democratic county committee. Then, on the morning of October 14, a lawsuit was filed to prevent the anti-Klan constable, Lee Petzel, from appearing on the ballot. That afternoon, Sheriff Robinson, furious about the lawsuit and accompanied by his deputy, Joe Acebo, stepped into the grocery store of G. E. Warren, a Klansman, on the corner of Railroad Avenue and Staples Street. Although the lawmen later claimed that they went to the store to stop a "Klan riot," that was hardly true. The sheriff asked Warren how business was, and the storekeeper replied that it was slow.

"That's how it is with you Ku Kluxers," Robinson declared. "You are a Ku Kluxer, aren't you, Warren? By God, you know you are." Then he slapped the storekeeper's face. As a crowd gathered, Warren's wife telephoned the chief of police, Frank's former captain Monroe Fox, who soon arrived on the scene. By this time Sheriff Robinson and his deputy had left the shop and were lounging in front of a drugstore across the street. Fox talked with Robinson but refused to arrest him unless Warren swore out a complaint. In a repeat of his often-abysmal performance as a Ranger captain, Fox then abandoned the volatile scene as Sheriff Robinson, Deputy Acebo, Constable Petzel, and a crony, Cleve Goff, loitered across the street. Warren telephoned Fred Roberts and asked him for help and advice. Roberts drove to the store, discussed the assault with Warren, then walked out and climbed into his auto. Just as he started the engine, Sheriff Robinson crossed the street, jerked his pistol, and pumped three slugs into the chest of the unarmed Roberts, killing him instantly. As the crowd scattered, Sheriff Robinson, Acebo, Petzel, and Goff fired several shots into the car and also at Warren in front of his store.

Monroe Fox raced back to the scene, where he arrested Petzel and Acebo. Fox found Robinson and Goff at the sheriff's office, and then, instead of jailing them, placed all four in the custody of the chief deputy sheriff inside the courthouse. The killing caused a frenzy of excitement, and townsfolk feared more violence between Klan and anti-Klan factions. Neither the mayor nor the county judge believed that Fox could handle the turmoil, so they telephoned Governor Neff for Rangers. That night, Frank Hamer boarded a train for Corpus Christi, where he was soon joined by Captain Roy Aldrich. To a reporter, Hamer made it clear that he, not Aldrich, was in charge, and that he was "empowered . . . to make a full investigation of the shooting." Frank was stunned to find that Monroe Fox had brought no charges against the killers and had not even jailed them. Hamer interviewed witnesses, then swore out warrants charging Robinson, Acebo, Petzel, and Goff with murder.[20]

Years later, Gladys Hamer said that when her husband arrived in Corpus Christi, the killers were barricaded inside the courthouse, protected by an armed band of thirty henchmen. Alone, Hamer kicked in the doors of a courtroom and confronted the crowd. "I'm Frank Hamer, Texas Ranger," he declared. "I have a warrant for the arrest of the men involved in the murder of Fred Roberts. The rest of you put up those guns and get the hell out of here." Gladys's account is largely confirmed by a contemporary newspaper, which reported, "When Captain Hamer reached Corpus Christi, the officers who did the shooting were lionized in the courthouse surrounded by a bunch of forty or fifty Catholic henchmen armed with shotguns and rifles. Captain Hamer went straight to the bunch and said, 'Here, you officers come with me to jail.' There was not a whimper; they trotted to the jail and were locked up by Frank Hamer."[21]

Captain Hamer read the warrants to the four prisoners in their cells. All refused to make any statements. Fred Roberts had been hugely popular; a crowd of more than six thousand attended his funeral, and feelings ran high. The next day, Captain Wright arrived from Brownsville with two privates. Hamer wired a report to the adjutant general's office describing the tension and excitement in Corpus Christi as "deplorable" but saying that "the situation is under control of state officers." Frank declared to a newspaperman, "You can tell the public and say I said it that the chief of police, Monroe Fox, hasn't been of the slightest assistance to us in securing evidence against the men who killed Mr. Roberts; on the other hand he seems to be spending his time looking for an excuse for them. Quote me as saying that, if you will." An indignant Fox told reporters that Hamer's comments "should have no weight." A petition was soon circulated by the Woman's Christian Temperance Union, signed by five hundred women, demanding Fox's resignation. The city council refused to fire him.

Frank ignored his former captain, concentrating instead on building the murder case and keeping the town quiet. Sheriff Robinson, Deputy

Hamer playing with his son Frank, Jr., about 1921. *Travis Hamer personal collection*

Acebo, and Constable Petzel promptly resigned from office. Given the strong feelings between the Klan and anti-Klan factions, a change of venue sent the case to Laredo, where the trial took place in January 1923. The district attorney in Laredo was Hamer's friend John A. Valls, a tough Hispanic prosecutor widely known as "the silver-tongued orator of the Rio Grande." When Monroe Fox took the stand as a defense witness, Valls raked him over the coals. Focusing on his performance as a Ranger captain, Valls pointed out that Fox was one of the men who posed for photographs dragging a dead Mexican raider at Norias and that his men had massacred Mexicans at Porvenir. Fox denied any culpability for the Porvenir massacre, insisting that he had been in Marfa, "eighty-five miles away from the scene of the alleged killing of the Mexicans."

Valls's efforts to get a conviction were in vain. Despite the fact that Roberts had been murdered in cold blood, a jury set the three former lawmen free. Sheriff Robinson testified that when he approached the automobile, he thought Roberts was trying to draw a gun. In November 1923, Petzel, Acebo, and Goff were tried in San Antonio for assault to murder the storekeeper, G. E. Warren, but again all were acquitted. The time-honored Texas tradition of self-defense, as we have seen, generally worked even if the case was clearly not self-defense.[22]

The Fred Roberts murder illustrated that strong anti-Klan sentiment existed, at least in parts of Texas. But just as Frank Hamer was no supporter of the Klan, he likewise would not tolerate the murder of a Klansman. Fred Roberts's widow was greatly appreciative. She had not forgotten that her husband had wanted to present special six-guns to Hamer and Captain Wright. Soon after his death, she ordered a pair of Colt Single-Action Army revolvers in .45 caliber. Each was nickel-plated, with profuse factory engraving. Hamer's gun was inscribed on the back strap: CAPT. FRANK HAMER, STATE RANGER, PRESENTED BY THE CITIZENS OF CORPUS CHRISTI, 7-22-22. Will Wright's Colt had a similar inscription, commemorating the date that the two captains had preserved order in the primary election. Hamer's pistol was presented to him when he returned to Corpus Christi with six other Rangers to maintain order during the general election on November 7. He was deeply moved by this gesture.[23]

During the early 1920s other Rangers—not just Hamer—repeatedly responded to stop Klan violence. But opposing the Klan was Hamer's specialty. Two weeks after leaving Corpus Christi, he was sent to Breckenridge in the wake of a Klan-influenced parade. An oil boomtown with a floating population of thirty thousand, Breckenridge was situated a hundred miles west of Fort Worth. On the night of November 14, three hundred local Klansmen, calling themselves the White Owls, marched through town demanding that black and Mexican laborers be fired. They handed out placards to businessmen reading, "We employ white people only." About two hundred Mexican and three hundred black laborers fled. Mexicans complained to their consul in Dallas, who in turn lodged a protest with Governor Neff. Humiliated city officials denounced the group and offered protection "to all law-abiding and employed negroes, Mexicans, or persons of any other race."

The manager of a local oil company was not assuaged and wired Governor Neff: "Lawless element at Breckenridge intimidating labor. County and city officials very seldom act until after damage is done. . . . Please send Frank Hamer or some other good reliable ranger to Breckenridge to protect labor before they all run off." The captain, with Sergeant John Gillon and Privates Bill Molesworth and Joe Orberg, arrived by train on November 17. For out-of-state oil roughnecks who had never seen a Texas Ranger, a local reporter described them in his newspaper: "All are men of large physique, and are above middle age and wear corduroy suits, boots, and large white hats. They are armed with six-shooters and large belts of cartridges and in addition carried rifles." When asked to comment by a journalist, Hamer had only one terse statement: "You can say that there is no occasion for any more Mexicans or negroes to leave town. They will be protected."[24]

Local officials told Hamer that the trouble had been caused by the Industrial Workers of the World—the Wobblies. That was virtually impossible, for the IWW, a radical labor organization, supported the employment rights of all races, especially blacks and Hispanics. Because Mexican citizens had been threatened, Hamer called in agents from the FBI. The Rangers and federal agents spent more than a week interrogating numerous witnesses and members of the White Owls, who denied any involvement. Several witnesses—probably to divert attention from the Klan—claimed that some members of the White Owls were Wobblies. The Rangers jailed one IWW organizer and a handful of bootleggers before General Barton ordered the lawmen to return home to spend Thanksgiving with their families. Hamer's cool handling of the trouble—reinforced by the fearsome reputation of the Texas Rangers—restored calm to Breckenridge and allowed blacks and Hispanics to return to their jobs.[25]

Investigations of the Klan were extremely difficult. Over the years,

Hamer had slowly developed a wide network of criminal informants. He became well known to underworld characters and earned a reputation for always living up to his word. If he made a deal with a criminal for information, he never violated that agreement. But Klansmen were not ordinary criminals who could be trapped in customary ways. Unlike career criminals, they did not associate with thieves, fences, or prostitutes, who, from the era of the thieftakers in eighteenth-century England, were a detective's most reliable source of information. Klansmen were often law-abiding, churchgoing men who organized privately, met at night, and took oaths of secrecy. They belonged to local klaverns, and their fellow Klansmen were often relatives or lifelong friends. Cracking open a Klan-related assault or murder case was more than difficult. Getting a conviction from a local jury, which might include Klan sympathizers, was even harder. But Frank Hamer was undeterred. As Captain Rogers had explained years before, "The harder the criminal and more dangerous and hazardous the work, the better he likes it."

In between his bouts with the Klan, Hamer continued to handle everything from murder investigations to moonshine raids. On March 16, 1923, he received a tip that an auto loaded with liquor would be coming into Austin from San Antonio. Frank got a good description of the vehicle: a Dodge touring car with disk wheels and a set of bull's horns mounted on the radiator. That morning, Hamer, with Deputy Sheriff Jim McCoy, Deputy Constable Barney Basford, and several other officers, set up a roadblock eight miles south of Austin on the Post Road, which connected the capital city with San Antonio. Before long, a high-powered Dodge approached from the south. When Hamer ordered the driver to stop, two rumrunners inside drew guns and opened up on him. Hamer and the rest returned the fire, and the car fled at what was a high rate of speed for the early 1920s—more than fifty miles an hour.

Basford and McCoy jumped onto the constable's motorcycle and raced off after the bootleggers, with Hamer and the others following in an auto. The fugitives veered off the Post Road and fled east on rough country byways. Basford fired several pistol shots at the Dodge and thought he hit the driver. During the wild chase, the rumrunners threw twenty gallons of liquor in bottles and jugs from the car. The pursuit took

them east through Webberville and toward Bastrop. Finally, the bootleggers managed to outrun Hamer and the rest and disappear. Frank
sent a wire to San Antonio police, telling them to be on the lookout for
the escaping vehicle. The next day, two young brothers, Jack and Joe
Adams, reported to San Antonio officers that they had rented the vehicle to a third man. They denied being the rumrunners, and neither bore
bullet wounds. Nonetheless, they were arrested, and Hamer brought
them to Austin to face bootlegging charges.[26]

The Ranger captain quickly returned to his investigations of the
Klan. The klavern in Burleson County, just west of Navasota, was especially troublesome. During the state primary election on July 22, 1922,
Klansmen had run off opposition voters from the polls, even stealing
ballot boxes at gunpoint and destroying their opponents' votes. Then,
on November 29, 1922, a white-hooded band shot and wounded a
prominent white citizen in Caldwell, the county seat. Subsequently,
several other whites, including a city marshal and a doctor, were flogged
or tarred and feathered. The final—and worst—outrage took place on
July 2, 1923, when three Klan members drove up to the farmhouse of a
white man, Otto Lange, near Somerville. They tried to kidnap him in
front of his mother, wife, and three-year-old daughter. Lange and his
wife resisted, and one of the Klansmen pulled a pistol and opened fire,
killing him and wounding the child. The anti-Klan sheriff, Clint
Lewis, promptly telephoned for assistance from the Rangers. Captain
Roy Aldrich announced that he would respond and declared to the
press, "Arrests will be made immediately in the murder of Otto Lange."

Yet Aldrich had little, if any, experience investigating homicides,
for his job as Ranger quartermaster was primarily clerical. He teamed
up with the Somerville constable, W. S. Houston, who helpfully announced to reporters, "I am a Klansman, and I told [Lieutenant] Governor Davidson that the Klan had absolutely nothing to do with the
killing of Lange, that it was a purely family affair." The gullible Aldrich
accepted the Klansman's theory. When Aldrich foolishly reported that
Lange's murder "resulted from family difficulties," General Barton relieved him and sent Frank Hamer to Somerville. Lieutenant Governor
Davidson assured the public that there would be no cover-up: "Captain

Hamer is in charge of the work and I have great faith in his ability and integrity as an officer." Frank spent a week in Somerville interviewing witnesses, then returned several times during the next three months to continue his investigation. Working with Sheriff Lewis, he developed evidence connecting two railroad workers and suspected Klan members, Kinch Shelburne and Charles Balke, with the murder. On November 4, 1923, Hamer presented his evidence to the Burleson County grand jury, but that body, perhaps in sympathy with—or in fear of—the Klan, failed to return indictments. Sheriff Lewis did not give up, and more than two years later, he and two other Rangers managed to get Kinch Shelburne's ex-wife to turn against him. In June 1926 Shelburne and Balke were indicted for the Lange murder. Four others, all members of the Klan, were charged with stealing the ballot boxes. A judge later dismissed the case against Balke, but Shelburne was convicted of murder and, to Hamer's disgust, sentenced to only five years in prison.[27]

Soon after the Otto Lange murder, Frank was called on to investigate Klan violence in Amarillo, the largest town in the Panhandle. Amarillo boasted fifteen thousand residents, a thousand of them members of the Klan, including Potter County's sheriff, Less Whitaker, and its prosecuting attorney, Henry L. Ford. On August 15, 1923, Klansmen

Frank Hamer's ornately engraved Colt single action revolver and gold Texas Ranger captain badge, carried in the 1920s. *Collection of Kurt House, San Antonio, Texas*

snatched E. T. "Little Mike" McDonald, a white railroad carpenter, from an Amarillo street. McDonald had a reputation as a womanizer and had been living with a local widow until she kicked him out of her house. He was taken out of town, savagely whipped, tarred and feathered, and ordered to leave the county on pain of death.

Hamer and Ranger Ollie B. Chessir arrived in Amarillo the next day, and this time they had a live, though badly injured, witness. From his hospital bed, McDonald told the captain that a month earlier, on July 9, Sheriff Whitaker had picked him up, drove him outside town, and delivered him to a band of hooded, white-robed men. They ordered McDonald to leave the county, but, though he stood only five foot tall, he was not easily cowed and refused to obey. On the fateful night of August 15, he attended a motion picture show with another woman, and on the way home was kidnapped by the Klansmen. Despite their masks, McDonald recognized several of his tormentors. Frank wasted little time, and on August 17 he arrested Sheriff Whitaker and three other members of the Klan. Whitaker admitted to Hamer that he "took McDonald to a committee of robed men for a lecture" but that he "was unable to identify any of them." Captain Hamer's arrest of the sheriff made front-page news in Texas, but the Klan, as was its custom, denied any involvement.

Hamer wired a report of the arrests to Lieutenant Governor Davidson, who responded by telegram: "Do your full duty—Texas is behind you." Frank's strongest case was against Klansman T. W. Stanford, who was tried in October and convicted of whitecapping. Numerous local Klan officials were forced to testify, and all claimed that McDonald's attackers had acted on their own, without Klan approval. Stanford got a two-year prison jolt, but his conviction was later overturned by an appellate court. Sheriff Whitaker went on trial in January 1924, with "Little Mike" McDonald the prime witness. McDonald described his first kidnapping but admitted that Sheriff Whitaker told the Klansmen to "return the man to him without hurt or injury." Though Hamer also testified, the jury acquitted Whitaker. Frank later insisted that the county attorney, Henry L. Ford, who was a Klansman, deliberately bungled the prosecution. A measure of justice was meted out, however, when the Ku Klux Klan sheriff was voted out of office in the election later that year.[28]

While many Texas lawmen sympathized with the Klan, and many were undoubtedly members, Frank Hamer thought they were cowards. His lifelong empathy for African Americans, coupled with a rabid hatred of bullies and lawbreakers, propelled his efforts against the "Invisible Empire." The firm stand taken by Hamer, the Rangers, and other peace officers worked. In 1922 seventeen victims were slain by fourteen different mobs in Texas. The next year, the state had just two lynchings; the following year, one. In 1925, for the first time since 1883, Texas had none.[29]

Hamer's struggles against the Klan, though completely unknown today, were among the most important of his career. The physical courage he displayed in dozens of gun battles with desperadoes paled in comparison to his moral courage, never so evident as when he investigated Klan murders, arrested prominent Klansmen, and protected blacks from Klan-led lynch mobs. In so doing, Hamer sought to replicate the principled bravery of Captain Rogers. The example Hamer set—consistently opposing lynchers and lawbreakers, no matter who they were or how powerful their support—was followed by fellow Rangers. Though it is doubtful that few of them believed in racial justice, they revered Hamer's absolute fearlessness. Other Rangers in turn sought to emulate his acts, and, as a result, the Ranger force became increasingly consistent in its efforts to combat racial strife. Frank Hamer's iron-fisted leadership in the fight to stop lynching in Texas was the brightest and most noble episode of his official life.

15

MA AND PA FERGUSON

The Democratic primary election of 1924 presented the Texas electorate with an unsavory choice: a Klan-backed judge or a return to the corruption of Jim Ferguson's regime. Because the impeached "Pa" Ferguson was prevented by law from holding state office, he had made a run for U.S. senator in 1922. He failed and then tried for the governor's office in 1924, but a judge struck his name from the primary ballot. He then ran his wife, Miriam A. "Ma" Ferguson, for governor in a strong anti-Klan campaign, with the popular slogan, "Me for Ma, and I ain't got a durned thing against Pa." Ma Ferguson insisted that her principal motivation was "to vindicate my husband's good name" and promised "two governors for the price of one." After narrowly winning the primary, she easily defeated her Republican opponent in the general election in November to become the nation's second elected female governor. But all Texans recognized that their real governor was Farmer Jim.

Taking office in January 1925, Ma Ferguson immediately set out to hamstring the Texas Rangers. Ostensibly to cut costs, she reduced the Rangers from fifty-one to twenty-eight, stationed most of the force along the Mexican border, and ordered that Rangers be sent to towns and cities only if requested by local officials. These changes were a direct repudiation of Governor Neff's policies. The Fergusons, to their great credit, strongly opposed the Klan and did not shy from sending in Rangers to stop lynchings.

On the night of May 20, 1925, a crowd of five thousand surrounded the Dallas County jail. Inside were two African American brothers, Frank and Lorenzo Noel, who had been arrested for robbing and killing two white men and raping their girlfriends. At first the crowd was good-natured. It was made up largely of curious young men and girls but had a hard inner core of determined lynchers who were probably Klansmen. A heavy guard of police and deputy sheriffs cordoned off the jail. Then the throng became unruly, and firemen were called in to turn their hoses on the crowd. This had little effect, and at one in the morning an enraged lynch mob of three hundred attacked the jail, hurling bricks, bottles, and rocks, which injured forty officers and firemen. When two of the mob opened fire, police and deputies sent 150 shots into the rabble, wounding five men, one fatally, and scattering the lynchers.

Captain Hamer and Sergeant Wheatley arrived in Dallas the following day and found a crowd of ten thousand, which filled Main Street near the jail. Thousands of automobiles crammed with spectators created a massive traffic jam. The Rangers joined local officers and a company of National Guard, which cordoned off the jail. After conferring with Hamer and the county sheriff, the presiding judge announced, "A demonstration by anyone will be tantamount to his committing suicide." The show of force had a salutary effect. *The Dallas Morning News* reported that the crowd "laughed and joked with the officers much as they would have done had they been along the side lines at a football game or witnessing a downtown parade." But the *News* also issued a caution to its readers: "Capt. Hamer . . . has established a long record of successes in combating mob violence in various sections of the State during his years of service."[1]

The next day, when Captain Tom Hickman arrived with several members of his company, the National Guard was relieved of duty. Adjutant General Mark McGee believed that the two captains and a handful of Rangers were equivalent to a company of guardsmen. The rape trials of Frank and Lorenzo Noel began on May 28, when Hamer, Hickman, and two fellow Rangers brought the Noel brothers into court. There was no violence, for, as *The Dallas Morning News* reported, "Orders to shoot to kill have been given [to] Texas Rangers." The brothers were quickly tried, back-to-back, in a single day. Both admitted raping one of the women, and in each case the juries deliberated less than five minutes. The judge sentenced them to die in the electric chair in the Huntsville prison. Rape was then a capital offense in Texas, and it remained so until 1972, when the U.S. Supreme Court struck down such laws as cruel and unusual punishment. Just before the Noels were executed on July 3, 1925, they confessed to the murders and rapes in front of state officials, including Captain Hickman and the prison chaplain.[2]

Meanwhile, Hamer returned to Austin to confront political trouble with the Ferguson regime. Ma and Pa were intent on remaking the Rangers and replacing many of them with political hacks. They retained Captains Hickman, Aldrich, and Roy Nichols and named three other captains, none of them Hamer. He was left with two choices: resign or get fired. And Frank was incensed to learn that Monroe Fox was to be his replacement. Pa Ferguson appreciated Fox's willingness to carry out his unlawful *ley de fuga* orders during the Bandit War, ignored his involvement in the Porvenir massacre of 1918, overlooked his inept performance as police chief of Corpus Christi, and repaid him with a captaincy. But Ferguson was no fool, and he decided that Tom Hickman, not Fox, would be senior captain.[3]

On June 4 *The Galveston Daily News* ran a front-page headline: DEAN OF TEXAS RANGERS RESIGNS. Calling Hamer "the oldest man in point of service," the *News* reported that he had handed in his resignation the day before and that Tom Hickman would take his place as senior captain in charge of Headquarters Company. "With the resignation of Captain Hamer one of the most spectacular peace officers in Texas passes from the ranger service," declared the *News*. "Captain Hamer has figured in many of the greatest battles against lawbreakers in Texas since he first entered the service. . . . A hero in handling mobs and an expert in trailing in the brush, he has always been a modest man, shunning publicity and tributes." The *News* account was picked up by wire services and published throughout Texas.[4]

Former Governor Pat Neff read about Hamer's resignation in the newspapers and sent him a grateful note: "I regret very much your resignation for the reason that I know full well the valuable, faithful, and efficient services you have rendered for so many years to the State. I want you to know that during the four years of my administration I appreciated and still appreciate the services rendered by you in behalf of law and order. When you went anywhere any time in the name of the State to uphold the law and maintain peace, I never lost any sleep, because I knew the work would be done just as it should be."[5]

Hamer's resignation did not take effect until June 30, and he continued his energetic service. To inquiring reporters he refused to state his plans, but said he would keep his home in Austin. Although Frank strongly disliked the Fergusons, they had no animosity toward him and fully recognized his ability. Because the law limited the Rangers to six captains, the Fergusons looked for a way to keep Hamer in state service. On July 1, Frank was commissioned a Ranger private. He was quickly appointed a special investigator for the adjutant general. His office was in Ranger headquarters, a whitewashed wood barracks in Camp Mabry, the Texas National Guard base, situated in the hills four miles northwest of the capitol.[6]

Much to Hamer's irritation, his desk was next to that of Captain Roy Aldrich. Frank never forgave Aldrich for his role in dropping him from the force in 1919 and could barely conceal his contempt. During the Canales hearings, when it was proposed that a private's monthly pay be increased from forty to ninety dollars, Aldrich had declared that he "could get all the Rangers he wanted for $75 a month." Hearing that, Frank snapped, "You could send off seventy-five tobacco tags and get a better Ranger than Aldrich." By the time Hamer became senior captain in charge of Headquarters Company, Aldrich was, next to the adjutant general, the most powerful man in the organization. Independently wealthy and politically connected, he lived in a large estate on the outskirts of Austin and got his younger brother Tod, who had no law-enforcement experience, appointed as a Ranger. Though nominally the quartermaster, Aldrich had usurped Hamer's position as senior captain, boasting, "I am the general 'ramrod' of the force." Under Texas law, however, his duties were clerical, and he had no authority to command Rangers. Frank had a mortgage, a wife, and four children and could ill afford to again become unemployed by bucking political forces. Accordingly, he had acquiesced in Aldrich's assumption of his role as chief of the Rangers, although Hamer never allowed him to participate in or interfere with his investigative work.[7]

In November 1925 Frank drove to Del Rio for a visit with Harrison and his family. For the previous two years, Harrison Hamer had been stationed there as a U.S. customs officer. He liked the border town, securing a house and moving there with his wife and large brood. Harrison, like his older brother, was a very active lawman and a deadly gunfighter. He saw a lot of action against smugglers along the Rio Grande, once recalling, "Every time you went to the river in those days, you would get shot at. But they were poor shots."[8]

When Frank visited Harrison, he must have been regaled with stories of his younger brother's shooting scrapes on the border. On the night of November 22, Frank decided to accompany Harrison and their old captain, William W. Taylor, then a Ranger sergeant, on a scout along the river. They drove to a spot near Jiménez, on the Rio Grande twenty miles south of Del Rio, where they hoped to catch smugglers trying to cross over. No sooner had they brought their motorcar to a halt than a barrage of gunfire exploded from the Mexican side. The three lawmen dove for cover and returned the fire with their rifles. The smugglers were concealed in the brush, so the officers aimed at their muzzle flashes. Scores of shots were fired in the cross-river shootout before the smugglers slipped away in the dark. Reported one Texas newspaper the next day, "Those Mexicans who fired on Frank Hamer just didn't know what they were doing. Good thing they were across the river border, for to even think of pointing a gun at Hamer in Texas means disaster."[9]

Hamer's principal duty as a Ranger was to investigate a number of old, unsolved murder cases. One of the most infamous was the Corpus Christi bombing of November 14, 1923. That morning, a messenger for the American Railway Express Company delivered a wood box marked "magazines" to the Corpus Christi home of J. A. Barnes, a prominent real estate broker. When he opened the box, it triggered a terrific explosion that wrecked the rear of the house and blew out windows in the neighborhood. The blast from the bomb—in the parlance of the day, an "infernal machine"—killed Barnes and his seven-year-old son Jesse and injured his wife and the family maid. An investigation quickly determined that the package had been sent from San Antonio. There, Rangers arrested Juan Morales, a fourteen-year-old newsboy. The youth said that a young white man in a Ford coupe had asked him to take the wood box to the American Railway Express office inside the Missouri, Kansas & Texas depot. Morales did not know how to handle an express shipment, so he first went to find someone who did. When he returned, the driver of the Ford coupe had left, taking the wood box with him. Rangers and detectives did not believe him and used "third degree" methods to get the youth to admit that he had shipped the bomb from San Antonio.[10]

It turned out that the young man in the Ford coupe had left the MK&T station and driven to the International & Great Northern terminal (now known as the MoPac depot), where he paid two other Hispanic youths twenty-five cents to ship the box for him. The boys were soon picked up, and they provided the same description of the man in the Ford. Despite a lengthy investigation by American Railway Express detectives, the Ford driver could not be identified, and the case stalled for several years. Then Frank Hamer took over. He rejected the coerced confession of young Morales and focused on the only person who had a motive to kill J. A. Barnes. At the time of Barnes's death, his oldest daughter, Dorothy, was a student at the University of Texas in Austin. Beautiful, popular, and a graceful dancer, she was enamored with twenty-five-year-old Frank H. Bonner, a fellow student at the university and former army lieutenant. The elder Barnes was strongly opposed to his daughter's romance. Several months after the bombing, the young couple eloped to New York City, where they were married. Under the stage name Dorothy Dale, she danced in numerous Broadway shows. With the passage of three years, the murders were all but forgotten by the public—but not by Hamer.

Assisted by Tom Hickman and the express detectives, Frank slowly and methodically developed a web of circumstantial evidence against

Bonner. Juan Morales and the other two Hispanic youths, when shown photographs of Bonner, were unable to positively identify him as the driver of the Ford coupe, but all agreed that Bonner looked like him. Hamer found that eleven days before the bombing, thirty-five sticks of dynamite and a box of blasting caps had been stolen from a construction site toolshed on the University of Texas campus. A young neighbor of Bonner's recalled that, several years earlier, Bonner had demonstrated how to detonate dynamite caps with an electric battery. Most tellingly, Hamer found that Bonner's name was missing from his university class roll on the day the package was shipped from San Antonio. It was the only time that semester that Frank Bonner had missed the class.[11]

In the summer of 1926, Frank and Dorothy Bonner, oblivious to the investigation, moved back to San Antonio, where they opened a dance studio. Hamer, as usual, kept his probe secret. On August 31, the *San Antonio Light* ran a front-page article claiming that Hamer was close to cracking the case. Hamer was livid at the report, telling newsmen that he "had not been in Corpus Christi for three years, had not been in the Ranger service for over a year and . . . was not working on the bomb case." Hamer saw nothing wrong with misleading the press in order to protect his investigation. On December 8, 1926, Hamer and Hickman presented their evidence to the Nueces County grand jury, which promptly indicted Frank Bonner for the murders. That night, he was arrested at his home in San Antonio and brought to the jail in Corpus Christi.

The Barnes family was shocked by the arrest. Both Dorothy and her mother stood by Bonner and insisted that he was not guilty. "Nothing on earth could ever make me believe Frank is not innocent," Dorothy declared. She visited her husband in jail twice a day. Bonner announced, "I really haven't anything to worry about. I am innocent and very few innocent men are convicted in this country. I shall not be one of them."[12]

His trial began in Corpus Christi on January 18, 1927. Barnes's widow took the stand and described the bombing, but she denied that there had been any friction between her husband and Frank Bonner. An explosives expert testified that the bomb had been constructed with dynamite. Other witnesses described Bonner's detonating dynamite caps and said that Bonner regularly drove Dorothy's Ford coupe. His landlady said that Dorothy had telephoned his rooming house the morning of the bombing but that Bonner and the auto were gone. He returned later that day in a "greatly excited" state. Bonner's university professor testified that he gave a quiz on the fateful day, and his class roll showed that Bonner did not turn in an answer to the exam. Juan Morales and the other two Hispanic youths from San Antonio swore that Bonner resembled the man in the Ford coupe. Prosecutors also presented evidence about the theft of explosives at the university and about the name listed as the shipper on the fatal box, which was that of a fellow student who knew Bonner. An express-company clerk identified Bonner as the man who came into his office a few weeks after the bombing, claiming to be with the company's legal department, and asked him to make a sketch of the fatal package. But on cross-examination, the defense lawyers showed that the same clerk had incorrectly identified Juan Morales as the youth who shipped the box.

In defense, Dorothy and a college friend both swore that Bonner was in Austin the morning the package was shipped in San Antonio. Bonner himself took the stand and claimed that he had been in class that morning and had not turned in his examination paper because he knew he would fail. The only strong evidence in Bonner's favor came from an Austin auto supply dealer, whose books showed that Bonner had made a payment on his account the day the bomb was shipped. The dealer did not know what time of day the transaction occurred, and it was evident that Bonner could have shipped the bomb from San Antonio and then driven to the Austin store the same day. Following three days of testimony, the jury deliberated for thirty-seven hours before they hung, ten to two in favor of acquittal. In May, much to Hamer's disgust, the state dismissed all charges against Frank Bonner. Hamer and other lawmen remained convinced of Bonner's guilt, and in 1931 they again had him indicted for the murders, but the case never came to trial. Frank and Dorothy Bonner stayed married, raising a family and living out their lives quietly in San Antonio, where he died in 1980 at the age of eighty-one. In the final analysis, the fact that the dead victims' own family stood by him during the trial had swayed the jury. Nonetheless, the prosecution had presented a strong circumstantial case, and Frank Bonner must forever remain the prime suspect in the Corpus Christi Bombing.[13]

While working on the bombing case, Hamer investigated a number of other perplexing homicides. One of the most difficult was a triple murder on the outskirts of Austin. On August 9, 1925, a prosperous farmer, Charles Engler, and his wife were found murdered in bed. Their twenty-five-year-old adopted daughter, Emma, had evidently been pursued from the house, savagely pistol-whipped, and then dragged back to the parlor and slain. Each had been shot in the head, and the parents died in their sleep. Nothing was taken from the home, and neither woman had been raped. The killer was no stranger, for the family watchdog, which always barked at visitors, would have awakened the Englers.

Sheriff W. D. Miller, of Travis County, sensibly called in Austin police detective Raymond D. "Boss" Thorp, the department's identification and fingerprint expert—and later the city's police chief for thirty years—to examine the crime scene. At the same time, the sheriff, favoring prejudice over forensics, conducted a botched investigation. As Thorp later recalled, "Sheriff Miller had ordered a search for any person, probably a negro, with blood on his clothing. The terrific battering Emma had suffered was typical of many negro horrors in the South, and the sheriff's first reaction was that she had been the victim of such an offense." Relying on the police dragnet, deputy sheriffs promptly arrested six men: two neighbors who had discovered the bodies and, for good measure, four more of the "usual suspects"—two Mexicans and two African Americans. There was no evidence against any of them, and all were soon released. Then Captain Tom Hickman took over the case, but he had no better success. Walter Prescott Webb called it "one of the most baffling murder cases in Texas."[14]

Although a large reward was offered, the investigation stalled. Months later, the Engler case presented two of the earliest usages of truth serum in an American murder investigation. Dr. Robert E. House, a rural obstetrician in Dallas County, had found that female patients, while in "twilight sleep" induced by the anesthetic scopolamine hydrobromide, could answer questions accurately, without inhibition, even though deeply unconscious. Apparently some pregnant but unmarried women, under the anesthetic during childbirth, would even reveal the father's name. Dr. House saw the drug as a way to free innocent defendants, and he first used it on prisoners in the Dallas County jail in 1922. His experiments created a public sensation, and scopolamine was soon dubbed "truth serum" by journalists, setting off a national debate about whether it was a great forensic discovery or quack science.[15]

In January 1926, two brothers, Otto and Willie Wolter, were picked up by a private detective. In a vain effort to induce a confession to the Engler murders, they were taken to Austin and forcibly administered truth serum by Dr. House. Both insisted they were innocent. In September a black suspect, Link Bookman, was arrested in Houston and brought to jail in Bastrop. After a long grilling by Boss Thorp, he agreed to allow Dr. House to administer truth serum. House gave him four injections, saying it was "the largest dose he had ever given a negro." While under the influence, Bookman proclaimed his innocence, and Dr. House announced, "He is either not guilty or the test was a failure."[16]

Now Frank Hamer was assigned to assist Boss Thorp in the year-old murder case. Hamer focused on Willie Giese, a decorated army veteran who had been wounded in France. Giese had been engaged to marry Emma Engler, and soon after the murders he had been questioned by the Travis County grand jury and declared he was not guilty. His mother and sister had claimed he was home the night of the slayings. In that era of scant government and paltry public coffers, the adjutant general could not afford an expensive investigation. It was necessary for the Texas state legislature to allocate $5,000 for the probe and to pay for out-of-state forensic experts. Willie Giese was arrested at his family home in late December 1926, and his .38 revolver confiscated. The American Legion came to his support, declaring that he was "unlawfully restrained and imprisoned." An Austin judge promptly released him.[17]

On January 22, 1927—while Frank Bonner was on trial in Corpus Christi—Hamer and Thorp presented their case to the Travis County grand jury. Their key evidence was a report from Calvin H. Goddard of

New York City, the father of modern ballistics. He would soon achieve national prominence in the famous Sacco and Vanzetti case in Massachusetts, where his ballistics testimony helped send the two anarchists to the electric chair. Several years later, his expertise would be crucial in unraveling the St. Valentine's Day massacre in Chicago. By using the newly invented comparison microscope, Goddard was able to definitively compare marks on bullets and cartridge cases to prove whether or not they had been fired from the same weapon. In his written report on the Engler murders, Goddard showed that the bullets removed from the dead bodies had been fired by Willie Giese's pistol. In response, Giese claimed that his revolver had been stolen and then somehow was mysteriously returned to his home. The grand jurors, influenced by Giese's war record, were unswayed by the newfangled technology. Hamer was not ready to give up, and in early February he and Thorp had Mrs. Engler's body exhumed and another bullet removed. This time, Calvin Goddard came personally to Austin. At Camp Mabry, he performed ballistics tests for the grand jury, showing that a round fired from Giese's revolver matched exactly the murder slugs. But Goddard, Hamer, and Thorp could not convince the recalcitrant grand jurors. The tight-lipped Ranger made no public comments, but Walter Prescott Webb discussed the case with him and later wrote that Hamer "solved the Engler murder case, but could not secure an indictment because a Travis County grand jury would not accept the evidence of a ballistic expert." In a gross miscarriage of justice, Willie Giese got away with a triple murder.[18]

While Hamer was busy untangling murder mysteries, his old enemy, Captain William M. Hanson, suffered an ignominious downfall. In 1923 Hanson's friend, Senator Albert B. Fall, got him appointed district director of the U.S. Immigration Service, supervising much of the Southwest and the Mexican border. Hanson was as treacherous as ever and supported any Mexican government that had the power to return his lost land. In 1926 Hanson, without a court order, transported a Mexican revolutionist to Mexico, even though the man was a political refugee and faced certain death. Six days later, the man was summarily executed by firing squad, and newspapers in Mexico City reported that

Hanson's El Conejo ranch in Tamaulipas had been returned to him. The news created a sensation, for it was evident that Hanson had made a secret deal with the Mexican government. Hanson publicly denied the reports, but a month later he was forced to appear before a U.S. Senate immigration committee in Washington, D.C. One senator accused him of having secret conferences with Mexican spies and of sending the revolutionist to his death, calling the deportation "a cowardly act." On April 28, 1926, no doubt to Hamer's immense satisfaction, Hanson resigned in disgrace. He managed to find work as a court bailiff in San Antonio, where he died in obscurity in 1931.[19]

As special investigator, Hamer spearheaded an extensive inquiry into the murder of Dr. James A. Ramsey, of Mathis, west of Corpus Christi, in 1926. This was one of the most sensational murder mysteries in Texas during the Roaring Twenties. Frank arrested an old acquaintance, Harry Leahy, who, Hamer showed, had kidnapped and killed the doctor and then tried to extort a $10,000 ransom. Hamer compiled overwhelming evidence against Leahy, who was convicted and received a life sentence. Leahy then appealed and got a new trial. Once again, he was convicted, but this time the jury sentenced him to death. Leahy's date with the Huntsville prison electric chair—later known as Old Sparky—was just after midnight on August 2, 1929. At Leahy's request, Frank attended the execution; before Leahy died, he made a full confession to Hamer.[20]

By 1926 Hamer was by far the most famous lawman in the Southwest. Reporters trumpeted his virtues. In one feature on the Rangers, a journalist used the breathless prose of the era: "There is the mighty Frank Hamer, senior captain at Austin, the hero of many a hot exchange of lead and perhaps the best shot in Texas. He is a living embodiment of Pinkerton and Kit Carson, a relentless, cunning, straight-shooting officer with the mind of a sleuth and the physical courage of a tiger." On February 16, 1926, Will Rogers, the celebrated humorist, visited Austin. He was greeted at the railroad station by the Texas Cowboys, a fraternal organization at the University of Texas. That afternoon, he gave a performance before an audience of three thousand at the university, but the Texan he was most eager to meet was Frank Hamer. Escorted to the enormous capitol building, Rogers gushed, "By golly, this is dern near Washington. I've seen a lot of capitols, but this is the prettiest." With Hamer, Roy Aldrich, and other dignitaries looking on, Adjutant General Dallas Matthews swore him in as a special Ranger. Quipped Rogers, "I hope they don't call me into service on this Ranger commission. I'd have to dig out my five or six words of Mexican if I went into service on the border." Then Rogers asked to "chat a while" privately with Hamer.[21]

Frank's newfound fame also had its disadvantages. For months, a charming, diminutive con man had been traveling across the country, claiming to be a Texas Ranger. At different times he professed to be Captain Frank Hamer, Captain Tom Hickman, or the fictitious Captain Buck Miller. Wearing a Shrine pin studded with diamonds and a thirty-second-degree Masonic charm, he preyed on Shriners and Masons, attending their conventions, borrowing money, and passing forged checks. In Virginia he swindled a victim by impersonating a Department of Justice official. On Christmas Eve 1925, he checked into the Benson Hotel in Portland, Oregon, claiming that he was in town to extradite a prisoner in the Walla Walla penitentiary. Local Shriners prepared a lavish banquet in his honor. He grew so bold he consented to an interview with *The Portland Oregonian*, which published a feature article about the bogus Ranger, even including his photograph. He told *The Portland Oregonian* that he was Captain P. W. Miller, of the Texas Rangers. Wrote the gullible reporter, "Captain Miller is no six-footer, but is one of those small-sized men who do not offer much of a target to shoot at, but have a penchant for giving a good account of themselves in a fight. For instance, Captain Miller took 75 men, went to Marfa and followed the orders of Pat Neff, then governor of Texas, to 'shoot first and inquire afterward.' When the captain's men had finished the job there were more than 300 dead Mexicans; the newspapers were filled with the exploit. General Squires of the regular army protested, but General Funston backed up the captain." The con artist claimed to have been a Ranger for twenty-seven years and earned $400 a month, more than the salary of Ma Ferguson.

As Walter Prescott Webb later pointed out, "This press reporter might have known that General Funston was long dead before Pat Neff was governor of Texas; he might have known that Marfa is a town far inland and entirely out of the danger zone of raiding Mexicans. At no time since the battle of San Jacinto have three hundred Mexicans been killed by Texans at one time." But a sucker is born every minute, and the bogus Ranger continued to drift from city to city, passing bad checks and skipping out on hotel bills. When Hamer got wind of the article in *The Oregonian,* he was not amused. He already knew much about the culprit, and from the adjutant general's office, he fired off a letter to Portland saying that "the fellow is an imposter, a swindler and a few other things" and that he "passes under the names of Captain Buck Burkett, Captain Buck Bowen, Captain Dan Haggerty, Captain Tom Hickman, Captain Frank Hamer, and other aliases." Hamer warned that "the police, hotels and Shrine bodies along the coast be notified immediately to look out for the 'hero.'"

The slippery imposter managed to elude a nationwide manhunt. Several months later, he brazenly showed up in Texas, appearing one afternoon at the Jefferson Hotel in Dallas. While signing the register, he told the clerk, "I'm Frank Hamer and I'm on a job. I may not be back tonight, but I'll be here for sure tomorrow and I want to be certain of a room." The hotel man had been forewarned and immediately called a real Ranger, who staked out the room. But the imposter got suspicious and boarded a train for San Antonio. He drew dozens of checks on Hamer's name, and Frank was forced to respond to bills and overdue notices sent to him from merchants all over Texas.

On July 15, 1926, the swindler went to the San Antonio campaign headquarters of Lynch Davidson, who was seeking the Democratic candidacy for governor in the primary election. He announced himself as Captain Frank Hamer, adding, "I, of course, want to keep my job on the force and I think Davidson is going to win. I thought I'd like to give a little something toward the campaign." He handed the campaign manager a check for $350 and asked that he cash it. That done, "Captain Hamer" handed the pleased manager a hundred dollars and departed with $250. The check, of course, proved worthless. During the next few days, he purchased clothes, hats, and meals, frequently using Hamer's name in passing bad checks along the way.

Ranger Captains Frank Hamer, left, and Tom Hickman, right, posing with the captured con man John Bernard Sawyer in 1926. *Author's collection*

From San Antonio he made the mistake of going to Austin. There he stepped into the American Railway Express office and asked the agent, E. I. Bodell, the cost of traveler's checks. When Bodell gave him the figure, he replied, "Might just as well get them here, I guess. Same price as I have to pay at the bank."

He ordered a thousand dollars' worth and began making out a check in payment. "What's the name?" Bodell asked, glancing across the counter at the check.

"Hamer, Ranger Captain Frank Hamer." He slid a shiny badge toward the agent. But, like many in Austin, Bodell was well acquainted with the big Ranger.

"You're not Hamer!" he exclaimed. The swindler grabbed the badge and fled out the door.

Frank and Boss Thorp began a hunt for the man. They traced him to New Orleans, then Dallas, and finally back to San Antonio. Hamer notified local and federal officers there, and a week later, on July 21, a federal agent picked him up on Houston Street and confiscated his Texas Ranger badge. He proved to be John Bernard Sawyer, a forty-one-year-old native of New Jersey and an escapee from the Texas state prison. His record of theft, forgery, and impersonation stretched back to 1909. Hamer was notified, and he and Thorp drove to the San Antonio jail to interview the phony Ranger. When Hamer entered the office, Sawyer, frightened out of his wits, cowered behind a desk. Frank laughed out loud, saying, "Come on out. I won't hurt you."

The two had a long chat, and Sawyer became increasingly amiable. Soon he even boasted of his exploits, proudly admitting to twenty-eight aliases and having forged checks all over the United States and even in Canada. He had served time in Texas, Pennsylvania, New York, Michigan, and Ohio. After the interview, Sawyer presented Hamer with a gold pocket watch, remarking, "Look at the back."

Hamer turned it over and saw that it was inscribed, "Frank Hamer, Captain of Texas Rangers."

Sawyer explained with a grin, "It was useful for identification purposes."

Frank kept the watch as a memento. Later, Sawyer sent Tom Hickman his gold Masonic charm. He was extradited to Virginia, convicted of impersonating a Department of Justice agent, and sent to federal prison. Before Hamer left the San Antonio jail, he was photographed standing next to Sawyer. Frank towered over the phony Ranger, who stood but five foot six and weighed 130 pounds. Other Rangers got copies of the photo, and they never stopped ribbing Hamer, insisting that the two were twins, with identical personalities. Frank took it all with a laugh, always saying, "'Captain Hamer' was the nicest crook I ever met."[22]

For the scrupulously honest Hamer, working for the Fergusons presented a moral dilemma. To remain on the force he loved so dearly, he turned a blind eye to the rampant graft of the Ferguson regime. The Fergusons were repeatedly accused of granting state highway contracts in exchange for kickbacks. Their corruption was never so evident as in the wholesale granting of pardons. Ma Ferguson averaged 150 a month; the total was 3,595 by the end of her two-year term. According to a popular joke, a man started to enter a door of the capitol building at the same time as Ma Ferguson. "Pardon me," he said politely. "Sure," she responded. "Come on in. It'll only take a minute or two to do the paperwork." Allegations of bribery were rampant, but nothing could be proved. No doubt some of the pardons were legitimate, but years later two of the Fergusons' secretaries admitted that Farmer Jim sold clemency in exchange for votes or cash. One described convicts' friends and relatives routinely bringing greenbacks concealed in newspapers to the governor's office. Pa Ferguson would scoop up the cash into a basket and lock it in the vault.[23]

Probably the Fergusons' most despicable pardon was that of J. Patrick Holmes, superintendent of the Eagle Pass school district. In 1925 Holmes pled guilty to sexually assaulting six schoolboys and was sentenced to six years in prison and a $3,000 fine. Despite a public uproar, his wealthy family had no trouble obtaining a pardon directly from Farmer Jim, who even sent a squad of Texas Rangers to escort Holmes from jail. Of all Ferguson pardons, the one that rankled Hamer the most was that of Felix R. Jones, the notorious assassin who had been hired to kill him and his father-in-law in 1917. Jones, who had been sentenced to twenty-five years for the murder of cattle baron Thomas Lyons in El Paso, was pardoned by Ma Ferguson on November 23, 1926, near the end of her term. News of the pardon did not leak out for three weeks, finally making newspaper headlines. Ma Ferguson, in her pardon proclamation, tried to defend her act, claiming that Jones had served "more than twelve years" of his sentence. In fact, he had served nine years. "Subsequent developments make it at least doubtful as to whether Jones was guilty," she declared, ignoring the fact that he had committed numerous Texas murders. Not only was Jones one of the most infamous professional assassins in Texas, the evidence against him in the Lyons case was overwhelming. Frank could only wonder what sums were paid to the Ferguson regime to bring about the release of Felix Jones.[24]

But on one occasion Hamer himself took advantage of the Fergusons' liberal pardon policy. Frank had long considered his ex-Ranger comrade, Elmer B. McClure, a fine, courageous officer. But McClure, who with Hamer had slain the band of smugglers near El Paso in 1921, was a controversial lawman who figured in several questionable shooting scrapes. In 1920, while serving as a Ranger in the Big Bend, he shot and killed an unarmed Mexican on the Rio Grande. McClure later worked in Wichita Falls as a railroad policeman. In 1924 he shot two black men dead in separate incidents in the Wichita Falls rail yards. The first shooting he claimed was self-defense; the second, an accident. Nonetheless, a young, crusading district attorney, James V. Allred, charged the railroad officer with murder. McClure was convicted in the second shooting and sentenced to the minimum punishment: five years in prison.[25]

This was one of the few times in the Jim Crow era that a white Texas lawman was convicted and imprisoned for killing a black suspect. The McClure prosecution reinforced Allred's reputation as "the fighting district attorney." Allred, only twenty-five years old, had achieved local prominence for opposing the Klan and statewide recognition for his murder prosecution of the mayor of Wichita Falls, who killed a youth who had eloped with his daughter.

Hamer did not concur with Allred's popular image as a fearless district attorney. Instead, he was infuriated by the prosecution of Elmer McClure. Frank believed that McClure's two killings in Wichita Falls were justifiable and considered Allred politically ambitious and overzealous. With his customary disregard for those who were prominent and powerful, Hamer openly and repeatedly denounced Allred and used his influence with the Fergusons to lobby for McClure's pardon. Hamer was joined in his quest by railroad officials, and in January 1927 Ma Ferguson issued McClure a full pardon. Lone Wolf Gonzaullas, in recalling this affair, commented, "Frank loved his friends and hated his enemies." Allred, who rose to state attorney general and eventually became governor of Texas, never forgave Hamer. Years later, the McClure pardon would have profound repercussions for the veteran Ranger.[26]

The graft and pardon scandals of the Ferguson regime prompted the state attorney general, Dan Moody, to run for governor. In the election that November, he overwhelmingly defeated Ma Ferguson. Hamer had proved to be a bright spot in the dreary panorama of the Fergusons' governership. He solved the Corpus Christi bombing, the Engler triple murder, and the killing of Dr. Ramsey. Although he failed to obtain convictions of Frank Bonner and Willie Giese, there can be no reasonable doubt of their guilt. The Texas press praised his tenacious investigations. His work with ballistics expert Calvin Goddard showed plainly that he had fully transitioned from Old West lawman to modern investigator. As ever, he led by example, trying to avoid the limelight and working quietly and closely with fellow Rangers, local police, and federal officers. Frank Hamer's dogged, even brilliant, investigative work firmly established his reputation as the most capable detective in the Southwest.

16

THE HINGES OF HELL

Christmas Eve of 1926 was a quiet one for Frank and Gladys Hamer as they busily decorated their yuletide tree. Trix was now married, and Beverly, seventeen, was out on a date. Frank Jr. and Billy slumbered in an upstairs bedroom. At a few minutes past eleven, a loud knock rattled the front door, and Gladys, thinking it was Bev, swung the door open and exclaimed, "Boo!"

She found herself staring into the midsection of a tall, young stranger.

"I want Hamer," he said.

Frank approached the doorway, extending a handshake. "I'm Frank Hamer."

As Frank stepped onto the front porch, the visitor shrank back into the shadows. Without another word he yanked out a small automatic pistol and raised it to fire. Instinctively, Hamer slapped him across the face. The heavy blow lifted the man off his feet. He fell backward and tumbled down the stairs to the street below. Gladys rushed onto the porch with Frank's six-shooter, calling to her husband, "Kill him! Kill him!"

"No," replied Frank, watching the assailant flee down Riverside Drive.

"There's his gun," he said, pointing to the pistol on the porch. "I won't shoot a man in the back. Let him run away if he wants to."

"But he'll lay for you again," Gladys insisted.

"If he does I'll attend to him," answered Frank, as he scooped up the handgun from the floor. At that, five-year-old Billy, awakened by the commotion, rushed downstairs crying, "Is it Santa Claus? Is it Santa Claus?"

Hamer never reported the incident to the Austin police, remarking, "There's no need to. With that kind of man you just let him run out enough rope and he'll hang himself." Many years later, Gladys recalled that the would-be assassin died soon afterward in an automobile accident.[1]

Frank, like many of his fellow Rangers, greeted the New Year and Dan Moody's election with optimism and anticipation. Exulted Walter Prescott Webb, "Law and order have returned to the state of Texas." Honest and conscientious, at thirty-three the redheaded Moody was Texas's youngest elected governor. He had served as an army officer in World War I, then as a prosecuting attorney in Williamson County. There he achieved a statewide reputation for prosecuting members of the Ku Klux Klan, which resulted in his election as Texas attorney general, a post he held from 1925 to 1927. While attorney general, he achieved prominence by bringing lawsuits to cancel unconscionable and unlawful highway contracts entered into by the Ferguson administration. Dan Moody was a fair man. As a private defense lawyer, he had represented both whites and blacks accused of crime. But in keeping with the times, he was also a Jim Crow racist. On one occasion, while cross-examining a black witness in court, he became enraged at the man's "impudent answers." Moody picked up a chair and smashed it over the witness's head, knocking him unconscious.[2]

Moody was inaugurated on January 17, 1927. Just as the Rangers were anxious to see what changes he would make to the force, Hamer was eager to regain his lost captaincy. But he had a lot of competition. As Roy Aldrich wrote to a friend, "We have a change of administration . . . and nobody knows what will happen. I am the oldest man on the Rangers force from point of service, about twelve years now, but I am just as liable to lose out as a new man. The position of Ranger captain is much in demand, and all the big politicians are backing some friend for the place." Reported the *San Antonio Express,* "Rumors have been persistent for several days that there is to be a general shakeup in the State ranger force."[3]

Governor Moody was determined to reenergize and professionalize the Texas Rangers. He retained Roy Aldrich and Tom Hickman and discharged the rest of the Ferguson captains, including Monroe Fox. Hamer was reinstated as senior captain in charge of Headquarters Company. Much to Frank's annoyance, Aldrich arranged to have his brother Tod transferred to Hamer's company so he could live in Austin. The new captains were Hamer's old friend William W. Sterling and the veterans Will Wright and John H. Rogers. Frank was especially pleased to serve again with his mentor. Rogers, now sixty-four, was the last of the Four Great Captains to see duty in the Rangers. Though Bill Sterling had the least law-enforcement experience of the bunch, he had strong political connections. The appointments of Hamer, Rogers, and Wright were a huge boost to Ranger morale and a clear public statement that the new force would return to the time-honored traditions of the horseback era: character, fairness, honesty, tenacity, and courage.[4]

Frank did not waste a minute in repaying Governor Moody's trust. At six o'clock in the evening of February 2, 1927, the very day he was sworn in as captain, Hamer and Tom Hickman were in the adjutant general's office in the capitol building when Willis Chamberlin, a Houston optometrist, walked in. Chamberlin told them a troubling story. He had come to Austin on behalf of the Texas Optometric Association to work against a new bill in the legislature that would place a fifty-dollar annual tax on all optometrists. He approached H. H. Moore, the representative from Delta County who had introduced the bill, but Moore told him he would have to talk with F. A. Dale, an attorney and representative from Fannin County. Chamberlin then met with Dale, who brazenly suggested that he could kill the bill in exchange for a payment of $1,000.

Chamberlin, convinced that the bill had been introduced merely to "shake down" the optometrists, returned to Houston and reported the scheme to the president of the Optometric Association. He went back to the capitol on February 1 and notified Robert L. Bobbitt, the Speaker of the House, who in turn consulted with Jake Wolters, the lawyer and National Guard general, and then with Dan Moody. The young governor, suspecting that the scandals of the Ferguson regime had resulted in permanent corruption in Austin, was outraged. He pounded his desk and exclaimed, "If the parties are guilty, they belong in the penitentiary and not in the legislature!" At Moody's suggestion, Bobbitt informed the House leadership, then told Chamberlin to report the scheme to Captains Hamer and Hickman.

By this time General Wolters had also met with Governor Moody and advised him that the case should be handled by Hamer. Wolters also suggested that Chamberlin obtain $1,000 in fifties and twenties, first having one of his bankers make a list of the serial numbers. Then Chamberlin met with Hamer and Hickman in the adjutant general's office. Frank immediately swung into action. Because the attorney general's office was closed, he first sought legal advice from General Wolters, who was staying in the Driskill Hotel. "I wanted to see just how far we could go legally," Frank later explained.

The two captains, accompanied by Chamberlin, walked to the Driskill Hotel and discussed the case with Wolters in his private room. In response to the Rangers' questions, Wolters advised them of the current state of the search and seizure law. He also confirmed that Chamberlin, by paying the bribe, would not be committing a crime because he was acting at the direction of the Rangers. Thus satisfied, Hamer and Hickman departed for the Stephen F. Austin Hotel, where the two crooked representatives were waiting to meet Chamberlin. While Hamer and Hickman took seats in the crowded lobby, Chamberlin went up the elevator to Moore's room. Both Representatives Moore and Dale were present, and the three ordered dinner and ate in the room. During the meal Chamberlin explained that he had managed to get the $1,000 from the Optometric Association, but Dale refused to accept it in the hotel room. After they finished eating, Dale told Chamberlin to meet him outside the hotel.

Chamberlin left the room and found Hamer and Hickman waiting by the elevator.

Chamberlin whispered, "They wouldn't take it in the room. Follow us."

The two Rangers took the elevator down to the lobby and waited a few minutes until Chamberlin and Dale stepped out of the elevator together. As Chamberlin passed Hamer, he said quietly, "Follow us. I am to deliver it to him on the outside of the hotel."

Hamer walked silently behind the pair, and just outside the door he saw Chamberlin hand a small packet to Dale, who put it in his left pants pocket. As Chamberlin crossed the street, Hamer followed Dale into an alley behind the hotel. There he stopped Dale, introduced himself, and announced, "I am an officer."

"Well, what's the trouble?" asked Dale.

"Possibly not anything," replied Hamer. "I have information that possibly you have recently accepted a bribe of a certain sum of money."

"Well," said Dale, "I just accepted a fee of a thousand dollars to represent a man."

"Well," Hamer parroted, "consider yourself under arrest. I want to search you."

"All right, go ahead."

Hamer reached into the representative's pocket and pulled out the wad of cash. As Tom Hickman walked up, Dale insisted that the money was an attorney fee and that Moore was in his hotel room and would confirm that.

"Go up there and I will prove it to you," exclaimed Dale.

"All right, we will go up in the hotel," Hamer answered. The two Rangers accompanied him back to his room. While Hickman waited in the hallway with Dale, Hamer entered the room alone and confronted Representative Moore.

"Was there any kind of a deal made in your room this evening in which a thousand dollars was involved?"

"Not that I know of," lied Moore.

"Do you know Mr. Dale?"

Moore stammered, then said, "Yes, I know him."

"When did you see him last?"

"Well, I saw him yesterday evening," Moore answered, then quickly corrected himself. "I believe he was in here a while ago."

"You didn't have any conversation with reference to a thousand dollars or any other sum?"

"No."

"All right," said Hamer quietly, then placed Moore under arrest. He and Hickman took their prisoners to the sheriff's office. There Frank matched the bills with the serial numbers on Chamberlin's list. In the morning newspaper headlines trumpeted the arrests. Immediately, a legislative investigation was held; just six days later, the House of Representatives voted overwhelmingly to expel both legislators. So brazen were Dale and Moore that they returned to their districts and announced themselves as candidates for reelection. They were both defeated by large majorities. A year later, Dale was brought to trial on criminal charges of bribery. His defense lawyer claimed that he had been entrapped by Chamberlin, and also that Chamberlin had paid Dale $1,000 as an attorney fee. Even though these two theories were totally inconsistent, a gullible jury in Austin acquitted him. Dale, in a display of unmitigated gall, then sued Hamer for return of the $1,000, but the Ranger captain had already donated the money to three Austin churches. It was yet another graphic example of the wildly uneven application of justice in Texas courts of that era. Despite the ignominious conclusion, Hamer's quick actions had done much to restore public faith in the Texas Rangers. One newspaper's editorial banner read, BRINGING THE RANGERS INTO GOOD SERVICE AGAIN.[5]

By the spring of 1927, the rowdiest oil town in Texas was Borger, located in Hutchinson County in the Panhandle, fifty miles northeast of Amarillo. The county had long been quiet and sparsely settled; the population in 1920 was little more than seven hundred, consisting mostly of the families of cowboys who worked the big ranches in the breaks and rugged canyons along the Canadian River. In the early 1920s, oil was discovered. It created the biggest excitement in the Panhandle since the 1874 Battle of Adobe Walls, when Billy Dixon, Bat Masterson, and twenty-six other buffalo hunters withstood repeated attacks by more than seven hundred Comanche, Cheyenne, and Kiowa warriors led by Chief Quanah Parker.

In March 1926 Asa "Ace" Borger bought 240 acres on the plains and laid out a town site. Borger, who had successfully promoted several boomtowns in Oklahoma, named the new settlement after himself. Within three months Borger had a railroad spur line and 45,000 people. Its rutted, two-mile-long main street was jammed with automobiles and lined with ramshackle buildings and tents. That sweltering summer, the booming, wide-open little city became, as Texans were fond of saying, hotter than the hinges of hell. Just as in Mexia and other boomtowns, oil roughnecks, gamblers, drug peddlers, prostitutes, and fugitives from justice flocked to the new Eden. Mayor John R. Miller, who was Ace Borger's crooked partner, and chief deputy sheriff Emerald "Two Gun Dick" Herwig ran a wide-open town that was under the control of organized crime. Bill Sterling said that it was called "Borger by day and 'Booger' by night." In response to complaints of violence, including the murder by bandits of a fifteen-year-old schoolgirl, Ma Ferguson sent in Rangers under Captain Roy Nichols in October 1926. Accompanied by Prohibition agent Lone Wolf Gonzaullas and a force of fellow "prohis," they made fifty arrests and shut down twenty dives, and by the end of the month Captain Nichols announced that Borger had been cleaned up. His proclamation was premature.[6]

Once the Rangers were gone, lawlessness promptly returned. Gambling halls and bordellos operated openly; the county sheriff was reportedly on the take. "Anything goes in Borger" became the popular refrain. In November 1926 a Borger police captain took part in a pitched gun battle that left him and his assailant dead. During a January 1927 filling-station robbery, a woman was shot to death. Weeks later, two men died in separate shooting frays in the Palisade Dance Hall. On March 19, 1927, a Borger policeman, Coke Buchanan, was shot dead by gangsters when he came to the aid of another officer. The suspected killers were the notorious Oklahoma outlaws Matt Kimes and Ray Terrill; a local desperado, William "Whitey" Walker and his brother Hugh; and Ed Bailey. Whitey Walker had been recently pardoned by

Ma Ferguson. The Walker brothers and Bailey were arrested for the officer's murder and then—in an almost unbelievable display of judicial laxity—promptly released on bond.[7]

A few days after Buchanan's murder, on March 31, five unmasked robbers held up a bank in Pampa, thirty miles east of Borger. Three of the robbers were later identified as Matt Kimes, Ray Terrill, and Ed Bailey; the Walker brothers were also suspected. The bandits fled toward Borger in an auto with $25,000 in loot. Early the next morning, two deputy sheriffs tried to stop them on the outskirts of Borger, but both officers were shot to death. Four Borger lawmen had been slain in four months. The local courts, which had just released several of the suspected killers, were either corrupt or incredibly incompetent. For Dan Moody, enough was enough. He sent in the Rangers.[8]

In contrast to Governor Neff's Mexia cleanup, Moody's efforts in Borger did not include mobilizing the National Guard. "I will not call martial law unless it is shown definitely that civil law has failed," he declared. "I believe the rangers will be sufficient. They will remain until the law wins out over the lawless—until the lawless unconditionally surrender." In Austin, Captain Hamer boarded a northbound Santa Fe passenger train with Bill Molesworth, Tod Aldrich, and four other privates. When the train stopped in Fort Worth, L. A. Wilke, city editor of the *Fort Worth Press*, climbed aboard. He and Hamer knew each other well. Recalled Wilke, "I didn't get along with Frank, and he didn't like me." The newspaperman had a permit to carry a small .25 caliber automatic, which he kept tucked in his vest pocket. Soon after the train left Fort Worth, Wilke fell fast asleep in his seat. Hamer, in a playful mood, quietly slipped the pistol from his pocket. Wilke awoke to see Hamer towering over him, flicking the pistol up and down in his ham-like fist. Said the captain with mock seriousness, "Wilke, you better not ever shoot me with this thing and let me find out about it. When I go to hub a little hell, I want a forty-five!"[9]

The Headquarters Company men arrived in Borger on April 2. They were soon joined by Tom Hickman and two more Rangers. They found that the Walker brothers and Bailey had been rearrested. Therefore, the Rangers' first job was to assist local officers in hunting Kimes and Terrill. Hamer and his men spent several days running down clues, but the Oklahoma desperadoes had vanished. The Rangers also investigated the city's recent election, arresting ten men for voting fraud. At first the underworld was confident, making bets that Hamer would be bumped off within thirty days. But as Frank later remarked, "A lot of people lost money."[10]

The Rangers now began their cleanup of Borger. On the night of April 6, Hamer, Hickman, and their men rounded up 260 "undesirables," most of them prostitutes, and issued a "sundown order" that they leave town by 6:00 P.M. the following day. Many departed for other Panhandle oil towns. A witness spotted more than a dozen of the girls, bundles on their backs, trying to hitch rides on the highway south of Borger. Then the Rangers seized 203 slot machines and arrested sixty drunks and vagrants, cramming them into the city's rickety clapboard jail. Recalled Bill Sterling, "This insecure building had a huge chain fastened to the main floor beam. Prisoners charged with the more serious crimes were shackled to it. The inmates dreaded this barbarous but necessary fetter, which from the multiple prisoners it held, was known as the 'trot-line.'" The only violence that night was when two Borger policemen tried to stop a suspicious car; the vehicle escaped in a hail of the officers' gunfire.[11]

Scores of vagrants were picked up and brought to the police station, where they were questioned by Hamer and Hickman. Each was either jailed or ordered out of town. The Rangers seized a five-hundred-gallon still near Borger. They piled up the confiscated slot machines in an empty lot at the corner of Fifth and Weatherly Streets. As large crowds gathered, Rangers, police, and volunteers wielding sledgehammers worked throughout the day to destroy all 203 of the one-armed bandits, valued at $150 to $200 each. The nickels and quarters taken from the machines were tossed into a large box for donation to United Charities of Borger. Next Hamer turned his attention to stolen autos. On April 9 Rangers and state highway inspectors headed by Louis G. Phares seized between seven and eight hundred cars that lacked either license plates or current registrations. They were stored in empty lots until their ownership could be proved.

The same day Hamer and Hickman issued a public announcement that Mayor John Miller was cooperating with them. The captains also declared, "But this final word of warning must be given: The presence of undesirables, not only in Borger but in the entire [oil] field, will not be tolerated. Those having no visible means of support will be dealt with as the law directs and no favorites will be played." Vagrancy laws had long been common in the United States. Idle persons who did not work could be arrested and fined. Since most had no money, their presence in jail, where they had to be fed, was an expense many communities could not afford. As a result, up to the 1960s rural police customarily ran "vags" out of town—the "bum's rush." In 1972 the U.S. Supreme Court ruled that vagrancy statutes were overbroad and thus unconstitutional, because they prohibited seemingly innocent conduct. Today's antiloitering acts and gang injunctions are a modern reincarnation of the old vagrancy laws.[12]

The Rangers kept up their raids, closing speakeasies, gambling halls, and brothels, including the notorious Palisade Dance Hall, scene of numerous brawls and shooting scrapes. Hamer and his men drove up to Stinnett, the Hutchinson County seat, where they arrested J. W. "Shine" Popejoy, the leading moonshiner in the Panhandle, seizing 105 gallons of whiskey in his home. While the raids went on, Borger citizens continued to patronize the town's movie theaters and spring fashion shows. Hamer even gave the go-ahead to a much-anticipated wrestling meet at the Jim-Jo Club. "I am heartily in favor of clean sports and will be glad to attend the wrestling match Monday night myself if it is possible to be there," Frank told reporters. The two Ranger captains, convinced that Borger's government was corrupt, pressured the police chief, three officers, the city judge, and five other officials to resign. The police department was then placed under the temporary control of Hamer and Hickman.[13]

Governor Moody ordered Captain Bill Sterling and more Rangers into Borger. Hamer greeted Sterling by quipping, "Judging from the time it took you to get here, you must have made the trip from Laredo on horseback and led your pack mule." The captains kept up their pressure on corrupt city and county officials. On April 16 they forced six deputy sheriffs and four more city police officers to quit. The Rangers recommended competent lawmen to take their places, including a new chief of police. Within a few days, another judge resigned, making a total of twenty-three city and county officials ousted by the Rangers. Hamer suspected that Sheriff Joe Ownbey was on the take, but neither he nor Governor Moody could force him to resign. However, the crooked mayor, John Miller, was soon indicted for accepting a $200 bribe to keep a gambling hall open, and in early May he also stepped down. In all, the Rangers ran 1,200 "undesirables" out of Borger.[14]

The Fort Worth journalist L. A. Wilke was a close friend of Tom Hickman and, much to Hamer's annoyance, got many scoops from the publicity-seeking Ranger captain. Wilke recalled an incident in Borger that spoke volumes about Hamer's good-natured, but ultimately distrustful, relationship with the media. When Frank spotted Wilke on the street talking with a reporter from the *Houston Press*, Frank's old adversary, he approached the pair. With a broad grin, the Ranger captain stepped between the two newspapermen, throwing a pair of massive arms over

Texas Rangers at the Adobe Walls monument during the Borger cleanup of 1927. Standing center, is Captain, and later Adjutant General, Bill Sterling. Frank Hamer is standing at right. At lower left is Special Ranger Jack DeGraftenreid. *Courtesy of the Texas Ranger Hall of Fame and Museum, Waco, Texas*

their shoulders, and exclaimed, "Now I know how Jesus Christ felt crucified between two thieves."[15]

By now Hamer and his men had a little time to relax. On one of their trips to the county seat in Stinnett, Hamer, Sterling, and several other lawmen drove seventeen miles northeast to visit Adobe Walls, scene of the celebrated Indian fight. The adobe ruins of the original fort and trading post had long since melted under winter rains, but in 1924, on the fiftieth anniversary of the battle, a monument was erected at the site. Frank and the rest posed in front of the newly built marker for several now-famous photographs. On another occasion, as Sterling recalled, "A Panhandle sheriff, who was the best marksman in that part of the country, came to Borger one day for a friendly shooting contest with Captain Hamer." Frank, with Sterling and the sheriff, drove out to the edge of town. Before the targets could be set up, Hamer spotted a small white rock, glistening in the sunlight a hundred yards distant. Drawing Old Lucky, he took aim and fired once, striking the pebble. The sheriff, said Sterling, "refused to take his gun out of the holster, declaring that he came to shoot at pistol distances, and that anything beyond forty yards was a range for rifles."[16]

On April 20 Hamer and Hickman were called to Austin to testify in criminal court against the crooked ex-legislators, Moore and Dale. Captain Sterling and the other Rangers stayed in Borger and continued aggressive raids on moonshiners. In early May Hamer and Hickman rejoined Sterling in Borger and oversaw even more resignations of local officials. Then Hamer, Hickman, and Sterling reported to Austin for a conference with Governor Moody, leaving Private A. P. "Sug" Cummings in charge. Cummings was one of the Rangers in the 1915 ambush by Chico Cano's band that killed Joe Sitter and Eugene Hulen. Though a veteran lawman, he sorely lacked good judgment. On May 6 Cummings arrested Victor Wagner, city editor of the *Borger Herald*, locked him in jail, and refused to allow him to post bail. When the editor's friends tried to send telegrams of complaint to Austin, Cummings seized and tore them to shreds. They then telephoned the governor's office and reported that Cummings had arrested Wagner because he was upset by an article that claimed that the Rangers had beaten a man during a raid and that Matt Kimes and Ray Terrill were hiding out in Borger. An outraged Moody ordered Wagner released from jail, declaring, "If Mr. Cummings does not know it, he ought to know that he has no authority to exercise a censorship over the press, and that he has no right to arrest people and place them in jail because they write things in the newspapers that are not pleasing to him." In keeping with his desire to professionalize the Rangers, Moody promptly suspended Cummings and sent Hamer back to Borger to investigate. Frank found that the charges were true, and on May 14 Sug Cummings was fired from the force.[17]

By this time Governor Moody was satisfied that the boomtown had been cleaned up. Hamer, before leaving, announced that Borger, "after being wild and wooly for a year is now as quiet as any Sunday school town. We have broken the backbone of the lawlessness and it will stay broken." To dispel commonly held notions that Texas Rangers were trigger happy, he added, "And we did it without firing a shot, and not a shot was fired at us. When we told the crooks they would have to get out, they moved and none of them has attempted to return." Frank's statement was not entirely accurate, for Special Ranger Jack DeGraftenreid had shot and slightly wounded a deputy sheriff during a quarrel over a prisoner in front of the Borger police station. And the captain's prediction proved all too wrong. Borger would fester like an open sore, and it had not seen the last of Frank Hamer.[18]

Upon his return to Austin, the Headquarters captain was kept busy with a plethora of assignments from Governor Moody. One was a hangover from the Fergusons' highway construction scandals. It turned out that $1,000,000 in state road-building equipment had been leased out and then misappropriated by private contractors. Hamer saw to it that the missing vehicles and machinery were returned to the state. Next he took three Rangers to Marshall in East Texas to investigate a series of floggings by whitecappers. Several arrests put a stop to the whippings. In September he helped hunt the men who robbed a bank in Buda, just south of Austin. Hamer and the county sheriff located the abandoned getaway car but found no trace of the bandits. A week later, he investigated the mysterious murder of a young girl of about twelve years whose body had been found buried in a shallow grave near Fredericksburg in the Hill Country. Despite his efforts, Frank and the local sheriff were unable to identify the girl or her killer. This case haunted Hamer, for the victim must have reminded him of his own stepdaughters. He would return to Fredericksburg several times in the ensuing years in a vain effort to solve the ghastly crime.[19]

At the same time, the big Ranger captain tackled one of the enduring mysteries of the Texas frontier. The Sam Bass gang of the 1870s had long since entered the halls of Texas myth. Bass and his young companions achieved great notoriety, robbing stagecoaches and trains in Texas, Dakota Territory, and Nebraska. In 1878 the gang rode into Round Rock, north of Austin, to rob the town bank. They were trapped by Texas Rangers who had been tipped off. In a pitched gun battle, Sam Bass and Seaborn Barnes died, and gang member Frank Jackson escaped. Dime novels and a popular ballad soon made Sam Bass a folk hero, but Frank Jackson had vanished. He was spotted in New Mexico in 1882, and repeated rumors over the years insisted that he had settled down, started a ranch, and fully reformed.

In 1927 the popular western author Eugene Manlove Rhodes learned that Jackson was living under an assumed name near Roswell, New Mexico, longing to return to Texas and see his family before he died. Rhodes contacted his friend James F. Hinkle, former governor of New Mexico, who in turn wrote to Dan Moody. The old outlaw was willing to come to Texas and surrender if all charges against him were dropped. Frank Hamer, assigned to investigate, concluded that the man in New Mexico was indeed the long-missing desperado. He saw this as an opportunity—not to bring in a fugitive but to preserve history. Hamer informed Walter Prescott Webb, then working on a history of the Texas Rangers, who jumped at the chance to interview the last surviving member of the Sam Bass gang.

"We ought to go pretty slow, because if we get this old bird into trouble, we'll have to get him out," Webb wrote to Hamer. "They can't prove anything on him, but they can deal him some misery if they get mean and lawyer-like enough." Hamer and Webb began a lengthy correspondence with Gene Rhodes and ex-governor Hinkle in New Mexico.

The Ranger captain had obtained an assurance from Governor Moody that Jackson would not be prosecuted if he returned to Texas. But as Rhodes wrote to Webb, "It isn't going to be easy to convince Jackson." Hamer then secured a letter from Governor Moody, promising that Jackson could "return to Texas without fear of arrest." But the elderly Jackson was unconvinced. As Rhodes later wrote to Bill Sterling, "You see it was the name of Frank Hamer and the Texas Rangers that did not reassure him." In the end Jackson never came back to Texas, and Frank never made contact with him. Whether or not Hamer was correct about the old man being Frank Jackson, the true fate of the last of the Sam Bass gang remains one of the baffling mysteries of Texas.[20]

Hamer's intuitive skill as a detective was never so evident as in his investigation that fall of a major car theft ring. Probably through his wide network of criminal informants, he learned that the ring's head-quarters were in Llano County. Frank, of course, knew the county well from his boyhood years. He arrived in Llano on October 24, 1927, accompanied by a local sheriff, and began poking around. Five days later, Hamer discovered a cache of cars hidden in a canyon near Llano. They had been stolen from all over the state. He soon arrested one of the culprits. Frank was certain that more stolen autos had been sold throughout Llano County, but he could not figure out a way to identify and recover them. At that time Texas autos were assigned a different license plate number every year, making it very difficult to determine whether they were stolen.

Hamer's investigation quickly became, as *The Llano News* reported, "the principal subject of conversation on the local streets." Frank stepped into a small café and pondered the problem over a bowl of hot chili. While reading a telegram about another case, he overheard one of the waitresses whisper, "I'd give ten bucks to know what that telegram's about."

His natural curiosity aroused, Hamer left the café and made quiet inquiries about the waitress. He found that she was the sweetheart of a man whom he suspected was in the gang. Frank went to the telegraph office, got a blank telegram, and wrote out the following message: "Do not prosecute innocent purchasers who turn in cars. Arrest all others and hold in jail for criminal prosecution." That evening he returned to the café for another bowl of chili. As he left, he pulled his handkerchief from his pocket, allowing the folded telegram to fall to the floor. Hamer later recalled, "As I went out the door, I cut my eye around and saw that gal land on that telegram like a duck on a junebug."

Early the next morning there was a knock on his hotel room door. The visitor introduced himself and said, "I understand you're looking for some stolen cars here."

"Yes, I am," the Ranger responded.

"Well, I think the car I bought several weeks ago was stolen and I'd like to turn it over to you."

"Come on in and I'll give you a receipt," replied Hamer. Within hours, as Walter Prescott Webb related the story, "the stolen automobiles were pouring in on Captain Hamer faster than he could write receipts for them." By the end of the day, he had recovered fifty-two purloined vehicles. The waitress had spread the word all over Llano. Frank soon picked up three more ringleaders, all local ranchers. To reporters he declared, "This is by far the worst situation of car theft I have ever known and many will be implicated in the matter before it is over." He explained that the autos had been stolen throughout Texas and brought to Llano for sale, adding that he "had been flooded with telephone calls from nearly every section of the state making inquiries about stolen cars." As usual, Hamer did not allow personal friendships to influence his work. He frankly admitted that one of the ringleaders "was a boyhood chum" and the two "grew up on a west Texas Ranch." Said Frank, "Many times we went in swimming together and also hunted in West Texas."

By the time the case was over, seventy stolen cars had been recovered, twenty-eight men were indicted for receiving stolen property, and the ringleaders were sent to prison. Hamer also appeared before the state legislature to lobby for a change in the licensing of motor vehicles, explaining, "The identification purpose of the license plate is almost entirely defeated by the annual changing of numbers." His commonsense proposal was rejected, and Texas vehicles were not assigned permanent license plate numbers until the 1970s.[21]

Not all of Hamer's cases ended so successfully. One of his greatest weaknesses was his temper, coupled with an occasional lack of tact and diplomacy. In February 1928, Governor Moody ordered Hamer into Wharton County, sixty miles southwest of Houston. A local cattleman, Forrest Damon, was refusing to allow cattle inspectors on his ranch. The inspectors worked for the Texas Livestock Sanitary Commission, charged with inspecting and dipping cattle to eradicate the tick that caused the deadly Texas Fever. Cattlemen lost millions of dollars a year from the devastating disease, and for thirty years the Livestock Sanitary Commission had made an aggressive and successful campaign against it. Infected cattle were dipped in vats of water mixed with tick poison.

Forrest Damon was, as Bill Sterling vividly recalled, "Wharton County's most bull headed citizen. Those who knew him best warned that he could not be handled without a fight, which they predicted would result in bloodshed." Explained Sterling, "He was a large red-muzzled man who wore a broad brimmed, uncreased hat which made the average cowboy sombrero look like a golf cap. When angry, which was at least half the time, he would pop his teeth like a wild hog and, altogether, presented a formidable picture." When tick inspectors came to examine Damon's small herd of thirty-eight head, he ordered them off his ranch. "Forrest Damon not only failed and refused to dip his cattle, he defied anyone to make him do it," said Sterling. "He announced that he did not believe in the law. Damon also threatened violence against the tick inspectors if they even dared set foot on his land." The inspectors got no assistance from Wharton County's sheriff, Anton Reitz, so the chairman of the Livestock Sanitary Commission appealed to Governor Moody for help.

On February 10 Hamer arrived at Damon's ranch with three tick inspectors. The officers were met with a locked gate, and when Frank demanded that Damon open it, the rancher claimed to have lost the key. They forced it open. Hamer knew that all stockmen fully understood the war on ticks, and he had no tolerance for Damon's refusal to cooperate.

Sterling said that Hamer "had little patience with the ranchman, as he disliked the overbearing type, and wasted no time trying to mollify him. Hamer told Damon to sit down and be quiet until the inspection was over, and that any monkey business on his part would get him a good booting. Ticks were found on the cattle and a dipping order duly issued." Frank apparently arrested Damon, for the rancher ended up in court that day and was ordered to post a $250 bond. Then the Ranger captain drove back to Austin. The next day, a brooding, angry Damon swore out a warrant against Captain Hamer and the tick inspectors, charging them with forcibly entering his property without a search warrant. Even though search warrants were not required under the tick law, a local judge appeased Damon and issued the arrest warrant.

When Sheriff Reitz sent the warrant to the sheriff in Austin for service, Frank was outraged. From his office he fired off a decidedly undiplomatic letter to Reitz: "I have just been informed that you have sent to the Sheriff here a warrant for my arrest. Also a bond, to be made for my appearance at some future date at Wharton. . . . Of course this is only an effort to humiliate me and not any effort by any means on your part to enforce the law. It seems that if you really want to do something to enforce the law, you should get busy and make an attempt to stop the wide open liquor traffic and gambling houses running rampant in your county. And I understand that they are running under protection. I am not a man to dodge any issue, and when it becomes my duty to go to Wharton County or to any other county, and am notified by the proper parties I will go. I know what my duties are and I have all the respect for the law that is necessary, but I refuse to be made a goat of by a bunch of disgruntled soreheads that hasn't got the guts to enforce the law. These officers here [in Austin] refuse to be made a party to your frameup, and I am awaiting your arrival here to escort me back to your city."[22]

Needless to say, Sheriff Reitz did not arrest Frank Hamer. Meanwhile, Captain Bill Sterling was sent to Wharton to ensure that Forrest Damon's cattle were dipped. In his memoirs, Sterling described in great detail how he placated Damon, who "was all riled up after the encounter with Captain Hamer." Sterling chatted amiably with the rancher, calmed him down, and even took a siesta in his front room. Damon liked him so much that while his cattle were being dipped, he gave the Ranger captain a ham from his smokehouse. Sterling's story may have been substantially true, but he did not succeed in getting Damon's cattle dipped. Six months later, when Damon's stock had still not been dipped, a judge ordered him arrested and locked in the county jail. Bill Sterling omitted that inconvenient detail from his memoir.[23]

Over the years, Frank Hamer's repeated contact with violence, corruption, vice, and depravity had made him hard and cynical. But his sardonic worldview was greatly offset by a keen interest in the gentler things in life: children, family, music, and reading. He liked nothing better than relaxing in an easy chair in the front room of his home, with a view of the Colorado River below, smoking a pipe or cigar and listening to the radio or reading western novels by his favorite author, Zane Grey. He kept a menagerie: a German shepherd, a coyote named Cactus, a pet wildcat, a javelina he called Porky Pig, and even a mischievous parrot. He loved to play with his two boys, and, when they were old enough, he taught them to hunt and fish. As was then the custom, seven-year-old Billy had long, golden curls extending to his shoulders; he never had a haircut until he started the first grade. Frank also developed a wide and diverse circle of friends beyond his fellow lawmen, including prominent lawyers Coke Stevenson, Jake Wolters, and John Valls; Governors Pat Neff and Dan Moody; ranchers Sam Hill and Caeser Kleberg; and card-playing cronies like Walter Prescott Webb. Eventually the ever-suspicious Hamer would even count a handful of newspaper reporters among his companions.

Yet none of this kept him as grounded as did his close relationship to God and nature. Never one to regularly attend church or to recite formal prayers, Hamer nonetheless spoke every night at bedtime to his Old Master. One of his good friends was Pierre B. Hill, a Presbyterian minister in San Antonio and chaplain of the Rangers for more than thirty years. In 1928 Hill authored the Ranger's Prayer, which began, "O God, whose end is justice, whose strength is all our stay, be near and bless my mission as I go forth today. Let wisdom guide my actions, let courage fill my heart, and help me, Lord, in every hour to do a Ranger's part." Hamer liked this poem so much he had it painted in block letters across the top of the walls in the hallway of his house. Later, it became a tradition for Rangers to have a framed copy displayed in their homes.[24]

And Frank never lost his boyhood love of wildlife. During the Borger cleanup, he and Bill Sterling had occasion to drive across the huge 6666 Ranch, a few miles south of the oil town. Sterling recalled that when a covey of quail ran across the road, "Captain Hamer stopped the car and said that he was going to call them. I was skeptical, but he proceeded to do this by making a chirping sound that is best described as a sort of cross between whistling and hissing. The partridges turned and came up to the automobile, some of them even getting under it. Of course we did not shoot the little fellows, and I was amazed and delighted to see and hear the plainsman talk to his feathered friends." Sterling never forgot the jarring, incongruous image of the toughest lawman in Texas playing gently with a flock of quail.[25]

17

THE MURDER MACHINE

The 1920s were the heyday of the bank robber, when swaggering, motorized bandits ranged across the Midwest, pillaging banks large and small. Americans were alternately thrilled and terrified by accounts of the brazen raids of Henry Starr, Al Spencer, Matt Kimes, Jake Fleagle, the Newton boys, and a host of imitators. Some were "burners"—torch men who cut into money vaults at night; others were daring daylight bank robbers. Brandishing the Thompson submachine gun, "the gun that made the Twenties roar," and escaping in high-powered motorcars, they defied rural sheriffs and big-city police, who lacked both the firepower to oppose them and the legal authority to pursue them across state lines. And laws making bank robbery a federal offense, thereby authorizing the FBI to hunt the bandits, were not enacted until 1934.

During the nineteenth century the term "bank robber" primarily referred to a bank burglar, and the vast majority of bank robberies were nighttime jobs committed by highly skilled safe crackers, most notably the infamous Jimmy Hope. During the 1870s and 1880s, Hope and his gang, using sophisticated tools and nitroglycerin, burglarized bank vaults on the East Coast and even in San Francisco, stealing hundreds of thousands of dollars. The James-Younger gang were rank amateurs compared to Jimmy Hope. Jesse James's gang, however, was responsible for the first of the western bank holdups—termed "daylight bank robberies" to distinguish them from burglaries—in Missouri in 1866.

In the Old West, bandit gangs were largely local, confining their operations to a single county, state, or territory. Bands like those of Jesse James and Butch Cassidy were highly unusual in that they ranged across multiple states. Nonetheless, before 1900 most bank robberies were pulled by two or three nondescript hobos or yegg burglars, who went anywhere there was a railroad. They hitched rides on freight trains, arrived in small towns at night, broke into the local bank, cracked or blew the safe, and slipped away on an outgoing railcar. Their nemesis was the Pinkerton National Detective Agency, which achieved prominence in the 1870s as a forerunner of the FBI. Employed by banks and express companies and unhampered by jurisdictional niceties, Pinkerton agents fanned out across the country to help local officers investigate and track down bank burglars and robbers. Because yeggs were restricted to travel by train, railroad "bulls" and local constables kept a close watch on the cars and rail yards, making it difficult for wandering burglars to ply their profession.

This all changed by the 1920s, when several factors caused an explosion of bank robberies. Automobiles were becoming bigger, faster, and more reliable. The booming postwar economy filled tax coffers—as well as bank vaults—and allowed state governments to build modern paved highways. The Federal Aid Highway Act of 1921 provided funds for national road building and mandated uniform highway numbers and clearly marked signs. For the first time, motorists could travel quickly and cheaply from county to county and state to state. This fact was not lost on highly mobile bank robbers, especially in Texas. Between 1920 and 1927, the state saw a wave of 140 successful bank holdups and burglaries; the culprits managed to escape punishment in all but thirty cases. The notorious Willis Newton later admitted that he and his brothers alone had burglarized between fifty and sixty banks, as many as forty of them in Texas.[1]

Captain Tom Hickman was the hero of one of the most spectacular of these holdups. On September 9, 1926, after receiving an underworld tip, Hickman, with three possemen, staked out the Red River National

Bank in Clarksville, near the Oklahoma line. When two gun-toting robbers, A. M. Slaton and D. L. Smallwood, emerged from the bank at noon carrying $33,000 in a gripsack, Hickman ordered them to halt. The bandits tried to make a dash for their car, but Hickman and his men opened fire, killing them. Two hours after the shooting, a telegram report was sent to Ranger headquarters in Austin. Although the dead bandits had not yet been identified, Hamer intuitively knew who they were. Hamer and Hickman had both suspected Slaton and Smallwood of a series of bank holdups. Frank stood up and announced to Roy Aldrich and the other Rangers, "Boys, here are the initials of the two men." Then, on the plaster wall above Aldrich's desk, he wrote the letters "S. S." It was a not-so-subtle reminder that he, not Aldrich, was the Rangers' chief investigator.[2]

The Texas Bankers Association promptly paid Hickman a $1,000 reward. The association's secretary pointed out that this was the first time in twenty years they had paid a bounty for the killing of a bank robber. The association then announced a new standing reward of $500 "for each dead bank robber, killed while in the act of robbing a member bank in Texas. The Association will not pay one penny for the arrest or conviction . . . of bank robbers."

Later, Hamer and Hickman got a tip that another bank would be held up. They staked out the bank, watching as the suspects' car cruised by several times. The two captains, puzzled by the would-be robbers' failure to strike, spotted a "lanky country boy" who had stopped in front of the bank, holding a gun he had brought into town for repairs. The bandits, thinking he was a bank guard, abandoned their scheme. It was the luckiest day of their lives.[3]

During the fall of 1927, Texas saw twenty-one daylight bank holdups and six burglaries, with a total loss of $75,000. The culprits in many cases were thought to be career criminals from out of state. As the wave of bank heists rolled on, the Texas Bankers Association, which boasted a membership of 1,600 banks, took drastic action. On November 10, 1927, it announced an increased reward of $5,000 for each bank robber or burglar slain. "Killing a few robbers is the only effective way to stop bank robberies in Texas," declared its secretary. "We want dead bank bandits and no other kind." All member banks prominently displayed a placard which read, "$5,000 in cash will be paid for the killing of any robber while robbing this bank. $5,000 for each Dead Robber—not one cent for a hundred live ones." This bounty—shocking by modern standards—was a vestige of the "dead or alive" rewards of frontier days and met with very little criticism in the Texas press.[4]

The new offer immediately began to bear fruit. Two weeks later, in the early morning hours of November 25, two men drove their auto into an alley behind a bank in Odessa in West Texas. Sheriff Reeder Webb, of Ector County, had been tipped off. Webb, with his deputy, Tom Jones, and two other lawmen, were concealed in an auto near the bank.

$5,000 REWARD

DEAD Bank Robbers Wanted

$5,000 Cash will be paid for each bank robber killed while robbing a Texas bank

THE Texas Bankers Association offers a standing reward of $5,000 for each dead Bank Robber, killed while in the act of robbing a member bank in Texas. No limit as to place of killing -- in the banking house, as the robber or robbers leave the bank, as they climb into their car, ten or twenty miles down the road as they flee, or while resisting a posse giving chase. This reward applies to night attacks as well as daylight holdups.

The Association will not give one cent for live robbers. They rarely are identified, more rarely convicted, and most rarely kept in the penitentiary when sent there -- all of which operations are troublesome and costly.

But the Association is prepared to pay for any number of dead Bank Robbers, killed while robbing its member banks, at $5,000 a piece.

$5,000 in cash will be paid for the killing of any robber while robbing

THIS BANK

$5,000 for each Dead Robber — not one cent for a hundred live ones!

The reward notice for dead bank robbers posted by the Texas Bankers Association. *Author's collection*

The officers later said that they watched as the two suspects unloaded explosives and a bag of tools. When the pair smashed open the bank's glass door with a crowbar, the lawmen opened fire with shotguns, killing them both. The lawmen were lionized in the press, and the Texas Bankers Association promptly paid the $10,000 reward.[5]

A month later, another bank shooting took place in Stanton, forty miles northeast of Odessa. On December 23, three Mexicans from Odessa were loitering in front of the town bank. A pair of would-be man hunters, Calvin Baze and Lee Smith, opened fire with rifles, killing two and wounding one. Next to the bodies were safe-cracking tools and a sack containing explosives. Baze and Smith boasted to townsfolk that they had killed two bank robbers and declared that they would claim the rewards. The wounded man, however, told officers that he and his companions had been promised work by Baze and Smith, who had brought them into Stanton and dropped them off in front of the bank just before they were shot. The powder and burglars' tools had been planted on the bodies. When Baze and Smith were charged with murder, the Texas Bankers Association refused to pay the rewards.[6]

Two weeks later, on the afternoon of January 10, 1928, three bandits held up the bank in Sylvester, north of Sweetwater, escaping with $2,500. A huge manhunt began. That night, an oil prospector was driving along the highway between Lubbock and Sweetwater, headed toward Post City, when a man stepped into the road and motioned him to halt. Thinking he was a hijacker, the prospector sped up. His Buick was riddled with buckshot from shotguns in the hands of a posse hoping to capture the bank robbers. The furious victim, wounded in the leg, told newspapers that the lawmen had shot him in hopes of claiming the dead bandit reward. Lone Wolf Gonzaullas investigated and found that the posse had fired so many rounds into the car—three hundred—that it was evident that they were trying to kill the driver rather than stop the vehicle.[7]

Meanwhile, Sheriff J. O. "Bud" Barfield got a tip that the First State Bank in Rankin would be burglarized. Rankin, the Upton County seat, was sixty-five miles south of Odessa. An oil town of about 1,500 people on the open prairie, its dirt streets were lined with cheap clapboard buildings. Sheriff Barfield, with his deputies, Clarence Shannon and

Hugh Gillespie, watched the bank for three nights from a hiding place in a nearby filling station. Then, at four in the morning on January 12, W. M. "Blackie" Miller and an accomplice, known only as Whitey, driving a roadster, pulled up to the rear door of the bank. While Miller jimmied open the door, Whitey unloaded an acetylene tank and torch from the car. Barfield and his deputies stepped forward, and the sheriff shouted, "Halt! Throw up your hands!"

Miller drew a pistol and fired at the officers. They opened up with shotguns, killing him. Whitey tried to flee, but he was struck with buckshot. He ran about two hundred yards before collapsing in the dirt street; in fifteen minutes he was dead. The acetylene tank and torch, as well as a second in the car, proved to have been stolen in recent burglaries. Miller turned out to be an ex-convict, just released from Huntsville. His partner's full identity was never learned. Sheriff Barfield and his deputies were praised for their quick actions, and the Texas Bankers Association paid them the $10,000 reward.[8]

But Frank Hamer was having none of it. The 1926 Clarksville bank job had been a real daylight holdup. The bandits were armed, had completed the robbery, and were attempting to escape when they were shot down. He fully supported Tom Hickman's role in that affair. However, Hamer found the fatal shootings at Odessa and Rankin as suspicious as the one in Stanton, where the killers had been arrested for murdering the supposed burglars. Walter Prescott Webb later wrote that Hamer determined "the men who were being killed were not real bank robbers, but simple-minded, half-drunken boys who had been induced to join pretending bank robbers, and lured to the spot where they had been shot down by officers who had been tipped. The officers then collected from the bankers the five thousand dollars, which they divided with the pretending bank robbers. In short, Frank Hamer learned that two or three men were making a profession of framing robberies for the purpose of killing men at the rate of five thousand dollars a head."[9]

It was a deadly version of the eighteenth-century English thieftakers' scam, in which corrupt officers induced young men to commit robberies on the King's highways and then arrested them to collect the standing rewards. Captain Hamer contacted local officials in Odessa and Rankin with his concerns, but they refused to believe that anything was amiss. Explained Webb, "He next approached the Bankers' Association, but with no better luck. The bankers refused to withdraw the reward, or even to modify it. Their position, and that of some officers, was that any man who could be induced to participate in a bank robbery ought to be killed. Frank Hamer does not believe in bank robbery, but he does believe in what he conceives to be right, and he holds steadfastly to the theory that every man, even a crook, is entitled to justice."[10]

Hamer met with William M. Massie, president of the Texas Bankers Association. "I went to Mr. Massie before he sent the check for the Rankin reward and laid before him such facts as I had at that time," Frank explained. "I suggested that before he paid this reward he should have a thorough investigation made. He asked me to make the investigation, and I told him that it would be necessary for me to receive authority to do this. He assured me that he would make a formal request to the proper authorities that I be sent to investigate. This request was never made, and in a short time the reward was paid."[11]

With Governor Moody's approval, Hamer then began his own investigation, assisted by Captain Will Wright and several other Rangers. Years later, he explained his recipe for success. "I know more criminals and characters of the underworld in the Southwest than any other man living. Every man and woman of them knows that. I never betrayed a criminal who put his confidence in me. And I never will. I kept every promise I ever made. And I never let a criminal be framed. Every crook in Texas knows that if he is my man he is going to get a fair trial, and if he gives me a tip-off about another man I am after, that confidence is sacred. Therefore, I can go among those people and get information that no other man can get. I don't say this boastfully. It is just a plain fact."[12]

Through his extensive network of criminal informants, Hamer learned that the Odessa and Rankin burglaries had been set up by two hardcases, James Dumas and Carl "Red" Wood. For the time being he kept their identities to himself, intending to compile enough evidence to convict them. Dumas, thirty-two, was a former cattle inspector from Lubbock. In 1923 he had received a two-year jolt in the Oklahoma State Penitentiary for stealing livestock. Wood, forty-eight, was a farmer from Oklahoma; in 1926 he had been arrested, but not convicted, of auto theft. Frank discovered that they were planning more "robberies," but he could not figure out how to stop them.[13]

As Webb pointed out, "Hamer for a time was at his rope's end. He knew . . . that other murders were being planned and that he must hurry to prevent them." The Ranger captain was so troubled that he did something that he had never done before, and would never do again. First he explained his plan to Dan Moody and obtained the governor's full support. Then, on the afternoon of March 12, 1928, he walked into the press room in the state capitol building and handed the assembled reporters a long, detailed statement exposing what he called the bankers' "murder machine." The story created a sensation when it hit the wire services, and overnight was published prominently in newspapers throughout the United States.[14]

Hamer began by saying, "My purpose . . . is to lay before the people of Texas, and the bankers of Texas, certain facts that they ought to know about the dead bandits and the rewards that have been paid for them in order to determine whether or not these rewards should be continued by the bankers or approved by the public in general. . . . I agree that bank robbing should be stopped, that bank robbers should be shown little consideration, and should be killed when caught in the act of robbing a bank. But I do not agree that the method adopted by the Bankers Association of Texas is either wise or just, because it is adding the crime of murder to the crime of robbery. There has come into existence in this state a murder machine."

The Ranger captain then drew on his knowledge of the Indian wars to remind Texans of a sorry episode from their own history. "The situation reminds me of a story that used to be told by the Indian fighters. The Apaches and Comanches spread such terror through northern Mexico that the government offered to pay $100 each for Apache and Comanche scalps. Some American adventurers went to Mexico and engaged in the business and made some money. But when Apaches and Comanches became scarce, the hunters took scalps from the natives that they were supposed to protect, there being a strong resemblance between the scalp of a Mexican Indian and a Texas Apache. This is exactly what has happened in the bank scalp war. Just as it was much safer to attack a Mexican sheep herder than it was an Apache warrior, so it is much safer in Texas to shoot down an inexperienced and weak character who has been lured into the game without understanding it than to shoot down the professional bank robber. The reward is the same in either case."

Hamer then proceeded to analyze the fatal bank shootings. "Supposed bank bandits have been killed since this reward was offered at Stanton, Odessa, Rankin, and Cisco." He described the recent Cisco job of December 23, 1927, which became renowned as the Santa Claus bank robbery. Four bandits, one wearing a Santa Claus disguise, held up the bank, and in the resulting shootout, two lawmen and one robber were slain, with the other three culprits captured alive. "Every peace officer and citizen in Texas should commend the good work done at Cisco," said Hamer. He then recounted the Stanton incident, in which the three Mexicans were set up and two of them killed. "This was a real case of getting the sheep herder and not the Apache," he declared.

Next Frank discussed the Odessa affair in which two men were shot dead and the $10,000 reward was paid to Sheriff Webb and his posse.

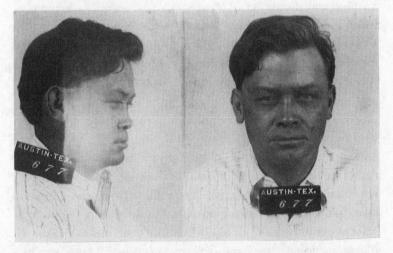

James Dumas, a former cattle inspector who helped set up the bloody bank jobs at Odessa and Rankin, Texas. Hamer got him to confess, which cracked open the Murder Machine case. *Travis Hamer personal collection*

Hamer first pointed out the obvious moral issue: "The job was pulled off at night. Now it so happens that it is not a capital offense to rob a bank at night, that is, without firearms and without endangering human life." Then he detailed the findings of his own investigation: "The two men who were killed in the Odessa job had nothing with them that would enable them to get into the vault of the bank, once they were inside the building. What they did have in their possession in the way of tools was planted there after they were killed by a man well known to me whose name I am ready to give to the proper authorities at the proper time. This man shared privately in the reward paid by the bankers." He explained that "the men who were killed at Odessa . . . were not professional bank robbers, nor were they even experienced criminals."

Hamer next turned his attention to the Rankin job, in which Blackie Miller and his partner were slain by Sheriff Barfield's posse. Declared Hamer, "These men did have in their possession an acetylene torch of the kind used by experienced bank robbers. But it was impossible to find, either on the person of the dead men, or anywhere about, tips for this torch. Without these tips the torch was as useless to them as a flashlight without battery or bulb, as a gun without ammunition. . . . The acetylene tank that was a part of the torch was stolen from a certain place which I know. The man who stole the tank left tracks made by high heeled boots. This can be proved. But the photographs of the two dead men, copies of which I have in my possession, show that both men had on well worn shoes. Where was the man with the boots? Was he probably not the expert who was to use the torch?"

Without naming James Dumas or Red Wood, Hamer declared that he knew who had set up the Odessa and Rankin jobs. "I could not afford to make the above statements unless I knew what I was talking about. An officer has many ways of gaining information, and he usually has information that he can not make public. I now have in my possession other facts and proofs which I am willing to lay before a grand jury or other proper authorities." He concluded with a direct plea to William M. Massie, president of the Texas Bankers Association: "I know it to be a positive fact that the man who shared in the Odessa and Rankin rewards is now framing two more bank robberies to be pulled in this state in the near future, not for the money that comes from the bank robbed but for the money that will come by way of reward for men killed. . . . Furthermore, regardless of what Mr. Massie has said in the newspapers and magazines to the contrary, the reward offered by the Bankers Association has not stopped bank robbing by the professional bank robbers. Since the reward was offered the following banks have been robbed: McCauley, Silvester, Killeen, Copperas Cove, Mullen, Grove, and Meridian."

The Ranger captain boldly focused his criticism on the bankers and their reward system. "Here is as perfect a murder machine as can be devised, supported by the Bankers Association, operated by the officers of the state and directed by the small group of greedy men who furnish the victims and take their cut of the money." Mincing no words, he called it "a disgrace to Texas and to civilization, and should not be tolerated."[15]

Hamer immediately received a groundswell of support from newspapers nationwide. The dramatic story—which pitted a lone Ranger against the powerful bankers of Texas—captured the public's attention more than any event up to that point in Hamer's career. A typical headline read, A TEXAS RANGER LEADS THE WAY IN DENOUNCING REWARDS FOR DEATH.

Declared *The New York Times*, "The entire southwest is watching the more or less single-handed fight which Ranger Captain Frank A. Hamer is waging on the standing reward of $5,000 offered by the Texas Banker's Association for dead bank bandits." His old antagonist, the *Houston Press*, proclaimed, "Capt. Frank Hamer has both physical and moral courage. When he thinks our state bankers are violating all rules of law, ethics, and decency, he doesn't hesitate to say so. Hamer is modest in demeanor, never strives for the limelight and when he makes a public statement he has the facts to back his statements." Added *The Galveston News*, "Texas Rangers are not given, as a rule, to vain loquacity, and for that reason, if for no other, the statement of Ranger Captain Frank Hamer concerning an alleged 'murder ring' in this state deserves . . . consideration. . . . Captain Hamer is justified in attempting to rally public opinion on his side of a question which has become an outstanding matter of public controversy. Should his charges be sustained . . . the

Bankers Association will be devoid of any excuse for continuing an inducement which results in the needless shedding of human blood."

When one of Frank's friends warned him of the danger in opposing "the greatest aggregation of wealth in the state," his response was simple: "When you go fishing, what kind of fish do you like to catch, little ones or big ones? The bigger they are, the better I like to catch 'em." Sheriff Bud Barfield, stung by Hamer's claims, demanded that he appear before the Upton County grand jury. Hamer replied, "I'm ready, anxious, and rarin' to go. If I can't prove what I have charged I'll sign a 'lie bill' as long as my leg." To reporters, Governor Moody announced his full support: "I have implicit confidence in Captain Hamer. He is a capable and trustworthy officer. I have some personal knowledge of the matter as Mr. Hamer had previously talked to me. I suggested to the captain that he present his facts to a grand jury."[16]

Frank Hamer did exactly that. He, along with Captain Will Wright, Sergeant Light Townsend, Special Ranger Graves Peeler, and two other Rangers, appeared before the Upton County grand jury in Rankin on April 5. They testified about their investigation into the Rankin shooting, and Hamer was on the stand for two days. Frank presented evidence that the supposed bank burglary had been cooked up by James Dumas, Red Wood, Sheriff Barfield, and his deputies, Clarence Shannon and Hugh Gillespie. Numerous other witnesses were sworn, including Massie and Sheriff Webb. The latter presumably testified that the Odessa job had not been a frame-up. The grand jurors indicted Dumas and Wood for murder but declined to charge Sheriff Barfield and his deputies. Because grand jury proceedings are secret, their reasoning is unknown. However, newspapers reported that the grand jurors "voted unanimously that under the circumstances the killing of the two men could not have been avoided and gave Sheriff Barfield and Deputies Clarence Shannon and Hugh Gillespie a clean bill in the matter, declaring the officers did their full duty."[17]

Red Wood had disappeared, but James Dumas was promptly picked up in Lubbock and brought to the Adjutant General's office in Austin. There, after Hamer and two state prosecutors grilled him for hours, he made a written confession. As usual, to protect the integrity of his investigation, Hamer refused to release any details. Even when the East Texas Sheriffs Association invited him to speak about the murder-machine case a few days later, he politely declined. On April 25 Red Wood was captured in Springfield, Missouri, and returned to Texas. Because the Upton County court ordered a change of venue to the state capitol, both were held in jail in Austin to await trial.[18]

Special Ranger Graves Peeler later provided a different story about the interrogation of Dumas and Wood. Peeler said that he was present in Austin when Hamer grilled the two suspects. According to Peeler, Hamer could get nothing out of them because he "went at them the wrong way." Peeler was an inspector for the Cattle Raisers Association, and Dumas, a former cattle inspector himself, asked for Peeler to come to their jail cell. "You bring him up here and I might talk to him," said Dumas. Peeler had a long talk with Dumas and Wood and finally managed to convince them that Hamer's main interest was in prosecuting the corrupt lawmen. "Hamer doesn't want you," explained Peeler. "He wants Reeder and that deputy." At that point Dumas made a full confession, implicating Reeder Webb and his deputy sheriff.

Frank then said, "Peeler, you've got in on this thing. I want you to go to Odessa with me to talk to Reeder Webb." Peeler accompanied Hamer to Odessa, where the two Rangers interrogated Sheriff Webb for several hours. The sheriff proclaimed his innocence, and Hamer then asked to interview his deputy, presumably Tom Jones, though Peeler did not identify him in his recollections. Sheriff Webb said that his deputy was at the jail in Rankin, so Hamer and Peeler piled into the captain's car for the sixty-five mile drive south. On the way, a large, powerful auto raced past them.

"That was Reeder in that car, Cap," exclaimed Peeler.

"The hell you say," Frank snapped.

"It was him all right."

"Well, we'll just set a little trap of our own and we won't walk into theirs," declared Hamer. "We'll go to the hotel and call them."

Instead of heading to the jail, Hamer and Peeler drove to the hotel in Rankin, a small brick building with two separate doors that led into the lobby. The captain then telephoned Webb and his deputy and asked them to meet him at the hotel. Hamer and Peeler waited in the lobby, hands on their six-guns while they eyeballed the two doorways. Suddenly, Webb and his deputy burst in, one through each door. The four lawmen faced off in a tense confrontation, bristling at each other. According to Peeler, Hamer dared Webb to draw, but the sheriff lost his nerve. "They turned and ran out of there like scalded cats," recalled Peeler.

"Let 'em go," ordered Hamer. "I've got all the information I need."[19]

But Sheriff Webb and his Odessa possemen were never prosecuted, probably because of their popularity and political connections in Ector County. The case against Dumas and Wood lingered for several years. Another change of venue was granted to San Marcos, but the trial was repeatedly continued. The delay may have been caused by Hamer's ongoing efforts to obtain immunity for Dumas and Wood to induce them to turn state's evidence. Finally, he was successful. In June 1931 the Ranger captain again appeared before the Upton County grand jury. This time he brought Dumas and Wood, who gave incriminating testimony against Bud Barfield, no longer sheriff, and his two former deputies. The grand jurors indicted Barfield, Shannon, and Gillespie for murder. It seemed that at last Frank Hamer had been fully vindicated, but his

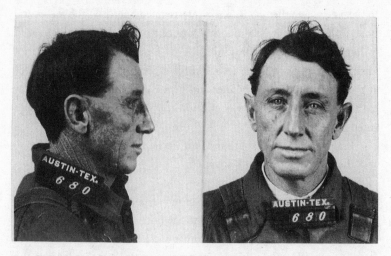

Carl "Red" Wood, partner of James Dumas. Hamer got them both to turn state's evidence against the corrupt lawmen involved in the Murder Machine case. *Travis Hamer personal collection*

triumph was short-lived. In September 1931, a judge in Rankin quashed the indictments on the grounds that at least three members of the grand jury were "not qualified to serve." The charges against Barfield, Shannon, and Gillespie were never refiled. For Hamer, it was yet another frustrating example of the vagaries of Texas justice.[20]

The Texas Bankers Association was unfazed by Hamer's campaign. Massie refused to eliminate or even modify the reward. When the wife of one victim filed a wrongful death lawsuit for $100,000 against the association and Sheriff Webb, the bankers vigorously defended the case. In 1928 the West Texas Sheriffs Association adopted a resolution demanding that the bankers alter the reward to read "dead or alive" and provide that it would not apply to night burglaries. Tom Hickman was one of the few who voted against it. Nonetheless, the Texas Bankers Association voted unanimously to continue the dead-bandit reward. Eventually, the bankers modified the reward to limit it to robbers "legally killed while robbing and holding up" a member bank "in the daytime." The reward program remained in effect until 1964, when it was finally withdrawn as a barbaric relic of the Wild West.[21]

Frank Hamer's campaign against the reward system revealed his strength of character coupled with a seemingly inconsistent set of beliefs. As he said, "I agree that . . . bank robbers should be shown little consideration, and should be killed when caught in the act of robbing a bank." In numerous gun battles over the years, he had demonstrated that he had little compunction about using deadly force against armed desperadoes. Yet, despite his abhorrence of crime and his contempt for criminals, he believed in justice and fair play. He thought that all men, regardless of race, were entitled to the protection of the law. Though he despised criminals, he often worked to obtain paroles or pardons for those who had reformed.

At the same time, he abhorred crooked officials, especially corrupt lawmen, and frequently exposed their crimes. Like his campaign against the Ku Klux Klan, Frank Hamer's struggle with the Texas Bankers Association was one of the most noble of his career. The moral leadership he displayed in his David and Goliath battle would long be remembered by the Texas public.

18

TOWN TAMER

In June 1928 all of Texas looked forward to one of the Lone Star State's most important events of the twentieth century: the Democratic National Convention in Houston. For Texans and Southerners it was especially significant, for this was the first national convention held by either party in the South since the Civil War. During the Roaring Twenties, Houston bypassed San Antonio and Dallas to become the largest city in Texas, a modern metropolis of almost 300,000, with 63,000 African Americans. The Bayou City's politicians and boosters raised $200,000 in its successful bid for the conclave. The convention showcased the presidential struggle between Democrat Al Smith, the Roman Catholic governor of New York who favored repeal of the Volstead Act, and Republican Herbert Hoover, who strongly backed Prohibition. Smith's Catholicism and his anti-Prohibitionist platform caused many southern Democrats to support Hoover's campaign for the presidency. Although Frank Hamer was not anti-Catholic, he favored Prohibition, which led him to vote for Hoover. This would be the first time that a Republican presidential candidate carried Texas. The Houston convention showcased something else that was just as important to Texans: that their state was no provincial backwater but a modern society and a powerful force in national affairs.[1]

But, once again, that fragile, genteel veneer of civic respectability was shattered by Judge Lynch. On June 17, less than a week before the convention, two Houston police detectives tried to arrest an African American, Robert Powell, and four other black men. Powell fled, and in an exchange of gunfire, one detective was slain. Police officers soon arrested Powell at his home. He had a bullet wound in his abdomen, which he claimed he got in a fight over a dice game. Powell was brought to Jefferson Davis Hospital and placed under guard. At two in the morning on June 20, eight armed, unmasked white men entered the hospital, overpowered a deputy sheriff, and looped a rope around Powell's neck as he lay in bed. "Oh Lord, have mercy on my soul!" he shrieked as they bound him hand and foot. Powell was dragged outside to two waiting autos, and the vigilantes drove off into the darkness.

Later that day, a pair of police detectives found Powell's badly bludgeoned corpse hanging from a bridge on the Post Oak cutoff road, eight miles from the city. A hospital nurse and an orderly, both black, said that one abductor wore a blue coat with gold braid on the sleeve. Governor Moody immediately sent Frank Hamer to Houston. Moody offered a $250 reward for each of the lynchers, the local branch of the NAACP added another $1,000 each, and Houston officials set aside a $10,000 fund to pay for the investigation. Civic leaders, deeply humiliated, insisted that this was the first lynching in Houston's history. In fact, there had been at least one, in 1859. The city's record of race relations had been poor, as demonstrated by the Houston riot of 1917, when black soldiers, subjected to discrimination and harassment by Houston citizens and police, rioted and killed sixteen whites, five of them police officers. The troopers were court-martialed, and nineteen died on the gallows.

The Powell lynching was more than embarrassing—given its timing on the eve of the national convention—and made newspaper headlines nationwide. As one editorialist pointed out, "It is a magnificent mockery of the very heart of the idea on which the Democratic party is supposed to stand. . . . But the murdered body of this man-forsaken and mob-destroyed negro prisoner, trailing at the end of a rope, will give the lie to every plea for justice and righteousness. Robert Powell, dead at the hands of a lynching gang, dominates the Houston scene." Just as Texans looked forward to the convention as a bellwether of the state's importance in national politics, Frank Hamer recognized the significance of his investigation. He was soon joined by Tom Hickman and three privates. While Houston newspapers issued scathing editorials condemning the lynching, the Rangers focused their probe on the local police, for the blue coat with gold braid worn by one of the lynchers resembled a police uniform. Fifty officers on duty that night were hauled before the grand jury. Within forty-eight hours, Hamer, Sheriff T. A. Binford, and Chief of Police Tom Goodson arrested seven suspects, none policemen but all of them friends of the dead officer. One turned state's evidence and the other six were indicted for murder.

This was one of the few serious efforts in Texas to prosecute the members of a lynch mob. The first of the culprits to come to trial was Charley Oldham. Although he had signed a written confession, Oldham now recanted. Not surprisingly, an all white jury acquitted him. A second member of the mob, Howard Minton, who had also confessed, was tried the following year and likewise acquitted. A disgusted Frank Hamer fully understood that the struggle to end lynching in Texas was far from over.[2]

But not all African Americans were victims; some struck back violently at Jim Crow. On the morning of October 9, 1928, Frank got a phone call with electrifying news. A black man, Armand Alexander, was on a murderous rampage in the neighborhood just south of the Hamers' home. The twenty-seven-year old Alexander, married with three young boys, had enjoyed a good reputation. But a month earlier, he had been fired from his work as a porter in the office of the state highway department for "insubordination and disrespect to white employees." Justifiably angry, he took a much harder job picking cotton on a farm outside town. On October 7, brooding over his problems, he went into a jealous rage when his wife, Lula, told him she had visited with his brother the evening before. Alexander kicked her and the children out of their house and forced them to sleep outside for two nights. On the morning of the ninth, he drove up to the home in a touring car and forced Lula and the boys to get inside. As they headed through south Austin, he threatened to shoot her, give the children to his relatives, and kill himself.

"I'm bound for hell and I'm going to take white folks and colored people with me," he declared.

When she struggled with him, he shoved her out of the car. With the children still inside, Alexander drove to the home and store of his aunt and uncle, Daniel and Catherine Pyburn. He evidently blamed Mrs. Pyburn for his troubles, because he called her and her twenty-four-year-old daughter, Ethel, to step outside. When they did so, he leaped from the auto with a twelve-gauge pump shotgun and fired a blast of buckshot at Catherine Pyburn, almost severing her head. She died instantly. A second charge of shot tore off half of Ethel's head. Daniel Pyburn and his son jumped for cover as the killer pumped five more rounds into the store. As Alexander's children screamed with terror, he tried to drive off, but his car had a flat tire. Leaving the boys in the auto, he took the shotgun and a .22 caliber rifle and started on foot west along Elizabeth Street. He passed the Brackenridge school for black students, half a block from the Pyburn home. A teacher, thinking a rabid dog had been shot, looked out and asked, "What are you shooting?"

"Getting rid of a bunch," was his angry response.

Telephone reports of the double murder quickly reached the police department, and Chief James Littlepage and five of his officers jumped into two autos and rushed to the scene. Littlepage, sixty-five, had been with the department for nine years, the last four as chief. The lawmen spotted Alexander fleeing south along the banks of East Bouldin Creek. While the other policemen pursued Alexander on foot, Chief Littlepage and Officer Jack Newman, in an effort to head him off, raced a mile south to the spot where the creek met Oltorf Street. After a quick search, they spotted Alexander just to the east, running down the 2400 block of Wilson Street. Littlepage, despite his age, leaped from the car and pursued the running killer. Overtaking Alexander, the chief tried to talk him into giving up.

"Don't you come near me," Alexander warned. "I'll kill you!"

At the same time, he swung up the .22 rifle and fired several times, striking the chief in the face. He started to run again, but then turned and fired a blast from the shotgun. Littlepage dropped with a load of buckshot in his stomach. Alexander fired twice more at the chief, picked up his pearl-handled .38 revolver, and fled. Officer Newman then pulled up in the auto, dragged his wounded chief inside, and rushed to the hospital. Littlepage died on the operating table half an hour later.

The crazed killer fled back north a half mile to the home of a black friend, Tom Shelby, at 1800 Newning Avenue, apparently to pick up some of his belongings. Finding a white carpenter, Joe Blunn, working at the rear of the house, he shot him dead. Then he spotted Shelby's wife, cowering on the front porch, and roared, "Guess I might as well kill you too!"

She shrieked and dove to the floor as Alexander's shot whined harmlessly above her. Alexander then raced a block west to South First Street, where he burst through the back door of the home of a white man, Ernest Arnold. He shot at the only occupant, Mrs. Arnold, who fled outside with her infant daughter in her arms. A teenager, Robert Pond, was passing by in a Ford roadster, and Mrs. Arnold flagged him down and jumped inside. The car stalled, and, as Alexander fired two shots at them, Pond got out and managed to crank the engine up and flee to safety. Alexander then ran back inside the house.

By this time Frank Hamer and other officers arrived on the scene. Drawn by the gunfire and the screams of Mrs. Arnold, Hamer and five Austin policemen quickly surrounded the Arnold house, a small white wood-frame building. Frank, armed with a six-gun, took a position overlooking the rear. Alexander, shotgun in hand, suddenly appeared at the front door.

"You damned sons of bitches," he shouted. "Stop or I'll kill all of you!"

As the killer ducked inside and slammed the door shut, two officers sent a dozen pistol shots splattering into the door. When Alexander retreated to the back of the house, Hamer and the others opened fire with six-shooters and shotguns. The assassin ran from window to window, screaming curses at the lawmen, who in turn riddled the house with forty to fifty rounds, blowing out the windows and door screens. Then Hamer and the policemen paused to determine whether any of their shots had taken effect. But the killer was not hit, for he responded with a shotgun blast from a window. It was evident that the officers' weapons could not pierce the walls of the house, so they sent for high-powered rifles.

As they waited, several long moments of silence were suddenly shattered by a single gunshot inside the house, followed by a heavy thud. Hamer cautiously approached the rear door, while several city detectives advanced toward the front. Frank kicked in the back door and burst inside. He found the gunman dead on the floor of the bathroom, a gaping wound in his throat. Alexander had shot himself with Chief Littlepage's revolver.

The five killings had all taken place within two miles of Hamer's Riverside Drive home. Frank's friend Boss Thorp was promptly named Austin's new police chief. The bloody rampage is all but forgotten today, but it would remain the most significant mass murder in Austin until 1966, when Charles Whitman opened fire from the clock tower at the University of Texas, killing sixteen people and wounding thirty-one.[3]

A month later, Hamer was sent to the Rio Grande Valley to investigate election frauds in Hidalgo County. A. Y. Baker, known as the "millionaire sheriff of Hidalgo County," was still in power as political boss. A former Ranger and protégé of the political boss Jim Wells, he had become wealthy by manipulation of public funds and powerful by controlling Hispanic votes. He commanded the county's politics, its businesses, and even its newspapers. In 1928 Republicans and anti-Baker Democrats formed the Good Government League to oppose him. Their complaints resulted in Governor Moody's sending Hamer, Bill Sterling, and seven Rangers to monitor the November 6 election. Due to widespread complaints of fraud, after the election Hamer seized the ballot box from the town of Mercedes and locked it in the courthouse in Edinburg for safekeeping. At the same time, the Good Government League appealed for martial law to enforce a fair vote count, but Moody refused because there had been no violence.[4]

The ballot counting in Hidalgo County took several days to complete and attracted national attention. Huge crowds surrounded the courthouse while Hamer, the Rangers, and deputy sheriffs stood guard.

On the third day, three men crawled underneath the room where the last ballot box was being counted. Frank caught them red-handed as they bored holes through the wood floor. When the tally was done, Sheriff Baker and his machine had won all but two of the county offices. This result sparked the Hidalgo County rebellion, a political and legal campaign against the Baker regime that eventually led to a federal grand jury investigation. In 1930 Baker and seven of his henchmen were indicted for voting fraud, but a jury acquitted them all. Baker's death from a stroke that November wrote finis to his machine. But as Frank Hamer was well aware, this hardly put an end to boss rule in South Texas.[5]

Meanwhile, Frank's Ranger duties were compounded by ongoing trouble with the quartermaster Roy Aldrich. "By paring the men's accounts, he made a great show of saving money for the state," said Bill Sterling of Aldrich, adding, "He dealt most generously with his brother and himself." Each captain was allocated fifty dollars a month for maintenance of an automobile, which was used by the entire company. "Aldrich allotted himself one of these allowances," Sterling complained. "His car was not used for state business, but to transport himself from the capitol to his suburban home." Sterling described an incident in which Hamer "decided to find out just how far the Aldriches would go with their intrigues." Frank arranged to have a telegram addressed to "Captain, Headquarters Company" sent to him from a distant city. It advised that a bank absconder was hiding out in a certain room in an Austin tourist motel and that a large reward was offered for his arrest. As Hamer anticipated, Roy Aldrich intercepted and read the telegram in the adjutant general's office. Saying nothing to the other Rangers present, he summoned his brother to the hallway outside. The two huddled briefly, then drove immediately to the motel. Barging into the room to make the arrest, they were shocked to find Hamer waiting for them inside. As Frank roared with laughter, the humiliated Aldrich brothers scampered away in chastened silence.[6]

By the spring of 1929, Borger, that open sore on the Panhandle prairie, was again in the news. After the Rangers left in 1927, the rough boomtown, surrounded by a forest of derricks, saw civic improvements.

Tents and ramshackle wood storefronts were replaced by brick and masonry buildings, sewage pipes were installed, and some of the muddy, auto-choked streets were paved. But those changes were cosmetic, for the city gradually fell under the rule of what Jake Wolters called "a strongly entrenched criminal ring that gave to Borger a real racketeering underworld." Known as "the Line," it controlled—to the extent there was a difference—both politics and vice. Gambling halls, again featuring hundreds of slot machines, as well as wide-open saloons and brothels, all paid rake-off to the Line. Those who didn't were roughed up by goons. Violence was endemic: thirty-two murders had taken place since the town was formed, and twenty remained unsolved. Most of the honest policemen who had been recommended by the Rangers in 1927 had left office. The new mayor, Glenn Pace, the police chief, John W. Crabtree, and the county sheriff, Joe Ownbey, whom Hamer had tried to pressure into resigning two years earlier, were all on the take, if not actual leaders of the Line.

In April the newly elected district attorney, Johnny Holmes, asked Governor Moody for the Rangers. His request was vigorously opposed by the local state representative, John H. White, who seems to either have been controlled by the Line or in sympathy with it. Finally, on June 28, Tom Hickman, Lone Wolf Gonzaullas, and sixteen more Rangers and Prohibition agents, disguised as country rubes in ragged straw hats and overalls, slipped into Borger and gathered evidence. Then they raided speakeasies, destroyed liquor and gambling devices, and lodged thirty-six men and women in the rickety jail. As soon as they left, Borger returned to its wicked ways. District Attorney Holmes could get no convictions in court. Explained Wolters, "He received no aid, no support, from the sheriff's department and interference from the constable and police departments of Borger." But Holmes was dedicated and fearless, and he pressed on with investigations of the underworld, the most important being the prosecution of Whitey Walker for the murders of the two deputy sheriffs in 1927.[7]

On Friday night, September 13, 1929, Johnny Holmes drove up to his Borger home, let his wife and mother-in-law out, and then pulled into the garage. As he exited the car, a hidden assassin opened fire with a .38 revolver, blasting two holes in his chest and one in his head. Holmes dropped dead, and neighbors, roused by five gunshots, rushed outside in time to see a dark figure flee on foot down an adjacent alley. Newspapers used their biggest, blackest type in headlining the story to a stunned readership. It was the first time that a Texas prosecutor had been slain in office since the murder of Cullen Higgins in 1918. Governor Moody, calling Holmes's assassination "one of the most atrocious and cowardly crimes in Texas history," immediately ordered his chief town tamer to Borger. Frank Hamer arrived at midnight on September 14, accompanied by Captain Hickman, Sergeant Jerome Wheatley, and two privates. As the Rangers swung down from the train, an ambulance roared past, taking the latest murder victim, mortally wounded in a brawl, to the city hospital.[8]

Two days later, a huge funeral was held in Borger for the slain prosecutor. Mrs. Holmes at first had refused to invite any of the city or county lawmen, whom she believed were complicit in her husband's murder. Although she subsequently relented, only one official, Judge H. M. Hood, attended the service. Incredibly, at the very time the funeral was underway, Borger lawmen posed with Whitey Walker for a notorious photograph at the courthouse in Stinnett. Walker, smiling broadly and without handcuffs, sat on the front steps of the courthouse. Surrounding him, each with broad grins, were Mayor Glenn Pace; Sheriff Joe Ownbey; the sheriff's chief deputy, Jim Crane; and Deputy Sheriffs Cal Baird and Berlin Millhollon. To the Texas public, this photo graphically confirmed the image of Borger officials in cahoots with gangsters.[9]

Hamer quickly found that Borger police had done very little to ferret out the Holmes killer except to round up twenty "suspicious characters," all of whom were released for lack of evidence. They had recovered five empty pistol cartridges and one unfired bullet near the garage. The assassin's tracks led down the alley and abruptly ended where he had jumped into an automobile. Yet Chief Crabtree had interviewed none of the neighbors and made no effort to locate other witnesses. Hamer learned that a year earlier, Johnny Holmes had obtained an indictment of Chief Crabtree for willfully allowing three prisoners to escape the city jail. Holmes also had charged Mayor Pace with election fraud and a Borger deputy constable, Sam Jones, with selling thirty-two gallons of confiscated liquor, and he had prosecuted another law officer for accepting a bribe from a prostitute.[10]

Hamer was assisted in his investigation by Clem Calhoun, district attorney at Abilene, whom Governor Moody appointed as special prosecutor to replace Holmes. He was also aided by a new Ranger, Benjamin Maney Gault, whose name was commonly, though incorrectly, spelled "Manny." Gault, two years younger than Frank, lived a few blocks from the Hamer home in Austin and worked as a mill foreman. After the pair first met in the mid-twenties, Frank had often recruited Gault as an undercover man in moonshine investigations. Though Maney Gault had no other law-enforcement experience, Hamer trusted his judgment. In 1929 Hamer got Gault commissioned as a Headquarters Company Ranger.[11]

In Borger, Frank and his men heard rumors that city and county officials had been involved in a conspiracy to murder Holmes. Once, when Chief Crabtree, Mayor Pace, and Sheriff Ownbey were drinking together, one of them had declared, "The dirty son of a bitch ought to be killed." The dead prosecutor's widow insisted that her husband's death had been ordered by Borger's criminal ring and that local officers had never given him any aid in his campaign against the gangsters. Hamer found a witness, Tex Thrower, who had seen a man he believed was Deputy Constable Sam Jones fleeing down the alley from the scene of the murder. The suspect escaped in an auto driven by Jim Hodges, a former Borger policeman and now the manager of a local boiler works.

Although many witnesses were too cowed to talk publicly, Hamer soon announced that he had "obtained affidavits concerning an alleged plot between city and county officials." In response, an infuriated Chief Crabtree declared that his department was fully investigating the Holmes murder. "City and county officials may not make the first arrest," he declared, "but I will bet a thousand dollars that when the right party is arrested the city and county officers will arrest him." It apparently never occurred to him to offer that $1,000 as a reward for the killer.[12]

Hamer had worked hard to control his temper and improve his diplomacy. A prosecuting attorney who worked with him in Borger commented, "One is impressed with his tact, ability, and energy." On the night of September 18, Hamer ran into Chief Crabtree in the Black Hotel. Frank told Crabtree "that he had heard certain rumors that the chief had threatened to kill him." This time Hamer, unlike in his angry confrontation with Sheriff Reeder Webb a year before, held his temper. The big captain issued a quiet but stern warning to the crooked police chief: "Now, I don't want to hear any more of that."

Crabtree vehemently denied making any threats, and the corrupt mayor, Glenn Pace, publicly denounced Hamer's charges of corruption. A few days later, Frank met with Governor Moody near Dallas to update him on the Borger investigation. On September 21 the governor announced that Hamer considered Borger "the worst organized crime ring he has observed in twenty-three years as a Texas Ranger." When reporters pressed Frank for details, all he would say was, "It is awfully bad." Hamer's comments hit the wire services and were reported in newspapers throughout the nation. After making a quick trip to Ranger headquarters in Austin and then to Brownsville to testify in another case, Frank returned to Borger to find that his remarks had created a firestorm of controversy. Sheriff Ownbey declared, "It's a lie, and you can quote me to that effect."[13]

Civic boosters in Borger, including the editor of its daily newspaper, denied that the town was controlled by racketeers or that its law officers were involved in the Holmes murder. As one journalist reported, "The rumor that Rangers knew the name of the assassin struck like a bombshell in the little boom town that has been attempting to silence all the stories of the brutal assassination of the diligent prosecutor who gave his life in performance of his duty. So far, there has been little cooperation between city and county officers and the ranger force." The *Borger Daily Herald*, in a front-page editorial, called on Hamer to prove his charges: "There never was a ring of criminals known to exist in a town the size of Borger that was not disbanded if capable officers worked on the case. If such a crime ring does exist here, Borger people demand the arrest of its leaders; if it does not exist, they demand a retraction of the information going out of the city to that effect."[14]

Hamer ignored the Borger newspaper and recommended to the governor that martial law be declared. Jake Wolters was now the nation's leading authority on the use of martial law, due to his training as a lawyer and National Guard general and his military leadership in the Longview race riot of 1919, the Galveston longshoreman's strike of 1920, and the Mexia cleanup in 1922. Governor Moody sent him to Borger to investigate the need for martial law. Hamer, Hickman, and Clem Calhoun wanted it, because martial law would allow the governor to summarily remove corrupt officials and force recalcitrant witnesses to testify before a military tribunal about the Holmes murder. Wolters met with prominent citizens, explaining that martial law could be avoided if Sheriff Ownbey, Chief Crabtree, Mayor Pace, and other officials resigned. An indignant Pace told Wolters that would never happen. General Wolters thereupon left Borger, seemingly with his tail between his legs. Three days later, on September 29, he returned on the evening train at the head of ninety-seven National Guardsmen and with Governor Moody's proclamation of martial law in hand.[15]

Wolters also brought a second decree from the governor, which suspended from office Sheriff Ownbey and

Frank Hamer, left, and Manuel "Lone Wolf" Gonzaullas in 1933. *Author's collection*

his deputies, Chief Crabtree and his entire department, local constables, and the Borger city judge. While a detachment of troops took over city hall, Hamer, Hickman, Lone Wolf Gonzaullas, and seven other Rangers began carrying out Moody's orders. Frank had been investigating Mayor Pace for forcing a witness in a murder case to leave town. He swore out a warrant against Pace and had Tod Aldrich lock him in the Borger jail, once again using a "trot-line" that the Rangers attached to a "snorting pole" buried in the ground. Then Hamer arrested Borger policeman Clint Millhollon for bootlegging while Maney Gault picked up Constable Sam Jones as a suspect in the Holmes murder. The Rangers disarmed all the law officers in Borger and in Stinnett, the county seat.[16]

Lone Wolf Gonzaullas described the arrests of Borger's lawmen: "Some of them tried to get smart with us, but we just smacked 'em around and hitched a few to the snortin' pole at the jail. That took the wind out of 'em and they didn't give us any more trouble. You just can't imagine the pile of guns that stacked up as we took them off the Borger officers, plus the run-of-the-mill gun-toters on the streets. It was just unbelievable. And, you should have seen how those fellows squirmed when the good people of the town came down to the jail to see 'em with the rings on 'em and chained to the snortin' pole. Why, those people laughed and laughed, because they knew that 'the Line' had come to the end of the line."[17]

On September 30 General Wolters convened a military court of inquiry into the Holmes murder and general corruption in Borger. He was assisted by six officials, including Hamer, Clem Calhoun, Judge H. M. Hood, and Colonel O. E. Roberts. The Rangers hauled in numerous witnesses for grilling, and their testimony, recorded by a stenographer, showed a sorry state of affairs. At the exact time of the Holmes assassination, all the Borger police were attending a prize fight at the Borger Coliseum. Officer Red Blasingame, the first to respond to the murder, arrived fifteen minutes later, after a large crowd had gathered. He immediately announced, "Well, they can't blame it on any of us policemen, because we were all at the fight."[18]

Other officers and their wives were also forced to testify and said that they had been at the boxing match. It was evident that some or all of them had advance knowledge of the plot and had attended the fight in order to establish an alibi. Borger policeman Clint Millhollon, an admitted bootlegger, testified that he went to the murder scene but claimed he had been too ill to help investigate the murder. He denied being "the official collector for the Line." His cousin, Deputy Sheriff Berlin Millhollon, disclaimed knowledge of any plot by local officials to murder Holmes. He swore that he had never heard of the Line and knew nothing about gambling, bootlegging, or prostitution in Borger. He insisted that he had helped investigate the Holmes murder, but when pressed for the names of witnesses he had questioned, he mentioned Sergeant Wheatley and Sheriff Ownbey, explaining, "I have talked to people, who I don't know. I think I have talked to people—brother officers—but could not tell you the names."

At that, an incredulous Colonel Roberts thundered, "Here's your district attorney of this county murdered, and the only people you can tell me you talked to are such people as Wheatley and the Rangers and other officers? Do you consider this efficiency in a peace officer?" Millhollon's lame response: Sheriff Ownbey had not assigned him to investigate the murder.[19]

When Sheriff Ownbey happened to drive past the Black Hotel, where the hearings were underway, National Guardsmen spotted him and hauled him inside. Not surprisingly, he was less than helpful. His interrogators confronted him with the report that a few nights before the murder he was with Chief Crabtree and Mayor Pace, when one of them said of Johnny Holmes, "The son of a bitch ought to be killed." Ownbey denied it, saying, "I don't think anyone had a feeling like that toward him." He swore that, soon after the killing, he had gone "up and down the alley" to find witnesses. He first claimed he could not recall the names of those he interviewed or what they had told him. After being pressed, he named several witnesses, saying, "All gave the same description pretty well. Said he was a big fellow with a big white hat. Most of them described him as being 190 [pounds]." When asked whom he suspected, he hemmed and hawed and finally responded, "Well, it looked to me for a while that it might be [Representative] John H. White but I don't think now he had a thing to do with it." When asked about the Line he said, "I heard of the Line and asked a time or two but did not have anything to do with it."[20]

The sheriff's denials were colorfully refuted by one witness, who described Ownbey: "He is not like the ordinary drinker. He stays in a pretty pickled state all the time." Louis Crim, widely believed to be one of the leaders of the Line, was also dragged in. A notorious bootlegger, he ran a Borger drugstore as a cover for his moonshining business. In 1927, after he savagely beat his wife, she shot and badly wounded him. He recovered, and they reconciled. Six months later, he shot and killed a night watchman in a personal quarrel in front of his drugstore. To the military court, he readily admitted to having been a professional bootlegger almost from the start of Prohibition. He also admitted that he had two prostitutes working for him but denied any knowledge of the Line. He insisted that he had been at home with his wife and two daughters on the night Holmes was slain and denied any knowledge of a murder plot or corruption of the city police.[21]

Frank Hamer brought in his prime witness, twenty-year-old Tex Thrower, an ice-truck driver. In answer to the captain's questions, Thrower said that, forty-five minutes before the shooting, he was parked in his ice wagon on Main Street when a dark green Buick Six sedan pulled up behind him. Two well-dressed men were inside, and the passenger got out and walked down the alley that led to the Holmes residence. The driver then took off. Thrower described the passenger: "He was a rather large fellow, heavy man about Sam Jones' build. . . . I didn't get to see his face, but seeing him walk down the street looked like the way he walked and looked like Sam Jones." He said that he thought the driver was a Borger police officer, but claimed he could not identify him. Colonel Roberts then took over the questioning, and it became evident that Thrower feared for his life if he gave more information, for he had previously told Judge Hood that the man in the alley was definitely Sam Jones.[22]

The military court grilled thirty-four witnesses over the next few days. Then, on October 4, the court reconvened and, during the following seven days, interviewed scores of people, most of them about bootlegging, corruption, and general lawlessness. The most important witness was Hoyt Embry, a neighbor of Johnny Holmes. He lived next to the alley, and, after hearing the fatal shots, he and his brother, A. C. Embry, looked outside and saw Sam Jones fleeing down the alley. Although he could only state that the man "looked like" Jones, he said that his brother was positive in the identification. Hamer then brought in Jim Hodges, the reputed getaway driver. Hodges claimed that he was at the Moose Hall at the time of the killing but admitted hearing rumors that he was involved in the murder and that money had been raised to hire an assassin.[23]

In the meantime, Rangers and troopers cleaned up Borger. Hundreds of prostitutes and criminals fled town "like rats running from a sinking ship," as one journalist reported. They closed at least thirty-six saloons, "blind tigers," gambling halls, and bordellos. According to wire reports, "The young solders usually stood guard outside while the grizzled rangers nonchalantly, and with quiet monosyllables, conducted the main business within." On October 7 Clem Calhoun announced that Officer Clint Millhollon, Deputy Sheriff Cal Baird, and five others had been arrested in "one of the largest liquor rings the Panhandle has seen." The jail held forty-six prisoners. Mayor Glenn Pace was under a $3,000 bail bond. Deputy Constable Sam Jones had been charged with receiving twenty dollars a week from a bootlegger. Borger's justice of the peace was jailed for investigation of corruption.[24]

On October 5 Hamer personally led what newspapers called "the biggest liquor haul since the establishment of martial law in Hutchinson County." With Tom Hickman, Lone Wolf Gonzaullas, Maney Gault, three other Rangers, and a detachment of National Guardsmen, he captured a pair of 250 gallon stills and arrested three moonshiners. This was the first raid he had led since the military court hearings had begun. Martial law resulted in the appointment of honest officials in Hutchinson County. Ranger C. O. Moore was named county sheriff with Ranger Marvin "Red" Burton as his deputy, and, at Hamer's urging, ex-Ranger Albert Mace, who had been installed as police chief in Mexia, was prevailed upon to take over as Borger police chief.[25]

After one moonshine raid in the Hutchinson County hills, National Guardsmen gathered to participate in a shooting exhibition. Hamer happened by and watched in amusement as Lone Wolf Gonzaullas practiced firing at a target with a small-bore semiautomatic rifle that a friend had given him. The mark was the size of a dime, thirty paces distant. Gonzaullas was not accustomed to the rifle's sights and repeatedly missed the mark. Finally, Hamer grunted in disgust, "I could beat that with a .45." Drawing Old Lucky, he fired once, tearing a hole through the bottom edge of the spot. The soldiers broke out in enthusiastic applause, but Frank feigned embarrassment. Patting Old Lucky in his holster, he said, "Carried it too long. The sight must be wearing off."[26]

Captains Hamer and Hickman, their work done, left a tamed Borger on October 12, and the National Guard troops withdrew six days later. The boomtown was left in the capable hands of its new lawmen. Red Burton, a crack officer, continued to investigate Sam Jones and Jim Hodges. In early November he arrested them for the murder of Johnny Holmes. Both were indicted by the grand jury, but their cases never came to trial, because Clem Calhoun did not believe there was sufficient evidence to convict them.[27]

While the Borger cleanup was going on, Frank's old friend, Captain Charles Stevens, met a violent end. "Cap'n Cholly" had spent much of the 1920s as a Prohibition agent. He brought his trademark aggressive energy to the job, making more than two thousand arrests. The work was hazardous in the extreme, and he made many enemies among bootleggers and crooked politicians. On September 24, the sixty-year-old Stevens and two of his men raided a huge still near Pleasanton, south of San Antonio. On the way back to San Antonio, members of the bootlegging gang ambushed his car and shot him to death. A grief-stricken Hamer immediately entrained for San Antonio. He arrived the next day, in time to serve as an honorary pallbearer at Stevens's funeral. Although numerous members of the gang were arrested, only the ringleader was convicted of the captain's murder.[28]

The cold-blooded assassination of Frank's close friend terrified Gladys Hamer. If a prominent former Ranger captain could be gunned down on a public highway, the same fate could befall her husband. Due to Gladys's worries, Frank began to consider quitting his beloved Ranger force. In late October, Texas newspapers first published rumors that he would resign. On November 6, he and Tom Hickman, with half a dozen Rangers plus local officers, were on hand to prevent wagering at the new Arlington Downs racetrack, located midway between Dallas and Fort Worth. While the gregarious Hickman was "meeting a dozen friends a minute," a reporter for *The Dallas Morning News* tried to interview Hamer about the rumors. Frank replied that he would "oil the old gun and put 'er in the bottom of the trunk," adding that he had been offered "something that is a lot better." He refused to elaborate, other than to say that the job "does not involve wearing a shining shield." Frank admitted that he did not want to leave the Rangers: "Well, I won't be happy, but there are other things." The newspaperman wrote that the "other things" he referred to were "Mrs. Hamer and their interesting children."[29]

But Frank could not bring himself to do it. His decision was a fortuitous one. A fateful day a week earlier, October 29, 1929, would be remembered in infamy as Black Tuesday. The public at first believed that the stock market crash would affect only stock speculators, but economic conditions steadily worsened. In Texas, the state's great wealth—in cotton, lumber, livestock, and oil—would stave off the worst effects of the Great Depression for several years. But eventually the Lone Star State, like the rest of the nation, succumbed to a decade of hardship and misery. The Depression quickly led to social unrest and racial strife, as well as a sharp increase in robberies and the rise of gangsters, resulting in some of the greatest challenges of Frank Hamer's career.

19

FUNERALS IN SHERMAN

Texans first felt the Great Depression in the cotton fields. In North and East Texas, where cotton was king, prices had been falling since the mid-1920s, caused by overproduction and decreasing demand as Americans turned to clothes made of rayon and other synthetic materials. After the stock market crash, cotton raising went from bad to worse. Less than half of the state's cotton growers owned their own farms; the rest—60 percent—were sharecroppers and tenant farmers, both white and black, whose bleak lives were marked by backbreaking work and grinding poverty. As cotton prices continued to fall and money became scarce, sharecroppers and tenant farmers bore the brunt. And to poor white sharecroppers, nothing was as threatening, or hateful, as cheap black labor.[1]

Sherman, seventy-five miles north of Dallas and the seat of Grayson County, was the center of a vast cotton-growing district. While its neighboring city of Denison was a rail hub for North Texas, Sherman was the county's political and agricultural center. With a population of almost sixteen thousand, Sherman boasted fine homes, a dozen parks, four private colleges, and vied with Waco for the title "Athens of Texas." It was served by five railroads plus the Interurban, a light electric railway with connections to Denison, Dallas, and Fort Worth. Despite the trappings of modernity, Sherman was very much of the Old South.

About two thousand of the town's residents were African American, and most lived in a segregated neighborhood centered on Mulberry Street, four blocks north of the courthouse. Jim Crow laws and customs were strictly enforced. The Ku Klux Klan first appeared in Sherman in 1921, when eight thousand people gathered to hear its imperial chaplain deliver a speech in a public park. Klavern number 105 was soon formed. Nonetheless, the black community thrived, with its own businesses and shops, even a movie theater and fraternal lodges: the Odd Fellows, Knights of Pythias, and Masons.[2]

During the late 1920s, the frequency of lynchings in Texas had remained low. The first lynch-free year was 1925. The following year saw four lynch-mob deaths. There was but one lynching in 1927, two in 1928, and three in 1929. Although Frank Hamer could be justifiably proud of his role in the fight against mob law, events in Sherman that May of 1930 would shake him to the core.[3]

Four miles southeast of Sherman stood the farm of Drew Farlow. In April 1930 Farlow hired George Hughes, a forty-one-year-old African American field hand and a newcomer to Grayson County. Two weeks later, on the morning of May 3, Hughes went to the farmhouse to ask for six dollars in wages. Farlow's pretty twenty-eight-year-old wife, Pearl, was home alone with their five-year-old son, Robert. Hughes's common-law wife later said that he had "commented several times" on Mrs. Farlow's "physical attractiveness and had indicated what he intended to do." Local blacks asserted that Hughes was a "half wit" and "crazy" and was subject to "spells." When Pearl Farlow told him that her husband was in Sherman and would return that evening, Hughes left. Forty-five minutes later, he returned to the kitchen door, armed with a double-barreled shotgun, and forced his way inside. He ripped off Pearl Farlow's clothing and dragged her into the bedroom, then raped her as the terrified child fled from the house. Hughes told the woman that "the white folks hated him and his race, and that was why he was assaulting her." Hughes, declaring that he "was not through with her and that he would be back in a little while," bound the woman to her bed with electric cord and went to the barn in search of the boy.

Pearl Farlow managed to untie herself and run to the farm of a neighbor, George Taylor, who telephoned Grayson County's sheriff, Arthur Vaughan. Taylor and other neighbors found the child crying on the road near the farmhouse. They spotted the gun-wielding Hughes inside the barn, but he fled on foot. Several men followed him, taking care to keep out of shotgun range. By then, a deputy sheriff, Bart Shipp, arrived on the scene. Taylor climbed into Deputy Shipp's auto, and the two raced off in search of George Hughes. They soon found him running through an alfalfa field toward Choctaw Creek. Shipp gunned his auto across the open field, and, as he closed in, Hughes fired two blasts with his shotgun, shattering the deputy's windshield. Shipp, seeing that Hughes's shotgun was empty, covered him with his pistol, and the desperado surrendered.[4]

Hughes was quietly locked up in the county jail, where he soon made a full confession. Within two days, however, false rumors circulated that he had mutilated Pearl Farlow and given her a venereal disease. Hughes was charged with rape, and his trial set for May 9, just six days after the crime, which was the earliest trial date allowed under Texas law. Sheriff Vaughan, rightly concerned about mob violence, secretly moved Hughes to the jail in McKinney, thirty miles south. On the evening of May 6, a crowd of rowdy youths in their late teens and early twenties gathered outside the Sherman jail and demanded the prisoner. One of their leaders was Jeff "Slim" Jones, a bootlegger and reputed Klansman. Officers fired warning shots over their heads, and they scattered. By eleven o'clock, the mob had regrouped, augmented by hundreds of onlookers. Many were drunk, and they planned to use a telephone pole as a battering ram to breach the jail. Sheriff Vaughan, Deputy Shipp, and a handful of local officers managed to quiet them by explaining that Hughes had been moved to another lockup. Instead of arresting the mob leaders, Sheriff Vaughan allowed Slim Jones, Raymond C. Hart, and three others to search the jail. This was a foolish decision, for in the end it only encouraged the mob. But for the moment it worked to pacify them. Then Pearl Farlow's father, Luther Atnip, accompanied by three men from his family, appeared at the jail, telling the mob that Hughes would be punished legally and urging them to go home. Finally, the would-be lynchers dispersed.[5]

George Hughes as he was being taken to court in Sherman on a charge of rape. *The Sherman Museum collection*

The next day, Judge R. M. Carter, fearing more trouble, made a telephone call to Governor Moody and requested aid from the Texas Rangers. Captain Hamer, with Sergeant Jerome Wheatley and Rangers Tod Aldrich and Jim McCoy, caught the 4:25 P.M. northbound train out of Austin. They arrived in Sherman the following morning, May 8. By this time Slim Jones had driven all over rural Grayson and adjacent counties, urging the country folk to attend the trial. Heavy rains had made it impossible to work the fields, so large numbers of white sharecroppers, tenant farmers, laborers, and their families flocked into Sherman to see the excitement. Frank Hamer found the streets teeming with spectators, many in an ugly mood. Though the air crackled with tension, it was a scene he had encountered many times. Hamer and his men, wielding rifles and shotguns, guarded a manacled Hughes as they brought him into the courthouse. He pled guilty to rape and agreed to accept any punishment a jury might affix. His trial, for the sole purpose of determining his punishment, was set for the following day.[6]

Sherman, like many Texas county seats, boasted a beautifully designed courthouse. Texans then and now are rightfully proud of their handsome nineteenth-century courthouses. Sherman's, a huge, elegant, two-story stone building set off by a towering cupola, had been erected in 1876 and was the most imposing structure in the county, situated at the center of the town square, and valued at the then-princely sum of $60,000. The main door opened into a lobby, from which a pair of curving staircases, one on each side of the lobby, led to the second floor. Besides the courts, it held the offices of the district attorney, tax collector, assessor, and other county officials. At nine o'clock the next morning, Friday, May 9, an angry, excited crowd began filling the courthouse square. A handcuffed George Hughes was brought into Judge Carter's second-floor courtroom, guarded by Hamer and his three Rangers, Sheriff Vaughan, and four deputy sheriffs. Pearl Farlow arrived at the courthouse in an ambulance and was carried inside on a stretcher. The sight of the rape victim enraged the huge throng of spectators. Many tried to follow her stretcher-bearers into the building, but deputy sheriffs kept them out.

Judge Carter opened court at 9:30. He had appointed a local attorney to represent Hughes and immediately began jury selection. The judge closed his courtroom to spectators, but the crowd, including women, packed into the first story, then into the corridors, the staircases, and finally the second story, hoping to get a glimpse of the trial. By eleven o'clock twelve jurors had been chosen, but the onlookers had grown so numerous and noisy that Judge Carter sent the jury out and ordered Hamer to clear the second floor. This infuriated the horde, which began to shout threats and obscenities. Hamer and his men managed to move the rowdy throng out of the hallway, down the stairs, and out the front door.

At half past noon, the first witness, the neighbor George Taylor, was called to the stand. Before he could finish testifying, the crowd, now an excited mob, tried to reenter the courthouse. Recalled Hamer, "I took one of my men and went to one foot of the winding stairs." He positioned his other two Rangers at the bottom of the opposite staircase. "Then the leaders of the mob appeared in the central doorway. I was surprised and worried to see women in the first group. I could tell they were agitating the men, urging them to take the negro from us." The mob, seeing the Rangers barring the way, hesitated. At that, Hamer barked, "The negro is upstairs, and there he stays. If you take him you'll have to come up these stairs. Don't try it."

Instead the mob pressed onward. "Then I cautioned them again, pleading with them to control themselves. There was a rush at both sides of the stairs. I had told my men to use their pistols as clubs and beat the crowd back. The mob surged forward. We swung our old-style frontier .45s, clubbing a man here and another there. This brought a pause. We followed the advantage through, forcing the mob back to the central door and out to the courthouse lawn."[7]

By now a mass of several thousand, including numerous women and children, jammed the courthouse square. Although some in the crowd were simply curiosity seekers, most of the onlookers shouted, screamed, and egged on a smaller number of determined lynchers. Their leaders, among them Slim Jones, were almost certainly Klansmen. To encourage the mob, Raymond C. Hart, a thirty-seven-year-old Sherman man who had previously helped search the jail, circulated a rumor that the Rangers had been ordered not to shoot. The story spread like wildfire and emboldened the rabble. A reporter for *The Denison Herald* overheard two women discussing the rumor and called it in to his newspaper without bothering to verify it. Within minutes the story was picked up by the Associated Press and republished as fact.[8]

From the courthouse windows, Hamer and his Rangers looked down onto the square, now an undulating sea of white straw hats and sun bonnets. The downtown streets were jammed with cars as spectators and lynchers swarmed around the building. At one o'clock the mob made a second assault on the courthouse, screaming, "We'll get the nigger!" Frank and his men again took up positions at the foot of the stairs. Said Hamer, "This time I saw fifteen or twenty women scattered about in the crowd, half a dozen of them to the very front of the wedge that was preparing to enter the front door. As the crowd neared the door I left my place on the stairs and walked to the entrance. This time I repeated in substance what I had said before. I did not tell the mob, of course, that I had instructed my men to use their pistols as clubs only, nor did I threaten to shoot into the crowd. I only cautioned them that they could not get to Hughes without climbing the stairs and explained that we were in the way. This warning had a slowing effect only; it did not stop them. The four of us prepared to withstand the assault and as the leaders came within reach we raised our pistols and swung down, hard, quick. I talked all the time I was swinging my pistol but I don't remember exactly what I said. I know that I continued to caution the crowd and suggest that they withdraw."

The mob forced Hamer and his men onto the two staircases. "After about twenty minutes in which the crowd would push us back two or three steps only to have us beat them down a step at a time until we reached the bottom again, the leaders lost courage, if mob leaders have courage. We pushed through the advantage again and for the second time the crowd trickled out through the door. I left Wheatley, Aldrich, and McCoy at the foot of the stairs and went back to the second floor to see how things were there." Frank then told Judge Carter that "the trial could not be held here without bloodshed." The judge decided to order a change of venue to another county. News of the change of venue further inflamed the mob, and repeated shouts of "Let's get the nigger right now!" filled the air.

Susie Crist and Ruth Jones, a pair of loudmouthed, seventeen-year-old girls from Denison, along with a woman who was a stranger in Sherman, egged on the rabble. They goaded the men by chiding them for "yellowness" in retreating from the Rangers, then urged a crowd of teenage boys to take over leadership. At that, an eighteen-year-old Sherman High School senior, J. R. Melton, tore down an American flag from the courthouse grounds and, with other boys, marched around the building, yelling for others to join them if they had "enough red blood to do something about a nigger who had raped a white woman." Led by the flag bearer, the mob reentered the courthouse and charged up the stairs. As Melton reached the upper story, Ranger Tod Aldrich struck him a heavy blow over the head with his pistol. The teenager fell backward and the other youths fled back down the stairs. Melton staggered outside, holding his bleeding head, which infuriated the mob even more.

Now the lynchers tried a different and much more dangerous tactic. In front of the courthouse, several men produced sticks of dynamite as makeshift hand grenades and tried to ignite them. But the Rangers were too quick for them, as Hamer later told reporters. "We grabbed a small fire hose and turned it on the dynamite, wetting it down so it was useless."[9]

Again the mob swarmed toward the front door. Said Frank, "Then we heard the rolling grumble again and knew that the third assault was to come. Meanwhile someone had found some tear gas bombs. As the mob approached the entrance several of these bombs were thrown." The corridor and stairways quickly filled with noxious fumes. Lynchers, choking and gasping, cleared out of the courthouse. The tear gas spread throughout the halls and seeped under the doors into the courtroom, which held about fifty people. The hallways were so full of gas that the only escape was through windows. A call was made to the fire department, which set up ladders so that witnesses, jurors, and court employees could escape the second story. Pearl Farlow, overcome by tear gas, was carried into the ambulance and whisked away.

As the fumes drifted away, the mob continued to surge through the front door. "I still had ordered pistols used only as clubs," said Hamer. "I was sure we could handle the situation that way and did not want to shoot anyone. On they came, and down swung our pistols. I wish I could remember what I said, but I can't." Frank added, "This attack was finally repulsed just like the others, and the mob withdrew to the lawn again. When I went back upstairs this time I got a shotgun. I hoped it would impress the crowd should they return."[10]

Instead, the mob began yelling at Hamer and his Rangers, "You can't shoot us!" Frank had no idea what they meant. He later reported, "I instructed my men that the next time they rushed the courthouse I would fire on the mob, but for them to hold their fire until I gave orders to shoot." Several minutes later a mass of lynchers charged through the door, yelling at the Rangers, "Nigger loving sons of bitches!"

Hamer recalled, "As the mob started entering the door I called to them to stop and leveled the shotgun at them. They stopped a minute and I explained that this time, if the charge were continued, I would shoot. They didn't believe me."

Two of the leaders were Dan Shero, thirty, of Sherman, and Jim Brown, an ex-soldier from Bells, twelve miles east of town. As Brown started toward the stairs, Hamer, standing on the stairway, barked, "If you put your foot on the step I will shoot it off."

The lynchers paid no heed and surged forward with Brown and Shero at the forefront. Hamer shouldered his shotgun and aimed low, firing a blast of buckshot into the onrushing mob. Jim Brown dropped with buckshot in his foot, and Dan Shero staggered with wounds in his leg. This terrified the frenzied mob, and they again fled outside.

Hamer now allowed a newspaperman to come up the stairs. He showed the Ranger captain a telegram from the Associated Press in Dallas that stated that Governor Moody had ordered, "Protect the negro if possible, but do not shoot anybody." Frank was surprised, telling the reporter, "I had received no such message." The Associated Press was the nation's largest wire service, with a strong reputation for honesty and reliability. Hamer had every reason to believe the report, but he knew Moody well enough to doubt it. He met again with Judge Carter. "I . . . told him about the report and informed him I didn't believe the governor would issue such orders, because we probably could not hold the prisoner if such order was issued." According to one journalist present, Hamer told the judge, "This means the mob will get the negro." Judge Carter replied, "Let's lock him in the big vault."

Frank recalled, "So we took Hughes into the vault and locked him in, putting in a big bucket of water so he could have a drink if his stay stretched out long as it looked like it might." The district court clerk's vault, located on the second floor, thirty by thirty feet in size and lined with walls of steel and concrete, was more than secure. Moments later, one of the emboldened mob leaders appeared at the foot of the stairway and demanded that the Rangers give up the prisoner. When Hamer refused, the lyncher shouted, "Well, we are coming up to get him!"

"Any time you feel lucky, come on," declared the captain. "But when you start up the stairway once more, there is going to be many funerals in Sherman."[11]

Hamer was dead serious, and the lynchers knew it. They made no further effort to invade the building. Frank began to breathe easy, believing, as he later said, that "we had them whipped off." He needed help in moving Hughes to the jail, so Judge Carter telephoned Governor Moody's office and asked for the National Guard. The adjutant general advised that a platoon would be immediately dispatched from Denison. After thirty minutes of quiet, a woman in the crowd began pelting the courthouse windows with rocks and bottles. Soon others joined her, quickly breaking out the lower windows. At 2:30 a seventeen-year-old Sherman high school student, J. B. "Screw" McCasland, accompanied by Alvin Gordon, fifteen, and a youth named Gross, rushed across the square and through the swarming crowd, carrying a five-gallon can of gasoline. McCasland threw it into the first floor window of the county clerk's office. Then Alvin Gordon lit several matches and tossed them inside. Jumping down from the window ledge, he exclaimed, "Now the damned old courthouse is on fire!"

The courthouse burns in Sherman, Texas. It was torched by the lynch mob on May 9, 1930. *The Sherman Museum collection*

The outer walls of the courthouse were stone, but the inside walls, flooring, and joists were all wood. The gasoline fire ignited the interior like a tinderbox. Sheriff Vaughan and his men were now outside, trying futilely to calm the mob. Deputy Bart Shipp spotted the flames and warned the Rangers upstairs. As the building filled with smoke, firemen began to evacuate by ladder the last occupants of the courtroom. Hamer asked Judge Carter to telephone Governor Moody about the alleged "do not shoot" order, but as the jurist later explained, his "efforts were cut short by the firing of the building." Frank later reported that "all at once the flames from the lower story of the courthouse swept up the stairways and on up to the ceiling over our heads to the second floor."

Outside, firemen unrolled their hoses to fight the flames. But one mob leader, a huge man carrying a long-bladed knife, began slashing the fire hoses. Another, Swafford Rolen, hacked open the hoses with an ax, while a third, Cleo Wolfe, pummeled a fireman with his fists. Others began pelting the firemen with rocks. Soon most of the fire department's hoses were useless. The sharecroppers and tenant farmers in the mob, who paid neither income nor property taxes, began yelling, "Let 'er burn down! The taxpayers will put 'er back!"

As flames roared out of the courthouse windows, the frenzied mob chanted, "Roast him! Roast him! Roast him! Burn him alive! Burn him alive!" Others screamed, "Burn that nigger! Then we'll get him!"

In all his experience in dealing with lynch mobs, Hamer had never seen a community burn down its own courthouse to get a prisoner. It was something he did not anticipate and had not prepared for. Amidst the searing flames and swirling smoke, he rushed frantically though the court offices, seeking any employee who might have the combination to the vault. But they had all been evacuated from the building. By then, said Hamer, it was too late to save George Hughes: "The flames cut us off from the vault and we could not have opened the vault if we could have gotten to it, as we did not know the combination." As the heat and smoke from the fire were about to consume them, Frank and his Rangers finally climbed down the fire ladder. As he later reported to Governor Moody, "myself and men barely escaped the burning building." They were the last to get out of the blazing inferno.[12]

At that moment, in the roaring flames of the Sherman courthouse, the "One Riot, One Ranger" ethos died. There was no way that four Texas Rangers could control a crazed mob of thousands. Briefly, Hamer and his men stood on the front steps of the courthouse, wielding their rifles and shotguns in the face of the infuriated rabble. Then the heat from the inferno pushed them off the steps and into the mass of people. By now George Hughes was dead or dying, and Frank had no further intention of firing on the mob. Lone Wolf Gonzaullas later said that Hamer "left Sherman immediately after the courthouse fire to avoid conflict with townspeople that might have led to shootings." In Hamer's official report to Governor Moody, he said, "Among the crowd were many women and children. We stood around a few minutes. I thought it necessary for me to communicate with you, as I heard the troops were on their way. Not caring to discuss this with you from Sherman, we were talking to a man and I asked him if he had a car, he said he did, I asked him to drive us to Howe, from which point I called you." Howe was a small town nine miles south of Sherman.

Frank's decision to make his phone call outside of Sherman was a wise one. In 1930 Grayson County did not yet have the newly developed dial telephone. Instead, every telephone call, whether local or long distance, was handled by an operator. And all long distance calls in the county had to be routed through the operator in Sherman. As one telephone operator of the day recalled, many calls were not confidential: "Because if something special—like the riot or phone call to the governor—was going on, then, of course the operator would stay on the line. You were not supposed to, but everyone did." Hamer at first was unable to reach Dan Moody, and as he waited on the line, he heard the snoopy Sherman operator say to someone, "Lynch the nigger," and "I am glad they burned the courthouse."

Frank angrily hung up the phone and proceeded with his men another twenty-five miles south, to McKinney, where he managed to connect with the governor on a different long distance line. Hamer recommended that a much larger detachment of National Guard be dispatched immediately. After delivering his report, Frank and his men began searching for a driver to take them back to Sherman. Governor

Moody tried unsuccessfully to contact Tom Hickman, then telephoned Sergeant Lone Wolf Gonzaullas in Dallas. Gonzaullas and Ranger Bob Goss left promptly for Sherman. Moody then ordered Guardsmen in Dallas to respond to the riot.[13]

Meanwhile, the heat from the inferno drove much of the crowd from the courthouse square. By four o'clock the flames subsided, leaving only the vault on the second floor and the stone walls of the courthouse standing. Spectators thronged into Sherman, increasing the crowd to five thousand. The city's ten police officers, unable to cope with the mob, were reduced to directing traffic as hundreds of cars jammed the downtown streets. Some residents later charged that the police took no action against the lynchers because Pearl Farlow was the niece of B. V. Atnip, an old and popular Sherman policeman. When Rangers Gonzaullas and Goss arrived late in the afternoon, Lone Wolf found the courthouse in smoldering ruins and said that Sherman was "in complete possession of the mob." He and Goss went to the county jail, a block west of the courthouse, and reported to Sheriff Vaughan.[14]

At 6:00 P.M. a platoon of fifteen or twenty National Guardsmen arrived on the Interurban car from Denison. With fixed bayonets, they marched on foot to the courthouse square. There they were surrounded by an infuriated mob of one thousand, which pressed so close the soldiers could not move forward. The front lines of the mass were women and children, protecting the rioters behind them, who were emboldened by the "do not shoot" rumor. Over the heads of the women and children, the rioters pelted the troops with bottles and rocks. One soldier and a rioter were seriously injured by flying bottles. The troopers, unwilling to risk harm to women and children, held their fire and retreated to the Interurban station, followed by the mob. The beleaguered soldiers boarded a car and escaped back to Denison.[15]

By this time wild rumors were circulating among the mob. Its frenzied leaders were desperate to locate George Hughes. They knew that he was not with Hamer and his Rangers, who were rumored to have left town by airplane. Some thought that Hughes was still alive in the vault; others believed that he had been spirited away to the county jail. From

Denton, Sheriff Ted Lewis rushed to Sherman at the head of a six-man posse. They arrived soon after the troopers had been driven from the square. "We received information that the mob was going to string up the Grayson County sheriff," Lewis later told reporters. At about 6:30 P.M. fifty-five National Guardsmen arrived on the Interurban from Dallas and reported to the jail. They found the Denton posse, Rangers, and local officers barricaded in the jail as it was surrounded by a huge mob. Several lynchers lit sticks of dynamite and threw them at the jail. They exploded but caused no injuries.[16]

Although Sheriff Lewis believed the AP's "do not shoot" report, Lone Wolf Gonzaullas was having none of it. Heavily armed with two pistols, a shotgun, and a Thompson submachine gun, he took up a position in front of the jail, while Bob Goss covered the rear. As the mob yelled taunts at Gonzaullas, he ordered them back, but they refused. Lone Wolf later gave differing versions of his response. In one account, he claimed that he fired buckshot over the heads of the rabble. However, in another, he said that he quickly singled out the leaders, drew a pistol, and shot "three or four" in the legs. The latter version may be substantially correct. Several of the mob surrounding the jail were wounded, among them a sixteen-year-old Sherman youth, Jed Brown, shot in the chest; a Sherman bricklayer, John L. Melton, wounded in the neck; and Howard Barker, seventeen, shot through the thigh. Melton had been hit by a metal-jacketed .45 round; the other two, by lead bullets. Later, National Guard officers denied shooting any of them, pointing out that their .30-06 rifles and .45 automatic pistols fired full-metal-jacket rounds. Only the Rangers and local officers carried guns that shot lead bullets. Although the Guard officers insisted that the three had been wounded by fellow lynchers, it seems evident that Melton had been shot by a trooper and the other two by Gonzaullas. Sheriff Lewis thought that even more rioters were wounded by the besieged lawmen at the jail. "Reports indicate that but few persons were injured by the bullets but I am of the opinion that a large number were hurt and that many injuries were not reported."[17]

At eight o'clock officials decided that the troopers should recover

George Hughes's body from the vault, for he could not possibly have survived the inferno. It was just after dark when they started for the courthouse. As the soldiers marched in formation down West Houston Street, between the jail and the courthouse ruins, they were assailed by the mob. A young girl running a soft drink stand handed out empty bottles to the rioters. A reporter said that "the air was filled with soda water bottles, bricks and timbers, showered on the troops." One of the mob, Gilbert Alsup, felled Private Perry McClain with a brick to the head. Rioters seized McClain's rifle and ammunition belt, yelling, "Take away his gun!"

Captains John Dunlap and Albert Sidney Johnson rushed to Mc-Clain's aid, but both were badly injured by flying missiles. The troopers were pushed back against the smoldering walls of the courthouse, which appeared ready to topple to the ground. Finally, the soldiers formed a column to retreat to the jail, but the shower of bottles and rocks continued unabated. They fired forty to fifty shots over the heads of the frenzied mob, which refused to scatter. Several rioters fired at the guardsmen, wounding two. The militia returned the fire, hitting one of the mob, Pink Hill. Followed by the horde, the soldiers made it to the safety of the jail, where six seriously injured troopers were taken inside. The rest set up a cordon around the building, with sharpshooters on the roof. As the crazed mob surrounded the jail, one woman held her infant child over her head and screamed, "Shoot it, you yellow, nigger lovin' soldiers! Shoot it!"[18]

By this time Hamer and his Rangers had returned to Sherman and joined the lawmen and soldiers at the jail. Tom Hickman and three of his men also arrived, as did several Dallas police officers. A call was made to the adjutant general, who ordered more troops sent from Dallas, but it would take hours for them to mobilize. For the first time in Hamer's career, he was utterly helpless. The forces at the jail, numbering about twenty law officers and fifty-five militia, plus the Rangers, were powerless against the mob. Because the courthouse had already been destroyed and George Hughes was certainly dead, it now seemed futile to use deadly force against the rioters. In addition, the large numbers of women and children in the mob made the officers loath to fire on them.

Though Hamer had already demonstrated that he would shoot white men to protect a black man, other lawmen and troopers may have had different scruples. Some of the local peace officers feared that if they attacked the mob, its members would torch downtown businesses. Hamer, Hickman, Sheriff Vaughan, and the National Guard officers elected to stay in the jail and bunker down until militia reinforcements arrived from Dallas and Fort Worth. It was a convenient but wrong decision, for it resulted in one of the most horrific displays in America's sorry history of racial conflict.

As radio stations as far away as Dallas spread news of the riot, highways into Sherman became jammed with vehicles. Between five and ten thousand spectators crowded around the jail and the courthouse square, where giant oak trees stood seared and blistered by the fire. Many of the mob had been waiting for the walls of the courthouse to cool down enough so they could open the vault. At nine o'clock, in a drizzling rain, lynchers turned a spotlight on the vault on the east side of the building and set up a ladder. Slim Jones and a teenage boy, "Duck" Roach, climbed the ladder to the vault. They set off several charges of dynamite, which failed to dent its two-inch outer steel wall. Then an ironworker, Horace Reynolds, pulled up in a truck with two large acetylene tanks in the bed. He scaled the ladder, put on his goggles, and went to work with his welding torch. It took two hours for Reynolds and another lyncher, C. B. Duckworth, to burn a small hole through the outer steel wall. Then the four ghouls, with a hammer and chisel, chipped away at the layer of concrete. Finally, Reynolds relit his torch and began burning through the inner steel wall. By this time it was 11:40 P.M. Growing impatient, Slim Jones climbed up the ladder with a stick of dynamite, put it in the hole, and yelled, "God damn it, stand back!"[19]

He lit the fuse, and the explosion blew chunks of concrete from the side of the vault. At that, the massive crowd began gleefully singing in unison the hit song, "Happy Days Are Here Again." Jones then inserted a huge charge of six dynamite sticks and struck a match. A terrific explosion blasted open a large hole in the vault. After waiting a few minutes for the dynamite fumes to clear, Duck Roach and Horace Reynolds crawled inside. One of them yelled, "Here he is!" and the mob broke into wild cheers. Dragging George Hughes's lifeless body through the hole, they tossed it outside. The limp body slid down the ladder, tumbling two stories to the ground below. As it hit the ground, two women fainted in their tracks. Although later reports claimed variously that Hughes had died from burns, smoke inhalation, or the dynamite blasts, an autopsy would show that he had suffocated when the fire sucked all the air from the vault.[20]

Now the mob, wild with bloodlust, converged like vultures on the corpse. One of them attached a chain to Hughes's neck, and several others hoisted it up on the limb of a hackberry tree next to the courthouse. At that, Slim Jones, from his perch at the top of the ladder, began shouting at the crowd, "Take him to niggertown! Take him to niggertown!"

The mob pulled the corpse down and dragged it across the lawn. One yelled, "Let's tie him on this car!" They attached the chain to the rear bumper of a Ford Model A roadster driven by Leo D. Luton, twenty-four, of Denison. Luton, who had two girls and a young man inside the car, started off. Bill Sofey, a twenty-two-year-old Sherman rowdy, jumped on the rear bumper, shouting in glee. Soon he was joined by more than a dozen, who crowded onto the Ford's running boards, hood, and roof. The mob began screaming, "Let's go to niggertown!"

With a hooting crowd of two thousand following, including women with babies in their arms, Luton dragged the body up Travis Street four blocks to Mulberry Street, the commercial center of the segregated black neighborhood. Going east on Mulberry, the mob came to a stop in front of the black-owned Smith Hotel, located at 219 East Mulberry. It housed Goodson's Drug Store, a beauty shop, undertaking parlor, tailor shop, and other African American businesses. Slim Jones and Bill Sofey, with other mob leaders, looped the chain over a limb of a cottonwood tree and hoisted the body up. Then Jones yelled, "Come on, gang!" as the rioters looted the hotel, taking chairs, display cases, and dry goods boxes, which they piled under the hanging body. In an ultimate act of degradation, Slim Jones drew a knife and cut off George Hughes's penis, then splattered coal oil on the corpse and the pile of wood. He lit a bonfire, and Hughes's remains slowly roasted on the leaping flames.

The climax of the Sherman riot: George Hughes on the funeral pyre on East Mulberry Street. *Author's collection*

As the gleeful, cheering mob crowded around, they enjoyed cigarettes, cigars, candy, and soft drinks that had been looted from the drugstore.

Not satisfied with the funeral pyre, Slim Jones stepped behind the Smith Hotel and set fire to a pile of rubbish. Within moments the building was afire, and as the flames reached skyward, the rabble burst into cheers. A newspaper reporter present described the scene: "Soon the sidewalks were covered with broken glass which, sparkling in the glare from torches, the flaming building and the moon, cast grotesque shadows on the dangling figure of the negro, hung to the tree by the chain which had dragged the body through the streets of Sherman."

By now more than a thousand African Americans had fled their homes. Several hundred hid in brush thickets on the outskirts of town, while many others took sanctuary in the houses of white friends and employers. Those blacks who owned automobiles, about one hundred, escaped to Dallas. As the Smith Hotel inferno died down, the mob, several thousand strong, moved west on Mulberry Street, breaking into and looting African American shops. Carrying gasoline and torches, they stopped at the two-story Andrews Building, also owned by blacks. In moments it too was aflame. The rioters pressed on to a nearby home owned by an African American doctor. The mob helped its white tenant move his possessions into the street, then torched the house. Next, in quick succession, they set fire to other black-owned businesses: another undertaking parlor, two restaurants, the Odd Fellows Hall, two barbershops, an attorney's office, the Capitol movie theater, the Knights of Pythias building, and several other buildings and residences. Sherman firefighters, with their hoses slashed, could do little to fight the flames.[21]

The mob now moved north across the railroad tracks to North Branch Street, where they were confronted by Sherman's bravest townsman. He was Salem Sofey, a sixty-five-year-old grocer, who had come to Sherman from Syria in 1888. His home and grocery store were located at the corner of North Branch and Brockett Streets. As the mob prepared to torch an entire block of houses, Sofey argued with the rioters, telling them that he owned every house on the block. It was a blatant lie—the homes were all owned by his African American neighbors. Sofey's ruse worked, and the mob left the houses alone. In an extraordinary irony, Bill Sofey—who prominently led the lynchers in the dragging and burning of the corpse—was his son. Salem Sofey, born and raised in the Middle East, possessed none of the racial hatred that consumed his Texas-bred boy.[22]

A detachment of the National Guard had finally arrived at 11:30 on the Interurban from Dallas. At 2:15 A.M. more troops came in from Fort Worth, and a final detachment disembarked from Interurban cars at 3:15 A.M. The total reinforcements numbered about three hundred. Carrying four heavy machine guns and thirty-two Browning automatic rifles, they set up a cordon around the jail. Upon the 2:15 A.M. arrival of the soldiers from Fort Worth, the reinforced Guard marched north into the black neighborhood, where seven hundred rioters were still running rampant. The troopers arrived at the corner of College and East Streets just as the mob was trying to torch the Fred Douglass Elementary School for black students. The rioters—for the first time faced with a large military force—hurriedly retreated. After posting a guard at the school, the militiamen marched to the cottonwood tree and took down George Hughes's body. Because both black undertakers had been burned out, one of the Guard commanders ordered a white funeral director to bury the body.

At 2:00 A.M., the Rangers under Captains Hamer and Hickman had left the jail and began interviewing witnesses on the street. Within two hours, they had managed to identify and arrest thirteen of the mob leaders. Hamer made the final arrest that night when he spotted a rioter, J. W. Jeffrey, carrying a stick of dynamite. Heavy rains, coupled with strong patrols by the National Guard, soon cleared Sherman of the crowds of lynchers and spectators. At daybreak Hamer and Hickman, with their Rangers and detachments of troops, began searching for blacks who had fled town. They found several hundred refugees cowering in the brush thickets and escorted them back to their homes.[23]

Newspapers that Saturday, May 10, trumpeted the hellish scenes in headlines nationwide. Governor Moody was excoriated in the northern press, and even in London, for giving the supposed "do not shoot" order. Moody, infuriated as much by the false reports as by the mob violence, declared the riot "treasonable" and a "shame to Texas" and declared martial law. Meanwhile, Hamer led the Rangers on a general roundup of the mob's leaders, arresting more rioters on Saturday and Sunday. His work was cut short when he got an emergency message that Gladys was seriously ill in Austin. When Frank caught a train home Sunday night, it marked the end of his investigation of the Sherman riot.[24]

Hickman, Gonzaullas, and the other Rangers stayed in Sherman, arresting forty-three suspected rioters and helping the National Guard conduct a military court of inquiry. Not surprisingly, many witnesses claimed that they recognized no one in the mob. All of the Sherman police officers and firemen were questioned; with but one exception, they too claimed ignorance. Sherman's public officials tried to distance the city from the violence. Mayor J. S. Eubank claimed that nine-tenths of the mob was not from Sherman. U.S. Attorney Randolph Bryant, while admitting that the courthouse fire was a result of "race prejudice," insisted that the burning of the black neighborhood was caused by "bolshevism" and "Sovietism." Those claims were false. Many of the mob leaders and members were Sherman townsfolk, and the Mulberry Street firestorm was motivated by unadulterated racial hatred.[25]

Based on testimony before the military court, the Grayson County grand jury indicted fourteen of the mob, including its principal leader, Slim Jones; arsonist "Screw" McCasland; the torch-man Horace Reynolds; Bill Sofey; and Cleo Wolfe. Ten of them were from Sherman. Although McCasland and his friend Alvin Gordon should both have been indicted for murder for starting the fire that killed George Hughes, Gordon was not charged at all, nor were many others who had been identified and implicated in the violence. Instead, the fourteen were indicted for arson, burglary, and inciting a riot, and the case was sent to Dallas on a change of venue. Six months later, Slim Jones was the first to be tried, but an impartial jury could not be found in Dallas County. Racism was so ingrained that at least three-fourths of prospective jurors declared that they would not convict anyone for taking part in the lynching or the riot. The judge ordered a change of venue to Austin, where in June 1931 Screw McCasland was convicted of arson and sentenced to two years in state prison. He was the only one of the mob ever punished; by 1932 the charges had been dismissed against Slim Jones and the rest of the lynchers.[26]

Following the riot, many wild stories circulated about the rape of Pearl Farlow. *The Afro-American,* published in Baltimore, Maryland, claimed that the victim had not been raped at all. Instead, it reported that George Hughes had fought with her husband over back wages, and she had been injured in the fray. This yarn is belied by the fact that Drew Farlow was four miles away, in Sherman, when the attack took place. Another African American newspaper claimed that "Hughes was lynched because he went to his employer's house asking for wages and that the employer, being unwilling to pay him, had his wife report that she had been assaulted." That scenario is hugely improbable. The stain of black-on-white rape was so severe that no white farmer would accept it in order to save six dollars. In later years, blacks in Sherman claimed that Hughes had a consensual relationship with Mrs. Farlow and that the affair was exposed when her boy found them in bed together. However, at the risk of stating the obvious, none of these versions explain why George Hughes went to the Farlow house armed with a shotgun.[27]

For Governor Moody, it was easier to disprove the Associated Press account that he had ordered the Rangers not to shoot. On May 14 he released Hamer's official report, in which the Ranger captain denied ever receiving such an order. The Sherman *Democrat* promptly reported that no such message had been received at either of the city's two telegraph offices. Subsequently, records from Southwestern Bell Telephone and Western Union showed that no communication occurred between Moody and Hamer before the assaults on the courthouse. The AP ran a retraction of the story, which was carried by many newspapers. Yet some editorial writers saw the larger problem: because of the long tradition of Judge Lynch in Texas and the South, the story was inherently believable. As the editor of the *Milwaukee Journal* pointed out, "The governor may well reflect, even as he takes the time and trouble to correct this statement, that the comment . . . had a historical basis in hundreds of acts in the south when the negro did not have equal protection before the law, even for his life."[28]

The Sherman riot was one of the most significant events of racial violence in America during the 1930s. Not surprisingly, it quickly spawned copycat lynchings. Seven days later, on May 16, a hundred-man posse shot and killed an accused black murderer who had holed up in a cabin near Honey Grove, about forty miles west of Sherman. They tied the body to the rear bumper of a truck and dragged it two miles into Honey Grove. After parading the corpse through the black neighborhood, they slung it from a tree in front of an African American church and torched it with gasoline. Two weeks later, at Chickasha, Oklahoma, a huge mob stormed the county jail, overcoming resistance by lawmen and National Guard troops, and shot to death an accused African American rapist. Soon after, on June 18, a black rape suspect, after managing to elude a manhunt near Bryan in East Texas, was found dead in a pasture, riddled with buckshot. The first two lynchings, at least, had been inspired by the Sherman riot.[29]

Judgments about Hamer's performance in Sherman are mixed.

Although wire service reports praised him as "the redoubtable Captain Frank Hamer, two-fisted, two-gun Texas Ranger who is known as the official 'mob buster' of the state," in truth he was the first and only Texas Ranger to lose a prisoner to a lynch mob. Years later, Lone Wolf Gonzaullas strongly criticized his Ranger friend, insisting that Hamer should have "shot the hell" out of the mob and then promptly called for reinforcements. He added, "Frank resented that he lost the courthouse and I held the jail." In Hamer's report to Governor Moody, he defended his actions, saying that "when I fired on the crowd in their last attempt to rush the courtroom, we had them whipped off and they could not have taken the prisoner from us in any way only by burning the courthouse as they did and we never dreamed of the gang doing that until the building was enveloped in flames." It is clear that he displayed great courage in defending George Hughes, for in a time and place where racial hatred ran rampant, Hamer stood unbowed before the mob. On the other hand, his failure to act while the mob destroyed the black neighborhood was no more defensible than Sherman police directing traffic while the lynchers blew open the vault. Although National Guard officers were in charge of the troopers, Hamer's ability and experience, to say nothing of his statewide prestige, made him the ad hoc leader of the forces at the jail. At a minimum, he should have made some effort to protect the African American neighborhood before reinforcements arrived. Instead, he, with the other lawmen and soldiers, hunkered down in the jail until 2:00 A.M., by which time George Hughes and the black-owned buildings had been roasted by fire. Only one conclusion can be drawn: Frank Hamer was willing to use force to defend black life, but not to defend black property.[30]

Hamer was more than frustrated by his inability to protect George Hughes. Ranger traditions were extremely important to him, and he felt shame and embarrassment to be the only Ranger who ever lost a prisoner to lynchers. It was a direct affront to his personal honor. Many American newspapers roundly criticized the leadership of both Hamer and Moody. Some Texans agreed. One citizen of Dallas wired Moody, "You should recall and dismiss your bunch of craven cowards known as the Texas Rangers." And despite all the racial violence the captain had seen in his career, he was deeply affected by the hatred and ferocity exhibited by the Sherman mob. As his family recalled in later years, "Hamer's disgust at the cowardly actions of the townspeople of Sherman never abated as long as he lived."[31]

During the ensuing decades, Sherman tried to live down its notoriety. Civic leaders continued to insist that most of the mob came from other parts of North Texas. The cottonwood tree on Mulberry Street was cut down; the black neighborhood was never rebuilt. Newspaper accounts in the Sherman library were defaced and the identities of the arrested rioters clipped out. But the names have not been lost, because they appeared in other Texas newspapers and, especially, in the transcript of the martial law hearing. Now, for the first time since 1932, they are identified in these pages so that the fiends can live in infamy. History—the unforgiving mistress of truth—will not allow us to forget that civilization, like George Hughes, perished for one hellish day on the funeral pyre in Sherman.[32]

20

BONNIE AND CLYDE

First there was utter stillness. Not even a humid morning breeze rustled the brush and the moss-covered pines. The six lawmen shifted restlessly in their hiding places, swatting away the mosquitoes and gnats. The younger officers nervously checked and rechecked their rifles and shotguns. Their leader carelessly fingered the grip of the old fashioned Colt .45 tucked into his waistband as he strained to hear the slightest sound.

Then, in the distance, he heard it. A low whine, like the hum of a sewing machine. It got closer and louder: the roar of a V-8 engine as the Ford sedan suddenly crested a low hill, racing at high speed along the rutted gravel road, then slowed to a stop just fifty feet in front of them. Sudden shouts were instantly drowned out by a deafening explosion of full-automatic and semiautomatic rifle and shotgun fire. Buckshot and steel-jacketed rounds ripped through the driver's door and windows. Bursting lead shredded clothes and flesh. Within seconds it was all over. The big Texas lawman lowered his empty rifle and stepped forward with his .45 in hand. He peered into the auto, then reached into his coat pocket for a rumpled pack of cigarettes. Striking a match, he took a long drag and exhaled slowly, as if in relief. Before him, slumped in the front seat, were the bloodied corpses of Clyde Barrow and Bonnie

Parker. In many ways, Frank Hamer's entire life had been in preparation for that single moment.

It was a great irony that he was not a Texas Ranger when he undertook his most famous exploit. Hamer's four-year journey from the fiery courthouse steps of Sherman to the bloody ambush on a gravel road in Louisiana in May of 1934 was a tortuous one. In 1930, Dan Moody, having served four years as governor, decided not to seek reelection. He was succeeded by Ross Sterling, a wealthy oilman, who had defeated Ma Ferguson in the 1930 primary. Just as Moody was a strong supporter of the Rangers, Sterling proved even more so. After taking office in January 1931, he strengthened the force by appointing Hamer's friend Bill Sterling—no relation to the new governor—as adjutant general.

Bill Sterling had a very high opinion of himself, and not without reason. He was tall, handsome, intelligent, college educated, and popular both in and out of the Ranger service. He loved publicity as much as he liked posing for photographs, often with his guns prominently displayed. One of his first acts was to fire Captain Roy Aldrich, the Ranger quartermaster, whom Sterling despised even more than did Hamer. He kept on the most experienced captains, Frank Hamer, Tom Hickman, and Will Wright, and appointed Hamer's capable friends Albert Mace and Light Townsend. For Frank, this good news was offset by the loss of his old mentor, John H. Rogers, who died the previous November, age sixty-seven, still in harness as a Ranger captain. Rogers had been one of the most important influences in Hamer's life, and Frank deeply mourned his death.[1]

As the Great Depression worsened, some idealistic Americans became interested in communism as an answer to economic woes. Its anti-capitalist, antireligious, and at the time pro-Soviet agenda, however, alienated most. Hamer, like all conservatives, saw the "Reds" as a threat to the nation's security. In February 1931 Communists and labor unions held demonstrations in the largest U.S. cities, demanding enactment of a federal unemployment insurance law. On February 10, as Bill Sterling, Hamer, and a handful of Rangers stood by, a group of seventy-five

Communists picketed the capitol building in Austin. Frank seized three of their placards, which read, "Equality for the Negro Masses," "Fight the Vagrancy Laws," and "Join the Communist Party." Neither he nor the Rangers confiscated any of the other signs, which they considered far less inflammatory. A committee of the protestors, after delivering speeches on the capitol grounds, was admitted to Governor Sterling's office so he could hear their grievances. As sympathetic as Hamer was to Texas blacks, he nonetheless believed in the doctrines of white supremacy and anticommunism. His action, an obvious infringement of the right to free speech and assembly, was altogether typical of the police response to social protest in that era.[2]

Hamer had quietly investigated the Communist Party in Texas and found that their activities were largely nonviolent. But soon after the demonstration at the capitol, he learned of the theft of a large supply of nitroglycerin, far more than any amount likely to be stolen by bank burglars. At the same time, he received tips that Communist terrorists planned to sabotage oil facilities in Texas, Oklahoma, and Kansas. On March 30, 1931, he began sending letters to thirty-eight major oil producers, warning them "that there is a movement on foot among the 'Communists' or 'Reds' to dynamite oil tank farms and pipelines." Hamer marked some, but not all, the letters "Strictly Confidential." On April 21 two nitroglycerin magazines in Oklahoma mysteriously exploded, and soon after, ninety quarts of the explosive were found buried in a field near Oklahoma City. Following a theft of nitroglycerin near Seminole, Oklahoma, the local police chief made Hamer's letter public.

The Ranger captain was livid, but as was his custom, he attempted to protect his investigation from snooping journalists. On April 24, when reporters asked him whether the letter was authentic, Frank was truthful but misleading: he denied sending any warning to the Seminole police. By the next day newspapermen learned that Hamer had written identical letters to numerous oil companies. When a reporter confronted Hamer in Austin, the captain admitted sending them, but angrily insisted that "the warnings were given in the strictest confidence." The journalist wrote, "He expressed regret, couched in unvarnished language, that the public generally had been taken into his secret." Hamer told the reporter that "enough dynamite and nitroglycerin had been stolen to make a dimple out of Pike's Peak," but refused to give any other details of the plot. Only one oil company, Texaco, dismissed Hamer's warning. "I take no stock in any such story," declared its superintendent, Fred P. Dodge. "Frankly, I think Captain Hamer is 'all wet.' I have received such warnings from him before." But Dodge admitted that he did not know what evidence the Ranger possessed. Although no sabotage took place, it seems clear that Hamer would not have taken the trouble to send out so many warnings unless he had compelling evidence of terrorism.[3]

Governor Sterling, like Moody before him, put implicit trust in Hamer's fairness and judgment. Frequently, when a plea for clemency was made, the governor would call Frank into his office and seek his

A group of famous Ranger captains in 1932. Standing center are Bill Sterling and Frank Hamer. At far left is John A. Brooks and at far right is John R. Hughes, two of the Four Great Captains. Seated is Captain Dan W. Roberts, who fought Indians and bandits in the 1870s. *Travis Hamer personal collection*

opinion. One journalist claimed that none of the convicts whom Hamer approved for pardon or parole ever reoffended. Frank's sense of justice extended to his testimony in court. As one criminal defense attorney pointed out, "I have found him uniformly fair and honest, always gentlemanly and courteous and willing to tell facts that benefit the defendant just as promptly and readily as those that benefit the State when he can truthfully do so."[4]

In February 1932 Hamer returned to Hidalgo County in the Rio Grande Valley to confront more political trouble. The 1930 death of A. Y. Baker, the county's political boss and millionaire sheriff, had put an end to his machine. However, when several of Baker's supporters were elected to the local irrigation district, leaders of the Good Government League paid a pistolero from Mexico $500 to assassinate six prominent Democrats. One of the plotters got cold feet and reported the scheme to Bill Sterling in Austin. Sterling sent Hamer, Captain Albert Mace, and several Rangers to investigate. Frank promptly arrested one of the conspirators, confiscating his pistol and $550 in cash. On February 19, 1932, Hamer and Mace picked up eight more suspects, three of whom immediately confessed. Frank called the plot "one of the coldest blooded things I ever ran across in all my years as a peace officer." Later that year, a jury convicted four of the plotters of conspiracy to commit murder and sentenced each to a two-year prison term. Nonetheless, bossism and electoral fraud would remain an ongoing problem in South Texas.[5]

By this time the Lone Star State was feeling the full brunt of the Depression. Drought and high winds caused massive soil erosion in the plains of West Texas and parts of New Mexico, Colorado, Oklahoma, and Kansas. The Dust Bowl resulted in enormous crop loss, unemployment, and human misery. President Herbert Hoover, who had been extremely popular in Texas, became a scapegoat for the nation's ills. Armadillos became "Hoover hogs," and homeless encampments were "Hoovervilles." When the Democrats chose Franklin D. Roosevelt and his Texan running mate, John N. "Cactus Jack" Garner, the outcome of the presidential election that year was a foregone conclusion. In the governor's race, the poor and uneducated flocked to that old charlatan,

Pa Ferguson, who once again fronted his wife for the office. As Bill Sterling pointed out, "1932 had all the earmarks of a 'Ferguson year.'" In July Ma Ferguson challenged Ross Sterling in the Democratic primary; the race was so tight it resulted in a runoff election. Governor Sterling had become unpopular because of his use of martial law to impose restrictions on drilling in the East Texas oil fields. That, coupled with the steadily declining economy, weakened his candidacy. During the campaign the Fergusons resorted to widespread ballot fraud. One half of all Texas counties registered a vote higher than the number of poll tax receipts, meaning that many voters were unregistered or they voted twice. In Gregg County, the heart of the East Texas oil field, the total ballot was 73 percent higher than the number of registered voters.

Hamer and the rest of the Rangers were apoplectic at the thought of the Fergusons returning to the governor's mansion. Although Frank had been willing to work for Ma Ferguson during her prior administration, he could no longer stomach the idea. He later gave reporters a sexist reason for his opposition, saying, "It's better not to be under the command of a woman." Bill Sterling openly campaigned for Governor Sterling, even authoring a pamphlet so critical of one of Ma Ferguson's pardons that she filed a lawsuit to suppress it. The runoff was scheduled for August 27, and the governor's supporters feared a repeat of the ballot fraud. Six days before the election, and without consulting the governor, Bill Sterling sent twenty-five Rangers under Captain Mace to Gregg County, ostensibly to raid dives and break up gambling and bootlegging gangs. In fact, as Sterling later admitted, the purpose was to break up the "horde of floaters" that, he charged, had been sent "to steal the election." But before the Rangers ever got to Gregg County, Governor Sterling learned of the scheme and called it off. He feared that the Fergusons would allege that the Rangers were attempting to influence the election, which indeed they were.[6]

With the help of extensive fraud, Ma Ferguson won the runoff by only 3,333 votes. Now Governor Sterling belatedly responded. Newspapers reported that on September 3, ten Rangers under Captains Hamer and Hickman arrived in the oil boomtown of Kilgore, "refusing to divulge the reason for their presence." In fact, they had come to investigate ballot fraud in Gregg County. One of the Rangers discovered a barrel of phony ballots in the Kilgore city hall. Others obtained witness affidavits showing that "great numbers of tramps were taken off freight trains passing through Gladewater . . . and were herded to the polls by election officials." Three days later, the governor's supporters tried to have the state legislature investigate, but they were rebuffed.[7]

Pa Ferguson issued a typical response, claiming that it was Governor Sterling, not he, who bought votes and stuffed ballot boxes. Farmer Jim lambasted the Texas Rangers, declaring, "Yes, the Ferguson campaign was one of the poor people and they had no big six-shooter Rangers to go out and intimidate [and] unlawfully arrest unoffending voters simply because they might want to vote for Ferguson." His supporters charged, "Rangers are intimidating voters and using duress to elicit affidavits." On September 11, Bill Sterling, Hamer, and several of their men arrived in Lubbock to attend the Democratic convention, hoping to block Ma Ferguson's nomination by proving to the delegates that ballot fraud had taken place in East Texas. Ferguson candidates insisted that the Rangers were there to intimidate them. As one journalist remarked, "A company of Texas Rangers headed by Captain Frank Hamer, seen in the downtown hotels, is causing much interest and comment." When one of Governor Sterling's lawyers admonished the Rangers to avoid trouble, Hamer wisecracked, "There will be no bloodshed. If we jump that bunch, the only thing that will be shed will be a lot of filth and corruption." Despite the Rangers' efforts, Ma Ferguson won the nomination. Governor Sterling filed an election lawsuit, but it was dismissed by the Texas Supreme Court. Ma Ferguson easily defeated her Republican opponent in November.[8]

The Texas Rangers' meddling in the 1932 campaign was profoundly improper, a direct violation of their rules and regulations, which prohibited taking sides in any elections. For the force to ever achieve true professionalism, it had to be entirely divorced from politics. Yet Hamer and the other Rangers believed they had little choice but to try to defeat the Fergusons. Farmer Jim would have fired most of them anyway and then packed the force with incompetents and political hacks, just as he had done twice before, in 1915 and 1925. By mid-October, newspapers were reporting that many of the Rangers would get the ax when Ma Ferguson took office in January. Frank Hamer was not willing to wait that long. For the past several months, his friends had been pressing him to apply for the post of U.S. marshal for the Western District of Texas, headquartered in El Paso. On November 1, 1932, he took an indefinite leave of absence so that he could lobby for the job.[9]

Frank was no self-promoter, but he believed that he, like Captain Rogers, had earned the right to be appointed U.S. marshal. For the first time in his life, he openly and energetically lobbied for a political job. By law, the appointment was made by the president, and, by custom, the choice was made by the senators of each state. During the next few months, Hamer got the support of scores of prominent Texans—politicians, state and federal judges, lawyers, businessmen, oilmen, and ranchers. He obtained at least a hundred letters of recommendation as well as the backing of the Sheep and Goat Raisers Association, the Live Stock Sanitary Commission, the Anti-Saloon League, and even the state legislature. But getting the marshal's job would prove more than difficult.[10]

Ma Ferguson took office in January 1933. One of her first acts was to fire the entire forty-four-man Ranger force, including Hamer, and replace them with political hacks. Much to Frank's disgust, she reappointed Roy Aldrich as quartermaster. Most surprisingly, in Hamer's place she commissioned his brother, Estill. Frank was unhappy with this turn of events, for Estill, formerly a police detective in El Paso and Tucson, had been out of law enforcement since 1920. Certainly, he considered it a measure of revenge, because Estill was a Republican and had no political connection to the Fergusons. According to family lore, it almost brought the two brothers to blows. However, unlike most of the Ferguson appointments, Estill performed well as the new senior captain. Frank and his older brother quickly patched up their differences, for their professional relationship would soon become crucial in the most sensational manhunt of Frank Hamer's career.[11]

Meanwhile, Frank continued to press the Roosevelt administration for the U.S. marshal post. In early April 1933, Frank entrained for Washington, D.C., where he personally lobbied both Texas senators,

Tom Connally and Morris Sheppard. Although the other applicants could not hold a candle to Hamer, President Roosevelt appointed Guy McNamara, former police chief of Waco. McNamara, during the Waco Horror of 1916, had watched the barbarity from his office window and had done nothing to stop it. Roosevelt's choice made Hamer especially bitter, and he would harbor a lifelong grudge against FDR. Always a political conservative, he came to oppose the New Deal and eventually joined the Republican Party. Years later, he recalled, "I was offered a position at one time under Franklin D. Roosevelt at $800 per month and unlimited expenses, a car and a chauffeur. I politely informed them that I would not work for the Roosevelt regime for $800 an hour."[12]

The finest lawman in the Southwest was now unemployed. From Governor Sterling Frank had obtained an unpaid commission as an officer with the newly formed Texas Highway Patrol. For the rest of the year, he performed sporadic private detective work, such as collecting a $200 bounty for capturing a fugitive in Del Rio. It was a far cry from the heady days of his Ranger career. In December he again lobbied Senators Connolly and Sheppard for a federal appointment, first with the U.S. customs service, and when that fell though, as a Prohibition agent. However, Prohibition was repealed that very month, and a political appointment was not to be Hamer's lot. By January 1934, Frank had been largely idle for a full year. His quest for a federal position had been a huge disappointment. Now he could only pray for the end of the Ferguson regime and hope for a Ranger commission. Then fate stepped in.[13]

On February 1, 1934, Lee Simmons, superintendent of the Texas Prison System, paid Frank a surprise visit at his Austin home. Simmons went directly to the point: would Hamer be willing to track down Clyde Barrow and Bonnie Parker? Frank was caught off guard, but the proposal interested him. Like everyone else in America, he had heard a great deal about the lovestruck duo, the most notorious Texas outlaws since Sam Bass. For almost two years they had been the subjects of a massive manhunt across the Midwest and Southwest. Murderous in the extreme, Bonnie and Clyde and their gang members had pulled countless holdups and slain nine men, six of them law officers. Driving night and day in high-powered stolen cars, they ranged from New Mexico to

Indiana and from Louisiana to Minnesota. Local police and sheriffs were not equipped to pursue motorized, multistate bandits. The FBI was staffed mainly with lawyers, not lawmen, and Ma Ferguson's Rangers were largely incompetent. Thus Bonnie and Clyde eluded capture, again and again.

Two weeks earlier, they had engineered a bloody break from the Eastham Prison Farm, which freed several of their gang, left one guard dead, and ignited the wrath of Lee Simmons. He approached the state prison board and obtained authority to hire a special investigator to capture or kill Bonnie and Clyde. Recalled Simmons, "I had my eye on one or two former Ranger captains. I weighed my choice strictly on the basis of who would be the best man for the job. Barrow was a desperado with no regard for human life, a man who despised the law and hated all peace officers. Whoever stopped Barrow would do so at the risk of his life. . . . My decision was for Frank Hamer. I talked to nobody about it, but my own mind kept telling me that Hamer was the man."[14]

Simmons knew he needed permission from Governor Ferguson to hire Hamer. "But I also knew," he later said, "that there was bad feeling politically between Hamer and the Governor." Simmons met with the Fergusons at the governor's office in Austin. "I told them of my need for a special investigator and that I was considering Frank Hamer. Did they have any objections?"

"Frank is all right with us," replied Mrs. Ferguson. "We don't hold anything against him."

Simmons declared that it would probably be necessary to use an informant to trap Bonnie and Clyde. "I might want to put somebody on the ground," he said, explaining, "I might want to promise someone clemency."

"Go ahead," Farmer Jim responded. "I told you we would do anything you want to assist you."

From the governor's office Simmons drove directly to Hamer's home. The two discussed Simmons's plan at length. "I told him that his name had been mentioned only to the Fergusons and that they were agreeable to the assignment," Simmons recalled. "I said I would put him completely in charge and back him to the limit."

"How long do you think it will take to do the job?" Hamer queried. He was not asking Simmons for manhunting advice, as the prison superintendent readily admitted: "That was his way of indicating that he had no intention of jumping into something that might peter out under him. He knew that the FBI, the Texas Rangers, and a great many peace officers had been trying unsuccessfully for years to run down, capture, or kill Clyde Barrow. Hamer was not about to accept an arrangement whereby after a few months I might say, 'Well, it looks like we are not getting anywhere, so we might as well call it off.'"

So Simmons answered, "That's something no man can guess. It might be six months; it might be longer. Probably it will take you thirty days to get your feet on the ground before you start to work. No matter how long it takes, I'll back you to the limit."

"Well, if that's the way you feel about it, I'll take the job."

"Captain, it is foolish for me to try to tell you anything," replied Simmons, "but in my judgment, the thing for you to do is put them on the spot, know you are right—and then shoot everybody in sight."[15]

Hamer did not reply, but he carefully considered Simmons's words. After all, he had done exactly the same thing before, in El Paso. Simmons left Frank's house to make formal arrangements to pay Hamer $180 a month as a special investigator. Frank already held his commission as a state highway patrolman, but it carried no salary. Getting on the state payroll would take a week or ten days, so Hamer used the time wisely. As he later explained, "It was necessary for me to make a close study of Barrow's habits. . . . An officer must know the mental habits of the outlaw, how he thinks, and how he will act in different situations." In his usual methodical way, he set out to learn everything he could about Bonnie and Clyde.[16]

While Frank was marshal of Navasota in 1909, a poor white sharecropper, Henry Barrow, and his wife, Cumie, produced a son, Clyde. The Barrows lived in Ellis County, just south of Dallas. Henry and Cumie Barrow turned out to be two of the worst parents in Texas history. Of their seven children, five became convicted felons; two of their sons died violently at the hands of lawmen. The Barrows' impoverished circumstances were little different than those faced by countless poor families in Texas, with one glaring exception. In 1922 they moved to crime-ridden West Dallas. Clyde's older sister Artie later recalled, "My brothers didn't get into bad trouble until we moved to Dallas. Living in West Dallas slums during the Depression was a bad environment." She explained, "One of Clyde's problems was that he was ashamed of being poor." In 1931 the older Barrow children bought their parents a gas station, with living quarters attached, on Eagle Ford Road.[17]

Bonnie and Clyde with part of their arsenal: two Browning Automatic Rifles. *Taronda Schulz collection*

When Clyde was thirteen, soon after the family settled in West Dallas, he joined a gang of youthful chicken thieves. Clyde's older brother Buck also became a petty thief. Dallas police first arrested Buck in 1925 for stealing tires, and in the following years he was repeatedly picked up for larceny. In December 1926 Clyde was charged with auto theft when he failed to return a rented car. During the next few years, Clyde held several minor jobs, but his principal occupation was auto thief and burglar. He bore several tattoos, one bearing the first name of his girlfriend, Grace Donegan, who was later described by an FBI agent as a "classy prostitute" and "dope fiend" and who was addicted to morphine. Clyde was again arrested, in Fort Worth in 1928, for stealing chickens, and in Dallas the following year, but the charges didn't stick. Buck Barrow was not so lucky. In December 1929 he was convicted of burglary and sentenced to four years in the Huntsville prison.[18]

A few weeks later, in January 1930, Clyde met Bonnie Parker at a friend's house in West Dallas. She was nineteen, petite, and intelligent, with pretty features that were often obscured by heavy makeup. But Bonnie was no Faye Dunaway. High school acquaintances recalled her as "real loud and vulgar." Just before she turned sixteen, she dropped out of high school and married Roy Thornton, who was a year older. Bonnie liked bad boys, and Thornton fit the bill; he was a career criminal, destined to die in a prison break. After Roy abandoned her in 1927, Bonnie began working as a waitress and part-time prostitute. Her mother later denied that "Bonnie was notorious in Dallas' night life, and the biggest 'hotcha' girl in town." Dallas police, however, knew Bonnie as a streetwalker but never arrested her. "We had bigger fish to fry than some ugly little half pint gal with dyed red hair," recalled one Dallas officer. "So long as she didn't roll her johns we let her alone."[19]

Bonnie fell hard for Clyde, and he for her. But just a month later, Clyde was arrested at the home of Bonnie's mother, Emma Parker. Lodged in jail in Waco on seven charges of burglary and auto theft, he pled guilty and received a sentence of fourteen years in prison. Bonnie, beside herself with worry, agreed to smuggle a gun into the jail. Clyde and two jail mates, using the smuggled pistol, escaped. They fled to

Ohio in a stolen car but were promptly retaken and returned to Texas. On April 21, 1930, Barrow entered the Huntsville prison and was later assigned to hard labor at nearby Eastham Prison Farm.[20]

A common myth holds that after Clyde entered Eastham, he was repeatedly raped by a fellow con, Ed Crowder. In revenge, Clyde beat Crowder to death with an iron bar. These purported events turned young Barrow into a violent criminal. Although conditions in Texas prisons were notoriously poor, there is no credible evidence that Clyde was raped in prison or that he murdered his attacker. In fact, Ed Crowder was stabbed to death by fellow con Aubrey Scalley in a knife fight in the prison dormitory on October 29, 1931. Clyde Barrow had no involvement. Numerous prisoners witnessed the fray; two knives were recovered at the scene. Scalley admitted the killing and pled self-defense; the county grand jury agreed with him.[21]

Clyde hated prison as much as he hated hard work. In the fall of 1932, he had a fellow convict chop off two of his toes with an ax in the hope he would be sent back to Huntsville, where the work was lighter. Six other Eastham cons did the same thing, but prison boss Lee Simmons recalled, "I made them stay there and we have had no epidemic of that kind since." Probably because of his injury, Clyde was paroled on February 2, 1933, and returned to West Dallas, still on crutches. Bonnie welcomed him with open arms.[22]

Barrow wasn't on crutches for long. He teamed up with Raymond Hamilton, an eighteen-year-old West Dallas thug, and Ralph Fults, twenty-two, whom Clyde had met in prison. They pulled a string of minor holdups in North Texas. On April 19 Bonnie was with Barrow and Fults when they tried to burglarize a hardware store in Kaufman. After a short manhunt, Bonnie and Fults were captured. Fults was sent back to prison, and Bonnie spent three months in jail before she was released. That meant she was not with Clyde when he committed his first murder.[23]

On the night of April 30, 1932, Clyde and Ray Hamilton drove up to the combination filling station and jewelry shop run by John Bucher in Hillsboro, sixty miles south of Dallas. Bucher, sixty-one, and his

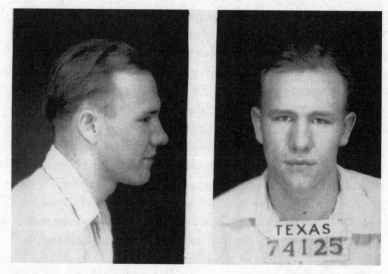

Raymond Hamilton, Clyde's partner in crime. *Travis Hamer personal collection*

wife were asleep in their rooms above the store. The desperadoes called Bucher to the front door, saying they wanted to buy a guitar string. Bucher invited them inside, where they offered to pay Bucher with a ten-dollar bill. He called his wife to come downstairs and open the safe to get change. As she did so, her husband, realizing it was a holdup, tried to grab a pistol, and one of the bandits shot him. Leaving Bucher to bleed to death on the floor, Barrow and Hamilton searched the store and the bedroom upstairs. Then they fled into the blackness with a paltry haul of $20 cash and some diamond rings.[24]

That summer, Clyde and Ray Hamilton kept up their spree of armed robberies. They held up an Interurban station on July 29 and robbed a meatpacking plant in Dallas four days later. Then, on the night of August 5, Clyde, Ray Hamilton, and two other desperadoes were driving through Stringtown, Oklahoma, about 150 miles north of Dallas, when they stopped to attend an open-air dance near the highway. The four Texans were not only drunk but also too well dressed for a country dance. The Atoka County sheriff, Charles Maxwell, and his undersheriff, Eugene Moore, spotted Barrow and Hamilton walking back and forth between parked cars and decided to investigate. As the officers approached, Clyde and his partner jerked their pistols and opened fire. Moore died instantly with a bullet in the heart. Sheriff Maxwell was wounded by six slugs but managed to return the fire. Barrow and Hamilton roared off in the car, leaving their comrades to flee on foot. The two desperadoes left a trail of stolen vehicles in their wake as they escaped back to Texas. Moore, survived by a widow and three small children, bore the dubious distinction of being the first of nine lawmen murdered by the Barrow gang.[25]

Clyde and Hamilton picked up Bonnie in Dallas and headed to Carlsbad, New Mexico, where they hoped to hide out with Bonnie's aunt, who was unaware they were robbers. After several days, she grew suspicious of the trio, and, thinking that their brand new Ford might be stolen, she telephoned the county sheriff on August 14. A local deputy responded, but the outlaws kidnapped him at gunpoint, then drove for twenty-four hours to San Antonio, where they let him go. Driving southeast to Victoria, they stole another Ford and then continued on to Wharton in two vehicles. In Wharton a pair of officers, following reports of the stolen Ford, set up a roadblock on a bridge over the Colorado River. The desperadoes ignored an order to halt and opened fire on the lawmen. As the officers shot back, the fugitives escaped in a hail of gunfire.[26]

Two months later, at 6:30 in the evening of October 11, Clyde walked into a grocery store in Sherman as butcher Howard Hall and clerk Homer Glaze were closing up. Just as he had done in Hillsboro, Barrow pretended to make a small purchase. He handed Glaze a dollar bill, and when the clerk opened the cash register, Clyde whipped out a .45 automatic. As Barrow emptied the till of sixty dollars, Hall exclaimed, "Young man, you can't do that." Cursing and brandishing his pistol, Clyde kicked Hall and struck him over the head with the gun. As Barrow forced the two men toward the front door, Hall tried to grab Clyde's gun hand. He fired three times into Hall, killing him. He then tried to shoot Glaze, but his pistol jammed. Barrow jumped into a waiting black sedan with two other men inside and escaped. Hall, fifty-seven, left a widow and son to mourn his death.[27]

In December 1932 sixteen-year-old William Daniel "W. D." Jones, a West Dallas friend of the Barrows, joined Bonnie and Clyde. On Christmas day the trio was in Temple, planning to rob a grocery store, but Jones got cold feet and refused to participate. Clyde called the teenager a coward, and Bonnie laughed at him. Soon afterward they spotted a Model A Ford roadster parked on the street. Clyde and W. D. climbed into the roadster and started it up. The owner, Doyle Johnson, rushed out of his house, yelling, "Wait a minute, that's my car!" As Johnson jumped onto the running board, Clyde shot him in the neck. Barrow raced off, with Jones clinging to the other running board and Bonnie following in a stolen Ford. They quickly abandoned the model A and fled Temple. Doyle Johnson, twenty-seven, died the next day, leaving a widow and child.[28]

Twelve days later, on the night of January 6, 1933, five lawmen went to the house of Raymond Hamilton's sister in West Dallas on a tip the gang might stop there. She lived just two blocks from the Barrow filling station. Three officers took positions in the front room of the small wood-frame house, and two others in a back room. At midnight, Clyde, Bonnie, and W. D. Jones drove up and parked in front. Clyde got out, carrying a semiautomatic shotgun, and approached the front porch. Hamilton's sister let out a scream, and Clyde, spotting an officer in the front window, opened up. The lawmen inside threw themselves to the floor and returned the fire. The two deputy sheriffs in the rear room raced out the back door and circled to the front yard. One, Malcolm Davis, was in the lead when Clyde dropped him at close range with two fatal blasts of buckshot in his heart. As Barrow raced back to the car, Bonnie fired two or three pistol shots to cover Clyde's retreat. Barrow leaped behind the wheel and roared off.[29]

Ten weeks later, on March 20, Ma Ferguson issued one of her most ill-considered pardons when she released Buck Barrow from the Huntsville prison. Buck and his wife, Blanche, joined Clyde, Bonnie, and W. D. Jones in Joplin, Missouri, where they rented a bungalow and hid out for two weeks. Their drinking and loud behavior caught the attention of neighbors, who thought they were bootleggers. On April 13 five local officers approached the house to investigate. The gang—including Bonnie—opened fire with shotguns and a Browning automatic rifle (BAR). Constable Wes Harryman died instantly, riddled with buckshot. The lawmen, caught by surprise and armed only with .38 service revolvers, were totally outgunned. As they took cover behind their cars and fired back, Detective Harry McGinnis was sieved with buckshot, a mortal wound. W. D. Jones, armed with the BAR, raked the officers with fire until he was stopped by a police bullet in his side. The gang jumped into their car and, with gun muzzles flaming, raced out of town and vanished. Inside the abandoned hideout, the officers found guns, a copy of Buck's pardon signed by Ma Ferguson, a poem written by Bonnie entitled "The Story of Suicide Sal," and a Brownie camera with a roll of undeveloped film. The photos were quickly developed and widely published, creating a sensation. They showed Bonnie and Clyde heavily armed and posing next to stolen cars. An image of Bonnie, destined to become one of the most famous in crime annals, showed her with revolver in one hand and a lit cigar clenched in her teeth. Ever after, and much to her chagrin, she would be known as a "cigar smoking gun moll."[30]

Yet Bonnie was indeed a gun moll. Contrary to recent myth, which holds that she never fired a gun, Bonnie took an active part in numerous shootings. A month after the Joplin gunfight, on May 12, Clyde and Buck tried to rob a bank in Lucerne, Indiana. Bonnie and Blanche waited nearby in their getaway car. When two bankers opened fire on the Barrows, the brothers raced outside and jumped into the auto. Clyde took the wheel while the gang fired a fusillade of rifle shots at unarmed citizens and wounded two women. Eyewitnesses said that a young blonde—Bonnie—had done most of the shooting. A week later, the gang pulled an identical bank robbery in Okabena, Minnesota. As they roared off in a stolen car, Bonnie, Clyde, and Buck fired at citizens with shotguns and BARs, narrowly missing a school bus full of children. Several townsfolk shot back, but the outlaws escaped.[31]

Despite a massive manhunt, Clyde Barrow had little trouble eluding lawmen. He would often drive a thousand miles straight, stopping only

Bonnie Parker, the quintessential cigar-smoking gun moll. This was one of the photos found after the gang's gunfight in Joplin, Missouri. *Taronda Schulz collection*

for gas and oil. Racing night and day at high speeds along back country roads, he stole cars, crossed state lines at will, and robbed numerous grocery stores and filling stations. But his luck changed on the night of June 10, 1933. Clyde, with Bonnie and W. D. Jones, was roaring down a road near Wellington, in the Texas Panhandle, when he missed a detour and his Ford coupe plunged into a dry riverbed. The car overturned and burst into flames. Bonnie, badly burned on her right leg, was brought to a nearby farmer's house. When two local officers came to investigate, Clyde covered them with a sawed-off BAR and took both hostage. They all crammed into one officer's car and drove north through the night to a bridge west of Sayre, Oklahoma. There they met Buck and Blanche, who were waiting for them in a parked auto. The outlaws tied up the two officers, then fled to Vinita, Oklahoma, where Bonnie got treatment for her wounds.[32]

The gang then moved to a tourist camp near Fort Smith, Arkansas, so Bonnie could rest and recover. Her younger sister Billie came from Texas to help nurse her. Like Bonnie, she had married a notorious thug, Fred Mace, who was now serving ten years for robbery. On June 23 Buck Barrow and W. D. Jones held up a grocery store in Fayetteville and headed south, toward the town of Alma, near Fort Smith. Henry Humphrey, city marshal of Alma, received a telephone report of the robbery. He and a deputy sheriff drove out to find the bandits. Two miles outside town, they spotted a Ford V-8 approaching at high speed. It suddenly crashed into a truck. As Humphrey and the deputy approached the wreck, Barrow and Jones opened fire. A blast of buckshot from Buck's shotgun slammed into the marshal, and he dropped, mortally wounded. After the deputy fled for cover, one of the desperadoes bent over Humphrey and snarled, "I ought to finish you now."

"Go ahead," the marshal gasped. "I think you have already finished me." But instead of shooting him again, Barrow and Jones left their wrecked Ford and fled in the deputy's car. Humphrey died three days later, leaving a widow and three adult children.[33]

Now the gang fled back to Oklahoma. Because most of their weapons had been left behind in the wrecked car, Clyde and Buck burglarized a National Guard armory in Enid on July 7. They made off with several BARs and forty-six Colt .45 automatic pistols. Eleven days later, Bonnie, Clyde, Buck, Blanche, and Jones holed up in the Red Crown Tourist Court outside Platte City, Missouri. Once again, their suspicious behavior attracted notice: two of the gang carried the bandaged Bonnie, they used small change to pay for their rooms and meals, and Clyde covered the windows with newspapers. To make things worse,

Blanche, who was a real looker, caught attention by wearing a sexy white blouse and riding breeches tucked into knee-high boots. Local officers, guessing they were the Barrow gang, readied for a raid. After midnight on July 20, twelve lawmen, supported by an armored sheriff's car from Kansas City, cordoned off two brick cabins occupied by the outlaws. At the order to surrender, the Barrow brothers and Jones opened up with BARs, unleashing forty-seven rounds of full automatic fire and wounding three of the posse. An FBI agent later reported that the supposedly armored car was "shot up like a sieve." The despera-does made a dash for their auto, with Bonnie and Blanche firing pistols to cover their retreat. Suddenly, a police bullet struck Buck Barrow in the head, tearing through his skull. Blanche dragged him into the Ford. The officers riddled the V-8 with gunfire, and exploding glass pierced Blanche's eyes. But, once again, the gang roared off into the night and escaped.[34]

The outlaws fled 175 miles north to Dexter, Iowa, and made camp in Dexfield Park, north of town. They tried to nurse Buck, but he was desperately wounded. A farmer spotted them on July 23, and that night a large posse of officers and volunteers quietly surrounded the wooded campsite. It seemed that at long last the Barrow gang had met its match. The posse moved in at daybreak, and the outlaws opened up with a barrage. One deputy sheriff reported that Bonnie fired repeatedly with automatic pistols. In a blistering exchange of shots, Buck took a bullet in the hip, while Clyde, Bonnie, Jones, and one deputy got minor wounds. Blanche was captured next to her fatally wounded husband, screaming, "Don't die, Daddy, don't die!" Incredibly, Bonnie, Clyde, and Jones escaped on foot into the woods, stole a car, and vanished. Buck died five days later, and Blanche got a ten-year jolt in the Missouri State Penitentiary. Before Buck died, an FBI agent asked him why the gang "so ruthlessly took human life." Barrow's cold-blooded reply: "Well, I had to see that I did not get hurt."[35]

Bonnie, Clyde, and Jones soon recovered from their wounds. To again replenish their lost weapons, Clyde broke into a National Guard armory in Illinois and stole three BARs and six .45 automatics. The trio pulled numerous minor robberies and frequently slipped into West

Dallas to visit their families. In November W. D. Jones was captured in Houston and jailed in Dallas. It may have been Jones who, in hopes of leniency, told deputy sheriffs that Bonnie and Clyde often visited their families at a spot near Sowers, northwest of Dallas. Richard "Smoot" Schmid, the newly elected sheriff of Dallas County, decided to lay a trap for the fugitives. A former bicycle-shop owner with no law-enforcement experience, Schmid had enough sense to bring along two of his top deputies, Bob Alcorn and Ed Caster, plus an energetic rookie, Ted Hinton. On the night of November 22, the lawmen hid in a roadside ditch near a Sowers dairy farm. They were well armed, with two Thompson submachine guns, a BAR, and a semiautomatic rifle. Sure enough, Bonnie and Clyde soon drove up in a Ford coupe, and the officers opened fire. Driving at just twenty-five miles an hour, Clyde shot back from the driver's window. Schmid and his deputies riddled the car, but the .45 caliber pistol bullets from the Tommy guns could not penetrate the Ford's steel body. Only the rifles pierced the car, wounding Clyde in the left arm and left leg. Undeterred, Barrow hit the gas and roared off. He and Bonnie quickly abandoned the damaged Ford, stole another car at gunpoint, and vanished.[36]

Clyde again quickly recovered from his gunshot wounds. In the meantime, Ray Hamilton, who had been captured and was serving a life term for the John Bucher murder and other crimes, began planning a breakout from the Eastham Prison Farm. When he was booked into prison, he had boasted, "I'll be back with Clyde before you know it." He offered $2,000 to an old con, James Mullen, who was soon to be released. Mullen got out of Eastham on January 10, 1934, and brought word of the plot to Ray's brother, Floyd Hamilton, in West Dallas. Floyd in turn recruited Bonnie and Clyde. Three days later, after dark, Mullen and Floyd hid two automatic pistols under a bridge on the unfenced prison farm. The next day, Floyd and his wife visited Ray Hamilton in Eastham and told him where the guns were hidden. Hamilton and a fellow con, Joe Palmer, retrieved the guns.

On the foggy morning of January 16, Bonnie parked a stolen Ford coupe on the outskirts of the prison farm. Clyde, armed with a BAR, and James Mullen, carrying a Browning semiautomatic shotgun, took

Bonnie pointing her sawed-off shotgun at Clyde. *Taronda Schulz collection*

up a position in a nearby ditch. Floyd and Palmer, with a group of cons on a brush-clearing detail, soon approached, guarded by Major Crowson, on horseback, and several prison officers. Suddenly, Palmer jerked his pistol and opened fire, wounding Crowson and another guard. At that, Barrow and Mullen laid down a barrage of almost a hundred rounds to cover the inmates' escape. As the remaining guards fled to safety, Bonnie began honking the horn to let the escapees know where the car was hidden. Floyd and Palmer started running, accompanied by two other cons, Henry Methvin and Hilton Bybee. A fifth prisoner fled into the brush alone. The prisoners piled into the coupe with Bonnie, Clyde, and Mullen, all four escapees crammed into the rumble seat, and sped to safety. Crowson died from his wound eleven days later.[37]

The Eastham breakout was the most brazen crime committed by the Barrow gang. Wire service reports called it "the most spectacular prison delivery in Texas history." The story was published on the front pages of newspapers nationwide, bringing the desperadoes even greater notoriety and redoubling the manhunt by federal and state lawmen. But the Eastham break was a fatal error, for it put Frank Hamer on the trail of Bonnie and Clyde. In three and a half months, he would accomplish what the FBI and the law-enforcement authorities of a dozen states had not been able to do in more than a year.

21

THE BARROW HUNT

Frank Hamer wasted no time in joining the Barrow hunt. On February 2, 1934, the day after Lee Simmons met with him at his Austin home, five robbers held up a bank in Coleman, Texas, taking $24,000 and fleeing south toward Austin. That night, a group of Texas Rangers spotted them in three automobiles near Blanco, west of Austin, but the bandits escaped in a storm of gunfire. The Rangers thought that three of the robbers were Clyde Barrow, Bonnie Parker, and Ray Hamilton. The next morning, Sheriff Lee Allen, of Travis County, deputized Hamer so he would have authority to assist the manhunt. Hamer, with Sheriff Allen and Deputy Sheriff Jim McCoy, rushed south to Gonzales, where they met Frank's brother Estill, senior captain of the Rangers. The four lawmen then headed north to Harwood, the home of Nellie Parker Gonzales, who was rumored to be Bonnie's married half-sister. They interviewed Nellie, and she vehemently, and truthfully, denied any kinship with Bonnie. Meanwhile, Rangers near Blanco stopped a car driven by a suspicious man and woman, seizing a German Luger pistol and one-third of the stolen cash. At first the Rangers thought they had Bonnie and Clyde, but the suspects proved to be John and Marie Newton from Oklahoma. Estill Hamer directed a huge manhunt for the rest of the holdup men, who were soon all captured. It turned out that they had no connection to the Barrow gang.[1]

Frank, on learning that Bonnie and Clyde had not been involved, returned to Austin, where he continued his quiet investigation. He recalled, "I soon learned that Barrow played a circle from Dallas to Joplin, Missouri, to Louisiana, and back to Dallas. Occasionally he would leave this beat, but he would always come back to it as most criminals do. One time he and Bonnie went as far east as North Carolina for no other purpose, it seems, than to visit a cigarette factory. Again they would go to Indiana, Iowa, or New Mexico, but like wild horses, they would circle to their old range."[2]

On February 10 Hamer got word from Lee Simmons that he was officially on the state payroll. Frank climbed into his black, four-door Ford V-8 sedan—the same favored by Clyde Barrow—and set out on one of the most epic manhunts in American history. He first went to Dallas and met with Sheriff Smoot Schmid. From the sheriff and his deputies Hamer gleaned much about Bonnie and Clyde, their families, and their habits. Frank recalled that he even learned "the kind of whiskey they drank, what they ate, and the color, size, and texture of their clothes." Schmid and Hamer agreed to work together to bring the gang to justice. As Lee Simmons later explained, "Schmid pledged himself to absolute secrecy and assigned Deputy Bob Alcorn to work with Hamer."[3]

Frank liked and respected his new partner. Alcorn, a highly experienced lawman, had served six years as a Dallas policeman and another six years as a deputy sheriff. He had taken part in at least two gunfights with desperadoes; in 1931 he received public praise for killing an armed robber who resisted arrest. Alcorn knew Clyde well and had once arrested him. He also knew Bonnie by sight; she had waited on him when she was a waitress in a café near the Dallas courthouse. Frank considered his knowledge invaluable. The warm feelings of respect were mutual. Alcorn called Hamer "one of the bravest men and the deadliest shots in the state."[4]

From Schmid and his deputy, Ed Caster, Hamer learned that a confidential informant had revealed that Bonnie and Clyde had been in

Frank Hamer and the 1934 Ford he drove during the manhunt for Bonnie and Clyde. *Taronda Schulz collection*

Louisiana in December. On the outskirts of Shreveport, they had robbed an A&P store manager of $500, and Clyde had been treated for a bullet wound in his left leg by a doctor in Cheneyville. This wound was the one he had received in his gunfight with Sheriff Schmid's posse on November 22. Frank believed that there was good reason to begin the manhunt in Louisiana: "Barrow was hot in Texas, Oklahoma, New Mexico, Arkansas, Kansas, Missouri, and Iowa because the long trail of murder he and Bonnie or he and his dead brother, Buck, had spread over those states. Louisiana was the one spot near his home state where he wasn't hot."

Hamer also knew of another Louisiana connection. Henry Methvin, whom Clyde had broken out of Eastham, hailed from northwestern Louisiana. Frank thought he might be riding with the gang. He and Deputy Alcorn set off in Hamer's Ford, and by February 15 they were in Shreveport, where they spent two nights at the Jefferson Hotel, running down leads. Recalled Hamer, "I first struck their trail at Texarkana. At Logansport they bought a half gallon of whiskey; near Keachi they bought gasoline, and then went in the night to a negro house and had the negroes cook them some cornbread and fry a chicken. In Shreveport they bought pants, underwear, gloves, and an automatic shotgun."[5]

Shreveport, with about eighty thousand residents, was the largest city in northern Louisiana. It was situated on the Red River, twenty-four miles from the Texas line. Because little attention would be paid to strangers in a city that size, Frank believed that Shreveport would be a good base for his manhunt. He and Alcorn met quietly with local officers, asking them to be on the lookout for Bonnie and Clyde, and explored the surrounding parishes. Hamer reported to Lee Simmons that he had met with "a free-talking sheriff with whom he was hesitant to work." This was Shreveport's veteran sheriff Tom Hughes, soon to be immortalized—in a negative light—by a popular song by bluesman Huddie "Leadbelly" Ledbetter. On February 19 the Texas lawmen drove fifty-three miles west to Arcadia, where they called on Henderson Jordan, sheriff of Bienville Parish. Although Jordan had been sheriff for less than two years and had no other law-enforcement experience, Frank thought him discreet and reliable. He recalled, "We visited Sheriff Jordan, sat on the courthouse lawn, and outlined to him why Barrow might reasonably be expected eventually to be found in that neighborhood."[6]

Hamer and Alcorn spent their last night in Shreveport at the New Inn hotel at 615 Milam Street. Of the lodgings in Shreveport, Frank liked the New Inn best because it had a garage under the hotel, where his Ford could be parked out of sight. The next morning, February 23, he and Alcorn made the 190 mile drive back to Dallas. There Frank took a room at the Sanger Hotel, located on the corner of Ervay and Canton Streets at the edge of downtown. He chose the Sanger because the hotel beauty shop was run by Clyde's sister, Nell, and the hotel barber was her husband, Luther Cowan. He could keep an eye on them as he quietly went about his business. Working out of the Sanger, Frank spent the next week in Dallas gathering information about the gang. During the previous two weeks he had driven almost 1,400 miles. No one in Dallas, except for Sheriff Schmid and a few of his deputies, knew of Hamer's assignment.[7]

In early March Frank drove to the Huntsville prison in East Texas to interview the escapee Hilton Bybee. After the Eastham breakout, Bybee had ridden with the Barrow gang for a couple of weeks until he was captured in Amarillo on January 30. He was sent to Huntsville for safekeeping. Lee Simmons undoubtedly arranged Hamer's interview. Although Amarillo lawmen had been unable to crack Bybee, Frank had better luck. He told the fugitive that he had accumulated enough evidence to convict him of several robberies. As Hamer later explained, "When you get the goods on a man, he'll talk about other things. You can force him to come through."

Bybee broke down and gave a detailed description of the gang's movements as they drove on isolated country roads through North Texas, Oklahoma, and Missouri, then south through Arkansas to Shreveport, Louisiana. In Hugo, Oklahoma, Joe Palmer and Henry Methvin robbed a filling station of a paltry seven dollars. Said Bybee, "Clyde raised sand about robbing it and getting them hot." Although Bybee did not specifically admit to the gang's bank robberies in Rembrandt, Iowa, or Poteau, Oklahoma, he said they had pulled a bank holdup and Bonnie divided the loot, about $400 each. She announced that she and Clyde "value friendship more than money, and will cut fair." Bybee told Hamer of various cars stolen by the gang and said they had abandoned a 1934 Ford near Electra, in North Texas. He revealed that in late January he and Palmer left the gang near Joplin and returned to Texas separately. Bybee said that he "wanted to rob banks and get some sure enough money," and Hamilton agreed with him, but "Clyde didn't care, [he] just wanted to ride around and get by." The desperado concluded by saying that he left Bonnie, Clyde, Methvin, and Hamilton together.[8]

Frank fully recognized the importance of Bybee's confession. It confirmed his belief that Clyde drove a circular route from Dallas to Joplin, then to Shreveport, and back to Dallas. More important, it showed that Henry Methvin and Ray Hamilton were with the gang. If he could locate Methvin or Hamilton, he might be able to find Bonnie and Clyde. First Hamer decided to recover the stolen Ford the gang had abandoned near Electra. With a transcript of the confession in hand, Frank drove

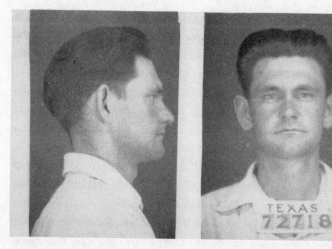

Hilton Bybee, who rode with Bonnie and Clyde after the Eastham breakout. Frank Hamer's interrogation of Bybee led him to Henry Methvin's family and ultimately to Bonnie and Clyde. *Travis Hamer personal collection*

back to Dallas, where he learned that Bob Alcorn had his hands full investigating a local bank robbery. Thereupon Hamer called on Frank J. Blake, the SAC—special agent in charge—of the Dallas office of the FBI. He told Blake that Methvin was with Bonnie and Clyde and provided him with a typewritten copy of Bybee's statement. Blake assigned the special agent Edward J. Dowd to work with him.[9]

On March 7, Hamer and Dowd headed out of Dallas. Their first task was to follow up on a tip that two relatives of the Barrow family lived in Grapevine, twenty-two miles northwest of Dallas. They interviewed the informant, who said that he had no further details and referred them to Grapevine's sixty-seven-year-old city marshal, Jim Daniel. Dowd reported that they found Daniel "quite talkative." However, said Dowd, "He claimed to have seen Clyde Barrow at Grapevine. When a photograph of Clyde Barrow and William Daniel Jones was exhibited to him, he immediately identified Jones as Barrow." The elderly marshal then incorrectly named several Grapevine residents as relatives of Clyde. Agent Dowd concluded: "In the conversation with

City Marshal Daniels [sic], he contradicted himself so many times that Captain Hamer and the writer are convinced that he knows little of the relatives and contacts of Clyde Barrow." This was but one of countless false leads Frank and fellow lawmen were forced to investigate.

From Grapevine, Hamer and Dowd drove 120 miles northwest to Wichita Falls, where that night they met with the police chief, county sheriff, and other local officers. Frank outlined a tip he had received that Clyde and Raymond Hamilton had made several visits to Wichita Falls, trying to contact Winnie Wolfe, a beauty shop operator and friend of gang member Gene O'Dare. Frank also revealed that Hilton Bybee had admitted that Clyde used a hideout in a hilly area near the Tenth Street Bridge, west of town and south of the Wichita River. The next day Hamer, Dowd, and two local lawmen explored rough dirt roads until they found the hideout. The only evidence left by the desperadoes was an abandoned, bullet-riddled auto that had been used for target practice. Scattered about were empty shells from rifles, revolvers, and BARs. The Wichita Falls lawmen promised to look out for the fugitives.[10]

Next, based on the confession of Hilton Bybee, Hamer and Dowd located the new Ford sedan that had been stolen in Fayetteville, Arkansas, and abandoned by Bonnie and Clyde near Electra, twenty-seven miles west of Wichita Falls. Inside were a number of shotgun shells and receipts for two women's dresses from Lord's department store in downtown Dallas. Frank learned that Clyde's relatives had bought the dresses for Bonnie. Hamer and Dowd also discovered that a local jailbird, Bob Russell, had been arrested in Wichita Falls, and in his pockets were two letters from Clyde's pal Ted Rogers. On questioning, Russell admitted that Clyde had visited his home in Wichita Falls soon after the Eastham raid. Clyde wanted Russell to help with a plot to break Ted Rogers out of the Huntsville prison. He asked Russell to contact Charles Mc-Donald, a Wichita Falls attorney and friend of Pa Ferguson, and offer him $200 to obtain a governor's reprieve. That would allow Rogers to be transferred to a minimum-security prison farm, where Clyde could break him out. Hamer immediately informed Lee Simmons of the plot.[11]

SAC Blake was pleased with Hamer's work and reported to J. Edgar Hoover in Washington that "we are rendering him every assistance possible, and he is working in close harmony with us." Blake urged that the FBI cooperate with Hamer: "It is quite probable that he will appear at Division offices in other districts, seeking information and assistance; and in my opinion he is an officer with whom agents of the Division can work with fullest confidence." Hoover, always suspicious of outsiders, did have his agents cooperate, but his innate jealousy would eventually lead him to forsake Hamer.[12]

While Hamer methodically tracked the gang's movements, Clyde continued his wild crime spree unabated. In the weeks following the Eastham breakout, the Barrow gang robbed two banks in Iowa, another in Oklahoma, and a fourth in Texas. They also broke into yet another National Guard armory, this one in Ranger, Texas, and stole more BARs and .45 automatics. The reality of their hardscrabble lives on the run was far removed from the glamour portrayed in films and popular books. Often hungry, they ate whatever they could get, slept in stolen cars, and bathed in muddy creeks. Clyde's stylish suits were all stolen in store burglaries. Bonnie and Clyde fought incessantly, and occasionally he beat her. Both were infected with gonorrhea, as was Bonnie's promiscuous sister Billie. In late January 1934, with her husband Fred Mace in prison, she joined up with the gang. In short order, Billie had sexual intercourse with Henry Methvin, Ray Hamilton, and Joe Palmer. When all three came down with gonorrhea, they began fighting over her, so Clyde sent her back to West Dallas.[13]

Meanwhile, FBI agents were following up on Hamer's information that Henry Methvin was with the gang. When Methvin had been arrested and sent to prison in 1930, he gave his home as Ashland, Louisiana, which is in Natchitoches Parish, fifty-five miles southwest of Shreveport. FBI agents quietly began searching the area to locate the Methvin family. Rhea Whitley, SAC in New Orleans, later recalled that he and his agents "lived for weeks in the swamps of Northern Louisiana" as they searched for any trace of the gang. On the afternoon of March 24, 1934, Agent Leslie A. Kindell visited Bienville Parish's sheriff, Henderson Jordan, at his office in Arcadia. Kindell was accompanied by Deputy Sheriff Steve Norris of adjacent Bossier Parish. Kindell, after explaining that they were on the trail of Bonnie and Clyde, asked Jordan, "Do you recall the Eastham, Texas, Prison Farm delivery last January? That was the raid in which a guard was killed. Five convicts were freed."

When Sheriff Henderson answered in the affirmative, Kindell continued, "We have established positively that Henry Methvin has been traveling with Barrow and Bonnie Parker. Working on the supposition that Methvin might attempt to visit relatives, we have been trying to locate his father. Ivan Methvin lived until recently in Bossier Parish, just west of your parish. He moved some time back. Our information is that he moved to a place about fifteen miles north of Coushatta, Red River Parish."

"That would put him just inside my parish, down in the southwest corner," Jordan responded. Although Hamer had asked him to keep an eye out for Bonnie and Clyde, this was the first information he had that the gang might have a hideout in Bienville Parish. Sheriff Jordan later recalled that the entire meeting lasted but fifteen minutes. "Before they left I had agreed to carry on a quiet investigation. I spent virtually every daylight hour of the following ten days traveling through the southwestern part of Bienville Parish. I stopped my car to talk to the farmers in the area. At no time did I ever make any reference to the purpose of my trips to the various communities. I talked to the merchants and police in the villages of the district. After the first week the task began to appear hopeless. I had spent hours listening to farmers discussing cotton prices, politics, and casual gossip. I had asked carefully worded questions about neighbors. A new neighbor is an event of importance in a rural community. Finally, I heard the name of Ivan Methvin! He had rented a place in the very tip of the parish, close to where Bienville Parish, Natchitoches, and Red River parishes meet at a common point." Sheriff Jordan quietly kept tabs on the Methvin family.[14]

Meanwhile, Hamer took a break from his manhunt. Contrary to myth, he did not spend the entire time on the road, sleeping in his car, but made frequent trips home to visit with his family. Gladys was relieved to see her husband. As she recalled, "I was scared to death about him, but he always said he'd be all right, and for me not to worry." They celebrated his fiftieth birthday on March 27 and observed Easter five days later. While in Austin, a reporter spotted him in the capitol building chatting with a fellow lawman, and Hamer remarked that he "recently turned down a position as detective for the Texas Railroad Commission." The tight-lipped ex-Ranger said nothing to the newspaperman about his manhunt for Bonnie and Clyde.[15]

On Easter Sunday, April 1, Texas radio stations broadcast electrifying news. That afternoon, Bonnie and Clyde murdered two Texas highway patrolmen in cold blood. Frank jumped into his car and raced to Dallas, where he quickly learned the grisly details. In the morning, the desperate couple had parked their black Ford V-8 sedan with yellow wire wheels on a dirt side road off Highway 114 near Grapevine, next to the farm of William Schieffer. Henry Methvin was with them, asleep in the backseat. Bonnie and Clyde planned to meet their families for an Easter picnic. Schieffer first saw the young couple in the car at 10:30 A.M., acting like lovers on a jaunt. From time to time, they would walk down to the highway, looking left and right, as if they were expecting someone. Schieffer, while hauling rock in his wagon after lunch, came within forty paces of the pair. Except for noticing that one was a petite woman and both wore khaki riding breeches, he paid them little heed.

At 3:30 Schieffer was at his house, a hundred yards distant, when he saw a pair of passing highway patrolmen, E. B. Wheeler and H. D. Murphy, approach the parked Ford. The officers, apparently thinking that Bonnie and Clyde were motorists in need of help, dismounted from their motorcycles twenty-five feet in front of the Barrow vehicle. Bonnie and Clyde, who were outside their car, reached down toward the running boards, picked up a pair of semiautomatic shotguns, and opened fire. The patrolmen didn't have a chance, and both dropped, riddled with buckshot. The outlaws fired their shotguns and a pistol into the prostrate bodies to be certain the officers were dead. Then they jumped into their Ford and roared off.[16]

A small army of law officers descended on the scene. The only evidence left behind was three sixteen-gauge shotgun shells; three twelve-gauge shotgun shells; five empty .45 caliber automatic cartridges; one .30-06 shell, apparently fired by a BAR; and an empty whiskey bottle. Two witnesses, Mr. and Mrs. Fred Giggal, told lawmen that they had driven by during the shooting. They reported looking through a grove of trees and seeing "the taller of two men" shoot into the body of one of the officers. Later, Barrow family members claimed that Clyde did not kill the patrolmen and blamed the murders on Henry Methvin. Clyde purportedly told Henry, "Let's take them," meaning that he wanted to kidnap the patrolmen. Methvin misunderstood and opened fire with a BAR. In order to believe this account, one has to assume that Clyde was not a murderer and that the Barrows—all of whom were either convicted felons or harborers of the gang—were credible.[17]

Bonnie and her sister Billie looked much alike. Schieffer later erroneously identified the killers as Billie Parker and Floyd Hamilton, and both were indicted. This despite the fact that, shortly after the murders, Schieffer told a Fort Worth homicide detective that he could not identify anyone. Although the farmer had been wrong in his identification, he consistently related that he had observed the Ford off and on for five hours and saw only two people around it—a young man and woman. Schieffer had a much better opportunity to observe the affair than the Giggals, who briefly glimpsed the killers and thought they were men, probably because both were wearing pants. Henry Methvin later insisted that he had been asleep in the back of the car until he was awakened by the gunfire. His statement is supported by both Schieffer and the Giggals, who said they saw only two killers. Six weeks later, Bonnie and Clyde were indicted for the murders.[18]

These cold-blooded killings were the most infamous of Bonnie and Clyde's career. Patrolman Murphy, only twenty-three, was to have been married in two weeks. In one of the most pathetic scenes in the history of American law enforcement, his fiancée wore her wedding gown to the funeral. The murders also illustrated the woefully inadequate training of Texas police in the 1930s. Grapevine was but twenty miles from West Dallas, home of the two most dangerous fugitives in Texas. Everyone in the Southwest knew that Bonnie and Clyde lived in their cars, parked in remote locations, and killed law officers. Those facts alone should have made the patrolmen alert. They paid with their lives for their lack of vigilance.[19]

The Grapevine murders sparked an even more frenzied manhunt. Louis G. Phares, chief of the highway patrol, rushed all of his officers to

North Texas, where they, with FBI agents and Dallas police, searched numerous farms owned by Barrow family members and friends. Deputy Sheriff Ted Hinton, of Dallas, later claimed that, two days after the Easter killings, he, Hamer, Bob Alcorn, and ex-Ranger Maney Gault, driving two autos, started tracking the gang north into Oklahoma. Hinton said that on April 4, he and Alcorn were in the lead car, passing through Durant, Oklahoma, when they spotted Bonnie and Clyde approaching in an auto. Instead of making a U-turn and pursuing them, Hinton pulled over, and while they waited for Hamer and Gault to drive up, the outlaws escaped. Hinton's story, like so many he told, appears on several counts to be fiction. First, he neglected to explain how Bonnie and Clyde got away; second, he gave no reason why they did not pursue the outlaws; and, third, Maney Gault was not assigned to the case until ten days later.[20]

That week, heavy rains and flooding turned the red dirt roads of Oklahoma into quagmires. On the morning of April 6, a citizen spotted two suspicious men and a young woman parked in a black Ford V-8 sedan with yellow wire wheels, just west of Commerce, a village in the northeastern corner of Oklahoma. Chief of Police Percy Boyd and the sixty-year-old constable, Cal Campbell, responded to the scene. As the officers approached the Ford, which was facing them, Bonnie threw it into reverse and backed away at high speed. The Ford slid off the road into a muddy ditch. Boyd and Campbell stepped forward and saw that the car's occupants were armed. Campbell drew his pistol and started shooting. At that, Bonnie fired two blasts with her sawed-off shotgun. Clyde Barrow and Henry Methvin leaped outside with BARs and opened up with a barrage of automatic rifle fire. Each man unloosed a twenty-round magazine, reloaded, and emptied a second. The two country policemen, armed with .38 caliber revolvers, were no match for such firepower. Campbell, who dropped to his belly and fired two more rounds, was instantly killed. Boyd fired four shots, two shattering the windshield. Then a bullet creased his scalp, knocking him to the ground, and he gave up.

At gunpoint, Clyde forced Boyd and several passersby, including the driver of a truck, to push and pull the Ford out of the ditch. He then ordered Chief Boyd into the car. Before driving off, Clyde told the by-standers, "Tell the other laws if they do not bother us we will turn this law loose, but if they bother us we will kill him." As they fled north into Kansas, Clyde berated Bonnie for shooting too quickly. Boyd later said, "Barrow told her that in the future she was not to do any shooting until he told her to."

Boyd noted that the desperadoes had three BARs, two semiautomatic shotguns, a Remington rifle, two .45 automatic pistols, and a suitcase full of ammunition hidden under a blanket on the backseat. He thought Henry Methvin was Ray Hamilton. Bonnie, a gun on her lap, played with a pet white rabbit and fed it carrots. The outlaws bandaged the officer's head and denied killing the two highway patrolmen at Grape-vine. Boyd recalled, "They said they were sorry they had to shoot Camp-bell, but they kept joking about it all afternoon." He added that Clyde "acted like he owned the earth. He thinks quite a bit of himself. Bonnie is a lot like him, but she thinks quite a bit of Barrow, you can tell that."

They kept the policeman hostage in the car all day, finally releasing him at midnight near Fort Scott. Before they drove off, Clyde told him, "You can tell the officers anything you want to, but be sure to tell them the truth. We would not have fired a shot if the old man had not come out of his car with a pistol." And Bonnie asked him to tell the public that she did not smoke cigars. "She said that the picture taken of her with a cigar in her mouth was a joke," explained Boyd later, "and that she took the cigar from Clyde for the photo."[21]

Hamer—probably with Bob Alcorn and possibly Ted Hinton—drove to Commerce, where he obtained details of the shootout and re-ported them to the FBI's agent Charlie Winstead. Frank attempted to track Clyde but later said that he had no success. "He and Bonnie would be heading west . . . and I would lose him. When I picked up the trail again he would be headed east or north, flying like a bat out of hell. He would simply stop, take a dirt side road, dodge up it 50 or 100 miles, strike east or north, wind around and pop up, maybe, in Joplin, pull two or three holdups to replenish his finances, and then be off again like the wind, spinning along the roads like a wild man."[22]

The manhunt for the Barrow gang was now enormous, involving

hundreds of deputy sheriffs and police officers throughout the Midwest, Southwest, and West. Officers patrolled roads from Iowa to Colorado and Wyoming, through Missouri and Kansas and south to Texas, Oklahoma, and Arkansas. The entire Texas Highway Patrol was assigned to the hunt. While patrolmen guarded roads and bridges leading into Oklahoma, Arkansas, and Louisiana, others donned plainclothes and ran down every lead, every sighting. Most turned out to be false. Two highway patrolmen and a redheaded stenographer, while on their way from Austin to Dallas, were pulled over six times by Tommy-gun-toting officers. Estill Hamer issued a plea for citizens to cooperate with the manhunt and to promptly identify themselves if they were stopped by lawmen. In Dallas, Estill and Sheriff Schmid coordinated the efforts of federal and state officers. A tap was placed on the Barrows' home telephone, and Bailey Tynes, a Barrow cousin and confidant, was paid to visit the Eagle Ford filling station and spy on the family.[23]

On one occasion, Clyde's mother was arrested at the family gas station, reportedly by Texas Rangers, and jailed for a night in Tyler. When interrogated, Cumie Barrow denied knowing Clyde's whereabouts. "I told them I didn't know anything," she said to reporters. In reality, Cumie was a principal supporter of the gang. She met regularly with Bonnie and Clyde at secret locations and gave them food, clothing, and information about police efforts to locate them. She and her husband accepted stolen money from Clyde. Nonetheless, Ma Ferguson was furious at Cumie's arrest, declaring that "any such unlawful practice of state rangers . . . is without my authority or consent. Some weeks ago, I had the adjutant general issue orders to prevent such practice." Estill Hamer quickly pointed out that the arrest had been made by a deputy sheriff and two highway patrolmen, not by his Rangers.[24]

On April 10 Frank Hamer telephoned Louis Phares, the bespectacled chief of the Texas Highway Patrol, to inform him that Bonnie and Clyde had abandoned their Ford V-8 and stolen a Pontiac sedan in Topeka, Kansas. Phares was eager to exact revenge for the killing of his two patrolmen, and he offered to lend Hamer one of his men. Recalled Frank, "I asked for B. M. Gault who had served with me in the Headquarters Ranger Company." Hamer knew that Phares was disliked in

Texas Highway Patrol commission carried by Frank Hamer in the manhunt for Bonnie and Clyde. *Author's collection*

many law-enforcement circles because of his dogmatic leadership style. To avoid conflict with Lee Simmons, Frank did not tell him how Phares found out he had been assigned to the Barrow hunt. Simmons was miffed when he got wind of Phares's offer to help. "How he learned that Hamer was representing me, I don't know. But he did learn it, and he summoned Hamer to meet him in Austin. Phares should have called me, of course. But he called Hamer, and Hamer then called me."

Frank met Simmons at an Austin hotel and told the prison boss that Phares wanted to assign one of his highway patrolmen to him. Simmons at first was unhappy. "Too many cooks spoil the broth for the law as in other affairs," he recalled. "I wanted secrecy maintained for Hamer's protection as well as for the success of his undertaking." He told Frank, "It's your job. I'm going to back up everything you do. Whatever you do about this is all right with me. Only I am depending upon you to run the show."

"I'll damn sure run it," Hamer replied.

"Whom does Phares have in mind?"

"Maney Gault."

"You want him?"

"Yes, I'd really like to have him."

"Well, you're running things," answered Simmons.

Gault met Hamer in Dallas four days later, and from that point on Frank worked almost exclusively with Gault and Alcorn.[25]

By this time the manhunt was coming to a head in Louisiana. The parents of Henry Methvin lived in the remote backwoods between Ashland and Black Lake Bayou, near the border of Bienville and Natchitoches Parishes. Hamer said it was "situated on the edge of the Black Lake swamp . . . on a dead [end] road which is rough and in places boggy." The Methvins were a hard bunch. Forty-nine-year-old Ivy T. Methvin, a mean drunk, eked out a living as a chair maker, freighter, and bootlegger. Ivy and his wife, Ava, were parents not only to Henry but also to two other boys: Terrell, twenty-four, and Cecil, twenty. Cecil, newly married, lived with his young bride at his parents' home. Like Henry, he had a larcenous streak and would soon be sent to the Louisiana state prison for auto theft. The Methvins were dirt poor and moved frequently, sometimes squatting in isolated cabins and farmhouses. It was no wonder that Sheriff Jordan had such a hard time trying to locate them. During the previous four years, they had moved from Logansport to Ashland to Bossier City and back to Ashland. Terrell, the eldest son,

was married with two small daughters and had his own place in Natchitoches Parish, five miles south of his parents' home. Ivy had many relations, most notably his older brother, Iverson, who was honest and
responsible. Iverson had a large family and worked a farm at Hall Summit, fifteen miles west of Ashland.[26]

On April 8, following the murder of Constable Campbell, wire service reports announced publicly for the first time what Hamer had
known for a month: the heretofore unidentified member of the Barrow
gang was Henry Methvin. In the southern tip of Bienville Parish, gos-
sips' tongues began wagging. Several tipsters told Sheriff Jordan and
Agent Kindell that Ivy and Terrell Methvin had recently moved from
Bossier City back to the Ashland area and "both had shown signs of
unusual and mysterious prosperity." Further, they said, strangers believed to be Bonnie, Clyde, and Henry Methvin, driving an auto with
Oklahoma license plates, visited the houses of Ivy and Terrell Methvin
on April 10. Three days later, on the afternoon of April 13, Kindell got
word from an informant that the fugitives were hiding out at either Ivy's
or Terrell's place.

Kindell immediately telephoned Shreveport and secured the assistance of Sheriff Tom Hughes and Chief of Police Dennis Bazer. That
afternoon, Hughes, with a large posse of deputies, and Bazer, with nine
of his policemen, raced to Arcadia. At the same time, Kindell had several FBI agents sent to Ringgold, twenty miles northwest of Ashland.
The lawmen were ready to move in on the Methvins' houses from two
directions. Late that afternoon, in preparation for a huge raid, Jordan
and Kindell drove to the Methvin neighborhood to confer with several
informants. They learned that the suspects in the Oklahoma car had left
on the tenth and had not returned. Jordan and Kindell decided to cancel the raid to avoid tipping off the gang.

The two lawmen drove back to Arcadia, where Jordan addressed
Sheriff Hughes, Chief Bazer, and the rest of the posse. "I want to ask
you men to say nothing about this affair. This is the first time in two
years that anything approaching a spot used as a permanent hideout by
Barrow has been found. If our plans should leak out the gang would be
scared out of the country. Please keep it quiet."

But Jordan's admonition was too late. Before Sheriff Hughes had left Shreveport, he foolishly boasted to newspaper reporters of his mission. The next morning, dailies in Louisiana and Texas gave prominent coverage to the planned raid. They announced that a large posse was about to descend on the gang's hideout near Ringgold and that Bonnie and Clyde had camped near Rocky Mountain Church in the Alabama Bend section just west of Ringgold. Agent Kindell was furious, and reported to his SAC that Sheriff Hughes had been obtaining private information from Smoot Schmid and spilling it to the newspapers. Kindell declared that Chief Bazer "was disgusted with the activities of Sheriff Hughes" in leaking news of the raid to the press.[27]

Hamer was flabbergasted at the amateurish way the raid had been planned. It should have been kept secret with no more than half a dozen officers involved; a large posse was sure to attract attention in a remote rural area. Frank later complained that "some local and federal officers made a drag on Ruston [Ringgold], Louisiana, and when Clyde heard of it, he quit the country and I had to wait for him to return." Hamer decided to interview Sheriff Hughes about the affair and what led up to it. He and Bob Alcorn drove to Shreveport and spoke with Hughes, who told them that the information for the raid had come from Sheriff Jordan. Hamer and Alcorn piled back into Frank's V-8 and continued on to Arcadia. In the sheriff's office they had a long interview with Jordan, who told them everything he knew. When Jordan was finished, Frank said, "That's the best information we have had on them. It looks like you have a fine chance of catching them. We would like to work with you, if you don't mind."

Sheriff Jordan, like every other lawman, had heard a great deal about Hamer, and later declared, "It should go without saying that I was more than glad to accept the offer of Frank Hamer." But the veteran Ranger had one condition. He insisted that Jordan "pay no attention to other officers, state or federal." At that time, the majority of the FBI's agents were lawyers with no prior detective or gunfighting experience. J. Edgar Hoover was acutely aware of that weakness, and to compensate he employed a small cadre of veteran Texas lawmen, among them James "Doc" White, Gus T. "Buster" Jones, the SAC at San Antonio, and Charlie

Winstead, who, a few months later, would shoot and kill John Dillinger in Chicago. Agent Kindell, thirty-two, had been an attorney before joining the FBI, and Frank considered him a lawyer, not a lawman. Hamer's prey were the most murderous bandits in America, and he was determined to capture or kill them without further loss of peace officers' lives. Despite his lack of faith in the Louisiana agents, he continued his cooperation with the FBI. But Hamer wanted no more blunders. He would be in full charge of the investigation.[28]

The abortive raid had one beneficial result. Soon after, Sheriff Jordan received a surprise visit from John Joyner, a friend and neighbor of Ivy Methvin. Joyner, thirty-five, was a hardcase like Ivy; nine years later, he would murder his wife and then kill himself. Joyner revealed that Methvin wanted a secret meeting with the sheriff. Several days later, Sheriff Jordan and his friend and chief deputy, Prentiss Oakley, met Ivy Methvin at an isolated spot in the piney woods. Methvin went immediately to the point. He said that his son Henry was constantly with Bonnie and Clyde. Since early February, they had made a number of visits to the Methvin home, sometimes staying for several days. They would suddenly leave, and days or weeks later would return unannounced. Ivy said that he and his wife were terrified of Bonnie and Clyde. He knew that, sooner or later, the duo would be killed, and he did not want his son to die with them. Ivy Methvin undoubtedly had an additional fear. The abortive raid showed that law officers were getting close to him and his family. If his neighbors' rumors were correct, the Methvins had been receiving money from Clyde, and they could face prosecution for harboring the outlaws.

Ivy told Sheriff Jordan that he would give up Bonnie and Clyde if Henry was pardoned. As Jordan later recalled, "Methvin said that his help should wipe his son's slate clean." Before the lawmen left, Ivy insisted on secrecy. "Methvin begged me to tell no one about our meeting," explained Jordan, "because Bonnie and Clyde had contacts everywhere and would find out about it. If they did, the Methvin family would be killed." Sheriff Jordan drove back to Arcadia and called Agent Kindell. The federal government had no authority to offer a Texas pardon, but Kindell knew that Frank Hamer did. Soon afterward, Kindell, Hamer, and Jordan met in Shreveport. Sheriff Jordan recalled, "Hamer agreed that a deal could be offered to the Methvin family. If Ivy Methvin would help capture Bonnie and Clyde, consideration would be given to Henry Methvin. While Hamer did not promise that all charges against Methvin would be dropped by the state of Texas, he came real close to saying that. Before the meeting was over, I came to realize that was the offer that I was to make to Methvin. If he would help capture Bonnie and Clyde, Henry would not have to go back to prison." Sheriff Jordan then relayed the offer to the middleman, John Joyner.[29]

Frank did not trust the Methvins and may have had concerns about meeting personally with them or Joyner. Thus far, his manhunt had remained a total secret, known only to a handful of lawmen and federal agents, and he did not want to risk exposure if the Methvins turned out to be unreliable or untrustworthy. He was also pursuing a lead that gang member Joe Palmer was in Amarillo and had a hideout in Corsicana. As a result, Frank's brother Estill went to Louisiana in his stead. On April 23 Estill, with Sheriff Jordan, Deputy Oakley, and Agent Kindell, drove from Arcadia to an isolated spot near Castor, a small village in the southern part of Bienville Parish. There the lawmen met with John Joyner and a local doctor, Chester Sledge.

Joyner told them that on the night of April 20, Henry Methvin had made a short visit to his parents' home. Before long, Bonnie appeared at the front door, armed with what the Methvins called a Tommy gun; it was undoubtedly a BAR, for Bonnie and Clyde did not use Thompson submachine guns. Bonnie impatiently told Henry that he had "stayed long enough" and ordered him, "Come on." The Methvins did not see Clyde but assumed he was outside, explaining, "Barrow never leaves his car for a moment." This visit had made the Methvins even more alarmed, and Ivy had asked Joyner to meet again with Sheriff Jordan. Joyner told Estill and the other officers that "the Methvins, including Henry, are now afraid of their lives as Barrow has threatened to kill the entire family if there is any treachery." Joyner said he had talked with Ivy Methvin and told him of the offer that "the state of Texas would wipe the slate 'clean'... provided the Methvins would place Barrow and Bonnie Parker on the spot." The Methvins had agreed, saying that if the deal was put in writing they would "finger" Bonnie and Clyde.[30]

Estill Hamer told Joyner that he would have no trouble getting written proof, because Lee Simmons had promised to secure a pardon for any gang member who turned in Bonnie and Clyde. After the meeting, Estill promptly telephoned Frank, who in turn contacted Lee Simmons. The prison chief later said, "I went at once to Austin, where I reminded Governors Miriam and Jim Ferguson of our former conversation, and I arranged with them that Methvin would be 'put on the ground' if he came through with the information that we needed. When next I saw Captain Hamer, I gave him a letter setting forth that, upon certain conditions involving certain assistance to the law, Henry Methvin would be granted a full pardon."[31]

The Texas lawmen had moved quickly. Simmons's letter to Frank Hamer was written April 24, only one day after Estill's meeting with the Methvins. Frank, with the letter in hand, waited impatiently in Dallas for Sheriff Jordan to set up a meeting with the Methvin family. Three days later, the arrangements were complete, and Hamer and Alcorn left again for Louisiana. The same day, SAC Blake sent a coded telegram from

Henry Methvin, who joined the Barrow gang after Bonnie and Clyde engineered the breakout from Eastham Prison Farm. *Taronda Schulz collection*

Dallas to the New Orleans office: "Have Agent Kindell meet Hamer tonight at Shreveport." Kindell promptly complied, and the next morning, April 28, Hamer, Alcorn, and the FBI agent drove to Arcadia, where they met with Sheriff Jordan at the courthouse. Jordan advised that John Joyner had made arrangements for them to meet with Ivy Methvin in a wooded area four miles from his house at ten o'clock that night. At the designated time, the lawmen met Methvin and Joyner in the woods. Ivy asked the officers to follow him to his house. There, they were introduced to his wife, Ava, and his sons Cecil and Terrell. As Agent Kindell later reported, "Mr. Hamer exhibited to those interested a letter which he had obtained from Mr. Simmons, Prison Manager, Texas State Prison at Huntsville, Texas, whereby Mr. Hamer was appointed as agent for the State of Texas and authorized to make any deal concerning Henry Methvin which would assist in causing the arrest of Clyde Champion Barrow and Bonnie Parker. The letter, in substance, granted Mr. Hamer permission to advise the Methvins that Henry Methvin's sentence in the State of Texas would be 'wiped out,' provided Methvin or his family would assist. Of course, Hamer was in no position to make any promises concerning what Henry Methvin may have done in the State of Texas or any other state since his escape."

At this point, Ivy's older brother, Iverson, arrived from his home at Hall Summit. The Methvins talked over the offer at great length and finally agreed to accept it. Ivy said he had no doubt he could finger Clyde, for the desperado trusted him and had recently asked him to go to Dallas and bring his mother to the Methvin home for a visit. Ivy explained that "no one knows just when Barrow is coming in and he remains only a very few hours and usually does not get out of his automobile." He added that Clyde might also stop at his son Terrell's house, that Joe Palmer had been riding with the gang, and that he expected another visit from them in six or seven days. At this meeting, or soon thereafter, Hamer paid Joyner $1,000 from his own pocket to secure his continued cooperation.

After a quick consultation, the lawmen devised a simple plan. For the time being, the Methvins would say nothing to Henry, for his own safety. As soon as Bonnie and Clyde reappeared, Ivy Methvin would send word to Sheriff Jordan, who in turn would telephone both Hamer and the FBI office in New Orleans. The officers would proceed to John Joyner's house and make ready for a raid on whichever Methvin home the gang visited. Agent Kindell described the difficulties they faced: "It is believed that not more than six men should be used in effecting the final arrest. While these homes are in an extremely isolated position, it would be almost impossible to rush any large number of men into the community without arousing the suspicion of the countryside. Further, Barrow remains in the vicinity for only a very few hours. There are no telephone facilities and it is impracticable to place any large number of men at given points for any period of time." Hamer and his possemen communicated by local and long distance telephone, for two-way police radios were not in common use until after World War II.[32]

Frank hoped against hope to capture Bonnie and Clyde alive. His natural instincts were to protect women and children at all costs; indeed, that ethic had led him to abandon the Sherman courthouse to the mob. The idea of having to shoot Bonnie Parker was repugnant to him. After all, Bonnie, misguided, perhaps even bloodthirsty, was the same age as his beloved stepdaughter Beverly. The two girls even resembled each other in their petite figures and pretty features. After the midnight meeting, Hamer, Alcorn, and Jordan discussed the possibility of a night raid on the Methvin homes. Recalled the sheriff, "In many respects I dreaded the thought. . . . It would endanger the lives of several women and children." Jordan told Hamer and Alcorn, "I don't like the idea of a night raid. I am sure that I can think out some way of avoiding it. Give me a little more time and we may be able to take them without killing or wounding innocent persons."[33]

Hamer and Alcorn returned to Texas. Frank was not willing to place all his eggs in the Methvin basket, and he continued following up on numerous leads about the gang. He later learned that Bonnie and Clyde were responsible for a bank robbery on May 3 in Everly, Iowa. Two days later, Bonnie and Clyde visited West Dallas but found that Cumie had gone to her sister's home near Nacogdoches. They followed and met her there the next day, but, by the time officers were notified, the outlaws were long gone.[34]

On the morning of May 9, Sheriff Jordan got word from Ivy Methvin that Bonnie, Clyde, and Henry had returned to Louisiana the night before. They arrived at Ivy's house at 11:00 P.M, then drove to Terrell's home, where they slumbered until 3:00 A.M. "This is the first time I have slept in a real bed for eight months," Clyde told them. Clyde liked Terrell's place, for, unlike Ivy's home, it had several access roads for easy escape. Bonnie and Clyde were driving a black Ford V-8 sedan and brought only two pistols into the house, leaving the rest of their arsenal in the car. Henry told his father that he wanted to stay at home for two or three days, but he feared neighboring farmers would get suspicious. As a result, Ivy decided to move to an even more isolated house in Bienville Parish. Later that night, Terrell told Henry privately about the plan to trap Bonnie and Clyde and the offer of clemency brought by Frank Hamer. Henry at first was suspicious but eventually agreed to cooperate, telling his brother that he "wanted more than anything in the world to get away from Barrow."

Sheriff Jordan immediately wired Hamer in Dallas. Frank, with Gault, Alcorn, and Deputy Ted Hinton, who also knew Clyde, left promptly for Arcadia, arriving at six that evening, May 9. Jordan told the Texas lawmen the latest developments, then quietly made arrangements for a meeting with the Methvins a few nights later. Hamer and his possemen returned to the New Inn in Shreveport. After two days of restless waiting, Frank penned a report to SAC Blake in Dallas. He detailed the gang's visit to the Methvins, a trip they made to Dallas on May 5, and Clyde's plans to pick up Billie Parker, who was infatuated with Henry Methvin. Hamer also mentioned rumors that Bonnie was pregnant, saying, "Bonnie as I told you before is in a delicate condition," and asked Blake to keep a close watch in West Dallas because he expected the duo to return for another visit to their parents. His closing words were prophetic: "I feel certain that we will sack the gang here."[35]

Late that night, May 11, Sheriff Jordan telephoned Hamer in Shreveport and asked him to bring his entire posse to Arcadia. At midnight, Jordan called Agent Kindell, who rushed by car fifty miles to Arcadia, where all six lawmen conferred with Ivy, Terrell, and Cecil. The Methvins promised that the next time Bonnie and Clyde returned, they would have Henry stay behind. Sheriff Jordan would notify Hamer and Kindell, then meet secretly with Henry to learn when and where Clyde would pick him up. "We expect to be waiting when Barrow appears," Kindell reported to his SAC. He added that Frank would stay in Shreveport, explaining that Hamer "does not intend to return to Texas feeling that the case has reached a critical point." The agent wanted desperately to be in on the final encounter. "It is essential that I remain in this general vicinity for the next two weeks," he pleaded to his SAC.[36]

Now, with the approval of Hamer and Jordan, Ivy Methvin moved twenty miles north to an isolated and abandoned farmhouse owned by John G. Cole. It was located at the end of what is now called the Otis Cole Road, a mile southwest of the little crossroads of Sailes. John Cole and his wife had died a few years before, leaving the home vacant. Local lore alleged that several family members had died from tuberculosis in the house, and thereafter no one was willing to live in it. Sheriff Jordan recalled that the house nestled deep in a pine forest and was an ideal hideout for Bonnie and Clyde. "The road leading to the house was winding, barely wide enough to accommodate a slowly moving car. . . . The house was occupied by Methvin without the permission of the owner."[37]

During the next week and a half, Bonnie and Clyde made several visits to the Cole house. Instead of staying inside with the Methvins, the ever-alert Clyde made camp in the adjacent woods. Several times, Terrell Methvin and his wife, Emma, invited Clyde, Bonnie, and Henry to dinner at their place. Bonnie liked playing with the couple's two little girls, and she and Clyde began to let their guard down. On at least one occasion, they all drove south to Black Lake, where they picnicked on the shore. During another visit to Ivy's house, Bonnie told Cecil's young wife that she was pregnant. The outlaws were constantly on the move, as Sheriff Jordan later explained: "Bonnie and Clyde traveled back and forth from the Cole house to Gibsland and on to Bossier City and Shreveport where they had a mail box at the post office. They also got their cleaning done in Bossier City and bought most of their groceries there." Trying to pin them down would not be easy.[38]

Meanwhile, Hamer and Maney Gault holed up at the New Inn, while Alcorn and Hinton returned to Dallas. Sheriff Jordan later said that all the possemen agreed that they "would be ready to leave on a minute's notice." During the following days, Hamer and Gault whiled away the monotony by playing poker in their hotel room. But Frank grew impatient. He decided to stake out the isolated Cole house and try to capture the outlaws. "On several occasions I went alone to this secret place," he later said. "It was my hope to take [Clyde] and Bonnie alive; this I could do only by finding them asleep. It would have been simple to tap each one on the head, kick their weapons out of reach, and handcuff them before they knew what it was all about. Once the plan came near succeeding, and would have succeeded but for those accidents which will happen over which the officer has no control. There was always plenty of sign in the camp: stubs of Bonnie's Camels—Clyde smoked Bull Durham—lettuce leaves for the white rabbit, pieces of sandwiches, and a button off Clyde's coat. I found where they had made their bed."[39]

Ivy Methvin feared that his family would be hurt or killed in a raid on the Cole house. As a result, Hamer and Sheriff Jordan decided that they would attempt to capture Bonnie and Clyde on the road between Gibsland and Sailes. The desperadoes would have to take this route to get to the Cole house from the north. The two officers drove up and down the gravel country road, looking for the perfect spot. They found it, at the top of a low hill about two miles north of Sailes. On the east side of the road was a ten-foot-high embankment, covered with pines and brush. It was a good place to conceal a posse. To the right, looking north, the highway could be seen clearly for a quarter mile as it rounded a curve and descended from a distant rise, then sloped up the hill. To the left, looking south, was a clear view for several hundred yards. The road was narrow, barely wide enough for two cars.

Now, Hamer returned to the New Inn and resumed the agonizing vigil. Finally, on the night of May 22, 1934, all the driving, hunting, planning, negotiating, and waiting paid off. At 8:30 he got a phone call from Sheriff Jordan, and the message was brief: "Come to Arcadia at once. Get your other men if you can."

It was the beginning of the end for Bonnie and Clyde.

22

"WE SHOT THE DEVIL
OUT OF THEM"

Hamer hung up the telephone, called Dallas, and asked Bob Alcorn and Ted Hinton to rush immediately to Gibsland. Then Frank phoned Lee Simmons in Huntsville, and, to evade snoopy long distance operators, he spoke in code: "The old hen is about ready to hatch. I think the chickens will come off tomorrow." Next he called home in Austin and told his wife, "The old hen's setting, and she's setting good." Gladys knew exactly what he meant, and she began a long, anxious wait through the night.[1]

Hamer and Gault immediately drove to Arcadia, where Sheriff Jordan filled them in. The previous day, May 21, 1934, Bonnie and Clyde had reappeared at Terrell's house and had driven with Henry and other members of the Methvin family down to Black Lake. They had another picnic and returned home that night. Bonnie, Clyde, and Henry went to their camp near the Cole house for some sleep, and at three in the morning they awoke and departed for Bossier City. Before they left, Ivy took Henry aside and warned him not to return with Bonnie and Clyde. The outlaws stopped outside Bossier City, situated on the east bank of the Red River, directly opposite Shreveport, and Henry walked into town to pick up some food. There was a long wait, and, when Henry did not return, Bonnie and Clyde drove back to the Cole house, arriving there between five and six o'clock that evening. They thought that Henry might have come back home on his own, but Ivy told them that his son was not there.

Clyde surmised that Henry might have gone to the former Methvin home near Ashland, so he ordered Ivy, "You go to the old place and see if Henry is there. We will go to Bossier Parish. He may have gone there." Clyde said that if they could not find Henry they would come back to the Cole house the next morning. Soon after Bonnie and Clyde left, Ivy Methvin told John Joyner to drive into Arcadia to inform Sheriff Jordan. By that time it was 8:30 P.M., and Jordan immediately telephoned Hamer in Shreveport. Jordan also made numerous calls in an effort to locate Leslie Kindell, but the FBI agent was investigating a kidnapping near Lake Charles and could not be found.[2]

At about midnight, Hamer, Gault, Jordan, and Deputy Oakley left Arcadia and drove west to Gibsland. Alcorn and Hinton arrived an hour or two later from Dallas. The officers carefully went over their plans and checked their weapons. Then they piled into their cars and proceeded south to the ambush site, eight miles below Gibsland, arriving between two and three in the morning on May 23. Bonnie and Clyde would have to pass this spot on their way back to the Cole house. Sheriff Jordan went on to the Cole house, where he instructed Ivy Methvin to drive his truck to the site. The lawmen had him park his truck on the west side of the road, facing north. At first light, they would take off a tire and pray that Bonnie and Clyde would stop to help him. Hamer expected that Clyde, as he drove up the rise, would have his attention focused on Ivy's truck to his right, and not on the posse on the embankment to his left. Said Jordan later, "Methvin was with us because he had gotten so scared I really did not trust him."

The officers secreted their autos in the nearby woods. Then Hamer positioned the men in a ragged, twenty-yard line along the brush-and pine-covered embankment. Each man was about ten feet apart, making it difficult for Clyde, if he spotted the posse, to hit them all. Said Hamer, "I held the position on the extreme left, and next was Gault, Jordan, Alcorn, Oakley, and Hinton in the order named. Gault, Jordan, and myself were to take care of the front seat, Oakley and Alcorn of the

Hamer and his posse in Arcadia, Louisiana, the day they killed Bonnie and Clyde. Left to right: Prentiss Oakley, Bob Alcorn, Henderson Jordan, Ted Hinton, Frank Hamer, and Maney Gault. *Taronda Schulz collection*

back seat, if occupied, while Ted Hinton was at the end of the line representing the reserves. If the car got past us, Hinton was to step out and bust the engine with a Browning Machine Gun." Hinton's BAR was the only fully automatic weapon in the posse. Hamer, Jordan, and Oakley carried Remington model 8 semiautomatic rifles. Gault and Alcorn hefted short-barreled Remington model 11 semiautomatic shotguns loaded with buckshot. Each man also wore a sidearm, while the officers brought along one or two extra Model 8s and at least one shotgun.[3]

Hamer and Jordan got along well, but they strongly disagreed about whether to give the outlaws a chance to surrender. As much as Frank did not want to harm Bonnie, he had no such feelings about Clyde. Recalled Sheriff Jordan, "Hamer and I argued about that for days. I wanted to step out in the road and demand their surrender, but Hamer said if I did, I was a dead man." Frank never forgot the death of Sergeant

Timberlake, and he did not want to bury another comrade. But he finally relented. As Hamer later explained, "We agreed to take Barrow and the woman alive if we could. We believed that when they stopped the car, both would be looking . . . away from us; such action on their part would enable us to escape observation until we demanded their surrender."

The posse's wait in the brush was a long one, said Hamer. "Waiting is about the hardest thing an officer has to do. Many men will stand up in a fight, but lose their nerve completely if required to wait long for the excitement. On this occasion I did not detect the slightest nervousness on the part of a single man." Bob Alcorn, on the other hand, frankly admitted his anxiety during the long wait: "Do you know how heavy your eyes get and how you get to imagining you see things that don't exist? How the noises of the forest magnify and how you can think of the thousand creeping, crawling things of the swamps? A score of times we jumped up on the alert, thinking our quarry was at hand and a score of times we settled down."

And the possemen forgot to bring food. "All of us were hungry," recalled Jordan. "The next meal was the principal topic of discussion, and we talked about food to lessen the monotony."

Just before daylight, Jordan called to Hinton, "How are the groceries holding out, Ted?"

"What groceries?" Hinton retorted. "I have eaten the stock off your rifle and am starting on the barrel."

At daybreak the lawmen had Ivy Methvin jack up his truck, remove the right front tire, and stand next to it. The drivers of several passing autos stopped to help, but Ivy told them he was almost finished replacing the tire. "After each car passed, Methvin would run over to us and beg us to call the whole thing off," recalled Jordan. "He said that we would all be killed. Each time I would patiently listen to him and then firmly send him back to his place on the road beside his truck. At one point I told him that if he did not get back to his truck and do what he was told to do, Bonnie and Clyde would not get the chance to kill him because I would."

Jordan added, "As the hour of 9 o'clock approached the strain increased. Two or three cars flashing down the highway from the north caused added tenseness as we awaited the word from Deputies Hinton and Alcorn. For each of these cars they shouted, 'No!'"[4]

By this time Hamer and his possemen began to think that Bonnie and Clyde were not going to appear. Recalled Alcorn, "By 9 o'clock we had just about decided to give up, but waited a few minutes. At 9:15 I saw a light tan Ford V-8 head south over the hill north of us. I knew that was the kind of car Clyde was driving." Hamer said that they heard it long before they saw it. "A car was coming from the north at a terrific speed, singing like a sewing machine. We heard it when it must have been three miles away. Finally, it came into view at a distance of a thousand yards, and though it was still coming rapidly, it began to slow down as it climbed the hill towards us." The Ford slowed to forty-five miles an hour. The driver must have seen Ivy Methvin, for the car continued to slow down. Bob Alcorn crouched low, shotgun in hand, peering through the brush. Suddenly, he raised his left arm out straight and called, "It's Barrow! The Parker woman's with him!"

The Ford was now a hundred yards distant. Clyde was driving, Bonnie in the front passenger seat. Sheriff Jordan quickly looked down the line of officers. "I could see most of the other men in the posse. None showed the slightest trace of nervousness." He called to Alcorn, "Be sure, man!"

"I know! It's Barrow and his woman. Steady!"

At that, Hinton chimed in, "It's them! I'd know Clyde Barrow anywhere!"

Just then a loud rumble from the south caused several of the posse to glance to their left. A truck loaded with logs was slowly approaching, operated by two black men. Then the tan Ford came to a stop on the highway between Methvin's truck and the posse, fifty feet distant.

"Hello. Got a flat?" Clyde called to Methvin.

"Yes," Ivy replied. "Did you find Henry?"

"No," answered Clyde. "Haven't you seen him?"

Ivy answered in the negative, then asked Bonnie, who was holding a sandwich in her lap, "Have you got a drink for me?"

Before she could answer, Clyde started to pull forward to allow the approaching logging truck to pass by on the narrow road. Suddenly, all the arguing about whether the lawmen would give Bonnie and Clyde a chance to surrender became moot. Prentiss Oakley, the most inexperienced man in the posse, thought the desperadoes were trying to escape. Just as several of the officers yelled, "Halt!," Oakley opened fire with his Remington. At that, the occupants of the lumber truck abandoned their vehicle and raced for the woods.

In that split second of tense excitement, just as the Ford lurched forward, each lawman perceived events with slight differences. Sheriff Jordan said that Clyde "picked up a gun with his right hand. Bonnie Parker was seen to raise a pistol." Bob Alcorn recalled, "Clyde's left hand left the wheel and darted to the seat beside him. Bonnie made a desperate clutch for something in her lap. I saw Clyde's hand when it came into sight again and it held a sawed-off shotgun, a terrible weapon at that range. Almost simultaneously Bonnie came up with a weapon that matched Clyde's." Hamer, with more than thirty years of gunfighting experience, was the coolest head with the most accurate perception: "I saw that his right hand was on an automatic rifle across his lap and Bonnie had an automatic pistol in her hand."

Hamer and the rest of the posse unloaded a thunderous volley. Ivy dove for cover as buckshot and rifle rounds raked the left side of the Ford, shattering the windshield and door windows and blowing dozens of holes in the doors. The car kept moving forward at slow speed as Clyde's foot slipped off the clutch. Ted Hinton, instead of busting the engine with his BAR, raked the front seat, emptying the twenty-round clip in seconds. The recoil caused the automatic rifle to climb up, and eight of Hinton's .30-06 steel-jacketed bullets stitched Bonnie in a parallel line on the left side of her body. "She screamed like a panther," one of the officers later declared. "The car continued to move," said Sheriff Jordan. "Gunfire was raking it from six angles. The glass in the rear left door was blown to bits. I saw black holes appear in the side of the car. The noise was deafening."

Hamer later said, "I hated to have to shoot her. But as they drove up . . . and I pulled down on Barrow, knowing that some of my rifle bullets were going to snuff out her life along with his, I recalled how she had helped Barrow kill nine peace officers. . . . Thinking of that as

Bonnie and Clyde's "death car" with three BARs and other firearms, taken at the scene shortly after the ambush. *Taronda Schulz collection*

I drew down on them and sighted down my rifle barrel, I gritted my teeth and pulled the trigger as quickly as I could—pulled it again and again. If you are an officer sworn to do your duty you can't afford to feel mercy for such murdering rats, whether they are male or female."

Added Alcorn, "I saw Barrow's face contort into a snarl and the shock of pain which went over him as the bullets struck. He made a desperate effort to bring that gun into play. He raised it to the edge of the windshield and he may have fired it once. But I don't think so. If he did the shot went wild. I saw his hands fall and his head drop to his chest. Then his body slumped forward over the steering wheel for a minute and then slowly slid to one side. Bonnie had likewise raised her weapon just as the storm of steel struck her and forced the gun from her nerveless fingers and then slowly slid to one side." Said Sheriff Jordan, "I saw Barrow's head fall against the back of the seat. Blood was gushing out. I saw Bonnie Parker slump forward as if to pick something off the floor of the car."

The Ford had rolled slowly across the road and come to a stop on the same side as the posse, just south of their position. There was a brief lull in the firing as the officers quickly reloaded empty rifles and shotguns or jerked out their pistols. Bob Alcorn seized an extra rifle and jumped down from the embankment. "We didn't know whether we had killed them or not," he said later. "I ran into the road and to the right side of the car. . . . I fired into the rear of the car and again into the right side of the car. The other officers fired again. Nothing happened. We waited. Still nothing happened."[5]

"I had no idea of time," said Jordan later. "It might have been an hour that I stood there on the firing line. Actually, everything was over in seconds."

Now the lawmen stepped carefully from the brush. Hamer was the first to approach the Barrow car, Old Lucky clutched in his right fist.

"Be careful, Cap!" called Maney Gault. "They may not be dead."

"If they're not they soon will be," Frank shouted back.

But nothing was left of Bonnie and Clyde except for their bullet-shredded corpses, slumped in the front seat. Bonnie was wearing a red dress, red shoes, and a red and white tam hat, splattered with blood and gore. Her head was between her knees, an automatic pistol on her lap. Hamer was sickened by the sight, for it was the first and only time in his life he had physically harmed a woman. He had no such feelings about Clyde, whose right hand was still curled around the stock of his BAR. The vehicle had been riddled with 167 bullets and buckshot. Both desperadoes had been peppered by shards of flying glass. Bonnie had been struck by at least forty-one slugs; Clyde, by seventeen or more. The driver's door had protected Barrow from much of the shooting.[6]

The possemen stepped forward and searched the Ford. It was an arsenal on wheels. Underneath a robe on the backseat were two BARs, nine Colt automatic pistols, and one revolver, all loaded. Three bags and a box held more than two thousand rounds of ammunition, and on the floor was a valise with forty magazines, twenty rounds each, for the BARs. As fellow officers searched the car, Ted Hinton pulled out a 16 mm movie camera and began filming the scene. His first frames caught Hamer exhaling cigarette smoke as Sheriff Jordan examined the contents of the Ford's trunk. With Hinton's camera rolling, the officers stacked up the guns and ammunition next to the car. Inside, they found Clyde's saxophone, Bonnie's makeup kit, blankets, suitcases filled with clothing, a couple of popular magazines, and fifteen stolen license plates. In Clyde's pockets was $507 in cash.[7]

Once the inventory was completed, Hamer and Alcorn drove back to Gibsland. There Frank telephoned the news to Lee Simmons while Alcorn called Sheriff Schmid. Frank then called Gladys, who was beside herself with worry, and told her it was all over. "I'll be home tomorrow," he said. "None of the officers got hurt." Deputy Oakley drove into Arcadia and reported to the coroner, who ordered that the bodies be brought into town. Then Hamer and Alcorn returned to the death scene, followed by a tow truck. By this time word of the killings had spread like wildfire, and a crowd rushed to the site. To Frank's astonishment, by the time he and Alcorn got back, two hundred cars lined the roadside and a crowd of spectators surrounded the death car. Souvenir hunters stole some minor items from the car before the officers could fend them off. Others busied themselves prying spent bullets from tree trunks.

The tow driver chained the bullet-riddled Ford to his truck and started north, the dead bodies still inside. The lawmen accompanied him in their cars, followed by a parade of 150 vehicles. They passed through Gibsland and continued east to Arcadia, arriving just before noon. Telephone and telegraph wires hummed with the news, while radio stations broadcast the event nationwide. Reporters were already racing to Arcadia by automobile and airplane. Frank stepped into the telephone office to call Louis Phares. His report was typically terse: "The job is done." As he turned to leave, a reporter for the *St. Louis Post-Dispatch* called long distance and asked if he would give a statement. "Sure," he replied. "I can tell you what happened this morning. We just shot the devil out of them, that's all. That's all there was to it. We just laid a trap for them. A steel trap. You know, Bessemer steel, like gun barrels are made of." Yet the killing of Bonnie preyed on him, and when a local newspaperman pressed for details, Frank responded, "I hate to bust a cap on a woman, especially when she was sitting down. However, if it wouldn't have been her, it would have been us."[8]

Arcadia was a sleepy country town of two thousand, but by early

Frank Hamer speaking to reporters next to the courthouse in Arcadia, Louisiana, May 23, 1934. *Taronda Schulz collection*

afternoon ten thousand gawkers flooded in. They were soon joined by Sheriff Schmid and Louis Phares, who arrived on chartered planes. Tom Simmons, a cub reporter who had also rushed from Dallas by airplane, found Hamer in front of the courthouse. "I can't recall the last time I slept," Frank told him. As he described the manhunt "in rambling sentences interspersed with his rough humor," Simmons noticed that Hamer's "eyes glistened with the thrill of the hunt." Frank pointed to the lawn on the side of the courthouse and remarked, "Two months ago I sat there and really mapped the plan by which we got Clyde and Bonnie this morning. I've been a long way in those two months, into half a dozen states, but I always thought we'd get them around here." When Simmons asked about rumors that Henry Methvin's father gave the tip, Hamer laughed out loud, declaring, "The idea's ridiculous."

At that point Lee Simmons drove up, having just arrived from Huntsville, and the two spoke briefly. Frank then turned back to the reporter and said, "They died with their guns in their hands." Referring to the Grapevine murders, he added, "We didn't get them like they've been getting us." Hamer turned toward Lee Simmons and declared, "I've always had a fear of shooting women and children, though I've been a peace officer a mighty long time. As guilty as I knew that girl to be and as well as I knew that she'd get me if I didn't get her, I had a funny feeling in the pit of my stomach when I saw her there, her head slumped between her knees and her body riddled with bullets. It got me."

A few minutes later, the death car was brought into the courthouse grounds, followed by a massive throng. The bodies had been removed to Conger's funeral parlor, where a crowd of three thousand gathered. The Ford was parked behind the jail fence to keep souvenir hunters away. Photographers took images of the lawmen as reporters pressed in for interviews. To all, Hamer praised his possemen and gave full credit to Lee Simmons for his support. Then he and Simmons walked over to the death car, and Hamer opened the trunk. "Here is what's in it," Frank said, pointing to the arsenal of weapons. "It's up to you to say what's to be done with it."

"No," Simmons answered. "You take what you want and then divide the souvenirs with the boys who did the job. I'm not entitled to any-thing. You take charge of it and handle it."9

Then Hamer and the other possemen attended the coroner's inquest. If Bonnie was in fact pregnant, no evidence of it surfaced in the autopsy. At three o'clock Henry Barrow arrived from Dallas by ambulance to take Clyde's body home. Sheriff Jordan gave him the $507 found in Clyde's pockets. To reporters Henry announced, "We hold no ill feel-ing. We realize that these men were officers of the law doing their duty, and what happened was something that had to be. Time and again Clyde told me that he would never be captured, regardless of odds. . . . Bonnie told me that if it ever got too tight for them, Clyde would kill her and then kill himself." Henry's sentiments were not shared by Emma Parker. When newspapermen called her asking for comments, she railed, "What do you think of a bunch of men that would shoot them up like that? Shot them from ambush, that's what they did. Didn't give them a chance. They got a signal when to start shooting and didn't even try to take them alive."10

Shortly after midnight an exhausted Hamer returned to his room at the New Inn in Shreveport. Though he hadn't slept in forty-eight hours, he allowed a visit by Charles H. Newell, a veteran Dallas newspaper-man. Frank, shedding his coat and shoes, collapsed in a chair, removed his necktie, and undid three buttons on his green shirt. In one of the few lengthy interviews he ever gave to a reporter, he detailed his man-hunt for Bonnie and Clyde. "This was one of the few times in my thirty years experience as a peace officer that I was put exclusively on the trail of a badly wanted outlaw. Thanks to Lee Simmons, who employed me to work for the prison board, I had unlimited authority and resources to devote to finding Barrow and Bonnie."

He tried to dispel some myths about the outlaw duo. "There has been a lot of rot printed about Barrow running around with [Thompson] machine guns. He knew what every intelligent officer knows—that a high-powered [Browning] automatic rifle, shooting 20 shots, is far bet-ter for quick and deadly work than any [sub]machine gun. His armament when killed proves it. He had two sawed off automatic shotguns, three

automatic rifles and ten pistols and about a thousand rounds of ammunition." Frank added, "Some wild reports about Clyde and Bonnie have
gained currency. Barrow drank very little and didn't use dope at all.
Bonnie . . . loved whisky and kept herself stimulated with it. She couldn't
carry it well, however. Every time she got too much her legs gave out.
She couldn't walk. Clyde had to carry her to their car many times. That
helped to identify the pair. Her love of cigars was fact and not fiction,
though when killed she had cigarettes and not cigars in her lap."

Yet Hamer was characteristically vague and misleading in explaining how he set up the ambush. "It was through belated knowledge of
Barrow's habits that we eventually trapped him. We covered his known
contacts one by one. This we narrowed to a mighty few the places he could
dash for help. The heat was kept on in all his old haunts. He shuttled back
and forth between Fort Smith, Arkansas, and Northern Louisiana many

The bullet-riddled death car in the jailyard at Arcadia, Louisiana. Hamer is at right with his
back to the camera. Sheriff Smoot Schmid is at the left, in coat and tie. *Taronda Schulz collection*

times. Eventually we discovered that Barrow picked Tuesdays to get his mail. It was always under a board alongside the highways, or rather byways, over which he traveled. He designated the spot. Finally, we baited the trap in Bienville Parish two weeks ago. It took a lot of patient waiting before we were sure of the approximate time he would drive into it. I am sorry that I can't explain for publication exactly how we were morally certain that we would catch him when we did."

Hamer's mailbox-under-the-board yarn, which he first spun in this interview, was the story he would publicly tell the rest of his life. It was his way of protecting the Methvin family, even though they were quickly identified as the informants by the press. The Methvins themselves later admitted in open court that they had fingered Bonnie and Clyde, but Frank kept his promise and never publicly revealed their role. Even in his discussion with Newell, Hamer acknowledged that he was not entirely truthful.[11]

After the interview concluded, Frank was called on by Lee Simmons. The two sat up late, discussing the case, when they were interrupted by the jingling of the telephone. It was a long distance operator from New York. Simmons heard Frank's side of the conversation: "Yes, this is Hamer. . . . Yes. . . . National Broadcasting Company? . . . How's that? . . . A thousand dollars for a few minutes' talk over the radio? . . . Hell no! . . . I won't do it. What do you think I am? . . . Hell no!" Recalled Simmons, "He slammed the receiver on the hook, cussing a blue streak and mad as a hornet. I know men who would have leaped at the publicity, to say nothing of the thousand dollars. But not Hamer; he's not built that way."[12]

Frank was willing to give newspaper interviews because he understood the importance of the Barrow case. But he found such money offers especially repugnant. In the morning, newspapers headlined the killing of Bonnie and Clyde nationwide. Although during their lifetimes they had never achieved the notoriety of John Dillinger, in death they exceeded it. And within days Frank Hamer became a nationally famous figure, widely praised in the press. Wire service reports offered accounts of his long career with varying accuracy. One wild claim, oft repeated thereafter, was that he had killed sixty-five outlaws in the line of duty. Hamer was forced to deny reports that he had offered his services to the FBI to track down Dillinger.

After returning to Austin, Frank rested but a day before returning to work on the Barrow case. This time he intended to help Billie Parker and Floyd Hamilton, for he was certain they were innocent of the Grapevine murders. To reporters he announced, "I know that Clyde Barrow and Bonnie Parker did it. They talked to people about the killing and described it." Frank was subpoenaed to appear in a habeas corpus hearing in Fort Worth, but in the end his testimony was not needed. A fingerprint expert revealed that the prints of Clyde Barrow and Henry Methvin matched those on an empty whiskey bottle found at the murder scene. Ballistics tests by Houston police proved that empty shotgun shells found next to the patrolmen's bodies had been fired by the sixteen-gauge shotgun taken from the death car. In a dramatic court hearing on May 31, a Fort Worth judge dismissed the charges and personally apologized to Billie Parker.[13]

That fall, a showman, Charles W. Stanley, who billed himself as the "Crime Doctor," rented the death car from its legal owner. He began touring the country with the Ford as an exhibit in his lecture and slide show about Bonnie and Clyde. His pitch was that the desperadoes had been set up by Henry Methvin and executed without mercy by Hamer's posse. On March 2, 1935, Stanley made the mistake of bringing his act to an auto dealer's showroom in downtown Austin. That night, while he was regaling his audience, Hamer and Gault walked into the showroom. According to Stanley, Hamer cursed him, knocked him down, and confiscated his slides. To reporters, the irate lawman gave a more graphic account: "I slapped that guy clean across the room and told him if he ever showed those pictures again I would crawl on my knees to South America to kill him." Again Frank denied that the Methvins had fingered Bonnie and Clyde: "I was out $2,400 from my own pocket on the Barrow case and neither Henry Methvin nor his old man got a penny of it." Stanley continued to tour the United States with the death car, but he never came back to Austin.[14]

Hamer was not reimbursed for many of his expenses because he had

Frank Hamer, right, and Maney Gault in front of the garage at Hamer's Austin home, the day they returned from Louisiana. Gault holds a sawed-off shotgun and a BAR taken from the death car. *Taronda Schulz collection*

failed to obtain receipts, something he could not have done without blowing his cover. It was not until 1941 that the penurious state legislature passed a special act reimbursing him $1,075 in costs he had paid from his own pocket. And it was 1945 when the legislature finally repaid the $1,000 he had given to John Joyner. In lieu of reimbursement, and with the permission of Lee Simmons, he kept many of the firearms found in the death car. Cumie Barrow and Emma Parker, in twin displays of unmitigated gall, wrote letters to Hamer demanding the weapons.

Incredibly, Cumie insisted, "I do know that my boy did buy most of the guns he had," and she berated Hamer: "I feel you should think you have caused me enough grief and hardships without trying to cause me more trouble now." He did not bother to respond.[15]

Countless messages of congratulations poured in, among them a letter from his old admirer, Tom Mix. His friends arranged for a testimonial dinner in Austin, with one newspaper running a headline, HAMER-GAULT HERO DAY IS SET. He responded by saying that "he did not consider it appropriate and that he could not attend." And he consistently refused to profit from the deaths of Bonnie and Clyde. Soon after the ambush, a publisher contacted him with a proposal to produce a book about his life. When he declined, the editor asked, "How much would $10,000 mean to you?"

Hamer's blunt response: "No more than a Mexican dime."[16]

23

FRANK HAMER VS.
LYNDON B. JOHNSON

There was only one person more unhappy with Frank Hamer's killing of Bonnie and Clyde than the Barrow and Parker families. That man was J. Edgar Hoover. Had Leslie Kindell been part of Hamer's posse, the FBI could have taken credit for the feat. Yet it was Hoover's own fault that Kindell was not present. Less than two weeks before the ambush, the agent had pleaded to be assigned full-time to the case. Instead, Kindell was ordered to investigate a kidnapping in southern Louisiana, and the important role he played in the manhunt was completely forgotten. Hoover, whose bizarre character traits would later be documented by numerous biographers, developed an abiding jealousy of Frank Hamer.

After the ambush, newspapers speculated that Hamer would be hired by the FBI to track down John Dillinger. Walter Prescott Webb, Bill Sterling, and other prominent Texans recommended to Hoover that he hire Hamer for the job. They were informed that Hamer was not qualified because an FBI agent had to be a lawyer or an accountant. Newspapers had a field day with that story. When Frank gave a lengthy interview to A. B. MacDonald of *The Kansas City Star*, he said, "I can deliver Dillinger in the same way I did Bonnie and Clyde." MacDonald's story was republished nationwide. Although Frank repeatedly denied that he ever offered his services to the FBI, Hoover was enraged. Knowing little of the veteran lawman's relationship with the press, he told his agents, "Hamer is publicity wild." He explained, "Hamer is very suspicious and critical, but thoroughly fearless and honest," and ordered, "We will take anything Hamer offers to give us, but we will not give him anything." Hoover compiled at least eighteen files related to Hamer, and as late as 1949 instructed his men, "Be cautious. . . . If Hamer wants to turn anything over to us we will of course receive it but in view of Hamer's reputation it would be unwise for [the] FBI to seek him out."[1]

Hoover's jealousy extended even to his own agents. He famously forced Melvin Purvis, the G-man who headed the squad that killed Dillinger, out of the FBI in 1935. But he had no such control over Frank Hamer, who Texas newspapers now touted as the man who should be in charge of the Rangers. Hamer should have had a lock on the job, but there was one problem: the new governor, James V. Allred, who took office in January 1935. He was the same "fighting district attorney" whom Hamer had criticized mercilessly in 1925 for prosecuting his ex-Ranger comrade, Elmer B. McClure, for murder. Ever since, Allred had despised Hamer. He fired all but three of the Ferguson Rangers and replaced Estill Hamer with Tom Hickman as senior captain. Frank Hamer was out, and Allred refused to appoint him throughout the four years he was governor. Hamer told a reporter that he would never be able to reenter the Ranger service.[2]

The Texas Rangers had reached a nadir under the Fergusons. In addition to widespread incompetency, one Ranger was convicted of murder, one captain was convicted of theft and embezzlement, and another captain committed suicide. Numerous proposals had been made to abolish the force and have the Highway Patrol take over its functions. Now, foremost in the public mind was Hamer's successful manhunt for Bonnie and Clyde. He had shown what a small group of experienced, well-armed, and properly funded lawmen could do against the most dangerous and elusive criminals imaginable. To the Texas public, he was still a Ranger. Newspaper reports consistently called him "Captain Hamer" and referred to him as a Ranger or ex-Ranger. He had restored the faded glory of the Texas Rangers. Dissolving the fabled force quickly became unthinkable. In August 1935 the state legislature created the Department of Public Safety, with three divisions: the Highway Patrol; a Headquarters Division, consisting of a statewide crime lab and radio system; and the Texas Rangers. For the first time, the Rangers were removed from politics and could not be fired by every new governor. It was a great irony that Hamer, although his career as a Ranger captain was over, had saved the Texas Rangers.[3]

With the deaths of Bonnie and Clyde and the killing of Pretty Boy Floyd five months later, Raymond Hamilton became the Southwest's public enemy number one. He and Joe Palmer had been captured and sentenced to die for the murder of Major Crowson in the Eastham breakout. On July 22, 1934, they took part in a spectacular break from the death house at Huntsville. Hamilton and Palmer managed to escape, but Whitey Walker, of Borger notoriety, was shot dead by guards. Newspapers announced that Hamer would take the trail; in October press reports had him hunting the fugitive in East Texas. On January 3, 1935, he was appointed a grand jury bailiff in Dallas County and paid $210 a month to track down Hamilton. Two months later, Hamilton boasted to a reporter, "Frank Hamer and Maney Gault are looking for me, but I don't think they'll catch up with me." He added that "if either of those catch me I'll be pretty much ashamed." His statement proved correct, for in April he was collared in Fort Worth, not by Hamer, but by Sheriff Schmid, Ted Hinton, and other officers. A month later, Ray Hamilton died on the Huntsville electric chair.[4]

In October 1935 Hamer was asked to organize a squad of special police to protect the Houston waterfront from labor violence. A longshoremen's strike had just begun, and bloodshed was expected. A common misconception is that strike violence was usually the fault of police or strikebreaking "goons." The fact is that, in Houston at least, labor violence in the 1930s was just as often provoked by union thugs. In May 1934, during a previous longshoremen's strike, four pickets were shot and wounded by company guards; two months later, three black strikebreakers were shot to death by white strikers. Houston was one of the nation's largest ports, and the port commission wanted Hamer to provide trained and disciplined officers to prevent the type of bloodshed that had occurred a year before. Frank quickly hired a force of about twenty ex-lawmen. Union leaders believed that he had been retained to intimidate them. One blasted the port authorities for hiring "Frank Hamer, that famous bandit-catcher, as head of the dock police, just like the longshoremen were a bunch of bandits." Another charged that Hamer's employment was an "insult to the American labor movement." At a union meeting on November 1, the crowd booed vociferously when Hamer's name was mentioned.[5]

Frank Hamer in a lighter moment, 1937. He is in the backyard of his Austin home, holding the plains rifle that belonged to Texas Ranger "Big Foot" Wallace. *Author's collection*

Frank little realized that this initial strike duty would become his full-time job for the next thirteen years. In July 1936, he and Roy T. Rogers, former night chief of the Houston police, formed a private guard company and hired fifty former law officers for duty in Houston. Their clients included Gulf Oil and the Texas Company (Texaco). Hamer was despised by the unions, but he enjoyed wide support from citizens and newspapers. It didn't hurt that *The Texas Rangers,* a bestselling book by his old friend Walter Prescott Webb, was released that year. Webb devoted a long, laudatory chapter to Hamer and his colorful career. When a seaman's strike hit in November, Hamer's men were active in protecting the property of shipping and trucking interests. As he had done so often over the years, Frank relied on informants to keep him posted on the strikers' activities. Complaints were made to the National Labor Relations Board alleging that he had created a spy ring for Houston ship owners. Labor spying was outlawed by the recently enacted National Labor Relations Act. If Hamer's informants provided information on union activity, that was illegal. However, if the informants were used to prevent violence by strikers, it was lawful. Though no charges were brought against him, it is unclear whether Hamer's actions were legal or not.[6]

For the next three years, Frank commuted back and forth between Austin and Houston. The work paid $500 a month, far more than he had ever earned. His actions were sometimes controversial. On the night of May 8, 1939, he, Rogers, and Frank's nephew Clint, Harrison's oldest son, were on strike duty in Galena, just east of Houston. R. J. Kennedy of the National Maritime Union was acting as captain of pickets when the Hamer party drove up in a car. According to Kennedy, Rogers and Clint Hamer kept the strikers at bay with shotguns while Frank jumped from the car and, without any provocation, beat him to the ground, then kicked him in the head and the groin. Kennedy brought assault charges against all three, and each posted a $400 bond.[7]

Years later, Rogers gave his own—and probably more accurate—version of the incident. He said that as they tried to cross the picket line in their auto, a "dock walloper" directed a stream of curses at Hamer. Frank cupped his hand to his ear and said, "What's that you said? I'm a little hard of hearing." When the union man repeated his language, Hamer remarked, "Well, I'm sorry, sir. I just can't seem to hear you in here." He swung open the door and stepped outside. As Rogers said, "The next thing I saw was the bottom of the man's feet going up in the air. When the man hit the ground, all those tough pickets started applauding, as the man had no cause to be that foul mouthed." Hamer and his party then drove through, and had no more trouble with the strikers. Rogers didn't mention that they were charged with assault.[8]

Frank was incensed by Kennedy's charges, telling newspapermen, "Gangsters from Chicago are trying to intimidate the public here. Squads have been sent here to kill me. That doesn't worry me. There is not a man in Texas who has as much blood in his body as I have lost in trying to protect the public." Two days later, he repeated his charges before the Houston grand jury, which was investigating labor violence. In response, The Chicago *Socialist Appeal,* a leftist journal, blasted Hamer as a "notorious anti-labor deputy, on the payroll of most of the town's largest concerns" and ridiculed his claims as "highly imaginary 'beef squads' imported from Chicago for various strikes." A generation of dockworkers would recall Frank Hamer as a company "goon" and "scab herder."[9]

With Rogers to help run his business, Frank had free time to pursue his favorite pastimes: hunting and fishing. He frequently visited the Hill Country with his sons and often spent time in Kimble County, hunting with his old friend Coke Stevenson. He socialized with ex-Ranger comrades and several newspapermen, as well as the three most famous historians in the Southwest: Webb, J. Frank Dobie, and J. Evetts Haley, all of whom found him a walking encyclopedia of Texas history. Yet he retained his deep-seated suspicion of the press. During one waterfront strike, a reporter from the New York office of the Associated Press telephoned to ask him for an interview. "That's just fine," answered Hamer with a laugh. "And would you please tell the New York office of the Associated Press that I kindly asked them to go to hell?"[10]

Even in middle age, Hamer remained a mass of contradictions. Like most Americans, he strongly opposed communism and socialism. He also disagreed with the social-welfare programs of Roosevelt's New

Deal. As he once remarked to a friend, "Free enterprise made this country what it is, didn't it? We are becoming altogether too socialistic and too paternalistic. They are becoming substitutes for real democracy." But he did not follow that philosophy in his personal life and often helped those in need. Once, he was in a shore store when a woman came in and ordered a large supply of children's shoes. Upon learning that the shoes were for an orphanage, he quietly told the sales clerk, "I want you to do me a favor. Put the shoes on my bill, and send them on out there now." On another occasion, a youth gave him a tip that led to an arrest and payment of a large reward. Hamer endorsed the check to the boy, saying, "Son, I want you to use the check and go to school." When Joe Fulbright, an ex-Ranger friend, died in 1940, he left a destitute wife with two young girls. Frank and Gladys gave them money, and Frank found Fulbright's widow a job with the county clerk's office in Austin. Though Hamer despised lawbreakers, he routinely assisted reformed criminals by using his influence to obtain pardons and paroles. As late as the 1970s, ex-convicts and their families would appear at his Austin home, seeking the help of Captain Hamer, only to be told that he was long dead.[11]

As World War II approached, Hamer took a keen interest in the rise of the Axis powers. He abhorred fascism in all its forms, whether home-grown like the Klan or the new terror of Nazism. In September 1939, two days after the United Kingdom declared war on Germany, he wired the King of England offering fifty Texas volunteers to provide waterfront protection against sabotage. He received a prompt reply: "The King greatly appreciates your offer. Please apply British embassy, Washington." Before Frank could complete the arrangements, the U.S. government stopped the plan in accordance with neutrality laws. In March 1941 he offered to organize a thousand-man voluntary defense unit made up of former law officers and servicemen. This too did not come to fruition, but for Hamer, the war would hit home in the cruelest way imaginable.[12]

His eldest boy, Frank Jr., joined the Marine Corps after Pearl Harbor and served as a pilot. Billy married and had a daughter in 1942, but the union was not a success. After divorcing in 1944, Billy also joined the Marine Corps. One night in May 1945, Hamer and Rogers were asleep in their room in Houston's Rice Hotel when the phone rang. Frank answered, and it was Gladys, telling him she had received a telegram from the War Department. On March 7, Billy had been killed in action on Iwo Jima. Recalled Rogers, "Cap told me what had happened, then pulled a chair over to a window and opened it, then looked out. He sat there for almost two days and nights, it seemed, and must have smoked a half carton of cigarettes. He didn't eat, or drink, or sleep during the whole time, and wouldn't even answer the telephone."[13]

The death of his son was the greatest shock of Hamer's life. By all accounts, he changed greatly. Photographs of him taken later in 1945 show a man who looked eighty-one, not sixty-one. Never much of an imbiber, he began to drink, sometimes heavily. One day, Lone Wolf Gonzaullas ran into Hamer at a convention in Houston and was stunned to smell liquor on his breath. Before that, Gonzaullas had never seen his former captain take a drink.[14]

On September 9, 1948, Frank received an urgent telephone call from Coke Stevenson. Hamer's friend needed him immediately in the little Hispanic community of Alice in South Texas. Stevenson, a candidate for U.S. senator, was embroiled in the closest senate primary race in American history. After serving as governor of Texas from 1941 to 1947, he ran for the senate against Lyndon B. Johnson in 1948. Stevenson represented the traditional wing of the party and advocated states' rights and a return to prewar isolationism; Johnson, a World War II veteran, was supported by a younger, less conservative base that included Mexican Americans and blacks. The Democratic primary resulted in a runoff election on August 28. When the final returns were tallied by September 2, almost a million ballots had been cast, and Stevenson was announced the victor by just 362 votes. But, as was customary in Texas elections, late returns trickled in, and Stevenson's lead began to drop. The next day, a corrected return came in from the heavily Mexican American precinct 13 in Alice, Jim Wells County, showing two hundred additional votes for Johnson. LBJ now appeared to be the victor by eighty-seven votes.[15]

Coke Stevenson smelled a rat. He well knew that boss rule still prevailed in South Texas. Archie Parr, the "Duke of Duval," had died in 1942 and was succeeded by his equally corrupt son, George. Parr's chief henchman in Jim Wells County from 1940 to 1950 was Luis Salas, a burly deputy sheriff. "We had the law to ourselves there," Salas later boasted. "It was a lawless son of a bitch. We had iron control. If a man was opposed to us, we'd put him out of business. We could tell any election judge, 'Give us 80 per cent of the vote, the other guy 20 per cent.' We had it made in every election." Though Stevenson was honest, he had nonetheless taken advantage of the Parr machine and its bloc voting. In his two gubernatorial campaigns, Parr had delivered to him the South Texas vote. But Stevenson defied the Parr machine by appointing an independent district attorney in Laredo County to clean up prostitution around the huge Laredo Army Airfield. George Parr, who had his own man earmarked for the post, was furious and withdrew his support. Parr threw all his efforts behind LBJ, whom he credited with obtaining a pardon from President Harry S. Truman for his 1932 conviction for income-tax evasion.[16]

During the 1948 runoff, the six counties controlled by George Parr delivered 93 percent of the vote to LBJ. Given the prevalence of bloc voting, this was not surprising. It was Parr's sudden discovery of two hundred new votes in precinct 13 that raised Stevenson's ire. He sent three lawyers to investigate: Callan Graham, James Gardner, and Kellis Dibrell, the latter two ex-FBI agents. Graham recalled that, before leaving Austin, they were warned "not to wear a suit coat because it might be dangerous, that they were known to kill people down there." In Alice they called on Tom Donald, the secretary of the Jim Wells County Democratic Committee, who worked at the town bank, owned by George Parr. They told Donald that they represented Coke Stevenson and asked to see the poll list from precinct 13. When he refused, they showed him a book on election law, saying, "Well's here's the law right here. It says any citizen has the right to see it."

"I know that," Donald replied. "But you can't see them because they're locked up in that vault, and I'm not going to unlock the vault. That's why you can't see them."

The lawyers were stymied, and they called Coke Stevenson in Austin. His decision was instantaneous: get Frank Hamer. Early the next morning, September 10, Stevenson and Hamer made the 150-mile drive from Austin south through the brush country to Alice. They met two of the lawyers, Dibrell and Gardner, in the Alice Hotel. At first Dibrell was unimpressed with Hamer, saying, "He appeared to be an old man." While they discussed the situation, rumors swirled through town. "Coke Stevenson's here! And Frank Hamer's with him!" Hamer had investigated electoral fraud and political violence in South Texas in 1918, 1922, 1928, and 1932. He knew exactly what to do.[17]

Frank told the others to take off their coats so the townsfolk could see that they weren't carrying guns. Hamer, on the other hand, removed his coat so people could see Old Lucky tucked into his waistband. He had a special Ranger commission that authorized him to carry a gun. It was nine in the morning when they stepped out of the hotel and began the two-hundred-yard walk to the bank. In a scene out of an Old West drama, he and Stevenson walked shoulder to shoulder, followed by the two lawyers. People clustered on the streets and sidewalks, gasping, "Hamer, Hamer!" Three gunmen toting Winchesters had taken up positions blocking the door of the bank. A group of Hispanic *pistoleros* gathered on the street in front of the bank. "The veteran captain was well known to every man there," said one witness. Dibrell recalled, "Everywhere you turned there were people with guns on. When Frank Hamer walked down the street, those clusters of people parted."

Hamer stepped up to the band of *pistoleros* in the street.

"Git!" was all he said. They immediately moved back. Then he approached the three riflemen in front of the door.

"Fall back," he ordered. They obeyed.

Stevenson and the lawyers went inside the bank, while Hamer stood in the doorway. Several Parr henchmen tried to enter, but he blocked the way. Frank never touched his Colt.

There was another *pistolero* inside the bank—Luis Salas, the deputy sheriff and election judge for precinct 13. Salas later said, "I was threatened by a man with Frank Hamer if I did not give them the returns." He explained that the man was not Stevenson, Hamer, or Dibrell, thus leaving only ex-FBI agent Gardner. Salas told Stevenson, "You're mad this time because the votes didn't go your way as before." Stevenson stepped into the office of Tom Donald and demanded to see the poll list and the tally sheet. This time Donald complied. Dibrell and Gardner immediately noted that the last 201 names were all in alphabetical order, written in the same hand and the same ink. When they started copying them down, Donald got cold feet and exclaimed, "No, you can't do that." He snatched the list away. Dibrell recalled, "We didn't have a court order or anything and legally there was nothing we could do about it." By this time Gardner had also looked at the tally list and noted that the total, showing 965 votes for Johnson, had been falsified. The actual number was 765, for someone had turned the seven into a nine.[18]

The two lawyers stepped outside and quickly wrote down as many names as they could remember from the poll list. Then, accompanied by Hamer, they set out to find the purported voters. They located several Hispanics who signed affidavits swearing that they had not voted. Three more people on the list turned out to be dead. With a few affidavits in hand, Hamer and Stevenson drove back to Austin, leaving the lawyers in Alice to seek additional proof of fraud. The visit by Stevenson and Hamer to Alice was widely reported in the press that evening. The next day, Johnson blasted the pair, declaring, "I am not surprised that Coke, accompanied by a major oil company special ranger, would be meddling with tally sheets in counties that he lost." He complained that Stevenson, "who announced a few days ago that he was going hunting and fishing, shows up with a pistol-packing pal, commissioned only to protect the properties of the Texas Company, and starts going over tally sheets."[19]

At the same time, LBJ's attorneys filed a civil action in Austin, naming Stevenson, Hamer, Dibrell, and the Jim Wells County Democratic Executive Committee as defendants. The lawsuit alleged that "Stevenson, together with Defendants Dibrell and Hamer, have gone into Jim Wells County and, by threats and intimidation, have attempted to have the votes of one or more of the voting boxes in said County eliminated from the official canvass and official returns and to have new returns forwarded to the State Executive Committee, taking votes from Plaintiff

George Parr's triumphant henchmen pose with Ballot Box 13 in 1948. *Author's collection*

in sufficient number to change the result of the election." The judge promptly granted a temporary restraining order stopping any recount of the vote.[20]

This began a battle royal between some of the state's most powerful lawyers.

By filing a lawsuit first, LBJ's attorneys managed to prevent a recount in Jim Wells County. Stevenson then challenged the election results before the Democratic State Central Committee, which rejected his claim by a vote of 29 to 28, a result that reflected the schism between the party's two wings. Stevenson next filed an election contest in federal court and obtained a preliminary injunction that allowed time for a full hearing into the balloting in Jim Wells County. Because the evidence of fraud was so persuasive, LBJ wanted to avoid that at all costs. His attorneys rushed to Washington, D.C., where they obtained a ruling from Supreme Court Justice Hugo Black that set aside the injunction. Stevenson appealed Black's order to the full Supreme Court, which later ruled that the federal courts had no jurisdiction over a state election for U.S. senator. This was a complete victory for Lyndon B. Johnson. In November his name appeared on the general ballot, and he was easily elected over his Republican opponent.[21]

Frank Hamer was furious. For a year, he seethed over the charges LBJ had brought against him and Stevenson. In October 1949 he filed a criminal action against Johnson for "false swearing." He alleged that LBJ had lied in his lawsuit by alleging that Hamer attempted to have the voting results changed by "threats and intimidation." Hamer appeared before the Travis County grand jury, which, after considering the evidence, refused to charge LBJ. Johnson told reporters that he was not surprised by Hamer's action, "because it's pretty much in keeping with the line that's been followed all along." Over the years, LBJ and his supporters insisted that Ballot Box 13 had never been falsified. That was the prevailing and accepted narrative until 1977, when Luis Salas, then seventy-six, was overcome with a tardy attack of guilt. To the Associated Press, he made a full confession of the election fraud, explaining how George Parr had ordered him to add two hundred extra votes. Stevenson and Hamer were finally vindicated.[22]

The 1948 campaign would ordinarily be remembered as just another dismal, crooked South Texas election—except for one critical fact. It turned out to be arguably the most important Senate race of the twentieth century. By paving the road for LBJ's journey to the White House, it changed the course of history. Americans' views of war, federal power, and civil rights changed profoundly under Johnson's presidency. And it was a double irony for Frank Hamer. As a white supremacist who nonetheless protected the rights of blacks in Texas, he had failed in his efforts to help Coke Stevenson, which in turn opened the way to LBJ's presidency and his success in passing the Civil Rights Act, which provided civil rights protections for all African Americans. Hamer's failure was one of his greatest triumphs.

For years, Gladys and Frank Jr. had been trying to persuade Frank to allow his life story to be written. Frank had long known Stuart N. Lake, the author of the bestselling 1931 biography *Wyatt Earp: Frontier Marshal*. Frank Jr. said that his father "read it from cover to cover many times." The book was so successful that it had been made into three films, the best known being *My Darling Clementine* in 1946. As early as 1940, Lake told a reporter that he was working with Hamer on his biography, but nothing came of it. In 1948 Frank Jr. began a correspondence with Lake, and his father soon signed a book contract with the author. Hamer didn't need the money, for his security business was lucrative: in 1944 he had grossed $67,500 from Texaco. Lake quickly realized that he could make more money from a film about Hamer. He had already helped write several screenplays, including the hugely popular *Wells Fargo* (1937) and *The Westerner* (1940). He began talking to actor Joel McCrea about starring as Hamer in a feature film, with Lake to provide the script. But Lake and McCrea were unable to interest any Hollywood producers in the project, and Lake soon began working on another blockbuster, *Winchester '73*, which was released in 1950. By this time, Hamer despaired of the book ever being written. His son wrote to Lake, "He has become more and more impatient as time wears on, and seems to worry about his not hearing from you. His friends have passed away one at a time and he always remarks, 'I guess I'll be next.'" By the end of 1950, Lake had lost interest and turned his attention to other projects, in particular the television series *The Life and Legend of Wyatt Earp*. He never wrote the life story of Frank Hamer.[23]

In 1948 Frank had turned the day-to-day operations of his security company over to Roy T. Rogers. He still remained active, and in March 1949 agreed to be chief of security for the grand opening of the luxurious Shamrock Hotel in Houston. The owner, oilman Glenn McCarthy, known as the King of the Wildcatters, threw one of the biggest parties Texas ever saw. McCarthy invited 150 film stars and Hollywood celebrities and sent Hamer and Rogers to escort them to Houston. Frank was accompanied to California by a friend, Paul Hochuli, an entertainment writer for the *Houston Press*. Hochuli recalled, "Captain Frank didn't like to fly, so we took the S.P. to Los Angeles." As they passed Marfa and El Paso, Hamer's thoughts drifted back to his early years. "He knew every foot of the country," wrote Hochuli, "and as we rode through in bourbon-and-branch-water comfort, he spun many a yarn. On that hill, some gunman holed up, had to be blasted out. Behind that rise, some horse thieves were surprised, and their loot recovered. Right along here, some *hombres malos* had crossed over from Mexico, killed and looted— and paid for their invasion." But, try as he might, Hochuli could not get him to talk abut the killing of Bonnie and Clyde.

In Hollywood, Frank had two wishes. He wanted to meet the boxer Jack Dempsey and the film star Roy Rogers. Hochuli arranged for them to visit Rogers's home. Said Hochuli, "Rogers was impressed with the sinewy, weather-leathered Frank Hamer, showed him his gun collection— and asked for an autograph." Rogers asked to see Old Lucky, and Hamer obligingly handed it over. "Captain Frank felt undressed without that pistol," said Hochuli. A special train was chartered for the trip back to Houston. Its passengers included Dorothy Lamour, Robert Ryan, Ward Bond, Van Heflin, and Stan Laurel. Hochuli had managed to loosen Hamer up, for a reporter spotted him in one car regaling actors Andy Devine and J. Carrol Naish with stories of his Ranger career. They arrived in Houston on St. Patrick's Day for the grand opening, which also happened to be Hamer's birthday. Three thousand partygoers, including the elite of Texas society, crammed into the hotel, and another fifty thousand crowded about outside. The bash made national news and became the basis for the climactic scenes in Edna Ferber's popular 1952 novel *Giant* and the film version of 1956.[24]

Despite advancing age, Hamer sought a post on the Texas Public Safety Commission in 1951, but he was unsuccessful. The following year, he campaigned for Dwight D. Eisenhower as president and later lobbied the Eisenhower administration for appointment as U.S. marshal of the Western District of Texas, insisting that he was qualified "physically, mentally, and morally." Again his efforts were in vain. As late as April 1954, he was protecting nonunion workers on an oil-pipeline job near Beaumont. He still had a special Ranger commission, and, when asked by reporters for his authority to carry a gun, he replied tersely, "Ask Governor Allan Shivers."[25]

Soon after, Hamer suffered a heat stroke, and his health began to fail. For the next year, he rarely left his home. On the night of July 10, 1955, he suffered a heart attack and died peacefully in his sleep. His funeral was conducted by Ranger chaplain P. B. Hill, and the pallbearers

Frank Hamer visiting Roy Rogers at the film star's Southern California home in 1949. *Courtesy of the Texas Ranger Hall of Fame and Museum, Waco, Texas*

included his old friends Bill Sterling, Lee Simmons, Tom Hickman, and Charlie Miller. He was laid to rest in Austin Memorial Park. The *Houston Chronicle* eulogized, "Captain Hamer was a man of action, not words," and pointed out that "many exciting events of his long career may never be known. He wouldn't talk about them." Commented another journal, "There were giants in those days. The passing of Frank Hamer is a melancholy reminder that we shall see few of his kind." Added *The Dallas Morning News*, "A man who dealt in jeopardy and death for forty years without either carelessness or malevolence could not escape legend while he lived. How much the less, then, can his fame escape it now."[26]

Though Hamer's celebrity in Texas remained constant during the next twelve years, his national fame gradually waned. Then, in 1967, Warner Brothers released the film *Bonnie and Clyde,* starring heartthrob Warren Beatty as Clyde and the glamorous Faye Dunaway as Bonnie.

A cinematic masterpiece, heavily fictionalized, it was a runaway hit, winning two Academy Awards. Yet Gladys Hamer was apoplectic at its portrayal of her beloved husband. Played by Denver Pyle, Hamer is the villain. After being captured by the gang and humiliated, he kills Bonnie and Clyde in revenge. The filmmakers foolishly used Hamer's real name in their screenplay. Gladys retained Joe Jamail, one of the top trial lawyers in Texas, to sue Warner Brothers for defamation, invasion of privacy, and unauthorized use of Hamer's name. The studio fought the lawsuit, but when Jamail insisted on taking Warren Beatty's deposition, Warner Brothers folded its tent. The studio paid $20,000 in settlement, a significant sum at the time.[27]

But the damage had been done. Succeeding generations would recall Frank Hamer as the bad guy who killed the romantic outlaw duo. Gladys tried to offset the hit movie by sponsoring a biography, *I'm Frank Hamer,* written by two Texas history buffs, John Jenkins and Gordon Frost. Hastily written and skimpily researched, it was a far cry from the film it was intended to rebut. Not surprisingly, it made no mention at all of Hamer's first marriage and ignored Gladys's sexual infidelities and her role in igniting the Johnson-Sims feud. It also ignored Hamer's struggles against lynchers and the Klan.

Frank Hamer played an important role in American history. He was part of the forces that dragged Texas—kicking and screaming—into the twentieth century. He started life as a humble cowboy and ended up the most extraordinary lawman of his era. His controversies had been many; his victories, even greater. From his ironfisted protection of African Americans to his war against the immoral Texas Bankers Association, he showed what a lone Ranger, armed with little but courage and a Colt .45, could accomplish. Yet even he had difficulty in reconciling his violent life with the scruples of modern society. As he once said, "When our boys are overseas, they are fighting for the safety of their country and people. Likewise, peace officers fight for the safety of the public. Yet if they have to kill a man in the line of duty, they are usually criticized severely by the people they are defending." Hamer's words ring just as true today.[28]

In 2013 a larger-than-life bronze statue depicting Hamer as a young lawman was unveiled in Navasota. It is one of the few tangible reminders of his epic life. As horseback lawman, border gunfighter, manhunter, outlaw killer, Ranger captain, town tamer, investigator, battler against the Klan, and gangbuster, he had no peer. One day he might be remembered as the greatest lawman of the twentieth century. But history can be cruel, casting a blinding light on some deeds while relegating others to the shadows of oblivion. In our collective memory, Frank Hamer still remains the man who killed Bonnie and Clyde. Perhaps this book can help restore him to his proper place in the American story.

ACKNOWLEDGMENTS

I was two years old when Frank Hamer died. Like most of my generation, I was introduced to him as the villain in *Bonnie and Clyde*. Fascinated by the outlaw duo, I read everything I could find about them, even sneaking home a copy of *Playboy* magazine in 1968 that contained an interview with W. D. Jones. When my local library got a copy of *I'm Frank Hamer*, I was surprised to read the truth about Hamer's career, or at least what its authors presented as the truth. As the years passed, I realized that an in-depth biography of Frank Hamer was long overdue.

My biggest disappointment in researching this book was that Frank's beloved stepdaughter Beverly Sims died at age 101 during the very week I was booking my flight to Texas to interview her. Fortunately, my friend Bill O'Neal had conducted a lengthy interview with Beverly in 2008 and was kind enough to share his notes with me. Many others helped me in my research. I owe special thanks to Harrison Hamer, great-nephew of Frank, for graciously hosting me at his home near San Saba and sharing with me his family archives and photos. I received similar assistance from Travis Hamer, great-grandson of Frank, and his wife, Morgan Taylor Hamer, who kindly provided me with copies of many letters, documents, and photographs. Without their generous help, this book could not have been written.

No book on Texas history could be completed without the assistance of Donaly Brice, historian and archivist at the Texas State Archives. I don't know anyone who has been credited by so many authors in so many books. Donaly left no stone unturned in his search for data about Hamer's Ranger career. I am grateful for his help, and proud to count him as a personal friend. Kathy Hatchett, niece of Frank Hamer's first wife, Mollie Cameron, turned out to be a gold mine of information about a heretofore unknown period of Hamer's life. She generously shared letters, photos, and family reminiscences about Frank and Mollie.

It is more than difficult to research a Texas lawman from California. Taronda Schulz has long studied Frank Hamer's life; her grandfather, Joe Fulbright, was one of Hamer's Rangers. Taronda was literally my boots on the ground. Despite my numerous research trips to Texas, I could not do it all. Taronda was always there for me to run down that missing document, visit that remote courthouse, or answer my never-ending questions. I cannot thank her enough for her unselfish help.

Many others deserve credit for their assistance with this book: Bob Alexander, Bob Berryman, Anne Collier, Russell Cushman, Paul Cool, Laura David, Kathy Day, Sam Dolan, Doug Dukes, L. J. "Boots" Hinton, Kurt House, Jacob Koff, Randy Lish, Jerry Lobdill, Bob McCubbin, Rick Miller, Chuck Parsons, Patterson Smith, Harold Weiss, Frederica Wyatt, and Roy Young. Special thanks to Byron Johnson and Christina Stopka, of the Texas Ranger Hall of Fame and Museum in Waco; Lisa Sharik, of the Texas Military Forces Museum in Austin; the staff of the Briscoe Center at the University of Texas; the staff of *The Junction Eagle* newspaper; Pat Faught, of the San Saba County Clerk's office; Kim Smith, associate director, Cattle Raisers Museum, Fort Worth; and Aimee L. Morgan, archivist, Special Collections at Stanford University.

I would also like to thank my fellow members of the Wild West History Association for their fellowship and support. The association's bimonthly journal and annual rendezvous are highly recommended. Anyone interested in the history of the Old West is encouraged to join this organization.

To my agent, Claire Gerus, and my editor, Peter Joseph, go my heartfelt thanks for making this book much better than I wrote it. And, lastly, my everlasting gratitude to my wife, Marta Diaz, for her love and support in all my endeavors.

NOTES

1. A COWBOY OF THE HILL COUNTRY

1. Bill Neal, *Vengeance is Mine: The Scandalous Love Triangle That Triggered the Boyce-Sneed Feud* (Denton: University of North Texas Press, 2011), p. 189. On Texas feuds, see C. L. Sonnichsen, *I'll Die Before I'll Run: The Story of the Great Feuds of Texas* (New York: Harper and Brothers, 1951) and *Ten Texas Feuds* (Albuquerque: University of New Mexico Press, 1957, 1971). On the Sutton-Taylor feud, see *Chuck Parsons, The Sutton-Taylor Feud: The Deadliest Blood Feud in Texas* (Denton: University of North Texas Press, 2009).

2. U.S. Army Pension File, Franklin A. Hamer, National Archives; H. Gordon Frost and John H. Jenkins, *I'm Frank Hamer, The Life of a Texas Peace Officer* (Austin: Pemberton Press, 1968), pp. 3–4; Texas State Genealogical Society Supplemental Form, Harrison L. Hamer collection.

3. J. Evetts Haley, interview with Frank Hamer, Houston, December 6, 1943, Haley Memorial Library.

4. Affidavit of Helena E. Hart, February 18, 1928, Franklin Hamer pension file; *San Saba News*, May 21, 1942; Frost and Jenkins, *I'm Frank Hamer*, p. 6; William Warren Sterling, *Trails and Trials of a Texas Ranger* (published by author, 1959), p. 421.

5. Clarke Newlon, "Outlaw Tamer of the New West," *Startling Detective Adventures*, vol. 13, no. 76 (November 1934), p. 38; Byron Utrecht, "Frank Hamer, Crusader," *Texas Parade* (November 1957), p. 51; Frost and Jenkins, *I'm Frank Hamer*, pp. 5–6, 66; Bill O'Neal, *The Johnson-Sims Feud: Romeo and Juliet, West Texas Style* (Denton: University of North Texas Press, 2010), p. 9.

6. Walter Prescott Webb, *The Texas Rangers: A Century of Frontier Defense* (Austin: University of Texas Press, 1935), p. 521.

7. Utrecht, "Frank Hamer, Crusader," p. 52.

8. Webb, *Texas Rangers*, pp. 521–22; Newlon, "Outlaw Tamer," p. 38.

9. Author interview with Harrison Hamer, May 23, 2011.

10. Newlon, "Outlaw Tamer," p. 63; author interview with Harrison Hamer, May 23,

2011; Robert M. Utley, *Lone Star Justice: The First Century of the Texas Rangers* (New York: Oxford University Press, 2002), pp. 8–10, 17.

11. Frost and Jenkins, *I'm Frank Hamer*, p. 7; Harrison Kinney, "Frank Hamer, Texas Ranger," *American Gun*, vol. 1, no. 2 (1961), p. 82. Kinney obtained much of the information in his article from Gladys Hamer and Frank Jr. Harrison Kinney to author, October 7, 2011.

12. Kinney, "Frank Hamer, Texas Ranger," p. 82; Sterling, *Trails and Trials of a Texas Ranger*, p. 421.

13. Studies of honor in the South are Bertram Wyatt Brown, *Southern Honor: Ethics and Behavior in the Old South* (New York: Oxford University Press, 1982), esp. chaps. 2, 6, and 13, and Edward L. Ayers, *Vengeance and Justice: Crime and Punishment in the 19th Century American South* (New York: Oxford University Press, 1984), 9–33, 263–68. On the legal doctrine of no duty to retreat, see Richard Maxwell Brown, *No Duty to Retreat: Violence and Values in American History and Society* (New York: Oxford University Press, 1991), pp. 3–37.

14. N. A. Jennings, *A Texas Ranger* (Norman: University of Oklahoma Press, 1997), p. 113; Glenn Shirley, *Shotgun for Hire: The Story of "Deacon" Jim Miller, Killer of Pat Garrett* (Norman: University of Oklahoma Press, 1970), p. 56.; Bill O'Neal, *Encyclopedia of Western Gunfighters* (Norman: University of Oklahoma Press, 1979), p. 231.

15. John Boessenecker, "Genesis of the Gunfighter: Two Accounts from the 1880s," *Wild West History Association Journal*, vol. 1, no. 1 (February 2008).

16. *Calgary Daily Herald*, June 9, 1934; Frost and Jenkins, *I'm Frank Hamer*, pp. 8–10; Lee Simmons, *Assignment Huntsville* (Austin: University of Texas Press, 1957), p. 177; Glen Alyn, ed., *I Say Me for a Parable: The Oral Autobiography of Mance Lipscomb, Texas Bluesman* (New York: W. W. Norton & Co., 1993), pp. 156–57. The only detailed account of this incident was provided by Frank's brother, Harrison Hamer, to authors Frost and Jenkins. No reference to it appears in the *San Saba News* of the period or in the San Saba or Mills County court records. Harrison called the assailant "Dan McSwain," but San Saba County property records show that his last name was McSween. San Saba Clerk, Deed Records, vol. 39, p. 265, vol. 40, p. 265.

17. Frost and Jenkins, *I'm Frank Hamer*, p. 15; *San Saba News*, June 10, 1954; San Saba Clerk, Deed Records, vol. 40, p. 265. Daniel McSween died on February 20, 1909, and is buried in Crandall cemetery in Kaufman County.

18. *El Paso Herald*, May 11, 1915; Mike Cox, *Texas Ranger Tales* (Lanham, MD: Republic of Texas Press, 1997), p. 230.

19. Frost and Jenkins, *I'm Frank Hamer*, p. 16; Jeffrey Burton, *The Deadliest Outlaws: The Ketchum Gang and the Wild Bunch* (Denton: University of North Texas Press, 2009), pp. 327–28, 449.

20. Webb, *Texas Rangers*, pp. 522–523.

21. Ibid., pp. 522, 524; Newlon, "Outlaw Tamer," p. 58.

22. Webb, *Texas Rangers*, pp. 530–31.

23. Sanford C. Hamer to Flavious Hamer, November 22, 1905, Harrison Hamer collection; Webb, *Texas Rangers*, p. 525; Frost and Jenkins, *I'm Frank Hamer*, p. 20.

24. Sterling, *Trails and Trials of a Texas Ranger*, p. 418.

25. Webb, *Texas Rangers*, pp. 525–26; Frost and Jenkins, *I'm Frank Hamer*, pp. 20–21.

26. Frost and Jenkins, *I'm Frank Hamer*, p. 22.

27. Descriptive List and Oaths of Service, Jim Moore; Enlistment, Oath of Service, and Description, E. S. McGee, October 7, 1905; Captain John H. Rogers, Scout Report, April 15, 1906. The Texas Ranger and adjutant general records and correspondence cited in the notes are from the Texas State Archives.

28. Enlistment, Oath of Service, and Description, Francis Augustus Hamer, April 21, 1906; "Captain Frank Hamer, A Deadly Shot," *Frontier Times*, vol. 7, no. 2 (November 1929), p. 53.

2. TEXAS RANGER

1. On the early history of the Texas Rangers, see Utley, *Lone Star Justice*. On the Texas State Police, see Barry A. Crouch and Donaly E. Brice, *The Governor's Hounds* (Austin: University of Texas Press, 2011).

2. *Everybody's Magazine*, vol. 34 (1916), p. 779; Webb, *Texas Rangers*, p. 458.

3. Paul N. Spellman, *Captain John H. Rogers, Texas Ranger* (Denton: University of North Texas Press, 2003); Sterling, *Trails and Trials of a Texas Ranger*, p. 381.

4. Kinney, "Frank Hamer, Texas Ranger," p. 83.

5. Rogers, Scout Report, July 2, 1906; Monthly Return, Company C, June 1906; *San Antonio Express*, September 18, 1905; *Fort Worth Star-Telegram*, September 20, 1905.

6. Rogers, Scout Report, August 31, 1906.

7. Rogers, Scout Report, August 31, 1906; Alyn, *I Say Me for a Parable*, pp. 164–75. Lipscomb recalled incorrectly that Hamer had arrested the whole bunch.

8. The *Victoria Advocate*, September 26, 1906; *Fort Worth Star-Telegram*, September 24, October 1, 1906, April 21, November 7, 1907; The *Dallas Morning News*, September 24, 1906, June 8, 1908.

9. *Austin American-Statesman*, July 18, 1948.

10. "Mule Not Monk, Hamer Protests," 1954 newspaper clipping, Frank Hamer scrapbook, author's collection; Cox, *Texas Ranger Tales*, pp. 183–90.

11. Rogers, Scout Report, November 13, 1906.

12. *Ibid.*

13. Rogers, Scout Report, December 1, 1906.

14. Ibid., *San Antonio Daily Light*, November 20, 22, 1906; The *Dallas Morning News*, November 24, 1906, January 7, 1907; The *Kansas City Star*, November 22, 1906; Lawrence D. Taylor, "The Magonista Revolt in Baja California," *Journal of San Diego History*, vol. 45, no. 1 (Winter 1999).

15. Rogers, Scout Report, December 1, 1906; *Del Rio Val Verde County Herald*, November 30, 1906; The *Galveston Daily News*, November 30, 1906; The *Dallas Morning News*, November 30, 1906.; *San Antonio Daily Light*, December 2, 1906.

16. *Del Rio Val Verde County Herald*, December 7, 1906; *San Angelo Press*, December 6, 1906; Thorndale *Thorn*, December 7, 1906; The *Galveston Daily News*, December 12, 1906.

17. John R. Rogers to John A. Hulen, December 8, 1906.

18. *Ibid.*; *San Angelo Press*, December 6, 1906.

19. Rogers to Hulen, December 8, 1906.

20. Ibid., Rogers, Scout Report, January 2, 1907; *Del Rio Val Verde County Herald*, December 7, 1906; The *Dallas Morning News*, December 3, 1906; J. Marvin Hunter and Noah H. Rose, *The Album of Gunfighters* (Bandera, TX: published by authors, 1951), p. 100.

21. Hunter and Rose, *Album of Gunfighters*, pp. 100, 200.

22. *San Angelo Press*, December 6, 1906; notarized statement by Frank A. Hamer Jr. to Raymond Brown, December 9, 1981, quoted in James D. Julia Catalog, Fall 2006 Firearms Auction.

23. Rogers, Scout Report, January 2, 1907; "Captain Frank Hamer, A Deadly Shot," p. 53; The *Dallas Morning News*, November 7, 1929. Wayne Gard also told this

story twice: first in The *Dallas Morning News,* June 28, 1948, and then in his popular book *Frontier Justice* (Norman: University of Oklahoma Press, 1949), p. 273.

24. Rogers, Scout Report, January 29, 1907.

25. Ibid., February 1, 1907; Kinney, "Frank Hamer, Texas Ranger," p. 86; Charles H. Harris III and Louis R. Sadler, *The Texas Rangers and the Mexican Revolution* (Albuquerque: University of New Mexico Press, 2004), p. 330; Sterling, *Trails and Trials of a Texas Ranger,* p. 426.

26. The *Galveston Daily News,* February 14, 1907; The *Dallas Morning News,* February 15, 1907; *Alpine Avalanche,* February 27, 1907, quoted in Kenneth Baxter Ragsdale, *Quicksilver: Terlingua and the Chisos Mining Company* (College Station: Texas A&M University Press, 1976), pp. 88–89.

27. Rogers, Scout Report, April 30, 1907.

28. Ibid., May 3, 1907; *San Antonio Daily Express,* June 14, 1907.

29. Rogers, Scout Report, May 15, 1907; Wells Fargo & Co. reward poster for David H. Barker, March 22, 1907; *Brownwood Bulletin,* June 25, 1909; *Fort Worth Star-Telegram,* June 25, 1909; The *Galveston Daily News,* June 26, 1909; Jonesboro (AR) *Daily News,* June 26, 1909; Newlon, "Outlaw Tamer," pp. 37, 62.

30. "Captain Frank Hamer, A Deadly Shot," p. 53.

3. ONE RIOT. ONE RANGER

1. Rogers, Scout Report, May 28, 1907; *San Antonio Gazette,* May 24, 1907; The *Galveston Daily News,* May 17, 1907; *City Directory of Austin* (Austin: J. B. Stephenson, 1907), p. 157.

2. Alwyn Barr, *Black Texans: A History of Negroes in Texas* (Norman: University of Oklahoma Press, 1996), p. 136; Darlene Clark Hine, Steven F. Lawson, Merline Pitre, *Black Victory: The Rise and Fall of the White Primary in Texas* (Columbia: University of Missouri Press, 2003), pp. 71–73; James W. Marquart, Sheldon Ekland-Olson, and Jonathan R. Sorensen, *The Rope, the Chair, and the Needle: Capital Punishment in Texas, 1923–1990* (Austin: University of Texas Press, 1994), pp. 6–7.

3. Bertram Wyatt-Brown, *The Shaping of Southern Culture: Honor, Grace, and War, 1760s–1880s* (Chapel Hill: University of North Carolina Press, 2001), pp. 282–93.

4. The *Dallas Morning News,* November 5, 1892; Fort Worth *Gazette,* November 5, 1892; The *Galveston Daily News,* November 5, 1892; *Muskogee* (OK) *Phoenix,* November 10, 1892.

5. The *Dallas Morning News,* December 2, 1903; October 12, November 17, 1906, June 18, 1907; *Fort Worth Star-Telegram,* October 10, 12, November 18, 1906, June 2, 1907.

6. The *Dallas Morning News,* April 27, 1907; *Fort Worth Star-Telegram,* April, 27, 1907; The *Shiner Gazette,* May 2, 1907; *San Antonio Light,* April 27, 1907; Sterling, *Trails and Trials of a Texas Ranger,* p. 360. On James Dunaway (1874–1924), see Bob Alexander, *Bad Company and Burnt Powder* (Denton: University of North Texas Press, 2014), chap. 9.

7. The *Dallas Morning News,* April 28, May 17, 1907; The *Galveston Daily News,* April 27, 1907, June 14, 1908; Chuck Parsons, *Captain John R. Hughes, Lone Star Ranger* (Denton: University of North Texas Press, 2011), pp. 201–02.

8. Rogers, Scout Report, August 1, 1907; The *Dallas Morning News,* May 3, 1907, June 17, 1908; The *Galveston Daily News,* June 13, 14, 16, 1908.

9. Rogers, Scout Report, October 8, 1907; The *Dallas Morning News,* September 15, 18, 1907.

10. Rogers, Scout Report, October 25, 1907; *San Antonio Light*, September 8, 1907; The *Dallas Morning News*, September 7, 1907; *Fort Worth Star-Telegram*, September 8, 1907.

11. The *Dallas Morning News*, August 9, 1897, November 10, 1900, February 2, 3, 1903, October 4, 1907; Fort Worth *Morning Register*, August 10, 1897. On the Jim Buchanan case, see Gary B. Borders, *A Hanging in Nacogdoches: Murder, Race, Politics, and Polemics in Texas's Oldest Town* (Austin: University of Texas Press, 2006).

12. Rogers, Scout Report, October 25, 1907; The *Dallas Morning News*, October 6, 1907. On Andrew Jackson Spradley (1853–1940), see Henry C. Fuller, *A Texas Sheriff: A. J. Spradley, Sheriff of Nacogdoches County for 30 Years* (Nacogdoches: Baker Printing, 1931).

13. Rogers, Scout Report, October 1, 25, 1907.

14. Ibid., October 25, 1907.

15. Rogers, Scout Report, October 25, 1907; The *Galveston Daily News*, October 6, 1907; Paul N. Spellman, *Captain John H. Rogers, Texas Ranger* (Denton: University of North Texas Press, 2006), pp. 145–46; Borders, *Hanging in Nacogdoches*, pp. 173–74.

16. The *Galveston Daily News*, October 27, 1907; Rogers, Scout Reports, May 20, June 21, 1908.

17. Rogers, Scout Report, October 25, 1907; The *Galveston Daily News*, November 26, 1906; The *Dallas Morning News*, November 26, 1906, October 27, 1907; Sonnichsen, *I'll Die Before I'll Run*, pp.234–41.

18. Rogers, Scout Report, October 25, 1907; *Fort Worth Star-Telegram*, October 27, 1907; The *Dallas Morning News*, October 25, 29, 1907; San Antonio *Light*, October 29, 1907; The *Galveston Daily News*, October 26, 1907, June 27, July 1, 1908.

19. Rogers, Scout Report, October 25, 1907.

20. Ibid., The *Galveston Daily News*, November 14, 16, 1907; The *Dallas Morning News*, November 16, 1907.

21. Rogers, Scout Report, December 27, 1907; Sonnichsen, *Ten Texas Feuds*, chap. 8.

22. Newlon, "Outlaw Tamer," p. 38.

23. Rogers, Scout Report, November 30, 1907; *Houston Post*, December 21, 1907.

24. Rogers, Scout Reports, January–April 1908; The *Dallas Morning News*, April 20, 1908.

25. The *Dallas Morning News*, August 11, 1892; Ranger service records of Oscar Latta, Texas State Library and Archives.

26. Rogers, Scout Reports, May–June 1908.

27. *Palestine Daily Herald*, June 23, 1908; The *Dallas Morning News*, June 22, 1908; *Fort Worth Star-Telegram*, June 22, 1908.

28. The *Dallas Morning News*, June 23, 1908; Galveston *Daily News*, June 22, 23, 1908.

29. Rogers, Scout Report, June 21, 1908; *Palestine Daily Herald*, June 23, 1908; The *Dallas Morning News*, June 23, 1908, December 18, 1909; *Fort Worth Star-Telegram*, December 17, 1909; *Wright v. State* (1909) 120 Southwestern Reporter 458.

30. Rogers, Scout Report, July 7, 1908; The *Dallas Morning News*, July 2, 4, November 9, 1908, January 14, 1926; The *Galveston Daily News*, June 23, 24, 26, 27, 28, 30, July 1, November 8, 9, 1908.

31. Rogers, Scout Report, July 9, 1908; The *Dallas Morning News*, July 13, 1908; The *Galveston Daily News*, July 12, 1908.

32. The *Galveston Daily News*, July 15, 1908.

33. *Davis v. Mississippi* (1969) 394 U.S. 721.

34. The *Galveston Daily News*, July 16, 1908.

35. The *Dallas Morning News*, July 15, 1908; The *Galveston Daily News*, July 17, 23, 1908.

36. The *Dallas Morning News,* July 16, 17, 1909; The *Galveston Daily News,* July 17, 1908.

37. Rogers, Scout Report, July 15, 1908.

38. The *Dallas Morning News,* August 29, December 3, 1908, February 13, 1909; The *Galveston Daily News,* July 23, 25, December 18, 1908, February 13, 1909.

39. Rogers, Scout Report, September 23, 1908; *Fort Worth Star-Telegram,* September 27, 1908; The *Galveston Daily News,* September 26, 1908.

40. "Captain Frank Hamer, A Deadly Shot," p. 53; William J. Chambliss, ed., *Police and Law Enforcement* (Los Angeles: Sage Publications, 2011), pp. 200–01; William A. Geller and Michael Scott, *Deadly Force* (Washington, D.C.: Police Executive Research Forum, 1992), pp. 248–49.

41. Rogers, Scout Reports, July 24, September 25, 1908.

42. Rogers, Scout Report, October 15, 1908; *Newton v. State* (1910) 125 *Southwestern Reporter* 908–09; The *Dallas Morning News,* September 14, 15, 17, 19, October 17, 1908, February 24, 1910; The *Galveston Daily News,* October 16, 1908.

43. The *Galveston Daily News,* October 30, 1908; *Big Spring Weekly Herald,* March 3, 1944; *Victoria Advocate,* January 27, 1912; Discharge paper, Oscar Latta, July 15, 1909; Harris and Sadler, *The Texas Rangers and the Mexican Revolution,* pp. 20, 580 n17.

44. J. W. Lennox to F. A. Hamer, July 22, 1908; Reilly Undertaking Co. to F. A. Hamer, July 31, 1908, Harrison Hamer collection; Pedigree Resource File, Sanford Clinton Hamer, familysearch.org; Census Population Schedules, Mason County, Texas, 1910.

45. Frank Hamer, Warrant of Authority and Descriptive List.

4. MARSHAL OF NAVASOTA

1. The *Dallas Morning News,* July 8, November 15, 1900; *Fort Worth Morning Register,* November 15, 1900; *Fort Worth Star-Telegram,* May 31, 1903; Lawrence C. Goodwyn, "Populist Dreams and Negro Rights: East Texas as a Case Study," in Daniel Pope, ed., *American Radicalism* (Malden, MA: Blackwell Publishers, 2001), pp. 174–90.

2. *Fort Worth Star-Telegram,* March 9, 1908; *Liberty Vindicator,* March 13, 1908; Kathy Day, "Frank Hamer," unpublished ms., p. 6.; Alyn, *I Say Me for a Parable,* pp. 143–47. According to Mance Lipscomb, the lynched man was named John Cameron, who stabbed his victim in self-defense and was shot dead in the jail by the mob, then strung up.

3. *Navasota Examiner-Review,* December 3, 1908; Webb, *Texas Rangers,* p. 526; Navasota city council minutes, cited in Day, "Frank Hamer," p. 6.

4. *Code of Criminal Procedure of the State of Texas* (1908), articles 506, 564, 568, 637, 807, and 1106.

5. Frost and Jenkins, *I'm Frank Hamer,* pp. 31–32; Day, "Frank Hamer," p. 7.

6. Kinney, "Frank Hamer, Texas Ranger," p. 83; Frost and Jenkins, *I'm Frank Hamer,* pp. 32, 37.

7. *Navasota Examiner,* May 3, 1979, quoted in Day, "Frank Hamer," p. 2.

8. Sterling, *Trails and Trials of a Texas Ranger,* pp. 420–21.

9. Alyn, *I Say Me for a Parable,* pp. 147, 158. Beau De Glen "Mance" Lipscomb (1895–1976) spent most of his life as a sharecropper and pioneer blues musician in Grimes County before achieving national prominence as a blues and folk artist in the 1960s.

10. *Ibid.,* p. 149.

11. *Ibid.,* pp. 148–49, 157.

12. Webb, *Texas Rangers,* p. 527; Frost and Jenkins, *I'm Frank Hamer,* pp. 37–38.

13. *Lynn v. State* (1894), 33 Tex. Crim. 153, 25 S.W. 779.

14. Webb, *Texas Rangers*, p. 527.
15. *Navasota Examiner-Review*, January 14, April 1, 29, June 3, October 14, 1909.
16. Alyn, *I Say Me for a Parable*, pp. 157–59.
17. Frost and Jenkins, *I'm Frank Hamer*, p. 42.
18. The *Galveston Daily News*, June 20, 1909; *Navasota Examiner-Review*, June 24, 1909.
19. *Navasota Examiner-Review*, August 5, September 16, 1909.
20. *Ibid.*, September 30, 1909. A year earlier, Oscar Coe had been shot and wounded in a Navasota pool-room fracas. *Victoria Advocate*, May 30, 1908.
21. Alyn, I *Say Me for a Parable*, p. 150, 153.
22. Webb, *Texas Rangers*, pp. 526–527.
23. Alyn, I *Say Me for a Parable*, pp. 154–55.
24. *Navasota Examiner-Review*, October 7, 1909. Frost and Jenkins in *I'm Frank Hamer*, p. 46, relying on an undated newspaper clipping from Hamer's scrapbook, incorrectly place this incident in Houston in 1912.
25. *Navasota Examiner-Review*, November 11, 18, 1909, July 28, September 15, 1910; Day, "Frank Hamer," pp. 10–11.
26. Mollie Cameron to F. A. Hamer, August 21, October 21, 1909, Kathy Hatchett collection; Bryan *Morning Eagle*, November 17, 1908; Alyn, *I Say Me for a Parable*, p. 153.
27. *Navasota Examiner-Review*, April 14, 1910; *Fort Worth Star-Telegram*, February 17, 1905, December 22, 1912; *Handbook of Texas Online*, Highway Development.
28. Galveston *Daily News*, May 26, 27, 1910; "Wreck Prevented by a Scratch," *Navasota Examiner-Review*, undated 1910 newspaper clipping, Frank Hamer scrapbook. Frost and Jenkins, in *I'm Frank Hamer*, pp. 40–41, incorrectly date this event as April 1, 1911.
29. Navasota city council minutes, cited in Day, "Frank Hamer," p. 11; Newlon, "Outlaw Tamer," p. 60; Little John's Auction Service Catalog, Charles Schreiner III collection, April 29, 2003, pp. 58–59.
30. Rogers, Scout Report, July 1910; *Navasota Examiner-Review*, July 28, 1910; *Beaumont Enterprise*, July 19, 1910.
31. Alyn, I *Say Me for a Parable*, pp. 155–56.
32. *Navasota Examiner-Review*, March 9, 1911; *Fort Worth Star-Telegram*, March 3, 1911; Frost and Jenkins, *I'm Frank Hamer*, pp. 41–42.
33. *Navasota Examiner-Review*, March 9, 1911.
34. Mollie Hamer to Mrs. Lou Emma Hamer, March 20, 1911, Harrison Hamer collection.
35. *Navasota Examiner-Review*, April 20, 1911; Alyn, I *Say Me for a Parable*, p. 161; Charles H. Harris III, Frances E. Harris, and Louis R. Sadler, *Texas Ranger Biographies* (Albuquerque: University of New Mexico Press, 2009), p. 14.
36. *Navasota Examiner-Review*, April 20, 1911.
37. A. P. Terrell, "To Whom It May Concern," May 10, 1911, Travis Hamer collection; Alyn, *I Say Me for a Parable*, p. 159.

5. FROM HOUSTON TO THE OPEN RANGE

1. *Houston: A History and Guide* (Houston: Anson Jones Press, 1942), pp. 105–08; Dwight Watson, *Race And the Houston Police Department, 1930–1990: A Change Did Come* (College Station: Texas A&M University Press, 2005), p. 14.
2. *Fort Worth Star-Telegram*, March 20, 1910; The *Galveston Daily News*, April 5, 1910, April 21, 1911; *Beaumont Enterprise*, May 16, 1910; Martin Friedland, *The*

Death of Old Man Rice: A True Story of Criminal Justice in America (New York: New York University Press, 1996), p. 349.

3. The *Galveston Daily News*, April 28, 1892, September 22, 1910, April 21, 1911; The *Dallas Morning News*, April 30, 1892; Harris, Harris, and Sadler, *Texas Ranger Biographies*, p. 315. On Henry Lee Ransom (1874–1918), see Pat Goodrich, *Captain Ransom, Texas Ranger: An American Hero* (Nappanee, IN: Evangel Press, 2007). Authored by Ransom's granddaughter, this is an uncritical biography that makes no mention of the many murders he committed during his bloody career.

4. The *Galveston Daily News*, October 26, November 5, 1910, April 20, 21, 22, 1911.

5. *Ibid.*, September 22, 1910, April 13, 21, 1911.

6. H. C. Waters, "History of the *Houston Press*," unpublished ms., circa 1935, Stanford University Library; J. Evetts Haley, interview with Frank Hamer, Austin, February 1, 1947, copy in Haley Memorial Library and History Center.

7. Alyn, *I Say Me for a Parable*, pp. 162–64.

8. John R. Hughes to Adjutant General J. O. Newton, April 11, 1909; J. O. Newton to Captain Thomas Ross, April 13, 1909; Thomas Ross to J. O. Newton, May 18, 1909; *San Antonio Light*, October 3, 1911; The *Galveston Daily News*, October 4, 1911; *Crockett Courier*, November 28, 1912; The *Llano News*, August 7, 1919, February 29, 1924.

9. *Houston Post*, February 6, 1912; The *Galveston Daily News*, February 7, 1912; Bryan *Daily Eagle and Pilot*, February 6, 1912.

10. The *Galveston Daily* News, February 29, March 2, 1912.

11. Templeton Peck, "Paul C. Edwards, from Newsman to Trustees' President," *Stanford Historical Society Bulletin*, vol. 11, no. 1 (Fall 1986), p. 5; Waters, "History of the *Houston Press*.

12. The *Galveston Daily News*, June 12, 18, 19, 20, 21, 22, July 1, 1912; *Muskogee Times Democrat*, June 14, 1912; The *Dallas Morning* News, June 30, 1912; Goodrich, *Captain Ransom, Texas Ranger*, pp. 112–20; Waters, "History of the *Houston Press*. Two former Rangers hired by Ransom as Houston police officers were Levi Davis and J. C. Stephenson. The *Galveston Daily News*, June 29, July 4, 1912.

13. *Crockett Courier*, November 28, 1912.

14. *Houston Press*, November 19, 1912.

15. *Houston Chronicle*, November 19, 1912. Errors in spelling of the participants' names in the newspaper accounts of this affair have been corrected.

16. "Accused Ex-Officer Still Out of City," undated 1912 Houston newspaper clipping, Frank Hamer scrapbook, author's collection; *Houston Press*, November 20, 1912.

17. *Houston Press*, November 21, 1912.

18. "Accused Ex-Officer Still Out of City," The *Galveston Daily News*, November 23, 1911, September 9, 1913.

19. *Beaumont Enterprise*, June 16, 1911; The *Dallas Morning News*, June 16, 1911; The *Galveston Daily News*, June 16, 1911; Elijah Clarence Branch, *Judge Lynch's Court in America* (Houston, published by author, 1913), p. 103.

20. *Houston Post*, January 6, 1913; Zarko Franks, "Saga of a Texas Ranger," 1955 *Houston Chronicle* clipping, in Frank Hamer scrapbook.

21. *Houston Post*, January 6, 1913; The *Galveston Daily News*, January 4, April 23, 1913.

22. *Houston Press*, April 15, 1913; "Noble Denied Story; Hamer Slapped Writer," undated 1911 newspaper clipping, Frank Hamer scrapbook; Waters, "History of the *Houston Press*."

23. "Waters Boys in Street Fight," "Waters Struck by Officer Hamer," "Hamer Re-

signed as Special Officer," undated 1913 newspaper clippings, Frank Hamer scrapbook; Waters, "History of the *Houston Press*."

24. Peck, "Paul C. Edwards, from Newsman to Trustees' President," p. 6; "Waters Boys in Street Fight," "Officer Hamer Resigns to Go to West Texas," Frank Hamer scrapbook; *San Antonio Light*, April 22, 1913.

25. Waters, "History of the Houston *Press*."

26. The *Galveston Daily News*, April 16, 1913; Bryan *Daily Eagle and Pilot*, June 12, 1913.

27. An Ordinance Appointing a Police Officer, December 2, 1913, Navasota City Archives; The *Dallas Morning News*, December 4, 5, 6; *Brazos and Colorado Rivers in Texas: Hearings Before the Committee on Flood Control of the House of Representatives* (Washington, D.C.: Government Printing Office, 1913), pp. 30–31.

28. Alyn, *I Say Me for a Parable*, pp. 175–79.

29. Bryan *Daily Eagle and Pilot*, March 16, 1914; The *Dallas Morning News*, April 9, 1914; The *Galveston Daily News*, April 10, June 13, August 31, 1914; *Burleson County Ledger and News-Chronicle*, June 19, December 11, 1914; The *Llano News*, September, 1, 1914; newspaper clippings, 1914, Frank Hamer scrapbook.

30. *Kimble County Citizen*, June 19, 1914, March 5, 1915; The *Galveston Daily News*, August 31, 1913.

31. *Proceedings of the Joint Committee of the Senate and the House in the Investigation of the Texas Ranger Force*, Texas State Archives, pp. 99–108.

32. Webb, *Texas Rangers*, pp. 527–28. On Sheriff Martin, see *Del Rio News Herald*, November 11, 1940.

33. Booth Mooney, *Mister Texas: The Story of Coke Stevenson* (Dallas: Texas Printing House, 1947), p. 10; Robert Caro, *The Years of Lyndon Johnson: Means of Ascent* (New York: Alfred A. Knopf, 1990), pp. 145–50.

34. *Kimble County Citizen*, January 15, 1915; "Coke Stevenson Was There," *The Sheep-Goat Raiser Ranch Magazine*, December 1965.

35. *Fort Worth Star-Telegram*, March 1, 1915.

36. Henry Hutchings to James E. Ferguson, March 19, 1915; Hutchings to James J. Sanders, April 6, 1915; J. M. Fox to Hutchings, July 15, 1915; *Fort Worth Star-Telegram*, February 24, March 26, 1915; Frost and Jenkins, *I'm Frank Hamer*, pp. 56–57; Harris and Sadler, *Texas Rangers and the Mexican Revolution*, pp. 196–198.

37. Hutchings to Sanders, April 6, 1915; Harris and Sadler, *Texas Rangers and the Mexican Revolution*, p. 198.

38. Hutchings to J. W. Almond, April 2, 1915; Hutchings to Hamer, April 2, 1915; Warrant of Authority and Descriptive List, March 29, 1915, Frank Hamer, James Dunaway; Harris and Sadler, *Texas Rangers and the Mexican Revolution*, p. 200.

39. *Comanche Chief*, October 15, 1915; "Coke Stevenson Was There," *The Sheep-Goat Raiser Ranch Magazine*, December 1965; Frederica Burt Wyatt, *Families of Kimble County*, vol. 1 (Junction: Kimble County Historical Commission, 1985), pp. 153–54.

40. Monthly Return, Company C, May 31, 1915; "Coke Stevenson Was There."

41. Mooney, *Mister Texas*, pp. 10–11; Caro, *Means of Ascent*, p. 150. Although Stevenson later recalled, "We sent him to the penitentiary," neither Gardner nor Cross went to prison. Apparently, Fletcher Gardner served only county jail time, according to Donaly Brice, of the Texas State Archives, to author, May 28, 2013.

42. *Comanche Chief*, October 15, 1915; The *Galveston Daily News*, October 17, 1915; Kerrville *Mountain Sun*, August 11, 1922.

43. J. M. Fox to Hutchings, June 15, July 6, 11, 15, 24, 1915; Hutchings to Hamer, July 6, 19, 1915; Hutchings to Fox, July 6, 7, 1915.

44. Author's interview with Harrison Hamer and Kathy Hatchett, niece of Mollie Cameron, Navasota, Texas, March 2, 2013. The author and researcher Taronda Schulz checked the clerk's offices in numerous Texas counties and have been unable to locate the Hamers' divorce case.

6. THE BANDIT WAR

1. The *Dallas Morning News,* May 13, 1902, May 29, June 9, 1915; Harris, Harris, and Sadler, *Texas Ranger Biographies,* p. 114; Robert M. Utley, *Lone Star Lawmen: The Second Century of the Texas Rangers* (New York: Oxford University Press, 2007), pp. 49–52; Harris and Sadler, *The Texas Rangers and the Mexican Revolution,* pp. 190–93.

2. *El Paso Herald-Post,* May 26, 1934.

3. Utley, *Lone Star Lawmen,* pp. 16–18. On James B. Wells, see Evan Anders, *Boss Rule in South Texas: The Progressive Era* (Austin: University of Texas Press, 1982.)

4. Utley, *Lone Star Lawmen,* p. 25; Parsons, *Captain John R. Hughes, Lone Star Ranger,* pp. 239–40.

5. Utley, *Lone Star Lawmen,* pp. 22–23; Harris and Sadler, *Texas Rangers and the Mexican Revolution,* pp. 210–21.

6. *Cleburne Morning Review,* July 10, 1915; The *Dallas Morning News,* July 6, 1915; *Investigation of Mexican Affairs: Hearing Before a Subcommittee of the Committee on Foreign Relations, United States Senate* (Washington: Government Printing Office, 1919), p. 1243–44, 1317; Harris and Sadler, *Texas Rangers and the Mexican Revolution,* pp. 250–51, 258, 276.

7. *San Antonio Light,* October 23, 1913; *Victoria Advocate,* October 25, 1913; The *Galveston Daily News,* October 24, 1913, April 9, 1914; The *Dallas Morning News,* September 29, 1914, July 21, 1915, April 3, 1918; Harris and Sadler, *Texas Rangers and the Mexican Revolution,* pp. 255, 259; Sterling, *Trails and Trials of a Texas Ranger,* p. 47.

8. *Fort Worth Star-Telegram,* August 3, 1915; Harris and Sadler, *Texas Rangers and the Mexican Revolution,* pp. 259–60; Utley, *Lone Star Lawmen,* pp. 27–28.

9. *Fort Worth Star-Telegram,* August 3, 6, 1915; The *Dallas Morning News,* August 7, 1915; Utley, *Lone Star Lawmen,* p.30.

10. Testimony of W. T. Vann, *Proceedings of the Joint Committee of the Senate and the House in the Investigation of the Texas Ranger Force,* Texas State Archives, pp. 560–62; *Brownsville Herald,* August 7, 1915; *San Antonio La Prensa,* August 11, 1915; *Fort Worth Star-Telegram,* August 7, 1915; The *Dallas Morning News,* August 8, 1915; Utley, *Lone Star Lawmen,* pp. 30–1, 348 n11; Tom Lea, *The King Ranch* (New York: Little Brown & Co.), pp. 583–84; Harris and Sadler, *Texas Rangers and the Mexican Revolution,* pp. 263–64.

11. D. P. Gay, "The Amazing Bare-Faced Facts of the Norias Fight," p. 2, typescript dated January 12, 1933, Walter Prescott Webb papers, Briscoe Center, University of Texas Library; *Brownsville Herald,* August 9, 1915; The *Dallas Morning News,* August 10, 1915, Lea, *King Ranch,* pp. 583–84.

12. Gay, "Norias Fight," p. 3; Roy W. Aldrich, "History of the Texas Rangers," typescript, July 21, 1937, Briscoe Center.

13. Gay, "Norias Fight," pp. 3–5; testimony of Marcus Hines, *Investigation of Mexican Affairs,* pp. 1309–11; The *Dallas Morning News,* August 10, 1915; Mike Cox, *Time of the Rangers* (New York: Tom Doherty Associates, 2009), pp. 67–69; Lauro F.

      Cavalos, *A Kineno Remembers: From the King Ranch to the White House* (College Station: Texas A&M University Press, 2008), pp. 8–12. Antonio Rocha committed several more murders until he was slain by Mexican troops in 1919. On Rocha, see testimony of Sheriff W. T. Vann, *Investigation of Mexican Affairs*, pp. 1296–1302, and *Brownsville Herald*, May 12, 1919.

14. Gay, "Norias Fight," p. 7; C. L. Douglas, *The Gentlemen in the White Hats* (Dallas: South-West Press, 1934), p. 178; Utley, *Lone Star Lawmen*, pp. 32–33; Harris and Sadler, *Texas Rangers and the Mexican Revolution*, pp. 264–65.

15. Gay, "Norias Fight," p. 7; Harris and Sadler, *Texas Rangers and the Mexican Revolution*, p. 266.

16. *Investigation of the Texas Ranger Force*, p. 1224; *Wichita Daily Times*, August 10, 1915; The *Galveston Daily News*, August 11, 1915; The *Dallas Morning News*, August 10, 11, 1915; Gay, "Norias Fight," p. 9; Harris and Sadler, *The Texas Rangers and the Mexican Revolution*, pp. 265–66.

17. *Investigation of the Texas Ranger Force*, p. 1225; The *Dallas Morning News*, August 13, 1915. The real photo postcard showing Frank Hamer and Jim Dunaway (incorrectly identified as Captain Fox) is in the author's collection.

18. Cavalos, *Kineno Remembers*, p. 13; Cox, *Time of the Rangers*, p. 396 n17.

19. *Fort Worth Star-Telegram*, September 6, 1915; Arnoldo de Leon, ed., *War Along the Border: The Mexican Revolution and Tejano Communities* (Houston: University of Houston, 2012), p. 119.

20. *San Antonio La Prensa*, August 11, 1915; *Brownsville Herald*, August 9, 1915.

21. The *Dallas Morning News*, August 14, 1915.

22. Douglas, *The Gentlemen in the White Hats*, pp. 178–79.

23. *Fort Worth Star-Telegram*, October 2, 1915; Harris, Harris, and Sadler, *Texas Ranger Biographies*, p. 361; Harris and Sadler, *Texas Rangers and the Mexican Revolution*, pp. 270–71; Sterling, *Trails and Trials of a Texas Ranger*, pp. 417, 419. While serving as a deputy sheriff in 1914–15, Sterling shot and killed two men in personal quarrels. Sterling, who had an enormous ego, said nothing in his book about those questionable killings.

24. The *Dallas Morning News*, August 11, 1915; *San Antonio Light*, August 15, 1915; The *Denver Post*, August 15, 1915; *Columbia* (SC) *State*, August 16, 1915.

25. J. M. Fox to Adjutant General Henry Hutchings, August 21, 1915; *San Antonio La Prensa*, August 24, 1915; *Kansas City* (MO) *Cosmopolita*, August 28, 1915.

26. The *New York Times*, October 31, 2004; *Investigation of the Texas Ranger Force*, pp. 906–07; Harris and Sadler, *Texas Rangers and the Mexican Revolution*, pp. 273–74, 287–91, 290–92; Utley, *Lone Star Lawmen*, pp. 35, 39–43.

27. Henry Hutchings to James E. Ferguson, November 16, 1915; James E. Ferguson to Henry Hutchings, November 19, 1915; Henry Hutchings to J. J. Sanders, J. M. Fox, and H. L. Ransom, November 20, 1915; Cox, *Time of the Rangers*, p. 92; Utley, *Lone Star Lawmen*, pp. 43–46. On the first use of the term "Rangered," see *San Antonio Light*, September 9, 1915.

28. Benjamin Heber Johnson, *Revolution in Texas: How a Forgotten Rebellion and Its Bloody Suppression Turned Mexicans into Americans* (New Haven: Yale University Press, 2003), pp. 176–78.

29. The *Dallas Morning News*, February 2, 1919; *Investigation of the Texas Ranger Force*, p. 679; *Investigation of Mexican Affairs*, pp. 1248–49; Webb, *Texas Rangers*, pp. 476, 478.

30. *Brownsville Herald*, January 21, 1937; Newlon, "Outlaw Tamer," p. 58; Kinney, "Frank Hamer, Texas Ranger," p. 82.

7. THE JOHNSON-SIMS FEUD

1. John H. Rogers to Cattle Raisers Association of Texas, quoted in Frost and Jenkins, *I'm Frank Hamer*, p. 66. The authors date this letter June 16, 1916, which must be an error, for at that time Hamer had already been employed by the association for six months.

2. E. B. Spiller to Henry Hutchings, November 1, 1915; *Investigation of the Texas Ranger Force*, p. 104.

3. E. B. Spiller to Henry Hutchings, November 4, 1915; Affidavit of F. A. Hamer, November 8, 1915; Enlistment and Oath of Service, F. A. Hamer, November 8, 1915; Lorie Rubenser and Gloria Priddy, *Constables, Marshals, and More: Forgotten Offices in Texas Law Enforcement* (Denton: University of North Texas Press, 2011), pp. 72–73; *Cattle Raisers Association of Texas, Official Souvenir Magazine* (Fort Worth: Cattle Raisers Association of Texas, 1912), pp. 23, 25, 27.

4. Henry Hutchings to E. B. Spiller, November 2, 1915; Utley, *Lone Star Justice*, pp. 228–229; Utley, *Lone Star Lawmen*, pp. 10–11.

5. Henry Hutchings to E. B. Spiller, November 11, 22, 1915; F. A. Hamer to Henry Hutchings, November 7, 19, 1915; *Fort Worth Star-Telegram*, September 4, 1916; Rubenser and Priddy, *Constables, Marshals, and More*, pp. 74–75.

6. Kinney, "Frank Hamer, Texas Ranger," p. 83; Frost and Jenkins, *I'm Frank Hamer*, pp. 66–67; O'Neal, *Johnson-Sims Feud*, p. 95.

7. O'Neal, *Johnson-Sims Feud*, pp. 16–22, 27, 153–54.

8. *Ibid.*, pp. 27, 54–56.

9. *Ibid.*, pp. 40, 58–59, 78–79.

10. *Ibid.*, pp. 80–82.

11. *Ibid.*, pp. 82–86.

12. Texas Adjutant General Service Records, Gee McMeans; Texas State Penitentiary Convict Ledger, inmate no. 20704; Texas State Penitentiary Conduct Ledger, inmate no. 20704; Sterling, *Trails and Trials of a Texas Ranger*, p. 425; The *Dallas Morning News*, September 1, June 22, 1906; *Fort Worth Star-Telegram*, October 15, 1905; El Paso *Herald*, July 25, 1910, May 24, 1911; Paul N. Spellman, *Captain J. A. Brooks, Texas Ranger* (Denton: University of North Texas Press, 2007), p. 174.

13. O'Neal, *Johnson-Sims Feud*, pp. 86–88; *Abilene Daily Reporter*, September 25, 1918.

14. O'Neal, *Johnson-Sims Feud*, pp. 88, 91.

15. Marriage record of Harrison Hamer and Freddie Rainey, August 10, 1907, Harrison Hamer collection; Frost and Jenkins, *I'm Frank Hamer*, pp. 66–67.

16. *San Antonio Light*, December 18, 1916; *Victoria Advocate*, December 18, 19, 1916; *Abilene Daily Reporter*, September 26, 1918; O'Neal, *Johnson-Sims Feud*, pp. 106–10.

17. Frank A. Hamer to Sam H. Hill, December 1, 1932; Frost and Jenkins, *I'm Frank Hamer*, p. 68; O'Neal, *Johnson-Sims Feud*, p. 118. On Horace L. Roberson, see Harris and Sadler, *Texas Rangers and the Mexican Revolution*, pp. 456–57; Bob Alexander, *Fearless Dave Allison: Border Lawman* (Silver City, NM: High-Lonesome Books, 2003), pp. 158–61, 217–65. In 1923 Roberson and Dave Allison were assassinated by the notorious outlaw Hill Loftis, alias Tom Ross, and an accomplice.

18. W. A. Merrill and O. P. Wolfe to James Ferguson, December 20, 1916; W. W. Weems et al. to James Ferguson, December 21, 1916.

19. Weems et al. to Ferguson, December 21, 1916; J. D. White to Henry Hutchings, December 27, 1916; John L. Wroe to Henry Hutchings, December 21, 1916.

20. Henry Hutchings to James Ferguson, December 29, 1916; James A. Ferguson to

Henry Hutchings, January 1, 1916; John L. Wroe to Henry Hutchings, January 3, 1916; Henry Hutchings to W.A. Merrill, January 5, 1916.

21. F. A. Hamer to Henry Hutchings, January 10, 1917.

22. Henry Hutchings to Sam H. Hill, January 10, 1917; Henry Hutchings to F. A. Hamer, January 11, 1917; Hamer to Hutchings, January 13, 1917.

23. Brown, *No Duty to Retreat*, pp. 3–6, 25–27.

24. *El Paso Herald*, February 15, 1918. On Felix Jones's bloody career, see affidavit of W. G. Clark, June 14, 1917, Travis Hamer collection; *Fort Worth Star-Telegram*, December 23, 1909, August 2, 1910, February 16, 1914, July 1, 1917; *Abilene Daily Reporter*, June 7, 1912; The *Dallas Morning News*, September 4, 1912, September 25, 1913, February 10, 1914, September 22, 1918. August 2, 1928; *Cleburne Morning Review*, August 22, 1913; *El Paso Herald*, February 19, 1918. On the career of W. G. Clark, see *Fort Worth Star-Telegram*, May 2, 1905, December 14, 1915, February 18, March 5, August 22, 1918; The *Dallas Morning News*. March 5, 1918; *El Paso Herald*, February 15, 1918; *W. G. Clark v. State of Texas* (1919) 85 Texas Criminal Reports 153–58.

25. Kinney, "Frank Hamer, Texas Ranger," p. 84; Frost and Jenkins, *I'm Frank Hamer*, p. 67; O'Neal, *Johnson-Sims Feud*, p. 111.

26. *El Paso Herald*, February 15, 1918; Frost and Jenkins, *I'm Frank Hamer*, pp. 67–68.

27. *El Paso Herald*, February 15, 18, 1918.

28. On the Thomas Lyons murder case, see Jerry J. Lobdill, *Last Train to El Paso* (Fort Worth: Cross Timbers Press, 2014).

29. *El Paso Herald*, June 4, 14, 1917; *El Paso Times*, June 14, 1927; The *Dallas Morning News*, August 23, 1918, February 13, 1919; *Felix R. Jones v. State of Texas* (1919) 85 Texas Criminal Reports 538–54.

30. O'Neal, *Johnson-Sims Feud*, pp. 119–20.

31. Frost and Jenkins, *I'm Frank Hamer*, pp. 69–70.

32. Hamer to Sam H. Hill, December 1, 1932; telegram, A. G. Beard to Adjutant General, October 1, 1917; author interview with Jerry McMeans, December 22, 2011; O'Neal, *Johnson-Sims Feud*, p. 120; Frost and Jenkins, *I'm Frank Hamer*, p. 70.

33. Hamer to Sam H. Hill, December 1, 1932; Kinney, "Frank Hamer, Texas Ranger," p. 86.

34. Hamer to Hill, December 1, 1932; The *Snyder Signal*, October 5, 1917; The *Dallas Morning News*, October 2, 1917; *Fort Worth Star-Telegram*, October 2, 1917; *Aspermont Star*, October 4, 1917; Kinney, "Frank Hamer, Texas Ranger," p. 84; Frost and Jenkins, *I'm Frank Hamer*, pp. 70–73. Perhaps the most detailed contemporary account appeared in the *Sweetwater Reporter* and was reprinted in its sister newspaper, the *Abilene Daily Reporter*, October 2, 1917, but according to the editor of The *Snyder Signal*, it was written hastily after the gunfight and contained numerous errors.

35. Walter Prescott Webb, "Texas Rangers Quell Troubles," *State Trooper*, vol. 5, no. 12 (August 1924), p. 13.

36. A. G. Beard to Adjutant General, October 1, 1917; E. J. Robinson to Judge A. R. Anderson, October 10, 1917; The *Dallas Morning News*, October 3, 1917; Kinney, "Frank Hamer, Texas Ranger," p. 84.

37. Sandra Lynn Myres, "S. D. Myres, Saddlemaker," M.A. thesis, Texas Technological College (1961).

38. Hamer to Hill, December 1, 1932; *Abilene Daily Reporter*, October 7, 1917; The *Dallas Morning News*, October 7, 1917; Frost and Jenkins, *I'm Frank Hamer*, pp. 72–73; Patti Neill, Nolan County District Court Clerk, to author, November 23, 2011.

39. Bill O'Neal, interview with Beverly Sims, March 5, 2008; Frost and Jenkins, *I'm Frank Hamer*, pp. 74, 80; O'Neal, *Johnson-Sims Feud*, p. 124.

40. *Investigation of the Texas Ranger Force*, pp. 288–93, 400–02, 422–32, 442–45, 459; The *Snyder Signal*, March 22, 1918; The *Dallas Morning News*, March 19, 1918; *Fort Worth Star-Telegram*, March 19, 20, 21, 22, 23, 1918; O'Neal, *Johnson-Sims Feud*, pp. 128, 132, 136–37.

41. Inquest into the Death of Captain Henry R. Ransom, April 1, 1918, Texas Ranger Hall of Fame and Museum; W. H. Koon to James A. Harley, April 16, 1918; The *Dallas Morning News*, April 3, 1918; *Fort Worth Star-Telegram*, April 2, 1918; *Houston Chronicle*, April 2, 1918; *Houston Post*, April 3, 1918; *San Saba News*, April 4, 1918; The *Galveston Daily News*, April 3, 1918; Waters, "History of the Houston Press"; Harris and Sadler, *Texas Rangers and the Mexican Revolution*, pp. 381–82. Goodrich, *Captain Ransom, Texas Ranger*, pp. 217–24, argues vaguely that Ransom's death was the result of some kind of conspiracy but does not state a cogent theory to support her claim or identify any of the alleged conspirators.

42. *Abilene Daily Reporter*, September 26, 1918; O'Neal, *Johnson-Sims Feud*, pp. 139–40.

43. Hamer to Hill, December 1, 1932; author interview with Jerry McMeans, December 22, 2011; *Odessa American*, January 29, 1957.

8. GUNSMOKE ON THE RIO GRANDE

1. O'Neal, *Johnson-Sims Feud*, p. 146.

2. Richard D. Jensen, *The Amazing Tom Mix: The Most Famous Cowboy of the Movies* (Lincoln, NE: iUniverse, 2005), pp. 1, 8–14; Mike Cox, *Texas Ranger Tales*, pp. 216–23.

3. Frost and Jenkins, *I'm Frank Hamer*, p. 74; O'Neal, *Johnson-Sims Feud*, p. 124.

4. Frost and Jenkins, *I'm Frank Hamer*, pp. 74, 79.

5. *Ibid.*, pp. 42, 80; Sterling, *Trails and Trials of a Texas Ranger*, pp.73–74.

6. The *Snyder Signal*, March 8, 1918, April 23, 1920; O'Neal, *Johnson-Sims Feud*, p. 142.

7. Robert H. Curnutte to J. C. Harris, September 5, 1918; James A. Harley to F. A. Hamer, September 7, 1918; Enlistment and Oath of Service, Frank A. Hamer, October 1, 1918; *Investigation of the Texas Ranger Force*, pp. 707–08; *Brownsville Herald*, August 22, 28, October 11, 1918; Harris and Sadler, *Texas Rangers and the Mexican Revolution*, pp. 409–10.

8. Enlistment and Oath of Service, Frank A. Hamer, October 1, 1918.

9. *El Paso Herald*, February 8, 1918; The *Dallas Morning News*, March 10, 1918; *Investigation of the Texas Ranger Force*, pp. 834–52. On the Porvenir massacre, see Utley, *Lone Star Lawmen*, pp. 58–66, and Harris and Sadler, *Texas Rangers and the Mexican Revolution*, pp. 351–56. For Lake's account of Porvenir, see San Diego *Union*, May 27, 1934, reprinted in *Time* magazine, June 25, 1934, p. 3. Lake wrote, "I never could get Frank Hamer to talk about the fight at El Porvenir," and then went on to describe a pitched gun battle in which Hamer and two other Rangers killed sixteen smugglers. Lake tended to embellish history, as demonstrated by his hugely popular book *Wyatt Earp: Frontier Marshal* (1931), which while beautifully written, contains invented dialogue and other fictional elements. Frost and Jenkins, in *I'm Frank Hamer*, p. 60, also have Hamer at Porvenir. They incorrectly place the site of the incident at "Candelia," meaning Candelaria, located about twenty miles downriver from Porvenir.

10. On William T. Vann, see The *Dallas Morning News*, September 16, 1927; *Madi-*

sonville Meteor, June 27, 1929; Parsons, *Captain John R. Hughes, Lone Star Ranger,* pp. 238–39.

11. Charles F. Stevens to Walter F. Woodul, June 12, 1918; *San Antonio Light,* March 15, 1925; Harris, Harris, and Sadler, *Texas Ranger Biographies,* pp. 361–62; Utley, *Lone Star Lawmen,* pp. 70–71. Utley, *Lone Star Lawmen,* p. 83, names Stevens and three other captains as "mediocrities or worse." With regard to Stevens, that judgment is overly harsh; the facts of the captain's long career showed he was a worthy and ethical officer.

12. Jonathan C. Brown, *Oil and Revolution in Mexico* (Berkeley: University of California Press, 1993), pp. 136, 242–43; Laton McCartney, *The Teapot Dome Scandal* (New York: Random House, 2008), pp. 53–54; Harris and Sadler, *Texas Rangers and the Mexican Revolution,* pp. 384–85.

13. Stevens's account appears in G. W. Sager, Special Agent, Bureau of Investigation, report to R. W. Tinsley, October 27, 1925, p. 4, FBI Teapot Dome file.

14. W. M. Hanson to James A. Harley, October 15, 1918, Walter Prescott Webb Papers, Briscoe Center, University of Texas Library; *Investigation of the Texas Ranger Force,* p. 565; *Brownsville Herald,* October 11, 15, 1918; *San Antonio La Prensa,* October 16, 1918; Harris, Harris, and Sadler, *Texas Ranger Biographies,* p. 379.

15. *Investigation of the Texas Ranger Force,* p. 565; *Brownsville Herald,* October 11, 15, 1918; *Floresville Chronicle Journal,* October 25, 1918; *San Antonio La Prensa,* October 16, 1918; *San Antonio La Epoca,* October 20, 1918; *Kerrville Mountain Sun,* July 21, 1938; undated 1918 newspaper clippings, Delbert Timberlake vertical file, Texas Ranger Hall of Fame and Museum; Webb, *Texas Rangers,* pp. 528–29; Frost and Jenkins, *I'm Frank Hamer,* pp. 81–83; Harris and Sadler, *Texas Rangers and the Mexican Revolution,* pp. 419–20. Several accounts incorrectly provide the date of Timberlake's death as October 11, 1918.

16. Hanson to Harley, October 15, 1918; Webb, *Texas Rangers,* pp. 529–30; Frost and Jenkins, *I'm Frank Hamer,* pp. 83–84.

17. Sterling, *Trails and Trials of a Texas Ranger,* p. 424; Maude T. Gilliland, *Wilson County Texas Rangers, 1837–1977* (Brownsville: Springman-King Co., 1977), p. 64.

18. *Brownsville Herald,* October 15, 1918; Webb, *Texas Rangers,* p. 529; Sterling, *Trails and Trials of a Texas Ranger,* pp. 423–24; Frost and Jenkins, *I'm Frank Hamer,* p. 83.

9. "THIS RUFFIAN HAYMER"

1. *Investigation of the Texas Ranger Force,* pp. 884–85; Harris and Sadler, *Texas Rangers and the Mexican Revolution,* pp. 414–15.

2. *Investigation of the Texas Ranger Force,* pp. 879, 1417–24. The Bureau of Investigation later became the Division of Investigation and, finally, in 1935, the Federal Bureau of Investigation. For simplicity's sake, it will be referred to in this book as the FBI.

3. *Investigation of the Texas Ranger Force,* pp. 879–81, 888, 893–94, 925–28.

4. W. M. Hanson to Captain H. M. Johnston, November 19, 1918; G. W. Sager to R. W. Tinsley, October 27, 1925, p. 1.

5. R. W. Aldrich to Frank A. Hamer, February 4, 1919; Harris and Sadler, *Texas Rangers and the Mexican Revolution,* pp. 423–25.

6. W. S. Adamson, W. A. Merrill, C. R. Buchanan to James A. Harley, September 12, 1918; Enlistment and Oath of Service, Harrison Hamer, October 23, 1918.

7. W. M. Hanson to Captain H. M. Johnston, November 19, 1918; Johnston to Hamer, November 22, 1918.

8. *Investigation of the Texas Ranger Force*, pp. 527–33, 885–87. Benjamin Heber Johnson writes that at the time of this incident, Hamer's "reputation as the 'Angel of Death' in Texas was already well established," *Revolution in Texas: How a Forgotten Rebellion and Its Bloody Suppression Turned Mexicans into Americans* (New Haven: Yale University Press, 2003), p. 174. That is incorrect. Frank Hamer was never called the "Angel of Death," and in 1918 he was still a relatively obscure figure, widely respected in law-enforcement circles but generally unknown to the Texas public.

9. *Investigation of the Texas Ranger Force*, pp. 549, 867–68; Utley, *Lone Star Lawmen*, pp. 68–69; Harris and Sadler, *Texas Rangers and the Mexican Revolution*, pp. 428, 460.

10. *Investigation of the Texas Ranger Force*, pp. 888–90.

11. *San Antonio Express*, May 21, 1902; Harris and Sadler, *Texas Rangers and the Mexican Revolution*, pp. 383–387; Richard Ribb, "La Rinchada: Revolution, Revenge, and the Rangers," in Arnoldo de Leon, ed., *War Along the Border*, pp. 59–63, 80–89.

12. *Investigation of the Texas Ranger Force*, pp. 891–92.

13. *Ibid.*, pp. 893–94.

14. *Ibid.*, pp. 149, 895.

15. Sterling, *Trails and Trials of a Texas Ranger*, pp. 419–20.

16. F. A. Hamer to R. W. Aldrich, January 5, 1919; *Investigation of the Texas Ranger Force*, pp. 899–900.

17. *Investigation of the Texas Ranger Force*, pp. 899–900.

18. Adjutant General Special Order no. 7, January 30, 1919, Frank Hamer Service File.

19. *Investigation of the Texas Ranger Force*, pp. 99–108.

20. *Ibid.*, pp. 1409–11, 1503–04.

21. The *Dallas Morning News*, February 8, 1919; *El Paso Herald*, February 11, 1919; *San Antonio Evening News*, February 11, 1919; Cox, *Time of the Rangers*, p. 89.

22. *Investigation of the Texas Ranger Force*, pp. 1235, 1243–47, 1569.

23. Canales's quote is from Harris and Sadler, *Texas Rangers and the Mexican Revolution*, p. 460.

24. William M. Hanson to F. A. Hamer, February 19, 1919; James R. Ward, "The Texas Rangers, 1919–1935," Ph.D. dissertation, Texas Christian University (1972), pp. 19–22; Cox, *Time of the Rangers*, pp. 95–96.

25. The *Dallas Morning News*, February 21, 1919; Utley, *Lone Star Lawmen*, pp. 82–84.[26] On national peace officers fatalities, see the website of the National Law Enforcement Memorial Fund.

10. THE LONE RANGER

1. Frost and Jenkins, *I'm Frank Hamer*, pp. 84, 89.

2. G. W. Sager to R. W. Tinsley, October 27, 1925, pp. 1–2, FBI Teapot Dome file.

3. Sager to Tinsley, October 27, 1925, p. 2; Special Order no. 37, December 27, 1918; Harris and Sadler, *Texas Rangers and the Mexican Revolution*, p. 408; Frost and Jenkins, *I'm Frank Hamer*, p. 61.

4. *Brownsville Herald*, December 31, 1918; Utrecht, "Frank Hamer," p. 51; Webb, *The Texas Rangers*, p. 532; Harris, Harris, and Sadler, *Texas Ranger Biographies*, p. 375, 428.

5. Sager to Tinsley, October 27, 1925, p. 2; James A. Harley, Special Order no. 37, December 27, 1918; The *Galveston Daily News,* February 21, 1919; The *Seattle Daily Times,* March 12, 1919; Webb, *Texas Rangers,* p. 532.

6. Frost and Jenkins, *I'm Frank Hamer,* p. 65.

7. *Albuquerque Journal,* February 23, 1919; *Duluth* (MN) *News-Tribune,* February 24, 1919; *San Antonio Evening News,* March 11, 1919; The *Seattle Daily Times,* March 12, 1919.

8. F. A. Hamer to James A. Harley, March 23, 1919; *Logansport* (IN) *Daily Tribune,* March 12, 1919; *Brownwood Bulletin,* March 22, 1919.

9. Caeser Kleberg and Charles H. Flato, Jr., to James A. Harley, March 28, 1919.

10. The *Dallas Morning News,* April 8, 1919.

11. R. W. Aldrich to Frank Hamer, March 26, 1919; *Brownsville Herald,* May 30, 1919; Frost and Jenkins, *I'm Frank Hamer,* p. 93.

12. James A. Harley to F. A. Hamer, August 8, 1919.

13. F. A. Hamer to James A. Harley, June 19, 1919.

14. Aldrich to Hamer, June 24, 1919; Frank Rabb to James A. Harley, June 26, 1919; Caesar Kleberg to James A. Harley, June 27, 1919; Oscar C. Dancy to James A. Harley, June 30, 1919.

15. James A. Harley to Frank Rabb, June 27, 1919; James A. Harley to Caesar Kleberg, June 28, 1919; James A. Harley to Oscar C. Dancy, July 5, 1919; *Investigation of the Texas Ranger Force,* pp. 99–108.

16. F. A. Hamer to James A. Harley, July 8, 1919.

17. R. W. Aldrich to Frank Hamer, June 6, 1919; James A. Harley to F. A. Hamer, August 8, 1919.

18. Hamer to Aldrich, July 14, 17, 1919; Aldrich to Hamer, July 18, 1919; Hamer to James A. Harley, August 16, 1919; Beverly Sims, interview with Bill O'Neal, March 5, 2008; O'Neal, *Johnson-Sims Feud,* p. 146.

19. F. A. Hamer to James A. Harley, August 16, 1919; W. M. Hanson to F. A. Hamer, August 26, 1919; John R. Rutledge to R. W. Aldrich, June 26, 1920; R. W. Aldrich to John R. Rutledge, June 28, 1920.

20. Enlistment and Oath of Service, F. A. Hamer, November 25, 1919; Sager to Tinsley, October 27, 1925, p. 2; The *Dallas Morning News,* September 4, October 2, 1919; Harris and Sadler, *Texas Rangers and the Mexican Revolution,* p. 475.

21. R. W. Aldrich to George Millard, December 3, 1919; H. C. Smith to Frank Hamer, December 4, 1919; R. W. Aldrich to Charles F. Stevens, December 10, 1919; Charles F. Stevens to Adjutant General Cope, December 10, 11, 12, 1919.

22. *El Paso Herald,* January 1, 1920; Frost and Jenkins, *I'm Frank Hamer,* pp. 53, 63.

23. *El Paso Herald,* December 10, 1919; *Boyd v. United States* (1886) 116 U.S. 616; *Carroll v. United States* (1925) 267 U.S. 132.

24. *El Paso Herald,* December 26, 1919.

25. *Ibid.,* December 26, 1919.

26. *Ibid.,* December 26, 1919.

27. *El Paso Herald,* December 27, 1919; Webb, *Texas Rangers,* p. 545.

28. *El Paso Herald,* December 30, 1919.

29. *Ibid.,* December 31, 1919.

30. Cope to Stevens, December 30, 1919; *El Paso Herald,* January 3, 1920; The *Dallas Morning News,* January 2, 4, 1920; *Fort Worth Star-Telegram,* January 3, 1920.

31. *Fort Worth Star-Telegram,* January 20, 21, 22, 24, 25, 27, 29, 30, 31, 1920; The *Dallas Morning News,* January 20, 23, 25, 27, 30, 1920; *Tulsa World,* January 21, 25, 27, 29, 30, 1920; *Big Spring Daily Herald,* May 30, June 13, 1934.

32. E. B. Clarkson to W. P. Hobby, January 22, 1920; H. C. Smith to W. D. Cope,

January 23, 1920; Ed Clarkson to H. C. Smith, January 28, 1920; H. C. Smith to Ed Clarkson, January 29, 1920; C. J. Blackwell to W. D. Cope, February 1, 1920; R. W. Aldrich to St. Joseph's Infirmary, March 1, 1920.

33. Charles F. Stevens to W. P. Hobby, February 3, 1920; R. W. Aldrich to T. J. Jackman, March 3, 1920; *Fort Worth Star-Telegram*, February 7, 1920; *Brownsville Herald*, February 8, 1920; The *Dallas Morning News*, February 8, 1920; Harris and Sadler, *Texas Rangers and the Mexican Revolution*, pp. 493–84; Cox, *Time of the Rangers*, pp. 103–05.

34. *Tulsa World*, January 30, February 2, 1920; *El Paso Herald*, March 11, 1920.

35. W.D. Cope, Special Order no. 6, March 16, 1920; *Fort Worth Star-Telegram*, March 12, 13, 15, 1921; *Tulsa World*, March 13, 1920.

36. *In Re Neagle* (1890) 135 U.S. 1.

37. The *Dallas Morning News*, March 18, 19, 23, 25, 1920; *Fort Worth Star-Telegram*, March 18, 25, April 1, 1920; *Tulsa World*, March 16, 23, 24, 1920; *El Paso Herald*, March 23, 1920; *Oklahoma v. Texas* (1921) 256 U.S. 70; Webb, *Texas Rangers*, p. 530.

11. HELL PASO

1. Frank Hamer, Prohibition Agent ID card, May 11, 1920, National Archives; Dianna Everett, "The Wettest Drought in the History of Texas: A Survey of the Enforcement of the Eighteenth Amendment and the Dean Act, 1920–1933," *Panhandle-Plains Historical Review*, vol. 52 (1979), pp. 39–45.

2. *Austin American*, May 16, 1920; "Gets Jail Sentence on Pro Law Charge in Court at Austin," undated news clipping, Frank Hamer scrapbook.

3. *San Antonio Express*, August 10, 11, 1920; *San Antonio Light*, April 20, 1921; *San Antonio Evening News*, August 19, December 14, 1920; Bartlett (TX) *Tribune and News*, August 13, 1920; The *Dallas Morning News*, December 26, 1920, January 21, April 17, 1921; *Fort Worth Star-Telegram*, April 17, 1921; The *Galveston Daily News*, January 20, 1921; Frost and Jenkins, *I'm Frank Hamer*, pp. 95–96; Robert M. Lombardo, *The Black Hand: Terror by Letter in Chicago* (Chicago: University of Illinois Press, 2010), pp. 107–08.

4. *San Antonio Light*, April 17, 20, 1921; The *Sandusky* (OH) *Star Journal*, August 27, 1923.

5. *El Paso Herald*, September 17, 1920; *Fort Worth Star-Telegram*, September 24, 1920; *Philadelphia Inquirer*, September 16, 1920; *Milwaukee Journal*, September 16, 1920; Cox, *Time of the Rangers*, p. 106.

6. *El Paso Herald*, August 7, November 3, 5, December 20, 1919, January 3, March 1, 2, April 9, June 5, September 23, 1920; The *Dallas Morning News*, December 20, 1919.

7. *Fort Worth Star-Telegram*, March 23, November 20, 1921; Mario T. García, *Desert Immigrants: The Mexicans of El Paso, 1880–1920* (New Haven: Yale University Press, 1981), pp. 31, 36; Frost and Jenkins, *I'm Frank Hamer*, p. 91.

8. *El Paso Herald*, January 10, 11, 1921; "Bootleggers Car Riddled in Battle with Dry Agents," undated El Paso newspaper clipping, Frank Hamer scrapbook; Frost and Jenkins, *I'm Frank Hamer*, pp. 92, 95.

9. "Customs Officer is Shot in Bullet Battle on Border With Band of Seven Whiskey Runners," undated 1921 newspaper clipping, Frank Hamer scrapbook; *Fort Worth Star-Telegram*, May 1, 1921; Frost and Jenkins, *I'm Frank Hamer*, pp. 91–92.

10. *Fort Worth Star-Telegram*, March 4, 6, 7, 22, 1921; "Prohibition Officer Is Shot in Fight with Smugglers on Border," undated 1921 news clipping, Frank Hamer scrapbook; Frost and Jenkins, *I'm Frank Hamer*, p. 92.

11. From an undated 1963 interview of Raithel by Zarko Franks in the *Houston Chronicle,* Harrison Hamer collection. Raithel recalled that Arch Wood was a member of the posse; this was incorrect, for Wood had already been slain. On the killing of Beckett and Wood, and the subsequent murder trials, see *El Paso Times,* March 23, 1921; *Fort Worth Star-Telegram,* March 22, 23, May 27, 29, 31, June 3, August 28, September 21, 22, 23, November 20, 1921; The *Dallas Morning News,* March 23, 24, May 28, 29, June 1, 4, September 20, 22, 1921.

12. *Fort Worth Star-Telegram,* May 1, 1921; author interview with Robert W. Stephens, October 7, 2013; Robert W. Stephens, *Lone Wolf: The Story of Texas Ranger Captain M. T. Gonzaullas* (Dallas: Taylor Publishing Co., 1979), p. 62.

13. J. Evetts Haley, interview with Frank Hamer, Austin, January 15, 1939.

14. The *Dallas Morning News,* May 3, June 15, 1921.

15. Sager to Tinsley, October 27, 1925, pp. 2–3, 5–7.

16. Undated transcript of radio program about Frank Hamer on "The Polar Hour," (which aired on KTBC radio in Austin in the late 1940s), Travis Hamer collection; The *Snyder Signal,* June 18, 1920; *Austin Statesman,* September 20, 1973; Newlon, "Outlaw Tamer," p. 58.

17. *Fort Worth Star-Telegram,* February 6, May 29, July 20, 1921; The *Bartlett Tribune and News,* July 22, 1921.

18. "Colonel Wants to Know Why George Nunelee Case Hasn't Been Tried in Austin," undated newspaper clipping, Frank Hamer scrapbook.

19. The *Dallas Morning News,* August 26, 1921; *Austin American,* August 25, 26, 30, 1921.

20. John H. Rogers to Pat M. Neff, January 1921, Travis Hamer collection.

21. The *Dallas Morning News,* February 11, August 13, 1921; *Fort Worth Star-Telegram,* February 15, August 13, 1921; Norman D. Brown, *Hood, Bonnet, and Little Brown Jug: Texas Politics, 1921–1928* (College Station: Texas A&M University Press, 1984), pp. 13–14; Cox, *Time of the Rangers,* p. 106; Frost and Jenkins, *I'm Frank Hamer,* p. 96.

22. *Austin American,* August 30, 1921.

12. GUNFIGHTER

1. Oath of Members, Ranger Force, Frank Hamer, September 1, 1921; R. W. Aldrich to W. A. Gray, August 20, 1921; *Austin American,* September 2, 1921; Ward, "The Texas Rangers," p. 66; Harris, Harris, and Sadler, *Texas Ranger Biographies,* pp. 253–54; Brownson Malsch, *Lone Wolf Gonzaullas, Texas Ranger* (Norman: University of Oklahoma Press, 1998), pp. 206–08; Leroy Thompson, *The Colt 1911 Pistol* (Westminster, MD: Osprey Publishing, 2011), p. 34.

2. The *Dallas Morning News,* June 21, 1951, May 25, 1963; Lewis Rigler, *In the Line of Duty: Reflections of a Texas Ranger Private* (Denton: University of North Texas Press, 1995), p. 162; Harris, Harris, and Sadler, *Texas Ranger Biographies,* pp. 126–28.

3. U.S. Census Population Schedules, El Paso (1920), Dallas (1930). The 1900 census, which was enumerated in Galveston three months before the flood, does not list his family there. His mother's name, which he claimed was Helen Von Droff, does not appear in Canadian vital statistics records. His purported middle name, Trazazas, is neither a name nor even a word in Spanish. In several accounts, however, he gave his middle name as Terrazas, which may have been a family name. Accordingly, it is possible that he was related to the large Terrazas family of El Paso. One of his biographers, Brownson Malsch, who wrote *Captain M. T. Gonzaullas: Lone*

Wolf, the Only Texas Ranger Captain of Spanish Descent (1980), reprinted as *"Lone Wolf" Gonzaullas, Texas Ranger* (1998), seems blithely unaware of his subject's background and makes no effort to detail his life before 1920. Robert W. Stephens, in *Lone Wolf: The Story of Texas Ranger Captain M. T. Gonzaullas* (Dallas: Taylor Publishing Co., 1979), which is based partly on the author's interviews with the captain, says that Gonzaullas "knew little about his early life and family background" and that he claimed he was named after General Luis Terrazas, the land baron of northern Mexico. See pp. 10–11.

4. The *Dallas Morning News*, January 1, 1926, July 13, 1969; Rick Casey, "Was First Hispanic Ranger Prejudiced?," San Antonio *Express-News*, August 9, 1996. Stories that Gonzaullas killed seventy-five outlaws are totally preposterous.

5. R. W. Aldrich to H. O. Monroe, September 14, 1921; R. W. Aldrich to M. T. Gonsaullas, September 9, 1921; interview, Captain M. T. "Lone Wolf" Gonzaullas, January 26, 1977, Texas Ranger Hall of Fame and Museum; Stephens, *Lone Wolf*, p. 25. Aldrich enlisted Lone Wolf in the Rangers in 1920 and consistently spelled his surname Gonsaullas, which again raises the question of his true name.

6. R. W. Aldrich to Frank Hamer, January 7, 1920; Stephens, *Lone Wolf*, pp. 25–26.

7. *Deseret News*, November 22, 1913; *Salt Lake Telegram*, November 22, 1913; Stephens, *Lone Wolf*, pp. 24–25. The Buffalo Bill story, at least, was not true. See *Denver Post*, December 3, 1913.

8. *Salt Lake Telegram*, November 22, 26, 1913; *Ogden Standard*, November 29, December 6, 1913; Laurence P. James, "The Great Underground Manhunt; or, One Mexican Versus the State of Utah," *Journal of the West*, vol. 18, no. 2 (April 1979), pp. 11–13.

9. *Deseret News*, November 23, 1913; *Eastern Utah Advocate*, January 08, 1914.

10. *Salt Lake Telegram*, November 22, 1913.

11. *Ibid.*, November 24, 25, 1913; *Ogden Standard*, December 6, 1913.

12. *Salt Lake Telegram*, November 26, 1913; *Ogden Standard*, November 28, 1913.

13. *Salt Lake Telegram*, November 28, 29, 1913; *Ogden Standard*, November 29, December 1, 1913; *Eastern Utah Advocate*, January 8, 1914.

14. *Ogden Standard*, December 1, 1913, February 9, 1914; *Salt Lake Telegram*, December 14, 15, 1913, February 9, 1914; *Deseret News*, April 18, 1995.

15. Frank Hamer described the Lopez gunfight in an interview with reporter Ed Kilman published in the *Houston Post*, August 5, 1945. Frank Hamer and Charlie Miller told the story of the gunfight to Frank Hamer Jr. See Randy Lish, interview with Frank Hamer Jr., October 26, 2002, and affidavit of Frank Hamer Jr., regarding death of Rafael Lopez, October 26, 2002, both in Randy Lish collection; also Frost and Jenkins, *I'm Frank Hamer*, pp. 98–101. The gold watch ended up in the collection of Hamer's friend Charlie Schreiner III and was sold at auction in 2003.

16. Newlon, "Outlaw Tamer," p. 62.

17. *Houston Post*, August 5, 1945; Randy Lish, interview with Frank Hamer Jr., October 26, 2002; Frost and Jenkins, *I'm Frank Hamer*, p. 100. Frank Hamer, in his 1945 *Houston Post* interview, referred to Rafael Lopez as "Red Lopez," a name he was occasionally, and incorrectly, called. Jenkins and Frost, *I'm Frank Hamer*, p. 98, confound Rafael Lopez with Arturo "Red" Lopez, a noted Mexican revolutionary leader who was executed in 1911. On Arturo "Red" Lopez, see *Tucson Daily Citizen*, March 24, 1911, and *Salt Lake Telegram*, June 6, 1911. Salt Lake County's deputy sheriff, Randy Lish, reopened the Rafael Lopez case in the late 1990s after learning that Lopez had been slain by Frank Hamer. Deputy Lish submitted his comprehensive report on December 2, 2002, and the case against Lopez was officially closed by the Salt Lake County district attorney on Janu-

ary 24, 2003. Randy Lish to Sheriff Aaron D. Kennard, investigation into the death of Rafael Lopez, December 2, 2002; David E. Yocum, Salt Lake County district attorney, to Sheriff Aaron Kennard, January 24, 2003; *Salt Lake Tribune*, February 17, 2003.

18. *Salt Lake Telegram*, November 22, 1913.
19. *Milwaukee Journal*, June 12, 1934; *Amarillo Sunday News Globe*, June 10, 1934.
20. J. Evetts Haley, interview with Frank Hamer, Houston, December 6, 1943.

13. BOOMTOWN

1. *Austin American*, January 19, 1949; Jenkins and Frost, *I'm Frank Hamer*, p. 101; O'Neal, *Johnson-Sims Feud*, p. 147.
2. Walter Prescott Webb, "Texas Rangers Quell Troubles," *State Trooper*, vol. 5 (August 1924), p. 13.
3. *Brownwood Bulletin*, September 17, 1919; *Rules and Regulations Governing the State Ranger Force* (Austin: Adjutant General's Department, 1919), p. 6; Jenkins and Frost, *I'm Frank Hamer*, p. 101.
4. *Fort Worth Star-Telegram*, February 24, 25, March 1, November 27, 1921; Utley, *Lone Star Lawmen*, pp. 91–92.
5. Deposition of Jim Wasson, February 20, 1922, Mexia Martial Law file, Texas Military Forces Museum; Monte Akers, *Flames After Midnight: Murder, Vengeance, and the Desolation of a Texas Community* (Austin: University of Texas Press, 2011), pp. 22, 74; Cox, *Time of the Rangers*, pp. 110–11.
6. Statement of Spencer Tarkington, Deposition of J. L Bell, January 25, 1922, Mexia Martial Law file, Texas Military Forces Museum; The *Dallas Morning News*, December 19, 1921; *Fort Worth Star-Telegram*, November 16, 19, 1921; *Mexia Daily News*, August 24, 1970.
7. The *Dallas Morning News*, January 9, 1922; *Fort Worth Star-Telegram*, January 9, 1922.
8. The Dallas *Morning News*, January 9, 1922; *Mexia Daily News*, January 9, 1922, August 24, 1970; Utley, *Lone Star Lawmen*, pp. 94–95.
9. The *Dallas Morning News*, January 9, 10, 1922; *Fort Worth Star-Telegram*, January 10, 1922; Jacob F. Wolters, *Martial Law and Its Administration* (Austin: Gammel Book Co., 1930), pp. 81–89; Utley, *Lone Star Lawmen*, p. 95.
10. The *Dallas Morning News*, January 11, 12, 1922; *Fort Worth Star-Telegram*, January 11, 1922.
11. The *Mexia Evening News* January 13, 1922; *San Antonio Express*, January 13, 1922; The *Dallas Morning News*, January 13, 14, 1922; *Fort Worth Star-Telegram*, January 13, 14, 1922.
12. The *Dallas Morning News*, January 14, 19, 20, 21, 1922; *Fort Worth Star-Telegram*, January 15, 1922; Galveston *Daily News*, January 14, 1922.
13. *Corsicana Daily Sun*, January 16, 1922.
14. Deposition of Walter Hahn, January 25, 1922, Deposition of J. L. Bell, January 26, 1922, Deposition of Johnny Johnson, January 19, 1922, Mexia Martial Law file.
15. Newlon, "Outlaw Tamer," p. 60.
16. The *Dallas Morning News*, January 26, 27, 29, 1922.
17. *Ibid.*, January 29, 1922.
18. Wolters to Adjutant General, February 3, 4, 1922, Mexia Martial Law file; The *Dallas Morning News*, February 4, 5, 1922; The *Fort Worth Star-Telegram*, February 4, 5, 1922; Utley, *Lone Star Lawmen*, pp. 95–96.

19. Jenkins and Frost, *I'm Frank Hamer,* pp. 113–18. Molesworth's account is hand-written on the back of an original photograph of Hamer firing the submachine gun, in the Briscoe Center collection.

20. The Petmecky Co. to Adjutant General, January 3, 1922; T. A. Clarke, Auto-Ordnance Corporation, to Adjutant General, January 7, 1922; R. W. Aldrich to The Petmecky Co., February 3, 24, October 6, 1922. On the Thompson submachine gun, see William J. Helmer, *The Gun That Made the Twenties Roar* (New York: Macmillan Publishing Co., 1969).

21. *Fort Worth Star-Telegram,* February 19, 1922; The *Dallas Morning News,* February 19, March 5, 1922; Utley, *Lone Star Lawmen,* p. 96. On Albert Mace (1872–1938), see Dallas *Morning News,* October 19, 1938.

22. The *Dallas Morning News,* January 18, 1922; Cox, *Time of the Rangers,* p. 110; Jenkins and Frost, *I'm Frank Hamer,* p. 111.

14. THE KU KLUX KLAN

1. The *Dallas Morning News,* May 27, 1922; *Fort Worth Star-Telegram,* May 27, 28, 1922; Newlon, "Outlaw Tamer," pp. 34–36.

2. Mexia Ku Klux Klan no. 47 to Mayor and City Commissioners, Mexia, February 28, 1922, Mexia Martial Law file; The *Dallas Morning News,* March 1, 1922; Brown, *Hood, Bonnet, and Little Brown Jug,* p. 70.

3. Brown, *Hood, Bonnet, and Little Brown Jug,* chap. 2; Richard Maxwell Brown, *Strain of Violence: Historical Studies of American Violence and Vigilantism* (New York: Oxford University Press, 1975), pp. 56–59.

4. *Wichita Falls Times,* December 30, 1962.

5. The *Dallas Morning News,* February 15, March 14, 15, 23, 24, 1922; *Fort Worth Star-Telegram,* November 5, 1921, February 21, March 22, 27, 30, 1922; Ella Marie Farmer, "The Phantom Killer of the Brazos," *True Detective Mysteries,* vol. 23, no. 3 (December 1934), pp. 38–39. On Sheriff Buchanan's bloody fight with the Klan, see Ben Procter, *Just One Riot: Episodes of Texas Rangers in the Twentieth Century* (Austin: Eakin Press, 1991), pp. 49–58.

6. *Fort Worth Star-Telegram,* January 18, March 26, 1922; The *Dallas Morning News,* March 21, 28, 31, 1922.

7. *Fort Worth Star-Telegram,* March 24, 25, April 2, 1922; The *Dallas Morning News,* April 1, 5, 8, 1922.

8. The *Dallas Morning News,* April 10, 1922; *Fort Worth Star-Telegram,* April 9, 1922.

9. The *Dallas Morning News,* May 5, June 3, 1922; *Fort Worth Star-Telegram,* May 5, 6, 7, 1922.

10. The *Dallas Morning News,* May 8, 9, 1922; *Fort Worth Star-Telegram,* May 5, 8, 1922; Akers, *Flames After Midnight,* chaps. 7 and 8.

11. The *Dallas Morning News,* March 28, April 29, May 11, June 25, July 2, 21, 1922; *Fort Worth Star-Telegram,* April 29, May 11, June 25, July 5, 1922; "Rangers Ordered Sent to Amarillo," 1922 newspaper clipping, Frank Hamer scrapbook; Brown, *Hood, Bonnet, and Little Brown Jug,* pp. 67–68, 70–71, 450 n50; Cox, *Time of the Rangers,* pp. 113, 407 n34.

12. The *Dallas Morning News,* May 11, 1922; Farmer, "Phantom Killer of the Brazos" (1934), p. 39.

13. David L. Lewis, "Sex and the Automobile," in David L. Lewis and Laurence Goldstein, *The Automobile and American Culture* (Ann Arbor: University of Michigan Press, 1983), pp. 123–29.

14. The *Dallas Morning News*, May 20, 27, 1922, *Fort Worth Star-Telegram*, May 9, 26, 1922. On the 1916 lynching, see Patricia Bernstein, *The First Waco Horror: The Lynching of Jesse Washington and the Rise of the NAACP* (College Station: Texas A&M University Press, 2005).

15. The *Dallas Morning News*, May 27, 1922; *Fort Worth Star-Telegram*, May 27, 28, 1922; *Wichita Daily Times*, May 26, 1922; Newlon, "Outlaw Tamer," pp. 34–36.

16. The *Dallas Morning News*, May 28, November 21, 1922, January 16, 1923, November 8, 1953; *Fort Worth Star-Telegram*, November 21, 1922; "Waco Is Quiet," undated 1922 news clipping, Frank Hamer scrapbook; Ella Marie Farmer, "Phantom Killer of the Brazos," *True Detective Mysteries*, vol. 23, no. 4 (January 1935), pp. 73–74.

17. The *Dallas Morning News*, January 22, February 1, 10, 21, July 31, 1923; *San Antonio Evening News*, February 9, 1923; Farmer, "Phantom Killer of the Brazos," (1935), pp. 76–78.

18. The *Dallas Morning News*, July 17, 22, 31, 1923, March 10, 1934; The *Galveston Daily News*, February 1, 10, 1923. Patricia Bernstein, in *The First Waco Horror*, p. 189, argues that Roy Mitchell may have been innocent, suggesting that the stolen property could have been planted in his house. That is most improbable. Based on Mitchell's admissions, evidence against him was collected in several other locations and a watch taken from one of the victims was even recovered from a friend of Mitchell's in Detroit, Michigan. One hour before he died, Mitchell again voluntarily confessed to all the murders. Mitchell's execution is often called the last legal hanging in Texas. That is incorrect. The last legal hanging was that of Nathan Lee in Angleton, Brazoria County, a month after Mitchell's execution. The *Dallas Morning News*, September 1, 1923, February 15, 1998.

19. *San Antonio Express*, July 23, 1922; The *Dallas Morning News*, July 23, 1922; *Fort Worth Star-Telegram*, July 22, 1922; "Corpus Christi Boys Won Hard Fight After Long, Bitter Struggle," July 26, 1922, newspaper clipping, Frank Hamer scrapbook.

20. *San Antonio Light*, October 15, 1922; The *Dallas Morning News*, October 15, 17, 1922; *Laredo Weekly Times*, January 14, 1923.

21. "Fusillade of Revolver Bullets Ends Life of Prominent Citizen of Corpus Christi While Unarmed," undated 1922 newspaper clipping, Frank Hamer scrapbook; Frost and Jenkins, *I'm Frank Hamer*, p. 122.

22. "Fusillade of Revolver Bullets Ends Life"; *San Antonio Express*, October 16, 27, 1922, January 9, 1923; The *Dallas Morning News*, October 15, 17, November 6, 1922, January 7, 14, 1923; *Bartlett Tribune and News*, October 20, 1922, November 16, 1923; *Fort Worth Star-Telegram*, October 15, 16, 17, 25, 1922; *Brownsville Herald*, October 16, 18, 1922; *Victoria Advocate*, October 24, 1922; *Laredo Times*, August 13, 1941; *Corpus Christi Caller Times*, July 21, 2010.

23. Frank Hamer to Herbert Mills, July 15, 1952. The Hamer presentation Colt is in a private collection; Captain Wright's identical gun is on display in the Texas Ranger Hall of Fame and Museum.

24. The *Breckenridge Daily American*, November 16, 17, 1922.

25. Ibid., November 16, 17, 21, 26, 28, 1922; The *Dallas Morning News*, November 16, 17, 21, 28, 1922; *Fort Worth Star-Telegram*, November 17, 19, 20, 21, 22, 1922.

26. The *Galveston Daily News*, March 18, 1923; *San Antonio Express*, March 18, 1923; *Austin Statesman*, March 16, 17, 18, 1923; *Austin American*, March 17, 1923.

27. The *Dallas Morning News*, July 4, 6, 7, 11, 13, 18, 19, 20, 23, 24, August 19, October 18, 23, 1923, June 13, 14, December 1, 1926, September 20, 1927; *Brownwood Bulletin*, July 14, 1923; *Corsicana Daily Sun*, July 9, 1923; *Weimar Mercury*, June 17, 1927; *Shelburne v. State* (1928) 11 Southwestern Reporter 520.

28. The *Dallas Morning News,* August 16, 17, 19, 23, October 10, 11, 12, 1923, January 4, 5, 1924, January 1, 1925, January 24, 1926; *Brownwood Bulletin,* January 5, 1924; J. Evetts Haley, interview with Frank Hamer, Austin, January 15, 1939; Mika Smith, "Hooded Crusaders: The Ku Klux Klan in the Panhandle and South Plains, 1921–1925," M.A. thesis, Texas Tech University (2008), pp. 24–29; Paul Howard Carlson, *Amarillo: The Story of a Western Town* (Lubbock: Texas Tech University Press, 2006), pp. 104–05.

29. The *Dallas Morning News,* January 1, 1925, March 7, 1926, February 4, 1928; David L. Chapman, "Lynching in Texas," M.A. thesis, Texas Tech University (1973), pp. 111–12.

15. MA AND PA FERGUSON

1. The *Dallas Morning News,* May 21, 22, 23, 1925; *Brownwood Bulletin* May 22, 1925.

2. The *Dallas Morning News,* May 24, 25, 26, 27, 28, July 3, 1925; *Furman v. Georgia* (1972) 408 U.S. 238.

3. *San Antonio Express,* March 27, 1925; The *Galveston Daily News,* June 14, 1925; Ward, "Texas Rangers," pp. 125–26; Sterling, *Trails and Trials of a Texas Ranger,* p. 115.

4. The *Galveston Daily News,* June 4, 1925; The *Dallas Morning News,* June 4, 1925.

5. Neff to Hamer, June 12, 1925, reproduced in Frost and Jenkins, *I'm Frank Hamer,* p. 128.

6. Oath of Service and Warrant of Authority, Frank Hamer, July 1, 1925; The *Galveston Daily News,* January 15, 1933; Walter Prescott Webb, "Rangers Reorganized," *State Trooper* July 1927, p. 13; Cox, *Time of the Rangers,* p. 127; Utley, *Lone Star Lawmen,* pp. 112, 359 n5.

7. Aldrich to Mrs. Josephine Davis, May 24, 1926, Roy Aldrich papers, Briscoe Center; The *Dallas Morning News,* July 17, 1921; *Rules and Regulations Governing the State Ranger Force,* pp. 9–10; Sterling, *Trails and Trials of a Texas Ranger,* pp. 194, 197.

8. *Austin American-Statesman,* February 17, 1976.

9. Clippings from Frank Hamer scrapbook, November 1922; The *Galveston Daily News,* November 23, 1925; Frost and Jenkins, *I'm Frank Hamer,* p. 126.

10. The *Dallas Morning News,* November 15, 24, 28, 1923; *San Antonio Express,* January 20, 1927.

11. *San Antonio Light,* October 18, 1926, January 2, 1927.

12. The *Galveston Daily News,* December 9, 11, 12, 1926; *Abilene Morning News,* December 10, 1926; *San Antonio Express,* January 2, 1927; *Mexia Daily News,* September 2, 1926; *San Antonio Light,* August 31, December 9, 1926.

13. The *Galveston Daily News,* January 19, 20, 1927; *San Antonio Light,* January 20, May 2, 1927; *San Antonio Express,* January 20, 21, 22, 23, 1927, October 22, November 3, 4, 1931; Social Security Death Index, Frank Bonner.

14. The *Dallas Morning News,* August 10, 12, 13, 1925; Ward, "Texas Rangers," p. 131; Walter Prescott Webb, "Larger Texas Force," *State Trooper* (February 1927), p. 17; R. D. Thorp, "$1000 for the Murder of the Three Englers," *True Detective Mysteries,* vol. 30, no. 1 (April 1938), pp. 4–7. Perhaps at Hamer's insistence, Thorp makes no mention of his role in the investigation.

15. Alison Winter, *Memory: Fragments of a Modern History* (Chicago: University of Chicago Press, 2012), pp. 33–47. By the 1930s the most popular truth serum was Sodium Pentothal.

16. *Mexia Daily News*, January 11, 1926; *Corpus Christi Times*, January 11, 1926; *San Antonio Express*, January 12, 1926; *San Antonio Light*, September 10, 1926.

17. The *Dallas Morning News*, January 2, 1927; *Laredo Daily Times*, January 1, 3, 1927; *Denton Record Chronicle*, January 3, 1927; The *Galveston Daily News*, January 4, 1927.

18. *San Antonio Light*, February 7, 1927; Thorp, "$1000 for the Murder of the Three Englers," pp. 9, 110–12; Webb, *Texas Rangers*, p. 530.

19. *Laredo Times*, January 14, 1926; *San Antonio Express*, January 17, February 2, 10, April 29, 1926; March 27, 1926; The *Dallas Morning News*, March 27, 1926; *Brownwood Bulletin*, March 26, 1926; The *Seattle Daily Times*, February 9, 1926; *Boston Herald*, March 27, 1926; *San Antonio Light*, February 19, 1931.

20. *San Antonio Light*, June 26, 1926, August 2, 1929; Mrs. J. A. Ramsey, "When Death Rode the Old Spanish Trail," *Master Detective*, vol. 11, no. 6 (February 1935), pp. 6–11, 67.

21. *Port Arthur News*, December 23, 1928; *San Antonio Express*, February 17, 1926; The *Dallas Morning News*, February 17, 1926; "Rogers Given Rough Ride," 1926 Austin newspaper clipping, Frank Hamer scrapbook; C. Richard King, "The Poet Lariat Comes to Town," *The Alcalde, University of Texas Alumni Magazine* (April 1960), p. 16.

22. Confession of John B. Sawyer, undated typescript, Travis Hamer collection; *Portland Oregonian*, December 27, 1925, February 2, August 16, 1926; *San Antonio Express*, February 8, 1926; *San Antonio Light*, July 22, 1926; The *Dallas Morning News*, July 22, 1926; *Prescott (AZ) Evening Courier*, July 22, 1926; Walter Prescott Webb, "Rangers Solve Mystery," *State Trooper*, October 1926, p. 10; Newlon, "Outlaw Tamer," pp. 61–62; Jenkins and Frost, *I'm Frank Hamer*, pp. 132–35.

23. The *Galveston Daily News*, January 19, 20, 1927; Carl McQueary and May Nelson Paulissen, *Miriam: The Southern Belle Who Became the First Woman Governor of Texas* (Waco: Eakin Press, 1994), pp. 161–62, 205; Brown, *Hood, Bonnet, and Little Brown Jug*, pp. 270–74.

24. Miriam A. Ferguson, Pardon Proclamation, Felix R. Jones, November 23, 1926, Texas State Archives; *Lubbock Morning Avalanche*, October 28, 1925; *San Antonio Express* July 21, October 28, 1925; The *Galveston Daily News*, November 23, December 16, 1926; The *Dallas Morning News*, December 16, 1926; *Abilene Morning News*, December 16, 1926.

25. *San Antonio Express*, June 1, 1924, January 8, 1925; *E. B. McClure v. State of Texas* (1926) 281 Southwest Reports 559; death certificates of Montie Mitchell and Wesley Lisk, accessed on familysearch.org; Harris and Sadler, *Texas Rangers and the Mexican Revolution*, p. 490.

26. Miriam A. Ferguson, Pardon Proclamation, E. B. McClure, January 4, 1927, Texas State Archives; The *Dallas Morning News*, February 15, March 27, 1925; The *Galveston Daily News*, December 31, 1926, January 6, 1927; Stephens, *Lone Wolf*, pp. 62–63.

16. THE HINGES OF HELL

1. *Amarillo Sunday News Globe*, June 10, 1934; Kinney, "Frank Hamer, Texas Ranger," p. 86; Frost and Jenkins, *I'm Frank Hamer*, pp. 123–24

2. The *Galveston Daily News*, March 18, 1923; *Corsicana Daily Sun*, January 14, 1928; Walter Prescott Webb, "Rangers Arrest Lawmakers," *State Trooper* (April 1927), p. 11.

3. Roy W. Aldrich to Add Magoffin, January 12, 1927, Aldrich Papers, Briscoe Center; *San Antonio Express*, January 22, 1927.

4. Oath of Service and Warrant of Authority, Frank Hamer, February 2, 1927; Oath of Service and Warrant of Authority, J. W. Aldrich, September 28, 1925; *Laredo Daily Times*, February 4, 1927; The *Galveston Daily News*, March 26, April 29, 1927; Utley, *Lone Star Lawmen*, pp. 119–21; Sterling, *Trails and Trials of a Texas Ranger*, p. 96.

5. *San Antonio Light*, April 17, 1928; *Lubbock Morning Avalanche*, April 18, 22, 1928; *Corsicana Semi-Weekly Light*, April 24, May 29, 1928; *Journal of the House of Representatives of the Regular Session of the Fortieth Legislature of the State of Texas* (1927), testimony of Willis Chamberlin, pp. 351–77, Frank Hamer, pp. 377–80, Thomas Hickman, pp. 382–85, Robert L. Bobbitt, pp. 423–28, Jacob F. Wolters, pp. 428–30; Webb, "Rangers Arrest Lawmakers," p. 11; Brown, *Hood, Bonnet, and Little Brown Jug*, pp. 346–47.

6. The *Dallas Morning News*, October 13, November 6, 1926; Utley, *Lone Star Lawmen*, pp. 115–17; Sterling, *Trails and Trials of a Texas Ranger*, p. 99; Malsch, *Lone Wolf Gonzaullas*, pp. 64–65.

7. The *Dallas Morning News*, December 1, 23, 1926, January 23, February 2, 27, 1927; *Borger Daily Herald*, March 21, 22, 29, April 1, November 27, 1927.

8. The *Dallas Morning News*, April 1, 2, 1927; *Borger Daily Herald*, December 16, 1927.

9. Mike Cox, "One Riot, One Ranger," in Mike Blakely, Mary Elizabeth Goldman, eds., *Forever Texas: Texas, The Way Those Who Lived It Wrote It* (New York: Forge Books, 2000), pp. 211–12.

10. The *Galveston Daily News*, April 2, 1927; *San Antonio Light*, April 2, 1927; *Borger Daily Herald*, April 5, 6, 1927; "Polar Hour," p. 8.

11. The *Dallas Morning News*, April 9, 1927; *Borger Daily Herald*, April 7, 8, 1927; Sterling, *Trails and Trials of a Texas Ranger*, p. 105.

12. *Borger Daily Herald*, April 8, 10, 1927; *Papachristou v. City of Jacksonville* (1972) 405 U.S. 156.

13. *Borger Daily Herald*, April 11, 12, 13, 14, 1927; John R. Erickson, "Panhandle Outlaw," *True West*, vol. 21, no. 3 (January–February 1974), p. 49–50.

14. *Borger Daily Herald*, April 17, 18, 1921; The *Dallas Morning News*, May 4, 1927; Sterling, *Trails and Trials of a Texas Ranger*, p. 99.

15. Cox, "One Riot, One Ranger," p. 213.

16. Sterling, *Trails and Trials of a Texas Ranger*, p. 100, 420.

17. *San Antonio Express*, April 21, 1927; The *Dallas Morning News*, May 5, 8, 15, 1927; *Borger Daily Herald*, April 19, 20, 21, May 9, 1927; A. P. Cummings Service File, Adjutant General Records.

18. The *Dallas Morning News*, April 23, 1927. Lone Wolf Gonzaullas told his biographer that a corrupt Borger official falsely charged Hamer with killing a man and that Hamer returned to Hutchinson County with Tom Hickman and Gonzaullas and threatened the grand jury not to indict him. Gonzaulla's memory was incorrect, for the story appears to be a garbled version of the prosecution of Special Ranger Jack DeGraftenreid for shooting the deputy on July 20, 1927. DeGraftenreid was indicted by the grand jury, but a trial jury found him not guilty on grounds of self-defense. Stephens, *Lone Wolf*, pp. 40–41; *Borger Daily Herald*, July 21, 22, 24, 1927; *Pampa Daily News*, August 7, 1927.

19. The *Galveston Daily News*, May 27, September 20, 1927; *Corsicana Daily Sun*, June 20, 1927; *Abilene Morning News*, June 21, 1927; *Port Arthur News*, September 25, 1927, September 6, 1929; *Mexia Daily News*, September 28, 1927; *San Antonio Light*, September 28, October 3, 1927; *Lubbock Morning Avalanche*, February 19, 1930.

20. The *Dallas Morning News*, January 2, 1927; *Roswell Daily Record*, January 27, 1928;

Laredo Daily Times, January 25, 1928; *Farmington Times-Hustler*, March 9, 1928; *Jefferson City News and Tribune*, February 25, 1934; Frost and Jenkins, *I'm Frank Hamer*, pp. 141–42; Sterling, *Trails and Trials of a Texas Ranger*, pp. 491–95; Rick Miller, *Sam Bass and Gang* (Austin: State House Press, 1999), pp. 301–03.

21. The *Llano News*, October 27, November 3, 1927; *San Antonio Light*, October 30, 31, 1927; *San Antonio Express*, November 1, 1927, November 24, 1928; *Corsicana Daily Sun*, May 21, 1928; The *Galveston Daily News*, November 1, 1927, February 5, 1928; *Sweetwater Daily Reporter*, October 31, 1927; *San Saba News*, November 24, 1927; *Kerrville Daily Times*, November 24, 1927; *Breckenridge Daily American*, January 15, 1928; Webb, *Texas Rangers*, p. 531; Frost and Jenkins, *I'm Frank Hamer*, pp. 136–38.

22. Frank A. Hamer to A. H. Reitz, February 13, 1928, Travis Hamer collection.

23. *Weimar Mercury*, February 3, 1928; *Corsicana Daily Sun*, February 11, 1928; *Avalanche Journal*, February 12, 1928; *Pampa Daily News*, February 13, 1928; *Bastrop Advertiser*, September 20, 1928; Sterling, *Trails and Trials of a Texas Ranger*, pp. 129–33.

24. Utrecht, "Frank Hamer," p. 50; author interview with Laura David, April 18, 2012.

25. Sterling, *Trails and Trials of a Texas Ranger*, p. 418.

17. THE MURDER MACHINE

1. On the number of Texas bank robberies in the 1920s, see Bob Alexander, *Lawmen, Outlaws, and S.O.B.s*, vol. 2 (Silver City, NM: High-Lonesome Books, 2007), p. 129. On the number of Newton-gang burglaries, see Willis Newton, interview, in the documentary film *The Newton Boys: Portrait of an Outlaw Gang* (1976).

2. The *Dallas Morning News*, September 10, 11, 17, 1926; Walter Prescott Webb, "Bank Robbers Slain," *State Trooper* (November 1926), pp. 7–8.

3. The *Dallas Morning News*, September 11, 1926; *Abilene Morning News*, September 11, 1926; *Grand Prairie Texan*, September 17, 1926; Webb, *Texas Rangers*, p. 533.

4. The *Dallas Morning News*, November 10, 1927, March 18, 1928; *Laredo Daily Times*, November 10, 1927; "When Homicide Committed to Prevent Commission of Crimes Is Justifiable," *Texas Law Review*, vol. 6 (1927–28), p. 184.

5. The *Dallas Morning News*, November 26, 27, 28, 1927; *Laredo Daily Times*, November 25, 1927; *Sweetwater Daily Reporter*, November 25, 1927.

6. The *Dallas Morning News*, December 24, 1927; The *Galveston Daily News*, December 24, 1927; T. Lindsay Baker, *Gangster Tour of Texas* (College Station: Texas A&M University Press, 2011), pp. 122–30.

7. The *Dallas Morning News*, January 11, 1928; *Lubbock Morning Avalanche*, January 13, 1928; Utley, *Lone Star Lawmen*, pp. 125–26.

8. The *Dallas Morning News*, January 13, 15, 1928; *Lubbock Morning Avalanche*, January 13, 1928; *Corsicana Semi Weekly Light*, January 13, 1928.

9. Webb, *Texas Rangers*, pp. 533–34.

10. *Ibid.*, p. 534.

11. Frank Hamer, "The Truth About the Bank Bandits and the Rewards," p. 1, typescript, Walter Prescott Webb papers. A condensed version of Hamer's statement appears in Webb, *Texas Rangers*, pp. 536–38.

12. *Milwaukee Journal*, June 11, 1934.

13. Austin Police Department identification cards, James Houston Dumas and Carl Fred Wood, April 23, 1928; Oklahoma State Penitentiary Record, J. H. Dumas; both in Travis Hamer collection.

14. Webb, *Texas Rangers*, p. 534.
15. Hamer, "The Truth About the Bank Bandits and the Rewards," pp. 3–9.
16. Webb, *Texas Rangers*, pp. 535–36; The *Galveston Daily News*, March 14, 1928; *Corsicana Semi-Weekly Light*, March 20, 1928. A "lie bill" was Southern slang for a false or libelous statement.
17. The *Dallas Morning News*, April 6, 7, 1928; *San Antonio Light*, April 8, 1928.
18. *Lubbock Morning Avalanche*, April 12, 27, 1928; *San Antonio Express*, April 12, 1928; *San Antonio Light*, April 16, 1928; *Port Arthur News*, April 25, 1928.
19. Interview with Graves Peeler, by W. K. Daetwyler, May 6, 1967, Cattle Raisers Museum, Fort Worth; Lawrence Clayton, *Longhorn Legacy, Graves Peeler and the Texas Cattle Trade* (Abilene: Cowboy Press, 1994); a digital copy can be found at www.ctlr.org, the Web site of the Cattlemen's Texas Longhorn Registry.
20. The *Dallas Morning News*, May 17, November 13, December 5, 1928, April 14, October 15, 1929, March 3, October 7, 1930, June 20, 1931; *San Antonio Express*, September 29, 1931.
21. The *Dallas Morning News*, March 18, 1928 April 12, 17, 18, 19, May 16, June 7, 1930; *Big Spring Herald*, February 24, 1928, April 17, 1930; *San Antonio Express*, November 28, 1929; *Lubbock Morning Avalanche*, January 5, 1929. A copy of the 1946 version of the reward poster appears in the *Texas Ranger Dispatch*, issue 31 (Winter 2010), p. 22.

18. TOWN TAMER

1. Frank A. Hamer to H. J. Porter, November 28, 1952, Travis Hamer collection.
2. *Houston Chronicle*, June 21, 1928; *San Antonio Light*, June 20, 21, 1928; The *Galveston Daily News*, June 18, 19, 21, 22, 23, 24, 1928; The *Dallas Morning News*, June 21, 22, October 1, 6, 1928, May 4, December 20, 21, 1929; *Greensboro* (NC) *Daily News*, June 21, 1928; Ward, "Texas Rangers," p. 158.
3. *Austin Statesman*, October 9, 10, 1928; *Austin American*, October 10, 1928; The *Galveston Daily News*, October 10, 1928; The *Dallas Morning News*, October 10, 1928; *New Orleans Times-Picayune*, October 10, 1928; Clifford R. Caldwell and Ron DeLord, *Texas Lawmen, 1900–1940: More of the Good and the Bad* (Charleston: History Press, 2012), pp. 25–26. Austin's worst serial murderer was the so-called Servant Girl Annihilator of 1885, with eight victims.
4. The *Dallas Morning News*, November 6, 7, 8, 9, 1928; *San Antonio Express*, November 8, 1928.
5. The *Dallas Morning News*, November 10, 1928; *Lubbock Morning Avalanche*, November 10, 1928; J. Gilberto Quezada, *Border Boss: Manuel B. Bravo and Zapata County* (College Station: Texas A&M University Press, 2001), pp. 18–19, 22–23.
6. Sterling, *Trails and Trials of a Texas Ranger*, pp. 196–97.
7. *Abilene Morning News*, June 11, 1929; The *Dallas Morning News*, June 29, 30, 1929; Wolters, *Martial Law and Its Administration*, pp. 92–93; Ward, "Texas Rangers," pp. 166–67; Malsch, *Lone Wolf Gonzaullas*, pp. 75–77; Utley, *Lone Star Lawmen*, pp. 129–30.
8. The *Dallas Morning News*, September 14, 15, 1929; *San Antonio Light*, September 14, 1929; The *Kansas City Star*, September 22, 1929; testimony of William H. Bates, p. 10, Borger Martial Law file, Texas State Military Forces Museum.
9. The *Dallas Morning News*, September 17, 1929; *Kansas City Journal-Post*, October 6, 1929.

10. *Lubbock Morning Avalanche,* November 3, 1928; The *Dallas Morning News,* January 13, 1929; testimony of Johnny Ford, p. 15, Borger Martial Law file.

11. Johnson Gault, "Benjamin Maney Gault—Texas Ranger," typescript dated April 19, 1978, author's collection.

12. Testimony of William H. Bates and Tex Thrower, Borger Martial Law file; *Abilene Morning News,* September 19, 1929; Ward, "Texas Rangers," p. 167; Cox, *Texas Ranger Tales,* p. 228.

13. Clifford Braley to Morris Sheppard, December 10, 1932, Travis Hamer collection; *Pampa Daily News,* September 22, 1929; The *Galveston Daily News,* September 23, 1929; *Lubbock Morning Avalanche,* September 24, 1929.

14. *Mexia Weekly Herald,* September 20, 1929; *San Antonio Express,* September 24, 1929; *Breckenridge American,* September 24, 1929.

15. Wolters, *Martial Law and Its Administration,* p. 94.

16. The *Dallas Morning News,* September 30, October 1, 1929; *Denton Record Chronicle,* September 30, October 2, 1929.

17. Malsch, *Lone Wolf Gonzaullas,* p. 78. Malsch mistakenly conflates the 1927 and 1929 Borger cleanups as a single event.

18. Testimony of William H. Bates and Johnny Ford, Borger Martial Law file.

19. Testimony of Clint Millhollon, Willie Mae Millhollon, Berlin Millhollon, Sam Jones, Mrs. Sam Jones, Borger Martial Law file.

20. Testimony of Joe Ownbey.

21. Testimony of William H. Bates, Louis Crim; *Borger Daily Herald,* July 1, December 20, 1927.

22. Testimony of Tex Thrower.

23. Testimony of Hoyt Embry, Martial Law Court Transcript, vol., 1, pp. 10–12, 36–37; testimony of Jim Hodges, vol. 1, pp. 182–85.

24. *Reno Evening Gazette,* October 4, 1929; *Denton Record Chronicle,* October 7, 1929.

25. *Denton Record Chronicle,* October 5, 1929; Wolters, *Martial Law and Its Administration,* pp. 89–119.

26. The *Dallas Morning News,* November 7, 1929.

27. *Ibid.,* November 3, 1929; *San Antonio Express,* November 4, 1929, May 15, 1930; The *Galveston Daily News,* November 17, 1929; Utley, *Lone Star Lawmen,* p. 133.

28. *San Antonio Light,* April 30, 1922, August 3, 4, September 25, 1929, November 19, 1944; *San Antonio Evening News,* July 17, 1922; "Hundreds Attend Stevens' Funeral," 1929 newspaper clipping, Frank Hamer scrapbook; Baker, *Gangster Tour of Texas,* pp. 161–79.

29. *San Antonio Express,* October 31, 1929; *Abilene Morning News,* October 31, 1929; The *Dallas Morning News,* November 7, 1929.

19. FUNERALS IN SHERMAN

1. Keith J. Volanto, *Texas, Cotton, and the New Deal* (College Station: Texas A&M University Press, 2004), pp. 4–6, 12–13.

2. The *Dallas Morning News,* August 26, 1921, May 19, 1922; Myra Elizabeth Crabb, "The Killing of a Black Man: The Case of George Hughes," M.A. thesis, East Texas State University (1990), pp. 1–11.

3. The *Dallas Morning News,* January 1, December 30, 1927, February 4, 1928, January 1, 1929, April 29, 1930; Chapman, "Lynching in Texas," pp. 112–13. Although the Tuskegee Institute reported that Texas had seven lynchings in 1926, that was

incorrect. The only lynching incident that year occurred near Raymondville, when local lawmen murdered four prisoners who had killed two deputy sheriffs. Three blacks were murdered by whites in another incident in Fort Bend County, but that resulted from a feud and was not a lynching. The *Dallas Morning News,* September 9, November 12, 25, 1926, January 1, 1927; Ward, "Texas Rangers," p. 142.

4. The *Dallas Morning News,* May 4, 1930; Crabb, "Killing of a Black Man," pp. 14–18; Arthur Franklin Raper, *The Tragedy of Lynching* (Chapel Hill: University of North Carolina Press, 1933), pp. 4, 319–20, 329.

5. *Lubbock Morning Avalanche,* May 9, 1930; testimony of R. C. Hart, Military Hearing at Sherman, Texas, vol. 2, pp. 250–51, 547–48; Texas Military Forces Museum; The *Dallas Morning News,* May 5, 7, 17, 1930; Crabb, "Killing of a Black Man," pp. 18–19.

6. The *Galveston Daily News,* May 10, 1930; Raper, *Tragedy of Lynching,* p. 321.

7. *Houston Press,* May 10, 1930.

8. Testimony of R. C. Hart, Military Hearing at Sherman, Texas, vol. 2, p. 250–52, Texas Military Forces Museum; J. Newell Johnston (ed., *Sherman Democrat*) to Dan Moody, May 16, 1930, Texas State Archives; The *Dallas Morning News,* May 18, 1930; Raper, *Tragedy of Lynching,* pp. 323–24; Crabb, "Killing of a Black Man," pp. 8–11.

9. Testimony of L. O. Blankenship, pp. 481–82, testimony of W. T. Mills, p. 491; Martial Law Jail Register, May 16, 1930, Texas Military Forces Museum; *Houston Press,* May 10, 1930; The *Dallas Morning News,* May 10, 13, 1930; The *Galveston Daily News,* May 10, 1930; *Greensburg* (PA) *Daily Tribune,* May 10, 1930; Raper, *Tragedy of Lynching,* pp. 323–24.

10. *Houston Press,* May 10, 1930.

11. Testimony of Jim Brown, pp. 617–27; Frank Hamer to Dan Moody, May 13, 1930, Texas State Archives; The *Dallas Morning News,* May 10, 1930; *Houston Press,* May 10, 1930.

12. *State of Texas v. J. B. McCasland,* no. A-20, 255, District Court, Travis County; testimony of Reagan H. Cooper, pp. 373–74; testimony of W. T. Spencer, pp. 408–09; testimony of H. L. Doggett, p. 456; testimony of T. W. McGraw, pp. 474–75; testimony of Robert Carter, pp. 593–95, all in Texas Military Forces Museum; Hamer to Moody, May 13, 1930; Dan Moody to F. A. Robinett, May 15, 1930; The *Dallas Morning News,* May 10, June 4, 5, 1930; *Houston Press,* May 10, 1930; *Greensburg* (PA) *Daily Tribune,* May 10, 1930; Crabb, "Killing of a Black Man," pp. 30–31; Raper, *Tragedy of Lynching,* pp. 11, 324–25.

13. Hamer to Moody, May 13, 1930; testimony of John Bruce, vol. 2, p. 415; Crabb, "Killing of a Black Man," pp. 32, 40–41; Ward, "Texas Rangers," p. 176; Stephens, *Lone Wolf,* pp. 46–47.

14. Raper, *Tragedy of Lynching,* p. 327; Ward, "Texas Rangers," p. 176; Stephens, *Lone Wolf,* pp. 46–47.

15. Testimony of John Bruce, vol. 2, p. 416; The *Dallas Morning News,* May 10, 1930.

16. Albert Sidney Johnson to Dan Moody, May 12, 1930, Texas State Archives; *Denton Record Chronicle,* May 10, 1930; Stephens, *Lone Wolf,* p. 48.

17. Testimony of John L. Melton, p. 523–24; *Denton Record Chronicle,* May 10, 1930; The *Galveston Daily News,* May 10, 1930; The *Dallas Morning News,* May 11, 1930; Stephens, *Lone Wolf,* pp. 47–48; Utley, *Lone Star Lawmen,* p. 137.

18. Testimony of Delmar Knox, pp. 384–85; Testimony of T. W. McGraw, p. 473; testimony of Robert Carter, pp. 601–02; Colonel Lawrence McGee, Final Report Re Martial Law Duty, Sherman, Texas, May 27, 1930, all in Texas Military Forces Museum; The *Dallas Morning News,* May 10, 1930; Raper, *Tragedy of Lynching,* p. 326.

19. Testimony of H. L. Doggett, p. 457; testimony of T. W. McGraw, pp. 470–71; testimony of Bill Sofey, pp. 505–06; Martial Law Jail Register, May 14, 1930.

20. Testimony of John Bruce, pp. 420–22; testimony of Bill Sofey, p. 507; testimony of Johnny Bryant, pp. 562, 572; The *Dallas Morning News*, May 10, 11, 1930; Raper, *Tragedy of Lynching*, p. 347.

21. Testimony of Jim Parker, pp. 461–63; testimony of T. W. McGraw, p. 472; testimony of Bill Sofey, pp. 508–09; testimony of R. H. Goff, p. 541; testimony of Johnny Bryant, pp. 562–80; testimony of Robert Carter, pp. 597–608; *Denton Record Chronicle*, May 10, 1930; The *Dallas Morning News*, May 11, 1930; *Trenton (NJ) Evening Times*, May 10, 1930; *Wyandotte (KS) Echo*, May 23, 1930; Raper, *Tragedy of Lynching*, pp. 326–28.

22. Testimony of Bill Sofey, p. 497; The *Dallas Morning News*, July 30, 1951; U.S. Census Population Schedules, Sherman, Texas, 1930; Raper, *Tragedy of Lynching*, pp. 328, 332; *Sherman City Directory* (Sioux City, IA: R. L. Polk & Co., 1925), pp. 242, 280, 346.

23. McGee, Final Report Re Martial Law Duty; The *Dallas Morning News*, May 11, 1930; The *Denton Record Chronicle*, May 10, 1930; *Trenton (NJ) Evening Times*, May 10, 1930.

24. The *Dallas Morning News*, May 11, 12, 1930; *London Evening Standard*, May 10, 1930.

25. Transcript, Military Hearing at Sherman, vol. 2, pp. 372–90, 396–98; The *Dallas Morning News*, May 16, 1930.

26. The *Dallas Morning News*, May 21, 31, November 16, 18, 1930, June 5, November 1, 3, 1931; *San Antonio Light*, June 3, 1932; Crabb, "Killing of a Black Man," pp. 47–48.

27. *Baltimore Afro-American*, June 7, 1930; Crabb, "Killing of a Black Man," p. 21; Raper, *Tragedy of Lynching*, p. 319. The *Afro-American* evidently got its story from Sherman sources, for it identified Pearl Farlow by her maiden name, Atnip.

28. Johnston to Moody, May 16, 1930; Moody to Johnston, May 20, 1930; *Sherman Democrat* to Dan Moody (telegram), May 16, 2013; The *Dallas Morning News*, May 15, 16, 18, 1930; *Sherman Democrat*, May 15, 1930.

29. The *Dallas Morning News*, May 17, June 1, 19, 1930; Raper, *Tragedy of Lynching*, pp. 125–29, 369–73.

30. Hamer to Moody, May 13, 1930; author interview with Robert W. Stephens, October 7, 2013; *Greensburg (PA) Daily Tribune*, May 10, 1930; Ward, "Texas Rangers," p. 176.

31. Sidney A. Stemmons to Dan Moody, May 14, 1930; The *Dallas Morning News*, May 16, 1930; Frost and Jenkins, *I'm Frank Hamer*, p. 168.

32. *Sherman Democrat*, March 17, 1996; Graham Landron, *Grayson County: An Illustrated History of Grayson County, Texas* (Fort Worth: University Supply & Equipment Co., 1960), p. 94.

20. BONNIE AND CLYDE

1. Sterling, *Trails and Trials of a Texas Ranger*, pp. 182–83, 197–204; Utley, *Lone Star Lawmen*, pp. 142–43; Spellman, *Captain John H. Rogers*, pp. 222–23.

2. The *Dallas Morning News*, February 11, 1931.

3. Frank Hamer, letter to oil companies, March 30, 1931; R. S. Ellison to Hamer, April 30, 1931, both in Travis Hamer collection; The *Dallas Morning News*, April 25, 26, 1931; *Denton Record Chronicle*, April 25, 1931; *Port Arthur News*, April 26, 1931; *San Antonio Light*, April 26, 1931; *Omaha World Herald*, April 25, 1931.

4. J. H. Baker to Tom Connally, December 6, 1932, Travis Hamer collection; *Seattle Daily Times*, July 15, 1934.

5. *San Antonio Express*, February 20, 21, 1932; *Denton Record-Chronicle*, February 20, 22, 1932; *Corsicana Daily Sun*, March 4, 1932; The *Galveston Daily News*, October 30, 1932.

6. The *Dallas Morning News*, August 14, 16, 17, 22, 23, 1932; *San Antonio Light*, July 10, 1932; *Corsicana Daily Sun*, August 22, 1932; *Brownsville Herald*, August 22, 1932; Newlon, "Outlaw Tamer," p. 39; Sterling, *Trails and Trials of a Texas Ranger*, pp. 252, 254–55, 264–66. Ward, "The Texas Rangers," p. 206, mistakenly states that the Gregg County raids were actually made.

7. *San Antonio Express*, September 5, 1932; The *Dallas Morning News*, September 7, 8, 1932; Sterling, *Trails and Trials of a Texas Ranger*, pp. 266–69; Ross S. Sterling and Ed Kilman, *Ross Sterling, Texan: A Memoir by the Founder of Humble Oil and Refining Company* (Austin: University of Texas Press, 2007), p. 216.

8. The *Dallas Morning News*, September 2, 10, 12, 1932; Sterling, *Trails and Trials of a Texas Ranger*, p. 270; Sterling and Kilman, *Ross Sterling, Texan*, pp. 209–10; Ward, "Texas Rangers," pp. 208–13.

9. *Rules and Regulations Governing State Ranger Force*, p. 5; Frank Hamer to Les Porter, August 20, 1932; W. W. Sterling, Special Order, November 1, 1932; The *Dallas Morning News*, October 16, 1932.

10. J. A. Whitten to Tom Connally, December 30, 1932; J. A. Whitten to Morris Sheppard, December 30, 1932; Sheep and Goat Raisers Association to Tom Connally, January 3, 1933; Atticus Webb to Morris Sheppard, March 14, 1933, all in Travis Hamer collection; *San Antonio Express*, March 19, 1933; *El Paso Herald-Post*, April 5, 1933; The *Dallas Morning News*, May 17, 1933.

11. The *Dallas Morning News*, January 15, 16, 1933; Utley, *Lone Star Lawmen*, pp. 152–55; Robert Nieman, "On the Trail of Bonnie and Clyde: Why Frank Hamer Wasn't Serving as a Texas Ranger," *Texas Ranger Dispatch Magazine*, no. 13 (Spring 2004), pp. 37–38; author interview with Harrison Hamer, May 23, 2011.

12. Frank Hamer to Jack Porter, November 28, 1952; Coke R. Stevenson to Jack Porter, December 21, 1952, Travis Hamer collection.

13. Frank Hamer, Texas Highway Patrol Commission, January 1, 1933, original in author's collection; Frank Hamer to Thomas Connally, December 27, 1933, and Frank Hamer to Morris Sheppard, December 27, 1933, Travis Hamer collection; *Laredo Times*, September 13, 1933; *Galveston Tribune*, May 24, 1934. Gladys Hamer later claimed that Frank was then employed as a security officer by a Houston oil company at a whopping $500 a month. Frost and Jenkins, *I'm Frank Hamer*, p. 209. Her memory was faulty; he did not begin working for Houston oil companies until 1935.

14. Simmons, *Assignment Huntsville*, p. 126; Webb, *The Texas Rangers*, p. 539; Newlon, "Outlaw Tamer," p. 58.

15. Simmons, *Assignment Huntsville*, pp. 126–28. Barrow gang member Ralph Fults later claimed that three lawmen, Tom Hickman, Lone Wolf Gonzaullas, and Ranger Captain Fred McDaniel, told him separately that each had been approached by Simmons prior to Hamer. Hickman and Gonzaullas had purportedly declined, stating, "We don't ambush people and we don't shoot women." Fults's claim is highly improbable for several reasons. Tom Hickman had already ambushed and killed two bank robbers at Clarksville in 1926. Gonzaullas, who had a huge ego, certainly would have mentioned such an offer to his biographer, but he never did (Robert Stephens to author, July 20, 2014). McDaniel did not even become a Ranger captain until more than a year after Bonnie and Clyde were killed. Lastly,

Simmons, in his memoir, said he only approached Hamer. Fults, a convicted felon, can hardly be considered a reliable source for Texas Ranger history. For Fults's claim, see John Neal Phillips, *Running with Bonnie and Clyde* (Norman: University of Oklahoma Press, 1996), p. 354 n3.

16. Webb, *Texas Rangers*, p. 540.

17. The *Dallas Morning News*, April 29, 1978, May 23, 1981. The Barrow filling station is still standing; the modern address is 1221 Singleton Blvd.

18. U.S. Department of Justice, Identification Order no. 1211, October 24, 1933; Report of Special Agent E. J. Dowd, April 21, 1934, pp. 1–3, FBI files; The *Dallas Morning News*, April 14, 1933, May 24, 1934; *Wichita Falls Daily Times*, May 23, 1934.

19. *Seguin Gazette-Enterprise*, September 18, 1991; Fortune, *Fugitives: The Story of Clyde Barrow and Bonnie Parker* (Dallas: Ranger Press, 1934), p. 49; Charley F. Eckhardt, *Tales of Badmen, Bad Women, and Bad Places: Four Centuries of Texas Outlawry* (Lubbock: Texas Tech University Press, 1999), p. 182.

20. The *Dallas Morning News*, March 12, 19, 23, 1930; Fortune, *Fugitives*, pp. 74–77.

21. The *Dallas Morning News*, October 31, November 21, 1931. The first published account of Clyde's alleged rape by and killing of Ed Crowder appeared in Phillips, *Running with Bonnie and Clyde*, pp. 52–54. Phillips's story came from Barrow gang member Ralph Fults, yet Fults does not explain why Clyde would ever admit to a fellow con that he was the victim of homosexual rape. The Fults account does not comport with contemporary newspaper reports that show that the knife fight took place in a crowded dormitory with two hundred prisoners scattering to escape the brawl. Since Fults was wrong about Clyde's killing Ed Crowder in revenge for being raped, it casts strong doubt on his claim that Clyde was raped by Crowder. Scalley himself later denied to an FBI agent that he and Clyde killed Crowder. See Report of Special Agent C. B. Winstead, February 5, 1934, p. 2, in FBI files.

22. The *Dallas Morning News*, December 17, 1933; Fortune, *Fugitives*, pp. 89–90; Simmons, *Assignment Huntsville*, pp. 119–20.

23. The *Dallas Morning News*, April 25, 1932; *Kaufman Herald*, August 11, 1932; Phillips, *Running with Bonnie and Clyde*, pp. 59–92.

24. The *Dallas Morning News*, May 1, 2, December 18, 19, 1932, June 3, 1933. Another current myth is that Clyde Barrow was innocent of the Bucher murder. However, Clyde admitted to his family that he took part in the robbery. He said that Ray Hamilton was not present and that two other youths whom he did not name had killed Bucher. Fortune, *Fugitives*, pp. 104–06. Ralph Fults claimed that the killers were Ted Rogers and Johnny Russell. Phillips, *Running with Bonnie and Clyde*, pp. 99–101; Jeff Guinn, *Go Down Together* (New York: Simon & Schuster, 2009), pp. 111–13. The fact is that Bucher's widow identified Hamilton, two of Bucher's employees identified Hamilton as a man who had cased the shop earlier that day, and another witness placed him near Hillsboro the day of the murder. Hamilton was later convicted and sentenced to life imprisonment. *Abilene Morning News*, May 31, June 3, 1933; *Amarillo Daily News*, June 1, 1933. Lastly, Clyde admitted the Bucher murder to gang member James Mullen. Report of Special Agent C. B. Winstead, May 3, 1934, p. 4, FBI files.

25. *Del Rio Evening News*, July 29, 1932; The *Dallas Morning News*, August 7, 1932; *Ada* (OK) *Weekly News*, August 11, 1932.

26. *San Antonio Express*, August 16, 1932; The *Dallas Morning News*, August 16, 1932, May 24, 1934. Guinn, *Go Down Together*, pp. 128–29, 136, states incorrectly that the Barrow gang did not fire at the officers at the Wharton bridge. In fact, the shootout was widely reported in the Texas press. See, for example, *Lubbock Morning*

Avalanche, August 17, 1932; *Abilene Morning News,* August 17, 1932; *Amarillo Daily News,* August 17, 1932; *San Antonio Express,* August 17, 1932.

27. *Sherman Daily Democrat,* October 12, 1932; *McKinney Daily Courier Gazette,* October 13, 1932; Death Certificate of Howard Hall, October 15, 1932; U.S. Census Population Schedules, Grayson County, Texas, 1920 and 1930. Guinn, *Go Down Together,* pp. 138–40, argues that Clyde did not kill Hall. However, the MO of the Hillsboro and Sherman holdups was identical, and the clerk, Glaze, positively identified Barrow from a mug shot a day after the murder. Though Guinn argues that the clerk's identification was wrong, the fact is that immediately after the murder, and a day before Clyde's photo was shown to him, Glaze gave a description of the killer that matched Clyde perfectly.

28. Confession of W. D. Jones, Dallas, November 18, 1933, pp. 2–3; The *Dallas Morning News,* December 26, 1932, November 26, 1933.

29. Confession of W. D. Jones, pp. 5–6; undated statement of J. F. Vannoy, Travis Hamer collection; The *Dallas Morning News,* January 7, 28, November 26, 1933.

30. Report of Special Agent Dwight W. Brantley, August 17, 1933, pp. 22–23, FBI files; The *Dallas Morning News,* April 14, 15, 1933; *San Antonio Light,* June 4, 1933; Ed Portley, "The Inside Story of Bonnie Parker and the Bloody Barrows, Part 2," *True Detective Mysteries* (July 1934), pp. 54–57, 73; Fortune, *Fugitives,* pp. 149–53.

31. Logansport (IN) *Pharos-Tribune,* May 12, 1933; Springfield *Daily Illinois State Journal,* May 20, 1933; *Moorhead* (MN) *Daily News,* May 19, 1933; Portley, "Inside Story, Part 2," p. 74.

32. George T. Corry to Special Agent F. J. Blake, June 30, 1933; Report of Special Agent E. J. Dowd, July 8, 1933; The *Dallas Morning News,* June 12, 1933.

33. Confession of W. D. Jones, pp. 13–14; *Fayetteville Daily Democrat,* June 24, 1933; *Miami* (OK) *Daily News Record,* June 26, 1933; The *Dallas Morning News,* November 26, 1933; Portley, "Inside Story, Part 2," pp. 76–77. Fred Mace was a friend of Bonnie's husband, Roy Thornton; Billie divorced him in 1935. The *Dallas Morning News,* November 28, 1931, November 10, 1932, December 4, 1934, March 8, 1935.

34. Report of Special Agent Dwight W. Brantley, August 17, 1933, pp. 3–4, 24–25, FBI files; The *Dallas Morning News,* November 26, 1933; Jefferson City (MO) *Post Tribune,* July 20, 1933; Ed Portley, "The Inside Story of Bonnie Parker and the Bloody Barrows, Part 3," *True Detective Mysteries* (August 1934).

35. Report of Special Agent Dwight W. Brantley, August 17, 1933, pp. 5–14, FBI files; Confession of W. D. Jones, pp. 15–16; Waterloo (IA) *Daily Courier,* July 24, 1933; New Orleans *Times-Picayune,* May 24, 1934; Portley, "Inside Story, Part 3," pp. 76–77.

36. Report of Special Agent Charles B. Winstead, November 27, 1933, pp. 1–2; Report of Special Agent E. J. Dowd, December 14, 1933, p. 4; Report of Special Agent Herman E. Hollis, December 23, 1933, p. 1–2, FBI files; The *Dallas Morning News,* November 23, 1933; Ted Hinton, *Ambush: The Real Story of Bonnie and Clyde* (Bryan, TX: Shoal Creek Publishers, 1979), pp. 103–07. Hinton claimed that Schmid insisted he would order the outlaws to halt and that the deputies objected to this plan. In fact, Schmid admitted to newspapers that his posse opened fire without warning. As we will see, Ted Hinton is an extremely unreliable source.

37. Reports of Special Agent C. B. Winstead, January 25, 1934, pp. 1–3, April 14, 1934, pp. 3–4, May 3, 1934, pp. 2–4; Indictment, *U.S. v. Mary Pitts, alias Mary O'Dare, et al.,* U.S. District Court, Northern District of Texas, case no. 8250, March 21, 1935, p. 7; The *Dallas Morning News,* January 17, June 13, 1934, February 23, 1935; San Antonio *Express,* January 28, 1934; James Mullen, "I Framed

Ray Hamilton's Prison Break," *Startling Detective Adventures* (November 1934), pp. 10–17, 75–76. "Major" was the first name of Crowson, the murdered guard.

21. THE BARROW HUNT

1. *San Antonio Light*, February 3, 1934; *Corsicana Daily Sun*, February 3, 1934; *Wichita Daily Times*, February 3, 1934; The *Gonzales Inquirer*, February 3, 1934; The *Paris News*, February 4, 1934; *Galveston Tribune*, February 5, 1934.

2. Webb, *Texas Rangers*, p. 540.

3. *Galveston Tribune*, May 24, 1934; Webb, *Texas Rangers*, p. 540.

4. The *Dallas Morning News*, November 11, 1924, September 14, 1931; The *Richardson Echo*, February 16, 1940; Bob Alcorn (with Clarke Newlon), "I Killed Clyde Barrow," *Startling Detective Adventures* (August 1934), pp. 6, 9.

5. D. L. McCormack to Special Agent in Charge, New Orleans, February 3, 1934; Memorandum of Special Agent Charles B. Winstead, February 2, 1934; Frank Hamer, Traveling Expense Account, March 23, 1934; Webb, *Texas Rangers*, p. 540. My story of Hamer's manhunt for Bonnie and Clyde is substantially different from previous published accounts. The reason is twofold: I have used the voluminous Dallas FBI file, which had been long lost until 2006 and not declassified until 2009, and I have also relied on a forgotten but detailed firsthand account by Sheriff Henderson Jordan, which appeared in the November 1934 issue of *True Detective Mysteries*.

6. Hamer, Traveling Expense Account; *El Paso Herald Post*, May 24, 1934; Simmons, *Assignment Huntsville*, p. 132. On Leadbelly's song, "Mr. Tom Hughes' Town," see Benjamin Filene, *Romancing the Folk: Public Memory and American Roots Music* (Chapel Hill: University of North Carolina Press, 2000), pp. 66–67.

7. Hamer, Traveling Expense Account; memo dated April 9, 1934, FBI file; Blanche Caldwell Barrow, *My Life with Bonnie and Clyde* (Norman: University of Oklahoma Press, 2004), p. 256 n6.

8. Special Agent E. J. Dowd to D. L. McCormack, February 7, 1934; Report of Special Agent E. J. Dowd, March 29, 1934; *Lubbock Morning Avalanche*, February 2, 1934; *Wichita Falls Daily Times*, May 24, 1934.

9. Report of E. J. Dowd, March 29, 1934; The *Dallas Morning News*, March 7, 8, 1934.

10. Memorandum of Special Agent E. J. Dowd, March 17, 1934; The *Dallas Morning News*, June 22, 1933.

11. Memorandum of Special Agent E. J. Dowd, March 17, 1934; Frank Hamer to Ed Portley, March 15, 1934, Joplin police files.

12. Frank J. Blake to J. Edgar Hoover, March 17, 1934.

13. Statement of James Mullen, in Report of Special Agent C. B. Winstead, May 3, 1934, pp. 5–7; Carroll Rich, "The Day They Shot Bonnie and Clyde," in Wilson M. Hudson, ed., *Hunters and Healers: Folklore Types and Topics* (Austin: Encino Press, 1971), p. 43.

14. *San Antonio Express*, September 21, 1930; Miami (FL) *Daily News*, January 12, 1938; Henderson Jordan, "The Inside Story of the Killing of Bonnie Parker and Clyde Barrow," *True Detective Mysteries* (November 1934), pp. 41–42. A number of writers incorrectly give Kindell's first name as Lester. Born in Ohio in 1901, he was a lawyer before joining the FBI.

15. *Big Spring Daily Herald*, April 8, 1934; interview with Gladys Hamer in the documentary film *Bonnie and Clyde: Myth or Madness* (1985).

16. Contrary to the claims of numerous writers, Schieffer gave fully consistent accounts of the double murders to the press and also in court. See *El Paso Herald Post*, April 2, 1934; *San Antonio Express*, April 2, May 25, 1934; The *Paris News*, April 2, 1934; The *Dallas Morning News*, April 2; *Wichita Daily Times*, May 26, 1934; *Corsicana Semi-Weekly Light*, May 29, 1934. Schieffer also gave a filmed statement: *Fox Movietone News Story 21-705: Hunt for Bonnie and Clyde*, which can be viewed at the Moving Images Research Collections on the University of South Carolina Library website.

17. For the statement of the Giggals, see The *Dallas Morning News*, April 2, 1934; *San Antonio Express*, April 2, 1934. For the Barrow family's earliest account, see Fortune, *Fugitives* pp. 230–33. In *Fugitives*, p. 236, Bonnie's mother claimed that Methvin confessed to her that he had killed both officers. Her statement is refuted by the eyewitness accounts and by ballistics tests, which showed that expended shotgun shells found at the scene had been fired by the sixteen-gauge shotgun later seized from the death car in Louisiana.

18. Henry Methvin's fingerprints, as well as Clyde's, were found on the empty whiskey bottle found at the scene. Methvin gave a written statement about the Grapevine murders to FBI Agent Leslie Kindell, The *Dallas Morning News*, February 24, 1935. Numerous writers have claimed that Bonnie was never charged with the Grapevine murders; that is incorrect. See The *Dallas Morning News*, May 19, 1934.

19. *San Antonio Express*, April 2, 1934; *Brownsville Herald*, April 14, 1968.

20. Hinton, *Ambush*, pp. 138–39.

21. Report of Special Agent Herman E. Hollis, April 19, 1934; Miami (OK) *Daily News-Record*, April 6, 8, 1934; *Galveston Tribune*, April 7, 1934. Agent Hollis was slain in a gun battle with Baby Face Nelson seven months after writing the foregoing report.

22. Report of Special Agent Charles B. Winstead, April 14, 1934; *Milwaukee Journal*, June 11, 1934.

23. Memorandum of L. G. Phares, Texas State Highway Patrol, April 11, 1934; Memorandum for SAC, unsigned, April 21, 1934; Special Agent Charles B. Winstead to Frank J. Blake, April 23, 1934; The *Dallas Morning News*, April 8, 10, 1934; *Galveston Tribune*, April 10, 1934.

24. *El Paso Herald Post*, May 12, 1934.

25. Webb, *Texas Rangers*, p. 541; Simmons, *Assignment Huntsville*, p. 131.

26. U.S. Census Population Schedules, De Soto Parish, Louisiana, 1930; Frank Hamer to Frank J. Blake, May 11, 1934; Rhea Whitley to J. Edgar Hoover, April 30, 1934; Baton Rouge *Advocate*, September 28, 1935; *Ruston Daily Leader*, October 25, 1935; Guinn, *Go Down Together*, pp. 272–73, 320.

27. Telegram, Rhea Whitley, Special Agent in Charge, New Orleans, to Special Agent F. J. Blake, April 13, 1934; report of James O. Peyronnin, Division of Investigation, April 16, 1934; Jordan, "Inside Story of the Killing of Bonnie Parker and Clyde Barrow," p. 42–43; Baton Rouge *Advocate*, April 14, 1934; The *Dallas Morning News*, April 14, 1934.

28. Jordan, "Inside Story of the Killing of Bonnie Parker and Clyde Barrow," p. 74; Webb, *Texas Rangers*, pp. 541–42.

29. Rhea Whitley, Special Agent in Charge, New Orleans, to J. Edgar Hoover, April 24, 1934; Statement of Henderson Jordan to Glenn Jordan, October 12, 1958; Jordan, "Inside Story of the Killing of Bonnie Parker and Clyde Barrow," p. 43. Henderson Jordan died on June 13, 1958, so the date of his statement, which appears on the author's typescript copy, is either incorrect or the statement was transcribed after his death. In Methvin's 1935 trial for murdering Constable

Campbell in Oklahoma, Henry and his mother testified that on March 1, 1934, Henry told his parents that he wanted to turn in Bonnie and Clyde. John Joyner testified that he informed Sheriff Jordan on March 1. That testimony was incorrect, either due to faulty memory or a desire to show that Henry was an unwilling member of the gang prior to the April 1 murders at Grapevine and the killing of Constable Campbell five days later. The special agents' reports of April 13 and 24, 1934, make it clear that the Methvins did not begin to cooperate with lawmen until after the abortive "drag" of April 13.

30. F. J. Blake, SAC, Dallas, to W. R. McDowell, April 14, 1934; Memo, F. J. Blake, April 17, 1934; Rhea Whitley, Special Agent in Charge, New Orleans, to J. Edgar Hoover, April 24, 1934.

31. Whitley to Hoover, April 24, 1934; Simmons, *Assignment Huntsville*, p. 132.

32. Telegram, F. J. Blake to Rhea Whitley, April 27, 1934; Rhea Whitley to J. Edgar Hoover, April 30, 1934; Simmons, *Assignment Huntsville*, p. 143. On Hamer's payment of $1,000 to the informant, see Declaration of Frank Hamer, March 13, 1941, Travis Hamer collection.

33. Jordan, "Inside Story of the Killing of Bonnie Parker and Clyde Barrow," p. 74.

34. Hamer to Frank J. Blake, May 11, 1934; Pat Murphy to SAC, Dallas, May 9, 1934.

35. Hamer to Frank J. Blake, May 11, 1934; Whitley to Hoover, May 14, 1934.

36. Rhea Whitley to J. Edgar Hoover, May 14, 1934; Jordan, "Inside Story of the Killing of Bonnie Parker and Clyde Barrow," p. 74.

37. Jordan, "Inside Story of the Killing of Bonnie Parker and Clyde Barrow," p. 74. Otis Cole was the son of John G. Cole. Ivy Methvin's move to the Cole house occurred after May 11, 1934. See Hamer to Blake, May 11, 1934. In order to protect the Methvins, Hamer gave a deliberately vague and misleading account to Walter Prescott Webb. He said that the lawmen "arranged to have Barrow's hideout moved into a parish where the officers were more reliable. In a comparatively short time the hideout was established in Bienville Parish at a place well known to me." He was referring to the Methvins' move to the Cole house and did not reveal that Ivy had relocated within the same parish. See Webb, *The Texas Rangers*, p. 541.

38. Statement of Henderson Jordan to Glenn Jordan, October 12, 1958; Guinn, *Go Down Together*, pp. 320–21.

39. Webb, *Texas Rangers*, p. 541.

22. "WE SHOT THE DEVIL OUT OF THEM"

1. Jordan, "Inside Story of the Killing of Bonnie Parker and Clyde Barrow," p. 75; *Galveston Tribune*, May 24, 1934; Simmons, *Assignment Huntsville*, p. 133.

2. Untitled FBI report on Bonnie and Clyde, September 14, 1934; Statement of Henderson Jordan to Glenn Jordan; Jordan, "Inside Story of the Killing of Bonnie Parker and Clyde Barrow," pp. 74–75.

3. A great deal of speculative fiction has been written about the weapons carried by Hamer's posse. This despite the fact that two photographs taken shortly after the shooting plainly show five of the posse's guns resting on the roof of the death car: a Remington Model 8, a BAR, and three Remington Model 11 shotguns. Frank Hamer Jr., in the documentary film *The Other Side of Bonnie and Clyde* (1968), displays a Remington semiautomatic rifle with a twenty-round clip that he claims was the one used by his father in the ambush; it is now in the Texas Ranger Hall of Fame and Museum. However, the rifle is a Remington model 81, manufactured in 1940, and therefore could not have been used in the ambush.

4. Statement of Henderson Jordan to Glenn Jordan; Jordan, "Inside Story of the Killing of Bonnie Parker and Clyde Barrow," p. 75; Webb, *Texas Rangers*, pp. 542–43.

5. Guinn, *Go Down Together*, p. 341, claims that Hamer, armed with a Colt Monitor rifle (a civilian version of the BAR), ran to the rear of the Barrow car and fired repeated bursts into the already-dead Bonnie. Guinn's sole source is an eight-page typescript prepared in 1998 by two gangster buffs. This fanciful report, based on its authors' reenactment of the ambush and their own purported forensic examination of the death car, lacks evidentiary and historical support. Its authors ignored the detailed accounts left by the posse and relied on their own chimerical ideas of what might have happened. For example, although the Colt Monitor on display at the Texas Ranger Hall of Fame and Museum in Waco was indeed Hamer's, there is no evidence that he used it in the ambush or even owned it in 1934. And the authors were either unaware of, or ignored, Bob Alcorn's statement in The *Dallas Morning News* of May 24, 1934, that it was he, not Hamer, who ran to the rear of the Barrow car and fired into it with his rifle.

6. Coroner's Report, Arcadia Parish, May 23, 1934; *Wichita Falls Daily Times*, May 24, 1934; Amarillo *Sunday News Globe*, June 10, 1934; Baton Rouge *Advocate*, May 24, 1934; Jordan, "Inside Story of the Killing of Bonnie Parker and Clyde Barrow," pp. 75–76; Alcorn, "I Killed Clyde Barrow," pp. 8–10; Webb, *Texas Rangers*, pp. 542–43; Frost and Jenkins, *I'm Frank Hamer*, pp. 232–23. Firsthand accounts by Bob Alcorn and Sheriff Jordan also appear in The *Dallas Morning News*, May 24, 1934. On Prentiss Oakley firing the first shot, see Statement of Henderson Jordan, October 12, 1958, and New Orleans *Times-Picayune*, May 29, 1934. The account of these events in Ted Hinton's book *Ambush: The Real Story of Bonnie and Clyde* (1979) is largely fictitious. Among his countless false claims, Hinton said that he knew Bonnie personally, that he was constantly on the Barrow hunt for months, that the posse lay in wait for two days, that the officers handcuffed an uncooperative Ivy Methvin to a tree, that all the possemen carried BARs, that he was cheated out of his share of the reward, and that Hamer revealed Ivy's role as informant. Hinton's untrue stories cannot be blamed on old age or on his coauthor, Larry Grove, for he was spinning many of the same wild yarns years before his book was written. See, for example, Hinton's statements in the Marietta (GA) *Journal*, September 26, 1969, The *Dallas Morning News*, June 7, 1971, and *Corsicana Daily Sun*, September 23, 1974. Hinton in fact received his full one-sixth share of the $1,000 reward for Clyde. L. G. Phares to Sam B. Dill, July 19, 1934, Travis Hamer collection.

7. *Austin American*, May 24, 1934. Guinn, *Go Down Together*, pp. 315–18, 343, relies on claims from the Barrow family to write that Sheriff Jordan stole a suitcase containing $18,000 in cash from the death car. Guinn's sole contemporary source is an account in The *Dallas Dispatch*, May 25, 1934, which reported that at the time of Clyde's death "negotiations were under way to pay Barrow $18,000" to break three robbers out of the Fort Worth jail. Contrary to Guinn's assertion, the *Dispatch* never reported that Clyde had actually been paid the money. There is no historical evidence that Clyde ever possessed $18,000 or that Sheriff Jordan stole anything from the death car.

8. *Wichita Daily Times*, May 23, 1934; *San Antonio Express*, May 24, 1934; The *Bienville Democrat*, May 24, 1934; *Austin American*, May 24, 1934; Frost and Jenkins, *I'm Frank Hamer*, pp. 235–36.

9. The *Dallas Morning News*, May 24, 1934; Baton Rouge *Advocate*, May 24, 1934; Simmons, *Assignment Huntsville*, p. 134.

10. *Lubbock Morning Avalanche*, May 25, 1934; New Orleans *Times-Picayune*, May 29, 1934; The *Bienville Democrat*, May 31, 1934; Baton Rouge *State Times*, June 1, 1934.

11. *Galveston Tribune,* May 24, 1934.

12. Simmons, *Assignment Huntsville,* pp. 176–77.

13. *El Paso Herald Post,* May 26, 31, 1934; The *Dallas Morning News,* May 27, June 1, 1934.

14. *Austin American Statesman,* March 3, 1935; The *Dallas Morning News,* March 3, 1935; Joseph L. Schott, "Bonnie and Clyde's Last Car," *Omaha World Herald Magazine,* May 4, 1980, pp. 28–29, 31.

15. Cumie Barrow to Frank Hamer, July 29, 1934, Emma Parker to Frank Hamer, October 16, 1934, copies in author's collection; *General and Special Laws of The State of Texas* (1941), p. 1361; The *Dallas Morning News,* June 19, 1941; *Austin American,* February 14, 1945; The *Paris News,* February 15, 1945; Frost and Jenkins, *I'm Frank Hamer,* pp. 256–58.

16. Newlon, "Outlaw Tamer," p. 36; Frost and Jenkins, *I'm Frank Hamer,* pp. 250, 254–55; Webb, *Texas Rangers,* p. 544.

23. FRANK HAMER VS. LYNDON B. JOHNSON

1. A. H. Carrigan to Frank Hamer, June 6, 1934, Barratt O'Hara to Walter Prescott Webb, June 15, 1934, Travis Hamer collection; J. Edgar Hoover Phone Logs, March 16, 1935, FBI files; J. Edgar Hoover, Memorandum, May 20, 1949, FBI file no. 100-355857; MacDonalds's The *Kansas City Star* article was reprinted in two parts in *Amarillo Daily News,* May 24, June 10, 1934; *El Paso Herald Post,* May 26, 1934; The *Dallas Morning News,* June 5, 1934. One FBI file on Hamer exists; the balance were destroyed in 1980. According to Ranger chaplain P. B. Hill, "J. Edgar Hoover said one time that Frank Hamer was one of the greatest law officers in American history." That is most improbable. For Hill's claim, see Frost and Jenkins, *I'm Frank Hamer,* p. 280.

2. *Amarillo Daily News,* January 11, 1935; *San Antonio Express,* September 4, 1935; Stephens, *Lone Wolf,* pp. 62–63.

3. *Big Spring Daily Herald,* May 31, 1934; Ward, "Texas Rangers," pp. 222–28; Utley, *Lone Star Lawmen,* pp. 156, 165, 171–72.

4. *Lubbock Morning Avalanche,* July 24, 1934; The *Dallas Morning News,* July 23, 1934, March 13, April 6, 10, 1935; *Taylor Daily Press,* October 23, 1934; *Chicago Tribune,* March 17, 1935; *Abilene Morning News,* March 20, 1935.

5. The *Dallas Morning News,* May 16, July 16, 1934; *Port Arthur News,* October 11, 12, November 1, 2, 1935; The *Galveston Daily News,* October 26, 1935.

6. Roy T. Rogers to Frank Hamer, August 4, 1941, Travis Hamer collection; *Amarillo Globe,* September 28, 1936; *San Antonio Express,* November 17, 1936; Rebecca Ann Montes, "Working for American Rights: Black, White, and Mexican American Dockworkers in Texas During the Great Depression," Ph.D. dissertation, University of Texas (2005), pp. 95–96.

7. *Abilene Morning Reporter News,* May 10, 1939; The *Dallas Morning News,* May 10, 1939.

8. Frost and Jenkins, *I'm Frank Hamer,* p. 264.

9. The *Dallas Morning News,* May 10, 1939; The *Galveston Daily News,* May 11, 1939; *Chicago Socialist Appeal,* June 20, 1939.

10. *Amarillo Daily News,* October 7, 1947.

11. Author interview with Laura David, April 18, 2012; Taronda Schulz to author, April 1, 2015; Utrecht, "Frank Hamer, Crusader," p. 51; Frost and Jenkins, *I'm Frank Hamer,* p. 280.

12. The *Dallas Morning News*, March 30, 1941; *Lubbock Morning Avalanche*, April 9, 1941; Frost and Jenkins, *I'm Frank Hamer*, p. 268.

13. *Hamer v. Hamer* (1945) 184 S.W. 2d 492; *Austin American*, January 19, 1949; Frost and Jenkins, *I'm Frank Hamer*, pp. 269–70.

14. Author interview with Robert Stephens, June 19, 2013.

15. Caro, *Means of Ascent*, p. 310–11, 316–17.

16. *Del Rio News-Herald*, July 31, 1977; Caro, *Means of Ascent*, pp. 189–91; Arthur Stehling, *L.B.J.'s Climb to the White House* (Chicago: Adams Press, 1987), pp. 12–15.

17. *Alice Daily Echo*, September 10, 1948; *El Paso Herald Post*, September 10, 1948; Caro, *Means of Ascent*, pp. 322–24, 327; Stehling, *L.B.J.'s Climb to the White House*, pp. 22–23.

18. *Abilene Reporter News*, October 29, 1962; *El Paso Herald Post*, September 29, 1948; *Del Rio News-Herald*, July 31, 1977; Caro, *Means of Ascent*, pp. 327–28; Frost and Jenkins, *I'm Frank Hamer*, p. 277; Mary Kahl, *Ballot Box Thirteen: How Lyndon Johnson Won His 1948 Senate Race by 87 Contested Votes* (Jefferson, NC: McFarland & Co., 1983), pp. 121–22.

19. Caro, *Means of Ascent*, p. 329; Kahl, *Ballot Box Thirteen*, pp. 129–30.

20. *Alice Daily Echo*, September 12, 1948; Josiah M. Daniel III, "LBJ v. Coke Stevenson: Lawyering for Control of the Disputed Texas Democratic Party Senatorial Primary Election of 1948," *Review of Litigation*, vol. 31, no. 1 (Winter 2012), p. 11.

21. Daniel, "LBJ v. Coke Stevenson," pp. 10–36. A detailed history and analysis of the 1948 election fraud is beyond the scope of this book. For a fuller discussion, see the sources cited in the foregoing notes.

22. *Brownsville Herald*, October 21, 1949; *Del Rio News-Herald*, July 31, 1977; Caro, *Means of Ascent*, pp. 388–90.

23. Frank Hamer Jr. to Stuart N. Lake, June 24, 1948; Lake to Captain Frank Hamer, June 29, 1948; Lake to Frank Hamer Jr., July 1, 12, 1948, June 6, 15, July 23, 1949, August 7, 1950, Stuart N. Lake collection, Huntington Library; *Brownsville Herald*, May 4, 1945.

24. *Lubbock Morning Avalanche*, March 16, 1949; *Amarillo Daily News*, March 18, 1949; *Houston Press*, July 12, 1955.

25. Frank Hamer to Jack Porter, November 28, 1952, and Coke R. Stevenson to Jack Porter, December 21, 1952, Travis Hamer collection; *Austin American Statesman*, March 11, 1951; *Lubbock Morning Avalanche*, April 2, 1954.

26. Mrs. Frank A. Hamer Jr. to Stuart N. Lake, May 19, 1955; *Austin American*, July 11, 1955; *Austin Statesman*, July 11, 1955; *Houston Chronicle*, July 12, 1955; The *Dallas Morning News*, July 12, 1955.

27. *Hamer v. Warner Brothers-Seven Arts, Inc.*, Travis Hamer collection; Travis Hamer to author, April 1, 2015; *New York Post*, January 6, 1968; *San Antonio Express*, October 8, 1968.

28. "Polar Hour."

INDEX